INSIGHTS in Biology

SECOND EDITION

EDC

KENDALL/HUNT PUBLISHING COMPANY
4050 Westmark Drive   Dubuque, Iowa 52002

EDC's Center for Science Education Development and Production Team

Jacqueline S. Miller, Principal Investigator
Kerry S. Ouellet, Production Editor
Christine Brown, Curriculum/Instruction Design Associate
Bettina Dembek, Research Associate
Silvia T. LaVita, Permissions Researcher
Anne Marie Walker, Senior Editor

Other Contributors
Robin Bryson, Content Reviewer
Janet Faley, Content Reviewer
Nicole Kooiker, Content Contributor
Cathrine Monson, Copyeditor/Content Reviewer
Sally Crissman, Content Contributor
Gilly Puttick, Content Contributor

Front cover image © 2007 iStock International Inc.
Back cover image © Walt Spitzmiller

ISBN 13: 978-0-7575-0863-9
ISBN 10: 0-7575-0863-4

This material is based on work supported by the National Science Foundation under Grant No. ESI-9255722. Any opinions, findings, conclusions, or recommendations expressed in this publication are those of the authors and do not necessarily reflect the views of the granting agency.

Printed in the United States of America

2 3 4 5 6 7 8 9 10   10 09 08

Contents

Dear Student:

Welcome to *Insights in Biology*. As the title of this book suggests, you are about to embark on a journey of discovery. Your journey will be an exploration of biological events and phenomena that take place in your world. Like any explorer worth his or her salt, success will depend on your curiosity, your enthusiasm, and your willingness to think about new ideas and develop new skills you may never have used before. As in most expeditions, success will also depend on teamwork—the ability to work together, communicate clearly, and take a few risks together to reach new heights. But the view of the world through understanding biology will be well worth the effort.

One of the main goals of *Insights in Biology* is to engage you in the excitement of biology. The study of biology is much more than just facts. It is a discipline that is as alive as the subjects it portrays. Everyday, new questions arise, new theories are proposed, and new understandings are achieved. As a result of these new insights, technologies are developed that affect the way you live and the kinds of decisions you need to make. We hope that this program encourages you to ask questions, to develop greater problem-solving and thinking skills, and to recognize the importance of science in your life.

Glance through the pages of your book. Your first instinct is correct: This is not a traditional biology textbook. Although textbooks provide a good deal of useful information, they are not the only way to discover science. In this student book, you will find that chapters have been replaced by learning experiences that include readings and activities. The activities include laboratory experimentation, role playing, concept mapping, model building, simulation exercises, and research projects. These learning experiences emphasize the processes of science and the connections among biological concepts. Much of the learning you will be doing will be in the context of stories. Some stories will be about everyday people and teenagers like you. Other stories will come from history, describing how discoveries were made and who made them. Still others are about cultures and countries that you may not know about. These stories are told not only to engage your interest but also to help you see how concepts in biology are involved in almost every aspect of life. Perhaps by the end of this course you will want to tell your own stories as a way of explaining the biological world around you.

Insights in Biology Staff

Safety Notes

Safety is your primary concern in conducting experiments and other activities in the biology classroom. Although all the investigations you will be doing in *Insights in Biology* are designed with safety in mind, you will be working with chemicals, living organisms, sharp objects, sources of heat, and other materials that can be hazardous to your health if you are careless or don't pay attention.

Therefore, always do the following:
- wash your hands before and after labs,
- wear safety goggles and an apron,
- tie back your hair if it is long (especially before lighting a burner) and roll up your sleeves,
- use caution with sharp objects and always cut away from yourself and your fingers,
- clean up your work space and after yourself following each investigation,
- follow the safety procedures described in the investigation, and
- report all accidents, no matter how small, to your teacher.

Never do the following:
- mix unknown chemicals just to see what happens;
- touch or taste any chemical unless specifically told to do so by your teacher;
- smoke, drink, or eat in the laboratory;
- touch your face, mouth, ears, or eyes while working with plants, animals, or chemicals;
- cut on an unstable surface or toward your body, particularly when using a razor blade or scalpels; and
- taste or smell any unknown substance. When you are asked to smell a substance, do so only by gently waving a hand over it to draw the scent toward your nose. Never pipette by mouth.

INSIGHTS in Biology

SECOND EDITION

UNIT 1

The Matter of Life
Cell Biology

Contents

The Matter of Life
Cell Biology

Introduction

Our world is dynamic; it moves and changes constantly. Electrons dash ceaselessly, but with some uncertainty around the nucleus of an atom. Molecules break down and rearrange their components to form new molecules. Cells in our bodies move, respond to stimuli, and reproduce themselves. The soil vibrates with the activities of millions and millions of microorganisms and insects; leaves on the trees flutter; and the sand on the beaches shifts from the action of the wind. Ocean waves beat unendingly on the shore; continents shift on the surface of Earth. And Earth itself rotates and spins around the sun at mind-boggling speeds.

Much of this movement is the result of external forces acting on inert substances. Wind and water erode rock, changing its shape; water moves as the result of wind and gravity. But other kinds of movement are the result of a different kind of force. This force is internal to the substance and drives the activities that possess it. This internal force is called life. Living substances have distinctive, universal characteristics and carry out specific chemical processes that enable these characteristics to take place.

What attributes distinguish living matter from nonliving matter? What does it mean to be alive? Can the nature of this life force be investigated? In this unit, you will identify the characteristics that define a substance as living. You also will explore the biological processes involved in maintaining these characteristics of life.

Living Proof

Prologue

Imagine sitting beside a pond in early autumn. A maple tree shades you from the hot sun, while blades of grass and newly fallen leaves form a soft cushion. A fish jumps, breaking through a green film that has recently formed on the pond's surface. Birds sing, and bees and butterflies dart in and around the colorful flowers, collecting the last nectar of summer. You toss a rock into the water, then watch concentric rings flow outward from the spot where the rock disappeared.

   Which of the things described above are living? This seemingly trivial question is not necessarily easy to answer. What are the characteristics that we can use to define something as living? Biologists have so far identified more than 3 million species of living things. These species occupy every nook and cranny of Earth's surface (not to mention a vast array of species that once occupied the planet but are now extinct). Their diversity in size, structure, and ways of living is astonishing. Yet all share specific and definable characteristics that distinguish them from nonliving things. Scientists are often confronted with the challenge of determining whether something is living or nonliving. Samples from geological expeditions, from the ocean bottom, and from other planets are brought back and analyzed for characteristics of life as we know it. Searching for signs of life can be quite a difficult task. For example, look carefully at Figure 1.1.

Brainstorming

Discuss the following questions with your partner, and record your thinking in your notebook. Be prepared to share your ideas with the class.

1. How do you know that a plant is a living organism? What characteristics or activities can you observe that would be evidence of life?
2. What characteristics or activities does the plant share with other living things? Are any of these characteristics unique to plants? to animals?
3. Choose one of these characteristics. Does this characteristic alone mean that something is a living organism? Explain.

Figure 1.1
Are these plants living? How do you know?

Living or Nonliving?

You will observe a sample of an unidentified substance. Then, using any approach you can devise, you will determine whether or not the substance is living. You must base your decision *only* on what you can observe in your sample. You also must be able to explain your decision.

Materials

For each pair of students:

- 2 hand lenses
- 1 glass stirring rod or dissecting needle
- 1 sample of unidentified substance

For the class:

- microscopes

PROCEDURE

1. Observe the sample closely, using available materials. Use your own observations to determine whether or not the sample is living. Record in your notebook the reasons why you believe it to be living or nonliving. Be prepared to discuss with the class the evidence you used to determine whether your substance is alive.
2. Refer to the class list of the characteristics of life. Describe how you used those characteristics to help determine whether or not you think your sample is living.
3. **STOP & THINK** What questions would you need to ask to gain more knowledge about whether your sample is living or nonliving?
4. **STOP & THINK** How might you go about answering your questions?

Whenever you see this **STOP & THINK** box, discuss the question with your partner or team member and record your thinking in your notebook.

Aliens: The Search for Extraterrestrial Life

READING

There are two possibilities. Maybe we are alone. Maybe we're not. Both are equally frightening.

—Isaac Asimov or Bertrand Russell as quoted in Search for Life on Other Planets, *1998, by Bruce Jakosky, Cambridge University Press*

Topic: Mars
Go to: www.scilinks.org
Code: INBIOH27

Humans have long wondered whether life as we know it on Earth exists elsewhere or whether we are alone in the universe. Life on planets in our own solar system, particularly Mars, has long been the subject of speculation and science fiction stories. The discovery in 1995 and 1996 of planets orbiting stars not unlike our own sun has further fueled the belief that other Earth-like planets might exist in the universe and, perhaps on them, the possibility of life.

In 1975, two spacecrafts—*Viking 1* and *Viking 2*—were sent to Mars with the mission of determining whether life, as we know it, was present on the red planet (see Figure 1.2). Samples from the Martian surface were collected and used in three different experiments and one analysis designed to detect the presence of living organisms.

The first experiment was designed to determine whether carbon, in the form of carbon dioxide (CO_2), was taken up by the soil sample. The first part of the experiment was carried out under conditions most like those of the Martian environment. The second part of the experiment involved heating the soil to 175°C (374°F) for 3 hours and then repeating the experiment. This experiment indicated that carbon was being incorporated into the soil. Heating the soil reduced but did not eliminate the uptake of carbon.

The second experiment tested for organisms that could take in nutrients from their environment and then release gas, either carbon dioxide (CO_2) or sulfur dioxide (SO_2), back into the atmosphere. Organisms on Earth will take in these nutrients, release gas over time, and gradually stop producing gas as the nutrients

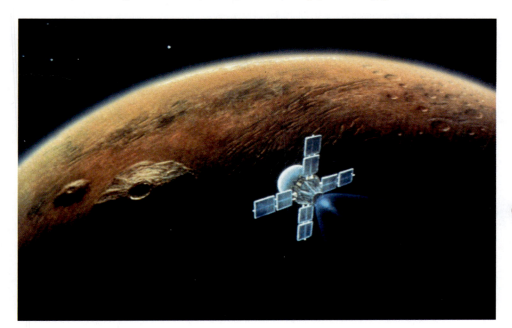

Figure 1.2

Viking fires its engines above Mars to become the first artificial object to orbit another planet.
Mars Orbit Insertion © 2004 Don Dixon/cosmographica.com

are used up. When this experiment was carried out on Martian soil, the Earth-like pattern of release was observed. Heating the soil to 160°C destroyed this activity.

The third experiment looked for exchange of gases. Nutrients were mixed with the Martian soil. The soil was then tested for the production of specific gases. These gases included hydrogen (H_2), nitrogen (N_2), oxygen (O_2), methane (CH_4), and carbon dioxide (CO_2). The exchange of gases would be indicative of the occurrence of biological processes. Gases were detected at various levels when the soil was tested. When the soil was heated to 160°C, gases continued to be produced.

The analysis of Martian soil indicated a complete absence of carbon-containing compounds. The conclusion of the Viking experiments was that there was no clear evidence of the presence of living organisms at the site of sampling by the Viking lander. Were the experiments carried out by the Viking lander the right experiments? Could there be other kinds of organisms that do not reflect our definition of life? How else might scientists look for life in other parts of the universe? These questions remain to be answered if humans are to continue their quest for extraterrestrial life.

 ANALYSIS

Record your responses to the following in your notebook.

1. What characteristics of life were the Viking experiments designed to test for?
2. Which tests suggested the possibility of life? Why?
3. If the soil had taken up carbon dioxide and released oxygen, what kind of organisms might be present in Martian soil? Explain your answer.
4. What was the significance of the fact that heating the soil to very high temperatures did not significantly change the results of the experiments? What was the significance of the lack of carbon-containing compounds?
5. What assumptions were made in the design of these experiments?
6. Do you agree with the conclusion that no life exists in the samples tested? Explain.
7. Suggest another kind of experiment that you would do if you were part of a team looking for life on another planet.

EXTENDING *Ideas*

▶ Set up a habitat for your organism. Research the natural habitats of the organism and any requirements it would need to stay alive. Determine what materials you would need, and identify the resources necessary for the organism to survive.

▶ Read or write your own story, poem, or song; examine a piece of art; or create a collage that develops the theme of life. In a short essay, explain what question this piece asks about life. Then describe how the question is answered for the reader, listener, or observer.

▶ Describe an experience you have had in which you found something and tried to determine whether it was living or nonliving.

Laboratory Assistant   "Our timeline is getting off track, and we might not be able to meet our deadline!" The scientists in the microbiology laboratory at GenPharms, Inc., are frantically looking for ways to streamline their lab processes for testing one of their new products. GenPharms, Inc., is a pharmaceutical company that manufactures generic drugs. The first person they turn to for advice is Jonathan, the microbiology lab assistant. Jonathan is the person most familiar with the detailed workings of the lab because he's involved with just about everything that happens.

On any given day, Jonathan can be found making detailed observations, analyzing data, interpreting results, or writing summaries of the protocols for an experiment. He maintains lab equipment, calibrates instruments, and monitors the inventory level for lab supplies. He has hands-on experience with all the lab processes. These include cleaning glassware, monitoring the robots that are part of the testing process, and working with the computers that organize the data files. Jonathan oversees the general organization and cleanliness of the lab.

Jonathan is pleased that the scientists have approached him with this challenge. He enjoys solving problems and finding ways to help improve the testing processes. In fact, he had been thinking of some modifications to achieve the best results. Together, the scientists and Jonathan examined their test protocol. They decided that they would save time and be more effective if they rearranged the steps involved in the testing process. Jonathan also suggested trying a new data management software program that he researched and thinks might help improve the lab's data analysis process.

Jonathan was drawn to a career as a laboratory assistant because he enjoyed science courses in high school, particularly the lab experiments. He also loved tinkering with computers and using programs to organize information. Based on Jonathan's detail-orientation, love for science and technology, and organization skills, a high school guidance counselor suggested a career as a laboratory assistant. Jonathan then researched the education and skills he would need to pursue such a career. Following high school, Jonathan attended a 2-year associate's degree program. He studied laboratory techniques and procedures as well as biology and computer science. After graduating from the associate's program, Jonathan began working at GenPharms, Inc., where he has been able to see the scientific process in action. He feels like it's a perfect fit!

Jonathan continues to learn about the latest laboratory equipment and techniques by reading trade magazines and by being a member of a national association for laboratory workers. His goal is to someday assume a laboratory manager position and continue his education by getting a bachelor's degree.

Which Way Do They Go?

Prologue

What do organisms need to stay alive? What are some basic resources? How might organisms obtain any of these resources? Because organisms depend on their environment for the resources they require to maintain life, they need ways to recognize and respond to these resources. For example, organisms can detect the presence of required nutrients and respond by moving toward them. You probably respond in this way when the aroma of a large pizza enters your environment.

As long as conditions remain constant, organisms may not need to respond any differently than usual. But what happens to an organism when its environment changes in a significant way? Say, for example, a change takes place within an organism's environment that makes the surroundings less hospitable. In that case, the organism will seek more favorable conditions. If the change is catastrophic and an organism can neither reach more favorable conditions nor adjust to the changed environment, it will die.

Brainstorming

Discuss the following questions with your partner, and record your thinking in your notebook. Be prepared to share your ideas with the class.

1. What resources might an organism require from its environment?
2. In what ways are these resources necessary to sustain life?
3. How might animals respond in order to obtain the resources that they require? If there were a drought, for example, how might animals get the water they need?
4. Think about an organism's ability to respond to the environment. Why might this characteristic of life be essential to living organisms?

Where Is the Light?

ACTIVITY

You will investigate the response of euglena (*Euglena*) to a change in their environment. Euglena are single-celled, photosynthetic organisms.

Materials

For each pair of students:

- 2 safety goggles
- 1 euglena phototaxis kit or culture
- 1 tall, straight, clear jar with screw cap
- spring water or filtered pond water
- 1 sheet black construction paper
- 1 eyedropper
- 1 microscope slide and coverslip
- 1 rubber band
- 1 scalpel or utility knife
- 1 sheet of cardboard (or other thick paper) as cutting surface
- 1 paper towel
- 1 dissecting needle
- access to a compound microscope

PROCEDURE

1. Pour about 15 mL (1 oz) of euglena culture into a straight-sided glass jar. Add spring water or filtered pond water to fill the jar to the top. Screw on the cap lightly; do not tighten. Observe the euglena and record their appearance in your notebook.
2. Use a scalpel to cut a strip of black construction paper. Make the strip the same height as the jar and long enough to wrap around the jar once, with the ends slightly overlapping (see Figure 1.3).
3. Choose a geometric shape, a letter of the alphabet, or other interesting design that is about 2 cm (1 in.) in diameter. Cut the design out of the center of the strip. (Place the black strip on a flat cutting surface and cut out the design using the scalpel.)
4. Wrap the construction paper around the jar and secure it with a rubber band.
5. Place the jar in a well-lit location so that the cut-out design is facing the light.
6. **STOP & THINK** What do you hope to find out about euglena by carrying out these steps? (That is, what question is being asked in this experiment?)
7. **STOP & THINK** Scientists often create a hypothesis to help plan an experiment. A **hypothesis** is an opinion or guess as to the probable answer to a question. In formulating a hypothesis, scientists rely on prior knowledge, observations, and experience. Some call this an "educated guess." Once a hypothesis is made, an experiment can be designed to determine whether the hypothesis is reasonable and correct. For example, an investigator may pose the question, "What resources do plants require in

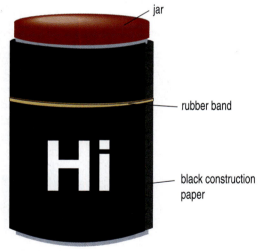

jar

rubber band

black construction paper

Figure 1.3

Setup for euglena experiment.

SAFETY NOTE

Do not allow the jar to overheat.

order to sustain life?" A hypothesis would then state, "Plants require sunlight, water, and air in order to sustain life." The investigator then designs an experiment or experiments to test this hypothesis. The experimental design is generally framed as, "If I do this (remove light, for example), then that (expected result) should happen." Create a hypothesis about the experiment you just set up. Base your hypothesis on your observations of euglena, your understanding of resources, and your prior knowledge.

8. Obtain a second, smaller sample of euglena for microscopic examination. Prepare a wet-mount slide as follows:

a. Using an eyedropper, place 1 drop of the culture in the middle of a microscope slide.

b. Place one edge of a coverslip on the slide near the specimen. Carefully lower the coverslip slowly over the specimen using a dissecting needle or other support (see Figure 1.4). (Do not drop the coverslip on top.)

c. Remove any excess fluid by touching the edge of a paper towel to the outer edge of the liquid under the coverslip. The coverslip should lie flat on the microscope slide. Press gently on the coverslip to remove any air bubbles.

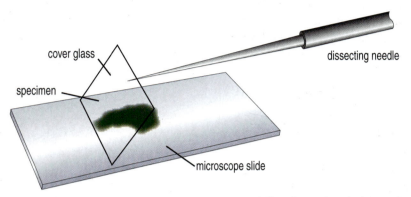

Figure 1.4

Preparation of microscope wet-mount slide.

9. Carefully place the slide on the center of the microscope stage. Observe the euglena under different powers of magnification.

10. Draw or describe any features of euglena that you observe with the microscope.

11. After making your observations, dispose of your euglena sample in the site designated by your teacher.

12. After 24 hours, pick up your jar setup gently and carefully slide the paper down. Be sure not to disturb the jar's contents. Describe the results of your experiment and respond to the following Analysis questions in your notebook.

ANALYSIS

1. Do the results of the experiment support or contradict the prediction from your hypothesis? Explain your answer.
2. What response have the euglena exhibited? Why do you think they responded this way?
3. What features of euglena enable them to respond in this way?
4. Do you think other organisms would respond the same way? Why or why not?
5. What do you think would happen if you placed the jar in complete darkness overnight? for 2 weeks?

READING

What's Your Response?

All living things have the capacity to react to their environment. Some of these reactions may be so subtle as to be invisible. But others may result in enormous changes in the responding organisms.

This ability to respond to the environment in a controlled way is one of the characteristics of life. When interacting with the world, all organisms must be able to sense and respond to continually changing conditions around them. Drought causes animals to migrate to habitats where water can be found more readily. A sense of danger causes prey to flee from predators. Cooler temperatures and shortening daylight are signals to migratory birds that it is time to move on. And as long as you continue to exhale carbon dioxide, that mosquito will find you for its next meal of blood.

Even *Escherichia coli*, a single-celled bacterium, can respond to changes in its environment. Inside the cell, several proteins continuously monitor the level of nutrients in the surrounding watery environment where the *E. coli* lives. If the nutrient levels remain steady or increase, the bacterium will move about in a random fashion. But when the levels begin to fall, the proteins interact with the flagellum. (The flagellum is the whiplike part of a bacterium that enables it to move.) This interaction causes the *E. coli* to move toward higher concentrations of nutrients.

Dictyostelium discoideum, a slime mold, uses a different strategy. This strategy is connected to the more complex life cycle of the slime mold. As long as nutrients are available and conditions remain constant, the slime mold can exist as a group of independent single-celled organisms called amoebae. When the food supply available to *D. discoideum* begins to dwindle, the cells stop dividing. The individual amoebae then start moving toward one another. Eventually, they clump together to form a sluglike, multicellular structure that moves along the surface of the soil. The slug develops into a new structure, called a fruiting body, that resembles a ball on a stalk. This fruiting body is the amoeba escape vehicle. Cells in the ball at the top of the fruiting body mature into spores, or reproductive cells. Each of these spores is capable of forming a new amoeba. These spores are scattered across the surface of the soil by wind, animals, or rain. In some cases, they end up in more favorable environmental conditions where nutrients are available (see Figure 1.5). The spores then give rise to individual amoebae. These amoebae continue to grow and divide independently of one another, thus continuing the cycle and ensuring the survival of this slime mold through its offspring.

Plants have ways of responding to stimuli in their environment as well. Sometimes plants are mistakenly regarded as nonliving. This happens partly because they do not display responses to their environment as rapidly or visibly as animals do. Animals seem to respond to their environment quickly and decisively. In comparison, trees and flowers may seem inanimate because they appear motionless; yet plants can and do respond to their environment. For example, grass responds to the amount of water in the soil by adjusting the depth of its roots. Infrequent light rain will cause the roots to spread out close to the surface to capture the small amount of moisture. Regular heavy rain, on the other hand, allows grass to sink its roots deeply, as the water penetrates deeper into the soil.

Humans, like most animals, are designed to move in response to detailed awareness of their environment. The bulk of the body is dedicated to sense, reaction, and motion. Cells in our eyes react to light; cells in our ears sense a myriad of sounds. These and other sensory organs provide data that are sent as messages to the brain, which processes these messages (within thousandths of a second). The brain, in turn, sends out signals to other parts of the body, such as to our muscles and organs, to respond appropriately. For example, our sense of smell will guide us to the source of that pizza delivery.

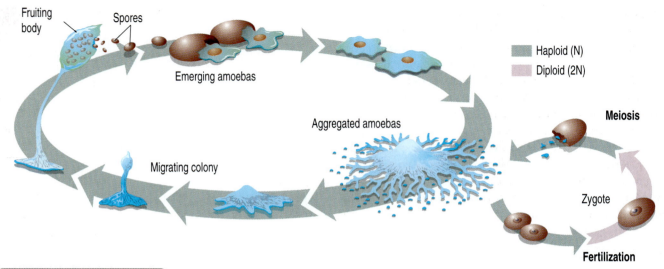

Fruiting body
Spores
Emerging amoebas
Aggregated amoebas
Migrating colony
Meiosis
Zygote
Fertilization

Haploid (N)
Diploid (2N)

Figure 1.5

A slime mold's responses to dwindling resources in the environment.

Organisms respond to their environment for many reasons besides obtaining resources. The responses include three important sets of factors:

- physical factors, which allow the organism to survive and reproduce (for example, level of salinity, pH, temperature, humidity, and type of soil);
- biological factors, which may interact with the organism (for example, predators, parasites, and any competitors for the same resources); and
- behavioral factors, which include the organism's feeding habits and its behavior when interacting with other organisms.

Some plants respond to factors in their environment in observable ways. Have you ever touched a sensitive plant? Heat from your hand causes it to react by folding in its leaves. Tulip petals open wide during the day and then close up each night. Evening primroses on the other hand open at dusk and close again when the hot sun begins to shine on them.

Animals have senses with which they perceive such conditions in their environment as light, sound, smell, temperature, and air. They respond by actively moving toward hospitable environments and away from hostile environments. The striped bass is one example of an animal that requires a specific temperature as an optimal environmental condition. Fish cannot control the temperature of their bodies; instead, they depend on the temperature of the water around them. Their metabolic processes function best at a specific temperature.

Metabolic processes are cellular processes that transform nutrients into the building blocks used to make new biomolecules and generate energy to sustain life. The fish move toward that temperature zone in the water. They sense changes in their environment and move when necessary toward the appropriate temperature (see Figure 1.6).

The ability to respond is a necessary characteristic for survival. That ability alone is not enough to define life. Without it, however, organisms would be unable to get necessary nutrients and resources or to seek out vital environmental conditions.

ANALYSIS

Record your responses to the following in your notebook.

1. What might cause an environment to change? Describe three changes that might alter the availability of resources in an environment.
2. Predict how these changes might affect the survival and behavior of organisms living in that environment. Explain your predictions.
3. How do the other responses described in the reading help an organism to maintain life?
4. Describe the relationship between the response of an organism and the requirements for maintaining life. Base your answer on the results of the experiment Where Is the Light?

Figure 1.6

Adult bass need temperatures below 25°C (77°F) in order to survive. When the sun heats the surface water, the bass move into areas that have more suitable conditions. If these suitable environments become too crowded, the bass may be forced into water that is warmer than they can tolerate, and they die.

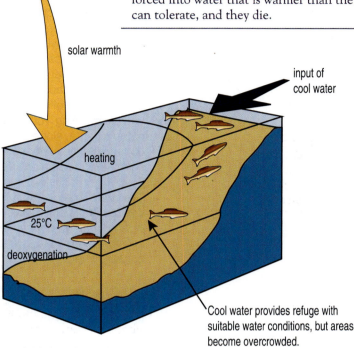

solar warmth

input of cool water

heating

25°C

deoxygenation

Cool water provides refuge with suitable water conditions, but areas become overcrowded.

EXTENDING *Ideas*

Organisms communicate within themselves and with each other in a number of fascinating ways. These include language, sophisticated mating dances, and chemical signaling, for example. These various types of communication allow organisms to communicate, thus enabling them to survive. Investigate methods of communication in more depth by researching one or more of the following:

- the biological basis of social behavior among bees or ants
- the development of language
- the biological basis of pheromones (and their role in human behavior)
- intracellular communication
- hormones
- the nervous system

SC*L*INKS®
NSTA

Topic: Responding to Stimuli
Go to: www.scilinks.org
Code: INBIOH215

CAREER FOCUS

Landscape Architect It's a chilly spring morning. Todd slowly walks through a wooded area, making notes, drawing pictures, and digging his hands into the soil. It's just another day on the job for Todd, a landscape architect hired by Superior Development, a real estate development firm that is building a new housing subdivision. Superior Development has just purchased 20 acres of land in Sunnyvale on which it plans to build 16 houses. Now that Superior Development has obtained all of the necessary permits and government approval for the subdivision, it is time to have Todd come in and assess the landscape architecture. Todd begins by examining the undeveloped land—a hilly, rocky, forested area that needs to be cleared for houses, roads, and utilities. This area will need to be designed to be beautiful as well. It's no small task, but this is what Todd loves to do!

This morning Todd analyzes the natural elements of the site. He makes note of the climate, slope of the land, drainage, and existing trees and shrubs. He observes and maps the land being developed and identifies the shady and sunny areas. He also takes soil samples, which he will send out to be analyzed. All of these tasks provide Todd with the information he needs to help Superior Development successfully build its subdivision. His next step will be to work with the architects, surveyors, and engineers to determine the most effective arrangement of houses and roads. He will also collaborate with environmental scientists, foresters, and other professionals to find the most efficient way to conserve natural resources. Todd's main goal as a landscape architect is to make the best use of the land and respect the needs of the natural environment.

Once these decisions are made and Todd has studied and analyzed the site, he will create detailed plans. These plans will indicate new topography, vegetation, walkways, and other landscaping details such as fountains and decorative features. Todd tries to design areas so that they are not only functional, but also beautiful and compatible with the natural environment. To account for the needs of Superior Development, government regulations, and the conditions at the site, he will probably make lots of changes before a final design is approved. That's just part of his job, and having computer-aided design (CAD) software helps this process tremendously. Sometimes, Todd uses video simulation to help clients envision the proposed ideas and plans. He also uses geographic information systems technology to map the site on his computer. His final proposal to Superior Development will include written reports, sketches, models, photographs, land-use studies, and cost estimates. When the plans are approved, he will prepare working drawings. These drawings will show all existing and proposed features, and outline the methods of construction and materials needed. At that point, Superior Development will take over, and its general contractor will direct the actual construction and installation of plantings.

As a child, Todd enjoyed the outdoors and nature. He loved to draw, but he also found that he was good at building things. He helped his father landscape their yard. After seeing a Japanese garden at a museum, Todd created a similar garden for his mother when he was in high school. As he got older, Todd realized that he just might be able to find a job that would combine his artistic, creative talent with his love for the outdoors.

After researching his options, Todd decided to attend a 4-year college to study landscape architecture. He enrolled in a program accredited by the Landscape Architecture Accreditation Board of the American Society of Landscape Architects. He took courses in surveying, landscape design and construction, urban and regional planning, plant and soil science, geology, mechanical and freehand drawing, management, English composition, and history. What Todd enjoyed most was that his program assigned students to real projects so they could get hands-on experience and make sure landscape architecture was for them. During his senior year of college, Todd interned for a residential development project where he learned firsthand how to organize all of the aspects of landscape architecture on a large-scale project.

Now that Todd is self-employed as a landscape architect, he regularly designs residential projects. Although he spends a lot of time in his office creating plans and designs, preparing models and cost estimates, doing research, and attending meetings, the rest of his time is spent outdoors at the site. Todd feels that his work in landscape architecture allows him to be an artist, scientist, architect, and an engineer, all rolled into one.

Agricultural Scientist

As the hot sun beats down on the vast expanse of the cotton farm, Maria kneels in the field, carefully examining cotton plants and the soil surrounding them. She doesn't have to search long before finding what she is looking for—a budworm. Maria has come to help CottonCorps, the firm that owns the farm, devise a plan for dealing with these cotton-eating pests that can ruin entire crops. Maria works with Duncan, the farm manager. As soon as he knew the cotton was infested, he contacted Maria's company, Agriculture Associates. Agriculture Associates is a biotechnology and genetic engineering corporation that specializes in developing crops that are resistant to pests like the budworm.

Maria and the other agriculture scientists at Agriculture Associates study plants and their growth in various soils. Their research helps farmers cultivate productive crops while conserving natural resources and maintaining the environment. They also study ways to increase the nutritional value of crops, improve seed quality, and develop crops resistant to insects and drought. Maria is a member of the Entomology department at a local university. Here staff members research and develop new technologies to control or eliminate pests in infested areas and prevent the spread of harmful pests to new areas.

In her preliminary meeting with Duncan, Maria suggests an alternative to chemical pesticides, which can be dangerous to the environment and kill off harmless insects in addition to pests. The bacterium *Bacillus thuringiensis,* or Bt, produces a toxin that is deadly to caterpillars like the budworm but is harmless to other insects. The gene for Bt toxin can be transferred from *Bacillus thuringiensis* to cotton. This produces cotton plants that make Bt toxin. These cotton plants can then be crossbred with other varieties. Because the Bt toxin is inside the plant instead of sprayed onto the plant, the only insects it can harm are those that eat the plant.

Maria grew up in a farming community and saw firsthand how a season of bad crops could devastate farmers. She loved spending time outdoors, investigating nature, and especially loved bugs. As a child, she participated in her local 4-H chapter and designed a project to learn about the effects that harmful insects can have on local corn crops. These experiences lead her to consider agriculture science as a career. She attended her state's land-grant college, which offered agricultural science degrees. During her college program, Maria took a variety of technical agricultural science courses as well as courses in communications, mathematics, economics, business, and the physical and life sciences.

Now Maria uses the principles of biology, chemistry, physics, mathematics, and other sciences to solve problems and apply biotechnology advances to agriculture. She spends time in the field conducting research, gathering samples, and collecting insects in their natural habitat. The rest of her time is spent meeting with clients and working in the lab at Agriculture Associates.

Before returning to Agriculture Associates, Maria takes some plant and worm samples from the CottonCorps site. She carefully labels and stores each, so she can further examine the samples when she returns to her lab. With her colleagues in the Entomology department, Maria will develop a detailed plan for the budworm problem CottonCorps is experiencing.

A Comfortable Place

Prologue

You will observe how an earthworm responds to the stimulus of light and then to the stimulus of water in its environment. Afterward, think about additional factors that you believe could cause a response.

Brainstorming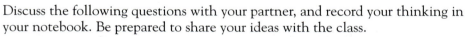

Discuss the following questions with your partner, and record your thinking in your notebook. Be prepared to share your ideas with the class.

1. When was the last time you saw an earthworm? Where can you find earthworms normally?
2. Under what conditions are you more likely to see earthworms on the surface? Why?
3. "It may be doubted whether there are many other creatures which have played so important a part in the history of the world." (Charles Darwin) Why are earthworms beneficial to the environment?

A Comfortable Place

Materials

For each pair of students:

- 1 or more earthworms
- 2 shallow boxes or trays
- 1 sheet black construction paper
- soil
- distilled water
- 1 spray bottle
- 1 ruler

PROCEDURE

Part A

1. Fill 1 shallow box or tray with soil and moisten with the spray bottle. Cover one-half of the box with construction paper and leave the other half exposed (see Figure 1.7).
2. Place a worm in the box at the border between the covered and uncovered parts. Which side do you think it will move toward? Why? Record your prediction and explain your reasoning in your notebook.
3. Continue to observe for 5–10 minutes (or until the worm has noticeably moved). Then record in your notebook where the worm has moved.
4. **STOP & THINK** While waiting for the earthworm to respond, think about other environmental factors (physical, biological, and behavioral) as described in the reading What's Your Response? Write responses to the following questions:

   a. Which factors do you think would have an effect on an earthworm?
   b. How could you set up an experiment that would test one of these factors?
   c. How might the earthworm respond?
   d. What might happen if it did not respond? Why?

Part B

1. Uncover the box from Part A and put aside the construction paper covering.
2. Take the second box and fill it with water. Place it next to the first box (long sides opposite each other). Balance the ruler as a bridge between the boxes and place the worm on the ruler (see Figure 1.8).
   To which environment do you predict the worm will move this time? Why?
3. Observe the worm's behavior again for a few minutes. Record your observations in your notebook.

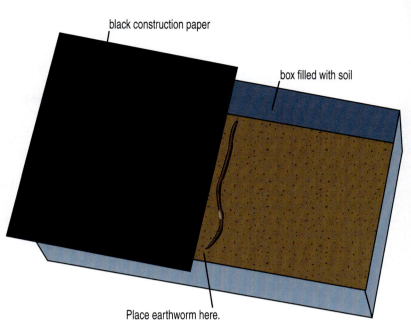

black construction paper

box filled with soil

Place earthworm here.

Figure 1.7

Setup for Part A.

SAFETY NOTE

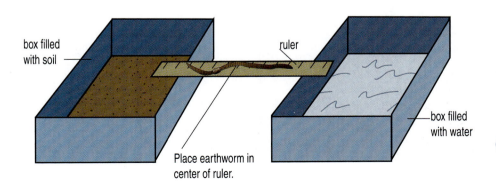

box filled with soil

ruler

box filled with water

Place earthworm in center of ruler.

Figure 1.8

Setup for Part B.

ANALYSIS

Record your responses to the following in your notebook.

1. How did the earthworm respond in Part A? in Part B? How did these responses compare with your predictions?
2. What did the two parts of the experiment tell you about the worm's ability to respond to the environment?
3. What factors in a natural environment could cause stimuli similar to what you simulated here?
4. What strategies do you have for testing additional factors?
5. What might cause factors in an environment to change?
6. What might be the effect on any organisms living in that environment?

Everything Under the Sun

Prologue

What kinds of substances in the environment are essential for life? In Learning Experience 2, you determined that euglena respond to light. What other resources in the environment are required to maintain the characteristics of life in organisms?

In this learning experience, you continue to identify resources that are essential to survival, specifically in the environment of a plant. Then you explore how a plant uses these resources.

Brainstorming

Discuss the following questions with your partner, and record your thinking in your notebook. Be prepared to share your ideas with the class. You will use the words and ideas discussed in class to construct a concept map. Your concept map will illustrate the resources plants require and how the resources might be obtained and used.

1. What kinds of resources do you think plants require to maintain the characteristics of life?
2. How do you think plants use each of these resources?
3. How do plants take in these resources from their environment?

TASK

1. Working with a partner, use the words identified in the class discussion to create a concept map. Identify which concept is the main idea. Decide how to group the remaining ideas based on how they relate to one another.
2. Pick linking words for the map that define the relationships between the concepts. Linking words should not be concepts themselves.
3. Start constructing a map by branching one or two general ideas from the main concept. Add other, more specific concepts to the general ones as the map progresses.

4. Enclose each of the concepts in a box or circle. Use lines to connect the concepts. Write a linking word on the line that tells why the concepts are connected.
5. Look for opportunities to draw cross-linkages to connect concepts from different branches of the map.
6. Be prepared to discuss your map with the class.

ACTIVITY

You Light Up My Life

You will use radish plants to investigate the resource requirements of a plant and to find out what happens if a plant does not obtain the resources it needs. You then use this information to examine the biochemical processes by which a plant obtains what it needs for survival.

What happens within a plant when it obtains the resources it requires? You may have already studied or examined photosynthesis in other classes. **Photosynthesis** is the process in which plants use the resources of sunlight, carbon dioxide (CO_2), and water (H_2O) to fulfill their needs for energy and food. The components of the word refer to its functions: "photo" means light, and "synthesis" means putting together.

What structural components of a plant are important in obtaining and using resources? Look at the drawing of a plant in Figure 1.9. Below the soil surface, a highly branched root system brings in water and minerals from the soil and anchors the plant in the ground. The stem contains a system of tubes that begins in the root and runs all the way to the top of the plant. One set of tubes (**xylem**) in the stem conducts water and dissolved materials drawn from the soil up to the leaves (Figure 1.10). Another set of tubes (**phloem**) in the stem transports sugars, the products of photosynthesis, and other molecules throughout the plant.

The leaf is the major site of photosynthetic activity (see Figure 1.11). Carbon dioxide enters the leaf through tiny holes in the leaf's surface called **stomata**. Water travels from the roots through the stem and enters the leaf. Special cells in the leaf can absorb energy from the sun using a molecule called **chlorophyll**. The water, carbon dioxide, and energy from the sun (**solar energy**) are all essential components in the photosynthetic reaction. They come together in special cells in the leaf. As you work with your radish plants, be sure to think about the relationship between the plant parts and the resources the plant needs.

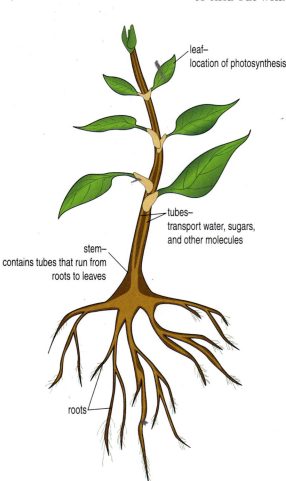

leaf–
location of photosynthesis

tubes–
transport water, sugars, and other molecules

stem–
contains tubes that run from roots to leaves

roots

Figure 1.9

A plant's structure enables it to take up resources.

Figure 1.10

The cross section of a stem showing the phloem and xylem.
© Clouds Hill Imaging Ltd./ Corbis

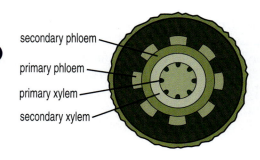

secondary phloem

primary phloem

primary xylem

secondary xylem

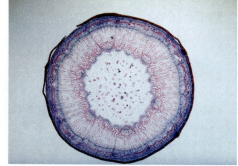

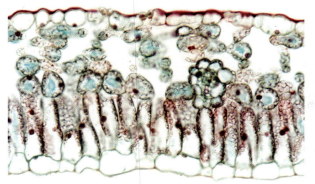
© Brad Mogen/Visuals Unlimited

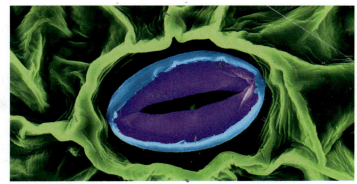
© Dr. Dennis Kunkel/Visuals Unlimited

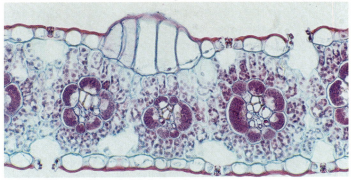
© Ken Wagner/Visuals Unlimited

Figure 1.11

Cross sections of a leaf showing stomata, phloem, xylem, and chlorophyll-containing cells (palisade mesophyll).

Materials

For each group of four students:

- 4 small pots of radish plants, each grown under one of these conditions:
  - in the light, under normal conditions
  - in the dark, under otherwise normal conditions
  - in a closed environment, under otherwise normal conditions
  - in a closed environment in the absence of carbon dioxide (CO_2)
- 4 safety goggles
- iodine solution
- 4 petri dishes
- 1 scalpel or utility knife
- 1 forceps or tweezers
- 1 beaker of distilled water
- 1 wax marking pencil

For the class:

- 4 plant pots, 5–8 cm (2–3 in.)
- potting soil
- 1 pkg radish seeds
- jars/beakers to cover plants and pots
- trays
- chart paper
- 2 boiling water baths

Topic: Plant Adaptations
Go to: www.scilinks.org
Code: INBIOH223

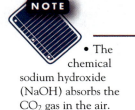

Sodium hydroxide can burn your skin. If it comes in contact with skin or clothing, rinse well with water.

NOTE

• The chemical sodium hydroxide (NaOH) absorbs the CO_2 gas in the air. Most of the CO_2 can be removed from the air by growing a plant in a closed system in the presence of NaOH.
• In your notebook, define the questions being asked in this experiment and your hypothesis.

• Boiling water can cause burns. Ethyl alcohol can catch fire.
• Iodine stains and is a poison. Be sure to clean any spills thoroughly and avoid contact with skin and clothing.

• 100 mL hot 95% ethyl alcohol
• 1 beaker (1000-mL) filled with tap water
• 100 g sodium hydroxide (flakes or pellets)
• medicine cups
• 1 beaker (1000-mL) for waste iodine

PROCEDURE

1. **STOP & THINK** At the beginning of this unit, you or your teacher germinated radish seeds under the following conditions:
    • in the presence of light, air, soil, and water
    • in the presence of air, soil, and water; in the absence of light
    • in the presence of light, air, soil, and water (in a closed environment)
    • in the presence of light, air, soil, and water; in the absence of CO_2 in the air (in a closed environment)
2. Compare the characteristics of the plants in each pot. Include height, color, ability to grow, and any other characteristics you may notice.
3. Label each of 4 petri dishes for one of the following: "light," "dark," "closed normal," or "closed no CO_2."
4. Take 1 leaf from a plant in each pot.
5. Identify each leaf you removed by notching it with a scalpel or knife. (For example, use no notches for those grown under normal conditions, 1 notch for those grown in the absence of CO_2, etc.) Be sure to record in your notebook how you marked each leaf (see Figure 1.12).
6. Immerse each leaf in boiling water for approximately 1 minute. Remove from boiling water with forceps.
7. Remove the pigments (chlorophyll and others) by immersing each leaf in hot 95% ethyl alcohol.
8. When most of the pigment (color) has been removed, use forceps to remove the leaf from the hot alcohol. Dip each leaf in hot water again for a few seconds. This will keep the leaf from becoming brittle.
9. Place each leaf in the proper petri dish and cover with iodine solution. Allow leaves to sit for a few minutes. Iodine is used to detect the presence of starch. Starch is a carbohydrate that is an essential substance found in all living things. Iodine changes from brown to black or blue black in the presence of starch.

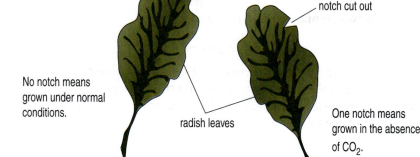

No notch means grown under normal conditions.

radish leaves

notch cut out

One notch means grown in the absence of CO_2.

Figure 1.12

Notching the leaves for identification.

10. Remove each leaf with forceps and dip it into the beaker of clear tap water to rinse it. Pour iodine into the designated iodine waste beaker. Rinse out the petri dish to remove any remaining iodine solution.
11. Place each leaf back in its petri dish.
12. Compare the staining of each leaf. Record in words and drawings what you observe.

NALYSIS

You may wish to discuss with your group the responses to the Analysis questions.

1. Prepare a laboratory report for this experiment in your notebook. Be sure to include the following:
   a. the questions being asked;
   b. your hypothesis;
   c. the experimental design, or how the experiment was set up;
   d. the data or observations you made; and
   e. the analysis and conclusions (include your responses to the Analysis questions that follow).
2. In an experimental design, the condition to be tested is a **variable**. That is, every condition in the experiment is held the same, or constant, except one—the variable. What was the variable in each of the experiments in the activity You Light Up My Life? What were the conditions that were held constant?
3. The experiment in which the effect of CO_2 was measured needed to be designed as a closed system. What is meant by a "closed system"? What would have happened if the system had not been closed?
4. In addition to having only one variable, a good experiment will also have a **positive control** or samples in which the outcome is known because there is no variable. Which plants served as your positive control? That is, which plants had all the appropriate resources? Which could be considered as having been grown under the best conditions regarding resources?
5. What do you think would eventually happen to the plants growing in the dark? to those growing without carbon dioxide? State your reasons.
6. Based on the experimental design, describe how you know starch is a product of photosynthesis. What would happen to those plants that were unable to synthesize starch?
7. A **chemical reaction** takes place when the interaction of two or more substances results in the formation of a different substance or substances. The new substances have different physical and chemical properties than the starting substances. Chemical reactions are often expressed as an equation. For example, the reaction that results in water can be expressed as the joining of two components to form a third:

$$\textbf{oxygen + hydrogen} \rightarrow \textbf{water}$$

Write a word equation based on what you have observed in this activity. Your word equation should describe what you think happens when plants are grown under appropriate environmental conditions with all the necessary resources for photosynthesis.

READING

How Does Your Garden Grow?

How do plants get what they need to survive? This question has intrigued people for centuries. Speculations about plants and their feeding habits have given rise to many stories; one such story follows.

> On the island of Madagascar, off the east coast of Africa, the natives tell of a strange tree. This tree is an eater of meat, so they say—human meat. The person who ventures too close to the tree is seized by the tree's long branches and imprisoned. The branches wrap themselves so tightly around the victim that no matter how hard he or she struggles, the trap holds fast. Then slowly, but with great strength, the tree pulls its victim into its hollow center. There the body is digested, except for the bones, and the tree is nourished until another victim comes along.

> From *Plants that Eat Insects: A Look at Carnivorous Plants* by Anabel Dean. Copyright 1977 by Lerner Publications Company, a division of Lerner Publishing Group. Used by permission. All rights reserved.

In the following article, Isaac Asimov, scientist and writer of science fiction, asks this question in greater detail. He presents one possible hypothesis based on an experiment carried out in the 1600s.

> Plants somehow supply the food. It must, somehow, come from somewhere. It can't really form "out of nothing." [Plants require soil, water, air, and sunlight to grow. How does a plant take these substances and use them?] . . .

> The man who had the thought [to find out] was Jan Baptiste van Helmont, an alchemist and physician of the Low Countries, who lived and worked in territory that is now Belgium, but was then part of the Spanish monarchy.

> Van Helmont had the notion that water was the fundamental substance of the universe (as, in fact, certain ancient Greek philosophers had maintained). If so, everything was really water, and substances that didn't look like water were nevertheless water that had merely changed its form in some fashion. For instance, water was necessary to plant life. Could it be then, that, unlikely as it might seem on the surface, plant tissue was formed out of water, rather than out of soil? Why not try and see?

> In 1648, van Helmont concluded his great experiment, great not only because it produced interesting and even crucial results, but because it was the first quantitative experiment ever conducted that involved a living organism. It was the first biological experiment . . . in which substances were weighed accurately and the carefully noted changes in weights supplied the answer being sought.

> Van Helmont had begun by transplanting a shoot of a young willow tree into a large bucket of soil. He weighed the willow tree and the soil separately. Now if the willow tree formed its tissues by absorbing substances from the soil, then, as the willow tree gained weight, the soil would lose weight. Van Helmont carefully kept the soil covered so that no materials could fall into the bucket and confuse the manner in which the soil lost that weight.

> Naturally, van Helmont had to water the willow tree; it wouldn't grow otherwise [see Figure 1.13].

> For five years, van Helmont watered his tree with rainwater. It grew and flourished and at the end of the time, he carefully removed it from the bucket, knocked the soil from its roots and weighed it. In five years of growing, the willow tree had added 164 pounds to its weight.

> Very good! Now to weigh the soil after it had been dried. Had it lost 164 pounds to the tree? Not at all. It had lost only two ounces!

willow tree

willow shoot

soil covered

1643

1648

Figure 1.13

Van Helmont's tree.

The willow tree had gained a great deal of weight—but not from the soil. What was the only other substance that made contact with the willow tree, van Helmont asked himself. The answer was: Water.

From this, he deduced that it was from water that the plant drew its substance, not from the soil. He used the results of this experiment to argue that water was indeed the fundamental substance of the universe, since if it could change to plant tissue it could surely change to anything else as well.

Excerpted from *Photosynthesis* by Isaac Asimov. Copyright © 1968 by Isaac Asimov. Reprinted by permission of BasicBooks, a member of Perseus Books, L.L.C.

ANALYSIS

Record your responses to the following in your notebook.

1. What question did van Helmont set out to investigate in his experiment?
2. Was van Helmont's experimental design a good one (based on what was known at the time)? Why or why not?
3. What conclusion did van Helmont reach about what constituted food for plants? Was his conclusion valid based on the data he collected? Why or why not?
4. How do van Helmont's conclusions compare to the conclusions you reached in your plant experiment? Are they the same, different, or unrelated? Explain.
5. Redesign van Helmont's experiment and predict the results.

Sunlight Becomes You

READING

What does sunlight provide for a plant? How does a plant use CO_2? What is "starch" and why does the plant need it?

The sunlight and air that a plant needs are used in the process of photosynthesis to generate food for a plant. **Food** is any substance that provides

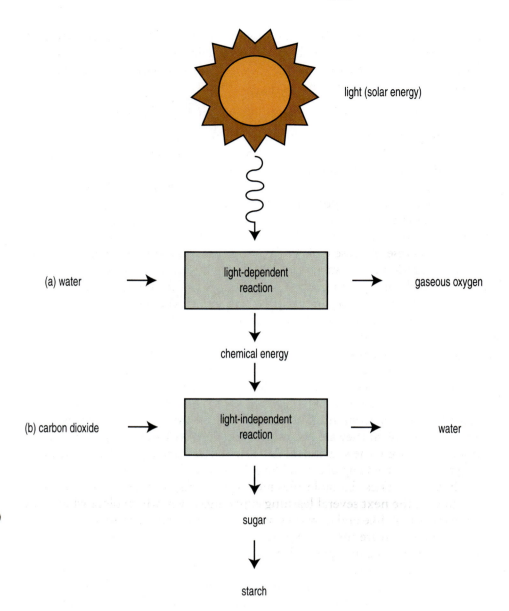

light (solar energy)

(a) water → | light-dependent reaction | → gaseous oxygen

chemical energy

(b) carbon dioxide → | light-independent reaction | → water

sugar

starch

Figure 1.14

Two related processes of photosynthesis: the "light-dependent" and "light-independent" reactions.

building blocks and energy for organisms. An example of food for a plant is the starch that you measured in the activity You Light Up My Life. The process of photosynthesis can actually be separated into two related biochemical processes. One process depends on the presence of light; the other can take place in the absence of light (see Figure 1.14). During the light-dependent reaction, energy in sunlight (solar energy) is absorbed by chlorophyll. Chlorophyll is the green pigment that gives plants their characteristic color. The chlorophyll, in turn, transfers this solar energy to another molecule. This molecule stores the solar energy as chemical energy.

The chemical energy obtained during the light-dependent part of photosynthesis (called the "light-dependent") is then used in the light-independent process (called the "light-independent"). During this process, the atoms in carbon dioxide and water are rearranged to form new molecules of sugar. Sugar is the substance that makes up starch. The sugar molecule contains carbon, oxygen, and hydrogen atoms; all of these were originally found in the carbon dioxide and water. In addition to sugar, this reaction also generates water and oxygen. The water and oxygen are formed from the hydrogen and oxygen atoms of the original water and carbon dioxide. The sugar molecule also contains chemical energy in the bonds between the atoms. Thus, the sugar molecule becomes the primary source of both energy and building materials for the plant.

The word equation that you created during the analysis of your experiment can now be converted into a chemical equation:

$$12\ H_2O + 6\ CO_2 + energy \rightarrow C_6H_{12}O_6 + 6\ H_2O + 6O_2$$

Plants require energy and building materials to carry out the processes of living. By the process of photosynthesis, plants obtain the nutrients and energy to grow, to respond to their environment, and to repair and maintain themselves. Without any one of the resources used in photosynthesis—air, water, sunlight—plants will "starve" to death. What happens to these molecules of $C_6H_{12}O_6$ sugar in the plant? Some of them remain as simple sugars such as fructose or glucose. Glucose, or grape sugar, gives that fruit its distinctly sugary taste. Another abundant sugar in plants is sucrose. Sucrose is also called table sugar or cane sugar because of its high concentration in the stems (canes) of plants, such as the sugar cane plant. Sucrose is synthesized when fructose and glucose are joined together to form a molecule containing two separate sugar molecules (**disaccharide**). Sucrose is the major sugar that is transported throughout a plant. It is the starting material for many other molecules in the plant.

Sugar molecules can also join together as links in long chains called **polysaccharides**. The starch that you tested for in the activity You Light Up My Life is an example of a polysaccharide. **Starch** consists of many glucose molecules joined together. Starch serves as food storage for the plant; when food is needed, the starch is broken down into simple sugars. The sugars can then be transported wherever in the plant they are needed as building blocks and energy sources.

Some sugars form the starting materials for other large molecules in the plant. Living things are made up of several large **biomolecules** in addition to sugars (carbohydrates). These biomolecules include proteins, lipids, nucleic acids, and fatty acids. In the next several learning experiences, you will explore what these biomolecules look like and how they are formed in living organisms.

Sugar and starch are the initial products of photosynthesis. They are produced in the cells that make up a plant's leaves. As described earlier in this learning experience, carbon dioxide from the air enters the leaf through tiny holes called stomata. The stomata also allow release of oxygen back to the environment. Oxygen is one of the by-products of photosynthesis. In the leaf cells surrounding the stomata, the interaction of carbon dioxide, water, and light forms sugars. (The water is brought to the leaf through the stem, and light energy is absorbed by the green pigment chlorophyll.) These sugars are transported through phloem in the stem to parts of the plant where they are needed. Some of the sugar is stored in the cells. Here it is converted into starch as a stored source of energy and building blocks.

All the nutritional needs of the plant are met between the photosynthetic activities of the leaf and the absorbing activities of the root (which bring in minerals needed by the plant from the soil). And by using these processes, plants can meet most of the nutritional needs of the rest of the living world.

 **NALYSIS**

Record your responses to the following in your notebook.

1. Concept maps have a number of uses. For example, you can use a concept map to analyze reading materials. Create a concept map from the reading "Sunlight Becomes You." Your map should show how photosynthesis takes

place and how its products enable a plant to survive and maintain the characteristics of life. Include the following terms: photosynthesis, plants, sunlight, energy, chlorophyll, carbon dioxide, water, sugar, starch, leaf, stem, oxygen, root, biomolecules. (Use additional terms from the reading as you need them.) Place each term in a circle and join the circles with linking words.

2. How might the plant and other organisms use the products of photosynthesis? Add these ideas to your map.

EXTENDING *Ideas*

- Hydroponics is a method for growing plants and crops in the absence of soil. Research hydroponics and describe how this method can supply all the resources that plants need. Describe why some agriculturists might choose this method over more conventional methods.

- If you have access to the Logal software program *Biology Explorer: Photosynthesis,* design and conduct your own extension of van Helmont's research.

- During the Vietnam War, defoliating agents were used as a form of warfare. These agents were designed to destroy plant life in areas where they were used. Research the nature of the defoliating agents and how they worked. Explain why this form of warfare was considered effective by some, inhumane by others. Base your explanation on your understanding of the role of photosynthesis in life.

- The Wetlands Protection Act limits actions such as cutting down trees in wetlands areas. Describe what would happen to the populations of smaller plants living under trees that were removed. Explain your predictions. If you have access to the Logal software program *Biology Explorer: Photosynthesis,* use the Independent Exploration "Sun and Shade Plants" to help you investigate the light requirements of different plants. Similarly, the Independent Exploration "Delicate Balance" may be helpful. This activity focuses on different levels of water availability and humidity.

- Changing climatic conditions alter the growth of plants. Explain how higher temperatures and greater concentrations of carbon dioxide influence the growth of plants and oxygen levels in the atmosphere. If you have access to the Logal software program *Biology Explorer: Photosynthesis,* use the Independent Exploration "Origin of Fossil Fuels" to help you investigate the role of climate in plant growth.

CAREER FOCUS

Landscaper and Grounds Manager   Devin checks his clipboard one last time before heading out with his crew. They have a busy day ahead of them. They have appointments at eight different homes in the Lakeland area to landscape residential grounds. Projects for the day include planting new shrubs, spreading mulch, and mowing and fertilizing grass. The crew will also plant a decorative flower garden and consult with a client about building a new front walkway.

It's mid-July and Devin is in the middle of his busiest season as a landscaper. Landscaping is a seasonal business, with steady work in the spring, summer, and fall. In the winter, Devin tries to keep busy by clearing snow from walkways and parking lots. Devin's landscaping business has boomed since he started 4 years ago. He's found that there is a lot of demand for residential landscapers, because many two-income families are too busy to landscape their yards.

After Devin graduated from high school, he wanted a career that combined his love of the outdoors and being physically active. So he found a job with a landscaper in Lakeland. His supervisor trained him to operate the mowers, trimmers, leaf blowers, and tractors, and to follow safety procedures and proper planting procedures. But Devin was also interested in the business end of landscaping. He discovered that most supervisors and owners have a formal education beyond high school. So he decided to go back to school for his associate's degree. He took courses in landscape maintenance and design, horticulture, botany, accounting, and English. That experience gave Devin the background he needed to start his own business.

Now Devin is self-employed, providing landscape maintenance directly to customers on a contract basis. Although the vast majority of his time is spent at the site, he does have to manage all of the accounting and billing for his business, which includes sending invoices and tracking payments. Someday Devin would like to become a Certified Landscape Professional. He can achieve his goal by taking an exam offered by the Associated Landscape Contractors of America (ALCA) and meeting certain education and experience standards.

At the end of the day, Devin checks off the last house on his list. He sends his crew home and heads to his home office to take care of the accounting. Completing some paperwork is actually a nice change after a tiring day of physically demanding work.

Botanist
Hannah uses DNA analyses to determine the evolutionary relationships of the cinchona tree. She conducts these tests to ensure that the tree's species name accurately reflects its genetic makeup. The cinchona tree is relatively well known for its use in making quinine sulfate to prevent malaria. But surprisingly little is known about where cinchonas fit in the evolutionary scheme. Hannah is on a mission to change that. Hannah works at a world-class botanic garden. Her work is similar to putting the pieces of a jigsaw puzzle together. She determines how different cinchona species evolved and their degree of relatedness. Because several species of cinchona trees exist, this is no easy task.

Traditionally, scientists used morphology or physical attributes, like leaf shape and texture, to classify plants. But for more useful and accurate classifications, Hannah compares their DNA sequences. The higher the number of base-sequence matches, the closer the evolutionary relationship. Hannah sees herself as an explorer. Knowing she is one of the first people to sequence a gene or a particular stretch of DNA energizes her. She feels privileged to be involved in such important and interesting work. Hannah's work as a botanist allows her to pose questions and find the answers.

Hannah comes from a family of avid gardeners. From an early age, she was fascinated by the life story of plants—how and why they grow from a seed to a mature plant. She found that a career in botany would combine her interest in plants with science. Hannah attended a 4-year college to get her bachelor's degree in plant biology. She then went on to get her master's degree in botany. Her classes focused on biology, math, chemistry, and physics. But she's also found her coursework in English, Latin, and history to be invaluable in her day-to-day work.

Hannah's day not only consists of research in the botanical lab, but she also helps run the lab. This involves doing the associated administrative tasks, such as ordering chemicals and equipment. She also does a lot of writing, including research papers, reports, and grant proposals.

To date, Hannah's research has uncovered the fact that one cinchona species is actually two distinct species. This finding will help scientists who are working with cinchona trees to assess their medicinal properties to treat malaria, which could potentially save lives. Ensuring that the name of a plant reflects its genetic makeup can have a huge impact on the production of pharmaceutical products such as quinine.

Learning Experience 4

Feeding Frenzy

Prologue

Why do we eat? Why do we eat what we eat? Using only air, sunlight, water, and a dash of minerals and vitamins, plants and other photosynthetic organisms can obtain all of the energy and manufacture all the materials they need to maintain the characteristics of life. Animals, however, are not so independent. They depend on plants to supply them with many of the resources required to sustain life. Animals may eat other animals, but every food chain originates with plants.

The sugars and other carbohydrates that plants synthesize serve as the source of energy and building blocks (that is, food) for the plant. Organisms that do not carry out photosynthesis must obtain all their nutritional needs by eating photosynthesizing organisms (plants) and other organisms. This allows them to obtain the building blocks and energy necessary to maintain the characteristics of life.

In the words of Isaac Asimov:

> If animals are to stay alive, then, they must find some source of food which doesn't have to eat, but which can produce its tissue substances seemingly "out of nothing."

> This would seem an impossibility (if we didn't know the answer in advance) but it isn't. The answer is plant life. All animals eat plants, or other animals that have eaten plants, or other animals that have eaten animals that have eaten plants, and so on. In the end, it all comes back to plants.

Excerpted from *Photosynthesis* by Isaac Asimov. Copyright © 1968 by Isaac Asimov. Reprinted by permission of BasicBooks, a member of Perseus Books, L.L.C.

SCLINKS®
NSTA

Topic: Food Chain/
Food Web
Go to: www.sclinks.org
Code: INBIOH233

Brainstorming

Discuss the following questions with your partner, and record your thinking in your notebook. Be prepared to share your ideas with the class.

1. What is a nutrient? Name some nutrients that you are familiar with.
2. What is meant by an **essential nutrient**?

3. What factors might influence the choices people make when deciding what to eat?
4. Do you think that a diet without meat can provide the same essential nutrients as a diet with meat? Explain your answer.

TASK

Your teacher will distribute nutrition labels. With your partner, examine the label and discuss the following questions.

1. What kind of information does this label give you?
2. Why do you think the government requires food packers to put these labels on food?
3. What does Percent Daily Value mean?
4. Which of the nutrients listed do you think are most important for maintaining good health? Explain your answers.
5. How do you think food producers and manufacturers determine what is in their products?

TASK

Imagine that aliens from another planet exploded a bomb containing an herbicide on the surface of Earth. The bomb extinguished all forms of plant life. Write a news article or create a series of drawings that explain the consequences of such an event to animal life on Earth.

ACTIVITY

What Am I Eating, Anyway?

Different cultures around the world have developed an assortment of diets that reflect their agricultural conditions, customs, and tastes. As different as they may seem at first glance, most of these diets supply the same nutritional requirements needed by humans to sustain life. What are these nutritional requirements? How can such different food sources as beef, rice, beans, insects, and vegetables all supply them?

How can we determine whether foods that seem so different in appearance are actually made up of the same or different components? In this activity, you will identify some of the components of food that are required to sustain life. These components that make up food are called **nutrients**. A nutrient is considered essential when it cannot be synthesized by the organism but must be obtained by the organism from its environment.

You will be using **indicators** as chemical detection tools to find out what nutrients are present in foods. Indicators are chemical compounds used to detect the presence of other compounds. Detection is based on observing a chemical change that is taking place. The substance being detected and the indicator together are involved in a chemical reaction that brings an observable change. Most often, this is a change in color.

Materials

For each group of four students:

- 4 safety goggles
- 4 pairs of disposable gloves (optional)
- 20 test tubes

- 1 test-tube clamp
- 1 test-tube rack
- 1 clean eyedropper
- 1 glass stirring rod
- distilled water in a beaker
- 1 wax marking pencil
- 3 food samples (or more if available)
- 3 beakers (250-mL)
- 1 small bottle Benedict's solution
- 1 small bottle iodine
- 1 small bottle Biuret reagent
- 1 small bottle Sudan III or IV reagent (or brown paper)
- forks
- plastic containers or mortar and pestle
- 1 graduated cylinder (50-mL) (optional)

For the class:

- positive test controls for
  - sugar
  - starch
  - protein
  - lipid
- boiling water bath
- blender (optional)

Pre-laboratory Analysis

Read the laboratory procedure carefully, and record your responses to the following in your notebook.

1. How would you go about finding out which nutrients foods have in common?
2. What do indicators tell us?
3. Before you do the experiment, in what ways are you treating the food? Why?
4. How will you know that each indicator has worked?
5. What is the positive control in this experiment? What is its purpose?
6. What is the **negative control** in this experiment? What is its purpose?

PROCEDURE

1. **STOP & THINK** Collect your group's food samples. Predict which nutrients are present in each sample you are about to test. Record your predictions in your notebook.
2. Set up 4 test tubes. With a wax marking pencil, label all 4 tubes with a minus sign (to indicate negative control). Then label each with one of the following indicator solutions:
   - sugar
   - starch
   - protein
   - lipid
3. After labeling the test tubes, place them in a test-tube rack.
4. Using an eyedropper, place 15 drops of each indicator in the appropriately labeled test tube (see Table 1.1). Be sure to rinse the eyedropper between

SAFETY NOTE

Biuret solution can burn your skin. If it comes in contact with skin or clothing, rinse thoroughly with water.

Table 1.1 Key for Nutrient Indicators	
Nutrient	**Solution**
sugar	Benedict's solution
starch	iodine solution
protein	Biuret solution
lipid	Sudan III (or IV) solution

NOTE

Known standards give you an opportunity to make sure indicators are working properly. Obtaining negative results with standard solutions can alert you to possible problems with the indicators.

solutions to reduce contamination. To rinse, draw water from one beaker into the dropper; then squirt the water into a second beaker. Repeat 2 or 3 times for a thorough rinse.

5. Add 15 drops of water to each test tube. These are the negative test controls.

6. Obtain 3 more sets of 4 test tubes. You will use these to identify the food nutrients in each food sample.
   a. Label the set 1 tubes as follows: 1/sugar, 1/starch, 1/protein, 1/lipid.
   b. Label set 2 as follows: 2/sugar, 2/starch, 2/protein, 2/lipid.
   c. Continue to label the tubes in this way and place them in your rack.

7. Obtain 4 more test tubes. Label them to indicate positive controls as follows:
   + sugar
   + starch
   + protein
   + lipid
   Place these test tubes in your rack. Be sure to have all the same indicators in one row. Start with the negative control at one end and finish with the positive control at the other end of the row. The samples to be tested should be in between (see Figure 1.15).

8. Record the name of each sample in your notebook. Assign each sample a number from 1 through 3. Copy Figure 1.15 into your notebook.

9. Take food sample 1 and mash, blend, or dissolve it in enough water to make it liquid. Use the glass rod to mash or crush the food (or mix it in a blender). Add about 10–20 drops of water, then stir with the glass rod. Place small amounts into each of the set 1 test tubes. Repeat with your second and third food samples. Add them to set 2 and set 3 test tubes respectively.

10. Obtain from your teacher the positive test controls—sugar, starch, protein, and lipid. Add 15 drops of each to the appropriately labeled tubes. Be sure that, if you are using the same eyedropper, you rinse it thoroughly in water between taking samples. The positive controls are your known standards. Because you know which nutrient each is composed of, the controls can be used to determine what a positive test for each indicator looks like. Chemical changes in indicator testing are not always obvious. So it is important to become familiar with exactly what a positive test looks like. In that way, you can be informed and experienced when you begin testing unknowns.

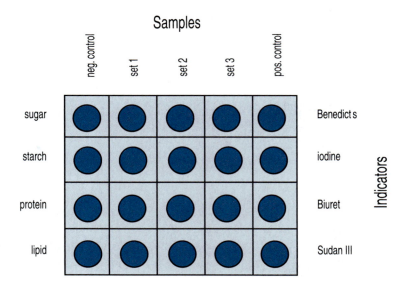

Figure 1.15

Test-tube setup for nutrient analysis test.

11. **STOP & THINK** Why is it important that you prepare your negative controls first and your positive controls last? Record your response in your notebook.

12. You are now ready to perform the first of your 4 indicator tests.
    a. Add 15 drops of Benedict's solution to each of the 3 tubes labeled "sugar." Benedict's indicates the presence of sugars (or simple carbohydrates). When you add your indicator to each tube, be careful not to touch the side of the test tube with the eyedropper. Hold the dropper over the tube mouth and let the drops "free fall" into the tube. After adding the indicator, give each tube a gentle tap with your forefinger to mix.
    b. Heat the tubes in a boiling water bath for 5 minutes without disturbing. (You may continue with the other tests using this same procedure while waiting for this test.) Use a test-tube clamp to lift the test tubes out of the boiling water bath in order to examine the contents (see Figure 1.16).
    c. Compare your results with the positive and negative test controls. Describe the results in your notebook.

13. Add 15 drops of iodine solution to each of the 3 test tubes labeled "starch." Examine the contents of each tube. Compare your results with the positive and negative test controls. Describe the results in your notebook. Is it positive or negative for that nutrient?

14. Add 15 drops of Biuret solution to each of the 3 test tubes labeled "protein." Examine the contents of each tube. Compare your results with the positive and negative test controls. Describe the results in your notebook.

15. Add 5 drops of Sudan III or IV to each of the 3 test tubes labeled "lipid." Examine the contents of each tube. Sudan III and IV indicate the presence of lipids (**fats**). Compare your results with the positive and negative test controls. Describe the results in your notebook.

NOTE
• For easier observation, you may want to hold the test tubes in front of a sheet of white paper.
• Be sure to rinse the eyedropper between your test of each solution.

SAFETY NOTE
Hot plates and boiling water can cause burns. Handle the test tube clamp carefully to avoid dropping the test tube or splashing the water.

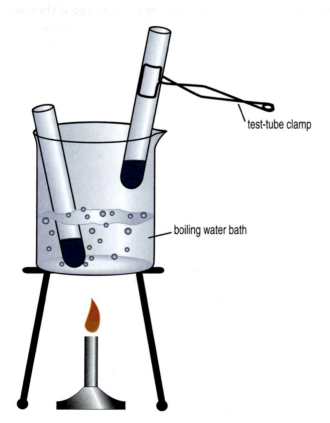

test-tube clamp

boiling water bath

Figure 1.16
Removing test tubes from a boiling water bath.

ANALYSIS

1. Prepare a laboratory report for this experiment in your notebook. Be sure to include the following:
   a. the question being asked and your predictions about the experimental results;
   b. a brief description of the procedure (include how indicators work);
   c. a data table showing the results of your experiment and the observations you recorded;
   d. a discussion (include your responses to the Analysis questions that follow); and
   e. your conclusions (do not repeat data results).
2. Describe any sources of error that might have affected your results.
3. Why was it important to rinse the eyedropper between tests?
4. What function did the negative control serve? the positive control?
5. Did some nutrients appear to be present in greater amounts than other nutrients?
6. Through reading and experimentation, you have identified certain nutrients that are present in food. Create a table listing these nutrients across the top. List the foods you have eaten today along the left side of the table. Decide which nutrient(s) you received from each of the foods you ate and place a check mark in the appropriate column. Base your decisions on the results from the class data about the nutrients in the samples tested and your own knowledge about nutrients. What, if anything, surprises you about your diet?
7. Do you think your diet adequately meets your nutritional requirements? Why or why not?
8. Do you take particular care about what you eat each day? If so, what kinds of food do you try to eat and why?

READING

The Missing Ingredients

Why are we encouraged by parents, teachers, and the U.S. government to eat well-balanced meals? What are these foods providing us? If an organism is to sustain life, it must be able to obtain building blocks and energy from the biomolecules that make up its food. As you have determined, nonphotosynthesizing organisms must obtain from their environment three basic types of nutrients: proteins, carbohydrates, and fats. In addition, they require certain amounts of vitamins and minerals. The following is an account of what happens when an organism, in this case a human, does not get an adequate balance and amount of nutrients.

MADELYN'S STORY

When I was 12, I put myself on a diet. I would drink one glass of powdered skim milk and eat one hard-boiled egg. I would eat an egg because that was a measured amount, and I used to agonize over the size of the egg after awhile. I stayed on that diet for a month and a half—it was my secret. I got a baby-sitting job after school just so that I would not have to eat with my family. If I was not baby-sitting, I was at the library.

I was up all night exercising. I would wear layers of clothes so no one had any idea of what I was doing. If anyone said I looked drawn, haggard, or pale I would redouble my attempt to appear normal, all the time keeping to my 150-Calorie-a-day diet. The next 20 years I spent trying to follow that diet and regain the feeling of control I had while on it.

One night I was dragged to a relative's house for dinner. I remember eating a piece of lettuce and feeling that the whole month and a half was for nothing, that my diet had been ruined. I wanted to kill myself. I felt very out of control. Later I realized that I thought then that my body and what I ate was the only thing I could control, and I was very good at that. As a typical perfectionist I did not want to do what I was not good at . . .

—An excerpt from *Eating Habits and Disorders* by Rachel Epstein, New York, Chelsea House Publishers, 1990

Madelyn was in the process of self-starvation. In drinking only one glass of skim milk and eating one hard-boiled egg, she severely limited her nutrient and Calorie uptake.

What does a person's body do when placed under this form of stress? The body has no way of storing proteins. Even after just one day without protein, the body will begin to break down the protein in nonessential tissues, such as muscles. The body will "recycle" the components for essential functions. Eventually, the body will begin to break down the protein in essential tissues, like the heart or the liver. Serious health problems result.

Carbohydrates are the major source of energy for the body. Studies have indicated that in a healthy diet, 60% of the energy we use should come from carbohydrates. The energy comes from the supply of glucose that the organism has stored as carbohydrate. In plants, the chief energy storage molecule is starch. Many organisms, including humans, use plant starch as a primary source of food. In humans, glucose is stored as **glycogen** in muscle tissue. Many long-distance runners "carbohydrate load" before a long race by eating enormous quantities of pasta. The pasta provides them with a ready source of energy. Carbohydrates also are important in forming structural components of organisms.

Fats form a fundamental part of an organism's structure and function. They are as essential to maintaining life as proteins and carbohydrates. Fats are also a major energy storage form, but the energy in fats is not as readily available as that of carbohydrates. Fats are a member of a class of nutrients called lipids. Hormones, cholesterol, and some vitamins are also members of the lipid family of molecules. **Lipids** form essential structural components of membranes, store and circulate certain vitamins, and store energy in reserve. Without an intake of a certain amount of fat, organisms cannot maintain these important functions.

Weight was the whole focus of my life. I [Madelyn] had been aware of it even before I began dieting. My older sister was very overweight and usually left the dinner table in tears. I felt very guilty about it, but I remember thinking I was glad I had an older sister like her so I would know I should never become that fat, that it was too painful. My older sister had no friends and was ridiculed by my father (Epstein, 1990).

The long-term consequences of Madelyn's disorder (anorexia) are frightening. Madelyn's symptoms show what can happen if appropriate nutrients are missing:

- generalized fatigue, lethargy, and lack of energy
- paleness or grayish tones to skin, becoming dark and scaly
- cramping of muscles—muscles eventually waste away, making all physical activity difficult
- numbness or tingling sensations in the hands or feet

- stomach bloating, constipation, and difficulty urinating; kidney and bladder infections
- periods of dizziness, light-headedness, and even amnesia
- shrinkage of internal organs, which may be irreversible in extreme cases
- kidney failure
- heart failure

Food plays an important role not only in maintaining health but in our social lives. We entertain with food, we signify certain events with food, we use food symbolically in cultural and religious events, we reward with food. In many societies, food is also associated with aiding performance and personal appearance. We eat certain things to do well at sports or to think better. (Weight lifters eat protein; fish is known as "brain food.") We may or may not eat certain things hoping to enhance our appearance. (For example, thinking that eating gelatin strengthens nails; drinking water clears the complexion, chocolate does the opposite; cheesecake goes right to the hips and thighs.) In some instances, this consciousness of what we "should or should not eat" can result in skewed and even dangerous eating habits.

Dieting is a hallmark of American culture. Books on how to take off unwanted pounds abound. Diet programs are everywhere. And fat-free foods and products to "take it off fast" fill our supermarket and pharmacy shelves. Most of these "get-thin-quick" approaches are destined to fail for most people. Losing weight, in most cases, is a matter of a consistent plan of increasing physical activity to a level that exceeds the daily intake of food. When this happens, the glycogen reserves in liver and muscle are reduced significantly, and the body will begin to use stored fats as a source of energy. Continued on a regular basis, this approach results in a slow but steady reduction in fat reserves and weight loss. For some, the solution is not so simple; metabolic rates and genetic heritage may override even the most dedicated dieter. But for most people, a well-balanced diet coupled with daily activity will ensure that the needs of the body will be met as weight is lost.

ANALYSIS

Using the reading and any previous knowledge, record your responses to the following in your notebook.

1. This reading describes some of the symptoms of anorexia nervosa. Describe what nutrients were lacking in Madelyn's diet and how this relates to the symptoms described.

2. What factors might contribute to a person severely limiting his or her intake of adequate amounts of nutritional substances?

3. The eating disorder described here is severe. At one time or another, many individuals limit their intake of certain foods for a variety of reasons without the serious consequences described. Yet limiting nutrients can have health consequences even when done in a less intensive fashion. Even if one is dieting to lose weight, nutrients should be obtained in a balanced fashion.

    a. Create a menu based on the following intake for an average person to maintain his or her weight (2,000 Calories for a female, 2,500 Calories for a male). Use the nutrient information from a variety of food labels, nutrition/diet books, or the table Nutrient Content of Food, found in Appendix A.

Daily Recommended Intake for an Adult Wishing to Maintain Weight	
fat	60 grams total*
protein	55 grams total
carbohydrate	250 grams total
calories	2,500 Calories

(*Calories obtained from fat are not exactly comparable to Calories obtained from carbohydrates. For this analysis, however, assume they are comparable.)

b. Using the same information, reduce the total Calorie intake by about one-third (for a new total of 1,500 Calories). What could you remove or change in the original diet to keep the diet balanced? What amounts and types of foods would constitute a balanced diet while allowing the person to lose weight?

c. Take this one more step by reducing the above intake by about half (800 Calories total daily). Could a balanced diet be maintained at this level? (This is now approaching an anorexic diet.)

EXTENDING *Ideas*

- Research the discovery of one of the nutrients. How was it identified? How did researchers determine its role in the body?

- The requirements for certain vitamins and minerals were determined by studying diseases that result from deficiencies. For example, the importance of vitamin C was determined by investigations that focused on scurvy, once a common disease of sailors. Research a disease caused by a vitamin or mineral deficiency. Describe what the symptoms are and why they happen. Base your descriptions on your understanding of the role of the substance in the body.

- Certain countries concentrate their agricultural efforts on a single crop—rice. These are often countries in which not much meat is consumed because of economics or dietary restrictions. Describe why this could create a health problem. Design a possible solution. Explore the economic, social, and health issues involved in such a solution.

- Research how the FDA (Food and Drug Administration) conducts its food testing. How are Calories measured? How are the amounts of protein, carbohydrates, fats, vitamins, and minerals determined? How many batches of each food need to be measured before an average is taken? Why do you think the government is interested in the nutritional state of its citizenry?

- Research the concept of a limiting nutrient. How do limiting nutrients affect populations? What happens when the limiting nutrient is supplied in excess?

- Research various commercial diet plans. What is the total nutrient value of each? Are any essential nutrients missing? Describe why each of the diets researched would or would not be good for the body on a long-term basis.

The diets of a group of individuals may be determined by factors other than what is best for them as living organisms. One factor in the United States is advertising. Find newspaper and magazine advertisements that are designed to influence eating habits. Determine whether their claims are accurate based on your understanding of the nutritional needs of humans. Describe why they are or are not appropriate.

At the other end of the dietary spectrum from anorexia is teenage obesity. The number of overweight teens has increased to the point that some health experts are calling it an epidemic. In 2004, 15% of the nation's children and teenagers were considered overweight. This figure is up from 6% in 1984. Overweight children are increasingly seen to suffer from adult diseases. These include high blood pressure, clogged arteries, and type-2 diabetes. Half of today's overweight children will never manage to shed the weight as adults. Several factors have been named as the cause of this health problem. These include lack of exercise, increase in fast-food eating, and supersized portions. Research factors in your community that might have contributed to an increase in teenage obesity in the past 20 years. For example, has your school decreased the number of hours for physical education or put soda machines in the cafeteria? Explain how these factors might affect weight.

Diet fads abound—low carb, no carb, low fat, protein only. Research the biochemical principles behind one of these diet fads. Decide whether you think this approach constitutes a sensible way to lose weight. Justify your decision with evidence.

CAREER FOCUS

Nutritionist and Dietitian   Jacob is working with a new patient who was recently admitted to Hillside Hospital. Barbara is an overweight diabetic woman with high blood pressure. Jacob is a nutritionist and registered dietitian. His challenge is to formulate a diet that will meet Barbara's complex health and nutritional needs. He uses his science background to examine the relationship between food composition and how the human body uses the nutrients found in food.

Jacob has spent considerable time gathering information about Barbara's medical status and working with Barbara and the doctors at Hillside Hospital to assess and coordinate her medical and nutritional needs. Jacob loves the time he spends talking with his clients and the doctors, and listening to their concerns. His next step is to develop and implement Barbara's specific nutrition program. By promoting healthy eating habits and making dietary modifications, this program may help to prevent and treat any future illnesses Barbara may be susceptible to.

When he was in high school, Jacob wasn't sure what he wanted to do when he "grew up." He enjoyed his biology classes but knew he didn't want to spend his time in a laboratory. What he really wanted to do was work with people. He wanted to help them to improve their lives in some way. Outside of school, Jacob loved to exercise and experiment with different recipes. He tried to make them more healthy but tasty as well. He wondered whether to major in biology, social work, or health science. A few weeks into his first semester, Jacob met with his academic adviser, who listened to his interests. She suggested that Jacob consider studying food science to become a nutritionist or dietitian. Once she described the career and job activities to him, Jacob knew he'd found the right fit! Becoming a dietitian would allow him to work with people, use his scientific knowledge, and help people improve their health.

Jacob worked toward a bachelor's degree in nutrition in a program approved by the Commission on Accreditation for Dietetics Education (CADE). He learned about a variety of career options available for nutritionists and dietitians. These included jobs at company cafeterias, schools, wellness programs, and nursing homes. Part of his training was to complete a professional internship with a registered dietitian. This experience would help him decide whether to pursue becoming a clinical dietitian where he could apply his biology, chemistry, nutrition physiology, institution management, and psychology courses in a hospital setting.

Working with Barbara and her doctors, Jacob can create a daily nutrition plan for Barbara during her hospital stay. By reducing the salt content in Barbara's food, he hopes to help lower her high blood pressure and help manage her diabetes by lowering her sugar intake. Jacob has also created a low-fat, reduced-Calorie meal plan to help her lose weight. Through his nutritional counseling at Hillside Hospital, Jacob gets a lot of satisfaction from being able to help people.

Learning Experience 5

The Lego® of Life

Prologue

What happens to food in living organisms? You may have heard the phrase, "You are what you eat." But what does what you eat have to do with what you are?

The diversity of foods is caused by different variations in the components that make up food. In any construction work, the kind of building materials you need is determined by the kind of structure you want to build. So it makes sense that foods should provide the right materials for building organisms. After all, foods are living, once-living, or at least made up in part of once-living organisms. Each day of photosynthesis by a plant, or each meal eaten by an animal, is a shipment of supplies for that organism's construction work. But how does that happen?

In Learning Experience 4, Feeding Frenzy, your work with chemical indicators demonstrated that most foods are actually composites of several different components. These components are nutrients, which include sugars and starches (carbohydrates), fats (lipids), and protein. Exactly what are these biomolecules? What are they made of? What do they contain that living organisms need? In this learning experience, you examine the chemical composition of the biomolecules that make up food. You also compare the chemical components and structures of these biomolecules.

Brainstorming

Discuss the following questions with your partner, and record your thinking in your notebook. Be prepared to share your ideas with the class.

1. Choose one item of food that you had for breakfast or lunch. What do you think is the major biomolecule in that food?
2. What do you think happens to that biomolecule in your body?
3. Why do you think that biomolecule is important in your diet?

Madam, I'm Atom

What happens to the hamburger and fries you ate at lunch? What are the steps that take place in your body that enable you to use those delicacies to maintain the characteristics of life? To make them accessible to you, these foods must be broken down into forms your body can work with. Food taken into your body gets broken down into smaller and smaller components. Beginning in your mouth, food is digested or broken down as it passes through your digestive system. This happens either mechanically by teeth, for example, or by chemicals designed to break down the biomolecules into their component parts.

What are these parts? What are they made of? How do scientists find out what things are made of? What is the smallest unit into which things can be subdivided?

More than 2,000 years ago, people were already wrestling with the idea of what the smallest unit of matter might be. A Greek philosopher named Democritus thought that you could keep cutting a material into smaller and smaller pieces until finally you would get to a piece so small it was uncuttable. He thought that any kind of matter—like an apple—could be divided only so many times. Each cut would take him closer to the smallest piece, which itself would be uncuttable. He called this uncuttable piece an atom.

Democritus never actually saw an atom. But it made sense to him that all matter was made up of smaller parts. What he did not know was whether those smaller parts were all identical. In other words, was an apple made up of "atoms of apple?" Or did an apple contain atoms that were also found in other substances such as water, wood, and soil?

Aristotle, another Greek philosopher, had a different take on what made up something like an apple. He thought that everything was made of the same four basic things, which he called "elements." Aristotle's elements were earth, water, air, and fire. How could this be? How can an apple be made of fire or air or soil? Aristotle might have explained it in this way. The apple tree roots carved into the soil, an apple tree grows from the earth, and the tree gained substances and water in the earth. With a few simple experiments, Aristotle might have observed that without air, the tree could not have survived. Finally, Aristotle might have held a torch to the tree and observed that the tree "gives off a lot of fire." Aristotle hypothesized that the apple tree must be made of earth, water, air, and fire.

Van Helmont (whose experiments you studied in Learning Experience 3) had many ideas that were similar to Aristotle's. He thought that whatever was taken in from the earth made up the plant. He turned to water to explain the plant's growth when he found that the soil only lost 2 ounces while the plant gained dozens of pounds. He thought that water must be what makes up the plant, even though water and the plant did not look at all alike. Neither Aristotle nor van Helmont considered that water, earth, and air might be composed of smaller pieces that could be rearranged into something else.

In the late 1700s, a scientist named Antoine Lavoisier demonstrated what Aristotle and van Helmont could not imagine. This was the idea that water could be divided into smaller pieces that were not themselves water. By applying enough energy to separate the component atoms, Lavoisier found that water was made up of two smaller components. These components were hydrogen and oxygen. He could not separate hydrogen and oxygen into any smaller components, at least in ways he could detect. Lavoisier's experiment demonstrated that one of

Aristotle's basic elements, water, was composed of smaller elements. His experiment also demonstrated that these elements could join together to make a substance very different from the starting material. Another scientist, Joseph Priestley, dismantled another of Aristotle's elements, air, into smaller pieces that included oxygen, a component of water.

In 1808, John Dalton, an English meteorologist, formally presented the modern atomic theory. His theory was a sort of modern-day version of Democritus's theory. Dalton proposed that for each chemical element such as oxygen or hydrogen, there was a unique type of indivisible object called an atom. In fact, **elements** are defined as substances that are composed of only one kind of atom. When two or more atoms join together, they form a **molecule**. Molecules make up most of the different kinds of material in the world.

The concept of one atom, indivisible, came tumbling down in 1897. The English physicist Joseph John Thomson identified a particle called an **electron**, which was smaller and lighter than any atom known. He concluded that atoms themselves were not the fundamental building block of matter. Instead, they were made up of even smaller and more fundamental particles. In the early 20th century, scientists discovered two more subatomic particles, the **proton** and the **neutron**. These were heavier than electrons and were in the center, or **nucleus**, of the atom (Figure 1.17). The number of protons in the nucleus determines the type of atom; for example, all hydrogen atoms have one proton, and all carbon atoms have six protons.

As scientists learned more about what matter was composed of, they began to learn that living matter and nonliving matter were very different. Nonliving matter, such as minerals in rocks, table salt, water, and air, can be made up of a wide variety of elements.

Living matter, however, seems to be composed of a very small number of elements. Six of these elements are present in great abundance. They are carbon, hydrogen, oxygen, nitrogen, sulfur, and phosphorus. And, as you will see, these six elements make up the major components of living organisms. Living organisms also contain other elements, but in much smaller amounts. For example, plants actually contain 17 different elements. They contain the six that are found most abundantly and 11 others.

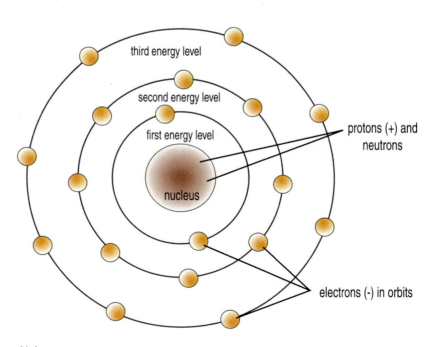

Figure 1.17

Structure of an atom.

Periodic Table of the Elements

1 **1A**																	**18** **8A**
1 **H** 1.008	**2** **2A**											**13** **3A**	**14** **4A**	**15** **5A**	**16** **6A**	**17** **7A**	2 **He** 4.003
3 **Li** 6.941	4 **Be** 9.012											5 **B** 10.81	6 **C** 12.011	7 **N** 14.007	8 **O** 15.999	9 **F** 18.998	10 **Ne** 20.179
11 **Na** 22.990	12 **Mg** 24.305	**3** **3B**	**4** **4B**	**5** **5B**	**6** **6B**	**7** **7B**	**8**	**9** **8B**	**10**	**11** **1B**	**12** **2B**	13 **Al** 26.982	14 **Si** 28.086	15 **P** 30.974	16 **S** 32.06	17 **Cl** 35.453	18 **Ar** 39.948
19 **K** 39.098	20 **Ca** 40.08	21 **Sc** 44.956	22 **Ti** 47.90	23 **V** 50.942	24 **Cr** 51.996	25 **Mn** 54.938	26 **Fe** 55.847	27 **Co** 58.933	28 **Ni** 58.71	29 **Cu** 63.546	30 **Zn** 65.38	31 **Ga** 69.72	32 **Ge** 72.59	33 **As** 74.922	34 **Se** 78.96	35 **Br** 79.904	36 **Kr** 83.80
37 **Rb** 85.468	38 **Sr** 87.62	39 **Y** 88.906	40 **Zr** 91.22	41 **Nb** 92.906	42 **Mo** 95.94	43 **Tc** 98.906	44 **Ru** 101.07	45 **Rh** 102.906	46 **Pd** 106.4	47 **Ag** 107.868	48 **Cd** 112.40	49 **In** 114.82	50 **Sn** 118.69	51 **Sb** 121.75	52 **Te** 127.60	53 **I** 126.904	54 **Xe** 131.30
55 **Cs** 132.905	56 **Ba** 137.34	57 **La** 138.906	72 **Hf** 178.49	73 **Ta** 180.948	74 **W** 183.85	75 **Re** 186.2	76 **Os** 190.2	77 **Ir** 192.22	78 **Pt** 195.09	79 **Au** 196.966	80 **Hg** 200.59	81 **Tl** 204.37	82 **Pb** 207.19	83 **Bi** 208.980	84 **Po** (210)	85 **At** (210)	86 **Rn** (222)
87 **Fr** (223)	88 **Ra** (226.025)	89 **Ac** (227)	104 **Unq** (261)	105 **Unp** (262)	106 **Unh** (263)	107 **Uns** (262)	108 **Uno** (265)	109 **Une** (266)									

Transition Metals

Key:
- 1 — Atomic number
- H — Symbol
- 1.008 — Atomic mass

Inner Transition Metals

Lanthanide Series

58 **Ce** 140.12	59 **Pr** 140.908	60 **Nd** 144.24	61 **Pm** (147)	62 **Sm** 150.4	63 **Eu** 151.96	64 **Gd** 157.25	65 **Tb** 158.925	66 **Dy** 162.50	67 **Ho** 164.930	68 **Er** 167.26	69 **Tm** 168.934	70 **Yb** 173.04	71 **Lu** 174.97
90 **Th** 232.038	91 **Pa** 231.036	92 **U** 238.029	93 **Np** 237.048	94 **Pu** (244)	95 **Am** (243)	96 **Cm** (247)	97 **Bk** (247)	98 **Cf** (251)	99 **Es** (254)	100 **Fm** (257)	101 **Md** (258)	102 **No** (255)	103 **Lr** (256)

Actinide Series

Figure 1.18

Periodic table of the elements.

Of the more than 100 elements known (see Figure 1.18), only 22 appear to be essential to life. This seems hard to believe when we observe the great diversity of living organisms around us. How could all living things be composed of just a few kinds of elements? What might be the reason?

ANALYSIS

Record your responses to the following in your notebook.

1. Create a diagram that flows from largest to smallest, using the following substances: atom, neutron, electron, carbohydrate, cow, sugar, element, proton, lipid, nucleic acid, protein, water molecule, corn, nucleus of an atom. You may use a word more than once. If you are not sure which of two items is larger, place them side by side in your flow diagram.
2. Describe any relationships that might exist among the various substances (for example, cow eats corn).

A Mere Six Ingredients

ACTIVITY

The fundamental driving force that determines what organisms take in from their environment is what they require in order to survive. What role do nutrients play in sustaining life? How do organisms use nutrients?

All living organisms must obtain building blocks for making new biomolecules and energy to carry out the essential processes of life. These building blocks and energy are found in the four biomolecules that make up food and that also make up all living things. These four biomolecules are carbohydrates, lipids, nucleic acids, and proteins. These nutrients in turn are made up of only six elements (carbon, hydrogen, oxygen, sulfur, phosphorus, and nitrogen). These six elements are used to build a tremendous diversity of living things by being arranged in different ways. In living organisms, atoms of the six elements are joined in different arrangements and in different quantities to form all of the different biomolecules.

How do different organisms obtain these nutrients? For most organisms, there are only two possible ways. They can construct the nutrients during photosynthesis, or they can obtain the nutrients by feeding on other organisms. During photosynthesis, plants take in water and carbon dioxide from their environment. Using solar energy, the elements in these molecules (hydrogen, oxygen, and carbon) are "recycled." They are used to make a new, energy-containing molecule: sugar. Plants do not "eat" and, therefore, do not take in biomolecules such as protein and lipid. So plants must use this sugar molecule to construct all the carbohydrates, lipids, and proteins they require to sustain life. The sugar, in conjunction with vitamins and minerals that the plant obtains from soil, provides all the essential nutrients a plant needs.

Organisms that do not carry on photosynthesis are required to take in complex biomolecules from their environment. They do this by eating plants (with the nutrients the plants have manufactured) or other animals (that have eaten plants or still other plant-eating animals). Ultimately, all the nutrients animals take in can be traced back to plants. Thus, the phrase, "You are what you eat" is a very literal one. In plants and other photosynthetic organisms, food is manufactured by the process of photosynthesis. In animals, complex biomolecules are taken in as food. The elements that make up the biomolecules are then recycled into biomolecules that make up the animal. Remember these six elements: carbon, hydrogen, oxygen, sulfur, phosphorus, and nitrogen. They are joined in different arrangements and in different quantities, and are the main ingredients of life.

How do living organisms rearrange the components of their food? What do the biomolecules of life look like? In this activity, your group becomes the expert on one of the major biomolecules of life. After learning about the structure and function of your biomolecule, you will share your knowledge with the class.

Topic: Biomolecules
Go to: www.scilinks.org
Code: INBIOH248

Materials

For each group of students:

- 1 biomolecule information sheet
- 1 set of molecular models (optional)
- biology textbooks (optional)

PROCEDURE

Prepare a brief (5-minute) presentation for the class about your biomolecule. Be sure to address each of the following questions and directives in your report.

1. What elements make up the biomolecules you examined?
2. What are some of the similarities among the different biomolecules? What are some of the differences?
3. Which element would you consider the central element in living organisms? Why?

4. With which atoms does carbon most frequently bond? With what other atoms does carbon bond?
5. What other atoms interact with each other?
6. Describe the subunit structure of your biomolecules. Explain how these subunits link together to form large molecules.
7. Describe several functions that your biomolecule fulfills in an organism.
8. If molecular models are available, build a three-dimensional model of your subunit.

ANALYSIS

After each group has presented its report to the class, record your responses to the following in your notebook.

1. Which element do you consider predominant in living organisms?
2. Which elements does the carbon bond with most frequently?
3. Identify at least three similarities that the four classes of biomolecules have in common.
4. Identify at least three differences among the four classes of biomolecules.
5. Describe any functions that these biomolecules might have in common.

EXTENDING *Ideas*

▸ Research the digestive system. Describe or draw how nutrients are broken down in the various organs. Describe the digestive enzymes involved and how they act.

▸ Some vegetarians assert that obtaining protein from animal products is economically very inefficient. They believe that greater amounts of protein can be obtained by consuming only plant products. Many in the beef and dairy industries disagree. Research the arguments used by each side. Decide which one you would support in a debate and explain why.

▸ During the Cultural Revolution in China in the 1960s, famine forced many people to try to supplement their diet by eating leaves from trees. In spite of that, many died. Cellulose and starch are both long-chain polysaccharides found in plants. Both are made up exclusively of glucose molecules. If the leaves of the trees were mainly cellulose, why could humans not survive on leaves? Describe and explain the difference between a human's ability to use starch and the ability to use cellulose.

CAREER
FOCUS

Chemical Technician   For some time now, the chemical engineers at Doggy Diet, Inc., have been studying a new chemical compound and its effect on the nutritional value of dog food. And for months, scientists and technicians have been running various lab tests to collect information on the compound and its effects. Dr. Atherton frequently stops in at the lab to meet with Natasha, one of the lab's chemical technicians. They discuss the next steps in their research process. These steps include analyzing the data to determine if the compound is beneficial to dog nutrition and at what levels it is most beneficial, and deciding whether the compound should be added to the line of Doggy Diet dog foods.

Natasha has been involved with every aspect of the lab research. She carefully conducted all of the chemical experiments and tests to gather data on the effectiveness of the compound. In some tests, Natasha was responsible for putting dogs on different diets that consisted of various levels of the test compound. She monitored the concentration of the compound present to make sure the animals were getting the proper dosage. She also documented any effects the diet had on the dogs. Natasha was extremely precise in how she collected the data and also in her computerized record-keeping. She needed the information in a format that made it easy to work with. Now that the testing phase is complete, Natasha spends her time updating the computerized data files and ensuring that they are accurate so that data analysis can begin. She will work with Dr. Atherton to perform computerized statistical analyses on the data and brainstorm possible interpretations.

Most positions as chemical technicians require a 2-year associate's degree. But Natasha was able to intern at Doggy Diet, Inc., when she was a high school senior. Natasha was a whiz at chemistry and computer science. So when she was preparing for her senior internship requirement, her chemistry teacher thought she should try to intern as a chemical technician. Her guidance counselor and chemistry teacher helped her research companies and arranged her placement at Doggy Diet, Inc. During her internship, Natasha learned many of the lab procedures, and she applied for a position as a chemical technician once she graduated from high school. After being hired, she worked as a trainee under the direct supervision of a more experienced technician who continues to be her mentor.

Even though she had her dream job, Natasha still felt that taking college-level math and science courses would help her advance professionally. She also wanted to develop her writing and communication skills for writing reports and making presentations. Now she's working toward her associate's degree by taking evening classes, which are paid by Doggy Diet, Inc. But even when she has completed her degree, Natasha would like to keep up with new technologies by taking continuing education seminars and workshops through the American Chemical Society. Natasha feels that she has a very rewarding career. She's involved in the exciting world of science and discovery, and she can help improve the health of animals without having to get an advanced scientific degree.

Historian   The invention of the telephone simplified life for 20th-century scientists. But it complicated life for Virginia, a science historian and the curator of the National Museum of Scientific Research. Virginia pieces together stories of scientific advances and discoveries. She looks at how they came to be, who did what, what accelerated progress, and what obstructed it.

Nineteenth-century scientists often wrote to each other every day. They described their results, tested their ideas, exchanged information, and proposed new hypotheses. Their letters are valuable resources for historians. But with access to telephones, scientists stopped writing informal letters to each other. As a result, many of the daily phone conversations and e-mail exchanges among 20th-century scientists are lost to cyberspace.

Virginia is writing a book about the history of AIDS and the progress scientists have made since its discovery. The book will include excerpts from dozens of personal interviews, or oral histories, with researchers who have been pioneers in AIDS research. It will explain how they attacked this illness and how their thinking evolved over time. Although the interviews Virginia conducted were expensive and time-consuming, they are extremely valuable for understanding why scientists did what they did. And that is Virginia's main objective. She wants to interpret evidence to draw conclusions about how cultural and social interactions affected the development of science.

Virginia compares her work as a science historian to that of a detective trying to solve crimes. She starts by considering the body of data available; she researches materials found in libraries, government institutions, periodicals, and online databases. Then Virginia rules out extraneous information, culls the critical materials, and identifies patterns to construct an interpretation. Virginia always loved history, but it wasn't until she was in college that she got hooked on science. While researching Albert Einstein for a report in an introductory history course, she became fascinated by his life, the scientific theories he developed, and the effect he had on the scientific community and society in general. Virginia suddenly viewed science in a whole new light. She sought out her adviser who explained to her that historians can specialize in science, technology, and medicine as easily as they can specialize in American history. After graduating from college, Virginia worked toward a Ph.D. in the history of science.

Virginia has to juggle the time she spends researching and writing her book with her day job as curator of the museum. There she collects and displays instruments and equipment used in scientific research. Virginia handles hundreds of instruments and memorabilia people send her. She determines which items will become part of the museum's collection. She hopes that her work at the museum and as a science historian will help present-day scientists learn from the past.

The Ins and Outs of the Digestive System

Prologue

Before you can convert that piece of pizza you had for lunch into more of you, the pizza must be broken down into increasingly smaller pieces. This breakdown is essential in order for the nutrients to be small enough to enter the cells where the metabolic processes of catabolism and anabolism take place. The process of breaking nutrients down into their biomolecular components is called digestion, and it takes place in the digestive system or tract of most animals.

The basic idea of the digestive system is simple and is the same in most animals. The basic steps in digestion are as follows:

1. Food from the environment enters the organism.
2. A combination of chemical and mechanical digestion by different parts of the digestive tract reduce the food into smaller pieces.
3. Nutrients released by this breakdown are transported into the bloodstream.
4. Blood carries nutrients to cells throughout the body.
5. Waste matter exits the organism.

Even though the idea is the same, the structure of these systems varies among different species and is determined in large part by the types of food the organism consumes. In this activity, you examine and model the structure of the digestive system of one kind of organism and compare it to that of other organisms.

Brainstorming

Discuss the following questions with your partner and record your thinking in your notebook. Be prepared to share your ideas with the class.

1. Why is it important for most organisms to be able to digest their food?
2. Identify some foods that one organism can digest and another cannot.
3. Why do you think a meal for one organism is a case of indigestion for another? In other words, why can some organisms digest certain foods, whereas others cannot?
4. What happens if an organism eats something it cannot digest?
5. Do plants have a digestive system? Explain your answer.

It's Alimentary (My Dear Watson)

ACTIVITY

Any organism that cannot produce its own food requires some method for ingesting (taking in) food from its environment and breaking it down by physical and/or chemical (enzymes and acid) means into smaller units that can be absorbed by cells. The kind of digestive system that an organism has is determined in large part by the food the organism eats.

Intracellular digestion takes place inside a cell. Single-celled organisms such as amoebae or paramecia take in small food particles across their cell membranes into a specialized membrane-bound sac or vacuole that contains enzymes to break down the food further. Essentially, these organisms have no digestive system and rely on their cells being in direct contact with their environment. Some organisms such as fungi release enzymes into their external environment, which break down their food into smaller particles that can then be absorbed across their cell membranes. This digestion is extracellular, taking place outside the body, and requires no structured digestive system.

You are probably most familiar with extracellular—but inside the body—digestion. This is what humans and many other animals have. Food digestion takes place outside the cell but within the body of the organism and requires a specialized digestive system for ingesting the food, breaking it down, and transporting it to cells.

In this following activity, you will research the digestive system of one organism using information provided and/or other available resources. Then your group will construct a model of an organism's digestive system and prepare a display to share with other students at a class fair.

Materials

For the class

- assorted model-building materials
  - construction paper
  - glue or tape
  - pipe cleaners
  - balloons
  - drinking straws
  - plastic or paper bags
  - plastic or wooden beads
  - yarn
  - cardboard sheets or boxes
  - clay in a variety of colors
  - tubing
  - water
  - food dye
- poster board
- chart paper
- markers
- textbooks on comparative anatomy, Internet access (optional)

PROCEDURE

1. Your teacher will assign you an organism and provide you with information about its digestive system. Your teacher may also ask you to do further research using textbooks and the Internet.
2. Using background information, you will construct a model of your organism's digestive system. First, however, you should:
   a. determine the structures that make up the system;
   b. identify the function of each component of the system and its role in the digestive process;
   c. determine a scale (such as 1:1) for your model; and
   d. choose materials that might reflect the structure and function of each component. Be created. You can use materials not on the list.
3. Build your model.
4. Decide how you will construct your display for the fair. Share the tasks so that each member of the group has a part to prepare. Your display must include
   a. the completed model,
   b. a diagram of how food is processed through the system,
   c. a description of the function of each component, and
   d. a step-by-step annotation of how food moves through the system.
5. Your display should also include
   a. the kind of digestion involved (one-way or two-way; simple or ruminant);
   b. how this system reflects the diet of the organism;
   c. the steps that involve physical (mechanical) breakdown;
   d. the steps that involve chemical or enzymatic breakdown;
   e. involvement of enzymes, their functions, where they are made, and where they function in the digestive system;
   f. mechanism by which nutrients reach cells once digestion is complete; and
   g. the fate of waste products.
6. Construct your display.
7. During the fair, visit other displays and take notes on the differences in the various systems related to the mechanisms of digestion, the structure and function of the parts, and the diet of the organism. It might be helpful to use the topics outlined in steps 4 and 5 as a guide to your note taking. One member of the group should remain with the display to answer questions. Be sure to rotate this person so that everyone gets a chance to observe the other displays.
8. Be prepared to discuss the similarities and differences in the systems in a class discussion.

Turning Corn into Milk: Alchemy or Biochemistry?

Prologue

A cow stands over the grain bin contentedly chewing on corn. In a few hours, the dairy farmer will come in to milk her. What is the relationship, if any, between the corn that provides the cow with nutrients and energy and the milk that she produces both for feeding her offspring and for the farmer to sell?

In this learning experience, you apply the concepts from Learning Experience 5 to examine how organisms use food resources to synthesize new materials for their own use. You identify the chemical relationship between the food that a cow uses (corn) and one of the products a cow synthesizes (milk). You determine how one can be turned into the other.

Brainstorming

Discuss the following questions with your partner, and record your thinking in your notebook. Be prepared to share your ideas with the class.

1. Remember the phrase, "You are what you eat." Explain what that means to you.
2. What do you think the relationship is between what you ate at lunch and the cells, tissues, and organs that make up your body?
3. Why might this relationship be considered a form of recycling?

Corn and Milk: So Different Yet So Similar

ACTIVITY

How can a cow use a food resource like corn to produce milk (see Figure 1.19)— a very different substance? In this activity, you will analyze the biomolecular composition of corn and milk. You will use indicators to determine whether corn can provide any of the components found in milk. The indicators Biuret reagent, Benedict's solution, iodine, and Sudan III will help you test for proteins, sugar,

Figure 1.19

Cow, a natural recycling center:
input corn—output milk.

starch, and lipids. Look at the experiment you conducted in Learning
Experience 4, Feeding Frenzy. Review the use of indicators and the general
procedure for conducting an experiment that uses indicators.

Materials

For each group of four students:

- nutrient label from a milk carton
- 4 safety goggles
- 4 pairs of disposable gloves (optional)
- 1 eyedropper or 10 disposable pipettes
- heat source
- 2 beakers (250-mL) or clean plastic margarine tubs or other containers
- 12 test tubes
- 1 test-tube clamp
- 1 test-tube rack
- 1 glass stirring rod
- 3 tsp canned whole-kernel corn
- 10 mL fresh, whole, pasteurized milk
- 1 small bottle Biuret reagent
- 1 small bottle Benedict's solution
- 1 small bottle iodine
- 1 small bottle Sudan III or IV reagent
- 1 fork or spoon (to mash corn)
- 1 wax marking pencil
- access to distilled water

For the class:

- 1 set positive test control solutions, 1 tsp
- boiling water bath
- heat source
- blender (optional)

PROCEDURE

1. **STOP & THINK** Identify the question being asked, and make a prediction about the outcome of this experiment. Record your response in your notebook.
2. **STOP & THINK** Read through the entire procedure and draw your experimental setup in your notebook. See Figure 1.15 in the Procedure section of Learning Experience 4 for an example.
3. **STOP & THINK** Why is it important to analyze milk even when you have access to information about milk from the nutrition label? Record your reasons.
4. Place 3 spoonfuls of corn with its juice in a 250-mL beaker (or clean plastic container). Mash up the kernels with the back of a fork (or you may use a blender).
5. Pour approximately 10 mL of fresh milk into a container.
6. Label a set of 4 test tubes: Water +, then label each with one of the following: "sugar," "starch," "protein," or "lipid." These are your negative controls. Place the test tubes in the test-tube rack. There will be a class set of positive controls.
7. Label a second set of 4 test tubes: Milk +, then label each with one of the following: "sugar," "starch," "protein," or "lipid."
8. Label 4 more test tubes: Corn +, then label each with one of the following: "sugar," "starch," "protein," or "lipid." Place the test tubes in the test-tube rack. These last two sets are your experimental unknowns.
9. Using a clean pipette or eyedropper, add 30 drops of water to each of the test tubes labeled "Water +."
10. Using a clean pipette or eyedropper, withdraw the corn mush from the beaker. Place 30 drops of the mush into each of the test tubes labeled "Corn +."
11. Using a clean pipette or eyedropper, place 30 drops of milk in each test tube labeled "Milk +." Wash the eyedropper.
12. Using a clean and separate pipette for each indicator (or a clean eyedropper), add 15 drops of the appropriate indicator to the appropriate test tubes (see Table 1.1, Learning Experience 4). You should have 3 test tubes for each indicator: 2 samples (corn and milk) and 1 negative control. Heat in boiling water those test tubes that contain Benedict's solution.
13. Examine all your test tubes for any color changes and record the results. You may need to hold the Biuret test tubes against white paper to see the color changes more clearly.
14. Record your results. Discuss them with your group.
15. Dispose of the contents of the test tubes and wash your glassware.

NOTE If you are using an eyedropper, be sure to rinse the eyedropper well between each step. To rinse, draw water from one beaker into the dropper; then squirt the water into a second beaker. Repeat 2 or 3 times for thorough rinsing.

SAFETY NOTE The hot plate and boiling water can cause burns. Biuret is caustic. If it comes in contact with skin, rinse thoroughly with water. If you should get any in your eyes, irrigate them immediately and inform your teacher.

ANALYSIS

1. Prepare a laboratory report for this experiment in your notebook. Be sure to include the following:
   a. the question(s) being asked;
   b. your predictions about the outcome;
   c. the experimental design and how the investigation was set up (include a rationale for testing the milk again);
   d. the data or observations you made (in a chart or table);
   e. your analysis (include your responses to the Analysis questions that follow); and
   f. your conclusion (your answer to the question being asked).

2. What biomolecules are present in milk and in corn?
3. What chemical elements (atoms) make up these biomolecules? Would it be possible to make protein if you didn't take in protein? lipids? carbohydrates? Explain your answers.
4. How can two such different substances—corn and milk—be composed of many or possibly all (depending on your results) of the same biomolecules?
5. Create a diagram using words or drawings that illustrates the pathway by which a cow converts corn to milk. Base your diagram on the results of your experiment.

READING

Haven't I Seen That Carbon Somewhere Before?

Julie Lewis walks on a dream come true. Since she was a teenager, inspired by the rallies of the first Earth Day in 1970, she yearned to turn waste into something worthwhile. Now the 38-year-old is vice president of a company she founded called Deja. She calls her recycled invention the Deja Shoe.

Its cotton-canvas fabric is rewoven from textile scraps. The foam padding was designed to cushion chairs. Factory-reject coffee filters and file folders go into the insole. Add recycled grocery bags, tire rubber, and plastic trimmings left over from the manufacture of disposable diapers.

The shoes look handsome, durable, and ready for the outdoors. . . . Her Portland, Oregon firm ships 100,000 pairs annually [to] stores across the country. And when they wear out? Send them back to Deja to be recycled.

—An excerpt from Noel Grove, "Recycling," *National Geographic,* July 1994, pp. 92–115

Julie Lewis's company takes trash and turns it into shoes. Cows take corn and use it to produce milk. Similarly, you eat pizza or salad and convert them into proteins, lipids, carbohydrates, nucleic acids, and energy. Your body uses these things to continue to grow and to maintain itself. Long before the first Earth Day, organisms were recycling materials.

USE IT AGAIN, SAM

How do living organisms recycle the resources they take in? How do they transform them into new materials that an organism can use? How can a cow use a food resource like corn to produce milk—a very different substance?

As you have been finding out, perhaps corn and milk are not totally different substances. At least they are not totally different in terms of the biomolecules and chemical elements they are composed of. The big differences are in how those elements are put together. For example, all biomolecules are composed of similar elements. But the biomolecules differ because each of their elements is put together into different subunit structures.

Because these subunits can also be varied, many possible kinds of carbohydrates, proteins, nucleic acids, and fats can be made. Single subunits can be different, and groups of subunits can be put together in lots of different ways. There are sometimes slight and sometimes more obvious differences in the way things are put together. These differences can produce materials with very different structures, chemical properties, and functions. The carbohydrate in milk, for instance, consists primarily of the disaccharide sugar lactose. The primary carbohydrate in corn, however, is the polysaccharide starch.

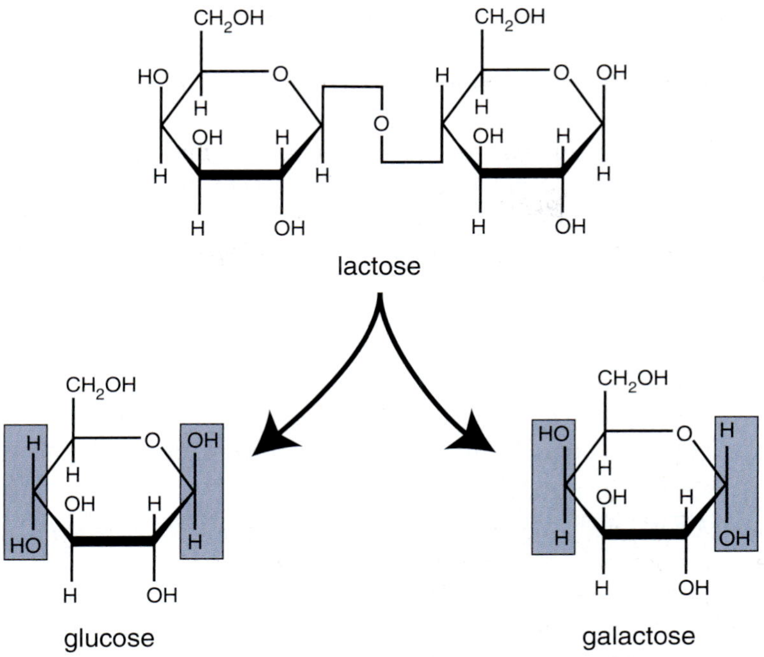

Figure 1.20

Lactose is a combination of glucose and galactose.

lactose

glucose

galactose

Grass, another food source for cows, has another polysaccharide, cellulose, as its major carbohydrate. Starch and cellulose are both composed of a long chain of linked glucose molecules. These two carbohydrates differ only in terms of how those glucose subunits are linked to one another. Lactose is a simpler carbohydrate. It is composed of a glucose molecule and a galactose molecule. Glucose and galactose are composed of exactly the same number of carbons (6), hydrogens (12), and oxygens (6)—($C_6H_{12}O_6$). But they differ in how these atoms are arranged (see Figure 1.20). This small difference in arrangement produces two sugars that are chemically different in nature. When these two sugars are joined by a chemical bond, yet a third and different sugar, lactose, is formed.

Imagine that you are an architect who has been hired to design a building constructed only of wood, ceramic, and glass. Using only these three materials, you have a tremendous variety of possibilities for how the final building might look. Just as carbon, hydrogen, and oxygen can be put together differently to make substances very different in nature from one another, you could design a variety of different buildings by changing the way building blocks are put together. All living organisms are made up of **organic** (carbon-containing) materials that have the same six elements. But life on Earth is diverse. This is due to the highly varied possibilities for design in how organic compounds can be put together. Think about the similarity in the elements that living things are made of and the variations in the structure of biomolecules. These characteristics suggest a start to responding to our questions, "How do living organisms recycle the resources they take in? How do they transform them into new materials that an organism can use?" If biomolecules differ in terms of how their elements are arranged, then perhaps one could be made into the other by reshuffling the chemical elements. If a cow could break down corn into smaller subunits, it could then rearrange them and build something new. This would be similar to Julie Lewis taking scrap pieces of textiles and weaving them together into a whole new shoe.

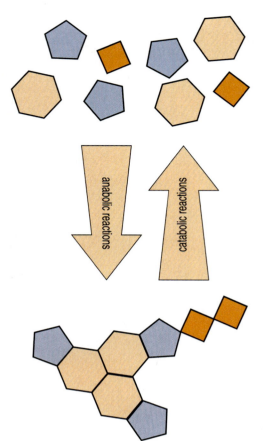

Figure 1.21

The cycle of catabolism and anabolism.

Break It Down, Building It Up

These chemical reactions of breakdown (**catabolism**) and synthesis (**anabolism**) are fundamental to how living organisms sustain life. One definition of a chemical reaction can be the transformation of molecules into other kinds of molecules. Anabolic reactions involve the building of biomolecules from other molecules. You have already seen an example of this in photosynthesis. Here carbon dioxide and water are transformed into sugar. The transformation of corn into milk actually involves many steps. The starch and other biomolecules are broken down (catabolized). Then the components are reassembled into the sugars and other biomolecules of milk. Figure 1.21 illustrates the relationship of anabolic reactions to catabolic reactions.

How do biomolecules get "broken down"? One of the major requirements is energy. If you have ever burned toast, you know that it turns black. The heat provided the energy that caused some of the bread to break down to carbon. This can also be seen when glucose is "burned." When heat energy is added in the presence of oxygen, the glucose molecule breaks. A great deal of energy in the form of heat is released. Chemically, electrons are transferred from the hydrogen atoms in the glucose molecule to oxygen. This results in the formation of water. When a molecule loses electrons, it is said to be **oxidized**. The chemical reaction for the burning of glucose can be written as the following equation:

$$C_6H_{12}O_6 + 6O_2 + energy \rightarrow 6CO_2 + 6H_2O + energy$$

In living organisms, a very similar reaction takes place. But this reaction happens in a much slower, controlled, series of small steps. The slower oxidation of glucose has several advantages for the organism. It (1) prevents the organism from burning up; (2) enables the energy in the bonds of the glucose molecule to be transferred to other molecules for use by the organism (rather than being released as heat); and (3) allows the products of the glucose molecule breakdown to be used by the organism to synthesize other biomolecules. In the next learning experience, you will be examining these energy transfers and the importance of oxygen in them.

Putting It All Together

Metabolism is the web of simultaneous and interrelated chemical reactions taking place at any given second of life. Within this web, complex chains of biomolecules are woven from simpler units or are dismantled piece by piece. Growth, movement, repair, and other life-sustaining activities depend on these collective chemical reactions.

Metabolic reactions are organized into pathways. Catabolic reactions are interconnected to anabolic pathways. The product or **intermediate** of a catabolic pathway may be the starting material for an anabolic pathway. The anabolic pathways consist of a number of individual steps. Through these steps, materials are progressively rearranged and built. These sets of reactions are called pathways. This is because they have a starting material (for example, starch), an end product (protein, nucleic acid, lipid, carbohydrate), and a series of reactions in between (steps along the path). At each step of a metabolic pathway, the

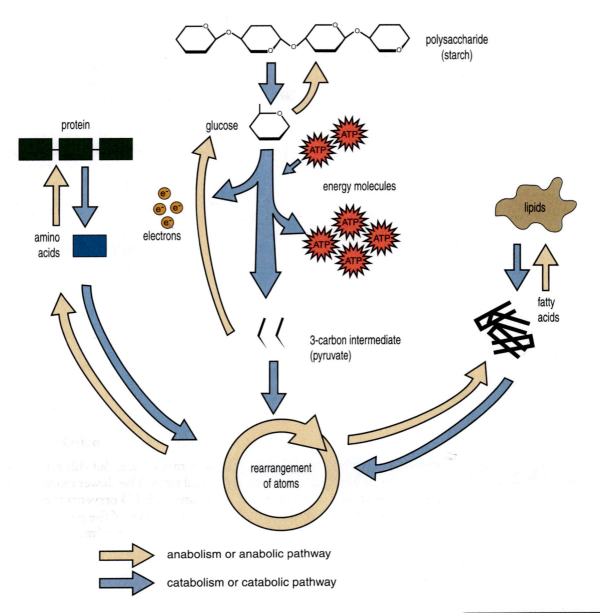

polysaccharide
(starch)

protein

glucose

energy molecules

lipids

amino
acids

electrons

fatty
acids

3-carbon intermediate
(pyruvate)

rearrangement
of atoms

anabolism or anabolic pathway

catabolism or catabolic pathway

Figure 1.22

Metabolic pathways.

starting material is changed a little more (see Figure 1.22). Sometimes a new pathway can begin in the middle of an ongoing pathway.

In your experiment, you determined that milk and corn contain the same kind of biomolecules. The cow ingests corn; the corn is broken down further and further. It is broken down first by the digestive processes into its biomolecular components. It is then broken down by the catabolic pathways, into intermediates. This process releases energy. This energy is then captured in a chemical form that the cow can use. These intermediates are then used as building materials to synthesize new biomolecules using the energy from catabolism. These materials are also used for the other life processes the cow must carry out. Figure 1.23 represents these transformations.

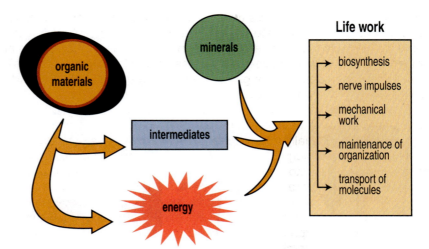

Life work

- biosynthesis
- nerve impulses
- mechanical work
- maintenance of organization
- transport of molecules

intermediates

energy

organic materials

minerals

Figure 1.23

Metabolic processes provide intermediates and energy needed to carry out the activities of life.

ANALYSIS

Record your responses to the following in your notebook.

Create a concept map using *corn* as the starting idea. Include at least 10 words or ideas from the reading. Use the illustrations to guide you in developing your concept map.

EXTENDING *Ideas*

Recycling is popular today. Whether it is making shoes out of garbage or finding uses for the packaging materials that enclose many items that we purchase. Blue or green bins in many cities contain various items for recycling. These include glass, aluminum, polystyrene foam, and plastic. Write or draw an analogy of the recycling of food packaging material as it compares to the breakdown and synthesis of food. Describe what happens to the package during the recycling process. Explain how this compares to the recycling of biomolecules.

CAREER FOCUS

Teacher Tyrell is the kind of teacher we all wish for. He's enthusiastic about the science he teaches, and he cares about his students. To an outsider, Tyrell's classroom probably looks chaotic. Students are busy investigating plant samples, talking to each other, and trying to solve the problem at hand. The walls are covered with colorful posters and samples of students' work. As a high school biology teacher, Tyrell has carefully created a learning environment where students can explore science firsthand.

Tyrell teaches classes in introductory biology, honors biology, microbiology, and genetics. His job involves planning which topics to cover, deciding which activities or labs to use to illustrate the topic, preparing the necessary materials, working with students as they do the activities, and writing and grading quizzes and tests. Tyrell wants to help students explore science concepts in depth and examine science within social, historical, ethical, and political contexts. He feels that as a teacher he can really make a difference in his students' lives. He loves to see the expression on his students' faces when they accomplish something or gain a new understanding. But he spends a lot of extra hours at home planning lessons and correcting work.

Tyrell was always interested in biology. As a child, he begged his parents for a plastic anatomy mannequin with removable organs. He would study it for hours and continually take it apart and put it together again. Given his interest in human biology, Tyrell thought that he would definitely become a doctor. But after volunteering at a local hospital during high school, Tyrell decided that health care wasn't the right field for him. When he was a senior taking AP biology, one of the introductory biology teachers became ill. Tyrell's teacher asked him to fill in and teach the Biology 1 class. He reluctantly agreed and to his surprise loved teaching the class.

That experience, combined with his interest in biology, prompted Tyrell to pursue a career as a biology teacher. He completed a Bachelor of Science/Bachelor of Education degree. He then spent an extra year after getting his bachelor's working as a student teacher and completing master's degree courses to become a certified teacher.

Tyrell is fascinated with the fact that so much is still unknown in the world of science and that there is always something new to discover. He conveys this excitement to his students. Being a school teacher has given Tyrell the opportunity to combine a career with his interests—science, psychology, and children—and to pass his enthusiasm on to the next generation.

For Further Study

Metabolic Managers

Prologue

Through your study of metabolism, you have been exploring the interconnected chemical reactions that constitute some of the essential processes of life. You know that as some reactions are breaking down complex biomolecules piece by piece, other reactions are transforming and restructuring the simple units into new materials.

One of the keys to diversity in the living world is the variety of different materials that organisms build from the nutrients they take in. A wide array of protein, fat, nucleic acids, and carbohydrate products are constructed by living organisms in hundreds of different types of chemical reactions. Maintaining the web of chemical reactions must be a well-organized operation if the living organism is to survive. All reactions require starting materials and involve a transfer of energy. Reactions also require efficiency to meet the extraordinary and continuous material and energy demands that take place at every second of an organism's life.

Brainstorming

Discuss the following questions with your partner, and record your thinking in your notebook. Be prepared to share your ideas with the class.

1. What happens to a soda cracker when you place it in your mouth for a while without chewing?
2. Why do you think this happens?
3. Do you think this would happen faster in water or saliva? Explain your answer.
4. Do you think there is a difference in what happens to the biomolecules in the cracker in water versus saliva?

READING

Critical Players

Enzymes are critical players in this need for efficiency. Enzymes are protein molecules built by living organisms from nutrient materials they take in. Enzymes **catalyze** (speed up) chemical reactions. They facilitate the transformation process by helping to convert materials from one form to another. Metabolic reactions would take place too slowly to sustain life if it were not for these catalytic proteins. If an enzyme is unavailable, the reaction will still proceed. But it will proceed at about one-millionth the speed. In humans, one meal would take about 50 years to be digested without digestive enzymes.

You may already be familiar with digestive enzymes. These enzymes help to break down food into forms that your body can use. Saliva contains the digestive enzyme amylase, which initiates the breakdown of starch. In the stomach, pepsin begins protein digestion. Other enzymes assist in the further breakdown of sugars, proteins, and lipids. If an organism does not have a specific enzyme, it may be unable to break down certain kinds of food.

Other enzymes throughout the body work specifically at each step along metabolic pathways. One example is the chemical reaction that transforms carbon dioxide into carbonic acid. Without enzymes, 200 molecules of carbonic acid can be produced in 1 hour. With the aid of an enzyme in the blood called carbonic anhydrase, however, the reaction rate is increased to 600,000 molecules per second.

Enzymes function at their best in certain conditions, such as within a certain pH range or a certain temperature range. Enzymes can cease to function or be destroyed by exposure to high temperatures. This, in turn, disrupts metabolism. That is why humans, for instance, cannot live when the body temperature exceeds 44°C (112°F). Beyond that temperature, too many metabolic processes become disrupted because the enzymes cannot function.

Topic: Enzymes
Go to: www.scilinks.org
Code: INBIOH265

ANALYSIS

Record your responses to the following in your notebook.

1. What is the role of enzymes in the cell? What other roles can you think of that enzymes might play in addition to those mentioned in the reading?
2. What might happen if enzymes did not function correctly or were missing?
3. Describe how enzymes might play a role in the relationship between the corn a cow takes in and the milk she produces.

Crisis at the Creamery

CASE STUDY

Before profits begin to fall at the esteemed milk producer, Sun Valley Creamery, you and your partner must determine whether Sun Valley or the complaining customers are at fault. In pairs, read through the following fictional scenario and answer the Analysis questions that follow.

Ms. Hatfield is the head of the Sun Valley Creamery. During the past several months, the company has received calls from customers who have repeatedly felt ill soon after drinking Sun Valley brand milk. They report suffering stomach cramps and bouts of diarrhea. Ms. Hatfield immediately runs a product check on all milk being shipped out from the company.

After scouring all facets of her operation and product testing the milk, Ms. Hatfield cannot find anything wrong with her production lines. Ms. Hatfield gathers data that compare her complaining customers with her noncomplaining customers (Table 1.2).

The complaining customers all drank from different batches. Thousands of other customers drank from all those same batches without suffering ill effects. Ms. Hatfield finds herself in a dilemma. The news of potential problems with Sun Valley products is spreading fast, and yet she cannot figure out where the problem lies. She needs to find out what is happening before any more people get sick and before Sun Valley's profits begin to disappear.

Ms. Hatfield starts to wonder what might tie all these cases together. Is there anything all these complaining customers have in common? Ms. Hatfield has a thought: Perhaps these complaining customers are having trouble with dairy foods in general. She recalls that many people lack the enzyme lactase, which converts lactose to glucose and galactose. Following the ingestion of certain dairy foods, people lacking lactase will experience stomach cramps and bouts of diarrhea. She decides to run an experiment. She asks several complaining and noncomplaining customers to participate. In this experiment, each participant is asked to consume (on separate occasions) a container of Sun Valley yogurt, a portion of Sun Valley cottage cheese, a portion of Sun Valley cheddar cheese, and a glass of Sun Valley milk.

HOW ARE DAIRY PRODUCTS MADE?

Ms. Hatfield chose the foods based on her experience with how dairy products are made. All dairy products begin with one basic ingredient: milk. Each of the cheese and yogurt products produced by Sun Valley, and tested by Ms. Hatfield, started out as milk. The transformation of milk into yogurt or cheese involves a transformation of the nutrients found in milk. These changes produce unique tastes, textures, and appearances.

The typical cheese-making process first involves separating fluid milk into curds (a white gel) and whey (a murky, watery liquid). Most of the nutrients are concentrated in the curd. (The nutrients are a high percentage of proteins and fats, and a smaller amount of sugar.) The Sun Valley Creamery makes cheese by adding bacteria to milk. As the bacteria grow in the milk, they produce acid (lactic acid). This causes the milk to curdle, or separate into curds and whey. The lactic acid is a product of the breakdown of the sugar lactose. Lactose is broken down by the enzyme lactase, which is produced by the bacteria. The lactic acid produced by the bacteria, as well as other changes in the nutrients caused by the bacteria, produces cheese with distinct tastes and textures.

Both cheddar and cottage cheeses are made from curds that have been acid-separated. However, cheddar cheese goes through an additional stage of preparation called ripening, or curing; cottage cheese does not. Ripening and curing describe the process in which the curd is exposed to another round of bacterial culturing. The bacteria, and more specifically the work of their enzymes, further transform the nutrients in the fresh curd. For instance, in this final stage of ripening, any remaining lactose in the curd is converted into lactic acid. Thus, ripened cheeses generally have no measurable amounts of lactose, whereas unripened cheeses may contain a small amount.

Unlike cheese, the yogurt products we eat contain live cultures. A spoonful of yogurt contains lots of bacteria. These bacteria work to metabolize the nutrients that you are also spooning into your mouth. Similar to the curd and whey separation in making cheese, yogurt cultures primarily consist of lactic acid–producing bacteria. These bacteria are converting the lactose in the milk into lactic acid. But because yogurt contains live cultures, these harmless bacteria can enter your stomach in a spoonful of yogurt. Here they continue to metabolize the lactose with the lactase enzymes they are producing.

The bacterial cultures in yogurt also build enzymes that break down proteins and lipids. As a result, the proteins and lipids clot. This "clotting" and the effect of the increasing concentration of lactic acid change the physical properties and chemical structure of milk into what we commonly recognize as yogurt.

Table 1.2 Ms. Hatfield's Test Results

Dairy Product	Complaining Customers	Noncomplaining Customers
milk	felt ill	felt fine
yogurt	felt fine	felt fine
cottage cheese	felt ill	felt fine
cheddar cheese	felt fine	felt fine

ANALYSIS

Record your responses to the following in your notebook.

1. Describe the similarities and the differences among yogurt, cottage cheese, and cheddar cheese.
2. Are the symptoms being experienced by some customers the result of a problem in the products being produced by Sun Valley? Explain your answer.
3. Explain why milk and cottage cheese cause some customers to feel ill, whereas yogurt and cheddar cheese do not.
4. Why do you think some customers have experienced these symptoms, whereas most of them do not?
5. Suggest ways that Sun Valley Creamery might help its customers.
6. How is the following scenario similar to Ms. Hatfield's dilemma? Describe the similarities and differences.
   A ruminant is an animal that "chews its cud." Animals such as cows, goats, and giraffes like to dine on grass and other vegetation that is made primarily of cellulose. Cellulose is a tough, fibrous substance; it is a long-chain polysaccharide. Animals cannot break down cellulose because they lack the necessary enzyme, cellulase. Cellulase breaks down cellulose to glucose. However, bacteria that inhabit the stomach of ruminants do produce cellulase. In exchange for room and board, these bacteria help cows and other ruminants break down the cellulose in grass to glucose. The glucose can then be used for energy and building blocks by the cow.
7. Why can ruminants eat grass, whereas humans cannot?

Learning Experience 7

A Breath of Fresh Air

Prologue

Take a deep breath. What did you just inhale? Air is made up of many different kinds of gases and is an essential resource for most living organisms. In searching for life on other planets, biologists use changes in atmospheric gases as one indicator of the presence of life. In Learning Experience 3, you determined that the plant grown in the absence of carbon dioxide could not carry out one of its central metabolic processes. This process was photosynthesis. Without carbon dioxide, the plant would eventually die. Many organisms that do not photosynthesize also require air. How do they use it? What does it have to do with their metabolic processes, if anything? In this learning experience, you explore how air is used by these organisms. You also examine how the role of air enables energy from the food you eat to drive the processes of life.

Brainstorming

Discuss the following questions with your partner, and record your thinking in your notebook. Be prepared to share your ideas with the class.

1. What resources have you explored so far? How are they used by living organisms?
2. What other resources are important to survival?
3. How long can humans survive without food? without water? without air? Why do you think the answers are so different?
4. What gas(es) in the air do you use when you take in a breath of air? Does the composition of air change when it is exhaled? If so, how?
5. How is the gas or gases used by your body?

ACTIVITY

What Goes In . . .

What happens when we take air into our bodies? Does it change composition or remain the same? The composition of air can be determined using indicators that detect different kinds of gases. In this activity, you will analyze data in which the gases of inhaled air and exhaled air are compared.

ANALYSIS

Using the data from Table 1.3, record your responses to the following in your notebook.

1. How do you think these data were obtained?
2. What do the data tell you about which component of air we use?
3. Why do you think the carbon dioxide content increased?
4. What do the nitrogen data tell you?
5. How might you design an experiment to answer the question, "What happens to air in the presence of living organisms?"

Table 1.3 Analysis of Air Inhaled and Exhaled by Humans		
Gas	Inhaled	Exhaled
oxygen	19.70%	15.70%
nitrogen	74.10%	74.50%
carbon dioxide	0.04%	3.60%

. . . Must Come Out

ACTIVITY

How can we measure changes in the composition of air as living organisms use it? What do living organisms use from the air they take in? In this experiment, you will determine which gases organisms use. You will use chemical indicators to observe changes in the air that take place in the presence of living things. You will also explore why these changes happen. The two indicators that you will use are

- phenol red, which changes color in the presence of an acid, and
- limewater, which forms a precipitate (gets cloudy) in the presence of carbonic acid. Carbonic acid is an acid that forms when carbon dioxide dissolves in water.

Materials

For each group of four students:

- 4 safety goggles
- 9 large test tubes
- 3 small test tubes that fit inside the larger tubes
- 3 cork stoppers to fit the large tubes
- 1 test-tube rack
- 2 wrapped straws
- paper towels
- 1 small bottle phenol red solution
- 1 small bottle limewater
- 1 small bottle carbonated water
- 1 small bottle vinegar
- 1 wax marking pencil
- 1 eyedropper
- 2 beakers (250-mL)

- distilled water
- one of the following pairs:
  - yeast-sugar solution
  - boiled yeast-sugar solution

OR
  - 1 small live insect
  - 1 small dead insect

PROCEDURE

1. Identify the question being asked in the experiment. Then create a hypothesis. Predict the results of the experiment in an if/then statement.
2. Read through the procedure and determine how you will record your data.

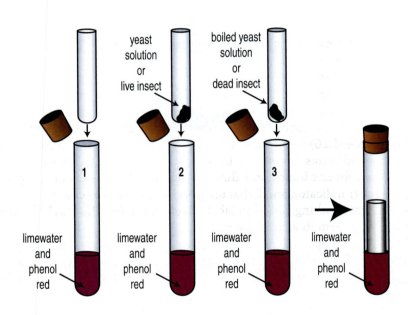

Figure 1.24

How to set up test tubes 1, 2, and 3.

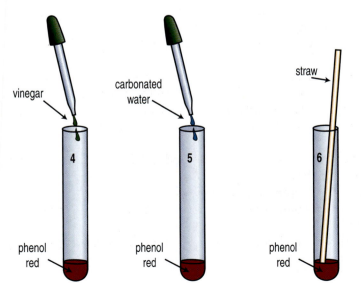

Figure 1.25

Setup for test tubes 4, 5, and 6.

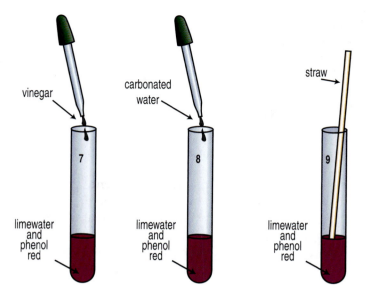

Figure 1.26

Setup for test tubes 7, 8, and 9.

3. Before beginning the experiment, record the following:
   a. the variable in the experiment, and
   b. the positive and negative controls.
   (Keep in mind that in many scientific investigations, there are many more controls than experimental samples. In this experiment, there are 7 controls. To identify each control, first copy the diagrams of the test-tube setups (Figures 1.24–1.26) into your notebook. Then indicate which ones are controls for which indicators. You should have 1 control that is negative for acids, 3 that are positive for one indicator, 1 that is negative for one indicator and positive for the other indicator, and 2 that are positive for both indicators.)
4. Use the wax marking pencil to label 9 large test tubes: "1," "2," "3," and so forth. Place them in a test-tube rack.
5. With an eyedropper, add 10 drops of phenol red solution to each of the 9 test tubes. Be careful not to touch the side of the test tube with the eyedropper. Hold the dropper over the mouth of the test tube and let the drops fall freely. Phenol red is an indicator that changes color in the presence of acids.
6. Rinse the eyedropper by drawing distilled water from one beaker into the dropper; then squirt the water into a second beaker. Repeat 2–3 times for thorough rinsing.
7. Pour limewater into tubes 1, 2, 3, 7, 8, and 9 until each is about one-quarter full.
   In the experiments in Learning Experiences 4 and 6, you used 1 indicator at a time. Here you will use 2 indicators in the same test tube. You will use phenol red to detect all acidic solutions (such as vinegar). And because limewater specifically detects carbonic acid, you will use it as your second indicator.
8. Label the small test tubes "1," "2," and "3." Place the following materials in these small tubes:
   Test tube 1: 10 drops of distilled water
   Test tube 2: a small, rolled piece of paper towel soaked in yeast-sugar solution
   Test tube 3: a small, rolled piece of paper towel soaked in boiled yeast-sugar solution
   OR

SAFETY NOTE

Limewater is an irritant. Avoid touching it. If it comes in contact with skin, rinse immediately with water.

Test tube 2: small live insect

Test tube 3: small dead insect

9. Gently slide the small test tubes into their like-numbered large test tubes (see Figure 1.24). Then place corks in all 3 large test tubes. Observe and record your initial observations in your notebook.

10. Add the following directly to the large test tubes labeled 4, 5, and 6 (see Figure 1.25). Be sure to rinse your eyedropper between *each* step.

Test tube 4: 5 drops of vinegar (3%–5% acetic acid)

Test tube 5: 5 drops of carbonated water (carbonated water contains dissolved carbon dioxide)

Test tube 6: your breath; blow through a straw for 30 seconds into the phenol red solution

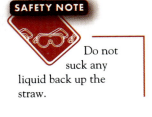

SAFETY NOTE

Do not suck any liquid back up the straw.

11. Add the following to test tubes 7, 8, and 9 (see Figure 1.26). Be sure to rinse your eyedropper between *each* step.

Test tube 7: 20 drops of vinegar

Test tube 8: 10 drops of carbonated water

Test tube 9: your breath; blow through a straw for about 30 seconds into the limewater and phenol red solution

12. Create a table in your notebook to record your observations of each test tube. Record the results from your indicators (color and other changes) from all 9 tubes. Compare your observations of tubes 2 and 3 with the other tubes. Compare your observations of tubes 2 and 3 with the initial observations you made in step 8. If there is a difference among these observations, explain why.

ANALYSIS

Record your responses to the following in your notebook.

1. Use your data to
   a. determine whether your hypothesis is correct. Explain why you think your hypothesis did or did not agree with your results.
   b. identify one characteristic of living organisms based on your experimental samples in test tubes 2 and 3. Explain your conclusion.

2. Use your data and the data in Table 1.3 to
   a. predict what kind of change might be observed in the oxygen content of the air in test tube 2. Explain your prediction.
   b. describe or diagram how you think these changes in the composition of air might take place in the presence of living organisms. Indicate what additional information you might need in order to explain what has caused the change in the composition of the air.

3. Where do you think the carbon dioxide in air comes from? Where do you think the carbon and the oxygen in carbon dioxide come from?

READING

Energy for All

What would happen if we left a living insect in a stoppered bottle for a while, even in the presence of food and water? Why does it need oxygen? Why does a lack of oxygen quickly lead to death? Clearly, oxygen is essential to life.

The following reading explores the role of oxygen in metabolism. It also examines how energy is obtained from the metabolism of the food you eat. As you read, keep track of what is happening to the biomolecules and where in the process energy is obtained. An analogy might help you understand energy in metabolism. Think about glucose as money in the bank and ATP, the molecule that cells use when they need energy, as money in your pocket that you can spend.

From Sun to Life

Much of your exploration so far has focused on the need of living organisms for energy and building blocks to sustain life. But where does this energy come from? As you learned in Learning Experience 3, the origin of energy on Earth comes from the sun. Plants transform solar energy into chemical energy (sugar). Plants then use this sugar to form carbohydrates, proteins, lipids, and nucleic acids. They do this through the processes of anabolism and catabolism.

During metabolic processes, the energy from the sun flows, in the form of chemical energy, from molecule to molecule. It is used to take molecules apart and build new molecules. During catabolism, larger molecules are broken down or oxidized. This reaction requires the input of some energy. But much more energy is released from the chemical energy stored in the chemical bonds in the molecules. During anabolism, energy is stored in chemical bonds. It remains there until the molecule is catabolized in another reaction. Thus, metabolism is two interconnected processes: (1) breaking down molecules to make building blocks that produce energy, and (2) building up molecules that store the energy needed to carry out functions in the cell.

It Takes Energy to Make Energy

As described in Learning Experience 6, the breakdown or oxidation of glucose is a multistepped process in living organisms. This multistepped process is facilitated by enzymes. Enzymes catalyze all the chemical reactions that take place during metabolism. Enzymes also catalyze the breakdown of glucose and the controlled release of energy. The bonds in glucose are broken, not in a single step as in the burning of glucose, but in nine steps. The bonds in the glucose molecule are broken using chemical energy. The products of this breakdown are rearranged in eight steps to form eight intermediate molecules. The end product of this breakdown of glucose is the generation of two new molecules. (This breakdown is called **glycolysis**; this means "glucose breaking.") These molecules contain three carbons each (**pyruvate**).

Topic: ATP
Go to: www.scilinks.org
Code: INBIOH273

They also contain energy that is released from the chemical bonds of glucose. This energy is transferred to a new molecule, **adenosine triphosphate** or **ATP**.

ATP is a very important molecule in living organisms. It is used widely as an energy "holding tank" in most living organisms. This molecule holds the energy released during the catabolism of glucose until it is needed by other processes in the cell such as anabolism and catabolism. Figure 1.27 is an overview of glycolysis. It shows the starting

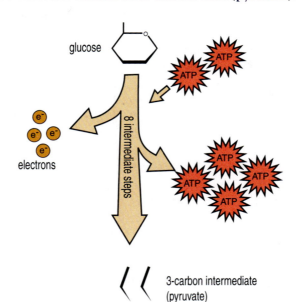

Figure 1.27

Energy transfer during glycolysis. To break the bonds in glucose, the energy of two ATP molecules is required. In the steps between the breakdown of the glucose and the formation of the two pyruvates, four ATP molecules are formed. This results in a net gain of two molecules.

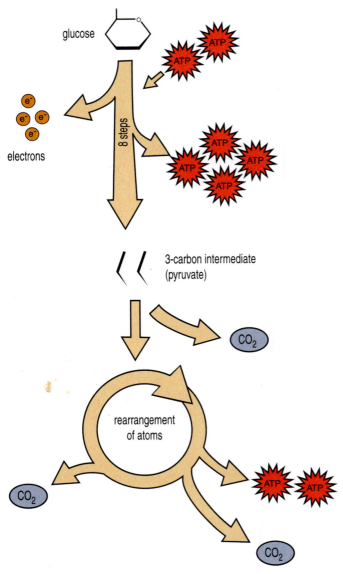

glucose

electrons

8 steps

ATP ATP

ATP ATP ATP ATP

3-carbon intermediate (pyruvate)

CO_2

rearrangement of atoms

CO_2

CO_2

ATP ATP

Figure 1.28

Pyruvate produced by glycolysis enters another metabolic pathway. Here it is transformed through a series of steps that result in the net gain of two more molecules of ATP and the release of two molecules of carbon dioxide as by-products.

material glucose and the eight intermediate products before the 3-carbon molecules are formed. In addition, it shows that the reaction requires an input of two ATP molecules. But four molecules of ATP are formed by the process. That means that there is a net gain of two ATP molecules available for other work of the organism. Although a net gain of two ATPs was made, in the bigger picture of the energy needs of a living organism, it is not nearly enough. In addition, the energy transferred from glucose at this stage to ATP represents only about 2% of the energy in the original glucose molecule. How does an organism tap into the rest of that energy?

The end products of glycolysis, those 3-carbon molecules called pyruvate, enter into yet another pathway. In this pathway, these pyruvate molecules are broken down, rearranged, and rejoined in a series of steps. These steps generate new molecules that form the starting material for other anabolic pathways. During the course of this pathway, electrons are transferred from molecule to molecule. (Remember, chemical reactions are actually the transfer of electrons.)

This transfer of electrons also involves the transfer of energy that is contained in the electrons. It is the energy in the electrons that is ultimately transferred to ATP. Carbon dioxide is released at this point as a waste product. From the beginning of the breakdown of glucose, a net gain of four ATP molecules has been made (see Figure 1.28). Still not enough! During this pathway, however, many high-energy electrons have changed "hands" (actually molecules). But there is still a lot of energy to be had. How can the organism get more of this energy converted into ATP?

Let's Get Oxidized!

Oxygen is the organism's key to finally obtaining the solar energy that was trapped in glucose. Look again at the rearrangement in the two pathways shown in Figure 1.28. High-energy-containing electrons were transferred to molecules whose main purpose is to pass them on, through a complex transport system. The energy that is present in these electrons when they enter this transport system is gradually transferred, in a series of steps, to form ATP. Oxygen, which organisms have taken from the air, is the final acceptor of the electrons. The net gain of ATPs from this transfer of electrons is 32. Much better!

At the end of these reactions, the electron has lost its high energy. It has lost this energy by passing it on to the molecule of ATP. Finally, we see a role for oxygen. In any system, the role of waste remover is essential. Oxygen serves that essential role for living organisms. It removes the spent electrons that are by-products or waste products of metabolic processes. The final product of this reaction is water (see Figure 1.29). Thus, two waste products, carbon dioxide and water, are generated by the catabolic reactions just examined. The products gained by these reactions are building materials for the anabolic reactions and energy in the form of 36 molecules of ATP. This transport of electrons to oxygen and the generation of ATP along the way is referred to as **cellular respiration**.

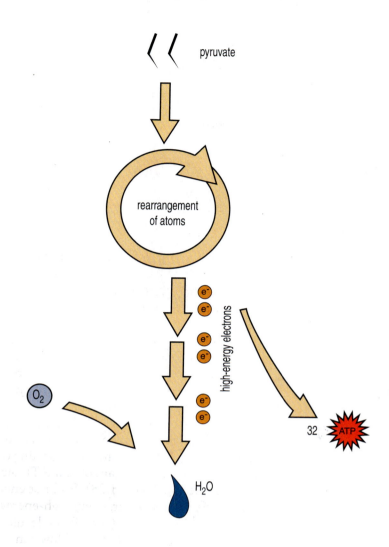

Figure 1.29
High-energy electrons are passed through a series of reactions in which oxygen serves as the final electron acceptor. Two more ATPs are formed, and water is formed as a by-product.

The rapid death of most living organisms when deprived of oxygen, then, is a direct result of the organism's need for an electron acceptor. If oxygen is not present, the flow of electrons is stopped. As a result, that large quantity of ATP cannot be made. Organisms need a constant supply of energy to continue to maintain the characteristics of life. In the absence of oxygen, the supply of energy is rapidly depleted. Thus, the organism can no longer carry out its energy-requiring life functions. Figure 1.30 presents an overview of metabolism. It shows the pathway's form, energy transfer, anabolism, and catabolism.

 **ANALYSIS**

Record your responses to the following in your notebook.

1. In Learning Experience 6, the chemical reaction for the burning of glucose was described as follows:

$$C_6H_{12}O_6 + 6O_2 + energy \rightarrow 6CO_2 + 6H_2O + energy$$

In words or drawings, explain how this reaction takes place metabolically. Include the following:
   a. where the glucose came from,
   b. where the oxygen came from,

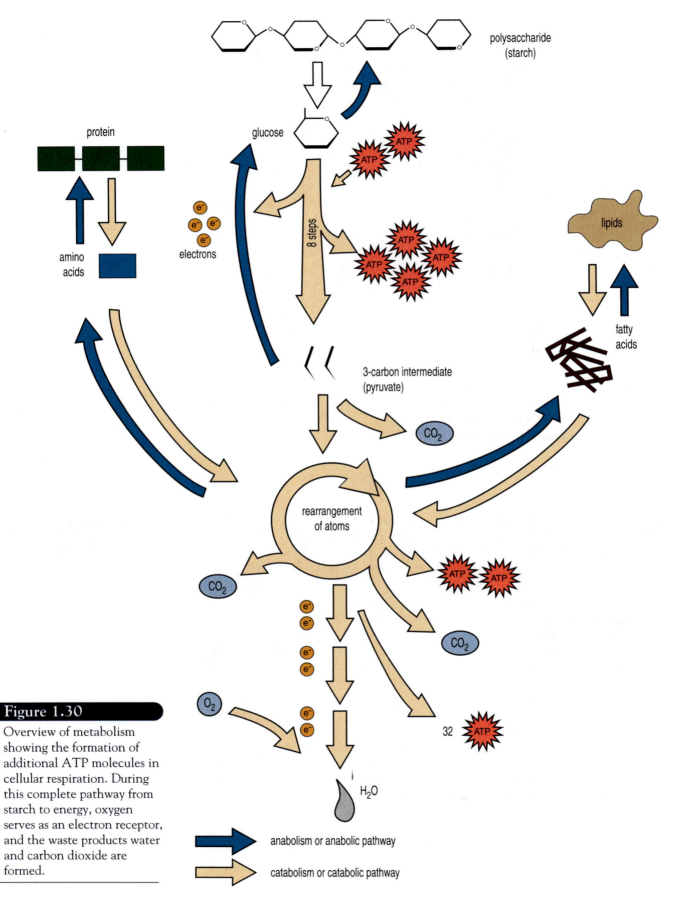

polysaccharide
(starch)

protein

glucose

ATP
ATP

amino
acids

electrons

8 steps

ATP
ATP
ATP
ATP

lipids

fatty
acids

3-carbon intermediate
(pyruvate)

CO_2

rearrangement
of atoms

CO_2

ATP   ATP

CO_2

O_2

32   ATP

H_2O

anabolism or anabolic pathway

catabolism or catabolic pathway

Figure 1.30

Overview of metabolism showing the formation of additional ATP molecules in cellular respiration. During this complete pathway from starch to energy, oxygen serves as an electron receptor, and the waste products water and carbon dioxide are formed.

c. the fate of the glucose molecule as it is catabolized,

d. the fate of the oxygen molecule,

e. products that are formed as a result of intermediate reactions,

f. where the energy for the catabolism is obtained,

g. an indication of the net energy gain, and

h. a comparison (differences and similarities) between burning glucose and catabolizing glucose.

2. Do you think that photosynthetic organisms carry out this process? Why or why not? Where would the glucose come from?

3. In 1772, Joseph Priestley observed that "good air" supported the burning of a candle flame. He also observed that good air supported the breathing of an animal. If a mouse was placed under a jar, it would live for a while and then die. If a plant was placed under a jar with a mouse, the animal would live longer than it would have without the plant. Explain the science in each of these results.

4. The poison cyanide binds tightly to a section of the electron transport system. This effectively blocks the transfer of electrons to oxygen. Explain why cyanide is deadly to living organisms.

5. Describe how the process of respiration might cause the changes in the air that you observed in the activities What Goes In . . . and . . . Must Come Out. Where do the carbon and oxygen atoms in the carbon dioxide come from?

6. Construct a concept map that describes the relationship among the concepts of metabolism, photosynthesis, and respiration. Use 10 or more words from the reading and previous learning experiences. Use the word *life* as your central concept. Be prepared to present your map in class.

EXTENDING *Ideas*

▶ Certain organisms can live and maintain life in the absence of oxygen. They do this by generating energy by a metabolic process called fermentation. Yeast cells carry out a fermentation process whose by-products are used in several ways. Describe the chemical reactions involved in the process of fermentation. Include the starting resources yeast use, how yeast obtain energy and building blocks during this process, and how the by-products of these reactions have been used by humans. Identify other organisms that provide products useful to humans through the process of fermentation.

▶ When the weather gets cold, water turtles head for the pond and settle in for a long winter's sleep. Burying themselves under layers of mud and dead leaves, they stop eating and breathing in a process called brummation. (Mammals hibernate; reptiles brummate.) Small amounts of oxygen are taken in through special skin cells in the turtle's tail. But oxygen levels are very low in the turtle during this period. Research this process and explain how turtles can survive for 2 to 3 months with very little oxygen.

Scientific Illustrator   Elise pulls out her first mock-up of a poster she is creating to show Dr. Brown, a measles researcher at the local university. The poster, titled "Have you ever had measles?," conveys, with the simplest of line drawings, the itchy, uncomfortable feeling of the disease. Elise drew a child's exasperated face dotted with spots. She then used computer design software to switch the background from white to black, convert the gray lines to green, and splatter the face with neon pink spots. Elise's job as a scientific illustrator is to turn scientific information into a dazzling picture, poster, chart, graph, book, flyer, kit, or other product that her client needs.

When Elise first met with Dr. Brown, her goal was to find out the story he wanted to tell, and discuss how best to illustrate it. She gathered information by talking to him, asking questions, and most important, listening to his ideas. Elise then set about translating the complex science and research findings into an easy-to-understand illustration. She researched the subject to make sure she understood the concepts. Understanding the scientific content is what separates scientific illustrators from other artists. Elise must be able to propose solutions the scientist hasn't considered and use her artistic training to suggest illustrations that will explain the concepts more clearly.

Elise starts every illustration by making a sketch using pencil and paper. She then has it checked by the doctor or scientist for accuracy. Computers are usually used to finalize the sketches and add color. Computers can speed up design, make artwork more precise, and allow you to look at more possibilities (such as color options). They also can be essential for animation and 3D molecular illustrations.

Growing up, Elise always loved art and she drew all the time. Although she loved to draw, she never considered art as a career. And by the time she got to high school, she also really liked biology. Her biology teacher made learning the structure and mechanisms of life fun. He gave bonus points for the drawings Elise included in her lab reports, and encouraged her to continue to improve.

In college, Elise decided to pursue medicine, and enrolled in a pre-med curriculum. She managed to sneak an art class into each semester just for fun. One afternoon while studying in the biology department, Elise saw a poster that asked, "What can you do with a biology degree?" A career as a scientific illustrator was on the poster's list. She'd never heard of it before but thought it sounded perfect. She found an old pamphlet in the campus career office and was amazed to discover that scientific illustration was the perfect union of the two seemingly unrelated areas she loved. Elise went on to get her bachelor's degree in biology and a master's degree in medical and biological illustration. Some day Elise would like to take more courses in 3D animation as well as in the biological fields that have expanded since she graduated from school.

Now Elise works for a small company that specializes in scientific art services. Its clients include scientific laboratories, magazines, newspapers, and publishing companies. Elise enjoys working with creative, intelligent people who she can learn from. She sees every project as an opportunity to learn and gets a kick out of helping to explain science to others. She's also thrilled that her job involves talking to accomplished scientists and doctors, each of whom challenges her to solve a puzzle. When Elise produces her creative solution, she is pleased to have solved the problem well.

Pollution Control Technician   Angelo and his co-worker Mikayla head out for a busy day on the job. Both men are pollution control technicians employed by the town of Santa Maria. They have a long list of sites they need to visit before the day is through. Some are sites where they will take water samples and others are facilities they need to inspect. Their first stop is Sampling Station #142 where they take a surface water sample to test for contaminants. Then they visit Leader Manufacturing to ensure that the company is complying with state and local health and water pollution regulations.

As part of Santa Maria's pollution control program, Angelo works with environmental specialists in the Santa Maria environmental health department. Angelo's primary job as a pollution control technician is to administer the town's water pollution control program. It's Angelo's responsibility to conduct inspections, tests, and field investigations to determine the extent of water contamination. He also tries to find ways to control and prevent contamination. He gathers and analyzes surface and groundwater samples for certain contaminants, tracks pollution sources, and ensures that they are abated. It's his job to set up, operate, and maintain environmental monitoring equipment and test instruments. Angelo and Mikayla share responsibility for maintaining the records and data they collect and for preparing reports that document their results. They also conduct inspections such as the one carried out at Leader Manufacturing.

Angelo grew up in the Midwest and loved exploring the outdoors. He also loved nature and the science that explained how nature works. By the time Angelo was a high school senior, he wanted to be a wildlife biologist. When he went to visit the coast for the first time, however, his interest changed. He became fascinated with the ocean. The marine environment was so mysterious that it triggered an interest Angelo felt he had to pursue. He researched several programs and decided on a 2-year physical science program offered in Santa Maria. The program allowed him to study marine biology, ecology, chemistry, physics, and computers, which he now uses in his daily work. While working toward his degree, Angelo took on a part-time internship with the town of Santa Maria where he received valuable on-the-job training.

After graduation, the environmental health department offered Angelo a full-time job as a pollution control technician. He feels that his career is relatively stable since environmental protection is a nationally legislated priority. Development pressures in coastal areas, habitat loss, and point and nonpoint sources of pollution are adversely affecting environmental quality almost everywhere. The need for pollution control technicians will continue, if not increase, as the complexity of environmental problems increases. Angelo truly enjoys being directly involved with, and responsible for, changes that make a positive difference in the natural environment.

Learning Experience 8

Reap the Spoils

Prologue

The very basics of sustaining life rely on a constant exchange of energy and chemical compounds among living organisms. There is a balance to this exchange; a product or waste of one organism may be a necessary resource for another. This flow of energy and matter links all living organisms. As a result, any change to any connection can alter the balance of the entire system.

During the next 2 weeks, you are going to observe and analyze these kinds of connections within a model environment. That model environment is milk. How is milk an "environment"? As you have seen in past learning experiences, foods contain nutrients that organisms use to sustain life. Milk has many nutrients, some of which you have identified. If milk is left open to the air, even for a short time, it can become the environment for many different kinds of microorganisms. These microorganisms float around in the air, searching for new environments with nutrients they can use as resources. As the organisms grow and live, dramatic changes can take place within this environment.

SCI
LINKS®
NSTA

Topic: Environment
Go to: www.scilinks.org
Code: INBIOH280

Brainstorming

Discuss the following questions with your partner, and record your thinking in your notebook. Be prepared to share your ideas with the class.

1. What do you think an environment is? What is in it? What does it provide to organisms that live in it?
2. How could different kinds of organisms live in the same environment?
3. What kinds of observations might you make if you wanted to study organisms in their environments?
4. What kinds of changes might take place in an environment as the result of organisms living in it?
5. What might cause these changes?
6. What kinds of indicators or tools of measurement would you use to determine whether changes had taken place in an environment?
7. How long might it take to observe changes in some environments?

8. How might we study the changes in an environment and the organisms in an environment in class over a reasonable amount of time?
9. What models of systems can you think of that might provide information about how environments change over time? What might be the limitations of using models?

Home Sweet Milk

You will begin the activity by setting up your model environment. Once you set up the environment, you need to design your investigative procedure. Your procedure will include careful observations over time and a method to record detailed and accurate data. The data should include kinds of organisms living in milk, how these populations alter the environment in which they live, and how they affect one another. This activity will continue over the course of the next 2 weeks. Every 2–3 days you will spend a class session sampling and testing your milk environment and talking with your group members about what you observe.

Materials

For each group of four students:

- 4 safety goggles
- 125 mL milk
- 1 beaker (250-mL) or clean plastic margarine tub or other container
- litmus or pH paper, or access to pH probe
- 1 thermometer
- 4 nutrient agar plates
- cellophane tape
- 4 sterile cotton swabs or 1 inoculating loop
- 8 microscope slides and coverslips
- 1 eyedropper
- distilled water
- 1 wax marking pencil
- plastic wrap
- 1 dissecting needle or fork
- 1 flame source (candle or Bunsen burner)
- 3 empty petri dishes or plastic containers for holding water
- crystal violet stain
- paper towels
- 1 forceps or tweezers

For the class:

- compound microscopes
- 1 pH probe (optional)
- 1 32°C–37°C incubator (optional—can be made from cardboard box)
- 1 pot holder or oven mitt
- 1 microwave oven or other heat source

PROCEDURE

1. **STOP & THINK** Determine the question being asked and write a hypothesis. Then predict the outcome of this activity.

2. **STOP & THINK** What kinds of tests and techniques would you need to carry out to determine what happens in the milk environment over time? Use your current understanding of metabolism to help determine some of the tests and techniques you might want to include. In the reading that follows, there are descriptions of techniques that might help you with this procedure. Use these techniques in addition to others you might include in your experimental design. Don't forget to use your senses as indicators of change in your experimental design.

3. **STOP & THINK** Develop ways to illustrate your observations and data-collecting system that are clear, accurate, and consistent. Also develop ways to keep track of questions that arise in the course of the experiment. Record any unexpected turn of events that may affect your outcome and results (for example, knocking over your container of milk). To complete your laboratory report and to prepare for a class presentation, you will need your data, illustrations, and the conclusions you draw.

4. Write a procedure that includes all of the necessary information described in steps 1–3 above. (Every member of the group will need to keep his or her own record of the data and his or her own illustrations.)

5. Ask your teacher to approve your proposed experimental design. Then obtain an empty 250-mL beaker (or margarine container). Label it with your group's name. Pour 125 mL of whole milk into the beaker.

6. Take any samples, conduct any tests, and record any measurements or observations your group has decided upon. Record your data in your notebook.

7. Find a storage location in the classroom where you can leave your milk sample undisturbed for several days. Confirm this location with your teacher. Note the characteristics of the area where your sample will be incubating. Is it sunny, cold, drafty, near a window, over a radiator?

8. Place both your milk sample, uncovered, and the covered agar plate (inverted, agar side up) in the designated storage location.

Techniques

Before you begin your experiment, carefully read all the steps listed in this reading. This information may be helpful in designing your experiment.

Population Studies

In this activity, you will want to observe what kinds of organisms are living in your milk now and during the course of your experiment. To help you do that, you will probably want to grow the organisms on nutrient agar plates. These plates contain nutrients that many kinds of bacteria can use to grow. They also contain a substance called agar, which is obtained from seaweed. Agar gives the nutrient mix a firmness that enables you to spread the organisms out on a surface and work with them. The procedure for preparing the plates is often

Figure 1.31
Streaking a plate.

called "streaking." Streaking enables you to examine more carefully what organisms are present at any point in time by amplifying their numbers. "Streaking out" your sample is actually a technique that permits separation of the different organisms that will grow on this plate. By spreading the sample across the large surface area of the plate, you can obtain isolated growths of microorganisms called colonies. Follow these steps to streak an agar plate:

1. Obtain a nutrient agar plate and a cotton swab or inoculating loop. Be careful not to touch the cotton end with your fingers. Place the nutrient agar plate on the table.
2. Dip the cotton end into the milk.
3. Remove the lid of the agar plate and continue to hold the lid in your hand. Be careful not to touch the inside.
4. Gently rub or streak the cotton swab or inoculating loop across the surface of the agar. Do not press too hard. It is best to move the swab in a zigzag pattern as shown in Figure 1.31. You may want to streak your initials in script.
5. Replace the lid on the agar plate and tape it closed. Use a wax marking pencil to label the plate on the bottom. Record your group name, the date, and the time. Place the agar plate upside down (agar side up) in a 37°C incubator or in the warmest spot in the room.
6. After a few days, check your agar plate for growth. Record any changes with an illustration.

Microscopic Population Studies

Now it's time to look carefully at and characterize the different kinds of organisms that might grow in your milk. To do that, you will probably want to examine samples taken from the agar plates under the microscope. Most bacteria are very small and difficult to see. Various stains will stain different kinds of bacteria and help in the identification process. For the purposes of this experiment, you will use one stain. When you take samples for viewing under the microscope, you may wish to sample from different-looking colonies. This will allow you to examine the different kinds of growth that may be taking place in your environment. Follow this procedure to stain each sample:

Prepare a Microbial Smear

1. Place a small drop of water on a microscope slide.
2. Remove a small amount of growth from your agar plate using the wooden end of a cotton swab. Mix it with the drop of water. You may wish to prepare several smears from different-looking colonies on your plate.
3. Air dry the slide for a few minutes. When it has dried, pass the slide briefly through a flame. (This is called heat fixing.) When fixing, be sure the side of the slide with the specimen is facing up, away from the flame.

SAFETY NOTE

Stain the Smear

1. Place several drops of crystal violet stain on the heat-fixed smear. Wait 2 minutes.
2. Rinse the slide with water and blot dry gently with a paper towel.
3. Examine your slide under a microscope. Start with low power, then increase magnification. Draw what you see.

Measuring pH

You may already be familiar with acidic and basic solutions. Vinegar, for example, is acidic; soapy water is basic. You can use pH paper or a pH meter to measure the pH changes that might take place in your environment. The pH scale found on pH paper or on a pH meter ranges from 1 to 14. These numbers indicate whether a solution is acidic (pH 1 to around 6), neutral (pH 7.0), or alkaline (basic, pH 8 to 14).

ACTIVITY

Continuing to Reap the Spoils

(Suggested days: 4, 7, 10)

PROCEDURE

1. Get your milk sample in the beaker from its storage (incubating) location.
2. Take careful notes that describe the conditions of the area where your sample has been incubating.
3. Sample and measure what you wish to measure. Record all of your observations. Then cover the milk sample container with a piece of clear plastic wrap. To aerate the container, pierce the plastic wrap with the tongs of a fork or other pointed tool.
4. Return your milk sample to the designated storage location.
5. If you have nutrient agar plates from previous sessions, check them for growth. If they have grown and you can observe the different organisms, prepare and stain your samples. Then make your observations.
6. If you wish to keep your bacterial smears, store them in a safe place.
7. In addition to recording your data, note any questions you may have or unusual observations you make.
8. Analyze your results and think about what has happened to the milk and why. Use the following questions as a guide:
   a. What do the changes you have observed suggest about what has happened in the milk over the last several days?
   b. How do these changes relate to metabolic processes that have taken place in organisms growing in the milk? Explain each change.
   c. Did you observe a change in the kind of microorganisms growing in the milk over time? If so, what might explain why this happened?
   d. Do you think the nutrient composition of the milk has changed? How? How would you go about verifying this?

Analyzing Reaping the Spoils

This is your final analysis for the extended activity on milk as an environment. Read the following Analysis section. You will need to write a final laboratory report and use the report for preparing a presentation.

ANALYSIS

1. Analyze your data with your group.
2. Discuss the results and draw your conclusions. (Take notes on the discussion for use in writing your laboratory report.)
3. Plan your presentation. Include in your planning, individual responsibility for preparing any illustrations, graphs, and text to be used in the presentation. The presentation should include the following:
   a. the observations and measurements your group chose to collect,
   b. the reasons your group chose to make those observations or collect the data,
   c. a summary of your results, and
   d. any conclusions your group was able to make based on your analysis.
4. Prepare an individual laboratory report for this experiment in your notebook. Be sure to include the following:
   a. the question or questions being asked,
   b. the design of the experiment,
   c. the procedures used to collect data,
   d. the data,
   e. the analysis and significance of the data,
   f. conclusions based on the data and your understanding of resource use and metabolic processes of living organisms,
   g. additional questions you might want to pursue and how you might go about answering them, and
   h. sources of possible errors.
5. Use material from your report to prepare your portion of the presentation.

EXTENDING *Ideas*

After the discovery of the existence of microorganisms by Anton van Leeuwenhoek in the 17th century, scientists began to investigate the origins of these life-forms. Some believed that the microorganisms were formed spontaneously from the nonliving matter present in their environment. Others believed that the "seeds" or "germs" of these microscopic creatures were always present in the air and in foods. They believed that these seeds could grow, provided that the conditions were suitable for their development. This argument over the theory of spontaneous generation raged for years. Scientists gathered some evidence that the latter theory was more likely. But it wasn't until 1861 that the spontaneous generation theory was dispelled. In that year, Louis Pasteur carried out a set of definitive experiments to prove that life only came from life. Pasteur boiled a broth and placed it in a flask connected to the outside air only by a piece of tubing. He bent the tubing in such a way that microorganisms could not pass through. After many weeks, this broth failed to show any microbial growth. Pasteur then broke off the neck of such a flask so that air entered. The broth rapidly became populated with microbes. State what you think Pasteur's conclusions were based on your understanding of the milk experiment.

Louis Pasteur was a French scientist who lived in the 1800s. He made many major contributions to the fields of microbiology and medicine. His germ theory of disease laid the foundation for understanding the nature of infectious disease. Using this understanding, he instituted major changes in hospital practices to limit the spread of infectious diseases. He discovered that weakened microbes could be used as vaccines. He also discovered that rabies was caused by agents so small that they were invisible under a microscope. These discoveries were one of the first indications of the existence of viruses and their ability to cause disease. A word derived from his name appears on almost every carton of milk as well as on many other products. Pasteurization refers to a process by which microbes that contaminate perishable foods can be destroyed by heat without affecting the food itself. Visit the grocery store and find as many pasteurized products as you can. Research the process to determine how microbes can be destroyed without destroying the food product.

CAREER FOCUS

Medical Technologist Marcus has just discovered that the lab results for a recent test performed in the chemistry section of the Department of Laboratory Medicine seem unusual. This is when Marcus transforms from a medical technologist into a detective. Because he is the team leader of the chemistry section at Memorial Hospital, Marcus needs to determine the reason for the unexpected results. The problem might be with the way a sample was drawn or with the lab equipment. So Marcus needs to rule out these possibilities. He talks with the patient's nurse and doctor about the results and looks for clues about how the results were obtained. Marcus reviews how the laboratory test was performed and checks the equipment used. After his investigations are complete, he concludes that the lab test must be repeated to ensure that the results are accurate.

Marcus is very conscientious of the quality of the lab's work. Many doctors depend on the results for diagnosis and other decisions about patient care. He routinely checks that test results are accurate, the instruments are working correctly, and all data are properly recorded. Marcus is also responsible for updating the protocols for the Laboratory Information System, the lab's computer database system for managing patient data.

Marcus feels that his job as a medical technologist allows him to have the best of both worlds. He performs laboratory bench work as a scientist and carries out administrative tasks. He handles daily staffing issues in the lab. These include making sure enough people are available to work in each subsection of the laboratory and training new employees on protocols and equipment use and care. He also helps to set up and test equipment, and performs lab tests on patient blood, urine, and other bodily fluids when the lab is short staffed.

When he was growing up, Marcus loved science and spent many hours experimenting with his chemistry set. After graduating from high school, Marcus attended a 4-year college to study biology and chemistry. But he wasn't sure which career path he would choose. While taking a freshman biology course, a classmate who was majoring in medical technology told Marcus about the profession. Through research at the college career office,

Marcus found out that the employment outlook was excellent and that a career as a medical technologist was both science and technically oriented. The first 3 years of his 4-year program consisted of academic study, which included courses in biology, chemistry, and computer and laboratory technology. The fourth year provided an internship at a local hospital where he did laboratory rotations through different departments.

After graduation, Marcus worked the evening shift as a medical technician at Memorial Hospital. He rotated through different laboratory departments and worked where he was needed most. The experience reinforced what he had learned during his internship and gave him a chance to see how health professionals work together. Marcus loved working in the chemistry lab, so he accepted a position at the first opening. After several years in that position, Marcus was promoted to medical technologist. Eventually he was designated the team leader for the chemistry lab.

Marcus takes pleasure in knowing that his work helps people. Lab tests help doctors make diagnostic decisions and figure out what is wrong with a patient. In the future, Marcus would like to help medical laboratory professionals continue their education by developing materials that they can use to update their skills. Medical technologists are required to maintain their skills through continuing education, which must be documented for hospital accreditation, professional certification, and/or state licensure. However, it is often difficult for people working in clinical laboratory science to attend outside training courses because of time, financial, or family constraints. Marcus would like to work with the staff at Memorial Hospital to develop online continuing education courses that are interesting and meaningful to medical technicians and technologists.

Microbiologist

It's 1:55 PM and Alexis just can't seem to tear herself away from the microscope. She's running late for her 2:00 introductory microbiology course that she teaches to undergraduates, and she can't wait to tell them what she has been learning in her lab. Alexis is a research microbiologist and professor at Whitcomb University. She runs a research laboratory where she studies bacteria and how they reproduce.

Alexis's first experience with microbes happened while growing up on her family's farm. She knew about many microbial diseases long before she knew about microbes because she saw how the animals on her farm were treated for illnesses. Little did she know that many of those diseases were caused by bacteria. Alexis enjoyed science, but it wasn't until high school biology that she really became captivated. Her teacher asked the class to bring in water samples from home to examine under the microscope. He suggested that the samples be taken from where the cows, chickens, or pets drank. Alexis thought the water from the pigpen would be a great source to sample. Looking at the water under the microscope, Alexis discovered that her sample was loaded with microbes. All of the students in her class took turns looking at the bacteria floating in her sample. That's when Alexis caught the bug for microbiology! She was fascinated and wanted to learn more about the bacteria she was seeing.

Based on Alexis's interest and enthusiasm, her teacher encouraged her to pursue microbiology at the college level. Alexis took courses in biology and bacteriology. She was able to experiment with different bacteria samples as well as with other organisms such as viruses, algae, mold, and yeast. During the summer between her junior and senior years, Alexis worked as a research assistant in one of the laboratories in the Bacteriology Department. During her senior year, she continued to work in the lab part time and really got hooked on research. She continued her lab work after graduation. But soon she realized that having only a bachelor's degree prevented her from being a major contributor in the lab. She just didn't have enough information to help the researchers come up with new ideas to pursue. Alexis felt that more class work and training was necessary. So she decided to earn a Ph.D. and learn how to become an independent researcher. With even more postdoctoral training and a lot of mentoring from experienced microbiology researchers, Alexis is now a professor of microbiology and runs her own laboratory.

Alexis loves making new scientific discoveries. She feels the changing world of microbiology helps her stay engaged in and energized about her work. She tries to pass on her energy and enthusiasm to the students she teaches. Alexis helps undergraduates and graduate students by mentoring them and giving them research assistant positions in her laboratory. In that way, she can show them what her work is really like and how they can contribute to scientific research.

How Did It All Begin?

Prologue

How did life begin? Did life arise from nonlife? How did the components of the molecules of life get organized into biomolecules and these biomolecules into cells? What is life? In the quest to answer those questions, the mystery of where and how life began inevitably follows. Attempts to learn how life began have been made through pursuits in the philosophy, religion, and science of every culture. The answers have inspired the creation of countless stories, poems, paintings, and musical scores. Ancient Egyptians thought that silt brought in by floods from the Nile gave rise to frogs and toads. The Greek philosopher Aristotle identified slime and drops of dew as the origin of insects, and mud as giving rise to fish and eels. Speculation about the events that brought about the transition from nonliving to living has resulted in many heated debates. Since no living thing existed to witness the beginnings of life, scientists rely on fossil evidence and on studies of the living descendants of the first life—life on Earth today—to help unravel this mystery. Scientific explanations for the origins of life have been proposed, discarded, and continue to change and evolve as evidence and data are gathered from many different fields including oceanography, molecular biology, geochemistry, paleobiology, and astronomy.

Brainstorming

Discuss the following questions with your partner, and record your thinking in your notebook. Be prepared to share your ideas with the class.

1. What stories, myths, or theories are you familiar with that account for the origins of life on Earth?
2. What do you think is meant by the statement, "Life arose from nonlife"?

A Long, Long Time Ago

ACTIVITY

Some theories propose that the transition from nonlife to life was a slow and measured event. In 1871, Charles Darwin proposed that life arose gradually over time in a "warm little pond." From a rich broth of organic chemicals, molecules coalesced (joined) to form the first stirrings of organisms. Other scientists have theorized that life exploded on the scene in a bubbling cauldron. It happened suddenly and in many different places. (A bubbling cauldron is a boiling kettle of soup that contained all the necessary ingredients of life.)

Another source of scientific exploration attempts to reproduce in the laboratory the actual beginnings. In 1953, Stanley Miller and Harold Urey recreated in a glass jar conditions that were believed to be present on Earth during its early formation. They used water (as oceans) and heat to form water vapor. They used methane (CH_4), ammonia (NH_3), and hydrogen for atmosphere. And finally, they used electrical sparks for the lightning and electrical discharges that probably punctuated the atmosphere. Within a week, a sticky sludge was collected in a beaker (see Figure 1.32). When analyzed, this sludge proved to contain organic molecules, including large quantities of amino acids. Using similar conditions, scientists have been able to generate nucleotides, lipids, carbohydrates, and ATP.

Were these conditions the same as those that prevailed during the formation of Earth? Was this how the molecules of life were formed 4 billion years ago? Exactly when did the planet Earth form? How long after the event did life appear? How long did it take from the formation of the first life to the appearance of humans? Conceptualizing numbers in the billions is often very difficult to do. In this activity, you will create a timeline of Earth's history using string to represent time and paper clips to represent events along the timeline.

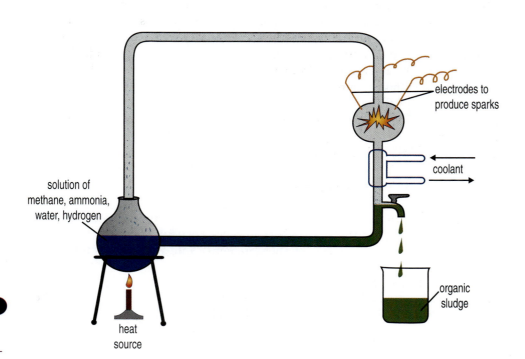

Figure 1.32

Setup of Miller and Urey's experiment.

Materials

For the class:

- 4–5 m (13–16 ft) of strong string
- marker or colored tape
- 20–30 paper clips (10–15 each of 2 different colors that represent either a geological event or a biological event)
- 20–30 event cards with 1 fact or piece of evidence on each
- box or hat

PROCEDURE

1. Several student volunteers will determine the length of string to use to represent a specific length of time. For example, 1 meter (about 3 feet) of string might represent 1 billion years.
2. Choose an event card and read the information on the outside of the card. Do not look inside the card until told to do so by your teacher.
3. Decide whether your information relates to a geological event or a biological event. Then select the paper clip with the appropriate color.
4. Decide when you think your event happened in the history of Earth. When it is your turn, use a paper clip to attach your card to the string at that point. Then open your card to see the actual time your event took place. If necessary, move your paper clip to the correct place on the timeline and reattach your card.

NOTE

Some cards may contain information that is bogus, or false. You must decide whether your information is real. If you think your information is false, tell the class when it is your turn and explain why.

The Bubbling Cauldron

Condensing from a cloud of dust and gases, Earth was formed approximately 4.6 billion years ago. Heat generated from the radioactive elements in the dust and from the pressure of gravity, which pulled Earth into a spherical shape, may have caused the interior of Earth to melt. Volcanic eruptions wracked the surface of Earth. The molten rock that spewed forth may have caused the atmospheric temperatures to reach fiery levels. The gravitational pull of Earth undoubtedly attracted meteors and asteroids from a heaven filled with celestial debris. This debris may have been remnants of the Big Bang that created the universe.

No one is sure of the composition of the air at that time. Recent evidence, however, suggests that it was not the atmosphere envisioned by Miller and Urey. Instead, the air over the surface of Earth was most likely made up of water vapor, carbon monoxide, carbon dioxide, nitrogen, hydrogen sulfide, and hydrogen cyanide (HCN). An inhospitable sphere bombarded by extraterrestrial missiles and having an atmosphere of cyanide and carbon monoxide. This does not sound exactly inviting for any form of life. Yet, from this hostile environment life apparently did arise.

ACTIVITY

SCLINKS®
NSTA

Topic: Evolution of the Earth
Go to: www.scilinks.org
Code: INBIOH291

PROCEDURE

1. Work with your partner to create a recipe for this "primordial soup" that would yield biomolecules. Use what you know about biomolecules and the information presented thus far in this learning experience.

2. Remember, you are limited to the materials and energy that were present on Earth at the time that it is believed life began. This is about 4.4 to 4.8 billion years ago.
3. Include the following in your recipe:
   - what elements are required,
   - which elements could bond together,
   - the role of energy and where the energy might have come from,
   - what the first biomolecules might have looked like, and
   - how larger molecules might have formed out of smaller molecules.

READING

The Spark of Life
Masses of Molecules

Did life arise in the calm of a pond, the warmth of a pool, slowly and steadily over millions of years, as Darwin proposed? Or did it arise frothing and spewing from a tumultuous, steaming environment? Recent discoveries near hydrothermal vents have revealed ecosystems teeming with life. (Hydrothermal vents are cracks leading to chambers of molten rock beneath the ocean floor.) These discoveries have lent support to the idea of a fiery origin of life. Mounting evidence indicates that life most likely began earlier than previously thought. This would have been before Earth began to cool and develop a more hospitable atmosphere. Other evidence suggests that the beginnings of life were brought to Earth by comets, asteroids, and meteorites colliding with Earth, or by the interplanetary dust that coated the newly forming planet. The meteorite that fell on Murchison, Australia, in 1969, was rich in an array of carbon-containing compounds. These compounds included several different amino acids, some of which have never been seen in organisms on Earth.

What did early biomolecules look like? Did they change over time? As you have investigated previously, all living things consist of primarily four kinds of biomolecules. Does that mean these were the only molecules that formed during this early period? Or is it possible that many arrangements of molecules came together but these were the only ones that, for whatever reasons, "survived" and were well suited for becoming "life"? This last idea reflects one of the great unifying principles of biology, evolution.

Evolution is the process by which changes take place in living things over time. Although these changes happen at random, certain of these changes persist. They do so because they offer some selective advantage for survival of a population. The biomolecules that are present today in all living things are the descendants of those early molecules. They are the result of changes that took place in the structure of biomolecules over time that made them well suited for survival.

The Importance of Being Organized

Let's assume that these biomolecules were formed and accumulated in a rich organic broth. The question then arises, how and why did they organize into larger structures? How did these biomolecules ultimately secede from their environment to form their own separate "union"?

For chemical reactions to occur efficiently, the reacting components must be in close proximity to one another. A chemist is more likely to carry out a reaction in a test tube than in a gallon vat or on a tabletop. Similarly, if life depends on a series of chemical reactions, the molecules of life must be close together. The next step on the road to living organisms was the encapsulation of the large molecules of life in a kind of living "test tube."

In 1923, a Russian scientist, Alexander Oparin, proposed that early organic molecules did not remain as simple compounds. He suggested that they formed large aggregates or clusters as a way of becoming more stable. Very early precursors of cells might then have been formed when aggregates of large molecules were surrounded by a membranelike structure. In 1960, American scientist Sidney Fox conducted an experiment. He demonstrated that large clusters of proteins or ribonucleic acids, when heated and allowed to cool under appropriate conditions, would form droplets or microspheres. These microspheres were able to grow, reproduce, and perform some of the basic life processes such as breaking down glucose.

Lipid molecules are likely candidates for this membranous kind of housing. Several theories exist about how biomolecules might have become encased in a lipid membrane. Experiments have shown that when a broth of concentrated organic molecules is dried, lipids spontaneously form droplets. It has also been shown that this drying process results in the chemical bonding of ribonucleotides to form large molecules of RNA. Could the association of these ribonucleotide molecules in primordial soup have led to the formation of membrane-bound ribonucleic acids?

Biologist David Deamer recently proposed another model. He suggested that molecules that formed membranes were also introduced by meteors. Deamer extracted organic compounds from the meteorite that had landed in Murchison, Australia. He demonstrated that among these compounds was a fatty acid chain, nine carbons long. This chain was capable of forming a membranous sack, a **liposome**. Further research with liposomes made in the laboratory has shown that these structures could take up RNA.

What is there about RNA that could make it a candidate for a component in the earliest life-form? In most organisms today, RNA is the nucleic acid that carries the information from DNA to the site in the cell where protein is synthesized. Some life-forms use RNA instead of DNA for information storage. One property of RNA is that it is highly changeable. That means that the information carried in RNA can change more easily than that in DNA. Another property of RNA is the ability to replicate or make copies of itself. The ability to make copies of oneself is a distinct advantage. The more copies, the more opportunity there is for change. The more opportunity there is for change, the more likely it is that some variant of the original molecule (or organism) will be better suited for survival.

Could RNA in a lipid shell have been the first cell-like structure? The association of self-replicating RNA inside a lipid membrane shell may not seem like much of a life. But it may have marked the beginnings of a line of cell-like structures that ultimately resulted in the structure of the cell as we know it. This would have happened through the process of change over time, evolution.

The ability to change with each new generation was an essential feature in the movement from the first cell-like structure to the complex organisms that have inhabited and continue to inhabit Earth. Without this ability to change, life on Earth today might still consist of little coalesced blobs of biomolecules. On a bigger scale, an additional characteristic of life is the ability to evolve. As living organisms reproduce themselves, their progeny (offspring) sometimes differ slightly from their parents. Sometimes these differences can give the offspring a slight advantage in surviving. This change is passed on to their progeny.

The change from blobs of biomolecules to prokaryotes then eukaryotes then multicellular organisms reflects a change from the simple to the more complex. Thus, another characteristic of life is complexity and the use of energy to maintain that complexity. In the next learning experience, you will investigate the cell and its complex structures. These structures enable the cell to carry out the biological processes of life.

ANALYSIS

Record your responses to the following in your notebook.

1. What events in the timeline of Earth's history and in your understanding of living organisms suggest that all life may have descended from common origins?

2. Could the droplets created by Sidney Fox be considered living? What about David Deamer's RNA-containing liposomes? Use your understanding of the characteristics of life to explain your responses.

3. Assume that many different kinds of molecules developed during the early time of the world. What might explain that only four kinds of molecules persisted?

4. Do you think life continues to be created from nonlife today? Does life continue to evolve? Explain your responses.

5. Create a concept map or a drawing that describes how life is thought to have begun. Start with primitive Earth and with the origins of life based on the readings. Include all of the components that you consider essential. Address how these might have organized into the biomolecules. Also propose how the biomolecules might have come together into a primitive organizational structure or cell.

Oceanographer   Dante and his fellow oceanographer are submerged more than a mile below the surface of the ocean. They're using the robotic arms of the submarine to take dozens of samples of deep sea sediments and rocks. It's part of the geological oceanography study they are conducting in their work for the federal agency that is responsible for the observation, measurement, assessment, and management of the country's ocean areas. Dante admits that being in a submarine and exploring depths seen by few humans is an amazing experience.

In total, Dante has spent months at sea during his career. He uses sound to map the ocean floor and sediment layers and takes air and water samples to monitor pollutants and carbon dioxide levels. He also uses optical devices to scan the deep ocean layers for evidence of underwater volcanoes and takes deep sea samples like he is doing today. But Dante also spends a considerable amount of time in his office and laboratory. Here he uses a computer and examines ocean samples. He writes proposals to formulate research plans, plots and analyzes data, and details the results of his work in documents to be published in scientific journals.

Growing up, Dante always wanted to be a scientist. By the time he finished elementary school, he had a telescope, microscope, and chemistry set. He also loved swimming and other water sports as well as watching

TV programs about the marine environment. In high school, Dante took an oceanography course that was offered as an elective. It was then that he began to entertain the idea of becoming an oceanographer. By setting up a classroom aquarium containing a variety of organisms, his teacher brought the subject into the classroom. Dante then volunteered at a local aquarium to learn more, and quickly became an oceanography aficionado. He decided to study oceanography in college and went on to receive his bachelor's degree. In addition to applying his coursework in physics, chemistry, and geology to his job, Dante also makes use of his coursework in English to write proposals and articles. His coursework in computers and mathematics helps him to manipulate and analyze data.

One aspect about studying oceanography that Dante appreciates is that so many branches of science are involved. Because oceanography is the study of the oceans, it includes all the basic sciences—physics, chemistry, geology, and biology. But when he was preparing to start his master's degree program, Dante wasn't sure whether to specialize in physical, chemical, geological, or biological oceanography. Physical oceanography involves studying the ocean tides, waves, currents, temperatures, density, and salinity. Chemical oceanography looks at the distribution of chemical compounds and chemical interactions that takes place in the ocean. In contrast, biological oceanographers, or marine biologists, study the diverse forms of sea life in the ocean. Dante decided to focus on geological oceanography because he was interested in the topographic features and physical makeup of the ocean floor.

After completing his master's degree, Dante began working for the agency. He enjoys tackling unsolved mysteries. He gets a thrill from working on research problems that are on the edge of new frontiers in scientific understanding. He realizes that little is known about the real workings of the marine environment, and that research constantly sheds light on new concepts. In addition to his job responsibilities, Dante is also involved with several national and international aquatic science societies. He helps review scientific manuscripts and coordinates research meetings. Dante loves being involved in the community of oceanographers that his organization provides.

Learning Experience 10

Night of the Living Cell

Prologue

In the past several learning experiences, you have been exploring the biochemical basis of life. You have examined how simple molecules such as carbon dioxide and water can be transformed into more complex molecules. You have also looked at how complex molecules can be broken down and rearranged by metabolic processes to produce a vast diversity of complex molecules that make up living organisms.

In essence, you have been examining the molecular architecture of life. This is how simple components can be combined to make complex and intricate structures. In this learning experience, you examine the next step in this organizational hierarchy. This is the cell. All of the components of a cell are composed of the biomolecules you have been examining. These biomolecules are organized into structures that have specific functions in the cell. They are the sites in the cell where the metabolic processes you have been studying take place.

Brainstorming

Discuss the following questions with your partner, and record your thinking in your notebook. Be prepared to share your ideas with the class.

1. As part of Learning Experience 8, you have been observing the growth of microorganisms. Describe some of the similarities and the differences between these single-celled organisms and the cells in your body.
2. Describe the fate of food once it has entered your body.
3. What is the final destination of nutrients obtained from food?
4. How do you think nutrients enter a cell?
5. How might a cell use nutrients?
6. How do you think the metabolic processes you have been studying relate to a cell?

Our Body, Our Cells

Organisms, from the simplest to the most complex (including humans), are composites of cells. This is not a very flattering image at first. We like to think of ourselves as highly evolved and complicated organisms, finely tuned to the business of living. On some levels we are. But the ways in which our cells function and interact with one another is what makes being human, or plant, or yeast, possible.

The human body has several trillion cells. Many of the fundamental processes of life that enable organisms to live are carried out at the cellular level. Cells take in resources such as nutrients, water, and gases from their environments. Cells use these resources to transform energy and to synthesize biomolecules that can be used to build new components of the cell. We see enormous diversity among animals, plants, and bacteria. But the functions and chemical composition of all cells are remarkably similar.

Cells may be the most complex units in existence. They may be even more complex in many ways than the bodies of which they are a part. The cell carries out many different activities. It coordinates the complex web of chemical reactions that make life happen. The work of all cells includes taking in nutrients from resources in the environment, then breaking them down and reconstructing them in different ways. This is just like the work of the living organisms that you have investigated so far. Individual cells also respond to their environment. They repair and maintain themselves. They replicate themselves. These are all the characteristics of life that you have been exploring.

The Whole Cell and Nothing but the Cell

What is in the cell that allows it to carry out metabolic processes? In the following activity, you are going to identify where in the cell these processes take place. You will research what structures are in a cell. Then you will determine the metabolic processes that take place within those structures. You will determine how structures within the cell work to ensure that these processes happen efficiently and effectively. Then, using available materials, you will build a large model of your cell. When the model is completed, each group will describe its cell in a presentation to the class.

Materials

For each student:

- 1 sheet of chart paper (optional)

For the class:

- assorted model-building materials
  - pipe cleaners
  - drinking straws
  - plastic or wooden beads

- polystyrene balls and other shapes
- pasta in a variety of shapes, sizes, colors
- clay in a variety of colors
- yarn
- construction paper
- cardboard sheets and boxes
- plastic or paper bags
- glue
- biology texts and other reference books
- access to Internet (optional)

PROCEDURE

1. Choose which cell type you would like to build: an animal, a plant, or a bacterial cell. You also may choose a specialized cell, such as a nerve cell, a blood cell, or a leaf cell.
2. Before building your model of the cell, you should
   a. find pictures in textbooks;
   b. determine the structures that are components of the cell;
   c. determine a scale for your model (such as 1:1000) and the approximate scale for the structures within (optional);
   d. identify what biomolecules make up the various components of your cell; and
   e. choose materials that reflect the structure and function of the cell components. (Be creative! You can use materials not on the list.)
3. Begin to build your group's model.
4. Discuss how your cell takes up nutrients and other essential resources and uses them to sustain life.
   a. Outline the metabolic processes. Use any notes and readings from this unit to assist in creating this outline.
   b. Label your model's structures (organelles) with the metabolic processes they perform.
   c. Create a diagram that shows the organelles of the cell and their metabolic functions. How might the function of one organelle affect another organelle?
   d. If you choose to model a specialized cell, be sure to research any specialized structures or molecules that enable the cell to carry out its specialized functions.
5. Visit other groups as work progresses. Observe their models, ask questions, and compare and contrast their models with that of your group.
6. Decide how your group will make its presentation. Split up the tasks so that each group member has a part to prepare for the presentation. Your group will have about 10–15 minutes to organize your presentation at the beginning of class. Each group will be given approximately 5 minutes. Your presentation must include the completed model, your diagram of the pathway that connects organelles through the metabolic process, and the following information:
   a. a description of the biomolecules that make up the various components of your cell;
   b. the structures involved in moving nutrients and other external resources from the outside environment of the cell to the inside of the cell, and those responsible for removing waste products;

For your presentation, you may want to prepare index cards with summarized notes. This way you can speak directly to your classmates instead of reading from your papers.

c. a description of how biomolecules might move around in the cell;

d. the relationships between breakdown and biosynthetic activities, where these activities take place, and how the products or intermediates might need to move to different places in the cell;

e. the structures within the cell that are involved in obtaining energy and transferring it into a form the cell can use; and

f. a description of how you think the organizational structure of the cell facilitates (makes easier) its ability to carry out the essential functions of life.

7. Present your model to the class.

As the Cell Turns

READING

"The cell is the basic unit of life." This is a definition that you may have heard at some time. What do you think it really means?

A Cell and Its Resources

As you have been investigating, living organisms must take up resources from their environment in order to maintain life. These resources include nutrients, water, gases, and energy. What happens to these resources within an organism? The processes for chemical and energy transfer take place primarily at the cellular level. But some processes, such as digestion of nutrients, begin outside the cell before other processes within cells can happen. Some single-celled organisms break down substances in the environment while they are still outside the cell using compounds that the organism secretes into its immediate environment. The nutrients are then absorbed through small holes (pores) in the surface of the cell or are engulfed by the cell, a wraparound eating process called **endocytosis** (see Figure 1.33). Waste products of metabolism are released in a reverse process called exocytosis.

Digestion of nutrients from food begins in multicellular animals when the animal ingests food. The breakdown process of complex carbohydrates starts in the mouth. Food continues to be digested in the stomach. The resulting products are passed on to the small intestine where further digestion takes place. By this

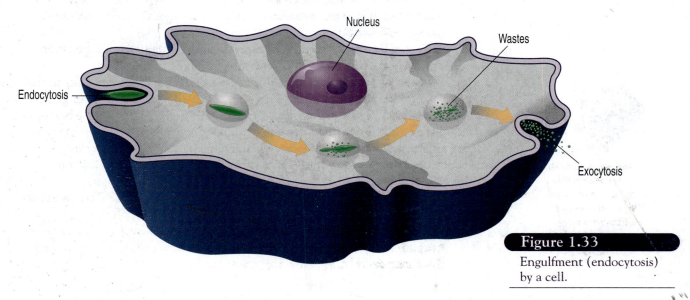

Nucleus

Wastes

Endocytosis

Exocytosis

Figure 1.33
Engulfment (endocytosis) by a cell.

time, the original food—though it has not yet entered any cells—has been broken down into its basic components such as **sugars**, amino acids, and fatty acids. These components are then absorbed into individual cells by mechanisms similar to those carried out by single-celled organisms.

Other resources, such as gases and water, are also taken into the organism. Little or no breakdown is necessary. These resources can be readily absorbed directly into cells for use. Plants also take in nutrients (in the form of minerals), gases, and water. These resources eventually make their way to the cells of the plant.

You Are What You Metabolize

Once the resources have entered the cell, the metabolic processes happen much in the way that you have been studying. A cell takes the resources from its environment and transforms (metabolizes) them into materials and energy it can use. The cell does this whether it is bacterial, plant, or animal. Animal and bacterial cells degrade complex biomolecules. They break them into building blocks, and transfer the chemical energy from the environment into a form of chemical energy they can use. (You determined this in Learning Experience 7, A Breath of Fresh Air.) Plant cells take in simpler molecules. They capture light energy from the sun, and using photosynthesis, transform these resources and light energy into materials the cells can use. All living organisms use this energy and these building blocks to synthesize the biomolecules every cell can use to build new parts of itself and to carry out the processes of life.

Cells are composed of biomolecules: proteins, lipids, carbohydrates, and nucleic acids. These complex chemical compounds join together with other biomolecules to form structures that make up the cell. Each of these molecules has chemical properties that are suited to its role in the cell. What roles do these biomolecules play in the cell? As you have seen, carbohydrates are used by the cell as an energy source and as starting materials for the synthesis of biomolecules. The ability of sugars to make long chain molecules enables them to form major structural supports in the cell. Fats also store energy. The fluid properties of lipids and the fact that they are insoluble in water make them well suited to be the major components in membranes. Nucleic acids are used to store and transmit the information in cells. Proteins are the main workhorses of the cell; they form important structural components of the cell and provide energy. In addition, enzymes, which are proteins, are responsible for facilitating all of the life processes you have been examining. You have learned about the breakdown of complex molecules, the release and capture of energy in new chemical forms, and the synthesis of new biomolecules from the building blocks. All of these processes are carried out by proteins.

Metabolism is a very dynamic activity. It is the capacity of cells to get energy and use it to build, break down, and store usable substances. The cells also use energy to get rid of waste substances. Remarkably, the cells do all of this in a controlled way. Metabolic processes make available the molecules that are required for the cell to do many things. The cell can make new parts for itself, repair itself when damaged, communicate with its environment and (in the case of multicellular organisms) with other cells, and ultimately replicate itself. These processes are taking place at every moment in the life of the cell. And each of these processes is multiplied by the trillions of cells in your body, even as you read this!

SC*LINKS*®
NSTA

Topic: The Cell
Go to: www.scilinks.org
Code: INBIOH2100

An Organelle with a View

One of the differences between different types of cells is the presence of structures within plant and animal cells that are absent in bacterial cells. The space inside plant and animal cells is divided by membranes into complicated structures known as **organelles**. Each organelle carries out a portion of the interconnected processes of metabolism. These structures give organization within the cell.

Another difference between bacterial cells (also called **prokaryotes**, see Figure 1.34) and plant and animal cells (called **eukaryotes**, see Figure 1.35) is the vast difference in size. You may or may not be aware of this difference (depending on whether you created your model to scale). Plant and animal cells are about 1,000 times bigger than the average bacterial cell. How do you think these differences in structure within cells and cell size might be related?

The following excerpt describes the differences between prokaryotic cells and eukaryotic cells. It explains why there came to be differences and why organelles contribute to the efficient functioning of eukaryotic cells. As you read, draw diagrams, create a table, or create separate concept maps of a prokaryotic cell and a eukaryotic cell. Compare the three main structural aspects that differentiate prokaryotic cells from eukaryotic cells.

Like most inventions, life started out simple and grew more complex with time. For their first three billion years on earth, living creatures were no larger than a single cell [prokaryotes]. Gradually, the forces of natural selection worked on these simple organisms until eventually they became bigger, more sophisticated and more intricate. Organisms increased in size not only because the individual cells grew but also because multiple cells—in some cases many millions—came together to form a cohesive whole. The crucial event in this transition was the emergence of a new cell type—the eukaryote. The eukaryote had structural features that allowed it to communicate better than did existing cells with the environment and with other cells, features that paved the way for cellular aggregation and multicellular life. In contrast, the more primitive prokaryotes were less well equipped for intercellular communication and could not readily organize into multicellular organisms . . .

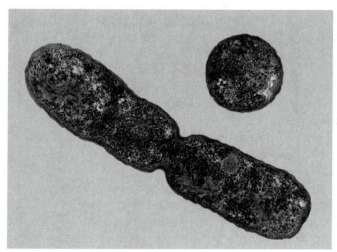

© Dr. Dennis Kunkel/Visuals Unlimited

Figure 1.34

A prokaryotic cell.

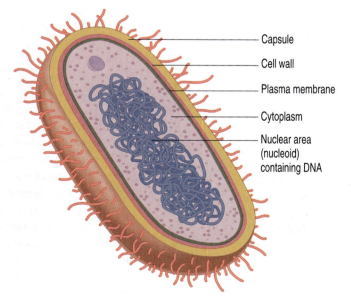

- Capsule
- Cell wall
- Plasma membrane
- Cytoplasm
- Nuclear area (nucleoid) containing DNA

Not only do eukaryotic cells allow larger and more complex organisms to be made, but they are themselves larger and more complex than prokaryotic cells. Whether eukaryotic cells live singly or as part of a multicellular organism, their activities can be much more complex and diversified than those of their prokaryotic counterparts. In prokaryotes, all internal cellular events take place within a single compartment, the cytoplasm. Eukaryotes contain many subcellular compartments called organelles. Even single-celled eukaryotes can display remarkable complexity of [structure and] function . . .

On a very fundamental level, eukaryotes and prokaryotes are similar. They share many aspects of their basic chemistry, physiology, and metabolism. Both cell types are constructed of and use similar kinds of molecules and macromolecules to accomplish their cellular work. In both, for example, membranes are constructed mainly of fatty substances called lipids, and molecules that perform the cell's biological and mechanical work are called proteins . . . Both types of cells use the same bricks and mortar, but the structures they build with these materials vary drastically.

The prokaryotic cell can be compared to a studio apartment: a one-room living space that has a kitchen area abutting the living room, which converts into a bedroom at night. All necessary items fit into their own locations in the one room. There is an everyday, washable rug. Room temperature is comfortable—not too hot, not too cold. Conditions are adequate for everything that must occur in the apartment, but not optimal for any specific activity.

In a similar way, all of the prokaryote's functions fit into a single compartment. The DNA is attached to the cell's membrane. [Structures for synthesizing proteins] float freely in the single compartment. Cellular respiration is carried out at the cell membrane; there is no dedicated compartment for respiration.

A eukaryotic cell can be compared to a mansion, where specific rooms are designed for particular activities. The mansion is more diverse in the activities it supports than the studio apartment. It can accommodate overnight guests comfortably and support social activities for the adults in the living room or dining room, for children in the playroom. The baby's room is warm and furnished with bright colors and a soft carpet. The kitchen has a stove, a refrigerator and a tile floor. Items are kept in the room that is most appropriate for them, under conditions ideal for the activities in that specific room. [However, items from one room may be needed in another room for the functions of both to be

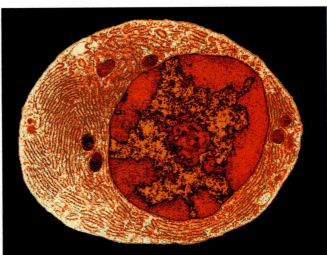

© Dr. Gopal Murti/Visuals Unlimited

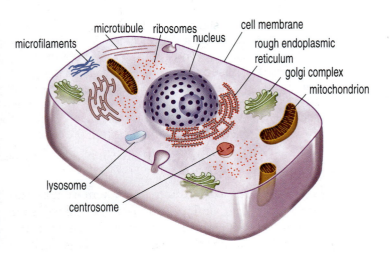

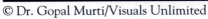

Figure 1.35

A eukaryotic cell.

carried out; for example, food prepared in the kitchen must be carried to the dining room in order to be consumed, and the waste generated in the kitchen must be removed to the trash cans outside.]

A eukaryotic cell resembles a mansion in that it is subdivided into many compartments. Each compartment is furnished with items and conditions suitable for a specific function, yet the compartments work together to allow the cell to maintain itself, to replicate [itself] and to perform more specialized activities.

Taking a closer look, we find three main structural aspects that differentiate prokaryotes from eukaryotes. The definitive difference is the presence of a true (eu) nucleus (karyon) in the eukaryotic cell. The nucleus [separates] the DNA in its own compartment . . . from the rest of the cell. In contrast, no such housing is provided for the DNA of a prokaryote. Instead, the genetic material is tethered to the cell membrane and is otherwise allowed to float freely in the cell's interior. . . .

The organelles of eukaryotes include membrane-bounded compartments such as the lysosome, a highly acidic compartment in which digestive enzymes break down food. The endoplasmic reticulum is an interconnected system of membranes in which lipids are synthesized. . . . [In] another membrane system called the golgi apparatus . . . proteins are . . . [transported to other places in the cell or to the outside of the cell]. Eukaryotic cells contain special energy centers. In animal cells these are the mitochondria; plant cells have chloroplasts as well as mitochondria. Within mitochondria, organic compounds are broken down to generate the energy-rich molecules [which] provide energy for the cell's biochemical reactions. [Prokaryotes do not have organelles, but some types have infoldings within their plasma membrane where some metabolic reactions may occur. Certain of these infoldings may have at some point extended so far into the cell's interior that they became channels to the surface of the cell. Perhaps some of these evolved into separate compartments that provided protection for certain components from foreign or harmful substances.]

The third distinguishing feature between the two cell types is the way in which the cell maintains its shape. Cells . . . have skeletons [plasma membranes] and . . . the cellular skeleton can be either internal or external. Prokaryotes have an external skeleton; a strong wall of cross-linked sugar and protein molecules surrounds the cell membrane and is made rigid by the [water] pressure of the cell. The wall lends structural support . . . and . . . helps to maintain a barrier between substances inside and outside the cell. Such an external skeleton . . . limits communications between cells. . . .

The skeleton of the eukaryotic cell is internal; it is formed by a complex of protein tubules. . . . The internal placement of the cytoskeleton means that the surface exposed to the environment is a pliable membrane rather than a rigid cell wall. The combination of an internal framework and a nonrigid outer membrane expands the repertory of motions and activity of the eukaryotic cell [and permits the cell greater communication with its environment and with other cells, which is a function of certain proteins].

—An excerpt from K. Kabnick and D. Peattie, "Giardia: A Missing Link Between Prokaryotes and Eukaryotes," *American Scientist* 79:34–43, 1990

Eukaryotic cells need their compartmentation because they are huge. A molecule drifting around inside a bacterial cell will sooner or later meet something suitable with which to react. In a eukaryotic cell, it could drift for its entire life. By walling off compartments, a larger cell keeps control over its content. It also provides the potential for diversity of function. This enables eukaryotic cells to come together, specialize, and form multicellular organisms.

ANALYSIS

Record your responses to the following in your notebook.

1. What structures does a eukaryote have that a prokaryote lacks? What structures do they have in common?
2. How do metabolic processes take place in each cell type? Where do these processes take place in eukaryotes? in prokaryotes?
3. "Organisms are not larger because they are more complex; they are more complex because they are larger." (J. B. S. Haldane) Write a paragraph that supports this statement. Use the information from the reading "An Organelle with a View," and any other ideas or concepts you have thought about during your research on cells.

EXTENDING *Ideas*

How did eukaryotic cells get organized into compartments? Did cell membranes come together as a way of being more efficient? Or are compartmentalized cells an example of cooperation among different cell types? Research the theory that suggests that organelles derived from prokaryotic organisms that got "organized"—mitochondria from bacteria and chloroplasts from blue-green algae. Describe the theory; then defend or refute it.

Do you own the cells in your body? Or can someone be allowed to use them to make a profit and not share the rewards with you? In 1976, John Moore, an engineer working in Alaska, was diagnosed with a rare and deadly form of cancer known as hairy-cell leukemia. This disease affects the spleen, an organ responsible for removing old and dead cells. In patients with hairy-cell leukemia, the spleen overproduces a type of white blood cell. This results in an increase in the size of the spleen. When John Moore's spleen was removed, it had increased in size from a normal 14 ounces to 14 pounds. The surgery was successful in putting the cancer into remission. But unbeknownst to Mr. Moore his spleen cells were taken and used to develop a "cell line." A cell line is a culture of living cells, placed in a growth medium, which continues to reproduce forever. This cell line had the potential of being very profitable for the pharmaceutical company that owned it. When Mr. Moore learned of this, he demanded in a court case to share the profits. Should Mr. Moore reap some of the profits from the use of his cells by a pharmaceutical company? If you were the judge, what would you decide? Write an opinion and explain your decision.

CAREER FOCUS

Pharmacologist It's almost time for Lauren's afternoon lecture to begin. Her lesson involves the effect of barbiturates on the nervous system. This is her area of research, so she has lots of information to share with her graduate students. Lauren is a research pharmacologist at Western College, where she also teaches pharmacology courses for graduate students. (Lauren is not a pharmacist who prepares and dispenses drugs to patients.)

After her lecture, Lauren returns to her lab on campus to continue working on her research. Like all pharmacologists, her goal is to study and understand the effects of drugs. She studies how they change the normal processes that take place in living animals. She also studies how drugs produce these effects by mimicking or interfering with the action of other substances normally found in the body. But Lauren specializes in clinical pharmacology. Clinical pharmacology is the study of therapeutic and toxic actions of drugs in humans. Lauren's lab research focuses on the effects of barbiturates on the human nervous system. (Barbiturates is a class of organic compounds.) Lauren explores how they can be used to create medications such as anesthetics and anticonvulsants. She studies how the chemical structure of the substance interacts at the cellular and molecular level in the brain. Lauren hopes that this research will help in standardizing drug dosages and discovering how they should be used most effectively.

As a student, Lauren excelled in biology. She particularly enjoyed learning about anatomy. Lauren was spellbound when a high school teacher taught a unit on neurobiology and explained how the different chemical properties of substances affect receptors in the brain. Lauren sought out her teacher after class and asked her what kind of scientists study such things for a living. Her teacher told her that the field of science was called pharmacology and that it required a lot of schooling. But she thought that it might be a good fit for Lauren.

While taking a pharmacology course in college, Lauren discovered that it was a fascinating field that would allow her to branch out into many different disciplines. The course required her to apply what she learned in her other courses in biochemistry, microbiology, microanatomy, and physiology. She decided that after graduation she would pursue a Ph.D. in clinical pharmacology from a medical school. To be considered a clinical pharmacologist, Lauren needed specialized training. This training involved using drugs for treatment, assessing their side effects, monitoring their levels in patients, preventing or treating overdoses, and determining the consequences of interactions with other drugs. While working toward her doctorate, Lauren assisted research pharmacologists. She learned how to design and carry out experiments to determine how drug concentrations in the body change over time. She also learned how to test newly discovered or manufactured substances for their safety, activity, and possible use as drugs.

After completing her graduate studies, Lauren had several career paths to choose from. Although she could have pursued positions in industry or in government, Lauren wanted to pass her knowledge on to others. She felt that working at a university would be the best fit for her. She began by doing several years of postdoctoral work for another pharmacology researcher before eventually taking a faculty position at Western College. Lauren loves working in a field that is challenging yet allows her to help others. She does this both through her pharmacological research and through the teaching and mentoring of students at the college.

Market Research Analyst
Joseph's current project is designing a questionnaire to identify the market for a new cough syrup. Joseph works in the marketing division of CVB, a biotechnology company that produces over-the-counter medications. As a market research analyst, it is his job to help CVB figure out whether people would buy this product and which other companies make similar products. Once the questionnaire is complete, Joseph will decide how to conduct the survey to best gather information. Should he survey people through the mail? via the Internet? over the phone? in person with a focus group, or rent a booth at the mall? Which method will reach the most people and give Joseph the best results? These are questions Joseph must consider.

As a market research analyst at a biotechnology company, Joseph uses his background in both science and business. He uses his marketing training to identify the market for CVB's products. He also identifies the competition, and then decides how to advertise these products to the customer so that the customer will purchase them. Once he gathers all of the market information, Joseph will compile the data, analyze them, and make recommendations to CVB based on his findings. These findings will help CVB's management team determine whether to produce the new cough syrup, and if so, how to promote it and what price to charge.

But Joseph's science background is just as important. It gives him the tools to understand CVB's products and what makes them unique when compared to the competitors' products. And science has been Joseph's main interest since he was a child. But he also finds people fascinating and enjoys trying to figure out why they behave the way they do. While studying biology in his first year of college, Joseph also took an introductory psychology course. On the last day of class, the professor talked about the different careers related to psychology. She mentioned how psychology is used in marketing to help companies sell their products. Given the success of the biotechnology field, Joseph believed he could combine his love of science and psychology by taking a marketing position in a biotechnology company. Joseph decided to pursue a major in biology and a minor in marketing.

Following college, Joseph wanted to get more business knowledge, so he attended a master's program in market research analysis. Those courses helped him develop his skills in marketing, survey design, and statistics. But he really learned the most from taking a part-time internship at a local biotechnology firm. There he was able to help gather and analyze data, conduct interviews, and write reports to gain experience that helped him land his job at CVB. Joseph is pleased that he can use a range of skills in his work—from statistics and science to psychology and teamwork.

Holding It All Together

Prologue

Living organisms must take in resources from their environment to continue their life processes. As you explored in Learning Experience 10, the cell is the site where the activities and life processes take place. It is where matter is rearranged and energy transferred into forms the cell can use to maintain the characteristics of life. Living cells, through metabolism, break down the resources into component parts. They then synthesize, or rearrange, them into new components the cells need for the activities of life.

The requirements of the cell present an interesting engineering problem. How does the cell both protect itself from hazards in its environment and allow resources from that environment into the cell in order to carry out its life-sustaining functions? For many years, biologists speculated about the nature of the material that separated a cell from its environment. Some even thought that no separating structure existed. They thought that the cell was like a droplet of oil in water, remaining separated because of its different properties. However, eventually the existence of a structure was demonstrated. As a result, the architecture and functions of the cell membrane became an area of active scientific investigation.

Every cell has a membrane that surrounds the cytoplasm. This membrane is a remarkable structure. It separates the internal metabolic action from the disordered and sometimes harsh external environment while permitting certain substances in selectively. This is called **selective permeability**. A cell must be able to take in the resources it needs in order to carry out the metabolic processes to sustain life. It must also be able to rid itself of wastes. In addition, it must keep out other substances that are harmful or otherwise not desired by the cell.

Consider for a moment a teabag placed in water. Water can flow into the bag and extract coloring and flavor from the tea leaves. The coloring and flavor dissolve in the water, and then tea flows out of the bag. Yet, the tea leaves are held inside the bag, which acts like a cell membrane. In this investigation, you examine the structure, components, and properties of the cell membrane. You also simulate the ways in which a cell regulates what can pass into and out of its interior domain.

Topic: Cell Membrane
Go to: www.scilinks.org
Code: INBIOH2107

Brainstorming

Discuss the following questions with your partner, and record your thinking in your notebook. Be prepared to share your ideas with the class.

1. If the cell is separate from its environment, how does it obtain the resources needed to perform metabolic processes?
2. Describe what you think might be important functions of the cell membrane.
3. What kinds of substances might be in the environment that the cell needs?
4. In what ways might a cell membrane be like skin? Does the skin let any substances in or out? How do you think skin might do this?
5. What might the structure of a cell membrane look like?
6. What would be some characteristics of a functional membrane?

ACTIVITY

Come into My Parlor . . .

This simulation is designed to demonstrate the structure and functions of a cell membrane, which allows certain materials to cross. You and your classmates will act as models for lipids. Groups of these "human lipids" will carry out a series of tasks. First, you will create and model a cell membrane. Then you will use that membrane structure to simulate the mechanisms by which different substances move across cell membranes.

Your teacher will divide the class into two large groups. Members of one group will be the molecules, and members of the other group will direct one of the tasks. Groups will switch roles as each task is solved.

For each of your group's tasks, read the task and the Science Information that relates to the biology of what will be simulated. Then try to solve each task. Use classmates in the role of lipid molecules and other materials as needed.

Materials

For the class:

- class members (to model human lipid molecules)
- several large sheets of stiff paper or cardboard
- tape (cellophane or masking)
- scissors
- 50 marbles
- 20 tennis balls, or balls of comparable size
- 30 table-tennis balls, or balls of comparable size
- 1 chair

TASK ONE

Create and form a model of a membrane structure that is composed of human lipid molecules. Include the following factors:
- one end of each molecule is hydrophobic, and one end is hydrophilic;
- the membrane structure is surrounded by water, both inside the cell and outside. (A watery environment exists on both sides of the membrane, but no water is present within the membrane structure itself.); and
- the membrane is flexible. Each lipid's tails can sway back and forth within the structure.

SCIENCE INFORMATION

Lipids are biological compounds that are not soluble in water. Some lipids are made from fatty acids. Fatty acids are long chains of hydrocarbon units joined together with a carboxyl group at one end. The lipid components of the cell membrane are actually phospholipids. A phospholipid is a molecule made of phosphorus and oxygen atoms attached to a glycerol molecule. This in turn is attached to two fatty acid chains (Figure 1.36). For simplicity, these phospholipid biomolecules are referred to as lipids.

The molecular structure of phospholipids is an essential characteristic of membrane architecture. Membranes form a separation, or demarcation, between the inside and the outside of the cell. Present both inside and outside the cell are fluids, primarily composed of water. Lipid molecules have two ends. One is a head end, which "loves" water (hydrophilic). The other end has two tail ends, which "fear," or repel, water (hydrophobic). Look at the lipid molecule shown in Figure 1.36. The polar end is the end that loves water. The other end, the fatty acid (nonpolar) end, is the water-fearing end. This end is not soluble in water. A group of lipids must start to form a membrane by means of a lipid bilayer. A membrane is composed of two rows of lipids with their nonpolar ends together. This arrangement gives structure to the membrane. It also serves to create a hydrophobic barrier between what is inside (the contents of the cell) and what is outside the membrane (the environment).

One way to envision this membrane structure is to imagine the following scenario. You have two slices of bread that are each buttered on one side and plain on the other side. Dunk one slice in a bowl of soup and the plain side will get wet, but the buttered side repels water. Take the second slice and place it against the first slice, buttered sides together. You have now formed a butter sandwich whose outsides can interact with the watery environment of the soup, but whose buttered interior does not permit water to enter. Thus, a double layer is formed—a lipid bilayer surrounded by water.

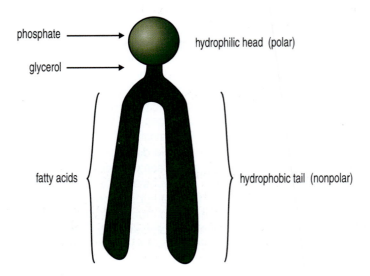

phosphate ⟶ hydrophilic head (polar)

glycerol ⟶

fatty acids { hydrophobic tail (nonpolar)

Figure 1.36

The main structural component of all cell membranes. A phospholid molecule has a glycerol that joins two fatty acid tails to a hydrophilic head of a phosphate group.

ANALYSIS

Record your responses to the following in your notebook.

1. Why does this arrangement allow for molecules with one hydrophobic end and one hydrophilic end to exist in an environment that has water on both sides?

2. You have modeled a section of the cell membrane (a "cutaway," used for the purpose of illustration). What would the configuration look like if you were to model a complete cell membrane? (Recall your cell model from Learning Experience 10, Night of the Living Cell.)

3. How might substances be able to make their way through this membrane?

TASK TWO

Create another human model of a lipid bilayer. Decide which side of the bilayer is inside the cell and which is outside the cell. Remember, you only need to model a portion of the cell membrane that surrounds a cell.

Outside the cell is a high concentration of other molecules. There are small molecules, such as oxygen, carbon dioxide, or water (represented by marbles). There are also larger molecules, such as glucose (represented by tennis balls). There is a much lower concentration of these molecules inside the cell. Arrange your human lipid bilayer so that

- a small molecule (represented by a marble) might pass through your membrane unimpeded,
- a larger molecule (represented by a tennis ball) would *not* be able to pass through, and
- the passage would require no energy or movement on the part of the membrane components.

SCIENCE INFORMATION

Have you ever added a drop of ink to a beaker of water? The ink particles slowly mix with the water. This movement is the result of the random movement of the ink particles and the water molecules. Gradually, the ink moves through the water to areas where there was no ink. At the same time, the water molecules also move randomly around to where there was less water (where there was ink). Small molecules tend to move unassisted across the lipid bilayer from a region of high concentration to a region of lower concentration. Movement of substances into the cell can happen by one of several different mechanisms. The mixing of two substances by the random motion of molecules is called simple diffusion. Some substances can pass through a cell membrane by this process of simple diffusion. Diffusion takes place when the concentration of a substance is greater on one side of the membrane than on the other side. The substance moves from the more concentrated side to the less concentrated side (the side with less of the substance). In general, only very small molecules such as water, oxygen, and carbon dioxide can move through a membrane by diffusion.

ANALYSIS

Record your responses to the following in your notebook.

1. What happens when the number of marbles on the inside of the cell equals the number of marbles on the outside of the cell?
2. How easy or difficult was it for marbles to pass through the membrane? What does this mean in terms of energy consumption for the cell? How much energy was used by the membrane to allow the marbles through?
3. Why were the tennis balls unable to enter?

TASK THREE

Your cell now needs more nutrients, in the form of glucose (represented by tennis balls). There are very few, if any, inside (low internal concentration). But the tennis balls are too big to pass through the cell membrane by simple diffusion. How might the cell membrane be modified to facilitate the passage of substances the size of tennis balls? This task requires additions to the existing structure of your model membrane. At this point, you may add channels to the lipid membrane structure that may allow larger molecules to enter. Design a membrane such that

- the tennis balls can pass through the membrane, and
- this transport requires no energy or movement on the part of the membrane components.

SCIENCE INFORMATION

Another mechanism for moving substances into and out of the cell is termed facilitated diffusion, or passive transport. As in simple diffusion, molecules move from an area of higher concentration to an area of lower concentration. However, there is an important difference between the two types of diffusion. This difference is the existence of channels made up of proteins that are part of the membrane itself. The membrane is a two-layered structure called a bilayer. Each layer is made up of a sheet of lipid molecules, with protein molecules embedded in it. Some of these proteins extend all the way through the bilayer. Others are located either on the inner or the outer face of the membrane (Figure 1.37).

Channels allow larger molecules to diffuse through the membrane, from high concentration to lower concentrations. These proteins may carry the molecules across the membrane or form channels or pores. These channels or pores allow the molecules to enter. In facilitated diffusion, as in simple diffusion, no energy is required. An example of a molecule that is carried into a cell by facilitated diffusion is glucose (Figure 1.38).

ANALYSIS

Record your responses to the following in your notebook.

1. Why can't glucose move by simple diffusion?
2. What components of the cell membrane allow for the movement of some small and some larger molecules? Why is no energy required by the membrane for this?
3. What might happen if the concentration of tennis-ball molecules were higher inside the cell than outside the cell?

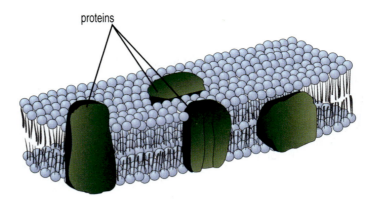

proteins

Figure 1.37

Fluid mosaic model of cell membrane.

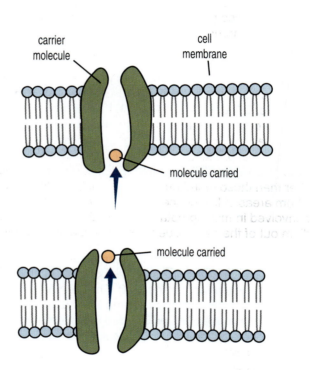

carrier molecule

cell membrane

molecule carried

molecule carried

Figure 1.38

Facilitated diffusion.

TASK FOUR

To carry out its metabolic processes, your cell needs many, many potassium molecules (represented by table-tennis balls). In fact, it needs a higher concentration of potassium molecules inside the cell than are in its environment outside. In other words, the cell must move these molecules across the membrane from a lower concentration to a higher concentration. Demonstrate how these table-tennis balls might get across a gradient. The lipid molecules in the model membrane created this time may add human "carrier protein" molecules to assist the membrane. Here the proteins may use any part of their "body" (hands, feet, shoulders, toes) to facilitate this transport.

SCIENCE INFORMATION

Molecular movement across a membrane that is aided by energy is known as active transport. Cells often require nutrients, such as minerals, that are scarce in the environment. If the concentration of this nutrient were higher in the cell than in its surroundings, you might expect that the cell would lose this nutrient by diffusion. The mechanism of active transport enables cells to retain these essential nutrients. Active transport moves molecules from areas of low concentration into areas of higher concentration through a carrier protein. But this requires energy. Unlike humans, actual lipid molecules of the cell membrane have no hands, feet, or shoulders with which to pass the molecules in. Instead, membrane proteins play an essential role in actively transporting substances across the membrane and into the cell. These carrier proteins lie across (transect) the membrane. One end of the protein is exposed on the exterior surface of the cell; the other end is on the interior surface of the cell. These proteins form the passageways by which certain molecules can move through the cell membrane. Membrane proteins are responsible for the selective nature of the cell membrane. That is, they determine which substances can enter the cell and which substances cannot enter. Specific substances can bind to the external portion of the carrier protein (the receptor site). This interaction results in a change in the shape of the carrier protein. This then results in the bound substance being moved across the cell membrane.

An example of active transport is shown in Figure 1.39. Potassium is essential for biological processes of cells, such as the conduction of nerve impulses through the body. It is required in concentrations inside the cell that are higher than those found outside the cell. Therefore, potassium ions must move from areas of low concentration to areas of higher concentration. The protein involved in moving potassium into the cell also moves excess sodium out of the cell. It does this against a concentration gradient as well.

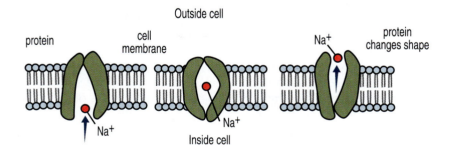

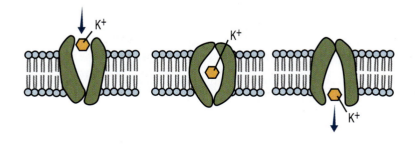

Figure 1.39

Sodium and potassium ions are moved from areas of higher concentration to areas of lower concentration. The same protein is involved in transporting both ions.

ANALYSIS

Record your responses to the following in your notebook.

1. In what ways might active transport be an advantage to the cell?
2. What could be some disadvantages to this type of transport?
3. How do proteins facilitate movement of substances in this type of transport?
4. Where might cells get the energy required for active transport?

TASK FIVE

Moving day! The cell needs to take in a very large molecule, such as a large food particle (represented by a chair). But this molecule can't pass through the channel or carrier proteins. Design a way to move this molecule into the cell in such a way that

- the integrity of the cell membrane remains intact (the lipid molecules don't break contact),
- more lipids may be added, and
- the large molecule (chair) must become entirely engulfed.

SCIENCE INFORMATION

Sometimes a cell needs to take in large substances, such as food particles. But these substances cannot pass through protein channels or move across the membrane by using carrier proteins. Some single-celled organisms ingest large food particles. White blood cells in animals can engulf bacterial cells and other substances as part of the body's defense system. These substances do not pass through the membrane. Instead, part of the cell membrane flows to extend out toward the particle and surrounds it. When the edges of the membrane meet, they fuse with each other and capture the particle in a little sac inside the cell. This process is called endocytosis. The sac, called a vesicle, is like a bag made of membrane. It contains some cytoplasm and the captured particle. Once inside the cell the sac may burst, releasing the particle into the cytoplasm. Alternatively, the sac may fuse with an organelle inside the cell, the **lysosome**, which contains digestive enzymes. These enzymes then digest the particle, breaking it down to smaller, simpler materials for the cell to use.

This ability of the cell membrane to extend itself and engulf particles demonstrates another important property of this structure. As described earlier, the membrane is fluid. The lipids and proteins that make up the membrane are not fixed in place. They are free, to some extent, to move about within the plane of the membrane. This fluidity is essential if the cell is to be flexible and able to apply its various mechanisms (Figure 1.40).

ANALYSIS

Record your responses to the following in your notebook.

1. What happens to the membrane during endocytosis?
2. What properties must the membrane have to accommodate such a substance?
3. How does this type of transport differ from the other types?

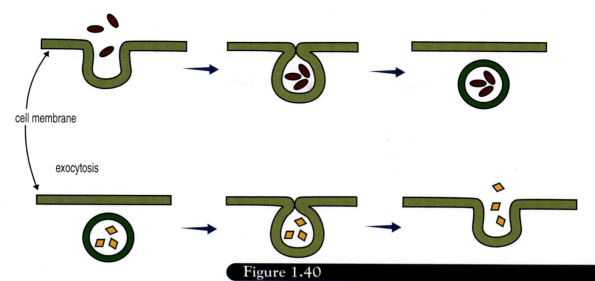

endocytosis

cell membrane

exocytosis

Figure 1.40

Particles too large to pass through the cell membrane are moved into the cell by the process of endocytosis. Large substances can be expelled from inside the cell by the reverse process of exocytosis.

A Mazing Membranes

In this investigation, you have been exploring the properties of the membrane that surround a cell. Membranes also play essential roles within the cell. Prokaryotic organisms have internal membranes. Many of the metabolic activities of these organisms, such as protein synthesis and photosynthesis, take place on these membranes. Eukaryotic organisms are characterized by their internal structures, which carry out specialized functions. Remember the compartments from Learning Experience 10, Night of the Living Cell. The nucleus, the mitochondria, the chloroplast, and the lysosome are all membrane-bound organelles. Within these organelles, many of the metabolic activities are carried out on internal membranes. The cytoplasm of eukaryotic cells is a maze of membrane systems. This maze includes the endoplasmic reticulum and the Golgi apparatus, two sets of membranes involved in the synthesis of proteins.

The membrane provides the cell with protection, support, and a carefully controlled means of moving things into and out of the cell. It also allows necessary chemical reactions to take place without "contamination." Without this elegant structure, the cell would die.

ANALYSIS

Draw on your responses to the questions from each task to answer the following.

1. What methods of transport does a cell membrane have? How do the different methods allow substances into or out of the cell? What substances might be transported by each method?
2. Why does a cell require certain substances? Why does it need to rid itself of certain substances? What kinds of substances might it remove? By what methods might they be removed?

3. Describe how a cell, using its membrane proteins, might specifically
   - recognize a substance it needs from its environment, and
   - bring it across its membrane.
4. Sometimes a cell mistakenly brings in a substance that is poisonous. Describe how you think that might be possible. What can happen to the cell?

EXTENDING *Ideas*

Long before understanding the principles behind osmosis, people preserved their food by salt curing. Research the principles of osmosis and the use of salt in the preservation of food. Explain the biological principles behind the use of salt.

The "kiss of life" is a term applied to one kind of diagnosis of cystic fibrosis. Parents and relatives who find their babies salty to the kiss may be detecting one of the consequences of this genetic disease. Cystic fibrosis patients have excess amounts of sodium and chloride ions in their sweat. This makes the sweat very salty. Another symptom of cystic fibrosis is the accumulation of thick mucus in the lungs of the patients. Research cystic fibrosis. Describe the relationship between the excess amounts of sodium and chloride ions and the excess fluid in these patients' lungs. Find out how this also offers resistance to cholera.

Biological systems can be viewed as systems that continually strive to maintain balance in a world that is constantly changing. To sustain their metabolic activities, cells must maintain temperature, nutrient content, and oxygen and salt concentration within a narrow range. The internal environment is controlled by a series of mechanisms. These mechanisms work to counterbalance changes in the cell's environment and keep the cellular environment constant. Homeostasis is the overall process by which this happens. Describe some of the systems of the cell that are involved in homeostasis.

The Great Divide

Prologue

Growth has been identified as one of the characteristics of life. But what does it mean "to grow"? Growth can be defined as an orderly increase of all the components of an organism. It is a process that depends on the efficient uptake of nutrients. The result of this growth is observable as an increase in the size of a living organism. Since living organisms are made up of cells, growth must be viewed as a process that takes place at the cellular level. Cells increase in size by taking in nutrients, breaking them down, and using the resulting energy and building blocks to make more cellular components.

The maximum size that many cells can reach is limited. At a certain size, they must replicate (or duplicate themselves). That is, they must divide. After a division, the two new cells, called daughter cells, will continue to grow. They will grow until the size limit is reached. Then division will take place again. Why can cells only grow to a certain size? What is the limitation on cell size? Most of this limitation has to do with the cell's ability to access its life-sustaining nutrients. As you saw in earlier learning experiences, the ability to move resources into and out of cells is essential for the cell to survive. Nutrients must enter and by-products must be removed. In fact, the ability to obtain building blocks and energy from resources is one of the characteristics of life. It enables the other characteristics of life to be maintained.

In this learning experience, you explore how another important life process, cell division, also depends on the process of metabolism. You see how it enables other characteristics of life to take place. These include the ability of an organism to grow, to maintain and repair itself, and to replicate. In the following activity, Soaking It All In, you relate cell size to the ability to obtain nutrients. You then determine the relationship of cell division to the maintenance of the characteristics of life.

Brainstorming

After your teacher has blown up a balloon and taken measurements, discuss the following questions with your partner. Record your thinking in your notebook, and be prepared to share your ideas with the class.

1. Do you think the balloon will increase in size indefinitely? If not, what might limit its size?
2. As the balloon gets bigger, what is happening to its skin? What is making the balloon get bigger?
3. Is the balloon growing? How might you define growth?
4. How do you think growth happens in organisms? Where does it take place?
5. If cells grow, how do you think that happens?
6. Do you think there is a limit to how big cells can get? If so, what might limit the size?
7. What is the role of nutrients in growth?

Soaking It All In

Efficient access to nutrients plays a role in determining how large a cell can grow. Using agar cubes to model the cell, you will examine the process of diffusion of substances through the cell membrane. You worked with agar earlier when you grew microorganisms on nutrient agar plates. The agar in this activity contains a chemical indicator similar to the phenol red you used to detect CO_2 in Learning Experience 7, A Breath of Fresh Air. Phenolphthalein is a chemical indicator that changes color in the presence of a basic or alkaline solution. You will place an agar block in a basic solution of sodium hydroxide (NaOH). This will prompt you to begin investigating the question, "How does the size of a cell affect its ability to obtain nutrients?"

Materials

For each pair of students:

- 2 safety goggles
- 2 pairs of disposable gloves (optional)
- 1 small block of phenolphthalein agar
- 1 petri dish
- solution of 0.1 molar (M) sodium hydroxide (NaOH)
- 1 beaker (250- or 500-mL)
- 1 metric ruler
- 1 scalpel or utility knife
- 1 spoon
- graph paper
- paper towels

PROCEDURE

1. **STOP & THINK** Make a prediction with your partner about the following. Record your thinking in your notebook.
   a. Which agar block will take up more liquid within a given period of time—a larger block or a smaller block? Explain.
   b. Will liquid penetrate farther into a small agar block or into a larger agar block?
2. Obtain a block of phenolphthalein agar from your teacher.
3. Carefully cut out 3 small agar cubes from this block. Make the cubes different sizes. One should be 3 cm on each side, one 1.5 cm on each side, and one 0.5 cm on each side.
4. Place the 3 cubes in a beaker; be sure that the cubes do not touch. Cover them with a solution of 0.1 M NaOH.
5. Every 2 minutes for a 6-minute period, turn the cubes over with a spoon so that all sides of each cube become exposed to the solution.
6. After 6 minutes, remove the cubes from the solution and place on a paper towel. Carefully pat the cubes dry with another paper towel.
7. Without touching the cubes with your hands, cut each cube in half with a scalpel or knife. It is important that you make 1 clean cut through each cube and that both halves are equal in size. Be sure to wash your hands at the end of this experiment.
8. Measure in centimeters how far from the edge the color change has occurred in each cube. What is the cause of this color change?
9. Compare how far the NaOH has diffused into each cube. Do this by calculating as follows the percentage of each block that has changed color.
   a. First determine the volume of each cube. Calculate the volume by multiplying the height (h) by the width (w) by the length (l). For example, in a cube that is 3 cm on each side, the volume of the cube would be 3 cm × 3 cm × 3 cm = 27 cm³ (see Figure 1.41). Calculate the volume of each of your cubes and record the volumes in your notebook.
   b. Determine the volume of the uncolored area. Do this by measuring 1 side of the uncolored area (for example, see Figure 1.42). In this example, 1 side of the uncolored area measures 2 cm. Therefore, the volume of the uncolored area is 2 cm × 2 cm × 2 cm = 8 cm³. Calculate and record the volume of the uncolored area of each of your cubes.
   c. Determine the volume of the colored area. Do this by subtracting the volume of the uncolored area from the total volume of your cube. In this example,

SAFETY NOTE

• Scalpels and knives are sharp. Cut the agar on a hard surface and cut away from yourself.
• NaOH is caustic. Avoid contact with your skin. If NaOH comes in contact with skin, rinse thoroughly with water. If you should get any in your eyes, irrigate them immediately and inform your teacher.

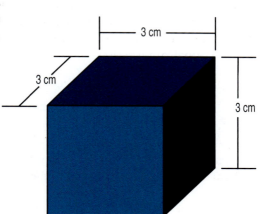

NOTE

Do not throw your cubes away!

Figure 1.41

Determine the volume of an agar cube.

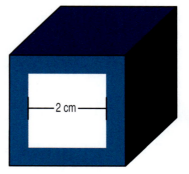

Figure 1.42

Determine the volume of the uncolored portion.

$$27 \text{ cm}^3 - 8 \text{ cm}^3 = \quad 19 \text{ cm}^3$$

total   uncolored   colored volume

Calculate and record the volumes of the colored area of each of your cubes.

10. Determine how much diffusion took place in the different cubes. Do this by calculating the percentage of each cube into which the NaOH solution has diffused. Divide the volume of the colored area by the volume of the total cube. For example,

$$\frac{19 \text{ cm}^3}{27 \text{ cm}^3} = .704 \times 100\% = 70.4\%$$

Calculate and record the percentage of diffusion in each of your cubes.

ANALYSIS

1. Prepare a laboratory report for this experiment in your notebook. Be sure to include the following:
   a. the question being asked,
   b. the procedure,
   c. the data, including all the calculations,
   d. a graph that plots the percentage of each cube that the NaOH solution entered versus the size of the cube (cm on 1 side), and
   e. your conclusions.
2. As part of the conclusion, address the following questions:
   a. Which cube has the greatest percentage of its volume reached by the NaOH?
   b. Do the data support your prediction? If not, why not?
   c. How does this experiment model cells and nutrients?
   d. Which size block would have an advantage for growth, the larger cell or the smaller cell? Why? Use the agar blocks and NaOH as cell models.
   e. What could the agar block that is disadvantaged for growth do to increase its ability to grow? Explain how this would help.
   f. What is the relationship between nutrients and growth?

 READING

Divide and Conquer: A First Look

One of the characteristics of life is the ability to grow. (You identified this characteristic in Learning Experience 1, Living Proof.) In multicellular organisms, growth is generally associated with getting "bigger." Physical changes that take place during the transition in life between a young organism to a mature organism may involve significant increases in size. How does this growth happen? Growth is the result of events that take place at the cellular level. Individual cells increase in size as they use nutrients and energy to build new cellular components. These nutrients are taken into the cell through the cell membrane and are metabolized.

When the cell is small, areas in the cell where metabolic activity takes place are very near to the membrane through which the materials are being transported.

As cells increase in size, however, the interior portions of the cell become farther and farther from the membrane. The distance from where nutrients enter the cell to where they are used increases. As a result, the functioning of the cell becomes inefficient. As in the agar block experiment, it takes much longer for substances to diffuse to the interior of a large cell than to that of a smaller one. Waste substances accumulate in the cells. They must be moved from the interior of the cell where they are formed to outside the cell. The larger the cell is, the longer that takes. And the longer that takes, the more energy is used.

For many types of cells, the method for dealing with this problem is to divide. The cells form two smaller cells (daughter cells) out of one oversized cell. By dividing into two smaller cells, the large cell increases its surface-to-volume ratio. This then increases the efficiency with which substances can reach all cellular components in the interior of the cell. Visually compare the surface-to-volume ratios of the cells in Figure 1.43. Think about how this affects the access of the metabolic pathways within the cell to nutrients in its environment.

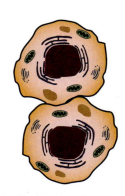

Figure 1.43

One large cell divides into two smaller cells. How does the surface-to-volume ratio change?

Divvying Up the Goods

The mechanism of cell division is a precisely orchestrated event that takes place in the same pattern in every eukaryotic cell. (There is, however, some variation in cells that eventually form eggs and sperm cells.) Cell division requires that the parent cell be able to do certain things. These include (1) duplicate all the information that the daughter cells will need to carry out the exact same metabolic activities and life-sustaining functions as the parent cell; (2) transfer this information to the daughter cells; and (3) provide the daughter cells with enough of the cellular machinery to be able to sustain themselves until they are making their own cellular parts and products. How does this happen?

In this activity, you will build a set of chromosomes for a mythical insect. This insect has three pairs of chromosomes that differ in length. In many organisms, chromosomes come in pairs. The chromosomes within a pair are copies of each other and carry the same information. (You will learn more about chromosomes in Unit 2.) After building your models, you will demonstrate cell division and mitosis, the process by which cells produce two identical daughter cells.

SC**L**INKS.
NSTA

Topic: Cell Cycle and Mitosis
Go to: www.scilinks.org
Code: INBIOH2121

Materials

For each group of four students:

- 24 pipe cleaners (chenille stems); 8 30 cm long, 8 15 cm long, 8 7.5 cm long
- 6 strips of Velcro®, 5 cm each
- 3 m of yarn
- scissors
- 1 metric ruler

PROCEDURE

Part A: Building the Chromosomes

1. Select 2 30-cm pipe cleaners and shape them into a double helix of DNA. Begin by twisting them together at one end to attach them; then twist them

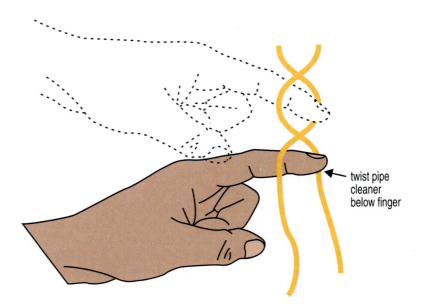

Figure 1.44

Creating a model of DNA.

around your index finger. Move your finger down the length of the pipe cleaner, twisting as you go (see Figure 1.44). When you have completed twisting the pipe cleaners together, join the ends by twisting them together.

2. Repeat step 1 with 2 more 30-cm pipe cleaners, 4 15-cm pipe cleaners, and 4 7.5-cm pipe cleaners. At the end of this step, you should have one pair each of a 30-cm, 15-cm, and 7.5-cm chromosome.

3. **STOP & THINK** What does each pipe cleaner represent?

Part B: Simulating Cell Division and Mitosis

As you work through this simulation, record in your notebook what you are doing at each stage. Explain how the stages represent the events that are happening in the cell. Table 1.4 describes and illustrates each stage of mitosis. Use this table as a reference to help you carry out the simulation.

 The first step in cell division involves the replication of the DNA within each chromosome. This ensures that the chromosomes are faithfully duplicated. These structures will carry all the required information to the daughter cells to ensure that they are exactly like the parent cell.

1. Cut the yarn into 2 pieces. Make 1 piece 2 m long and the other piece 1 m long. Use the larger piece to form a circle on a tabletop. This represents the cell membrane of the cell. Use the smaller piece to form a circle within the cell membrane. This represents the nucleus.

2. Place your pairs of 30-cm and 15-cm chromosomes in the nucleus in any position.

3. Take 2 of the remaining 30-cm pipe cleaners and make another chromosome as you did in Part A, step 1. Join these 2 chromosomes together by wrapping Velcro around each chromosome. Wrap the hook portion around one chromosome and the latch portion around the other chromosome so that the 2 chromosomes will stick together.

4. **STOP & THINK** What does this model represent?

5. Repeat step 3 with the remaining 30-cm, 15-cm, and 7.5-cm pipe cleaners. Place all of the chromosomes randomly in the nucleus of your cell and remove the inner circle of yarn (stage 2, Table 1.4)

6. **STOP & THINK** How many pairs of identical chromosomes are present in the cell? What does the removal of the inner circle of yarn represent?

7. Line up the matching or homologous pairs of chromosomes (same length) along the center or equator of the cell (stage 3, Table 1.4).

Table 1.4 The Stages of Mitosis and Cell Division

Stage 1	When the cell is not dividing, it experiences a period of growth as the result of metabolic activity. This part of the cell's life is called interphase. Before initiating cell division, the DNA in the cell makes copies of itself. The cell now contains two identical copies of the information in its DNA. At this stage, no chromosomes are visible within the cell nucleus.	
Stage 2	The membrane around the nucleus breaks down and spindle fibers start to form. Spindle fibers are protein structures in the cell that serve to guide the chromosomes around the cell. These protein wires or fibers form around the chromosomes to aid in the proper distribution of the chromosomes to the daughter cells. This stage is called prophase.	
Stage 3	The pairs of chromosomes align along the center or equator of the cell along the spindle fibers. This stage is called metaphase.	
Stage 4	The duplicate chromosome pairs separate and move to opposite sides of the cell. This is anaphase.	
Stage 5	When the chromosomes reach the ends of the cell, the cell begins to divide to form two daughter cells. Each daughter cell has one copy of the chromosome pairs. The spindle fiber scaffolding disassembles and a new nuclear membrane begins to form. This stage is called telophase.	
Stage 6	Cell division is complete, the nuclear membrane reforms, and the chromosomes become less discrete in the cells. The cells reenter interphase.	

8. Separate the homologous attached chromosomes into 2 rows. Each row should consist of 1 of each size chromosome pairs (stage 4, Table 1.4). Move them to opposite sides of the cell.

9. Cut the outer yarn in half, and close each half around 1 set of chromosomes. Cut the inner circle of yarn that you removed in step 5 (the nuclear membrane) in half. Place it around the chromosomes inside the cells (stages 5 and 6, Table 1.4).

10. **STOP & THINK** Explain what is happening at this stage of mitosis.

Divide and Conquer: A Second Look

Cell division in prokaryotic organisms is much less complex. The DNA of these organisms is not confined to a nucleus. Instead, it floats, weblike, throughout much of the cell and is attached at various points to the cell membrane. When the cell has grown to a size where it must divide, DNA replicates. Using the sites of attachment as anchors, the replicated DNA moves apart from the original DNA. A small fissure begins to grow inward from the cell membrane. New membrane and cell walls form between the DNA copies and eventually split the cell into two cells. Each cell contains the required DNA information and necessary cytoplasmic machinery (see Figure 1.45).

Cell division in prokaryotic organisms is also the process by which bacteria reproduce. Some eukaryotic organisms, such as amoebae and certain fungi, also reproduce themselves by simple cell division. This is known as asexual reproduction.

Repair and maintenance of a healthy organism relies on the ability of cells to divide in order to replace worn-out or damaged structures. When overexposure to the sun causes skin damage, for example, the injured and dead skin cells are sloughed off and cell division replaces the lost cells. Similarly, cell division is essential in healing wounds. In a human adult, cell division replaces approximately 200 million worn-out cells per minute.

Cell division is an essential process for the growth, repair, and reproduction of cells. For many years, however, scientists believed that muscle and nerve cells had a limited capacity to regenerate themselves when damaged or destroyed. They also believed that the number of these cells remained fixed. Muscle cells were known to grow by increasing their size. This can be seen in body builders. Their muscle mass would increase not as a result of cell division but rather because of an increase in the size of the individual cells in the tissue. But if these cells and tissues were damaged, research suggested that they could not be repaired by cell division of healthy cells. Rather, damaged tissue generally was replaced with fibrous connective tissue instead of muscle tissue. As a result, some or all function carried out by that tissue was lost. Similarly, scientists believed that damage to nerve cells almost always resulted in the permanent loss of essential functions. Recent research, however, indicates that by activating certain signals (or inactivating them in the case of nerve cells), these cells might be stimulated to divide. This gives new hope to individuals who suffer damage to nerves or muscles.

ANALYSIS

Record your responses to the following in your notebook.

1. Why is it important that DNA copies are distributed equally to the daughter cells?
2. Why is it important that each daughter cell receive all of the cellular organelles? (These include mitochondria, chloroplasts,

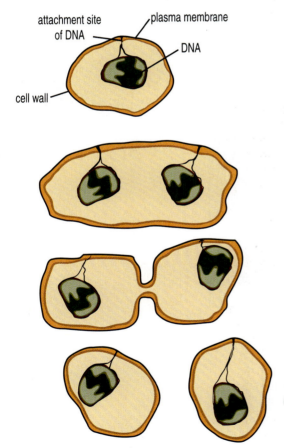

attachment site of DNA

plasma membrane

DNA

cell wall

Figure 1.45

Bacterial cell division.

Golgi apparatus, and endoplasmic reticulum.) Describe which processes might be affected if a daughter cell did not receive one of these organelles.

3. Cells need nutrients as building blocks for new biomolecules. What other product of metabolism do nutrients provide for the cell? At what points during the stages of cell division are these products required?

4. What difficulties might arise for an organism if muscle cells or nerve cells are damaged?

EXTENDING *Ideas*

Cancer is a disease that has a wide variety of symptoms and can affect one or more organs in the body. One common feature of all cancers is the loss of control over cell division. Research a specific form of cancer. Describe what we know about changes that have taken place at the cellular level. Also explain how the treatment reflects what we understand about how these changes cause the disease.

Extensive research is being conducted to develop ways to stimulate nerve cells to divide. Scientists hope that this will help patients with spinal cord injuries regain mobility in paralyzed limbs. Research why scientists believe that they can stimulate normally nondividing cells to divide. How might this help these people?

CAREER FOCUS

Cell Biologist Lily's major career objective is admirable and ambitious. Lily wants to find a cure for cancer. She is a cell biologist at Solution Pharmaceuticals. Here she studies cancerous cells, observing and analyzing patterns of growth and division. Along with a team of 20 other cell biologists, Lily conducts experiments to identify what might cause a cell to change from a normal growth pattern to an abnormal growth pattern. They hope this understanding will help them devise new treatments to prevent or cure cancer.

Most of Lily's time is spent with other cell biologists in the Department of Cell Biology. Solution Pharmaceuticals, however, encourages an interdisciplinary approach to science. Cell biologists, chemists, and cellular, molecular, and structural biologists working in conjunction. In this way, they can each appreciate problems from a unique perspective.

Lily grew up in a household of scientists. She was always fascinated with the world around her as well as with as the scientific explanations for how things worked. Because her parents were scientists, she was introduced to her first microscope at a young age. She could often be found looking for items to examine under the microscope, frequently confiscating the moldy bread forgotten on the kitchen counter. Lily knew she would go to college to study science but she wasn't sure what career path she would pursue. Upon entering college, she decided to major in medical technology because of the many career opportunities it offered, such as working in a lab and teaching. One summer, Lily found a job working in a medical school lab studying different diseases. Her experiences there convinced her that she could handle the intellectual aspects of research.

Lily changed her major to biology and started on a path that would prepare her for graduate school. Through her undergraduate work, she learned about the many types of biology and continued her fascination of examining cells under a microscope. She then enrolled in a graduate program in cell biology. Here she designed her own research project, worked with other students, and was mentored by a cell biology researcher. Lily's adviser provided crucial advice and direction that helped her gain confidence in her skills as an independent scientist. Lily still follows her advice—to focus on the data and the science—whenever she is faced with a challenging situation. Lily then went on to a postdoctoral fellowship where she spent several years working with a renowned cell biologist.

Lily could have followed an academic route and become a university researcher and professor. Instead, she chose to accept a job at Solution Pharmaceuticals. She was excited about helping to cure a human disease. She also wanted to learn about treating disease through numerous types of therapies, which had changed due to the growth of the biotechnology industry. Lily felt that the pharmaceutical industry had significant resources to create therapies. She also thought that the industry was more open to new ideas for treating human disease. Although her research applies what she learned in her graduate and postgraduate work, Lily feels that she is exploring a broader field of science than she would have in an academic lab. And by working in industry rather than in an academic position, Lily doesn't have to spend time away from data, writing grants for money to do experiments. But most important, Lily feels that there is nothing more exciting than believing your ideas may someday alleviate human suffering.

On Becoming a Specialist

Prologue

You are made up of an impressive collection of different kinds of cells. You share that characteristic with all multicellular organisms. In humans, this collection includes nerve, blood, skin, muscle, and bone cells (to name a few). All of these cells carry out the same basic activities that are required for maintaining life. In addition to these "housekeeping" functions, these cells also carry out specialized activities. These specialized activities enable them to perform specific functions such as carrying oxygen around the body (in the blood) or protecting the organism from the external environment (the skin). This is cell specialization.

Early in the development of an embryo, all cells are identical. A fertilized egg divides to produce many daughter cells. Each daughter cell contains the same information in the DNA as the original fertilized egg. At some point in development, cells begin to specialize. They assume the structures and functions of specific kinds of cells. What is the origin of this vast variety of cells? When and how do these cells that were identical start to become different? Scientific evidence indicates that at some point in the development process choices are made about which set of instructions in the DNA is to be followed. This happens even though all the information is present. For example, in a cell that is to become a muscle cell, one set of instructions is followed. In a cell destined to become a nerve cell, a different set of instructions is followed.

How does that happen? If a cell contains all the information in its DNA required by the entire organism, how might it be possible to express only some of this information? In this investigation, you examine propagation in plants and regeneration in planarians, a flatworm, as models for exploring how differentiation takes place.

Brainstorming

Discuss the following questions with your partner, and record your thinking in your notebook. Be prepared to share your ideas with the class.

1. Earthworms are good for the soil. Gardening lore recommends cutting earthworms in half when you find them in your garden. What do you think happens to the worm when you do that?
2. What do you think needs to happen at the level of the worm's cells?

Regenerate Thyself

You and your partner will be given a plant cutting or a planarian. Your teacher will explain how each specimen was prepared. Examine each organism carefully. Discuss with your partner your observations using these questions as guidelines. Be prepared to share your ideas with the class.

- Describe how your specimen was prepared. What, if anything, has happened to the original plant cutting or planarian?
- Are these results surprising? Why or why not?
- Where do you think the new plant structures or planarians came from?

Hold That Milk

Specialized cells in the lining of the small intestine of mammals produce the enzyme lactase. Lactase breaks down lactose (the sugar in milk). Lactase is produced at birth. It enables the offspring to digest its mother's milk. The production of lactase begins to decline as the animal ages. In humans, this begins to take place between the ages of 2 and 7. By young adulthood, lactase levels are generally about 10% of what they were during infancy. Despite these lowered levels, most adults can digest lactose. They can enjoy ice cream, cheese, and other dairy products. However, an inability to digest lactose occurs in many adults whose lactase levels may be just too low for that extra slice of cheese pizza. An intolerance for lactose is very common among certain ethnic groups. Fifty percent of the adults of Hispanic descent, and 75% of the adults of African, Asian, and Native American heritage suffer from this problem.

Symptoms of lactose intolerance include abdominal cramping, gas, and diarrhea. Normally, lactose is broken down in the small intestine. The resulting sugars, glucose, and galactose are used by cells to synthesize other biomolecules required to sustain life. However, if the lactase levels are low, lactose can pass undigested into the colon. Here intestinal bacteria use it as a resource for their own metabolic processes. These bacteria metabolize the lactose to fatty acids, hydrogen, carbon dioxide, and methane. A side effect of this bacterial feast is the retention of water and sodium. Water and sodium can combine with the gases generated and produce the symptoms characteristic of lactose intolerance.

ANALYSIS

Record your responses to the following in your notebook.

1. What can you infer about the information in the DNA for producing the enzyme (protein) lactase in a juvenile?
2. What can you infer about the lactase-producing information in the DNA of a lactose-intolerant adult?
3. One way lactose-intolerant adults can enjoy milk products again is to add the enzyme lactase to the milk product they want to eat before ingesting it. Can you think of other ways that science might help adults with this problem?

Learning Experience 12

Where Will It All End?

Prologue

In previous learning experiences, you have focused on the characteristics of life and the resources and processes required to maintain life. A critical question that seems to follow naturally from this study of life is, "What happens when these resources are not accessible and these processes no longer take place?" For example, what if food were no longer available? The characteristics of life that depend on the uptake and transformation of the nutrients into materials and energy for the organism would disappear. Unless the organism could find a way to locate and get food, that organism would perish. Death marks the end of the complex chemical reactions and transfer of energy that enable organisms to grow, respond, reproduce, and maintain themselves. Is death an end to life or an integral part of the cycle of life?

Brainstorming

Discuss the following questions with your partner, and record your thinking in your notebook. Be prepared to share your ideas with the class. This discussion revisits some of the questions you explored at the beginning of this unit. Use the understandings that you have gained in this unit to rethink these ideas and address new questions.

1. What is the difference between living things and nonliving things?
2. What is the difference between things that are alive and things that are no longer alive?
3. What do things that are alive and things that are dead have in common?
4. How would you determine that something was no longer alive? Use examples from this unit.
5. Do you know of any living things that never die?
6. Could something that was no longer alive have the characteristics of life? How could that happen?

7. Describe circumstances that might cause death for different organisms. Use examples of the kinds of organisms you have investigated in this unit. Explain why these circumstances would cause death.
8. How might the death of organisms be necessary for sustaining the life of other organisms?

When Organisms Die

When organisms die, the process of decomposition returns the biomolecules that had made up the living organism to the soil and air. Microorganisms called decomposers break down the proteins, fats, carbohydrates, and other complex organic substances. They then transform these substances into smaller molecules of carbon dioxide, ammonia, and other simple inorganic compounds. Thus, decomposers both rid Earth of no-longer-living organic debris. They return to the air and soil the simple compounds that plants require for the synthesis of their food and biomolecules. Life then goes full circle. Plants use carbon dioxide from the air, minerals from the soil, and energy from the sun. They use these things to generate the food that they and other organisms require to synthesize the biomolecules they use to maintain the characteristics of life. When these organisms die, they return these simple molecules to the soil and air for reuse. If it were not for that cycle, the world would be filled with the fossilized remains of once-living plants and animals.

Examine the diagram in Figure 1.46. Record your responses to the following in your notebook.

1. For millions of years, plants and animals have been living on Earth and using resources. Explain why Earth has not exhausted its supply of nutrients, minerals, carbon dioxide, water, and oxygen. Include information from Figure 1.46, from the reading "When Organisms Die," and from other material and your experience with this unit.
2. What do you think might happen if living things did not die?
3. Explain the following statement: The atoms of carbon in your body may have been part of a *Tyrannosaurus rex*; the oxygen you breathe may have been breathed by Julius Caesar.

Never Say Die

If there were an endless supply of resources, could an organism live forever? Is death inevitable? Is death the only outcome of life? Is there such a state as immortality? Is immortality a desirable state?

Science fiction is filled with stories of quests for immortality and the consequences of achieving it. What would it be like to live forever or for at least 500 or 600 years? What would it be like if everyone in the world could live forever? What might you look like? How would you plan your life? How might the quality of life change? What would the world be like?

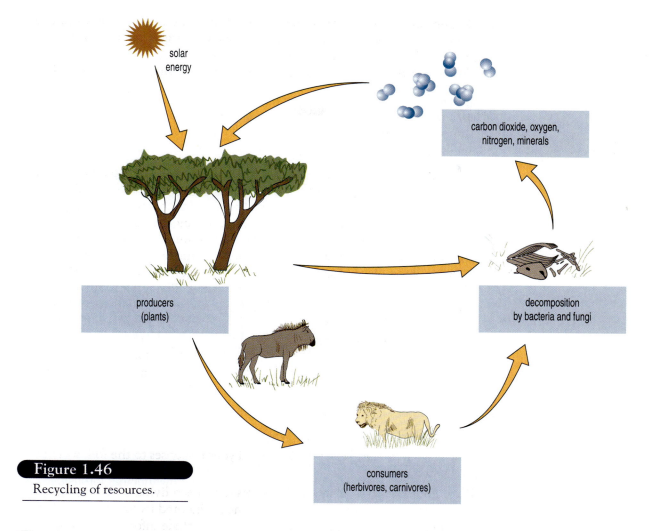

Figure 1.46
Recycling of resources.

Labels in figure:
solar energy
carbon dioxide, oxygen, nitrogen, minerals
producers (plants)
decomposition by bacteria and fungi
consumers (herbivores, carnivores)

TASK

Imagine that the year is 2120. You and many other people have decided to undergo a treatment that might allow you to live forever, or at least for a very long time. No one is sure how long you will survive after the treatment since it only recently has been made available to humans. Prolonged testing on mice, however, has indicated that human life expectancy could be extended for at least 500 years.

Write a short science fiction story describing what your life will be like in the coming 500 years. Be sure to think about all of the ramifications of living for 500 years. These would include personal; biological (characteristics to maintain life); social (economic and political); environmental; and ethical issues, as well as any other consequences that may result from such an extended lifetime.

EXTENDING *Ideas*

A recent theory in developmental biology suggests that the lives of humans and other multicellular organisms depend in a variety of ways on the programmed death of our own cells. Through a process called apoptosis, healthy cells prepare the means for their own destruction. They then commit suicide. In development, this healthy suicide is the process behind the loss of the tail of the tadpole as it turns into a frog. It is responsible for the loss of the juvenile tissues of the caterpillar when the time comes for metamorphosis into a butterfly. In humans, apoptosis deletes cells from the embryo's developing limbs, leaving behind 10 little fingers and 10 toes. In our immune system, apoptosis plays a number of crucial roles. Dying white blood cells self-destruct so that they can be cleaned up by other cells in the body's defense system. Cells infected by viruses may actually self-destruct so that the body's immune system can clean up the mess. Today, researchers wonder if apoptosis may hold the key to stopping certain cancers. If cancer represents uncontrolled cell growth, could the growth be halted by triggering programmed cell death? Does the discovery of apoptosis affect our understanding of what life itself means?

Are there any organisms that do not die? In an article titled "The Immortal Microorganism" (*New Scientist,* May 20, 1989), microbiologist John Postgate states the following: "When [bacterial] cell division takes place, there is no way of telling which of the two short rods is the mother and which is the daughter. Indeed, such evidence as is available tells us that no mother-daughter relationship exists; both progeny are of equal age. . . . Did the parent cell grow old and die? Of course not. So, do klebsiellae [a kind of bacterium] have any equivalent of aging and death, analogous to these processes in, for example, ourselves?" How would you answer that question?

CAREER FOCUS

Biological Technician   What do potato chips, the contents of a vacuum cleaner, and a knife recovered from a lake have in common? They can contain traces of DNA that can be used as evidence to convict criminals. In fact, the tools of molecular biology are now so powerful that forensic biology technicians like Ahmad can find DNA in the most surprising places. The potato chips were discovered in a location where a burglary had been committed; the perpetrator, it seems, decided to have a snack before leaving. Ahmad's job as the forensic biology technician is to try to find enough DNA in minute amounts of saliva on the chips to create a DNA profile—a personal signature—of the offender.

Ahmad is a biological technician who works for the state in a forensics facility. He's responsible for analyzing DNA samples sent to the lab. DNA profiles are unique to every individual, except identical twins. So if Ahmad can get a DNA profile from a piece of evidence, it can be used as hard evidence that a suspect was—or was not—at the scene of a crime. Working as a forensic biology technician allows Ahmad to use his scientific interests and skills in a way that contributes to the greater good of society, which he finds very satisfying. Although Ahmad's work may sound glamorous, he does have to be extremely meticulous. He has to check his work several times to ensure its accuracy since a police investigation or prosecution may depend on the quality of the forensic evidence. In addition, most samples sent to the laboratory need immediate results. This puts pressure on technicians to test the samples as quickly and as accurately as possible.

Growing up, Ahmad was motivated by all things related to science. He took great pleasure in carefully conducting experiments in the school lab. He also loved reading, particularly crime mysteries. But he didn't realize that that interest could one day play a major role in his career choice. When his biology course in high school sparked his interest in biology, he asked his teacher about what kinds of careers he might pursue. One of the careers his teacher recommended was as a biological technician. Ahmad researched his options and decided to enroll in a technical training program after high school. He chose to major in biotechnology and really enjoyed learning about genetics. At that time, he thought he would become a biological technician in a genetic engineering lab. But as he learned more, he realized that he was fascinated with DNA and wanted to find a career where he could do lots of DNA analysis. Forensics seemed like a great fit since analyzing DNA is such a big part of the job of a forensic biology technician. Ahmad took many courses specific to forensics. But he also tried to broaden his background by taking subjects such as writing, computers, statistics, and chemistry.

Part of Ahmad's program was to complete a year-long internship, which he did at the state lab. Following graduation, he was hired as a full-time employee. The forensic biology technicians in the state laboratory are encouraged to further their qualifications and attend conferences. So Ahmad plans on furthering his training in forensic science because the field is constantly changing due to continuous improvements in technology. He gets a lot of satisfaction from learning new techniques, which better help police solve crimes and capture criminals. Ahmad would also like to get enough experience to one day be promoted to a supervisory position. In that position, he can help other technicians develop and expand their careers.

Ecologist

It's daybreak and Rory is getting ready to head out to do some field research. She has a lot on her plate today. After spending a few hours collecting data for her research on the effects of air pollutants on ecosystems, she will head to Rocky University where she'll teach an ecology class. She will finish up her day back at her office, analyzing data. Rory takes on many different roles in her work as an ecologist. She's part researcher, part teacher, and part outdoor adventurer.

As an ecologist, Rory studies the relationships between organisms and their environment. She also studies the factors that influence these relationships. Rory focuses on understanding the implications of environmental problems, such as pollution and acid rain, and proposing practical solutions. She works part-time for a large research organization run by the government. That position gives her the flexibility to work on her research projects in the field instead of working in the central office. It also allows her to be a government employee while also holding a faculty position at the university. In addition to her research, Rory is responsible for teaching university classes, such as ecology, evolution, and environmental conservation.

Rory grew up in the mountains and developed a great interest in nature. She spent hours walking in the woods observing wildlife and the environment. She became interested in ecology in high school when her biology teacher organized class trips to study and explore other ecosystems. This helped Rory develop a respect for the environment and a desire to protect natural surroundings and environmental processes. Her teacher encouraged her to join the National High School Biology Honor Society. As a member, she would be involved in service projects with local elementary schools, such as teaching and leading field trips. Because she loved studying ecology, examining different environments, and working with kids, she decided to study environmental science in college.

During her sophomore year of college, Rory became a volunteer researcher in a local national park so that she could spend more time outdoors. She quickly got involved in a research project on acid rain. Although it was hard work, Rory really enjoyed doing field research. She decided that she wanted to pursue a Ph.D. so she could conduct her own ecological research. Sponsored by the Park Service, Rory conducted her graduate research in the ecosystem ecology of a national park. After completing her Ph.D., she was hired as a seasonal employee for the Park Service. In this position, she was able to conduct her own research and carry it through to publications and presentations. After several years, she accepted a position at the national office of the Park Service. This was a big break for her, since moving from seasonal to permanent employment is challenging.

Eventually, Rory accepted her current government and university positions. She finds the work to be a perfect mix of fieldwork, analytical work in the laboratory, teaching, and collaboration with others. She tries to inspire her students in the same way that her high school biology teacher inspired her. And knowing that her work helps to preserve the environment and solve ecological problems, greatly satisfies Rory.

Suspended Between Life and Death

Prologue

In the late 20th century, the ethics, the economics, and the humanity of extending a human life when the quality of that life had been compromised became a pressing issue. Today, huge numbers of Alzheimer's patients survive long after they have lost the capacity to think for themselves. Victims of total paralysis can be sustained through the application of respirators and feeding tubes. Modern medicine is often able to extend lives at the threshold of death.

Modern technology is forcing us to rethink our understanding of life and death. Just as old definitions of life have been challenged by new discoveries in science, so old definitions of death no longer apply. For example, in an 1890 law, the U.S. courts defined death as the cessation of the circulation of blood, of the pulse, and of respiration. But as we all know, in the modern world of emergency medicine many thousands of Americans whose respiration and/or circulation has stopped have been restored and then returned to productive, healthy lives.

There is one group of patients in which the number of compromised survivors has increased dramatically. These patients are those whose heartbeats or respiration have been restored after their brains have already been damaged. Today, in the United States, there are between 5,000 and 10,000 brain-damaged patients kept alive by artificial life support. These patients are unconscious and, for the most part, have no hope of full recovery. The nation's medical bill to sustain comatose and vegetative patients amounts to approximately $1 billion per year. (These two diagnoses are somewhat different.) It is these types of patients who will be the focus of the final learning experience in this unit.

Brainstorming

Discuss the following questions with your partner, and record your thinking in your notebook. Be prepared to share your ideas with the class.

1. What is your definition of life from a biological perspective? from a social perspective? Answer this question using your own experiences, including what you have learned in this unit.

2. Is an organism considered alive if it can no longer feed itself? What if it has a feeding tube to sustain its life?

135

3. Is an individual considered alive if he can no longer breathe? What if there is a respirator breathing for the individual?
4. How is the definition of life different when an organism sustains life itself than when machines or other apparatus are used to sustain life? What does the inclusion of modern technology mean in defining life or death?
5. Why do you think humans go to great lengths to extend their own lives and not the lives of other animals?

ACTIVITY

The Problem Defined

Thus far in this unit, you have constructed a scientific definition of life. One facet of that definition is that all living things must die. There are certain life processes without which life cannot be sustained. The question arises, then, is a person alive if he is unable to sustain his life processes on his own but medical technology can perform those processes for him?

What remains is to reflect upon the definition of human life and the quality of life. If the technical question of what makes a living thing alive is a topic for biologists, then the question of what makes a human life worth living is more a question of philosophy, of ethics, and of religion. Perhaps there is no better place to clarify our views about life than around the question of death, because it urges the living to reflect upon the experience of life.

To reflect about what constitutes human life, you are going to simulate an academic conference on the bioethics of life and death. Each of you will be given a role to play at the conference.

Topic: Characteristics of Life
Go to: www.scilinks.org
Code: INBIOH2136

TASK

Prior to the Conference

For your role, do all of the following:

- As background, read the fictional news article "A Difficult Choice." (This article follows the conference instructions.) Also read the role profile notes that your teacher gives you. Keep your role profile a secret. Prior to the conference, nobody else should know who you are or what your point of view will be. Maintain a little suspense and mystery before the conference.
- Take on the role you have been assigned. From the perspective of that role, write a thoughtful 2–3-minute opening statement. You will read or recite this statement during the conference. Treat the information provided to you about your role as only an outline for the character you will create. Go beyond what is given to you on the role description sheet. Expand on the rationales for your opinions and develop a personality for the role. Take some time to consider what your character would think about issues not covered in your character outline. For example, your role description states that your character is interested in saving money. By extension, what do you think such a character would think about using heroic measures to save a life? It is important that you give some thought to the general worldview of your character. Your character's viewpoint should remain logical and consistent throughout the simulation.
- Bring your notes to the simulation; they will be collected after the conference ends.

During the Conference

You will be evaluated not only for your opening remarks but also for your thoughtful attention to the ideas of other conference attendees. It is expected that you will rebut those who disagree with your character's point of view. It is likewise expected that you will ask questions and challenge the other speakers when you think doing so will broaden or deepen the conference discussion.

Rules for Conference Debate

- Your teacher is the conference moderator. Please respect the moderator's role.
- Raise your hand when you wish to speak. If the moderator calls for order in the conference, please respect this request.
- Fill out a name card with your character's name. Place this card in front of your chair at the conference. During the conference, address other conference participants by their formal titles.
- Feel free to raise questions in response to the opening remarks of other participants. However, respect the moderator's responsibility for time management. It is important that all conference attendees have a chance to make their opening remarks. To ensure this, it may be necessary for the moderator to limit questions and debate at some points.
- During the simulation, your performance may be evaluated by visiting guests.

Following the Conference

After the conference, you will prepare a policy-position essay. In this essay, you will decide whether a person should be sustained on life support. To write your essay, you will want to draw from all of the information and statements made during the conference and from your own research. Explain the reasoning behind your decision. Be sure to address all of these issues in your essay.

- Based on what you have learned from this unit, do you feel that a brain-damaged person on life-support machines is alive? Use the biology from this unit to defend your answer. Describe where biology may or may not be sufficient in answering this question.
- Should a brain-damaged, unconscious patient be left on life support? If so, for how long? At what cost? Should there be limits to such life-support care? Why or why not?
- Should there be national legislation that limits medical care for people whose consciousness has been compromised? If so, what should those limits be, and why? If not, why not?
- What are the societal implications of your answers to these questions? What do your answers suggest about how our society should invest its resources?
- How has your response to the preceding questions been influenced by your family's attitudes? by your friends? by your experiences? by the American culture around you?
- Conclude by reflecting upon how this simulated experience has deepened your thinking about what, if anything, makes human life unique.

Your essay will be evaluated on the following criteria:

- completeness (have you addressed all six parts of the essay question?),
- organization of ideas,
- reasoned basis for your responses,
- thought-provoking conclusion, and
- clarity of writing.

A DIFFICULT CHOICE

January 20, 2010

CITY NEWS—This week, following months of unusually well-publicized preparation, the City University Department of Bioethics will convene a conference to discuss the ethics of long-term life support. For a variety of reasons, this conference is receiving more than its share of national press attention. Several senators prominent in the resurfacing national debate over health care are expected to attend. For weeks there have been rumors that key members of Congress are considering new legislation on the right-to-die issue. Speculation centers on whether one or another senator may use this conference as an opportunity to propose new legislation. Expected to attend are a wide range of health care professionals, several legal scholars, and the family members of several comatose patients. All of these people hope to influence any legislation that may make it to a vote in Congress.

In addition, the focus of discussions at the day-long conference is the fate of Mark Vorst. If the celebrity status of many of the conference's attendees weren't enough to draw a media blitz, the conference's focus on Mr. Vorst's tragic story would itself be certain to turn many heads. By now, the story of Mark Vorst is familiar to many Americans. Mr. Vorst was a rising star in the Senate and a leading advocate of health care reform back in 1994. He suffered severe brain damage when his car careened off a bridge during an ice storm. Since that time, Vorst has been kept alive by surgically implanted feeding tubes and a respirator. Medical experts agree that he is in a "persistent vegetative state," with no chance of regaining consciousness. However, his face does occasionally register a smile or a grimace, and from time to time his eyes produce tears.

Unfortunately, the health care advocate himself had neglected to fill out either a health care proxy or a living will. As a result, Mr. Vorst's own wishes in the event of such a catastrophe are not known. Instead, his fate has become the subject of a bitter 5-year court battle. Mr. Vorst's parents have fought for the right to maintain their son on life support. His insurer and his wife have both been fighting for the right to remove the support. This case is almost a mirror image of the Nancy Cruzan case, settled by the Supreme Court in 1990. In that case, over the protests of Cruzan's doctors, the family won the right to stop life support.

To date, the life-support care for Mr. Vorst has cost the U.S. taxpayers approximately $650,000. This amount is on top of the $200,000 in emergency and intensive care treatment Mr. Vorst received at the time of his injury. (As a member of the U.S. Senate, Mr. Vorst's health insurance is provided by the federal government.) The court battle is now scheduled for a spring hearing before the Supreme Court. This has inspired a nationwide debate about the role of medicine and the question of setting limits in health care spending. The case may never receive a hearing before the Supreme Court if Congress chooses to legislate the issue before the court's spring session.

At the conference, participants will be asked to join in a dialogue about the same questions that the Supreme Court or Congress may soon debate: Should Mark Vorst be left on life support? Should there be national legislation setting limits to medical care? If so, what should those limits be? What are the ethical, economic, and social implications of our answers to those questions?

EXTENDING *Ideas*

To many physicians, death is the enemy to be held at bay. They believe that their role is to sustain the lives of their patients by any measure at their disposal. Dr. Jack Kevorkian has a different perspective. He feels that physicians have another obligation. This is to help patients avoid a lingering and sometimes painful death by assisting them in ending their own lives and ensuring that they die peacefully. In the late 1980s, he actually built a machine that would assist patients in committing suicide. The machine enabled patients to inject a lethal dosage of a narcotic at the moment of their own choosing. In 1998, however, he challenged the legal system by administering the lethal dose to a patient himself rather than simply providing the man with the means to kill himself. This was an act called active euthanasia. The state had another name for it, homicide. Dr. Kevorkian was sentenced to 10–25 years in prison. He is currently incarcerated in a correctional facility in Michigan. Murder or compassion? You decide. Back up your decision with biological, legal, and ethical evidence.

CAREER FOCUS

Lawyer A research scientist approaches Grady for advice about a unique antibody that another research institution wants to use in its experiments. Both Grady and the scientist work at a government research institute. As the technology transfer specialist (TTS), Grady uses his background knowledge in science and the law to help the researcher complete the appropriate legal documents.

Research scientists often form collaborations with scientists at other institutions to further their research goals. Even though Grady has a law degree, his work varies from that of a typical lawyer. Technology transfer is a relatively new field that involves the legal transfer of materials between organizations. A TTS facilitates the transfer of these materials by preparing the appropriate legal documents. Grady must understand the science, legal, and business aspects of the transaction so that the interests of all parties are understood and protected. The types of materials transferred can be anything used in research. These include proteins, chemicals, computer software, and equipment. Today, it is the research scientist's unique antibody.

In his day-to-day work, Grady prepares legal documents, such as agreements for material transfers, confidentiality, cooperative research, and clinical trials. But before he can complete these documents, he spends a lot of time reading research proposals and speaking with scientists. He needs to make sure he understands the nature of the research and the science involved. Once the agreements have been drafted, it's Grady's job to negotiate the final agreement with the lawyer representing the other research institute, university, or private company.

Grady always had an interest science. He liked asking questions and taking on the challenge of finding answers in the laboratory. He decided to study biochemistry in college and landed a laboratory position after graduation.

Although he enjoyed research, eventually he wanted to explore other types of work. One day while he was reading a science journal, he came across an article about scientists who became patent lawyers and technology transfer specialists. Becoming a lawyer specializing in technology transfer seemed to be the perfect way to stay in touch with the latest research while developing new skills and taking on new challenges. Grady did a lot of networking and research. Eventually, he found a law clerk position at a practice that specialized in biotechnology. Through the practice's clerk program, Grady was able to study law at night and have his schooling costs covered while gaining valuable work experience.

Once he finished his law degree, Grady began working at the research institute under the supervision of an experienced TTS. Grady loves that being a TTS allows him to carry out a variety of tasks every day. He enjoys reading about the cutting edge scientific research that is going on at his organization. He likes being able to research and read about legal issues as well. He gets to spend a lot of time working with people, whether they are scientific researchers or his technology transfer colleagues.

Nurse   Diego met Keisha by chance. He was in a car accident and was rushed by ambulance to County Hospital, where Keisha is a registered nurse (RN) in the emergency room. When Diego was brought in, it was Keisha's job to work with other nurses and doctors to observe and assess his injuries and decide on a course of action to help treat him.

Keisha got right to work. She monitored Diego's vital signs, took his temperature, monitored his pulse and blood pressure, administered pain medication, and carefully recorded all of her findings in a chart she created for him. Once she and the other doctors determined that he just had a broken arm, Keisha helped another doctor set it in a cast and helped make Diego comfortable.

As an RN, Keisha's goal with all of her patients is to promote health, prevent disease, and help patients cope with illness. Before Diego is discharged from the emergency room, Keisha will spend time with him and his family. She will teach them how to take care of his arm properly and discuss when he should return to have the cast removed. She will also spend time answering any questions they may have.

Keisha has wanted to be a nurse from the time she was very young. Her mother was a nurse. Keisha noticed that people shared their stories with her, and in turn, her mother was able to support them. Keisha's parents always encouraged her to select a career that had a lot of growth potential and that would allow her to make a difference in people's lives. When she was in high school, Keisha's father brought her to the library. He helped her research career choices based on her interests and the job outlook data. Nursing was Keisha's top choice. She felt that her caring, nurturing, and sensitive personality qualities would fit perfectly in the nursing role.

After high school, Keisha attended the College of Nursing and graduated with a Bachelor of Science degree in nursing. During her undergraduate work, she also interned at the Memorial Medical Center as a nurse technician. Before graduating from her program, Keisha had to pass a licensing exam to become an RN and practice nursing. Following college, Keisha had a lot of options open to her. In addition to working in a hospital, nursing opportunities were available at a doctor's office, a public health agency, a school, a camp, or a Health Maintenance Organization (HMO).

Keisha decided that working in the emergency room would allow her to meet many different people every day, so she pursued a position at County Hospital.

Keisha has been an RN in the emergency room at County Hospital for 3 years now. She finds it very satisfying when a patient's health improves, and when she is thanked by patients and their families. She knows that nursing allows her to make a real difference in other people's lives. She's proud of how she has touched the lives of so many others. She gets to meet interesting people every day and leaves work with a sense of accomplishment and fulfillment. Keisha enjoys being able to continuously learn on the job and feels that nursing is a profession that allows for many opportunities and career paths.

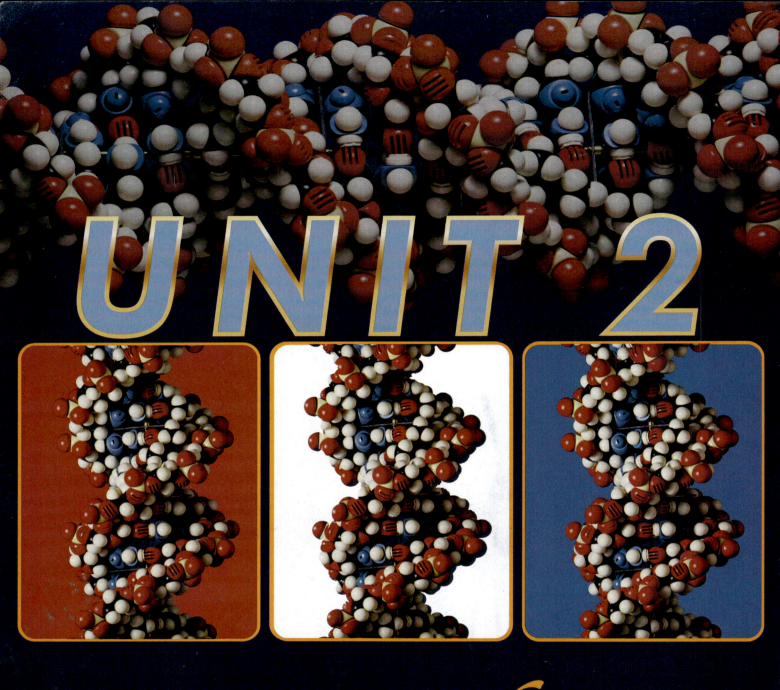

UNIT 2

Traits and Fates

Contents

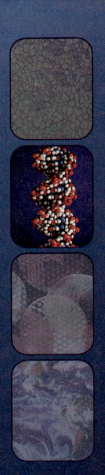

Traits and Fates

Introduction

At noon on July 1, 2004, the world's population reached 6,377,641,642. Think about that number. More than 6 billion people and no two are alike. Even identical twins who inherit the exact same genetic legacy have different fingerprints and different personalities. How does this variation in individuals happen? What are the factors that influence what you look like, how you behave, and how healthy you will or will not be?

The variation we observe in humans is due, in large part, to the differences in their genes. Genes also play a major role in the diversity of organisms that exist on Earth—in the past, present, and future. How does this diversity happen? Are genes the only cause? How much of "you" is determined by your biological inheritance? How much is influenced by the environment? How much of yourself can you shape by your own actions and choices?

In this unit, you will explore traits. Traits are those characteristics that make you you. You will examine the mechanisms by which traits are expressed. You will discover how they vary and how they are inherited. You will also observe the interplay between genetic inheritance and environmental influences. This interplay results in variation over generations and over vast expanses of evolutionary time. Using your understandings of these genetic principles, you will assess the effect and the value of new genetic research and technologies on your life.

Finding the "Gene" in Genetics

Prologue

The word **gene** is often seen in newspapers and magazines, and heard on television. You may have used it yourself in conversation or in the classroom. As is true of many words from science, this word has several levels of meaning. It can be used from the casual to the biochemical. In this learning experience, you begin to determine what you and your classmates mean by the word gene. You compare your meaning with the way the word is used by others, such as science writers and scientists.

Topic: Genes
Go to: www.scilinks.org
Code: INBIOH2145

Brainstorming

Discuss the following questions with your partner, and record your thinking in your notebook. Be prepared to share your ideas with the class.

1. Examine the headlines in Figure 2.1. Think about these headlines and about what you currently know about genes. Then write a definition for the word gene. Be prepared to explain how you came up with your definition.
2. With your classmates, develop a class definition of gene. Record it in your notebook.

TASK

Your teacher will assign your group one headline from Figure 2.1. Discuss with your group what you think the article is about. Then write your group's version of an opening paragraph for the article. Your paragraph should reflect the information in the headline as well as the class definition of a gene. You may be asked to read your headline and paragraph aloud. Your teacher will then provide the actual article. Read through it and compare the paragraph that you and your group wrote with the actual article.

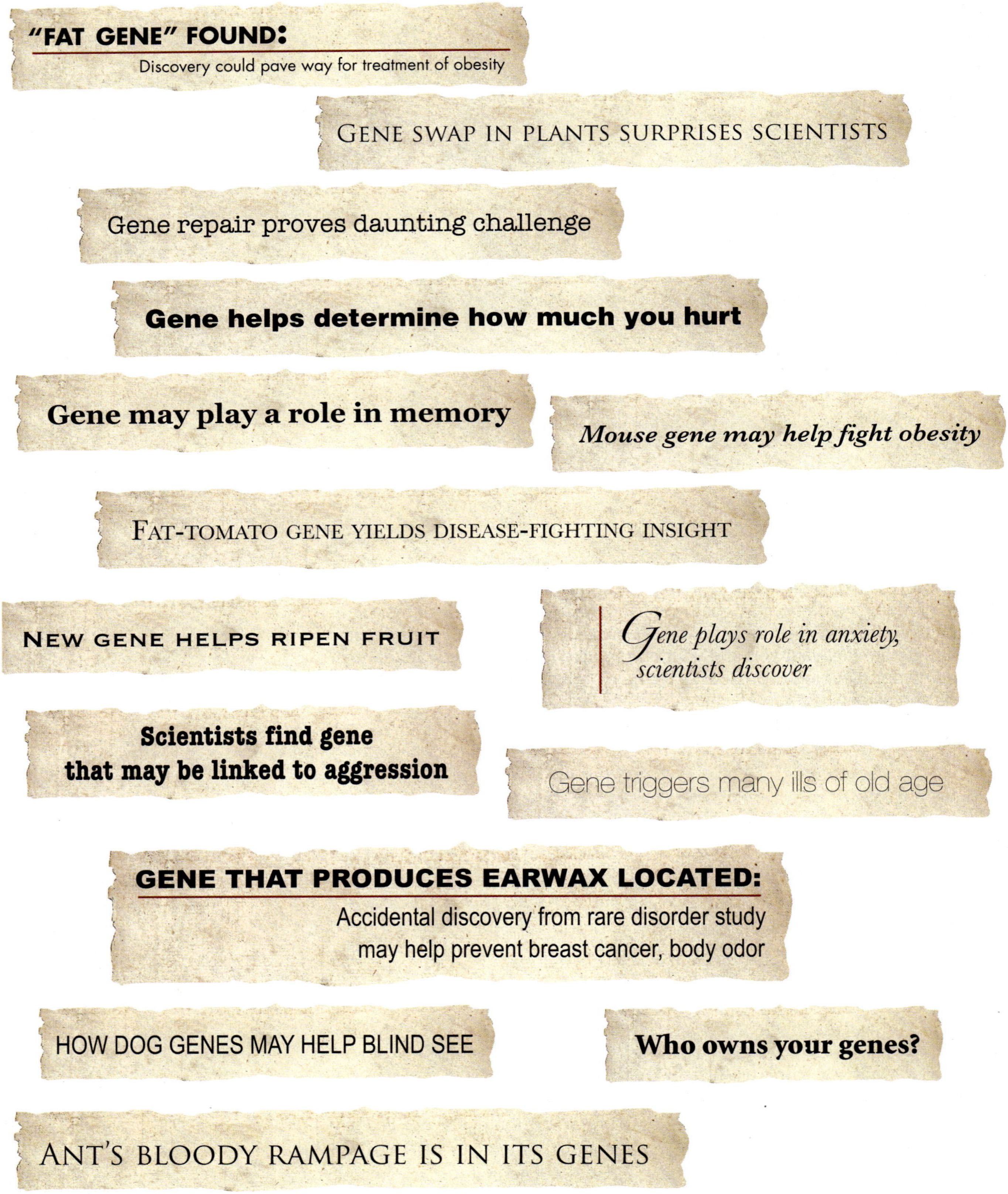

"FAT GENE" FOUND:
Discovery could pave way for treatment of obesity

GENE SWAP IN PLANTS SURPRISES SCIENTISTS

Gene repair proves daunting challenge

Gene helps determine how much you hurt

Gene may play a role in memory

Mouse gene may help fight obesity

FAT-TOMATO GENE YIELDS DISEASE-FIGHTING INSIGHT

NEW GENE HELPS RIPEN FRUIT

Gene plays role in anxiety, scientists discover

Scientists find gene that may be linked to aggression

Gene triggers many ills of old age

GENE THAT PRODUCES EARWAX LOCATED:
Accidental discovery from rare disorder study
may help prevent breast cancer, body odor

HOW DOG GENES MAY HELP BLIND SEE

Who owns your genes?

ANT'S BLOODY RAMPAGE IS IN ITS GENES

Figure 2.1

Genes in the news.

The Blue People of Troublesome Creek

THE STORY OF AN APPALACHIAN MALADY, AN INQUISITIVE DOCTOR, AND A PARADOXICAL CURE.

By Cathy Trost, *Science 82,* November 1982, pp. 35–39. Illustration by Walt Spitzmiller.

Six generations after a French orphan named Martin Fugate settled on the banks of eastern Kentucky's Troublesome Creek with his red-headed American bride, his great-great-great-great grandson was born in a modern hospital not far from where the creek still runs.

The boy inherited his father's lankiness and his mother's slightly nasal way of speaking.

What he got from Martin Fugate was dark blue skin. "It was almost purple," his father recalls.

Doctors were so astonished by the color of Benjy Stacy's skin that they raced him by ambulance from the maternity ward in the hospital near Hazard to a medical clinic in Lexington. Two days of tests produced no explanation for skin the color of a bruised plum.

A transfusion was being prepared when Benjy's grandmother spoke up. "Have you ever heard of the blue Fugates of Troublesome Creek?" she asked the doctors.

"My grandmother Luna on my dad's side was a blue Fugate. It was real bad in her," Alva Stacy, the boy's father, explained. "The doctors finally came to the conclusion that Benjy's color was due to blood inherited from generations back."

Benjy lost his blue tint within a few weeks, and now he is about as normal looking a seven-year-old boy as you could hope to find. His lips and fingernails still turn a shade of purple-blue when he gets cold or angry—a quirk that so intrigued medical students after Benjy's birth that they would crowd around the baby and try to make him cry. "Benjy was a pretty big item in the hospital," his mother says with a grin.

Dark blue lips and fingernails are the only traces of Martin Fugate's legacy left in the boy; that, and the recessive gene that has shaded many of the Fugates and their kin blue for the past 162 years.

They're known simply as the "blue people" in the hills and the hollows around Troublesome and Ball Creeks. Most lived to their 80s and 90s without serious illness associated with the skin discoloration. For some, though, there was a pain not seen in lab tests. That was the pain of being blue in a world that is mostly shades of white to black.

There was always speculation in the hollows about what made the blue people blue—heart disease, a lung disorder, the possibility proposed by one old-timer that "their blood is just a little closer to their skin." But no one knew for sure, and doctors rarely paid visits to the remote creekside settlements where most of the "blue Fugates" lived until well into the 1950s. By the time a young

hematologist from the University of Kentucky came down to Troublesome Creek in the 1960s to cure the blue people, Martin Fugate's descendants had multiplied their recessive genes all over the Cumberland Plateau.

Madison Cawein began hearing rumors about the blue people when he went to work at the University of Kentucky's Lexington medical clinic in 1960. "I'm a hematologist, so something like that perks up my ears," Cawein says, sipping on whiskey sours and letting his mind slip back to the summer he spent "tromping around the hills looking for blue people."

Cawein is no stranger to eccentricities of the body. He helped isolate an antidote for cholera, and he did some of the early work on L-dopa, the drug for Parkinson's disease. But his first love, which he developed as an Army medical technician in World War II, was hematology. "Blood cells always looked so beautiful to me," he says.

Cawein would drive back and forth between Lexington and Hazard—an eight-hour ordeal before the tollway was built—and scour the hills looking for the blue people he'd heard rumors about. The American Heart Association had a clinic in Hazard, and it was there that Cawein met "a great big nurse" who offered to help.

Her name was Ruth Pendergrass, and she had been trying to stir up medical interest in the blue people ever since a dark blue woman walked into the county health department one bitterly cold afternoon and asked for a blood test.

"She had been out in the cold and she was just blue!" recalls Pendergrass, who is now 69 and retired from nursing. "Her face and her fingernails were almost indigo blue. It like scared me to death. She looked like she was having a heart attack. I just knew that patient was going to die right there in the health department, but she wasn't a'tall alarmed. She told me that her family was the blue Combses who lived up on Ball Creek. She was a sister to one of the Fugate women."

About this same time, another of the blue Combses, named Luke, had taken his sick wife up to the clinic at Lexington. One look at Luke was enough to "get those doctors down here in a hurry," says Pendergrass, who joined Cawein to look for more blue people.

Trudging up and down the hollows, fending off "the two mean dogs that everyone had in their front yard," the doctor and the nurse would spot someone at the top of a hill who looked blue and take off in wild pursuit. By the time they'd get to the top, the person would be gone. Finally, one day when the frustrated doctor was milling inside the Hazard clinic, Patrick and Rachel Ritchie walked in.

"They were bluer'n hell," Cawein says. "Well, as you can imagine, I really examined them. After concluding that there was no evidence of heart disease, I said, 'Aha!' I started asking them questions: 'Do you have any relatives who are blue?' Then I sat down and we began to chart the family."

Cawein remembers the pain that showed on the Ritchie brother's and sister's faces. "They were really embarrassed about being blue," he said. "Patrick was all hunched down in the hall. Rachel was leaning against the wall. They wouldn't come into the waiting room. You could tell how much it bothered them to be blue."

After ruling out heart and lung diseases, the doctor suspected methemoglobinemia, a rare hereditary blood disorder that results from excess levels of methemoglobin in the blood. Methemoglobin, which is blue, is a nonfunctional form of the red hemoglobin that carries oxygen. It is the color of oxygen-depleted blood seen in the blue veins just below the skin.

If the blue people did have methemoglobinemia, the next step was to find out the cause. It can be brought on by several things: abnormal hemoglobin formation, an enzyme deficiency, and taking too much of certain drugs, including vitamin K, which is essential for blood clotting and is abundant in pork liver and vegetable oil.

Cawein drew "lots of blood" from the Ritchies and hurried back to his lab. He tested first for abnormal hemoglobin, but the results were negative.

Stumped, the doctor turned to the medical literature for a clue. He found references to methemoglobinemia dating to the turn of the century, but it wasn't until he came across E. M. Scott's 1960 report in the *Journal of Clinical Investigation* that the answer began to emerge.

Scott was a Public Health Service doctor at the Arctic Health Research Center in Anchorage who had discovered hereditary methemoglobinemia among Alaskan Eskimos and Indians. It was caused, Scott speculated, by an absence of the enzyme diaphorase from their red blood cells. In normal people hemoglobin is converted to methemoglobin at a very slow rate. If this conversion continued, all the body's hemoglobin would eventually be rendered useless. Normally, diaphorase converts methemoglobin back to hemoglobin. Scott also concluded that the condition was inherited as a simple recessive **trait.** In other words, to get the disorder, a person would have to inherit two genes for it, one from each parent. Somebody with only one gene would not have the condition but could pass the gene to a child.

Scott's Alaskans seemed to match Cawein's blue people. If the condition were inherited as a recessive trait, it would appear most often in an inbred line.

Cawein needed fresh blood to do an enzyme assay. He had to drive eight hours back to Hazard to search out the Ritchies, who lived in a tapped-out mining town called Hardburly. They took the doctor to see their uncle, who was blue, too. While in the hills, Cawein drove over to see Zach (Big Man) Fugate, the 76-year-old patriarch of the clan on Troublesome Creek. His car gave out on the dirt road to Zach's house, and the doctor had to borrow a Jeep from a filling station.

Zach took the doctor even farther up Copperhead Hollow to see his Aunt Bessie Fugate, who was blue. Bessie had an iron pot of clothes boiling in her front yard, but she graciously allowed the doctor to draw some of her blood.

"So I brought back the new blood and set up my enzyme assay," Cawein continued. "And by God, they didn't have the enzyme diaphorase. I looked at other enzymes and nothing was wrong with them. So I knew we had the defect defined."

Just like the Alaskans, their blood had accumulated so much of the blue molecule that it overwhelmed the red of normal hemoglobin that shows through as pink in the skin of most Caucasians.

Once he had the enzyme deficiency isolated, methylene blue sprang to Cawein's mind as the "perfectly obvious" antidote. Some of the blue people thought the doctor was slightly addled for suggesting that a blue dye could turn them pink. But Cawein knew from earlier studies that the body has an alternative method of converting methemoglobin back to normal. Activating it required adding to the blood a substance that acts as an "electron donor." Many substances do this, but Cawein chose methylene blue because it had been used successfully and safely in other cases and because it acts quickly.

Cawein packed his black bag and rounded up Nurse Pendergrass for the big event. They went over to Patrick and Rachel Ritchie's house and injected each of them with 100 milligrams of methylene blue.

"Within a few minutes, the blue color was gone from their skin," the doctor said. "For the first time in their lives, they were pink. They were delighted."

"They changed colors!" remembered Pendergrass. "It was really something exciting to see."

The doctor gave each blue family a supply of methylene blue tablets to take as a daily pill. The drug's effects are temporary, as methylene blue is normally excreted in the urine. One day, one of the older

mountain men cornered the doctor. "I can see that old blue running out of my skin," he confided.

Before Cawein ended his study of the blue people, he returned to the mountains to patch together the long and twisted journey of Martin Fugate's recessive gene. From a history of Perry County and some Fugate family Bibles listing ancestors, Cawein has constructed a fairly complete story.

Martin Fugate was a French orphan who emigrated to Kentucky in 1820 to claim a land grant on the wilderness banks of Troublesome Creek. No mention of his skin color is made in the early histories of the area, but family lore has it that Martin himself was blue.

The odds against it were incalculable, but Martin Fugate managed to find and marry a woman who carried the same recessive gene. Elizabeth Smith, apparently, was as pale-skinned as the mountain laurel that blooms every spring around the creek hollows.

Martin and Elizabeth set up housekeeping on the banks of Troublesome and began a family. Of their seven children, four were reported to be blue.

The clan kept multiplying. Fugates married other Fugates. Sometimes they married first cousins. And they married the people who lived closest to them, the Combses, Smiths, Ritchies, and Stacys. All lived in isolation from the world, bunched in log cabins up and down the hollows, and so it was only natural that a boy married the girl next door, even if she had the same last name.

"When they settled this country back then, there was no roads. It was hard to get out, so they intermarried," says Dennis Stacy, a 51-year-old coal miner and amateur genealogist who has filled a loose-leaf notebook with the laboriously traced blood lines of several local families.

Stacy counts Fugate blood in his own veins. "If you'll notice," he observes, tracing lines on his family's chart, which lists his mother's and his father's great grandfather as Henley Fugate, "I'm kin to myself."

The railroad didn't come through eastern Kentucky until the coal mines were developed around 1912, and it took another 30 or 40 years to lay down roads along the local creeks.

Martin and Elizabeth Fugate's blue children multiplied in this natural isolation tank. The marriage of one of their blue boys, Zachariah, to his mother's sister triggered the line of succession that would result in the birth, more than 100 years later, of Benjy Stacy.

When Benjy was born with purple skin, his relatives told the perplexed doctors about his great grandmother

Luna Fugate. One relative describes her as "blue all over," and another calls Luna "the bluest woman I ever saw."

Luna's father, Levy Fugate, was one of Zachariah Fugate's sons. Levy married a Ritchie girl and bought 200 acres of rolling land along Ball Creek. The couple had eight children, including Luna.

A fellow by the name of John E. Stacy spotted Luna at Sunday services of the Old Regular Baptist Church back before the century turned. Stacy courted her, married her, and moved over from Troublesome Creek to make a living in timber on her daddy's land.

Luna has been dead nearly 20 years now, but her widower survives. John Stacy still lives on Lick Branch of Ball Creek. His two-room log cabin sits in the middle of Laurel Fork Hollow. Luna is buried at the top of the hollow. Stacy's son has built a modern house next door, but the old logger won't hear of leaving the cabin he built with timber he personally cut and hewed for Luna and their 13 children.

Stacy recalls that his father-in-law, Levy Fugate, was "part of the family that showed blue. All them old fellers way back then was blue. One of 'em—I remember seein' him when I was just a boy—Blue Anze, they called him. Most of them old people went by that name—the blue Fugates. It run in the generation who lived up and down Ball [Creek]."

"They looked like anybody else 'cept they had the blue color," Stacy says, sitting in a chair in his plaid flannel shirt and suspenders, next to a cardboard box where a small black piglet, kept as a pet, is squealing for his bottle. "I couldn't tell you what caused it."

The only thing Stacy can't—or won't—remember is that his wife Luna was blue. When asked about it, he shakes his head and stares steadfastly ahead. It would be hard to doubt this gracious man except that you can't find another person who knew Luna who doesn't remember her as being blue.

"The bluest Fugates I ever saw was Luna and her kin," says Carrie Lee Kilburn, a nurse who works at the rural medical center called Homeplace Clinic. "Luna was bluish all over. Her lips were as dark as a bruise. She was as blue a woman as I ever saw."

Luna Stacy possessed the good health common to the blue people, bearing at least 13 children before she died at 84. The clinic doctors only saw her a few times in her life and never for anything serious.

As coal mining and the railroads brought progress to Kentucky, the blue Fugates started moving out of their communities and marrying other people. The strain of inherited blue began to disappear as the recessive gene spread to families where it was unlikely to be paired with a similar gene.

Benjy Stacy is one of the last of the blue Fugates. With Fugate blood on both his mother's and his father's side, the boy could have received genes for the enzyme deficiency from either direction. Because the boy was intensely blue at birth but then recovered his normal skin tones, Benjy is assumed to have inherited only one gene for the condition. Such people tend to be very blue only at birth, probably because newborns normally have smaller amounts of diaphorase. The enzyme eventually builds to normal levels in most children and to almost normal levels in those like Benjy, who carry one gene.

Hilda Stacy is fiercely protective of her son. She gets upset at all the talk of inbreeding among the Fugates. One of the supermarket tabloids once sent a reporter to find out about the blue people, and she was distressed with his preoccupation with intermarriages.

She and her husband Alva have a strong sense of family. They sing in the Stacy Family Gospel Band and have provided their children with a beautiful home and a menagerie of pets, including horses.

"Everyone around here knows about the blue Fugates," says Hilda Stacy who, at 26, looks more like a sister than a mother to her children. "It's common. It's nothing."

Cawein and his colleagues published their research on hereditary diaphorase deficiency in the *Archives of Internal Medicine* in 1964. He hasn't studied the condition for years. Even so, Cawein still gets calls for advice. One came from a blue Fugate who'd joined the Army and been sent to Panama, where his son was born bright blue. Cawein advised giving the child methylene blue and not worrying about it.

The doctor was recently approached by the producers of the television show "That's Incredible." They wanted to parade the blue people across the screen in their weekly display of human oddities. Cawein would have no part of it, and he related with glee the news that a film crew sent to Kentucky from Hollywood fled the "two mean dogs in every front yard" without any film. Cawein cheers their bad luck not out of malice but out of a deep respect for the blue people of Troublesome Creek.

"They were poor people," concurs Nurse Pendergrass, "but they were good."

ANALYSIS

Record your responses to the following in your notebook.

1. What physical trait did Martin Fugate and his wife pass on to their many generations of offspring?
2. What caused this condition?
3. How might you begin to define the term **genetics**? Base your answer on the reading and on your responses to the preceding questions.

CAREER
Focus

Genealogist   Recently Philip was approached by a woman who was trying to piece together some information she had about a once-hidden family secret. Louisa Kay, his client's great-aunt, had had an affair with a married man. She became pregnant, and her family suddenly moved to another state. Here Louisa gave birth to a girl named Sally. The client knew some information about Sally, but very little. There were two things she wanted to find out. Who was Sally's father? And if Sally had any children, where were they now?

Philip is a genealogist, that is, he puts together people's family trees. Philip knew that parents' names were usually listed on birth and death certificates as well as on marriage certificates. At that time, though, Louisa and her family may not have wanted to identify the father. Regardless, Philip needed to get his hands on copies of those certificates. He started with a couple of clues provided by his client. He knew that Louisa Kay originally lived in St. Paul, Minnesota. He also knew that Sally had grown up in Topeka, Kansas. Here she married a man named Brown, and later died there.

Philip started in St. Paul. He checked the 1900 census records, which are kept at branches of the National Archives in each state. Here he figured out that Louisa was living at home with her parents at that time. She had no children then. The 1910 census records had no listing of a Kay family.

Philip then traveled to Topeka. Here he checked the 1910 census records of that city. Louisa was listed, along with a 2-year-old daughter named Sally. Bingo! He then estimated the date of birth and went to the city hall in Topeka for Sally's birth certificate. No birth certificate existed for a Sally Kay in that city, which meant she was born somewhere else. He next decided to look at her death certificate. He traveled around Topeka speaking with cemetery administrators until he found her grave. The gravestone gave her date of death. With that, he returned to the city hall and retrieved her death certificate. The father was listed on the death certificate as "unknown." But that wasn't a dead end. The death certificate listed a place of birth—Wichita.

Philip flew to Wichita. Here he was able to get a copy of Sally's birth certificate. Again, no name was listed for her father. It was possible that there would be no way of knowing.

Philip proceeded to look for Sally's children. Since he had already found her date of death, he went to the Topeka Public Library and checked out the obituaries on microfiche. Listed in Sally's obituary were five children: Richard of Topeka, Robert of San Francisco, Nancy of Topeka, Louisa of Wichita, and Mary of Topeka. Philip had solved one puzzle. And a single phone call to one of her children solved the other. All of the children knew the name of their grandfather.

Philip enjoys his job. To him, his job is like following a mystery whose solution is constantly evolving. He likes making contact with people of widely different backgrounds. He especially enjoys the feeling of accomplishment after solving a puzzle. Some clients are interested in the in-depth creation of a family tree. This could mean going back many generations. Philip finds the names of relatives, their children, dates of major life events, and so on. Others are more interested in a specific piece of information. This could be the location of an heir, the date of someone's U.S. citizenship, or the place in America where ancestors first set foot.

Finding this information, as Philip is well aware, involves a lot of investigation and research. Experience is very important when becoming a professional genealogist. Philip learned much of what he knows from reading books and attending lectures by other professional genealogists and other workshops. He also learns a lot by asking questions while visiting the different branches of the National Archives. Philip prefers to work independently, although there are companies worldwide that specialize in genealogy.

Learning Experience 2

Inherit the Trait

Prologue

Much of what is written about genetics in the media relates to human genetics. Most of the basic research, however, is carried out in other animals and in plants. Examples of these organisms include peas, corn, bacteria, bread mold, yeast, fruit flies, and mice. The study of these organisms has provided insights into the most fundamental principles of genetics. Scientists use these organisms because they have short life cycles and produce many generations of offspring in a short time.

As you have already determined, traits run in families. All organisms pass on their traits to their offspring and to their offspring's offspring. In this learning experience, you carry out an extended laboratory experiment that you will revisit throughout this unit. You will investigate one kind of organism (either an insect or a plant) often used by geneticists in their research. You will characterize specific traits of these organisms and make crosses (mate them). You will then follow one or more generations of offspring to determine the patterns in which these traits are inherited.

In this learning experience, you will have another opportunity to experience a real scientific investigation. Here your ability to answer the research question will depend on several things. These include careful planning, skillful observation, meticulous data collection, application of concepts from the unit, information sharing, and other ideas from your group. At the end of the extended project, you will write the results of your experiment in a laboratory report.

Brainstorming

Discuss the following questions with your partner, and record your thinking in your notebook. Be prepared to share your ideas with the class.

1. Why do you think geneticists might want to understand how traits are inherited?
2. How do you think a geneticist might study patterns of inheritance?
3. What skills do you think might be important in these kinds of experiments?

Peanut, Peanut, Where's My Peanut?

In the late 19th and early 20th centuries, scientists depended greatly on their powers of observation to help them make sense of the natural world. This was the time when the foundations of genetics were being laid. "Most of us tend to look at things without really seeing what is there. In everyday life, this lack of observation may not be noticed, but in science it is a serious failing." (An excerpt from "Take This Fish and Look at It" by Samuel H. Scudder in *Readings for Writers*, Jo Ray McCuen and Anthony C. Winkler, eds., Harcourt Brace Jovanovich, San Diego, 1974, pp. 201–205.)

This statement highlights the difference between just looking and observing. How carefully do you observe the things around you? In this activity, you will find out. You will look at a peanut to help you improve on two important skills of science: observation and communication.

Materials

For each group of eight students:

- 1 paper bag containing 10 peanuts in shells
- 8 index cards (3 × 5-inch)

PROCEDURE

1. Have 1 person from your group hand out 1 index card to each group member.
2. Remove 1 peanut from the bag and pass the bag to the next person. Examine your peanut closely for 1 minute.
3. Allow time for everyone in your group to examine their peanut. Then return all the peanuts to the bag. Shake the bag to mix the peanuts.
4. Pour the contents of the bag onto a table or flat surface. Try to pick out your peanut.
5. Return all the peanuts to the bag and shake it again.
6. Take a new peanut and examine it closely for 1 minute.
7. Write a complete description of this peanut on the index card. Return your peanut to the bag.
8. Pass your index card to the person on your left. Take the index card from the person on your right.
9. Shake the bag again and pour its contents onto a table or flat surface.
10. Try to pick out the peanut described on the index card you are now holding.
11. When your group has finished, determine whether your identification was successful. Ask the person from whom you received the card whether you selected the correct peanut.

ANALYSIS

Record your responses to the following in your notebook.

1. Were you successful in identifying your own peanut? Describe how you identified the peanut. Were you successful in identifying the peanut described on the index card?

2. Was there a difference in what you looked for in step 2 and then in step 6? If there were differences, what were they? Why do you think there were differences between your first and second peanut observations?
3. What specific characteristics did you think would help identify the peanut? What did you discover about those peanut characteristics on your second look?

Date, Mate?

Humans used the principles of genetics long before the patterns of inheritance were defined, and the roles of DNA and genes in heredity determined. They used genetics to breed better plants and animals. Early farmers found that they could increase the yield, improve the taste of their crops, and cultivate resistance to disease. They could do all that by using the seeds from plants that showed these characteristics. They could create cows that produced high milk yields, had good temperaments, and could thrive on scrub brush. They did that by carefully crossbreeding cows and bulls with these characteristics. Through years of careful seed selection and breeding, farmers could maintain and enhance certain desirable traits.

OPTION ONE: FRUIT FLIES

The fruit fly, *Drosophila melanogaster,* is a small flying insect about 3 mm long (about 1/8 in.). It is known to most people as the pesky fly that circles fruit left too long in the fruit bowl. But fruit flies are also very popular with biologists as a powerful model system for understanding genetics. They have been used in genetics research for almost a century. As a result, we have gained many fundamental understandings about inheritance.

Fruit flies are popular research organisms for many reasons. They are easy to grow and handle in large numbers (if you don't mind flies buzzing around your head). They are inexpensive to maintain. They have a short life cycle of about 2 weeks at 25°C (77°F). This allows for the production of many generations in a short period of time. Because of the long history of their use, it is easy to obtain *Drosophila* with many variants of traits (such as eye color and wing shape) for use in genetic research.

Scientists experiment with crosses of *Drosophila* with different traits to help them determine offspring traits and to identify different patterns of inheritance. It is possible to observe the transmission of physical traits through several generations. One can also determine mathematically the patterns of inheritance for these traits.

The *Drosophila* life cycle is an example of complete metamorphosis (see Figure 2.2). The egg, about 0.5 mm long, matures and hatches a mere 1 day after fertilization. A wormlike larva emerges, growing and eating continuously. It molts (shedding to allow for increase in size) three times—at days one, two, and four after hatching. These stages are referred to as the first, second, and third instars. Two days into the third instar, the larva molts to form a pupa. During the pupal stage, which lasts 4 days, the body of the fruit fly undergoes a complete remodeling. The winged adult develops and breaks out from the pupa. The adult is then reproductively mature and ready to mate in less than 1 day.

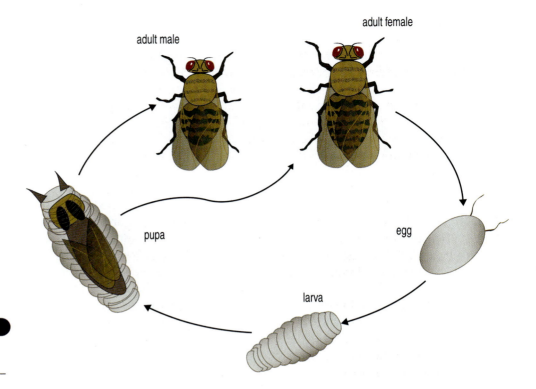

adult male

adult female

pupa

egg

larva

Figure 2.2

Life cycle of the fruit fly,
Drosophila melanogaster.

Materials

For each student:

- 1 small laboratory notebook (optional)

For each group of four students:

- 4 pairs of safety goggles
- 1 or more vials *Drosophila* wild type (winged)
- 1 or more vials *Drosophila* vestigial (short-winged) type
- 12 or more anesthetic wands
- 4 or more prepared vials with culture media (minimum)
- 1 fine-tipped paintbrush
- 1 book
- 1 white index card
- white paper
- 1 reanesthetizer (petri dish with gauze or cotton ball)
- 1 forceps or tweezers
- labels or masking tape
- 1 morgue (small jar with vegetable oil)
- 1 hand lens or access to a dissecting microscope
- 1 incubator (if available)

For the class:

- 100 mL fly anesthetic (e.g., FlyNap™)
- prepared slide of "giant" *Drosophila* salivary gland chromosome (optional)
- aceto-orcein stain (optional)

PROCEDURE

SAFETY NOTE

Part A: Anesthetizing and Observing Fruit Flies

1. Obtain a vial of flies. Tap it on a book to force the flies to the bottom of the vial.
2. Dip the applicator wand into the anesthetic and pull the plug partway out. Insert the wand into the culture vial just below the plug (see Figure 2.3a).
3. Lay the vial on its side in the groove of an open book. This way the flies will not get stuck in the media. Within 4 minutes, all flies should be anesthetized.
4. Immediately transfer the flies to a white index card. Examine them under the dissecting microscope or with a hand lens. Use the brush to move the flies on the card (see Figure 2.3b).
5. If the flies start to recover, use the reanesthetizer. Place a drop of the anesthetizer on the gauze or cotton ball and invert the petri dish over the card (see Figure 2.3c). Do not allow the flies to escape. They will become an annoyance and may interfere with or contaminate other experiments in the class.
6. Flies that have come in contact with too much anesthetic or that have been anesthetized too quickly die. Dead flies have wings that stick out straight from the body. Use forceps to place dead flies in the morgue.
7. Return flies to the vial. Do this by first placing them on a small piece of paper. Then transfer the flies to the vial while it is on its side. Replace the plug. Do not dump anesthetized flies back into the media; they will get stuck and drown. Place the vial upright when the flies have recovered.

Part B: Making a Cross (Mating)

1. Obtain a culture of wild type or mutant (vestigial-winged) fruit flies. Look on the surface of the media for examples of 3 life stages: the egg, the larva, and the pupa. Draw and describe each stage in your laboratory notebook.
2. Anesthetize the flies in the vial and transfer them to the index card. Observe the characteristics that distinguish males from females (see Figure 2.4).

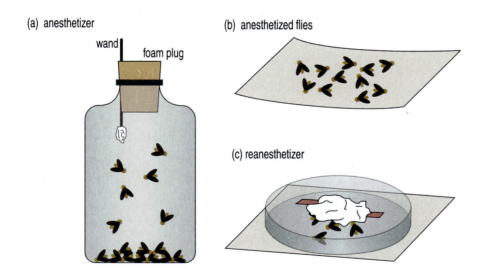

(a) anesthetizer
wand
foam plug

(b) anesthetized flies

(c) reanesthetizer

Figure 2.3

Anesthetizing techniques.

male

female

short, round
abdomen

long, pointed
abdomen

sex comb

male foreleg

female foreleg

Figure 2.4

Physical traits of male and
female fruit flies.

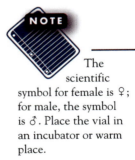

The
scientific
symbol for female is ♀;
for male, the symbol
is ♂. Place the vial in
an incubator or warm
place.

3. Separate 2 (or 3) vestigial-winged virgin females and 2 (or 3) wild type males. Brush them onto a piece of paper. The females must be virgins to ensure that the offspring are the result of the mating with the wild type males. (Females can store sperm in receptacles and fertilize the eggs as they lay them.) The virgin females will be light colored and hold their wings close to their bodies.

4. Place paper and flies into a fresh vial of media that has been placed on its side in the groove of an open book. Label your vial with the mating, the date, and the group name.

5. Follow the same procedure as described in step 3. But use virgin wild female and vestigial-winged male flies. Place in another fresh vial and label as before.

6. Observe your vials regularly. Record what you are observing. Be sure to also record the date.

7. After about the fifth day, anesthetize and remove the parents. Your teacher may direct you to place them into a fresh vial or into the morgue. Return the experimental vials to their warm place.

8. **STOP & THINK** Create a hypothesis for the type of wing you expect in the first generation of each mating. Record this in your notebook.

9. About 2 weeks after the matings, begin to anesthetize and count the first generation of adult flies in each vial. Record the sex and wing trait of each of the offspring. As you record your data, consider what conclusions can be drawn from these data. You should continue to anesthetize and record over a 3- or 4-day period as new flies emerge from their pupae.

10. Place at least 3 male and female pairs of the first generation of flies from the first vial in a fresh culture vial. Repeat with the flies from the second vial in a fresh culture vial. The females do not need to be virgins for these matings. Label the vials and place them in a warm place.

11. After about the fifth day, anesthetize and remove the adult flies to the morgue. Return the vials to their warm place.

12. **STOP & THINK** Create a hypothesis for the type(s) of wing that will appear in the second generation of flies in each of these vials. Your hypothesis may predict how many of each type of characteristic will happen. For example, you might predict a 3:1 ratio in wing traits.

13. As the second generation of flies emerges, anesthetize and record the sex and trait of each of the offspring. The more flies collected, the more reliable your data will be. You may have to collect flies over a 3- to 4-day period.

14. Record your group's data for the first and second generation (sexes and traits) on the class data chart.

OPTION TWO: MUSTARD PLANTS

The availability of rapidly developing plants has provided an excellent tool for investigating principles of genetics. Plants are easy to work with, easy to maintain, and easy to observe. The *Brassicaceae* family consists of more than 3,000 types. These include mustard, cabbage, broccoli, watercress, turnip, and others (see Figure 2.5). Two varieties that are most commonly used for genetics experiments are *Brassica rapa* and *Arabidopsis thaliana*. These varieties have a very rapid life cycle. They flower within 18–25 days after sowing. And they produce seeds, the next generation, within 28–45 days (under appropriate light

Figure 2.5

Some members of the family *Brassicaceae*.
© David Liebman

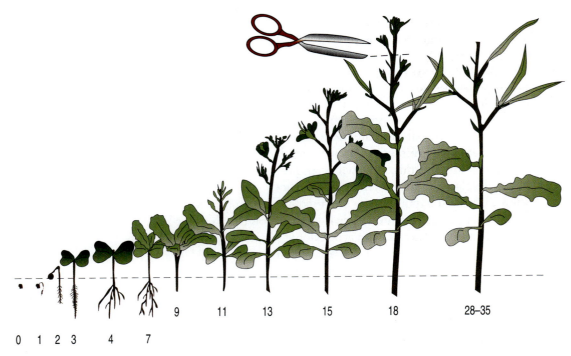

9   11   13   15   18   28–35

0 1 2 3   4   7

days after planting

Figure 2.6

Growth cycle of a rapidly developing plant in the *Brassicaceae* family.

and temperature conditions) (see Figure 2.6). This rapid development allows these plants to produce five or six generations within one school year. The plants are also small. This permits high densities of plants to be grown (up to 2,500 plants per square meter).

You will work with one variety of mustard plant. *Brassica rapa* is a small plant with alternating leaves along a single stem and bright yellow flowers. It has 10 chromosomes and has more than 100 distinctive genetic traits that have been studied.

Arabidopsis thaliana, another mustard plant, is also a small plant from the *Brassicaceae* family. It usually grows a rosette of leaves, from the center of which grows a single stem with white flowers.

Materials

For each student:

- 1 small laboratory notebook (optional)

For each group of four students:

- 4 pairs of safety goggles
- 4 small plastic plant pots (individual or connected in a growing tray)
- shallow trays or saucers for plant pots
- 4 labels
- 1 wax marking pencil
- 1 thermometer
- scissors (optional)
- 1 metric ruler or meterstick
- 2 small paintbrushes

- 2 small envelopes or paper bags
- plant stakes or bamboo skewers (optional)
- twist ties (optional)
- plastic bag or large jar (optional)
- sheet of paper or tray

For the class:

- 1 package of seeds (wild type)
- 1 package of seeds (mutant)
- growing medium (vermiculite, peat, or light potting soil)
- all-purpose plant fertilizer (such as 5-10-5)
- 1 adjustable plant stand
- 6 cool-white 40W fluorescent light tubes (4 ft) per light stand
- 1 watering can or other container
- distilled water

PROCEDURE

Part A: Growing Plants

1. Moisten growing medium until it has absorbed the water and feels damp.
2. Fill plant pots with the growing medium. Press down lightly to get rid of any air pockets. (Air pockets could dry out the roots of developing seedlings.)
3. Use 2 variants of 1 seed variety (such as wild type and mutant). Make 2 labels of each type and place 1 label in each pot.
4. Place 3–5 seeds of 1 variant in each of the first 2 pots. Place seeds of the other variant in the other 2 pots. Then press seeds down for solid contact with growing medium. Seeds should be covered with more growing medium to a depth of twice their diameter for best germination. For example, small seeds, such as radishes, need only about 0.25 cm (about 1/8 in.) of covering.
5. Water the pots using a gentle stream of water. Then set them in a warm location, about 17°–25°C (63°F–77°F). Place the pots on a light stand with lights no more than 5–8 cm (2–3 in.) above the pots.
6. Observe daily. Water when the growing medium begins to feel dry.
7. Record all observations in your laboratory notebook. Remember, always include the date.
8. Add an all-purpose fertilizer (such as 5-10-5) to the water about 1 watering each week. This ensures plant health and speed of growth to maturity. To avoid burning tender young roots, dilute fertilizer to one-fourth the strength recommended in the manufacturer's directions.
9. As you observe the seedlings, record the following information as available:
   a. When do differences between variants first become apparent?
   b. What are those differences?
   c. How do different plants compare with each other?
   d. What measurements can be taken of the differences?
10. Note when seedlings are about 6–8 cm tall (about 2.5–3 in.), or when they sprout their first set of true leaves. At that time, use scissors or fingernails to snip back all except 1 seedling in each pot. This seedling should be the hardiest- or sturdiest-looking one. Doing this will allow that 1 plant full use of the water and other nutrients in the growing medium. (If more plants are left in the pot, they will have to compete for the nutrients. This will generally produce less healthy, often spindly, plants.)

SAFETY NOTE

Do not allow the seeds to dry out; lack of water will inhibit germination. Be sure to water seedlings. They are susceptible to dehydration and the plants may die. Regular watering may be a problem, especially over weekends or longer periods. If this is the case, the pots may be enclosed in a large, clear plastic bag or an overturned clear, widemouthed jar. This will keep moisture inside the container "greenhouse." As a result, this closed system will need water much less frequently. On the other hand, too much water can cause the roots to rot or promote mold growth. (If you use this type of greenhouse, check the temperature within to make sure it does not overheat the plant.) As the plants grow, any covering should be removed or enlarged for proper growth to continue.

11. As plants grow, raise the lights so they are near, but not touching, the plants.
12. Continue to water the plants whenever the growing medium gets dry. If desired, insert plant stakes into pots; secure each plant to a stake with a twist tie. If favorable conditions prevail, the plants will grow. For the rapidly developing plants being used, flowering should begin within 15–20 days. Once flowers are produced, pollination and seed formation can take place.

Part B: Pollinating Plants

1. When plants begin to flower, use a small paintbrush to cross-pollinate them. Lightly touch the tip of the brush to 1 flower of 1 plant. Then gently shake that pollen over all the flowers on another plant that you have designated as the recipient. Use a second paintbrush to cross-pollinate the second pair of plants in this same manner.
2. After pollination is complete, pinch or cut off the top of each plant. Include any unopened flower buds. This allows each plant to use its energy on seed production of already-pollinated flowers rather than on overall plant growth.
3. **STOP & THINK** Create a hypothesis for the appearance you expect in the offspring of the next generation.

Part C: Harvesting Seeds

1. Note when seed pods have formed and begin to turn brown. They are now ripe and may be removed from the plant. Pods may be broken open with your fingers or rolled between your hands. Do this over a sheet of paper or a tray to collect the seeds.
2. Place seeds of each variant in a separate small envelope or paper bag and label. These seeds may be used to grow the next generation of plants.
3. Plant a second generation using the harvested seeds. Observe at least until the seedlings begin to grow and you can record the traits of each plant. Record traits through the growth and development of this generation. If time allows, pollinate and harvest the seeds as described earlier.
4. Record on the class data chart your group's data of the traits in the first generation.

ANALYSIS

Prepare a laboratory report for one of these experiments in your notebook. Be sure to include the following:

a. the project title;
b. the question being asked;
c. your hypothesis;
d. materials used;
e. abbreviated procedure;
f. data chart of results;
g. analysis of results (group and class);
h. possible sources of error;
i. conclusion (include explanations of your results based on your understanding of inheritance); and
j. further questions for experimentation.

Huntington's disease (HD) is a neurological disorder that affects 25,000 to 30,000 in the United States. Another 150,000 individuals are at risk of inheriting the disease. HD usually strikes young adults between the ages of 35 and 45. Symptoms of the disease include clumsiness, slurred speech, difficulty in swallowing, chorea (involuntary movements), personality changes such as irritability, temper tantrums, violent outbursts, paranoia, loss of memory, and the inability to communicate with others. There is no cure; HD is ultimately fatal. Understanding the patterns of inheritance for this disease was the result of the work carried out by Dr. Nancy Wexler. Dr. Wexler studied natives in Lake Maracaibo, Venezuela, many of whom suffered from this disease. All were related to one woman who died of the disease. Dr. Wexler's work led to the development of a complex chromosomal test. This test can determine if patients will develop the disease. Research Dr. Wexler's work. Describe how she determined the patterns of inheritance.

Topic: Genetic Diseases/
Genetic Screening/
Genetic Counseling
Go to: www.scilinks.org
Code: INBIOH2163

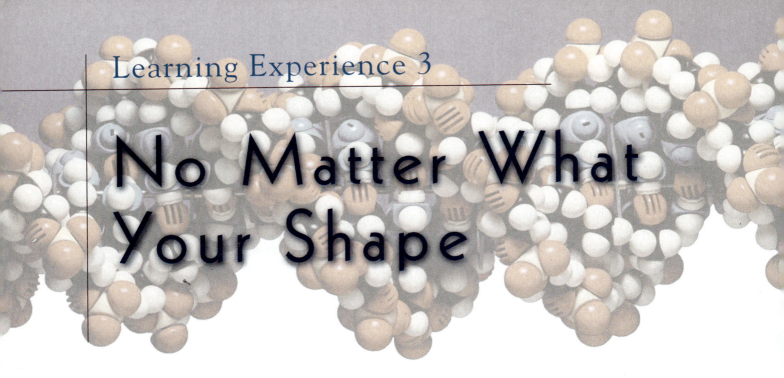

No Matter What Your Shape

Prologue

The easiest traits to describe in an organism are the visible traits. For instance, think about distinguishing between two people. You might use the texture of their hair as an easily identifiable trait. One might have curly hair, and the other straight hair. By using differences in hair texture, you have described **variants** of a single trait. In this case, that trait is hair texture.

What is responsible for variants in traits? Are traits and their variants only characteristics that are directly observable? Or are there underlying causes for these variants? In this learning experience, you use variations in the shape of peas as a simple model for investigating the answers to these questions. You then explore a trait in humans, sickle-cell trait, as another example of variations in traits.

Brainstorming

Your teacher will distribute two different kinds of peas to you and your partner. Examine them carefully. Discuss the following questions with your partner, and record your thinking in your notebook. Be prepared to discuss your ideas with the class.

1. List the traits you can observe in each kind of pea.
2. Describe the variations, if any, in each trait you have listed for the two kinds of peas.
3. What do you think might cause the variations in these traits?
4. What if you were to soak these peas in water? Do you think there would be a difference in the amount of water they absorbed? Explain your answer.

A Pea by Any Other Name Is Still a Seed

How might you begin to answer the question, "Why is one pea wrinkled and another round?" Think about ways you could find out more about the differences between round and wrinkled peas. Are there differences in how the peas are constructed? How might these differences produce a wrinkled shape instead of a round shape? Are there differences in what the seed is made of? How would this affect the shape?

In this learning experience, you will investigate the causes of variations in traits of organisms. Using these pea variants as a model, you will look at the differences between wrinkled peas and round peas (which are actually seeds). But first, you need to understand the general structure of a seed (shown in Figure 2.7). A seed is the part of a plant that results from the **fertilization** of the female egg by the male pollen. Following fertilization, the embryonic plant develops within a protective seed coat. In addition to the embryonic plant and the seed coat, the seed also contains a source of food. The germinating seedling will use this food until it can carry out photosynthesis. In one type of plant, this food source is in a separate structure within the seed called the **endosperm**. In another type of plant, the protein, starch, and fats are stored in two large seed leaves. Regardless of the system of storage, the newly sprouted plant depends on these stored food sources until it can make its own.

Seeds have a very low water content. During the final stages of the development of the seed, cells within the seed dehydrate. In other words, most of the water in the seed is removed. The resulting low water content in the seed causes most cellular processes to slow down or stop. In this dehydrated state, the embryonic plant can remain dormant (inactive) but viable (alive) within the seed. It can stay this way for long periods of time without growing or developing. This process enables the seed to delay germination until environmental conditions are suitable for its growth. **Germination** is the start of growth and development of a plant. This is when the embryonic plant breaks out of its seed coat. When conditions become favorable, water enters the seed. Rehydration triggers the reactivation of normal metabolic processes, and germination begins (see Figure 2.8).

As the plant begins to develop, it uses the starch stored in the endosperm or seed leaves as an energy source. A plant can use photosynthesis to provide its required food and energy only after breaking free of the soil and receiving sunlight.

In this activity, you will determine why some seeds (peas) are wrinkled at the end of their development and some are round.

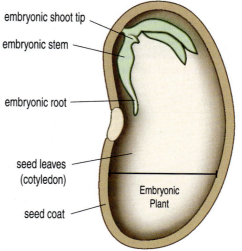

embryonic shoot tip

embryonic stem

embryonic root

seed leaves (cotyledon)

Embryonic Plant

seed coat

Figure 2.7

Structure of a seed.

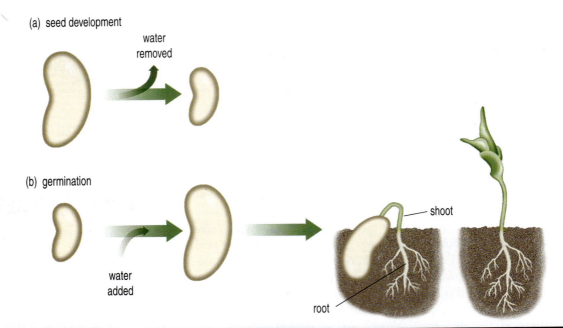

(a) seed development

water removed

(b) germination

water added

shoot

root

Figure 2.8

(a) During seed development, water is lost from cells. This dehydration slows down metabolic processes. (b) During germination, water enters the seed and the metabolic processes are reactivated. As a result, the embryonic plant begins to grow.

Materials

For each pair of students:

- 2 pairs of safety goggles
- 10 round peas
- 10 wrinkled peas
- 1 balance
- 2 small beakers or containers (50-mL)
- 1 wax marking pencil
- 2 microscope slides with coverslips
- access to a compound microscope
- 1 razor blade or scalpel
- 1 forceps
- 1 dropping bottle of dilute Lugol's iodine
- paper towels
- distilled water

PROCEDURE

Part A

1. **STOP & THINK** Develop a hypothesis that explains why some peas are wrinkled and some are round. Record your hypothesis in your notebook.
2. Read steps 3–8. Then create a data chart in your notebook. Fill it in as you carry out this part of the experiment.
3. Weigh all 10 round peas together. Record the weight of the peas on your data chart. Weigh all 10 wrinkled peas together. Record the weight of the peas on your data chart.

SAFETY NOTE

Figure 2.9

Lab setup.

4. Use a wax marking pencil to label one beaker "R" and the other beaker "W." Also mark the beakers with your group name. Place the dried round peas in the R beaker and the dried wrinkled peas in the W beaker. Add water until the beakers are three-quarters full (see Figure 2.9).

5. Place the beakers in the location designated by your teacher until the next class session.

6. After soaking the peas overnight, retrieve your 2 beakers. Label one paper towel "R" and another "W." Pour off the excess water from each beaker carefully. Then empty the peas from each beaker in a pile on the appropriately labeled paper towel.

7. Weigh each pile of peas again to determine the weight after soaking. Record the weights in your table.

8. Determine the weight difference for each kind of pea. Calculate the percentage of increase in weight for each kind of pea. Record the results in your table.

9. **STOP & THINK** Think about this experiment and your understanding of seed formation. Do you want to change your hypothesis as to why some peas wrinkle and others remain round when they are dried? Record your response in your notebook.

Part B

1. Use a wax marking pencil to label one microscope slide "R" and another "W."

2. Place 1 drop of dilute iodine on each slide.

3. Hold a soaked wrinkled pea with forceps. Cut the pea in half with a scalpel or razor blade. Cut a very thin segment or slice from the inside of the pea. Gently place the slice into the drop of dilute iodine on the slide labeled W (see Figure 2.10).

4. Carefully wipe the blade of the scalpel or razor blade clean with a paper towel. Repeat step 3 with a soaked round pea. Drop the slice on the slide labeled R.

5. Place a coverslip at an angle over each drop and gently lower it. Observe each slice under the microscope.

6. **STOP & THINK** Describe and draw in your notebook what you see. Compare the shapes, colors, patterns, and densities of the starch grains. Look at a few slides prepared by other class members and compare them with yours.

SAFETY NOTE

Avoid staining your skin with iodine. If iodine is accidentally ingested, seek immediate medical attention.

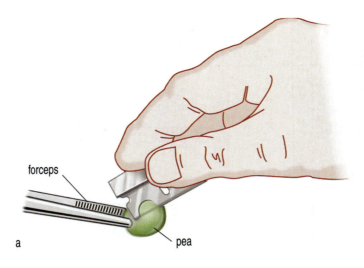

forceps

pea

a

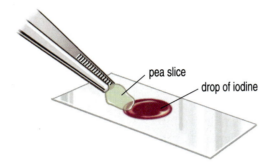

pea slice

drop of iodine

b

Figure 2.10

Hold the pea firmly with the forceps. Carefully slice several sections (a) until a very thin section is obtained. Using the forceps, transfer the section to the drop of iodine on the microscope slide (b).

 **ANALYSIS**

Prepare a laboratory report for this experiment in your notebook. Be sure to include the following:

a. your initial hypothesis (step 1 in the procedure);
b. your revised hypothesis (step 9), if you changed it (if you changed it, explain why);
c. your experimental procedure;
d. the purpose of each part of the experiment;
e. your data (show all your calculations where appropriate); and
f. any conclusions you can draw, based on your data.

Decide whether you have enough data and knowledge to identify the cause of the shape difference between the two different kinds of peas. Explain your answer.

 READING

Adding a New Wrinkle to the Picture

You have gathered a great deal of information about the differences between wrinkled and round peas. You know some things about these peas at both the visible and the biochemical levels. But you still may not be able to reach a conclusion about the exact cause of the difference in shape. To identify the exact cause of this difference, you need to understand more about the biochemistry of seed development.

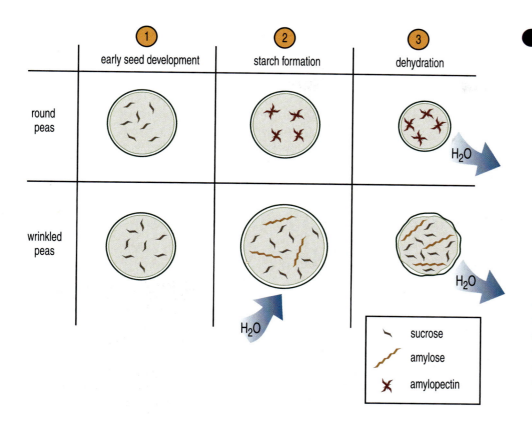

Figure 2.11

Sucrose changes to starch in seed development: A comparison of round and wrinkled peas. (1) Sucrose is made during early seed development. (2) In round seeds, SBEI converts sucrose to amylopectin (branched starch). In wrinkled peas, the SBEI does not function correctly. So no amylopectin is made. Instead, a different enzyme converts some sucrose to amylose (unbranched starch). The high concentration of unconverted sucrose in the wrinkled seed causes the seed to take up water and swell. This stretches the seed coat. (3) When the seed undergoes dehydration, the coat of the round seed remains smooth. But the coat of the wrinkled seed wrinkles because of its stretched seed coat.

In a developing seed, sucrose (a sugar) is converted to a highly branched form of starch. This starch is called amylopectin. It serves as a source of food for the developing plant. The conversion from sucrose to starch is facilitated by an enzyme. This enzyme is called starch-branching enzyme I (SBEI). Scientists used methods similar to the ones you carried out in class. They were able to demonstrate that the characteristic of wrinkled shape was the result of the pea's inability to synthesize amylopectin from sucrose. As a result of a faulty SBEI enzyme, these peas cannot make amylopectin. The unchanged sucrose concentrates in the developing seed. Using a different enzyme, wrinkled peas can synthesize a different, unbranched form of starch. This form of starch is called amylose. Amylose serves as the seed's food source.

What does this inability to make branched starch from sucrose have to do with shape? During the seed's development, the high concentration of sucrose caused water to accumulate inside the seed. The water, as in a water balloon, stretched the seed coat much more than it normally would stretch without the concentrated sucrose. During the final stages of seed development, dehydration takes place. The accumulated water is lost from the seed. This causes the stretched seed coat to collapse, somewhat creating a wrinkled pea. In the pea with the functional SBEI enzyme, sucrose did not accumulate. Thus, the seed coat was not stretched by excess water. So when the water was lost during dehydration, the seed coat remained round (see Figure 2.11).

Do round peas have only functional SBEI? Do wrinkled peas have only nonfunctional SBEI? Would a pea having both kinds of enzymes be a little bit wrinkled? Biochemical analysis demonstrates that peas that have both kinds of enzymes still appear round. You cannot see any difference from those peas that have only functional SBEI. Some of the enzyme cannot make amylopectin from sucrose in these seeds. Even so, the enzyme that can function can convert enough sucrose to amylopectin to prevent water from being retained and stretching the seed coat. They therefore appear round.

Think about an enzyme that can function efficiently even in the presence of a nonfunctional or dysfunctional enzyme of the same kind. Its activity is considered dominant to the activity of the nonfunctional (or recessive) enzyme. An organism that has both kinds of enzymes and displays the trait of the dominant activity (in this case, round) is considered **heterozygous** for that trait. An organism with only one kind of enzyme is said to be **homozygous**. A wrinkled pea is always homozygous for the nonfunctional enzyme. But a round pea could be either homozygous or heterozygous. In this case, you cannot necessarily judge a pea by its cover.

CASE STUDY

Am I a Carrier, and What Does That Mean?

It was Health Day at Denzel Jones's high school. "Career Day, Health Day, Environment Day," fumed Denzel. "When am I going to hear about stuff that matters to me?" Denzel's class filed into the auditorium. The air was buzzing with conversation about music, friends, the last biology exam—everything except the topic of health. Who cared, anyway? Well, at least it got them out of fifth period.

As several individuals from the local health clinic talked, Denzel found himself drawn in by some topics. These included exercise, smoking, and methods for the prevention of infectious diseases. One topic in particular caught his attention because he actually knew a couple of people with the problem. A physician's assistant began to talk about something called "hemoglobinopathies." He described one in particular, **sickle-cell anemia**. Denzel's uncle Jamal (his father's brother) had the disorder. He suffered from fatigue and bouts of intense joint pain. Because it bothered him to watch his uncle suffer, Denzel was curious about the cause.

Denzel learned that sickle-cell anemia is a disorder of red blood cells that can run in families. It causes the red blood cells to collapse into shapes resembling sickles (see Figure 2.12). This happens when the oxygen level of the blood is low.

Red blood cells sickle because they contain **hemoglobin** that is biochemically a little different from the normal hemoglobin protein. Normal hemoglobin (or hemoglobin A) is found in solution in red blood cells. It binds oxygen and transports it throughout the body. Once it releases the oxygen, the hemoglobin remains in solution in the red blood cell. Sickling hemoglobin (designated S) is a variant form of hemoglobin. It differs from normal hemoglobin by only a single amino acid. That slight difference in structure, however, alters its function. Hemoglobin S binds oxygen and carries it to where it is needed. But a problem arises when the oxygen is released and the concentration of oxygen around the hemoglobin is reduced. Normal hemoglobin remains in solution under these conditions. But the sickling hemoglobin comes out of solution. Its molecules bind together into long fibrous chains (crystallizes). These fibers push out against the inside of the membrane of the red blood cell. This produces the characteristic sickle shape (see Figure 2.13).

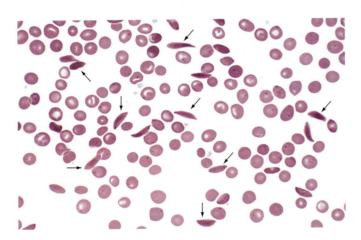

Figure 2.12

Normal red blood cells are shaped like disks. Some red blood cells of sickle-cell patients become stiff and sickled (see arrows). The misshapen cells often get stuck in small blood vessels. This causes extreme pain and damage.
© Dr. Gladden Willis/Visuals Unlimited

Because of their shape, these cells cannot flow easily through the tiny capillaries. (Capillaries are the smallest passageways of the circulatory system.) The cells get stuck and clog the flow of blood. This blockage decreases the blood supply to the vital organs—such as the heart, spleen, kidneys, and brain. These organs can be damaged. The buildup of pressure behind the blockage also can cause small blood vessels to burst. This results in internal bleeding and pain.

The symptoms of sickle-cell anemia are quite variable. But some general features include jaundice, anemia, and pain. (Jaundice is yellowing of the skin and other tissues due to the breakdown products of red blood cells.) Infants and children may have a predisposition to infection. In later years, blood-rich organs such as the heart, spleen, and liver are damaged by the restricted blood flow. The disease may cause leg ulcers, anemia, kidney failure, stroke, and heart failure. The severity of the symptoms varies from individual to individual. Some show few symptoms; others die young.

The physician's assistant explained that sickle-cell anemia is an inherited disease. The variant can run in families. Individuals can pass the variant to their children without having symptoms themselves. Parents who do not have sickle-cell anemia can have children with the disorder and children without the disorder. About 2.5 million, or one in every 12 African Americans carry the sickling trait without having the disease. (This group is the most affected population in the United States.) They have both kinds of hemoglobin in their red blood cells. Individuals who have both kinds of proteins are called **carriers**. Approximately 80,000 African Americans have only sickling hemoglobin. These people demonstrate the characteristics or symptoms of sickle-cell anemia.

Denzel began to wonder whether anyone else in his family besides Uncle Jamal had sickle-cell anemia. Could he be one of the individuals who had the sickle hemoglobin variant but didn't show it? The physician's assistant told the group that an easy test for sickling hemoglobin could be done at the clinic. He encouraged the students to have it done.

Denzel decided he wanted to be tested.

After the assembly, Denzel approached the physician's assistant to ask questions about the test. He told Denzel that there is a test to distinguish normal hemoglobin (hemoglobin A) from sickling hemoglobin (hemoglobin S). This test is based on the understanding that the difference between the two types of hemoglobin is only one amino acid. This amino acid changes the electrical charge on the molecule. This charge difference causes the two different forms of hemoglobin to separate in an electric field. In a solution through which an electrical current is passed, hemoglobin A will move in one direction; hemoglobin S will travel the opposite way.

Denzel was amazed. The difference between being healthy and having the symptoms of sickle-cell anemia was a single amino acid. And, through a fairly simple blood test, Denzel could learn whether he had any hemoglobin S.

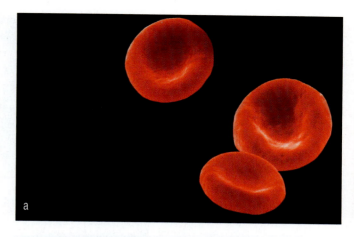

a

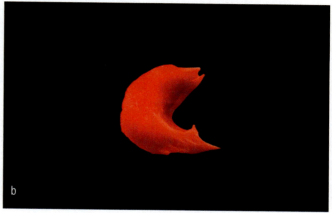

b

Figure 2.13

(a) Normal hemoglobin (A) remains dissolved in the cell after the release of oxygen. Cells remain disk-shaped. (b) Sickling hemoglobin (S) comes out of solution after the release of oxygen. It forms long crystals and distorts the cell shape.
© Dr. Stanley Flegler/Visuals Unlimited

Table 2.1 Hemoglobin Data		
Individual	**Hemoglobin A**	**Hemoglobin S**
Grandpa Jones	+	+
Grandma Jones	+	+
Grandpa Beausejour	+	−
Grandma Beausejour	+	−
Mr. Jones	+	+
Mrs. Beausejour-Jones	+	−
Uncle Jamal Jones	−	+
Tara Jones	+	+
Tabitha Jones	+	−
Denzel Jones	+	−
Carlos Jackson	+	+

At dinner that night, Denzel told his family what he had learned that day about the sickle-cell trait. He said he would like to be tested. He also thought that it might be a good idea for everyone to be tested, to know whether they carried the trait. Denzel's father was not so sure. He worried that if he carried the trait and someone at work found out, they might think he wasn't healthy enough to operate the forklift he drove every day. And what if he applied for more health insurance? What impact would being a carrier have on that? Denzel assured him that the physician's assistant said that individuals who carried the trait rarely exhibited any symptoms of the disease and were never considered "sick." Anyway, the results of the test were confidential. No one was ever supposed to know.

Tara, Denzel's older sister, was worried for a different reason. She was planning to be married soon and very much wanted to have children. What if she and her fiancé, Carlos Jackson, were both carriers? What would that mean for the children they might have? She wasn't sure she wanted to know.

In the end, everyone in the family decided to be tested. This included Denzel's four grandparents, Grandpa and Grandma Jones and Grandma and Grandpa Beausejour; his sisters, Tara and Tabitha; and Uncle Jamal. Even Tara's fiancé, Carlos, wanted to find out whether he carried the trait.

Everyone nervously waited a week for the blood test results. The data in Table 2.1 were collected on the Jones and Beausejour families. (A + sign indicates the individual has that form of hemoglobin; a − sign indicates it was not present.)

 **ANALYSIS**

Record your responses to questions 1–5 in your notebook.

1. Earlier in this learning experience, you found out that the difference in the shape of peas is the result of a difference in a single enzyme that functions during pea development. Explain the differences in the biochemistry of sickling and normal hemoglobin. How do these differences result in the visible trait (as seen under the microscope)?

2. The results of Tara's test, as well as some of the others tested, indicate that some of her red blood cells carry hemoglobin S as well as normal hemoglobin. These individuals are carriers of this variant form of protein. Yet none of them has shown any symptoms of sickle-cell anemia under normal circumstances. How do you explain this?

3. Carlos enjoys mountain climbing. On occasion, at very high altitudes he has suffered fatigue and severe cramps in his joints. What do you think is the reason for this? Base your answer on his test results.

4. Scientists use family trees or **pedigrees** as a tool to record and track inherited characteristics in families. What specific characteristics have you seen in members of a family that help identify them as belonging to that family?

5. Create a pedigree for Denzel's family. Indicate how members are related and how the sickle-cell trait runs in the family. Use the test results shown in Table 2.1.

To help you diagram the trait of sickle cell in Denzel's family, you will need to use the symbols shown in Figure 2.14 to create a pedigree of his family.

The generations of a family are marked with Roman numerals. Begin with the first generation listed in Table 2.1. Each individual within a generation is labeled with an Arabic numeral (1, 2, 3, 4, etc.). Within the children of a particular couple, the first born child is usually placed to the far left. Subsequent children follow to the right. Figure 2.15 is one example of a pedigree. Examine the pedigree. What can you tell about the relationships in this family? Who has the disease? Who are the carriers?

6. Tara and Carlos hope to marry soon and to have children. What do you think the test results mean for them? Write responses to the following:
   a. List all of the choices that Tara and Carlos have with respect to having children.
   b. Describe all of the consequences for each of the choices you listed in item 6a.
   c. Describe in a short paragraph what choice you might make if you were in the same situation as Tara and Carlos. Include your reasons for making that choice.
   d. What do you think would happen if everyone who was confronted with this situation made the same choice you made? Write a short paragraph describing what this future might look like.
   e. List four important values that influenced your decision. Explain how they influenced you. For example, some values might include religious reasons, your view of community, your sense of responsibility, your own personal health issues, and your sense of family.

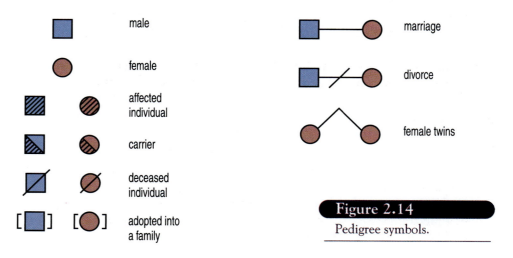

Figure 2.14
Pedigree symbols.

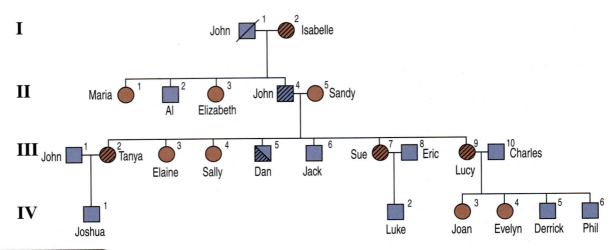

Figure 2.15

An example of a pedigree.

In the 1970s, Susan Perrine was a young doctor working in Saudi Arabia. She observed that many of the Arab patients who came to her clinic had surprisingly mild cases of sickle-cell anemia. In fact, many of them displayed no symptoms, even though their blood showed the characteristic sickling effect under conditions of low oxygen. When their hemoglobin was examined, the patients displayed high levels of fetal hemoglobin. Fetal hemoglobin is the kind of hemoglobin that all humans produce before birth but generally is replaced after birth by adult hemoglobin. Fetal hemoglobin has a higher affinity for oxygen. That means it binds oxygen more tightly than adult hemoglobin does. Apparently in these Arab patients for some reason the red blood cells had not completely switched from making fetal hemoglobin to adult hemoglobin. And surprisingly, the presence of this fetal hemoglobin reduced or eliminated the problem found when an individual makes only hemoglobin S. Explain why the presence of fetal hemoglobin may mask or dominate the effects of the sickling hemoglobin. Describe how this information might be used to treat sickle-cell patients.

The study of genealogy, that is, tracing a family's history, can be fascinating. Some people track their ancestors when an unfortunate illness shows up in the immediate family. They are concerned about whether they or their children may inherit the disease. Others search for the names and places of origin in their mother's and father's pasts for clues to their heritage. Create your own family tree. You may want to interview your oldest relatives. Ask them for their views of life and of family in past times to help you recapture family history that is often lost.

CAREER FOCUS

Phlebotomist   It's early in the morning, but the hospital is already busy. Metal trays covered with vials, syringes, tourniquets, and doctors' orders are being wheeled from room to room. One of these trays is followed closely by Arzu, a phlebotomist. On her morning rounds, she has orders to draw blood from an elderly woman being treated for a blood clot. She will also take a blood sample from a middle-aged man needing tests to find out why he has been feeling so ill and a young girl who is in the hospital for gall bladder surgery.

Arzu loves meeting new people. Many of those she deals with aren't too happy to see her, because it is common for people to be afraid of needles. But Arzu comforts them by educating them about what is going to happen and describing each step. She can usually quell patients' fears and take samples of their blood without any problem. Long-time patients are relieved when they see her face in the morning. They know she cares.

Patients are thankful for Arzu's gentle touch, but they are often unaware of her great range of knowledge. She is very skilled. To complete her certificate program in phlebotomy, Arzu was trained in collecting, transporting, handling, and processing blood samples; identifying and selecting equipment, supplies, and additives used in blood collection; recognizing and adhering to infection control and safety procedures; and recognizing the importance of each step from drawing blood to analysis and seeing how her part fits into the whole picture of a specific person's medical care.

Arzu's expertise in the field is in drawing blood for analysis. She translates the doctors' orders for the lab technicians who do the analysis. When doctors, physician's assistants, and nurses receive the results, they use the data from these blood tests to prescribe medication and a plan for care. By being specifically trained in bloodletting procedures, Arzu allows doctors and nurses the time to complete important paperwork, update records, and continue patient care toward a speedy recovery.

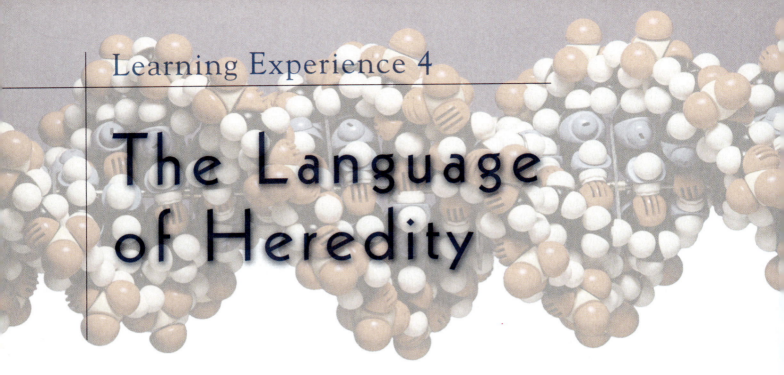

The Language of Heredity

Prologue

In the previous learning experience, you saw that the variations in the trait of pea shape are the result of the ability of an enzyme to function. When the starch-branching enzyme (SBEI) catalyzes the bonding of smaller sucrose molecules into the larger amylopectin molecule, the pea is round. If it cannot carry out this activity, the pea is wrinkled.

This protein is responsible for the expression of a trait in an organism. But what is the blueprint that directs the formation of the protein? Where is this blueprint found in the cell? You may already be familiar with the molecule **deoxyribonucleic acid (DNA)** as the agent of heredity. In this learning experience, you explore in detail the structure and function of DNA.

Brainstorming

Working with a partner, brainstorm everything you think you know about DNA. Record your thinking in your notebook. Be prepared to share your ideas with the class.

READING

The Twisted Molecule of Life

Part I: Identifying the Molecule of Heredity

In 1866, an Austrian monk by the name of Gregor Mendel had collected an enormous body of data on the inheritance patterns of various traits in peas. From the data, he concluded that some units he called "factors" were responsible for the passage of traits from one generation to the next. The science community started to look for the factors. In 1909, Wilhelm Johannsen renamed the factors genes (meaning "give birth to" in Greek). Soon after, William Bateson coined the term genetics as the study of inheritance.

What was this genetic substance that passed on information, determined an offspring's visible traits, and also accounted for the incredible diversity to be found among living things? Some scientists thought it must be a protein. They knew that proteins are present in large quantities in the cell and that they carry on numerous functions. Proteins are made of 20 different subunits called amino acids. These subunits can be joined in a great variety of combinations. Supporters of proteins as the molecule of heredity thought that this variety would allow for the diversity we see in organisms. They imagined this in much the same way as the 26 letters of the English alphabet. These letters can be placed in a variety of ways to produce an immense quantity of words.

Other scientists noted that large amounts of DNA were also present in cells. They thought that DNA was the molecule of heredity. However, it seemed too simple a molecule. It only has six subunits: deoxyribose (a sugar), phosphate, and four nitrogenous bases (see Figure 2.16). The bases **adenine** (A) and **guanine** (G) were characterized by two nitrogen rings (**purines**). **Cytosine** (C) and **thymine** (T) were characterized by one nitrogen ring (**pyrimidines**). The debate raged hot and heavy. Which was the molecule of heredity?

In 1928, Frederick Griffith demonstrated that a trait could be transferred from one kind of bacteria to another. He called the substance that carried this information a "transforming factor." But he was unclear as to its nature. In 1943, after many years of chemical analysis and experimentation, Oswald Avery and his co-workers reached a conclusion. They showed that it is DNA that directs the expression of traits within an organism and their transmission from generation to generation. But their experimental work and conclusion still did not satisfy all scientists.

Alfred Hershey and Martha Chase ended the controversy in 1952 with their experiments on bacteriophages. **Bacteriophages** are viruses that infect bacteria and that are made of only protein and DNA. Upon infecting a bacterium, a bacteriophage produces many copies of itself (**progeny**). The progeny have all the characteristics of the original infecting virus. But was it the DNA or the protein that transmitted the information for these characteristics to the progeny?

SC*i*LINKS
NSTA

Topic: Amino Acids
Go to: www.scilinks.org
Code: INBIOH2177

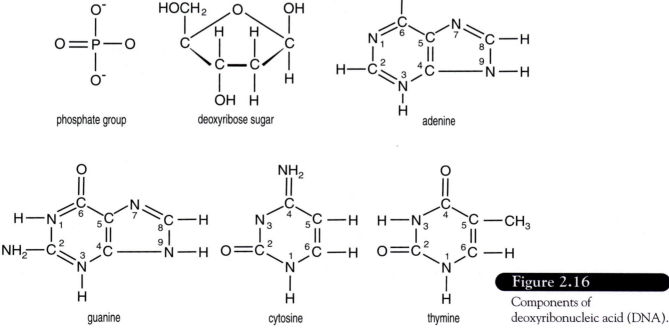

Figure 2.16

Components of deoxyribonucleic acid (DNA).

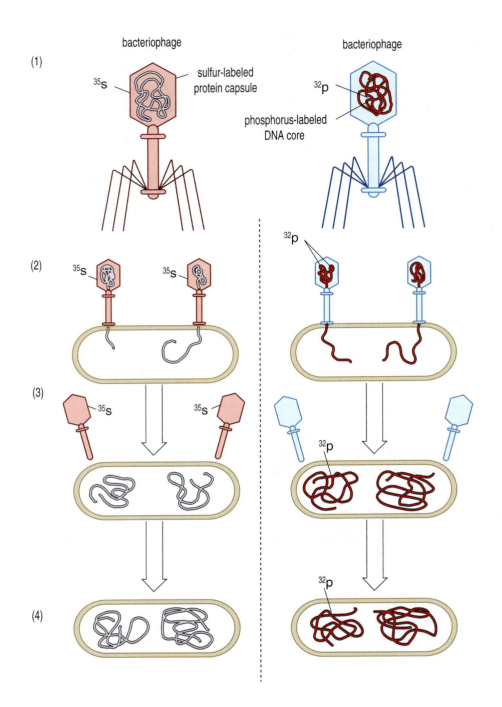

(1) bacteriophage

^{35}S — sulfur-labeled protein capsule

bacteriophage

^{32}P

phosphorus-labeled DNA core

(2) ^{35}S ^{35}S ^{32}P

(3) ^{35}S ^{35}S ^{32}P

(4) ^{32}P

Figure 2.17

The Hershey-Chase experiment.

To determine the answer to that question, Hershey and Chase conducted the following pivotal experiment (see Figure 2.17). They knew that the element sulfur is found only in the protein of the bacteriophage and phosphorus only in the DNA. So they infected one dish of bacteria with a virus containing radioactive sulfur and a second dish with a virus containing radioactive phosphorus. They reasoned that these radioactive labels could distinguish DNA from proteins. The two samples of infected bacteria were then assayed to see which radioactive substance was taken into the bacterial cells and used to make more viral progeny. Hershey and Chase found that the phosphorus entered the bacteria, whereas the sulfur remained outside. Since only the DNA entered the cell, they proved conclusively that DNA was the molecule used by the virus to make more of itself.

Table 2.2 Composition of DNA in Several Species

Source	Purines		Pyrimidines	
	Adenine	Guanine	Cytosine	Thymine
human	30.4%	19.6%	19.9%	30.1%
ox	29.0%	21.2%	21.2%	28.7%
salmon sperm	29.7%	20.8%	20.4%	29.1%
wheat germ	28.1%	21.8%	22.7%	27.4%
E. coli	24.7%	26.0%	25.7%	23.6%
sea urchin	32.8%	17.7%	17.3%	32.1%

Scientists now knew that DNA functioned as the storage site and transmitter of information for traits. But what was its structure? How were those six subunits arranged in the molecule so that DNA could be the bearer of vast amounts of information and code for the incredible diversity seen in living things? Erwin Chargaff added an important piece to the puzzle with his experiments. He showed that the proportions of nitrogenous bases found in DNA were the same in every cell of an organism in a given species. But he showed that the proportions varied from species to species. He also provided an important piece of data about the ratios of nitrogenous bases as indicated in Table 2.2.

 **ANALYSIS**

Examine Chargaff's results in Table 2.2. Record your responses to the following in your notebook.

1. What does this table tell you about the DNA of all organisms?
2. Note the proportion (the ratios) of each nitrogenous base to other nitrogenous bases in DNA in humans. What do you notice about the relative (not exact) proportions of the four nitrogenous bases?
3. Does this observation hold true for the other species as well? What conclusion might you draw about which nitrogenous base might be joined to another nitrogenous base?

Building the Twisted Molecule of Life

ACTIVITY

What is the arrangement of subunits in DNA? What are the special features of this molecule? In this activity, you construct a paper model of DNA. As you piece the molecule together, keep this question in mind: How might this molecule encode all the information necessary for determining the biochemical activities and specific characteristics of all organisms?

Materials

For each group of four students:

- 1 large envelope containing 4 small envelopes and copies of the following model pieces to cut out:
  - 10 each of 4 bases
  - 20 phosphates
  - 20 sugars
- 2 paper strips (1 cm × 30 cm)
- masking tape (or drafting or other removable tape)
- white glue
- 4 scissors

PROCEDURE

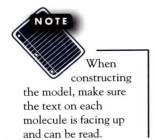

When constructing the model, make sure the text on each molecule is facing up and can be read.

1. Place your group's cutouts into 4 separate piles. Make 1 pile for the sugar molecules and 1 pile for the phosphate groups. Combine the adenine and thymine bases into a third pile. And combine the cytosine and guanine bases into a fourth pile. Note that each molecule has a right and left version.

2. **STOP & THINK** Why are you combining the adenines and thymines? the cytosines and guanines?

3. Remove 5 bases from the third pile and 5 bases from the fourth pile. Scramble them to make a random order. Place them in a line on the left side of your lab table.

4. Remove 1 sugar molecule from the sugar pile. Attach it to 1 of the bases. Glue the tab on the sugar (as a bond) to the lower corner of the base. (Look for the letter S at the corner of the base; see Figure 2.18.)

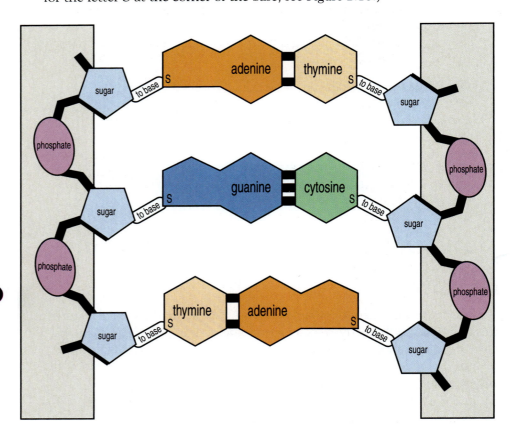

Figure 2.18

Model of a section of DNA. This model shows the bonds between the sugar and phosphate molecules, the bases and the sugar-phosphate background, and the bases themselves.

5. Remove 1 phosphate group from its pile. Attach it to the bonded sugar molecule. Glue the tabs.
6. Locate the appropriate matching base from the third or fourth piles. Attach them to the model. Attach the 2 bases by taping the "hydrogen bond" tabs together. (There are 2 bonds between adenine and thymine, and 3 bonds between cytosine and guanine.)
7. **STOP & THINK** Discuss questions 1 and 2 of the Analysis with your group as you construct your model. Record your responses in your notebook.
8. Repeat steps 3–6 for each of the bases lined up on the left side of your table. Make 10 complete sets of base pairs.
9. Complete the model by gluing the model to the 2 paper strips (see Figure 2.18).

ANALYSIS

As you and your group construct the model, discuss your responses to the following. Record your responses in your notebook.

1. Describe the basic features of a DNA molecule. What information do the letter symbols give you?
2. What features of the DNA molecule remain constant in various organisms? What features differ?
3. How might the order or the placement of bases affect the information in the DNA?
4. Write the sequence of bases for the DNA strand you constructed.
5. Say 27% of the bases in a certain segment of DNA were adenine. What would be the percentages of thymine, cytosine, and guanine?
6. DNA determines the characteristics of an organism. This means that DNA has to be able to carry an enormous amount of information. How can a molecule composed of only four different kinds of subunits carry large amounts of diverse information?
7. How might DNA differ among different organisms? For example, how do you think mouse DNA or bacterial DNA differ from human DNA?

The Twisted Molecule of Life

Part II: Determining the Structure of DNA

In the early 1950s, James Watson, an American, and Francis Crick, an Englishman, set out together to discover the structure of the DNA molecule. They wanted to know in what molecular configuration the six subunits were arranged. They did not carry out laboratory experiments themselves, but based their hypothesis on data accumulated by others. These data included the X-ray work of Rosalind Franklin. Dr. Franklin showed that DNA had a double helical (or spiral) form (see Figure 2.19).

From this information, Watson and Crick were able to build a model that satisfied all the known data. They worried that the structure would be "dull," that is, that it could not explain the many functions of a hereditary molecule. They knew that the

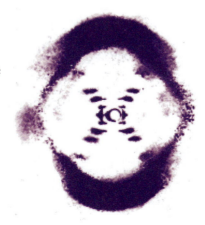

Figure 2.19

X-ray diffraction pattern of DNA produced by Rosalind Franklin.

Topic: DNA
Go to: www.scilinks.org
Code: INBIOH2182

molecular structure must be varied, carry a huge amount of information, replicate itself before cell division, and code for traits. To their excitement, as Watson said in his book *The Double Helix*, DNA's molecular structure turned out to be very "interesting." Their paper, published in 1953, set off great excitement in the biology community. Their ideas initiated the explosion of DNA research that continues to this day. Watson, Crick, and Maurice Wilkins (in whose laboratory Franklin had worked) were awarded the Nobel Prize in Medicine in 1962.

We now know that DNA is a very long, thin double helix made up of linked nucleotides. Each nucleotide consists of one phosphate group, one sugar (deoxyribose) molecule, and one attached nitrogenous base. This base can be either adenine, cytosine, guanine, or thymine. The alternating phosphate and sugar molecules provide the sides of the helix (similar to the sides of a ladder). The "rungs" of the helix are made of pairs of nitrogen and carbon-ringed bases (see Figure 2.20). As you determined from Table 2.2, the bases adenine and thymine are present in equal amounts and are joined together. The bases cytosine and guanine are also present in equal amounts and are joined together. Each rung is made of a pair of these **complementary** (matching) nitrogenous bases. These bases are always linked as A with T and C with G. Each of these bases is attached to the sugar molecule in the alternating sugar-phosphate sidepiece or strand. The two bases are held together by hydrogen bonds. This configuration, in turn, keeps the double strands of the DNA molecule together (see Figures 2.20 and 2.21).

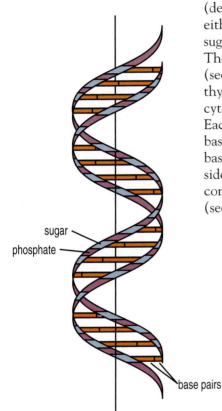

sugar

phosphate

base pairs

Figure 2.20

Illustration of a section of the DNA molecule showing the sugar-phosphate backbone. The rungs are formed by the four nitrogenous bases.

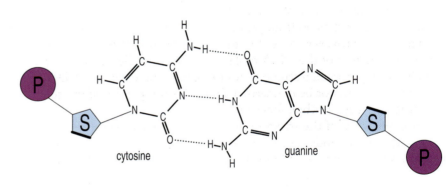

cytosine   guanine

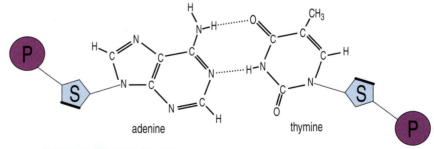

adenine   thymine

Figure 2.21

Chemical structure and arrangement of the subunits in DNA.

1. Create a DNA discovery timeline that charts the research that led to the discovery of the structure of DNA. Base your timeline on the reading "The Twisted Molecule of Life." This timeline should begin with Mendel and include
   - the scientist(s);
   - a time frame;
   - the experimental organism(s), (if one is described); and
   - conclusions or ideas that added to the scientific knowledge of the time.

   Be prepared to share your timeline with the class.

2. In carrying out their experiments, scientists usually build on the discoveries of other scientists. Explain how each experiment in the reading built upon the earlier discoveries described.

In Their Own Words

READING

The article that follows is one of the classic papers in scientific literature in the 20th century. It represents the culmination of 40 years of intense scientific research. It bridged the gap between earlier discoveries about traits and patterns of inheritance of traits and our modern understanding of how genes code for proteins and how proteins result in traits. In 1953, scientists knew that DNA was the molecule responsible for conferring traits within an organism and for passing characteristics on from generation to generation. What was not yet known was how this was done. In order to understand how, it was crucial to know the structure of the DNA molecule. In this article, James Watson and Francis Crick proposed a structure for deoxyribonucleic acid, DNA.

As you read, do not be concerned about the complexity of the science or the scientific language. Rather, focus on
- the description of the structure itself and its composition,
- how the two strands are held together, and
- what Watson and Crick felt was the significance of their model.

MOLECULAR STRUCTURE OF NUCLEIC ACIDS

Reprinted by permission from *Nature*, volume 171, April 25, 1953, pp. 737–738. Copyright

A STRUCTURE FOR DEOXYRIBOSE NUCLEIC ACID

We wish to suggest a structure for the salt of deoxyribose nucleic acid (DNA). This structure has novel features which are of considerable biological interest.

A structure for nucleic acid has already been proposed by Pauling and Corey.[1] They kindly made their manuscript available to us in advance of publication. Their model consists of three intertwined chains, with the phosphates near the fibre axis, and the bases on the outside. In our opinion, this structure is unsatisfactory for two reasons: (1) We believe that the material which gives the X-ray diagrams is the salt, not the free acid. Without the acidic hydrogen atoms it is not clear what forces would hold the structure together, especially as the negatively charged phosphates near the axis will repel each other. (2) Some of the van der Waals distances appear to be too small.

Another three-chain structure has also been suggested by Fraser (in the press). In his model the phosphates are on the outside and the bases on the inside, linked together by hydrogen bonds. This structure as described is rather ill-defined, and for this reason we shall not comment on it.

This figure is purely diagrammatic. The two ribbons symbolize the two phosphate—sugar chains, and the horizontal rods are the pairs of bases holding the chains together. The vertical line marks the fibre axis.

We wish to put forward a radically different structure for the salt of deoxyribose nucleic acid. This structure has two helical chains each coiled round the same axis (see diagram).

We have made the usual chemical assumptions, namely, that each chain consists of phosphate diester groups joining β-d-deoxyribofuranose residues with 3′,5′ linkages. The two chains (but not their bases) are related by a dyad perpendicular to the fibre axis. Both chains follow right-handed helices, but owing to the dyad the sequences of the atoms in the two chains run in opposite directions. Each chain loosely resembles Furberg's[2] model No. 1; that is, the bases are on the inside of the helix and the phosphates on the outside. The configuration of the sugar and the atoms near it is close to Furberg's 'standard configuration,' the sugar being roughly perpendicular to the attached base. There is a residue on each chain every 3.4 Å [angstroms] in the z-direction. We have assumed an angle of 36° between adjacent residues in the same chain, so that the structure repeats after 10 residues on each chain, that is, after 34 Å. The distance of a phosphorus atom from the fibre axis is 10 Å. As the phosphates are on the outside, cations have easy access to them.

The structure is an open one, and its water content is rather high. At lower water contents we would expect the bases to tilt so that the structure could become more compact. The novel feature of the structure is the manner in which the two chains are held together by the purine and pyrimidine bases. The planes of the bases are perpendicular to the fibre axis. They are joined together in pairs, a single base from one chain being hydrogen-bonded to a single base from the other chain, so that the two lie side by side with identical z-coordinates. One of the pair must be a purine and the other a pyrimidine for bonding to occur. The hydrogen bonds are made as follows: purine position 1 to pyrimidine position 1; purine position 6 to pyrimidine position 6.

If it is assumed that the bases only occur in the structure in the most plausible tautomeric forms (that is, with the keto rather than the enol configurations) it is found that only specific pairs of bases can bond together. These pairs are: adenine (purine) with thymine (pyrimidine), and guanine (purine) with cytosine (pyrimidine).

In other words, if an adenine forms one member of a pair, on either chain, then on these assumptions the other member must be thymine; similarly for guanine and cytosine. The sequence of bases on a single chain does not appear to be restricted in any way. However, if only specific pairs of bases can be formed, it follows that if the sequence of bases on one chain is given, then the sequence on the other chain is automatically determined.

It has been found experimentally[3,4] that the ratio of the amounts of adenine to thymine, and the ratio of guanine to cytosine, are always very close to unity for deoxyribose nucleic acid.

It is probably impossible to build this structure with a ribose sugar in place of the deoxyribose, as the extra oxygen atom would make too close a van der Waals contact.

The previously published X-ray data[5,6] on deoxyribose nucleic acid are insufficient for a rigorous test of our structure. So far as we can tell, it is roughly compatible with the experimental data, but it must be regarded as unproved until it has been checked against more exact results. Some of these are given in the following communications. We were not aware of the details of the results presented there when we devised our structure, which rests mainly though not entirely on published experimental data and stereo-chemical arguments.

It has not escaped our notice that the specific pairing we have postulated immediately suggests a possible copying mechanism for the genetic material.

Full details of the structure, including the conditions assumed in building it, together with a set of coordinates for the atoms, will be published elsewhere.

We are much indebted to Dr. Jerry Donohue for constant advice and criticism, especially on interatomic distances. We have also been stimulated by a knowledge of the general nature of the unpublished experimental results and ideas of Dr. M. H. F. Wilkins, Dr. R. E. Franklin and their co-workers at King's College, London. One of us (J. D. W.) has been aided by a fellowship from the National Foundation for Infantile Paralysis.

J. D. Watson
F. H. C. Crick

Medical Research Council Unit for the Study of the Molecular Structure of Biological Systems, Cavendish Laboratory, Cambridge. April 2.

NOTES

1. Pauling, L., and Corey, R. B., *Nature*, 171, 346 (1953); Proc. U.S. Nat. Acad. Sci., 39, 84 (1953).
2. Furberg, S., Acta Chem. Scand., 6, 634 (1952).
3. Chargaff, E., for references see Zamenhof, S., Brawerman, G., and Chargaff, E., Biochim. et Biophys. Acta, 9, 402 (1952).
4. Wyatt, G. R., J. Gen. Physiol., 36, 201 (1952).
5. Astbury, W. T., Symp. Soc. Exp. Biol. 1, Nucleic Acid, 66 (Camb. Univ. Press, 1947).
6. Wilkins, M. H. F., and Randall, J. T., Biochim. et Biophys. Acta, 10, 192 (1953).

ANALYSIS

1. Describe the approach that Watson and Crick took to develop a model of DNA. How does this approach fit with your understanding of how scientific research is done?
2. What about their model did Watson and Crick find significant?

Read *The Double Helix* by James Watson or *Rosalind Franklin* by Anne Sayre. Write an essay describing your view of how this major discovery was made. Include the nature of the approach, the importance of collaborative work, and the roles that luck or imagination might have played.

CAREER FOCUS

Criminalist   The courtroom was silent. The most important piece of evidence linking Jason Benton to the attempted murder of a state university student had been placed before the jury. That evidence came from forensic science, the practical application of science and medicine to law.

On a warm day in autumn, Missy, a freshman in college, was at a campus party with her roommate. She decided to leave early and walk back to the dormitory alone. When her roommate returned, it was obvious that Missy had not made it back. Her roommate and other friends retraced the path that Missy was assumed to have taken home. They found her lying just off the road, obviously terrified and suffering from severe trauma. She was coherent and said that she had been mugged and beaten on her way home. When police arrived, she explained that her attacker had grabbed her from behind. She never clearly saw his face, but she recalled that he had spoken with an angry stutter and a foreign-sounding accent. Because of the stutter and accent, the police suspected a well-known, recently paroled criminal, Jason Benton. They picked him up for questioning.

A forensics team that included the state's senior criminalist immediately studied the area for evidence. The team found little. But Missy had scratched her attacker and gotten some of his skin beneath her fingernails. It was just the break the forensics team needed. The skin scrapings were carefully extracted and sent to a nearby forensics lab, along with all of the other physical evidence. There, criminalists began DNA testing on the tissue sample.

The scientific principle behind the DNA test is that each person (except for identical twins) has his or her own unique DNA "fingerprint." If the DNA in the tissue Missy scratched from her attacker matched that of Jason Benton's blood, he would more than likely be found guilty. With a suspect's life at stake, it is vital to have accurate tests, and to avoid any contamination of the samples by other DNA. When the case went to trial, the jury would want to be positive that the DNA test was reliable.

Since the early 1980s, DNA analysis has been the most reliable tool for identifying criminals of violent crimes, particularly sexual assaults. DNA can also be used to identify serial criminals, prove paternity, and identify human remains.

DNA is just one of the many substances criminalists work with. They must have a knowledge of crime scene investigations, trace evidence examinations, physiological fluid analysis (including blood, urine, semen, and saliva), controlled substance analysis, and blood alcohol analysis. When evidence from a crime comes to the laboratory, criminalists must be able to decide which tests should be done. They must be able to conduct analyses or examinations on hair, fiber, soil, paint, glass, building materials, projectiles, and footwear. Once all the evidence has been tested and examined, it must be presented to local law enforcement personnel for possible use in a trial.

There are many different routes to becoming a criminalist. Colleges offer majors in biology and chemistry; some universities have more specialized majors in forensic science. Once a bachelor's degree is acquired, a student can enter the field or continue his or her education through the doctoral level.

Back in the courtroom, the DNA evidence was presented to the jury. The DNA fingerprints from the tissue and from Jason Benton's blood matched perfectly. After 10 hours of deliberating, the jury delivered its verdict: "We, the jury, hereby find Jason Benton guilty of assault and attempted murder."

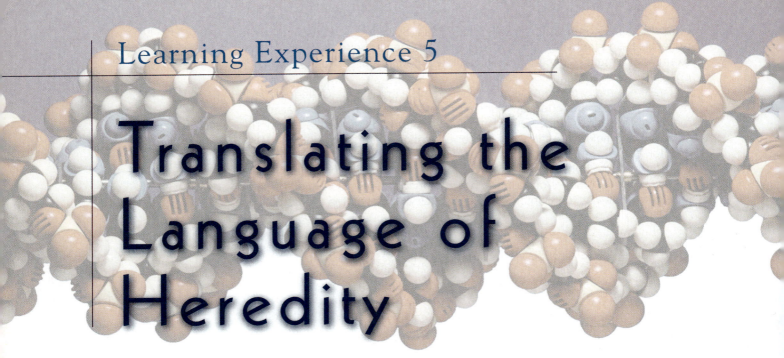

Translating the Language of Heredity

Prologue

How does information in DNA become the proteins that are responsible for traits? What is the relationship between nucleic acids, proteins, and traits? In this learning experience, you model the cellular processes that take the information stored in DNA and translate it into proteins.

Brainstorming

Working with a partner, develop three problems or issues involved in moving information from DNA to protein. Record your thinking in your notebook. Be prepared to share your ideas with the class.

READING

Deciphering the Code

After the discovery of the structure of DNA, intriguing questions arose. How can such a simple molecule be the basis of all the traits we see in living things? Remember, it is made of only four nitrogenous bases or "letters." What is the code these letters make? How can this code translate into heritable traits? You discovered that round peas are the result of the action of an enzyme (protein). So there must be a relationship between the sequence of the nucleotides (the code) and the production or synthesis of protein. What is this relationship?

Almost immediately after proposing a model for the DNA molecule, Crick hypothesized the following. He thought that there must be a molecule that carries the information from the DNA in the nucleus to the cytoplasm where protein was made. The discovery of a **ribonucleic acid**, called **messenger RNA**, confirmed this hypothesis. The process that copies the information from DNA into RNA is called **transcription**.

SCI**LINKS**®
NSTA

Topic: Transcription
Go to: www.scilinks.org
Code: INBIOH2188

Ribonucleic acid (RNA) is a single-strand molecule made of a backbone of alternating sugar (**ribose**) and phosphate groups. Its unpaired nitrogenous bases are attached to the sugar. These bases are adenine (A), cytosine (C), and guanine (G). **Uracil** (U) pairs with adenine; it is a pyrimidine similar to thymine. In 1961, Marshall Nirenberg tested the hypothesis that RNA was involved in making protein. He made a mixture from cells (cell extract) that was capable of making protein. Using this mixture, he demonstrated that in the absence of RNA, no proteins were made. But when he added RNA, proteins were made. He then made an RNA molecule composed entirely of one kind of nitrogenous base, uracil (U). When he added this RNA to a cellular extract, he found it made a protein that contained only one kind of amino acid. This amino acid was phenylalanine.

Nirenberg concluded that U-U-U coded for phenylalanine. Using this method, the codes for each of the amino acids were found. Further experiments showed that the code in DNA is a triplet. Three nucleotides (together called a **codon**) are required to code for an amino acid. This codon is transcribed into messenger RNA (mRNA). The mRNA is then translated into an amino acid. Soon, all the codes for the 20 amino acids were deciphered. In addition, codons also signal where the protein starts and where it ends. AUG, which codes for methionine, is the start codon. It signals the beginning of the protein **translation** process. For the stop codon, there are actually three different options: UAA, UGA, and UAG.

The connections among DNA, genes, and proteins had begun in 1941 with a classic experiment by George Beadle and Edward Tatum. Beadle and Tatum determined that a gene in an organism contains the information to synthesize a protein. Research continued on the mechanics of how the DNA blueprint is transcribed into the mRNA code and how the mRNA code is translated into a protein. This research sharpened the definition of a gene to mean a segment of the DNA molecule that codes for an enzyme or protein.

Examine Table 2.3. You will notice that a couple of amino acids have only one codon (for example, tryptophan and methionine). But others have several codons. (For example, lysine has two and leucine has six.) This variation in codon sequence is called "wobble."

ANALYSIS

Record your responses to the following in your notebook.

1. Describe the relationship between the nucleotides that make up DNA and the amino acids that make up protein.
2. Say Nirenberg had added an RNA molecule made up of only adenine to a cellular extract. He would have made a protein containing which amino acid? What kind of RNA molecule would he have needed to make a protein containing only the amino acid methionine? isoleucine? Explain your answer.

Table 2.3 Codons Coding for Amino Acids

codons	GCA GCC GCG GCU	AGA AGG CGA CGC CGG CGU	AAC AAU	GAC GAU	UGC UGU	CAA CAG	GAA GAG
abbreviations for amino acids	ala	arg	asn	asp	cys	gln	glu

codons	GGA GGC GGG GGU	CAC CAU	AUA AUC AUU	UUA UUG CUA CUC CUG CUU	AAA AAG	AUG	UUC UUU
abbreviations for amino acids	gly	his	ile	leu	lys	met	phe

codons	CCA CCC CCG CCU	AGC AGU UCA UCC UCG UCU	ACA ACC ACG ACU	UGG	UAC UAU	GUA GUC GUG GUU	UAA UAG UGA
abbreviations for amino acids	pro	ser	thr	trp	tyr	val	stop

For ease of writing, the amino acids are abbreviated as follows:

ala	alanine
arg	arginine
asn	asparagine
asp	aspartic acid
cys	cysteine
gln	glutamine
glu	glutamic acid
gly	glycine
his	histidine
ile	isoleucine
leu	leucine
lys	lysine
met	methionine
phe	phenylalanine
pro	proline
ser	serine
thr	threonine
trp	tryptophan
tyr	tyrosine
val	valine

The DNA Shuffle

ACTIVITY

In Learning Experience 3, No Matter What Your Shape, you found that the shape of peas (round or wrinkled) is determined by whether a single enzyme, SBEI, is functioning correctly. Similarly, whether an individual suffers from sickle-cell disorder depends on whether he or she has normal or sickling hemoglobin protein. Where does a pea or a human get the information for making proteins? In the following activities, you will investigate DNA as the molecule that contains all the information for the traits of organisms. You will determine how this information is transferred into protein.

After transcription, the mRNA leaves the nucleus and moves into the cytoplasm. There it binds to a structure called a ribosome. A **ribosome** is made up of protein and is a third kind of ribonucleic acid (rRNA). This is where the actual translation to protein takes place. The mRNA moves along the ribosome, "exposing" each codon. Another type of RNA molecule called a **transfer RNA (tRNA)** binds to the exposed codon. At one end of this tRNA are three exposed nucleotides (called an **anticodon**). These nucleotides are complementary to the mRNA codon exposed. At the other end of the tRNA is the specific amino acid that is encoded by the codon. The tRNA binds to the mRNA by matching nucleotides (C–G, A–U, etc.). The amino acid attaches to the preceding amino acid. This forms a growing chain of the **polypeptide** (see Figure 2.22).

In this activity, you will role-play the complete process of protein synthesis. You and your classmates will take on three roles. You will act as codons (mRNA triplet bases), anticodons (tRNA triplet bases), and amino acids. The steps in the Procedure describe the process in detail. Make sure you understand each

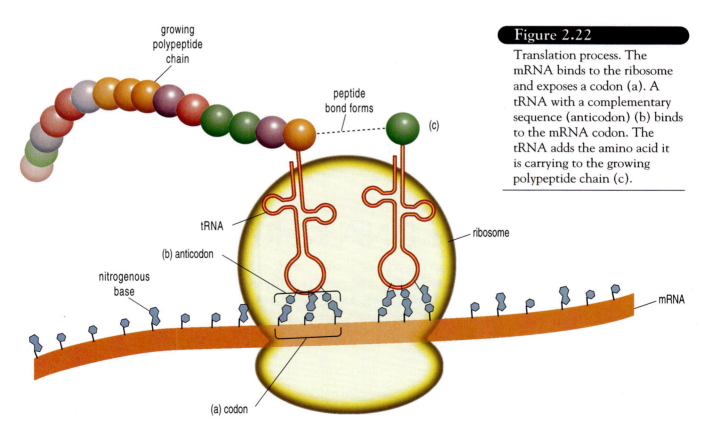

growing polypeptide chain

peptide bond forms

tRNA

(b) anticodon

nitrogenous base

(a) codon

(c)

ribosome

mRNA

Figure 2.22

Translation process. The mRNA binds to the ribosome and exposes a codon (a). A tRNA with a complementary sequence (anticodon) (b) binds to the mRNA codon. The tRNA adds the amino acid it is carrying to the growing polypeptide chain (c).

step, not just your role. These interactions are essential to all living things. The information stored in DNA is transcribed to mRNA, which codes for the assembling of a polypeptide chain. The actions of proteins determine the traits or characteristics of all organisms.

Materials

For the class:

- DNA sequence paper model
- index cards representing codons, anticodons, and amino acids
- tape
- plastic DNA model (optional)

PROCEDURE

1. Read through the entire Procedure before beginning the role-play activity.
2. Take 1 index card from the stack your teacher has prepared. Read the card. Identify to which of the groups—codons, anticodons, or amino acids—it belongs. When everyone has a card, form 3 groups of students (codons, anticodons, and amino acids).
3. Look at the gene (DNA sequence model) taped to the board. Determine who has the mRNA card that matches the first codon on the gene. That person should line up by the board in front of that codon.
4. Repeat step 3 for each codon. When all codons are in order, the process of transcription is complete.
5. Students representing the mRNA codon strand should then move away from the DNA to the center of the room (or other designated open area).
6. Students in the remaining 2 groups now pair up. Each person with an anticodon card (CAC, for example) pairs up with the matching person from the amino acid group (valine).
7. These pairs move to the mRNA strand (of students). The anticodon attaches to the appropriate codon.
8. One by one, the anticodons move away from the mRNA strand and go to one side of the room. As they do, each amino acid joins hands with the preceding amino acid.
9. This amino acid chain is called a polypeptide chain or a protein. As a group, this protein should move away from the mRNA strand to another part of the room. This completes the process of translation.

ACTIVITY

From DNA to RNA to Protein

In this activity, you will model the processes of transcription (DNA → mRNA) and translation in a different way (mRNA → polypeptide chain or protein). You will use pushpins to represent the nitrogenous bases of an actual DNA sequence.

Materials

For each group of four students:

- 54 pushpins in assorted colors
- 4 strips of corrugated cardboard (24 × 4 cm)

- 1 metric ruler
- 1 felt-tip marker
- 1 scissors
- masking tape

PROCEDURE

1. Select 18 pushpins to represent the nitrogenous bases of the DNA sequence that follows. Choose colors that correspond to the following color key. For example, for this sequence you will need 5 red pushpins to represent the 5 adenines.

   red pushpin   = adenine or A
   blue pushpin   = guanine or G
   yellow pushpin   = cytosine or C
   green pushpin   = thymine or T
   clear pushpin   = uracil or U

   DNA sequence: TACCACGTGGACTGAGGA

2. Arrange your 18 pushpins vertically down the center of 1 of the long cardboard strips. Make sure the colors of the pushpins match the order of the DNA sequence in step 1. This is your "sense" strand.
3. To the left of each pushpin, write the letter S. This represents the sugar that is attached to each nitrogenous base. Then write the letter P between each S. The arrangement of the S and P illustrate the alternating sugar-phosphate backbone.
4. To the right of each pushpin, write the letter of the complementary base in the second strand of this DNA segment. Refer to Figure 2.21 in Learning Experience 4 for how nitrogenous bases pair. (This written strand is the "antisense" DNA strand. However, we will not use this strand in this simulation.) Label this cardboard strip "DNA."
5. Place a second cardboard strip next to your sense strand of DNA pushpins (see step 2). Use this strand as the code to make a complementary mRNA strand. You may first wish to write out the mRNA sequence strand on paper. This process of transcription takes place in the nucleus of the cell (see Figure 2.23). Collect 18 more pushpins in the appropriate key colors. Place them in order along the strip.
6. Set up the cardboard strip of your mRNA sequence as you did in step 2. Write the letter S to the left of each pushpin and the letter P between each S. Label this cardboard strip "mRNA."
7. Use a marker to draw a line under every third nucleotide (base, sugar, and phosphate). For example, your first underline would be the codon AUG.
8. Model what happens after transcription. Move the mRNA cardboard strip away from the DNA strip. (This simulates that the mRNA is moving from the nucleus to the cytoplasm.)
9. Measure and cut the third cardboard strip into 6 equal sections (each 4 × 4 cm). Place the sections along the mRNA strand. Place pushpins on each of these sections to represent the complementary tRNA anticodon. For example, the first anticodon would be UAC attached to the AUG codon.

NOTE

Remember from the reading "Deciphering the Code" that three nucleotides are a codon. This codon determines which tRNA will bind to the codon and, therefore, which amino acid will be added.

Remember, it is the codon AUG that codes for the amino acid methionine. Methionine is the first amino acid of a protein chain; it is considered the "start" codon. tRNA is the carrier of the amino acid to the mRNA strand.

10. Measure and cut the fourth cardboard strip into 6 equal sections (each now 4 × 4 cm). Use the genetic code in Table 2.3 to determine the amino acid for each of the 6 mRNA codons. With your marker, write the name of each amino acid on a separate cardboard section.

11. Line up the amino acids next to the appropriate tRNA anticodon. Join the 6 amino acids together with tape. This series of amino acids is a polypeptide chain or protein.

ANALYSIS

Record your responses to the following in your notebook.

1. Explain in your own words how information in DNA codes for a protein.

2. Why do you think Crick hypothesized that there had to be another molecule involved in moving the information from DNA to protein synthesis?

3. The DNA sequence that you used in the last activity is the first 18 nucleotides that code for beta-hemoglobin. How many amino acids of the hemoglobin molecule does this sequence code for?

4. Define a gene. Use the understandings you gained from the readings and activities in this learning experience.

5. Create a concept map that describes the relationship between DNA and traits. Be sure to use at least 10 relevant words. Include words that relate to the biomolecules and processes involved in transferring the information from DNA to traits. Also include the terms you recorded in your notebook during the Brainstorming session in Learning Experience 4.

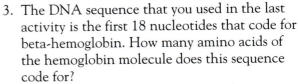

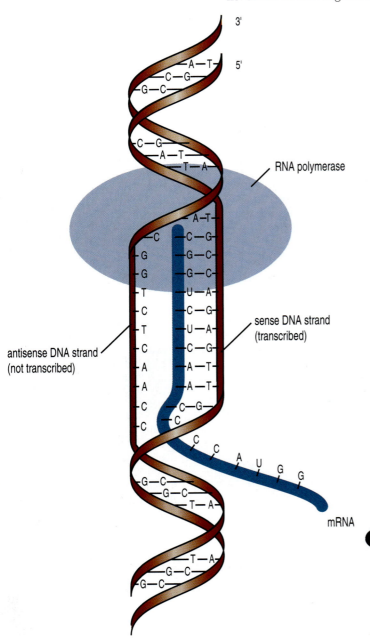

Figure 2.23

Representation of transcription showing DNA "unzipping." RNA nucleotides form a new strand of mRNA with the aid of RNA polymerase, an enzyme.

To Err Is Human . . . and the Way of All Living Things

Is nature perfect? If humans were to design an information transfer system, would they try to make it error proof? And, if they did that for DNA, would it be a good idea? In the following reading, Lewis Thomas considers this idea and the consequences of too perfect a system. After you have read the essay, write a one-paragraph explanation in your notebook summarizing the idea he is presenting. Then decide whether you agree or disagree with his idea. Explain your reasoning in a second paragraph.

As you prepare your essay, consider the following:

- What did Lewis Thomas think was the "greatest single achievement of nature to date"?
- What were his reasons for saying that?
- Why is it beneficial for DNA not to be "perfect," that is, to be subject to mistakes?
- According to Thomas's thesis, what would the world be like today if DNA were not subject to mistakes?

THE WONDERFUL MISTAKE

The greatest single achievement of nature to date was surely the invention of the molecule of DNA. We have had it from the very beginning, built into the first cell to emerge, membranes and all, somewhere in the soupy water of the cooling planet three thousand million years or so ago. All of today's DNA, strung through all the cells of the earth, is simply an extension and elaboration of that first molecule. In a fundamental sense we cannot claim to have made progress, since the method used for growth and replication is essentially unchanged.

But we have made progress in all kinds of other ways. Although it is out of fashion today to talk of progress in evolution if you use that word to mean anything like improvement, implying some sort of value judgment beyond the reach of science, I cannot think of a better term to describe what has happened. After all, to have come all the way from a system of life possessing only one kind of primitive microbial cell, living out colorless lives in hummocks of algal mats, to what we see around us today—the City of Paris, the State of Iowa, Cambridge University, Woods Hole, the succession of travertine-lined waterfalls and lakes like flights of great stairs in Yugoslavia's Plitvice, the horse-chestnut tree in my backyard, and the columns of neurones arranged in modules in the cerebral cortex of vertebrates—has to represent improvement. We have come a long way on that old molecule.

We could never have done it with human intelligence, even if molecular biologists had been flown in by satellite at the beginning, laboratories and all, from some other solar system. We have evolved scientists, to be sure, and so we know a lot about DNA, but if our kind of mind had been confronted with the problem of designing a similar replicating molecule, starting from scratch, we'd never have succeeded. We would have made one fatal mistake: our molecule would have been perfect. Given enough time, we would have figured out how to do this, nucleotides, enzymes, and all, to make flawless, exact copies, but it would never have occurred to us, thinking as we do, that the thing had to be able to make errors.

The capacity to blunder slightly is the real marvel of DNA. Without this special attribute, we would still be anaerobic bacteria and there would be no music. Viewed individually, one by one, each of the mutations that have brought us along represents a random, totally spontaneous accident, but it is no accident at all that mutations occur; the molecule of DNA was ordained from the beginning to make small mistakes.

If we had been doing it, we would have found some way to correct this, and evolution would have been stopped in its tracks. Imagine the consternation of human scientists, successfully engaged in the letter-perfect replication of prokaryotes, nonnucleated cells like bacteria, when nucleated cells suddenly turned up. Think of the agitated commissions assembled to explain the scandalous proliferations of trilobites all over the place, the mass firings, the withdrawal of tenure.

To err is human, we say, but we don't like the idea much, and it is harder still to accept the fact that erring is biological as well. We prefer sticking to the point, and insuring ourselves against change. But there it is: we are here by the purest chance, and by mistake at that. Somewhere along the line, nucleotides were edged apart to let new ones in; maybe viruses moved in, carrying along bits of other, foreign genomes; radiation from the sun or from outer space caused tiny cracks in the molecule, and humanity was conceived.

And maybe, given the fundamental instability of the molecule, it had to turn out this way. After all, if you have a mechanism designed to keep changing the ways of living, and if all the new forms have to fit together as they plainly do, and if every improvised new gene representing an embellishment in an individual is likely to be selected for the species, and if you have enough time, maybe the system is simply bound to develop brains sooner or later, and awareness.

Biology needs a better word than "error" for the driving force in evolution. Or maybe "error" will do after all, when you remember that it came from an old root meaning to wander about, looking for something.

EXTENDING *Ideas*

▶ After they are synthesized, many proteins require further processing before they are functional. In some instances, the proteins are cut or cleaved to form the mature protein. Sometimes, this final processing fails to take place correctly. As a result, the protein may not function properly, and disease symptoms may occur. Recent research suggests that a mistake in protein processing of an amyloid protein (a transmembrane protein) may be involved in Alzheimer's disease. Studies indicate that abnormal processing of this protein may lead to the formation of a toxic protein. This toxic protein can cause neurodegeneration, one of the main symptoms of Alzheimer's. Research this amyloid protein. Explain how failure to process this protein correctly can lead to symptoms of debilitating disease.

▶ To function properly, many proteins must be folded into a three-dimensional active form after they are synthesized. Mad cow disease (bovine spongiform encephalopathy) is characterized by the loss of thought and motor functions; it often results in death. This disease is caused by a novel infectious protein called a prion. This protein can be found in normal cells of the brain. But it is believed to become pathogenic when it misfolds after being synthesized. Research what we know about prions. What is the current thinking about how failure to fold properly can cause this disease?

Learning Experience 6

Change in Sequence, Change in Trait

Prologue

An excerpt from "Why So Many Errors in Our DNA?" *Blazing a Genetic Trail* by Maya Pines, Howard Hughes Medical Institute, 1991, p. 17.

As scientists learn to read the instructions in our genes, they are discovering that much of our DNA is riddled with errors.

Fortunately, most of these errors are harmless. Considering the difficulties involved—the 6 feet of DNA in a human cell consists of 6 billion subunits, or base pairs, coiled and tightly packed into 46 chromosomes, all of which must be duplicated every time a cell divides—our general state of health is something of a miracle.

We each inherit hundreds of genetic mutations from our parents, as they did from their forebears. In addition, the DNA in our own cells undergoes an estimated 30 new mutations during our lifetime, either through mistakes during DNA copying or cell division or, more often, because of damage from the environment. Bits of our DNA may be deleted, inserted, broken, or substituted. But most of these changes affect only the parts of DNA that do not contain a gene's instructions, so we need not worry about them.

Mutations are changes that take place in the sequence of DNA of an organism. In this learning experience, you explore what happens when different kinds of mutations happen in the sequence of a gene. You also look at how these changes are reflected in the traits that are determined by that gene.

Brainstorming

Discuss the following questions with your partner, and record your thinking in your notebook. Be prepared to share your ideas with the class.

1. If our DNA is riddled with errors, why do they not always manifest as visible changes in traits?
2. Some mutations do take place that may show up as changes in an individual. But these changes are not necessarily passed on to future generations. How does that happen?
3. How might a change in the sequence of DNA affect the encoded protein?

197

ACTIVITY

Simple Mistake, Serious Consequences

Think back to Health Day at Denzel Jones's high school in Learning Experience 3, No Matter What Your Shape. Denzel learned that a single change in an amino acid in the hemoglobin protein can mean the difference between being healthy and having a life-threatening disease. He knew that proteins were made up of amino acid subunits. He also learned that the kind and arrangement of amino acids in a protein determine its function. But Denzel did not know how changes in a protein take place.

In the following activity, you will determine how a change or mutation in the DNA sequence that codes for hemoglobin can cause a change in the protein. In this case, the change results in sickling hemoglobin.

TASK

1. Obtain a copy from your teacher of the mRNA sequences for
   - normal hemoglobin (hemoglobin A)
   - sickling hemoglobin (hemoglobin S)
2. Draw a line under every three nucleotides. For example, your first line would be under AUG. This is the first codon. Complete for the sequence of both normal and sickling hemoglobin.
3. Determine the amino acid sequence of the protein encoded in each RNA codon. Use the codon codes in Table 2.3 (Learning Experience 5). List the amino acids in each sequence in your notebook.

ANALYSIS

Record your responses to the following in your notebook.

1. What is the difference between the mRNA sequences for normal and sickling hemoglobin? How does this affect the protein?
2. What effect does the change have on the function of the protein? (Use information from Learning Experience 3.)
3. How does this change affect the individual who carries the DNA sequence for hemoglobin S (sickling)?
4. Write the sequences for each of the strands of normal and sickling DNA. Use the two mRNA sequences as guides. What difference do you note?
5. Explain in a short paragraph the relationships among DNA, protein, and trait.

The Error of Our DNA

ACTIVITY

As you read in the article "The Wonderful Mistake" in Learning Experience 5, many errors in DNA sequence take place during the process of DNA replication. Some mutations happen because of environmental influences. (Radiation and certain chemicals can cause changes in the bases in DNA.) Most mutations occur at random or by chance. Most happen in regions that do not contain the instructions for encoding a protein. Problems only arise when an error in DNA alters the information needed to synthesize a functional protein. A mutation may involve the deletion, insertion, or duplication of a portion of a DNA molecule. It may also involve the substitution of one or more nucleotides in the molecule.

In this activity, you will alter a DNA sequence and describe how that error may affect the protein the DNA is coding for.

TASK

1. Write the following DNA sequence of a gene in your notebook:
   TACCGTCTGAAAGGT
2. Transcribe the DNA sequence into RNA. Then use Table 2.3 to translate the sequence into protein.
3. Depending on your group number, alter the DNA sequence from step 1 as follows:
   a. If your group number is 1, substitute one base for another.
   b. If your group number is 2, insert one new base.
   c. If your group number is 3, insert two new bases.
   d. If your group number is 4, insert three new bases.
   e. If your group number is 5, delete one base.
   f. If your group number is 6, delete two bases.
   g. If your group number is 7, delete three bases.
4. Transcribe the new sequence into mRNA. Then translate the resulting sequence into protein.
5. Be prepared to present to the class the results of your particular mutation. Describe what your group did, how your actions altered the amino acid sequence, and what implications this may have.

ANALYSIS

Discuss the following with your group, and record your responses in your notebook.

1. When might a change in the DNA sequence have no effect on the traits of an organism?
2. Where would a change in the DNA sequence make the greatest difference in the protein sequence?
3. The quotation at the beginning of this learning experience suggests that the DNA in our own cells undergoes an estimated 30 mutations during our lifetime. What might be the results of these mutations?
4. How do you think these changes might affect your life? Will these changes be passed on to your children? Explain your response.

Living with Gauchers Disease

Gauchers disease (pronounced go-shayz) is caused by mutations in the gene that codes for the enzyme glucocerebrosidase. This is a protein that normally breaks down a fatty substance called glucocerebroside. In the disease, the mutated glucocerebrosidase gene produces a nonfunctional enzyme. As a result, the fatty substance accumulates in the liver, spleen, and bone marrow, and on rare occasions, in the brain.

Typical symptoms of Gauchers disease include an enlarged spleen and/or liver, bone deterioration, and loss of bone density with multiple fractures and "bone crisis" (bone pain). In some patients, there is also progressive nervous system degeneration. Other symptoms include general fatigue, decreased ability to provide oxygen to the blood, disruption of kidney functions, and increased bleeding. Most people do not develop all of the possible symptoms, and the severity of the disease varies enormously.

Fewer than one in 40,000 people in the general population have Gauchers disease. The incidence is significantly higher among Jews of Eastern European descent. The higher frequency of this disease among this population has led to the mistaken notion that this disease is a "Jewish disease." In fact, individuals of any ethnic or racial background may be affected. The following story describes one person's experience with the disease.

Until recently, patient care and therapy for Gauchers disease was directed at managing (that is, relieving) the symptoms. Depending on symptoms, therapy includes the following measures, either alone or in combination: bed rest, anti-inflammatory medicines for acute pain, biofeedback techniques for pain management, hyperbaric oxygen therapy for the treatment of bone crisis, splenectomy (removal of the spleen), and oxygen therapy. None of these approaches is totally satisfactory. Spleen removal increases the susceptibility to bacterial disease and may lead to increased liver and bone symptoms.

Recently, researchers have made progress in the development of treatments that go beyond dealing with symptoms. Modified or variant glucocerebrosidase enzyme has been evaluated in clinical trials. These trials showed that repeated infusions of the enzyme reduced the signs and symptoms of the disease, and reversed the disease progression. The modified enzyme is called Ceredase. It is believed to be the first true therapeutic breakthrough. The administration of Ceredase will be required at regular intervals (usually several times a week as an infusion) throughout an individual's lifetime. Ceredase costs $150,000 a year for each patient. It would be an effective therapy for those who can get it, but not a cure for the underlying disease. (The cost is usually covered by health insurance.)

Researchers are also pursuing avenues of genetic investigations that may point to a possible cure for the disease. Efforts are underway to develop ways to introduce normal genes for glucocerebrosidase into cells of the affected person. These cells would then produce sufficient normal amounts of active glucocerebrosidase. This approach is highly experimental at present, and technical hurdles have to be overcome to demonstrate that it is safe.

SANDY'S STORY: MY SPLEEN WAS NOW ENORMOUS

Source: *Gauchers News,* September 1995 © Gauchers Association, 25 West Cottages, London, NW6 1RJ, UK.

I was diagnosed at the age of four at St. Thomas's Hospital in London after numerous blood tests and a bone marrow sample. My parents were told that it was a very rare disease and there was no cure or treatment available apart from removing my spleen if it became too enlarged. I come from a non-Jewish family of five girls—the disease was found in three of us.

Apart from nosebleeds, tiredness causing me to fall asleep in school and aching legs, it didn't present much of a problem for me until the age of 13 when I suffered what is now known as a bone crisis, but at that stage it was a mystery as nothing showed up on the X-rays. I was given 3 weeks' traction in an orthopaedic hospital. This occurred again at the age of 18 but this time 2 weeks' bed rest was the advice and it worked.

BONE MARROW TEST

I was again reviewed by the local hematologist who repeated the bone marrow test in my chest. This is not a pleasant experience and it would now appear that it is not even necessary. I was told although my spleen was enlarged, I should keep it as long as possible as evidence showed that once the spleen was gone, my bones would degenerate more rapidly.

I gave birth to my son at the age of 23 without too many problems. My spleen had enlarged quite a lot during the pregnancy but I was told that there was no reason why I should not have more children. Six weeks before the birth of my daughter, I was taken into the hospital for total bed rest as again it seemed that the pregnancy had accelerated the growth of my spleen and it was possible that it may rupture. I was now told no more children as it would be far too dangerous.

From this time on I continuously looked pregnant. I never had a waistline in the past but it was even more pronounced by my very large spleen . . .

TIME TO FIND OUT

In 1991 I decided that it was about time I found out about Gauchers disease. A friend saw an article in a national Sunday paper about a young boy who had this rare disease and was flying backwards and forwards to the USA to receive a life saving drug. She recognised the name of the disease and gave me the article.

After having the disease for all these years and meeting many different doctors who have never heard of it, apart from in their reference books, here it was in the papers, another person with Gauchers. This was my opportunity to follow it up and enquire about the treatment and see if I could be of help towards any research into it. I contacted the newspaper editor who . . . gave me the address of the National Gaucher Foundation in America who I wrote to immediately. They contacted me and asked if I would be interested in taking part in trials [that may lead to the possible cure of the disease.] . . .

 **ANALYSIS**

Record your responses to the following in your notebook.

1. Should Sandy go to America for treatment? List three reasons why she should go. Then list three reasons why she should not go.
2. If Sandy were to be part of this test, what should the doctors tell her about the treatment?
3. Should Sandy sign a permission form that says she will not sue the doctors if the treatment harms her in some way? Why or why not?
4. In a short paragraph, explain what choice you would make if you were Sandy. Include in your paragraph who should pay for the treatments you chose to get.

EXTENDING *Ideas*

Topic: Carcinogen
Go to: www.scilinks.org
Code: INBIOH2202

 Great concern is being expressed in the media about the rise in "environmentally induced" cancers. What is the role of mutagens, such as chemicals and radiation, in the environment in causing cancer? Mutagens are chemicals known to cause mutations.

Identify three mutagens that are known to be carcinogens (agents known to cause cancer). Research the relationship between carcinogens and mutagens.

CAREER FOCUS

Lobbyist   Jay is preparing for his afternoon appointment with one of his state's representatives in Congress. He is reading literature and background data about the latest legislation regarding health. More specifically, he is checking on life insurance companies' access to results of testing for genetic disorders.

Jay is a lobbyist. He was hired by a well-known insurance provider to convince members of Congress that companies dealing in life and health insurance must have access to certain health records. These companies feel that this access is necessary in order to protect themselves against high-risk consumers. They think that this extra protection will also allow them to keep rates affordable for their lower-risk customers. This then allows more people to acquire better coverage. Jay will try to meet with numerous members of Congress and pass out literature to people having political influence.

To do his job, Jay must keep one step ahead of the latest information regarding genetic testing. He needs to come across as believable and knowledgeable in the field. This may involve hours of research, and not only on genetic testing. Jay must investigate the insurance industry, general medicine, and even the running of our government. He has to be aware of all issues that might somehow affect the company he works for. One such issue is socialized medicine as practiced in areas such as Great Britain and Scandinavia. Here the governments control health insurance as well as health services.

At the same time, Christine is making similar appointments and reading similar reports. She is a lobbyist for a small special-interest group that strongly opposes genetic testing results being made available to insurance companies. Many in this group feel that some people will be unfairly penalized. Those people could be charged higher premiums because of hereditary diseases that may never appear, or they may even be turned down completely for insurance. This group is using the right to privacy as their main argument. Christine has collected data from a couple who had a genetics test for Down's syndrome on their unborn child. The child was born with only a very slight case of the syndrome. Even so, the parents have had to pay a much higher premium than is usual, a premium far above what they can afford.

Jay first learned about lobbying in his political science class in high school. He majored in political science in college, and gained most of his knowledge of genetics after being hired by the insurance company. Christine, on the other hand, has a good background in genetics from her college classes. After taking a trip to Washington, DC, during her senior year, she became interested in government and lobbying. She researched companies and nonprofit organizations that might be able to use her services. She also spent time researching the political process. It was important for her to find out who influences legislation and how different members of Congress have voted in the past on medical issues.

Jay and Christine have similar jobs, and they are interested in the same issues. But they have hopes for opposite outcomes. By informing members of Congress about issues from different perspectives, however, they help busy legislators make informed choices among complex alternatives.

A Gene for Everything and Every Gene in Its Place

Prologue

In 1820, an Augustinian monk, Gregor Mendel, theorized that traits in peas were the result of distinct, **heritable** entities he called "factors." This was long before DNA became a household word and scientists understood the biochemistry of genes. For many years, Mendel's theory of factors was disregarded and ignored. In the early 1900s, however, researchers started to pay attention. These researchers included Hugo de Vries of Holland, Carl Correns of Germany, and Erich von Tschermak of Austria. They realized that Mendel's factors could be used to explain many of their own observations about the ways in which traits were inherited in other plants.

The concept of a gene as the unit of inheritance was acknowledged at this time. But little was known about its physical nature. In 1902, Walter Sutton, a scientist at Columbia University in New York City, observed structures arranged in patterns in the nuclei of grasshopper sperm cells. He felt that these patterns could explain much of the data on the inheritance of characteristics. His discovery of these structures, called **chromosomes**, laid the foundation for fundamental research into the molecular basis of genetics. In the next two decades, the structure of chromosomes was determined.

Between 1915 and 1926, Thomas Hunt Morgan, an American zoologist, published two books, *The Mechanism of Mendelian Heredity* and *The Theory of the Gene.* In these books, he supported Mendel's idea of a gene being the unit responsible for heritable traits. He further extended the concept by concluding that all the genes of an organism existed on chromosomes. He then proposed that the patterns in which traits were inherited could be explained by how genes were connected to one another on these chromosomes.

All these scientists conducted their research prior to Watson and Crick's discovery of DNA. In this learning experience, you explore the structure of the chromosome. You will use this understanding as a start to determining the mechanisms by which traits are inherited.

Topic: Chromosomes
Go to: www.scilinks.org
Code: INBIOH2204

Discuss the following questions with your partner, and record your thinking in your notebook. Be prepared to share your ideas with the class.

1. What is a chromosome?
2. In what context have you heard the word?
3. What is the relationship between DNA and chromosomes? between genes and chromosomes?
4. Draw what you think a chromosome looks like.

DNA, DNA, Wherefore Art Thou, DNA?

What is a chromosome? What is it made of? What is the relationship of a chromosome to DNA and genes? What did Sutton see when he first made his critical observation? Looking at a chromosome under a microscope is a little like looking at a building from the street. When you view a building from the outside, you see only the external structure. You see the shape of the building, and you notice the parts that make up the outside components: windows, doors, brickwork, and decorations. A cross section of that same building would give you a very different perspective. It would reveal to you what the interior of the building was made of. You could see how it was put together and even what kind of activities were going on inside.

If you want to use a microscope to look at a chromosome that has been stained with a dye, you would see a striped, rod-shaped structure (see Figure 2.24). This first view might not tell you much about a chromosome. Like the building, you would have to look deeper to determine exactly what it was made of, how it was put together, and what kind of activities were going on.

Chromosomes are found in the nucleus of cells. They are composed of long strands of DNA tightly packed with proteins. The DNA within the chromosome is highly coiled and entwined with protein structures called **histones**. The chromosome also contains other proteins (regulatory proteins). These proteins are involved in transcribing and regulating the expression of the information in the DNA. Emerging from DNA within a chromosome is the RNA that is being transcribed from genes on the chromosome (see Figure 2.25).

Remember the stripes or banding patterns that you observed on the stained chromosome. These patterns are the result of the dyes binding to specific types of proteins. Each chromosome pair in an organism has a unique banding pattern.

In this activity, you will construct a chromosome. You will then examine the relationships among DNA, genes, and chromosomes. Read through the entire procedure before you begin.

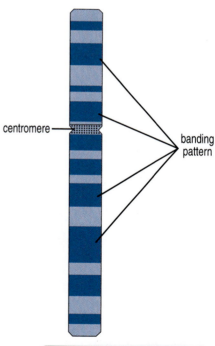

centromere —

banding pattern

Figure 2.24

Diagram of a stained chromosome as if viewed through a microscope.

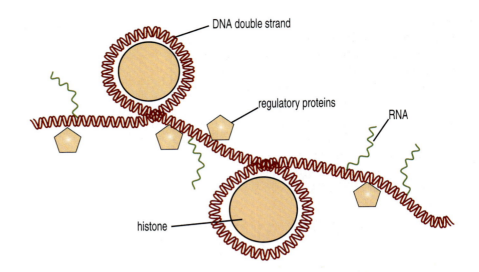

DNA double strand

regulatory proteins

RNA

histone

Materials

For each pair of students:

- 4 white or yellow pipe cleaners (also called chenille stems), 30-cm (12 in.) lengths
- 4 cotton balls
- 3 felt-tip markers (green, blue, and brown)
- string or thread, approximately 16-cm (6 in.) lengths
- cellophane tape

- 1 strip of Velcro, 5-cm (2 in.) wide
- 1 scissors
- 1 large plastic storage bag (1-gal)
- masking tape

PROCEDURE

Part A: Building the Model

1. Shape 2 white or yellow pipe cleaners to represent a double helix (double strand) of a DNA molecule. (You may recall doing this in Unit 1.) First twist the pipe cleaners together at one end to attach them. Then twist them around your index finger to make 1 turn of the helix. Move your finger down the length of the pipe cleaner, twisting as you go (see Figure 2.26). When you have used up the length of the pipe cleaner, you should have a double helix with at least 5 turns.

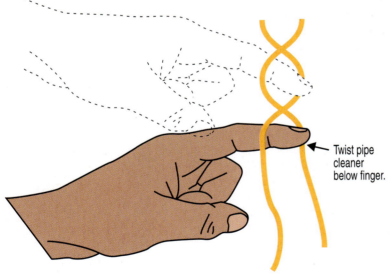

Twist pipe cleaner below finger.

Figure 2.26

Creating a model of DNA.

2. Mark the location of genes on your DNA molecule. Use different-colored felt-tip markers and Figure 2.27 as a guide. The blue and green marks represent genes whose functions have been identified. The brown marks represent genes whose functions are not known. (This will become important in the next learning experience.)

3. Place 3 or 4 cotton balls, which represent histones, along the DNA helix. Do this by twisting the pipe cleaners around the cotton balls, as DNA twists around histones (shown in Figure 2.25). You may wish to use cellophane tape to secure the histones to the DNA helix.

4. Cut the string or thread into lengths of 2 cm (about 1 in.). These threads represent RNA. Tape them onto your chromosome. Remember that mRNA is transcribed from genes. This is now your model of a chromosome because the DNA has histones attached. (Review the opening paragraphs to the activity and Figure 2.25.)

Part B: Duplicating the Chromosome

One of the major characteristics of life is the ability to reproduce or replicate. Think back to Unit 1: Learning Experience 11, The Great Divide. You will remember that before a cell divides, it must duplicate all of its chromosomes faithfully. Chromosome duplication begins with DNA replication.

1. Remove the histones and RNA from your model. (A simplified model is easier to work with.) Take 2 more pipe cleaners of the same color as your model and demonstrate how a chromosome duplicates or makes an identical copy of itself.

2. As you work through the model, draw each stage of the DNA replication process. Describe briefly the events that take place at each step. You may want to review Watson and Crick's ideas about the structure of DNA (Learning Experience 4, The Language of Heredity). You may also want to review what you learned about mitosis and chromosome replication in Unit 1: Learning Experience 11, The Great Divide.

3. **STOP & THINK** You learned in Unit 1 that during mitosis it is essential that each daughter cell receives all the information contained in the DNA of the original cell. How does this relate to DNA replication? Why is that important?

4. Mark the location of the genes on your replicated DNA molecules. Use the appropriate-colored felt-tip marker. Remember, the new DNA molecules are identical copies of the original DNA molecules.

5. Draw a diagram of your replicated DNA molecules. Label all the important parts of each molecule.

6. **STOP & THINK** DNA replication is usually accurate and produces identical copies of the original DNA. But sometimes mistakes happen. Think about what you learned in the previous learning experience and about your understanding of DNA replication. Explain what could happen during replication to produce a mutation.

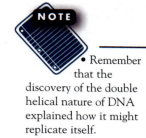

- Remember that the discovery of the double helical nature of DNA explained how it might replicate itself.
- Remember what the end result of replication must be.

SAFETY NOTE

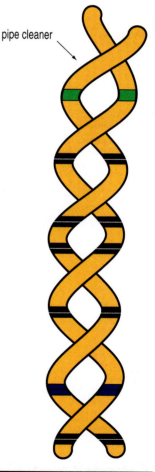

pipe cleaner

Figure 2.27
Placement of genes on chromosome.

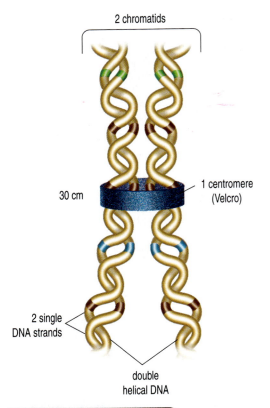

2 chromatids

30 cm

1 centromere
(Velcro)

2 single
DNA strands

double
helical DNA

Figure 2.28
A duplicated chromosome.

7. The 2 double-stranded DNA helices of a single chromosome are attached at a region called a **centromere**. The centromere is located at different places on different chromosomes. Each double-stranded DNA is called a **chromatid**. Wrap the Velcro strip around each chromatid so that the hook portion wraps around one chromatid and the latch portion wraps around the other chromatid. This represents a centromere. Attach the chromatids by sticking the Velcro strips together (see Figure 2.28). Add cotton balls to represent the histones. You now have a chromosome that has *duplicated* itself.

8. **STOP & THINK** How many centromeres and chromatids are represented on your chromosome? Label them on your diagram. Indicate in your drawing of the replicated DNA molecules where the histones and RNA would be on your chromosome. Explain the difference between DNA replication and chromosome duplication.

9. Place a piece of masking tape on a plastic bag. With a felttip marker, label the bag with your names. Place your model in the plastic bag for use in Learning Experience 8, Legacy of Heredity.

ACTIVITY

Characterizing Chromosomes

By the 1920s, the concept of the chromosome was well accepted. But direct examination of chromosomes was not easy. The available dyes and stains did not reveal much detail. Even locating and counting the chromosomes in a cell was chancy at best. Geneticists were not certain about the number of chromosomes in human cells.

In 1956, two geneticists developed a simple and reliable procedure that allowed us to see an organism's chromosomes. At that time, we knew that when cells were in the quiescent or nondividing state, chromosomes are spread out and diffuse. In fact, chromosomes seem to disappear in nondividing cells. During cell division, however, they form discrete structures within the cell. Geneticists Joe Hin Tijo and Albert Levan took advantage of this understanding. They created a method for "catching chromosomes." They did this when the DNA was tightly coiled and the chromosomes were most organized or condensed. Tijo and Levan treated human cells with a drug to stop cell division at that point. Using pressure to squash the cells, they spread them across a glass microscope slide. They stained the cells to make the chromosomes more visible. The researchers then photographed the chromosomes through the microscope. The final step was to clip each chromosomal image from the photograph, sort the images according to length, pair any matching sets of chromosomes, and paste them into a composite known as a **karyotype**.

Using this approach, Tijo and Levan were able to settle once and for all the matter of how many chromosomes were in a human cell. We now know that there are 46 chromosomes in a human cell. In addition, Tijo and Levan confirmed for humans an observation made by Walter Sutton in grasshoppers in 1902. In most cells, chromosomes come in matched pairs. That is, humans have 23 pairs of distinctly different chromosomes.

Investigations into a wide variety of organisms have found that most (but not all) organisms are **diploid**. This means that most of their cells carry two copies of each chromosome. We know that the number of chromosomes in different organisms varies widely (see Table 2.4). But nearly every cell in a specific type of organism has the same set of chromosomes as every other cell.

In this activity, you will identify all the important features in a human karyotype.

Table 2.4	Number of Chromosomes in Various Species
Species	**Number**
alligator	32
amoeba	50
carrot	18
chicken	78
chimpanzee	48
corn	20
earthworm	36
fruit fly	8
garden pea	14
goldfish	94
grasshopper	24
horse	64
human	46
sand dollar	52

Materials

For each student:

- 1 sheet of plain white paper

For each pair of students:

- 1 *Human Karyotype* sheet
- 2 scissors
- 1 glue stick or cellophane tape

PROCEDURE

1. Obtain from your teacher a sheet with 1 example of a human karyotype. Carefully examine the karyotype. Note the banding patterns and any other distinctive features that you can identify on the chromosomes.

2. Cut out each chromosome. Match the pairs based on their identifying features.
3. Glue or tape the pairs in rows on a new sheet of paper. Start with the longest chromosome pair, and arrange them by size to the shortest. Number your chromosome pairs; start with 1 for the longest pair.

ANALYSIS

Record your responses to the following in your notebook.

1. Describe several features that all the chromosomes in the karyotype have in common.
2. Describe the features of chromosomes that helped you to identify the matching pairs.
3. Did every chromosome have a match? If not, why do you think this is so?
4. This karyotype was made from the cells of a 14-year-old person. Will a karyotype look any different when this person is 60 years old? Explain your answer.
5. How many copies of the gene for hemoglobin does Denzel have (Learning Experience 3)? Base your answer on your understanding of chromosomes and sickle cell. Explain your response.

ACTIVITY

Reading the Future? Analyzing Chromosomes and Explaining the Consequences

Is knowing what the future holds for you a good thing? What about knowing the future of the children you may have one day? What would you like to know about your future if you could? Some people would like to know who their friends and partners might be. Others might want to know what kind of jobs they will hold or whether they will have money. Still others would like to know whether they will have good health.

There is no way to predict one's love life or financial status. But chromosome and DNA analysis have opened up the possibilities of predicting, to some degree, a person's likely future health problems. A genetic counselor is a person who analyzes this information and helps individuals understand the science behind the analysis. He or she also explains the complex implications of the results, including possible choices and outcomes.

Information about an individual's biological prospects is encoded in his or her DNA. An individual whose family has a history of a certain disorder might wish to know whether the information for this disorder is encoded in his or her genetic makeup. In Learning Experience 3, for example, Denzel Jones wanted to know whether he carried the sickling hemoglobin. One way to check for this is to have a test that checks for the variant protein. That's what Denzel did. Another option open to Denzel was to have his DNA analyzed. In this case, the DNA in Denzel's blood would have been isolated and then examined for the single base change that results in the sickling hemoglobin.

Using a karyotype is another way to determine whether a person has a predisposition toward a genetic disease. In his investigations of fruit flies, T. H. Morgan observed that certain changes in the characteristics of organisms correlated with specific changes in chromosome structure or number. Today, many genetic diseases have been correlated with changes in chromosomes that can be identified through karyotyping. Such changes may include a deletion of part of the chromosome or the addition of an extra chromosome (a **trisomy**). A part of one chromosome also may be exchanged with or added to another chromosome (a **translocation**).

Individuals may elect to have genetic testing done if there is a history of genetic abnormalities in their family. Since all cells in an organism (except red blood cells) have the same set of chromosomes, any cell sample can be used for a karyotype. (Red blood cells lack nuclei.) Normally, white blood cells are used. They are easy to collect, and good karyotypes can be obtained from them.

Expectant parents may wish to acquire information about their future child. This is especially true if they have reason to believe that the child might someday develop a disorder. (Their concern may come from family history or the birth of other children with inherited disorders.) In this case, samples are taken from the area of the developing fetus. They come from either the fluid surrounding the fetus (the **amniotic fluid**) or from one of the membranes (**chorion**) surrounding the fetus. These samples contain fetal cells. The fetal cells can be used to create a karyotype of the developing fetus. Technicians then examine the karyotype for **chromosomal aberrations** that might result in disorders in physical and mental characteristics of the child. The fetal cells can also be tested for disorders that result from mutations in the DNA. These are disorders such as sickle-cell anemia, cystic fibrosis, and Huntington's disease.

The role of the genetic counselor is to present the results of genetic analysis to individuals who have undergone testing. The counselor provides information in careful, clear, nonjudgmental, and informative terms. This helps individuals who are confronted with possible indicators of their own or their baby's future health to make well-informed personal decisions.

In this activity, you will assume the role of a genetic counselor. The expectant parents have had prenatal testing done on their developing fetus because the mother is over age 40. They know that the probability of chromosomal aberrations goes up with increased age. The results have come in. Your job is to determine, based on the karyotype, whether there is a problem. Generally, a genetic counselor would give the parents the information in person. But for this activity, you will write them a letter.

Materials

For each pair of students:

- 1 *Karyotype Placement Grid*
- 1 chromosome smear
- 2 scissors
- 1 glue stick or cellophane tape

PROCEDURE

1. Obtain from your teacher your "photograph" of a chromosome smear and a copy of the *Karyotype Placement Grid*.

2. Cut out the chromosomes from the chromosome smear. Arrange them in pairs to create a karyotype on the *Karyotype Placement Grid*. Use the normal karyotype you constructed as a guide to match and arrange your chromosome pairs. Use their banding patterns and sizes.

3. Write the number of your chromosome smear on the top of your *Karyotype Placement Grid*. Glue or tape your chromosomes to the appropriate place on the sheet.

4. You may wish to determine the sex of the fetus. (But remember, not all parents want to know ahead of time whether they will have a boy or a girl.)

5. Your teacher will hand you a sheet titled *Information on Chromosome Disorders*. Determine whether the karyotype is normal or has any errors. If an error is apparent, identify the problem.

6. Discuss with your partner the presentation you will make to the class on your karyotype, the disorder, and its possible consequences.

7. Write a letter to the parents of the fetus that includes the following:

   a. a basic introduction to chromosomes in which you describe what they are;

   b. what information the DNA in the chromosome carries;

   c. how this information is transferred into protein;

   d. why functional proteins are important, and what role they play for living things;

   e. why an error in the DNA or chromosome number or structure can result in variants in traits that can cause problems to the organism;

   f. how the karyotype was done;

   g. what information the karyotype can give;

   h. what the results of their fetus's karyotype have shown; and

   i. if the results show a problem, how this problem might manifest itself in a child carrying this genetic makeup.

Conclude your letter by inviting the parents to come see you. Explain that you would like to discuss what alternatives they have and the personal decisions they might make in light of the results. Remember, your letter must be clear, explain things simply yet completely, and be sensitive to the parents.

EXTENDING *Ideas*

● Why Y? Why does the presence of the Y chromosome result in maleness in mammals? Scientists used to think that the male chromosome originally had many genes in common with the X chromosome (the other sex chromosome). But they thought that in the course of evolution, the Y began to lose many of its genes, and in a sense, degenerate. Recent studies, however, present another, more "macho" possibility. Researchers have found evidence that the Y chromosome may actually be a refuge for genes that are beneficial to male fitness and fertility (J. Travis, "The Y Copies Another Chromosome's Genes," *Science News,* November 16, 1996). Research the data for each of these theories and describe the evidence. Explain whether one theory is more convincing than the other and why you think this.

● During the Olympic games in 1994, women competitors received gender verification cards when they passed a sex test. This test was required of all women athletes to authenticate the fact that they were actually women, not men masquerading as women. Karyotyping is done when there is a question of sexual identity. If any Y chromosomes are present, the athlete is declared ineligible to compete in women's events. The rationale behind the testing is that maleness, as indicated by the presence of a Y chromosome, indicates the presence of androgens. Androgens are hormones that cause an increase in muscle mass and strength. Many individuals have protested that sex testing is unethical and may not be a true indicator of sex. Find out about sex testing and the controversy surrounding it. Decide whether you think it is a valid determination of sex. Do you think sex testing is ethical? Explain your thinking.

CAREER FOCUS

Genetic Counselor   Jeanine and Richard Jensen have been married for 6 years. They had always planned on having a large family. Three years ago they were blessed with the birth of their daughter Michelle. Michelle seemed perfectly normal at birth. But after being home for a few weeks, Jeanine noticed that Michelle had stopped gaining weight and was coughing up large amounts of mucus. They brought Michelle in for a full physical. After some tests, she was diagnosed with cystic fibrosis (CF). CF is a genetic disease whose symptoms include the malfunction of the pancreas, and frequent lung infections.

Michelle was very sick. Jeanine and Richard were heartbroken, but they were also relatively lucky. With daily medication and a special diet, Michelle has been able to survive for 3 years and there is hope for a long future. But the Jensens are concerned about the possibility that a second child could be born with the same condition. They love Michelle. But they do not want to submit another child to the trials of CF even though the outlook for curing and for alleviating symptoms for the genetic disease seems brighter.

Jeanine and Richard made an appointment to see Maya Mani, a genetic counselor with the local medical center. Maya sat down with the Jensens to help them consider the possible consequences of having another child. CF is a recessive gene. That means that both parents are carriers. The chances that one of their children would be born with the disease is one in four. Maya helped the Jensens discuss their fears and their hopes. The presence of CF in a fetus can be detected by a genetic test during pregnancy. Should the Jensens decide to get pregnant, they had the option of this test. But a positive result could create great distress and bring about other decisions that would have to be made.

As a genetic counselor, Maya spends most of her time working with individuals and families. These are usually people with a family history of disease. Some families contact her to find out if a particular disease is genetic. If it is, they ask Maya if they will be able to have healthy children. Others see her after finding out that they are destined to develop a disease, such as Huntington's disease. Huntington's is a disabling condition of the nervous system that does not usually develop until later in adulthood. Maya is there to help people make critical decisions in their lives. She ensures that people with little or no scientific background can make informed decisions as they are offered their first glimpse of DNA.

While in high school, Maya knew she wanted to work with people and she had a love of medicine. After going to college to major in biology, she was introduced to the science of genetics and found it very exciting. She soon learned that genetic counseling would combine her two interests. After graduating from a master's program in genetic counseling, Maya went on to work in a medical center known for its expertise in this field. Genetic counselors are presently in high demand. They can be found on the staffs of universities, and in state offices, departments of social services, and bureaus of maternal and child health. They are employed in nursing homes, large hospitals, and many other institutions.

The Jensens decided to try to have another baby after their counseling sessions with Maya Mani. They also made the decision to forgo any further testing. But Maya was one of the first people they contacted with the good news of a healthy baby boy!

Learning Experience 8

Legacy of Heredity

Prologue

Sex. What's it all about? Contrary to movies, the news, the Internet, and most popular opinion, the main purpose of sex (biologically speaking) is to produce offspring for the continuation of the species. To achieve that result, animals use sexual reproduction. But they also have evolved elaborate behaviors, such as courtship displays, fighting for mates, and sending candy and flowers on Valentine's Day. Why is all of that necessary? Many single-celled organisms can reproduce with incredible speed and little fuss by simple cell division (**asexual reproduction**). A single bacterium can give rise to billions of cells in a few days—cells that are genetically identical to it. As well as being speedy, this form of reproduction is very efficient. Even the most isolated cell can reproduce.

So why do organisms invest so much time, effort, and physical and even mental energy to reproduce sexually? Why has sex evolved? Several theories exist. The cells specialized for reproduction (sex cells or **gametes**) are the link to the future. Gametes pass information stored in their DNA from one generation to the next. As you saw in Learning Experience 6, mutations in the sequence of DNA sometimes happen. Gametes are endowed with mechanisms that enable them to repair many of these mutations more efficiently than other cells can. Reproducing through sex cells rather than by cell division is one way to ensure that random errors are passed on to offspring less frequently.

Another explanation for the evolution of sexual reproduction is that this kind of reproduction allows for much greater variation in the characteristics of the offspring. The progeny of organisms that reproduce by asexual reproduction are almost identical to the parent (with a few mutations here and there). The progeny of sexually reproducing organisms, however, show both variation from the parents and diversity among siblings.

In this learning experience, you explore the processes by which information in chromosomes is passed from parent to progeny during sexual reproduction. You determine how this process can result in variation.

Brainstorming

Discuss the following questions with your partner, and record your thinking in your notebook. Be prepared to share your ideas with the class.

1. In the previous learning experiences, you explored the relationships among DNA, genes, chromosomes, and traits. You learned that children inherit traits carried on chromosomes from their parents. How do you think the chromosomes are passed on from parent to child?
2. What kinds of aberrations or changes did you observe as you analyzed your karyotype in Learning Experience 7?
3. Do you think that you would be able to see a mutation in the DNA sequence in a karyotype?
4. How do you think chromosomal errors happen?

In the next few sessions, you will explore the processes by which the information for traits is passed on from generation to generation. You will see the ways variation among siblings can happen.

Task

Your teacher will return the chromosome you and your partner built in Learning Experience 7. Partner with another pair of students who made a different color chromosome than you. In a group of four, you should have one yellow chromosome and one white chromosome. The two chromosomes together represent the chromosomes in every cell of a mythical mosquito. One chromosome comes from the "father" or **paternal** parent of this mosquito. The other chromosome comes from the "mother" or **maternal** parent.

Review the parts of the chromosome with your group. Then record your responses to the following in your notebook:

1. How many double-stranded DNA molecules are in each chromatid?
2. How many double-stranded DNA molecules are in each chromosome?
3. What do the blue, green, and brown marks represent?
4. Are the marks on the maternal chromosome in the same place as the marks on the paternal chromosome? Why or why not?
5. Assume the yellow chromosome is from the father and the white chromosome is from the mother. In what way are they the same? How are they different?

READING

The Cells of Genetic Continuity

What, exactly, do we get from our parents? And how does it get from them to us? The legacy given to us by our parents is their chromosomes. Their chromosomes come to us packaged in their gametes. To understand sexual reproduction, we need to explore where gametes originate, how they develop, and what their purpose is.

During development of an organism, cells take on special functions in addition to their "housekeeping" functions of metabolism. Muscle cells make proteins that enable the cells to expand and contract. Brain cells make proteins that enable them to communicate by chemical and electrical interactions. Similarly, certain cells in the reproductive organs (ovaries or testes) become sex cells and develop the capacity to carry out the reproductive functions. Males develop sperm cells; females develop egg cells. Within these cells is all the information needed to create the next generation.

What do these sperm and egg cells look like? How do they form? All human body cells, except sex cells, contain 46 chromosomes. **Meiosis** is the process that produces sex cells. This process reduces the chromosome number to half.

The female reproductive cell (**ovum** or egg) develops by a process called **oogenesis**. At birth, a human female contains about 400,000 primary **oocytes** in her ovary. These oocytes contain 46 chromosomes (the diploid or full chromosome number) or 23 pairs. This is the same number of chromosomes as every other cell in the body. Maturation of the primary oocyte involves several steps as illustrated in Figure 2.29. First, the chromosomes (Figure 2.29a) duplicate; they form two chromatids in each chromosome (Figure 2.29b). The cell now contains a complete set of paired or homologous chromosomes. Next, the chromosomes separate, and the oocyte divides. This results in two cells; each cell contains one complete set of unpaired chromosomes (Figure 2.29c). The cytoplasm of the oocyte is distributed unequally. This results in one large cell and one smaller cell. Now, the two chromatids of each chromosome separate and cell division takes place. This results in three small cells and one large cell; each cell contains one set of unpaired chromosomes (Figure 2.29d). In the final step,

Topic: Meiosis
Go to: www.scilinks.org
Code: INBIOH2217

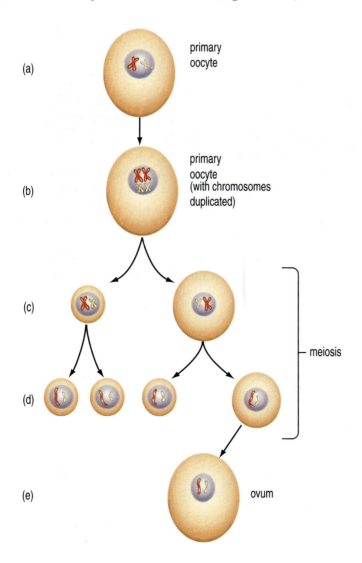

(a) primary oocyte

(b) primary oocyte (with chromosomes duplicated)

(c)

meiosis

(d)

(e) ovum

Figure 2.29

During oogenesis, eggs mature in the ovary of the female. Primary oocytes, which contain 46 chromosomes, undergo meiosis to produce ova or mature eggs. (Only four out of 46 chromosomes are shown.)

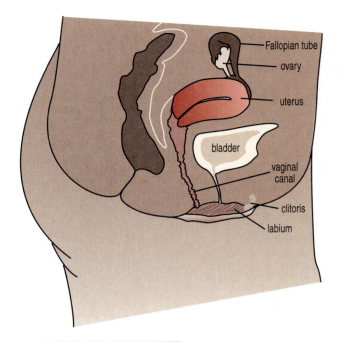

Figure 2.30

Once a month, an egg makes its way from the ovary through the Fallopian tube to the uterus.

the large cell matures to become the ovum or egg. It contains one copy of each chromosome of the woman and is ready to be fertilized by the sperm (Figure 2.29e). Thus, during maturation of the egg the chromosome number is reduced from 46 to 23. This is the **haploid** number.

At monthly intervals after puberty, one egg is released from the **ovary** (**ovulation**) and makes its way down the **Fallopian tube** to the **uterus** (see Figure 2.30). If the egg is fertilized, it will attach to the uterine wall and develop. Otherwise, it will travel down the vaginal canal and be released in the monthly menses (**menstruation**). During a woman's reproductive life, approximately 400 eggs will make this journey.

A similar process of chromosome reduction or meiosis takes place during sperm development or **spermatogenesis**. The primary **spermatocyte** also has 46 chromosomes. Development takes place in the male sex organ, the **testis**, and involves several steps as shown in Figure 2.31. First, the chromosomes (Figure 2.31a) duplicate; they form two chromatids in each chromosome (Figure 2.31b). The cell now contains a complete set of paired or homologous chromosomes. Next, the chromosomes separate, and the spermatocyte divides. This results in two cells; each cell contains one complete set of unpaired chromosomes (Figure 2.31c). Now, the two chromatids of each chromosome separate and cell division takes place. This results in four cells; each cell contains one set of unpaired chromosomes (Figure 2.31d). In the final step, these cells mature to become the sperm. Each sperm contains a complete set of unpaired chromosomes (23) of the man, a compacted head, and a long powerful **flagellum** (tail) that enables the sperm to move (Figure 2.31e).

In the female, only one mature egg is produced for each oocyte. But a primary spermatocyte will produce four mature sperm. After maturation is complete, sperm leave the testes and travel through a system of ducts or tubules. These ducts produce fluids to help move the sperm to the opening of the penis where they are released (see Figure 2.32). After puberty, males continually produce vast numbers of sperm—approximately 200 million per day.

When egg and sperm meet and fuse in the process called fertilization, a new kind of cell is formed. This cell is called a **zygote**. The zygote contains a full complement of 46 chromosomes. It is the starting place for the development of a complex, multicellular organism.

ANALYSIS

Record your responses to the following in your notebook.

1. Compare and contrast oogenesis and spermatogenesis. Do this in chart form or in a labeled diagram.
2. Do you think each of the four resulting gametes gets an identical set of 23 chromosomes? Why or why not?
3. What would be the result if meiosis did not take place?
4. Fertilization is the joining of the male and female gametes. Draw or describe the chromosomal composition that results from this union. Why is this result important? (If you draw your zygote, use different colors for the chromosomes from the sperm and the egg.)

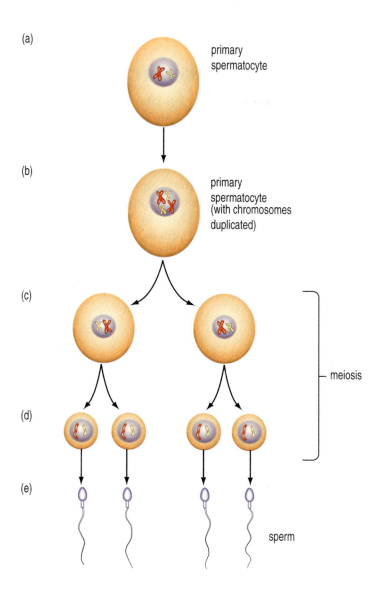

(a) primary spermatocyte

(b) primary spermatocyte (with chromosomes duplicated)

(c)

(d)

meiosis

(e)

sperm

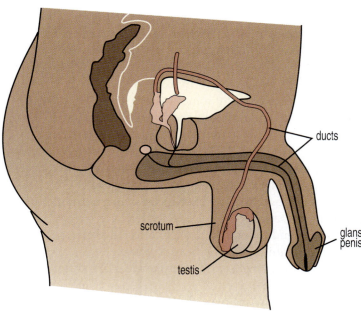

ducts

scrotum

testis

glans penis

Dance of the Chromosomes

The process of meiosis has been referred to as "the dance of the chromosomes." This is because of the way the chromosomes move and sort. The movement of chromosomes has also been compared to marionettes dancing and moving on strings.

In this activity, you will revisit the mythical mosquito and build two more sets of chromosome models to complete its chromosomal makeup. A karyotype of this mosquito has revealed that it has three pairs of chromosomes. (This is the normal number of chromosomes for mosquitoes.) After building your models, you will demonstrate the process of meiosis and determine which genes will be in the mosquito gametes. The genes that an organism has are called its **genotype**. From the genotype, you will determine the phenotype of these offspring. A **phenotype** is what an organism looks like as a result of the expression of the genes.

Materials

For each group of four students:

- 2 models of chromosomes (1 white and 1 yellow, 30-cm lengths) with 2 chromatids (from Learning Experience 7)
- 16 pipe cleaners
  - 4 yellow and 4 white (22-cm lengths)
  - 4 yellow and 4 white (15-cm lengths)
- 3 felt-tip markers (red, black, and brown)
- 4 strips of Velcro, 5-cm (2 in.) lengths
- masking tape
- 1 coin
- 1 large plastic storage bag (1-gal)

PROCEDURE

Part A

For this activity, you do not need to add histones, other proteins, or the RNA. But be sure to keep in mind that these are always present.

1. Gather all the materials for your group. (Your group will consist of 1 pair of students that constructed a yellow chromosome and 1 pair of students that constructed a white chromosome.)
2. Place your group's yellow and white chromosomes from Learning Experience 7 on the table.
3. Construct 4 duplicated chromosomes (as you did in Learning Experience 7). Use Figure 2.33 as a guide. Build 2 models that are 22 cm long (Figure 2.33b: 1 white and 1 yellow). Build another 2 models that are 15 cm long (Figure 2.33c: 1 white and 1 yellow). Each chromosome model should
   - consist of 2 intertwined pipe cleaners (the pipe cleaners represent the double-helical DNA molecule of each chromatid);
   - be either yellow or white (white indicates chromosomes from the mother; yellow from the father);
   - have colored bands drawn on the DNA to represent specific genes (use Figure 2.33 as a guide to gene location); and
   - be surrounded by a single centromere made of 2 loops of Velcro (2 loops equals 1 centromere).

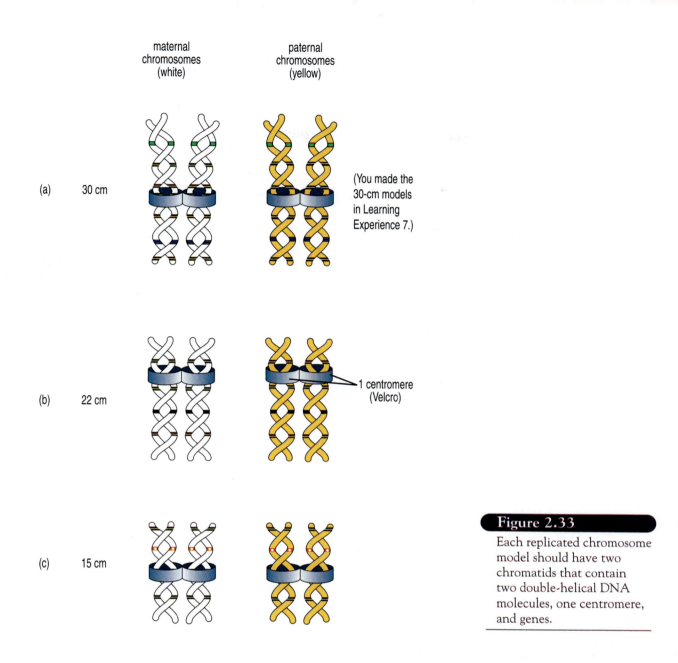

maternal chromosomes (white)

paternal chromosomes (yellow)

(a) 30 cm

(You made the 30-cm models in Learning Experience 7.)

(b) 22 cm

1 centromere (Velcro)

(c) 15 cm

Figure 2.33

Each replicated chromosome model should have two chromatids that contain two double-helical DNA molecules, one centromere, and genes.

4. Genetic studies of this mythical mosquito have identified 4 genes that are responsible for 4 of its traits. Use Figure 2.33 to mark the 2 remaining genes on the 22- and 15-cm chromosomes. Remember, the function of the brown genes is unknown.

Part B

Your group now has 6 mosquito chromosome models. These models represent 3 pairs of homologous chromosomes. **Homologous chromosomes** are chromosomes that have genes for the same trait at the same location. We also have 3 maternal and 3 paternal sets. Genes that code for the same trait on the

Table 2.5 Information Summary: Traits of the Mosquitoes

Trait	Phenotype	Symbol for Allele	Band Color	Chromosome (cm)
antenna texture	hairy smooth	H h	red	15
wing shape	round square	R r	green	30
wing length	long short	L l	black	22
abdomen color	black orange	B b	blue	30
unknown	not available	not available	brown	on all chromosomes

chromosomes from the mother and the father are called **alleles**. Each chromosome pair contains 1 or 2 genes whose traits are known and several genes whose functions are not known. This information is described below and summarized in Table 2.5.

- Red bands represent the genes that encode a protein responsible for antenna texture. This can be either hairy (represented by an *H*) or smooth (represented by an *h*).
- Green bands represent the genes that encode a protein that determines wing shape. Round is *R*; square is *r*.
- Black bands represent the genes that encode a protein that determines wing length. Long is *L*; short is *l*.
- Blue bands represent the genes that encode a protein that determines abdomen color. Black is *B*; orange is *b*.
- The brown bands indicate other genes on the DNA. These genes encode functions that are either unknown or not of interest in this study.

Table 2.5 provides a summary of the traits, the 2 possible phenotypes of the alleles, the symbol for each different allele, the band color that represents that trait, and on which chromosome it is located.

The labeling of the genes in this activity reflects the convention used by geneticists. The uppercase letter represents the dominant trait; the lowercase letter represents the recessive trait. (For example, in peas, the gene for the trait of pea shape can be *R* for round. This means it encodes a functional SBEI. Or it can be *r* for wrinkled, meaning the gene encodes a faulty or nonfunctional SBEI.) An allele is a different form or variant of a gene for a specific trait. For example, the gene for shape has two alleles. One allele results in wrinkled shape and the other allele results in round shape.

In this activity, each gene has 2 possible alleles. You will determine which allele is present on the chromosome by flipping a coin. To assign the allele of your 4 genes, your group must make a total of 8 coin flips. Both chromatids on a chromosome will have an identical allele.

Part C

1. Locate the red bands on your white 15-cm chromosomes. These bands represent the allele *H* or *h*.
2. Flip the coin once for the white 15-cm chromosome. If the coin lands on heads, write the letter *H* on 2 small pieces of masking tape. Attach the tapes to the red bands on the 2 chromatids of this chromosome. If the coin lands on tails, write the letter *h* on 2 pieces of masking tape and attach to the red bands on the 2 chromatids.
3. Flip the coin a second time for the yellow 15-cm chromosome. Label the alleles (*H* or *h*) as described in step 2.
4. Repeat steps 1–3 to determine the allele on each chromosome for the 3 other traits. These are wing shape (*R* or *r*), wing length (*L* or *l*), and abdomen color (*B* or *b*). Use Table 2.5 as a reference for gene location.
5. **STOP & THINK** Your group now has alleles for each of the 4 known genes on your 6 mosquito chromosomes. These alleles represent the genotype of your mosquito. Figure 2.34 shows an example of one possible result of the coin flips. The genotype for this mosquito is listed in the caption. Record the genotype of your mosquito in your notebook. Use this example as a guide.
6. **STOP & THINK** Record in your notebook all the parts of the 6 chromosome models. Describe or label diagrams where appropriate. Include the following:
   a. what each different color chromosome represents,
   b. why there are 2 chromatids in each of the chromosomes,
   c. what *R* and *r* represent,
   d. the relationship between *H* and hairy antennae,

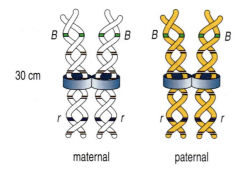

30 cm

maternal   paternal

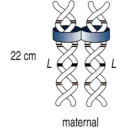  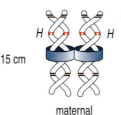 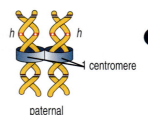

22 cm

15 cm

centromere

maternal   paternal   maternal   paternal

Figure 2.34

One possible mosquito genotype resulting from the coin flips. The genotype for this mosquito would be *BB, rr, Ll, Hh*.

e. why the alleles for each gene in each chromatid are identical within the same chromosome,

f. why the alleles in the homologous chromosomes might be different, and

g. what the difference is between an organism's genotype and its phenotype.

7. At the end of this activity, store your models in the bags for use in the next activity.

Simulating the Stages of Meiosis

In this activity, you will model the events that take place in sex cells as your mosquito becomes sexually mature. The chromosomes you have built are found in the primary oocytes or primary spermatocytes. Recall from your reading that when an organism matures sexually, its gametes or sex cells develop from their precursor cells—oocytes or spermatocytes—into eggs or sperm. They do this through the process of meiosis. In this activity, you will examine how the chromosomes move and sort themselves. Table 2.6 describes and illustrates each stage of meiosis. Use the table as a reference to help you model the process of meiosis.

Materials

For each group of four students:

- 6 complete chromosome models from Dance of the Chromosomes
- 1 piece of yarn, 6–8 m (20–26 ft)
- 1 scissors
- 1 measuring tape or meterstick

PROCEDURE

Part A: Meiosis I

1. Cut 3 pieces of yarn. Make 2 pieces 1 m long and the other piece 2 m long. Use the larger piece to form a circle on a tabletop. This represents the cell membrane of your sex cell. Use 1 smaller piece to form a circle within the large circle. This represents the nuclear membrane.

2. Be sure the chromatids in each chromosome are joined by their Velcro centromere. Then place all of your chromosomes anywhere within the inner circle. This represents the beginning of meiosis. At this stage, the chromosomes have duplicated and formed chromatids (Table 2.6, row A).

3. Pair each chromosome with its homologous chromosome (same size, same genes). Remove the inner circle. The nuclear membrane breaks down at this point in meiosis (row B).

4. Place your chromosomes in a straight line within the cell (row C).

5. Separate your homologous chromosome pairs into 2 rows. Each row consists of 1 each of the different chromosomes. Move the rows apart to opposite sides of the cell (row D).

6. At this point, a new cell membrane is formed (row E). Two daughter cells result. Model this by cutting the outer yarn (cell membrane) in half. Close each half around 1 set of 3 chromosomes. (You may wish to attach additional pieces of yarn to enlarge each cell membrane. This represents growth.) Place an inner circle of yarn (nuclear membrane) around each of the 2 newly formed nuclei in the daughter cells. During this stage, the chromosomes become less visible (row F).

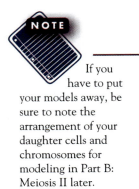

NOTE

If you have to put your models away, be sure to note the arrangement of your daughter cells and chromosomes for modeling in Part B: Meiosis II later.

ANALYSIS

Record your responses to the following in your notebook.

1. Describe in your own words the events of this first meiotic division. Explain how the chromosomes from each parent have been distributed.
2. What other chromosomal patterns might have resulted in the daughter cells? (You may wish to move your model pieces around to help illustrate the possibilities.)
3. How many chromosomes does each daughter cell have at the end of meiosis I? What helped you determine that number?
4. How many alleles for each trait does each daughter cell have?

PROCEDURE

Part B: Meiosis II

1. At the end of meiosis I, 2 complete daughter cells have formed (Table 2.6, row F). At this stage, chromosomes condense and become visible again (row G). Remove the inner circle of yarn. (The nuclear membrane breaks down.) Line up the 3 chromosomes vertically in the middle of each cell within your 2 daughter cells (row H).
2. Within each cell, separate the chromatids by detaching the Velcro. Move the separated chromatids away from the middle, toward opposite sides of the cell (row I).
3. Use your pieces of yarn to represent cell membranes that form as each cell divides. A total of 4 gametes have formed from each of the starting sex cells. Each gamete contains 1 copy of each chromatid, which now looks like a chromosome (rows J and K). The nuclear membrane re-forms. Use more yarn to represent the daughter cells.
4. Store your models in a bag for use in the next session.

ANALYSIS

Record your responses to the following in your notebook.

1. Describe in your own words what has taken place in meiosis II. Indicate which chromosome came from which parent in each of the resulting cells.
2. What is the difference between the starting cell and the cells at the end of meiosis I? (The starting cell is the primary spermatocyte or oocyte.) What is the difference between the cells at the end of meiosis I and the cells at the end of meiosis II?
3. What other maternal and paternal chromosomal combinations might have resulted?
4. Write the genotype of each of the four gametes in your group's model. Use the symbols for the alleles for each chromosome.

Table 2.6 Stages of Meiosis

Stages of Meiosis I

A	The oocytes or spermatocytes (precursors to the gametes) have undergone mitosis (cell division) and are ready to mature. In the mosquito cell, there are six chromosomes (or three pairs). At this point, the DNA within the chromosomes has replicated (or doubled). Each chromosome has two double-helical DNA molecules (called chromatids). These molecules are joined together by a centromere. The nuclear membrane begins to break down. This stage is called interphase I.	
B	The homologous pairs of chromosomes line up and spindle fibers start to form. (Spindle fibers are protein structures in the cell that guide the chromosomes around the cell.) This stage is called prophase I.	
C	The pairs of chromosomes align along the equatorial plane of the cell. This stage is called metaphase I. Each different-length pair consists of two homologous chromosomes (four chromatids).	
D	During anaphase I, the chromosomes move away from the center of the cell.	
E	When the chromosomes reach the edges of the cell, the cell begins to divide. It forms two daughter cells. Each cell has one copy of each chromosome. This stage is called telophase I.	
F	Cell division is complete. The nuclear membrane reforms, and the chromosomes become less discrete in the cell. This stage is called interphase II.	

G	In each of the two cells formed at the end of Meiosis I, chromosomes condense into discrete units and spindle fibers form. This is prophase II.	
H	During metaphase II, chromosomes line up along the center of the cell.	
I	The attachment between the two chromatids of each chromosome breaks. Chromatids move away from each other along the spindle. This phase is called anaphase II.	
J	In telophase II, cell division begins. Two new daughter cells—gametes—form.	
K	Cell division (**cytokinesis**) is complete. The nuclear membrane re-forms. Proteins associate with the chromatids to form new chromosomes. Chromosomes become less discrete.	

The Mating Game

When fertilization takes place, gametes fuse and the genes from two individuals join. It is this new combination of genes that results in the formation of a unique individual—be it an insect, animal, or plant.

Fertilization in humans takes place in the Fallopian tube. Males release millions of sperm into the vaginal canal of the female. These sperm squirm and thrash their way through the uterus and enter the Fallopian tube. Here they encounter a mature egg that has been released from the ovary. Sperm compete to donate DNA to the female egg. Millions of sperm surround the egg, which is approximately 75,000 times larger than a sperm cell. But only one sperm may bind, penetrate, and insert its DNA into the egg (Figure 2.35). The fertilized egg (or zygote) continues its journey through the Fallopian tube to the uterus; eventually, it attaches to the uterine wall. Here it continues to develop into a multicellular organism.

Joining the chromosomes of the egg and sperm results in restoring the full complement of DNA for the zygote. Now that it has the complete number of chromosomes, the zygote can begin development.

In this activity, you will simulate fertilization. You will combine the genetic material from the male and female gametes of your mythical mosquito. You will then determine the genotypes and phenotypes of the offspring.

Materials

For each group of four students:

- 1 large plastic bag containing chromosome models from Simulating the Stages of Meiosis

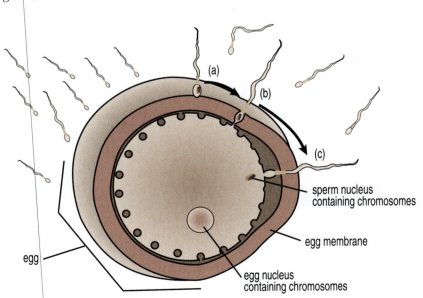

Figure 2.35

Fertilization of an egg. A single sperm (a) binds to the egg. (b) The sperm penetrates and injects its DNA (c).

egg

sperm nucleus containing chromosomes

egg membrane

egg nucleus containing chromosomes

PROCEDURE

1. Place your group's chromosomes on the table.
2. Choose 1 chromosome of each length (15-cm, 22-cm, 30-cm). Return the remaining chromosomes to the plastic bag.
3. Your teacher will designate half the groups as male and half the groups as female. Each group designated as male should join a group designated as female.
4. Copy Table 2.7 into your notebook. Write in the genotypes of the "sperm" and the "egg" of the fertilized mosquito cell.

NOTE

Choose any color. You do not need the sister chromatids.

Table 2.7 Potential Genotype of Fertilized Mosquito Cell

Genotype	Antenna Texture *H* or *h*	Wing Shape *R* or *r*	Wing Length *L* or *l*	Abdomen Color *B* or *b*
egg				
sperm				
offspring				

5. Use your chromosome models to model fertilization between the 2 gametes. Pair up the homologous chromosomes.
6. Record the genotype of the resulting offspring.
7. **STOP & THINK** Based on the genotype, what is the offspring's phenotype? Record the characteristic for all 4 traits. (You may wish to refer to Table 2.5.) Explain the variation in traits among siblings. Use your understanding of meiosis and fertilization. Why do some siblings have common characteristics? Record your responses in your notebook.

Mistakes of Meiosis

ACTIVITY

The human karyotype in Figure 2.36 shows three copies of chromosome 21. This is called a trisomy. Write two or three paragraphs in your notebook to explain, in detail, how this individual might have received chromosome 21 in triplicate. Use your knowledge of how chromosomes move and sort during meiosis and what you know about fertilization. Include diagrams that show the following:

- how chromosome 21 moved and sorted to result in the trisomy,
- which gametes were involved in the fertilization,
- the other gametes produced at the same time, and
- the effects on the other gametes, if any.

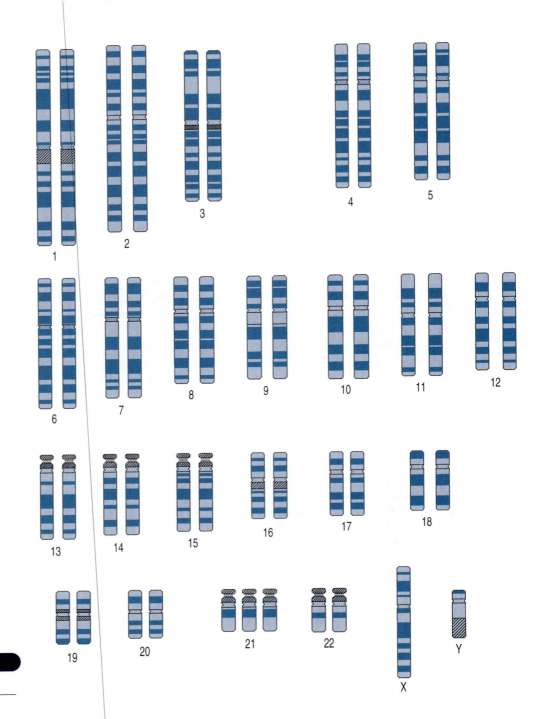

Figure 2.36

A trisomy 21 karyotype.

Cloning of the Lamb: Silence of the Man?

In February 1997, the scientific world was taken by surprise. Dr. Ian Wilmut of the Roslin Institute outside of Edinburgh, Scotland, announced that his group had cloned a sheep. They had done this by using the cells of the mammary gland of another sheep. The cloned sheep was an identical copy of the sheep from which the cells were taken. She was born in July 1996 and named "Dolly" (after the singer Dolly Parton).

The techniques involved were remarkably simple considering the momentous achievement. The scientists took cells from the udder of a 6-year-old Finn Dorset ewe. They placed the cells in an extract low in nutrients. By starving the cells, scientists were able to switch off the genes being expressed. Then they took an oocyte from the ovary of a Blackface ewe and removed its nucleus. This left the cytoplasmic material from the egg intact, with all its proteins required to produce an embryo.

The mammary cell was placed next to the enucleated oocyte in a dish. The cells were stimulated with an electric pulse. This caused the two cells to fuse together. The nucleus of the mammary cell—with its DNA—entered the oocyte. A second pulse caused the cell to start to divide and begin embryonic development. Six days later, the ball of embryonic cells was implanted into the uterus of a Blackface ewe. Here it continued to develop. The birth of Dolly took place on the 277th try. (Only 29 implemented embryos had developed enough to reach the implantation stage.)

Since the landmark cloning experiment that resulted in the birth of Dolly, a wide variety of animals has been cloned. The animals range from mice to kittens to horses. The ability to clone organisms will help scientists understand a great deal about disease, growth, and development. It will also help us to understand the nature of life itself. But it also opens the door to a number of potential uses and misuses of cloning. Cloning is currently the source of much public discussion and debate.

Topic: Cloning
Go to: www.scilinks.org
Code: INBIOH2231

ANALYSIS

Record your responses to the following in your notebook.

1. Is Dolly a Finn Dorset or a Blackface sheep? Explain your response.
2. At the announcement of this feat, was Dolly 7 months old or more than 6 years old? Explain your reasoning.
3. Do you think this experiment could have been done successfully in the other direction? Would scientists have been successful if they had placed the oocyte nucleus into an enucleated mammary cell? Explain your response.
4. What concerns do you think have surfaced since the news of this cloning? What concerns do you have, if any?
5. What benefits do you think might result from this type of experiment?
6. Describe the implications that cloning may have for the role of the male of the species. What implications might this have for biological variation?

In March 1997, there were reports that a group of scientists in Oregon had produced monkeys from cloned embryos. This is the first time a species so closely related to humans had been cloned. The scientists used a technique similar to the one that the Scottish scientists used to clone Dolly, the sheep. Two monkeys were born in August 1996. They were cloned from cells taken from embryos, not an adult as in the case of Dolly. Therefore, the cloned monkeys were not genetically identical to any adult monkey.

Research both experiments (Dolly and the cloned monkeys). Examine the science and the ethical issues. Write a position statement on the moral and ethical considerations of these experiments. If you feel that there are ramifications evident in one, but not the other, state your reasons for the difference.

Since the cloning of Dolly, many different kinds of organisms have been cloned. Scientists have cloned cats, mice, goats, rabbits, pigs, cows, and mules. Some scientists believe that these animals are perfectly normal and healthy. Others believe that certain genes of these organisms are expressed abnormally. They think this results in an array of apparent and hidden abnormalities. Research the experiments that support or refute the idea that these organisms are normal. Using the data as evidence, decide which experiments you believe and why. Discuss the implications for future cloning.

CAREER FOCUS

Recreational Therapist Manuel's two o'clock class will start shortly. On this particular day, Manuel will be leading his class in learning the latest new line dance. He's had a busy day already, working with numerous young adults at a school for the mentally disabled. This particular class includes 10-year-old Lucinda. Lucinda was born with Down's syndrome. Like others in the class, Lucinda feels clumsy and has difficulty performing certain tasks. She was very shy and withdrawn when she met Manuel a few months ago.

Manuel is a recreational therapist. His job is to help children like Lucinda have fun while learning coordination, increasing their self-esteem, and socializing effectively through physical activities. He does this by engaging students in music and dance, arts and crafts, cooking, and playing different sports. Much of his time is spent in a class situation. But he also spends time with each student separately. Some of the children Manuel works with will grow up to be semi-independent adults. Others will remain dependent upon others for care. Manuel uses information from medical records, medical staff, family, and the patients themselves to help individual students. He works with them at their personal skill levels. This may include something as basic as tossing a ball back and forth or as complicated as playing volleyball. He helps train a number of his students for the annual Special Olympics and has seen many of them win medals.

While in college to complete a bachelor's degree in recreational therapy, Manuel learned about the many positions that would be available to him. He could work in hospitals, adult day care centers, nursing homes, and retirement facilities, as well as residential facilities for the disabled. He could have found work in a nursing home by getting an associate's degree. But Manuel always enjoyed the thought of working with children in a residential setting. This required more education.

The class has ended. Lucinda loved the music and picked up the moves right away. Manuel chose her as his special assistant to help others learn the dance. Manuel loves his job. He likes feeling that he makes a difference in people's lives while bringing smiles to their faces and giving them a sense of accomplishment.

Sex and the Single Sea Urchin

Prologue

How do egg and sperm "get it together"? The initiation of new life in many plants and animals starts with the fusion of two gamete cells. An egg and a sperm meet and fuse to form a zygote. In organisms, such as humans, fertilization takes place internally within the female. (For in vitro fertilization, however, these steps are carried out in the laboratory.) In many other organisms, fertilization takes place externally, outside the body of the female. This happens in sea urchins and frogs.

Have you ever walked along an ocean shoreline? If you have, you may have seen sea urchins in tidal pools or along a beach. These animals are relatives of sand dollars and starfish (family Echinoidae). Sea urchins have an external skeleton, which forms a rigid shell. This shell is fitted with long movable spines. The mouth is located at one pole of the sea urchin's spherical body; its anus is at the other pole. There are no limbs or other protuberances (such as a head). All of the animal's major organs are located within the shell.

Most sea urchins are vegetarians or scavengers. They feed on plant materials and small animals on the seafloor. Many kinds of sea urchins have five sharp teeth in their mouths. They use these teeth to scrape food from rocks and other objects. Small pincerlike organs between the spines serve functions such as cleaning the urchin's shell. Some of these organs contain venom and are useful in warding off predators.

Sea urchins' gametes are easy to obtain and their eggs are relatively large and transparent. As a result, sea urchins have been used extensively in scientific research on fertilization and development processes. The eggs are also considered a delicacy in many cultures, appreciated for their delicate flavor.

Topic: Fertilization
Go to: www.scilinks.org
Code: INBIOH2233

Brainstorming

Discuss the following questions with your partner, and record your thinking in your notebook. Be prepared to share your ideas with the class.

1. Have you ever seen a sea urchin? If you have, describe one to your partner.
2. What other marine animals do you know about? Have you seen other marine animals when walking along the shorelines of an ocean or a lake?
3. What is a tidal pool?
4. Describe the living conditions of those animals that inhabit tidal pools?

It Takes Two to Fuse

In this activity, you will collect the eggs and sperm from sea urchins. You will mix them together and observe the process of fertilization under the microscope.

Materials

For each group of four students:

- 4 safety goggles
- 1 sea urchin
- 1 large container
- 1 beaker (500-mL)
- 500 mL seawater (or Instant Ocean®); 100 mL should be kept cold
- 1 syringe filled with 2 mL 4% potassium chloride (KCl) solution
- 2 petri dishes
- 1 glass stirring rod
- 2 eyedroppers
- 1 small medicine bottle
- 1 depression slide
- 1 small beaker (50–100 mL)
- compound microscope(s)
- coverslips or plastic wrap
- tap water
- latex gloves (optional)

PROCEDURE

Part A: Harvesting Sea Urchin Gametes

1. Fill 1 large container with seawater. Have available a small (empty) beaker and a syringe with 2 mL 4% solution of potassium chloride (KCl). KCl is a salt found in seawater. When injected into the sea urchin, this solution will cause the release of the gametes (egg and sperm).
2. Carefully collect 1 sea urchin from the class aquarium. Handle it very gently. Locate the mouth using Figure 2.37. (The area around the mouth is not spiny.)

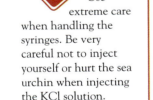

Mouth

Spines

Figure 2.37

Sea urchin. Shows location of spines and mouth. Anus is located in opposite side of animal from the mouth. © David Wrobel/Visuals Unlimited

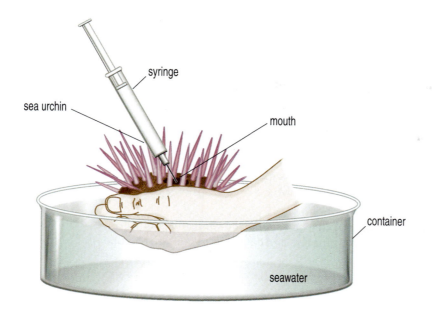

syringe

sea urchin

mouth

container

seawater

Figure 2.38

Injecting the sea urchin with
KCl solution.

3. Hold the sea urchin with its mouth upward. Place the bottom half of the animal in seawater. (Be sure that its anus is submerged.) Inject the KCl solution into the nonspiny membrane around the sea urchin's mouth (see Figure 2.38).

4. After the injection, remove the sea urchin from the seawater. Hold it, anus down, over the empty beaker. Within 2–3 minutes, the sea urchin will begin to shed its gametes. If your sea urchin releases clouds of thick, white fluid, it is male and is releasing sperm. If your sea urchin releases golden or red fluid, your sea urchin is female and is releasing eggs.

5. Depending on the kind of fluid released, do one of the following:
   a. If eggs were released, quickly rinse the eggs in seawater as follows:
      • Pour 150 mL of seawater over the eggs in the beaker. Use the stirring rod to gently stir the eggs; allow them to settle to the bottom of the beaker. Then carefully pour off the liquid, leaving the eggs at the bottom of the beaker. Repeat 3 times. This procedure removes debris and fecal matter.
      • Resuspend the eggs in 10 mL of cold seawater in a petri dish.
   b. If sperm were released, collect them with a clean eyedropper. Place them in a medicine bottle.

6. Place the sea urchin back into the saltwater aquarium.

7. **STOP & THINK** Describe in your notebook the appearance of the fluid, what it is, and the sex of your animal.

Part B: Fertilization

For this part, you will use the sperm and eggs harvested from the urchins.

1. Obtain a depression slide and a clean eyedropper. Carefully dip the eyedropper in the medicine bottle containing the sperm. Draw up some of the sperm. Place 2 drops of sperm into the well of the depression slide. Empty any remaining sperm back into the medicine bottle.

2. **STOP & THINK** Examine the sperm through a microscope under both low and high power. Describe in your notebook what you observe. Use words and/or drawings. Make sure that the sperm are alive and swimming.

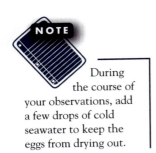

NOTE
During the course of your observations, add a few drops of cold seawater to keep the eggs from drying out.

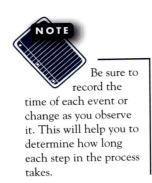

NOTE
Be sure to record the time of each event or change as you observe it. This will help you to determine how long each step in the process takes.

3. Rinse the slide and the eyedropper in clean water. Carefully swish the solution containing the eggs to resuspend them. Then dip the eyedropper into solution and draw up a sample. Place 2 drops in the well of the depression slide.

4. **STOP & THINK** Examine the eggs through a microscope under both low and high power. Describe in your notebook what you observe. Use words and/or drawings. After you have recorded your observations, leave the eggs on the slide under high power.

5. To ensure good activity on the part of the sperm, first mix the sperm with seawater. Carefully dip a clean eyedropper in the medicine bottle and draw up some of the sperm. Mix 3 or 4 drops of sperm with 25 mL of cold seawater in a petri dish.

6. Place 1 drop of the sperm and seawater mixture in the well of the depression slide that contains the egg cells. Focus the microscope on 1 or 2 of the egg cells.

7. **STOP & THINK** Observe, describe, and record the following:

   a. movements of the sperm around the egg
   b. how the sperm approach the egg
   c. how many sperm attach to the egg
   d. how many sperm enter the egg
   e. changes in the egg when a sperm binds
   f. changes in the egg after a sperm penetrates

8. Follow the changes in the egg for the remainder of the class session. Your teacher may allow time for you to continue your observations for several days. If so, add more seawater to the depression slide. Carefully cover with a coverslip or plastic wrap to prevent evaporation. Then store flat in a cool place between sessions.

ANALYSIS

Record your responses to the following in your notebook.

1. Why do you think it was important for the fertilization process to take place in seawater?

2. Eggs are designed to provide protection from the environment in which the embryo will be developing. What features of the sea urchin egg might help fulfill this function?

3. How do you think the sperm finds the egg? How might you determine this?

4. How many sperm did you observe entering a single egg? An egg controls the number of sperm that can enter. How do you think it does that? Why do you think that the number of sperm entering an egg is controlled by the egg?

5. What do you think happens to a sperm once it enters the egg?

6. What other factors besides the presence of seawater might affect the fertilization process? Describe an experiment that you could do to test the effects of a variable on fertilization.

7. Scientists have carefully characterized many of the events of fertilization. How do you think this information might be used?

Those Raging Hormones

Prologue

Growth, development and maturation in most organisms involve dramatic changes that are highly regulated and controlled. In plants, seeds germinate, cells differentiate to form new structures, stems elongate and bend toward the sun, flowers bloom and fruit ripens. During human embryogenesis and early childhood limbs, head and torso grow proportionately and organs and organ systems develop. Adolescence is a time of sexual maturation, marking the ability to reproduce with the production of eggs in girls and sperm in boys. What triggers these events and controls these processes so that they occur when and how they should?

In this learning experience, you will explore the role of hormones in regulating growth and sexual maturity. You will also learn about the endocrine system in humans, which produces hormones.

Brainstorming

Discuss the following questions with your partner, and record your thinking in your notebook. Be prepared to share your ideas with the class.

1. How would you define the word "hormone"?
2. What kinds of body processes might hormones control?
3. What hormones do you know about? What do these do?
4. How do you think hormones work?

Will My Investment Grow?

ACTIVITY

In most organisms, growth is a carefully controlled process. But what controls the rates and patterns of growth, and can these patterns be altered? How could you investigate these questions?

Imagine the following scenario: A small biotechnology company claims that it has developed a substance that, when applied near the growing (**apical**) tip of the plant, stimulates plant growth significantly. The company asserts that this is an important and profitable finding; the taller the plants, the greater will be the profits to be made from the plant. A group of investors has hired you to determine whether the company's claims are accurate.

With your background in biology, you decide that you will test the efficacy of the compound. The company has given you a small sample of the compound to test. You elicit the help of three friends (your group) to design and carry out an experiment using available materials.

Materials

For each group of four students:

- 4 safety goggles
- 2 two-week-old seedlings of variety A pea plants
- 2 two-week-old seedlings of variety B pea plants
- 4 toothpicks
- graph paper or graphing software
- metric measuring tape

For the class:

- lanolin paste with the substance to be tested gibberellic acid (500 ppm)
- lanolin paste
- chart paper
- felt-tip markers

PROCEDURE

1. Design an experiment that will determine the effectiveness of the compound on plant growth. Discuss the components of the experiment with your group, and write up your design in your notebook. Be sure to include the following:
   - the question being asked
   - a hypothesis
   - the procedure to be used to carry out the experiment (list the steps and the materials used)
   - controls (positive or negative)
   - the method to be used for measuring growth
   - the type of data to be collected
   - how you will collect your data and how often
   - how you will record your data
   - how you will analyze your data
   - any safety precautions to be taken
2. When you have designed your experiment, have your teacher check it. Be prepared to explain your reasoning for the procedure and the data collection, and be prepared, if necessary, to make changes or adjustments.
3. Set up your experiment according to your design. Since you will be collecting data over the next several days, design tables in which to record that data. Take your first measurements according to your experimental design and record the data.
4. At the conclusion of your experiment (3–5 days):
   a. discuss your data with your group, and decide how you will analyze and present it.
   b. determine the conclusions that you can make from your data.

5. In preparation for writing your final report, read "Shoot to Root, Are You There?"

6. Prepare a report for the group of investors who hired you. Your report should contain the following information:
   - the purpose of the experiment (that is, the scientific question being addressed)
   - your hypothesis
   - the procedure your group used for the experiment, including materials and procedure
   - the data (the numbers as recorded each day)
   - a graph of growth curves
   - analysis of the data (including growth rate (cm/day))
   - possible sources of error
   - discussion about the way this compound affected the plants and why it might have affected the plants differently
   - conclusions about the effectiveness of this compound as a growth promoter, including your conclusions about the veracity (truthfulness) of the biotechnology company's claims
   - your recommendation as to whether the investors should invest in this company's product and your rationale.

I Won't Grow Up Without My Hormones

READING

You may have been told that teenagers are ruled by "raging hormones." Yet you feel your life is ruled by you and your thought processes. What do hormones have to do with it?

In a single-celled organism, most communication takes place within the cell, or between the cell and its environment, across the cell membrane. One of the consequences of being multicellular, however, is that the methods for communicating within an organism become more complex. In multicellular organisms, communication within the organism is required for many reasons: for the organisms to continue to grow and develop; to maintain temperature and internal balance within an environment that may be changing; and to communicate within itself concerning what different parts are doing and what is happening in its environment.

A multicellular organism communicates internally by using two organ systems: the nervous system and the **endocrine system**. The nervous system enables a multicellular organism to send messages around the body and to respond to internal and external signals. It can signal hunger, danger, and the need for rest and repair, and it enables the body to respond to its environment.

The other organ system responsible for internal communication is the endocrine system. Made up of seemingly independent organs (**glands**) found throughout the body, the endocrine system produces a remarkable array of chemical substances called hormones, which can be either lipids or small proteins, that are responsible for regulating growth and development, maintaining the stability of the body's internal environment, regulating cell metabolism, and triggering sexual maturity. Figure 2.39 shows the glands of the endocrine system. Although widely separated in the body, these glands form an integrated system by producing hormones that can work with other hormones to

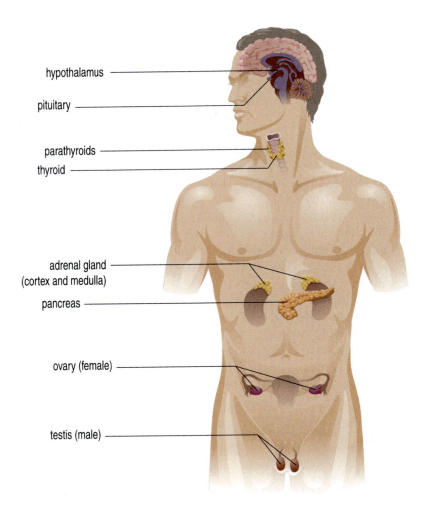

hypothalamus

pituitary

parathyroids

thyroid

adrenal gland
(cortex and medulla)

pancreas

ovary (female)

testis (male)

Figure 2.39

Endocrine system in humans.

affect a specific action. For example, this concerted action takes place when the hormones glucocorticoids from the adrenal cortex, thyroxine from the thyroid gland, and somatotropin from the pituitary gland all work together to regulate metabolic activity, which is the breakdown and synthesis of biomolecules in cells.

Hormones travel from the gland in which they are produced through the bloodstream to **target cells** in tissues, and regulate the activity of those cells. The human endocrine system can be compared to a radio broadcast system in that it is capable of communicating via a signal with millions of listeners (cells) that may be located at some distance away from the origin of the signal. Just as a radio has a set of filters that allow you (by turning a dial or pushing a button) to choose to receive only certain broadcast frequencies, these target cells have specific proteins on their surfaces called receptors that will receive or bind only certain hormones. Once the hormones bind to the receptors on the surface of their target cells, they may stimulate the cells to divide or initiate a new function.

Hormones play vital roles in growth and development. In animals, they contribute to the growth of the embryo within the womb, stimulate the body's growth from infancy to adolescence, and stimulate and guide the transformation from adolescent to adult. In insects, juvenile hormones control changes that occur between hatching and adulthood. In plants, hormones regulate plant growth, when a plant will flower and fruit, and when the leaves will turn color in autumn.

Certain hormones have the specific function of regulating growth. In most vertebrate animals, growth is regulated by the hormone **somatotropin** (generally referred to as growth hormone), which is produced in the pituitary gland located near the base of the brain (see Figure 2.40). This hormone exerts its primary effects on the long bones of the limbs where significant growth occurs. Growth hormone acts by binding to receptors on the surface of cells and stimulating the cells to divide. To coordinate bodily growth, somatotropin must affect bone and organ growth in a controlled manner.

In plants, growth hormone determines how tall a plant may get, its rate of growth, and its direction of growth in response to environmental influences (such as light, gravity, wind direction, and moisture). Plants make different kinds of growth hormone, several of which are made in the apical stem of the plant.

How tall will you be? When will you be fully grown? The answer to these questions is determined by several factors: the information in your DNA inherited from your parents, your hormones, and certain external factors such as nutrition. Growth may happen early in some, later in others. There may be a lot of growth or a little, but inevitably for most individuals, growth happens.

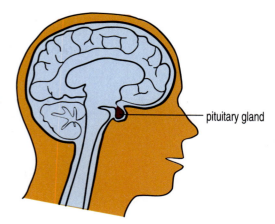

Figure 2.40

Site of the pituitary gland below the brain.

 **ANALYSIS**

Write responses to the following questions in your notebook.

1. What important functions of an organism do hormones help regulate?
2. How do you think hormones regulate bodily functions?
3. How do hormones move around in the body? Why is it necessary that hormones travel?
4. What might happen to an organism that has no growth-regulating hormones? Could this be an advantage? a disadvantage? Explain your answer.

Puberty: The Metamorphosis to Maturity

Humans become sexually mature and capable of reproduction during the period of adolescence called **puberty**. The age at which an individual "enters" puberty varies from individual to individual. External factors, such as general nutritional health, may be involved as well as family history (inherited characteristics). In girls, the onset of puberty is marked by the beginning of menstruation (the menarche); in boys, by a growth spurt. Further changes, such as the development of secondary sex characteristics, happen around the same time. What initiates such dramatic changes in a juvenile's body? Why does it happen when it does? Why does puberty occur?

PROCEDURE

The sequence of events during development can be shown most clearly with graphs. The following graphs indicate when specific events of puberty and adolescence take place.

1. Study Figures 2.41 and 2.42, which show the sequence of visible indications of puberty, collectively referred to as secondary sex characteristics. (The primary sex characteristic is the gonad—testes or ovaries—which determines gender.)
2. Working with your partner, discuss the following Analysis questions and write responses in your notebook.

ANALYSIS

1. Identify the changes that occur during puberty for boys and for girls.
2. What are the differences in changes between boys and girls? The similarities?
3. Describe the meaning of "variability of onset."
4. Identify any factors that might influence the timing of the onset of puberty.

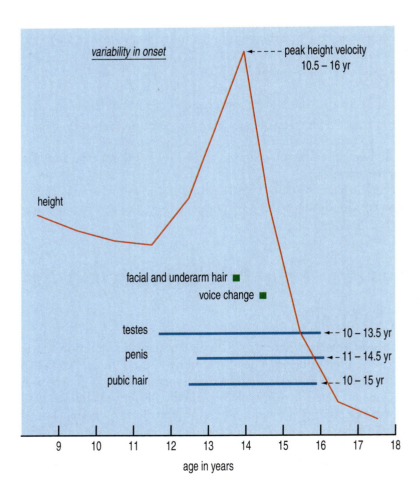

Figure 2.41

Sequence of development in boys.

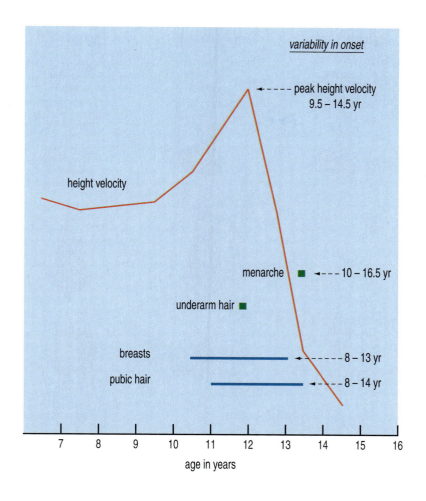

variability in onset

height velocity

peak height velocity
9.5 – 14.5 yr

menarche ■ ◄---- 10 – 16.5 yr

underarm hair ■

breasts _____ ◄----- 8 – 13 yr
pubic hair _____ ◄----- 8 – 14 yr

7   8   9   10   11   12   13   14   15   16
age in years

Figure 2.42

Sequence of development in girls.

What's Happening

Before puberty, girls and boys have about the same proportions of muscle mass, skeletal mass, and body fat. By the end of puberty, women have twice as much body fat as men, whereas men have one and a half times the skeletal and muscle mass of women. What controls these changes during puberty? The pituitary gland is a major endocrine structure involved in the cascade of hormones that streams through the body during puberty. Located beneath and controlled by the hypothalamus region of the brain, the pituitary gland produces many different hormones. When stimulated by **luteinizing hormone releasing factor (LRF)** from the hypothalamus, the anterior lobe of the pituitary produces the **follicle-stimulating hormone (FSH)** and **luteinizing hormone (LH)** that initiate changes during puberty.

FSH and LH act on the gonads or sex organ; FSH is involved in sperm production in the male and stimulates egg-producing follicles to grow and develop in the ovary of the female. In males, LH stimulates cells in the testes to produce testosterone whereas, in the female, LH stimulates follicles to release eggs. The joint action of LH and FSH cause the follicles of the ovary to secrete estrogen. Figure 2.43 shows the cascade of hormone production and the changes in the hormone levels from the juvenile stage to the adult stage.

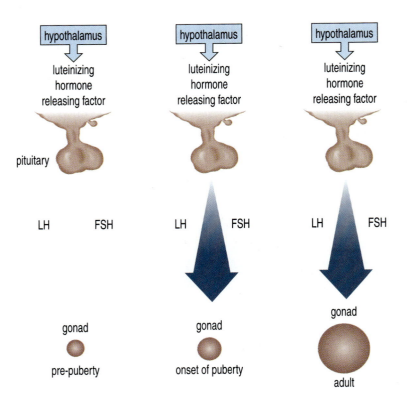

Figure 2.43

Hormones involved in the onset of puberty. The production of luteinizing hormone (LH) and follicle-stimulating hormone (FSH).

Testosterone and estrogen are involved in the production of sperm and egg respectively, and are also responsible for the appearance of secondary sex characteristics that mark the change from the juvenile stage to the sexually mature adult. In males, the testosterone produced by the testes (and in small amounts by the adrenal glands) is the main male hormone of puberty and adulthood. Testosterone targets many kinds of cells in the body and is involved in the maturation of the penis, the maintenance of the testes and the reproductive tract, sperm production, changes in the larynx, patterns of body hair, patterns of behavior, and general body configuration. Testosterone also stimulates muscle development. The testosterone molecule, a shortened version of the cholesterol molecule, is one of the organic compounds known as steroids. Males also secrete small amounts of estrogen.

In females, estrogen, produced by the ovaries, is the principal female hormone. Like testosterone, estrogen is also a steroid that binds to many kinds of cells in the body. Estrogen stimulates the development of breasts, the widening of hips, maturation of the reproductive tract allowing for the ability to bear children, and changes in patterns of body hair. Secretion of estrogen causes the maturation and maintenance of the ovaries and the reproductive tract. Figure 2.44 summarizes the interactions that result in the production of estrogen and testosterone. Females also secrete a small amount of testosterone, produced by the adrenal glands, which regulates pubic and axillary hair development.

Along with estrogen, LH and FSH are responsible for stimulating and maintaining the menstrual cycle. During that cycle, an ovum (egg) is produced and released approximately once every 28 days. Other hormones cause the thickening and increased blood supply of the uterine lining in preparation for

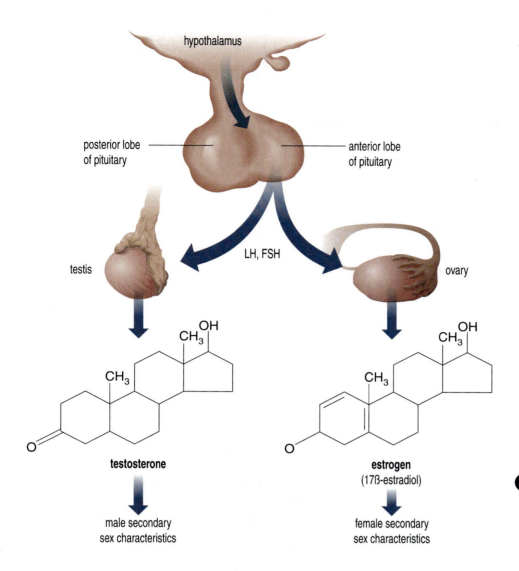

hypothalamus

posterior lobe
of pituitary

anterior lobe
of pituitary

testis

LH, FSH

ovary

OH
CH₃

CH₃

O

testosterone

male secondary
sex characteristics

OH
CH₃

CH₃

O

estrogen
(17ß-estradiol)

female secondary
sex characteristics

Figure 2.44

Hypothalamus-pituitary-
gonad interaction in human
puberty.

receiving the fertilized egg. If the egg is not fertilized, the uterus sheds its lining
(referred to as menstrual fluid), and the cycle begins again. These cycles of egg
production and shedding continue for approximately 40 years at which time
hormonal production slows and ovulation ceases (menopause).

Puberty can be considered analogous to metamorphosis, which marks the
transition from the juvenile to adult stage in insects and amphibians and is also
controlled by hormones. In *Alice's Adventures in Wonderland*, written by Lewis
Carroll, Alice complains to the Caterpillar that she is very confused by the
changes in size she has undergone. The Caterpillar finds nothing confusing
about it at all.

> *"Well, perhaps you haven't found it so yet," said Alice, "but when you have to
> turn into a chrysalis—you will some day, you know—and then after that into a
> butterfly, I should think you'll feel it a little bit queer, won't you?"*
> *"Not a bit," said the Caterpillar.*
> *"Well, perhaps your feelings may be different," said Alice, "all I know is it would
> feel very queer to me."*

ANALYSIS

Use the information in the reading to write an essay about the events of puberty. Your essay should include:

- a description of the sequence of events in (male and female) puberty,
- discussion of how puberty is similar or different in males and females,
- an explanation of the sequence of hormonal events that bring on these changes in either boys or girls (you may wish to do this as a diagram or series of drawings),
- a discussion of how the changes that occur during puberty might impact cultural perspective of men and women and their roles in society.

READING

Making Decisions

What problems and choices confront teenagers in their quest for excellence and perfection? The following reading, "Teen Choices," discusses anorexia, bulimia, and steroid use as consequences of this quest. Be prepared to discuss these and other ideas presented in the reading in class.

TEEN CHOICES

When Christy Henrich died in 1994 at the age of 22, she weighed only 61 pounds. How could this happen to a world class gymnast? In 1988, she had narrowly missed being named to the United States Olympic team. When a gymnast judge told her she was "fat," although she then weighed only 95 pounds, she became obsessed about losing weight. Her eating habits became so extreme that finally she was eating only an apple a day, then only an apple slice a day, all the while training for hours in the gym.

Christy had become the victim of two eating disorders: **anorexia nervosa**, a form of self-starvation, and **bulimia nervosa**, characterized by binge eating followed by vomiting and/or the use of laxatives. Although Christy was hospitalized in 1993 when her weight fell to 52 pounds and gained back some weight in the hospital, the year of starvation had already caused destruction of muscle—including her heart muscle—and organ shrinkage. Her body finally gave out.

It is too simplistic to accept the official cause of Christy's death as "multiple organ failure." The pressures that many gymnasts, ballet dancers, and models feel to be unrealistically thin must also play a causal role. But eating disorders are also a problem outside the sports arena. Women as well as men, from all walks of life and of all ages, can be drawn to anorexic behavior for various reasons. Statistics show that 1 in 100 women are anorexic; however, the majority of anorexics are girls between the ages of 12 and 18. (About five percent of all anorexics are men.)

ANOREXIA NERVOSA

In this serious physiological and psychological disease, a change in eating patterns results in the body weight being about 20 percent below the expected weight for a healthy person of the same age and height. The anorexic refuses to maintain a healthful body weight, is generally afraid to gain weight, and has a distorted perception of her body size or shape. Studying her image in the mirror, the anorexic sees a fat person, even if she is seriously underweight.

As in the case of Christy Henrich, the effects of anorexia nervosa may be severe and irreversible. External changes are emaciation, dry skin, hair loss, and the growth of fine body hair. Internal changes include the cessation of the menstrual cycle (**amenorrhea**), infertility, low blood pressure, edemic (water retention) swelling, loss in bone density, liver damage, dental problems, cramps, diarrhea, and heart irregularities.

Anorexia nervosa is a growing disorder in our weight-conscious society. Exploring the underlying causes is key to successful recovery and to helping women avoid the illness altogether. A common reason that older people become anorexic is depression. For a teenager, the most obvious and superficial cause may be the desire to be accepted and popular, and to wear stylish clothes; but, the deeper, subconscious causes may not even be realized. These may include the need to be perfect and to feel control over life, undefined feelings of being powerless, a need for attention and admiration on having self-control, and deep emotional conflicts that often arise from family issues. As a young girl develops into an adolescent, her hips begin to widen, and fat is deposited in places where it never was before, at just the time when appearance seems to be most important; so, she begins a diet that becomes uncontrollable.

BULIMIA NERVOSA

Bulimia nervosa is characterized by binge eating followed by inappropriate methods to prevent weight gain, such as self-induced vomiting or abuse of laxatives. If such behavior occurs at least twice a week for three months, it is classified as bulimia. The type of food consumed during binges varies, but typically it includes sweet, high-calorie foods such as ice cream and other desserts. Binge eating and the resulting purging generally occur in secret, amid feelings of loss of control.

The physical effects on the bulimic include fluid and electrolyte (mineral) abnormalities, which may, in turn, lead to heart problems; significant loss of dental enamel and increase in cavities; menstrual irregularities; and metabolic disorders resulting from the loss of stomach acid.

Individuals with bulimia place an excessive emphasis on body shape and weight, and these features become the most important ones in measuring self-esteem. Compulsive exercising to compensate for the binge eating and to achieve the desired shape and weight often occurs. Statistics show that from one to three percent of adolescent and young adult females are bulimic. The rate of occurrence in males is approximately one-tenth that in females, and the disorder is primarily found in whites.

ANABOLIC STEROIDS

Steroids actually include many lipids in the body, such as testosterone, estrogen, hormones made in the adrenal glands, and cholesterol. However, the statement that someone is "taking steroids" refers, in general, to the use of sex hormones that stimulate secondary sex characteristics, especially muscle size. When steroids are present in excess amounts, as in the case of steroid use by athletes, the results can be startling. Steroids can increase muscle mass significantly, increase muscle strength, and improve muscle definition, resulting in a faster, stronger, more durable athlete.

But using steroids is also dangerous. They can stop the growth of long bones, an important determinant of future height. They can also cause testicle shrinkage, liver tumors, abnormal liver metabolism, alterations in tendons, and increase in total cholesterol. Behavioral abnormalities often occur, including excessive irritability, hostility, and mood swings. Steroid use may also provoke anger, distractibility, violent feelings, insomnia, confusion, forgetfulness, and headaches. Before taking steroids, athletes, both professional and amateur, must weigh the trade-offs and the consequences of enhancing performance by this method.

There has been a dramatic rise in steroid use throughout the world. It is a complex problem with social, physiological, psychological, economic, and political variables. Just how many American teenagers are taking steroids? Although it is difficult to obtain accurate numbers, a University of Michigan study, released in December 1994, reported that more than 200,000 high school males took steroids during that year. Other estimates range as high as 500,000 teens a year with confirmed reports of some starting as early as 10 years of age. At the high school level, teens may get mixed messages from some adults about the importance of muscle mass. After teammates and friends, coaches and teachers ranked second as the source for these mostly illegal drugs.

ANALYSIS

1. What are the social pressures from one's peers?
2. What are potential influences from society and the media that could lead to these disorders?
3. What distinguishes dieting from anorexia?
4. What are the biological consequences of these disorders?
5. How might those trapped in these cycles be helped?

READING

Shoot to Root, Are You There?

Like all multicellular organisms, plants need to communicate. To be well formed and to function effectively, each part of the plant must be in communication with the other parts. Otherwise, the plant would be incapable of carrying out its life functions, such as growth.

Plant growth is indeterminate; that is, unlike many organisms whose size ranges are fixed by heredity, there are no absolute restrictions on the precise size a plant may reach or the precise shape it might assume. But growth is not random. Plants produce predictable structures and patterns that are characteristic of each species, indicating that plant growth is regulated. The controls on growth rate and the patterns of growth ensure that a plant will grow in a coordinated fashion. In addition, these controls enable a plant to respond to environmental conditions—light, gravity, wind direction, and moisture—which are essential for an organism that cannot move to different locations. As in other organisms, the controlling factors are hormones.

Evidence that plants contain hormones was first suggested in experiments by Charles Darwin and his son Francis in the late 1880s. It was a common observation that plants curve toward the sun or other source of light (phototropism). When the Darwins covered the tip of a growing plant with an opaque barrier, the plant no longer bent toward the light. This suggested to the Darwins that some influence from the tip, probably a chemical substance, caused one side of the plant to grow faster than the other side of the plant, resulting in curvature. This hypothesis was greeted with skepticism by other plant scientists, largely because Darwin (while known for his theory of evolution) was not recognized as a plant biologist. In that field, he was considered an outsider.

Fifty years passed before Frits Went (a plant biologist) carried out the definitive experiment to prove the existence of this chemical substance. Went removed the tip of a plant and placed it on an agar block for several hours. He then placed the agar block on one side of the plant from which the tip had been removed and kept the plant in the dark. Even in the dark, the stem began to move away from the block as if it were responding to a light source on the side away from the block (see Figure 2.45). Went's experiment demonstrated that a diffusible substance (a substance able to move from the tip through the agar block) able to stimulate growth was present in the tip of a plant. This substance stimulated cell growth in the cells on the side of the plant next to the block, causing this side of the plant to grow faster than the other side and inducing a curvature of the plant. Subsequently, this chemical substance was identified as **indole acetic acid**, or **auxin**, which promotes growth by causing cells to elongate.

In the late nineteenth century, Japanese rice farmers noted extraordinarily tall seedlings rising out of their fields of otherwise uniform plants. Hoping that these tall plants might result in a strain of giant rice, the farmers tended the tall plants carefully, only to find that they died before flowering. Many years later, scientists discovered that the source of this tall growth was actually an infection of the rice plants by a fungus that produced a substance they called **gibberellic acid**. Since then, gibberellic acid has been found in many plants. It stimulates plants to grow taller by causing stem elongation. Another attempt to use gibberellic acid for improving crop production was in the cereal industry. It was hoped that by applying tiny quantities of this hormone to cereal and grass crops, farmers might accelerate crop growth and obtain greater yields at harvest. The results of this have been disappointing: while gibberellic acid does promote growth during early development, the untreated plants eventually catch up with the

(a) (b)

hormone diffuses

(c)

Figure 2.45

The Went Experiment (a) The growing tip of the plant is removed and placed on an agar block for several hours. (b) The agar block is then placed on one side of the plant from which the tip has been removed. (c) The plant is placed in the dark and the response is observed.

gibberellic-acid-treated plants, so that both groups ultimately reach the same size and, therefore, result in similar crop yields.

Since these first experiments, many plant hormones have been identified. Hormones are involved in seed germination, growth, flowering, reproduction, and aging of plants. They also play a role in the ability of seeds to remain dormant for long periods of time. In both plants and animals, hormones play a variety of different but essential roles in the growth, development, and maintenance of the organism.

EXTENDING *Ideas*

- Hormones play many roles in the body; in addition to physical effects, hormones appear to be involved in influencing social behavior. Oxytocin and vasopressin are two such hormones. Similar in structure and produced by the posterior pituitary gland, these two polypeptides seem to be involved in producing monogamous and maternal (in females) and paternal (in males) behavior. These effects are described engagingly in "What Makes a Parent Put up With It All?" by Natalie Angier in *The Beauty of the Beastly,* Houghton Mifflin Co., NY, 1995, p. 27. Research these hormones and determine their structures, sites of action, and roles in influencing behavior.

- Regular supplementation of a cow's diet with small doses of a bovine growth hormone (bovine somatotropin) has been shown to increase milk production by 10–25%. Controversy has arisen as to whether or not the use of a growth hormone to animals used in food production poses a health risk to humans. Obtain literature from groups that hold opposing views (such as the American Dairy Association and the Cancer Prevention Coalition), analyze their presentation of the information, and decide with whom you agree, and why.

- Research studies have shown that when growth hormone injections are given to elderly males, many of the ravages of age are reduced; muscle tone returns, hair growth is enhanced, and testosterone levels rise. When the injections are stopped, the gains made are lost. Research these studies and decide whether growth hormone should be provided to anyone who wants them. Explain your thinking.

- There is a chronological discrepancy between when humans are biologically mature enough to procreate and when current Western society deems individuals mature enough to procreate. In this country many years ago, and in many cultures today, it was expected that young adults in their mid- (for girls) to late teens would wed and have children. This may be related to the life expectancy at the time or to the role of young adults in society. You may want to have students research cultures in which this is still the case and present their findings in terms of the relationship between biological evolution and cultural evolution.

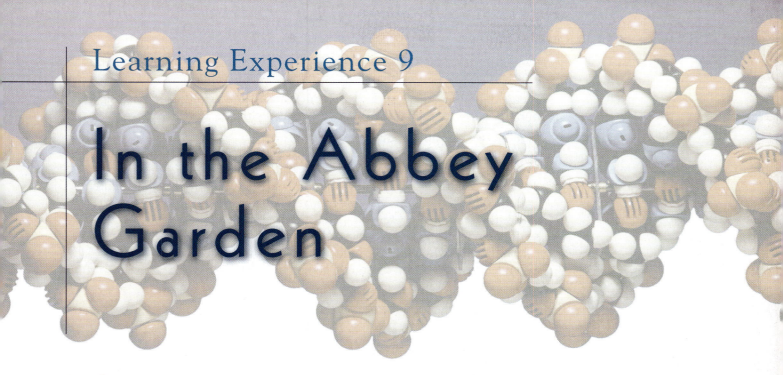

Learning Experience 9

In the Abbey Garden

Prologue

An old adage says that in life, we have to "play the cards we've been dealt." To rephrase that saying from a molecular perspective you might say in life, "we play the DNA we've been dealt." In many ways, the cards (or DNA) you get in life depend on two things. These are your starting deck (the genes from your parents) and the way the cards have been shuffled (variation taking place in meiosis). The deal may be random and the cards seem to come up by chance. But there is a certain predictability, as any gambler or magician knows!

Imagine you were to arrange a deck of cards in the following specific order—the aces of hearts, clubs, diamonds, and spades; then the twos of hearts, clubs, diamonds, and spades; and so forth through the kings. Then you dealt the cards out into four piles. You put the ace of hearts in the first pile, the ace of clubs in the second pile, and so forth in order. When you are done, you would have 100% certainty (or **probability**) that each pile contains the ace through the king of a single suit.

But, if you shuffled the original deck before making the piles, the four piles would look quite different from each other. The order and suits in each pile would be random; no two stacks would be alike. However, the probability of a single card ending up in any one pile could be calculated mathematically.

The assortment and recombining of chromosomes during meiosis and fertilization are very similar to the shuffling and distributing of cards from a deck. In this learning experience, you explore how the distribution of chromosomes to offspring is a random process. You also look at how distribution can be predicted by the laws of probability. To do this, you will examine the experiments of Gregor Mendel. Mendel's investigations into the inheritance patterns of peas led to the establishment of several fundamental principles of inheritance. Mendel also helped us understand the variation in the traits that are observed between parents and offspring, and among siblings. To understand Mendel's experiments, you first investigate how plants reproduce.

Brainstorming

Discuss the following questions with your partner, and record your thinking in your notebook. Be prepared to share your ideas with the class.

1. How do you think plants reproduce?
2. What parts of the plant are involved in reproduction? What function does each part have?
3. Think about your own family or other families you know. Do the children look like their parents? Do the brothers and sisters look alike? In what ways are they similar? In what ways are they different?
4. Propose an explanation about why children do not look exactly like their parents and why siblings can look similar or very different. Use your understanding of chromosomes, genes, and meiosis.

ACTIVITY

The Flowers That Bloom in the Spring

In every flowering plant, the flower is the reproductive organ that allows for the continuation of the species. This is the case whether the plant is an apple tree or a dandelion. Despite the extraordinary diversity in their shape, coloration, and size, flowers (like the plants that bear them) demonstrate simplicity and similarity in structure and function.

Within flowers, gametes are produced, fertilization takes place, and the seeds develop. Some plants, such as a lily, have flowers that contain both male and female parts. Other plants have flowers that contain either only male or only female sexual structures. The female structure, the **pistil**, is in the center of the flower. It consists of a vase-shaped ovary. The ovary is where the eggs are produced. The **stigma** is also part of the pistil. It connects to the ovary through a tubular **style** (see Figure 2.39). The more numerous male parts of the flower are contained in the **stamen**. These parts usually surround the female parts. They

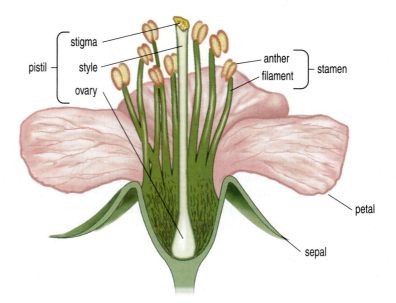

Figure 2.39

Reproductive structures in a flower.

include the **anther**, which produces the pollen (or sperm), and the **filament**, which supports the anther. Surrounding these male and female parts are the petals and **sepals**. These flower parts are attractive to birds and other animals that play an important role in plant fertilization.

During fertilization, the pollen from either the same plant (**self-pollination**) or from another plant of the same kind (**cross-fertilization**) attaches to the stigma. Pollen from other flowers can be carried by the wind, on the bodies of insects, or by birds feeding on the nectar of the flower. Thousands of pollen grains make their way down the style to fertilize the eggs in the ovary. Seeds develop from these fertilized eggs. When mature, the seeds are released from the ovary with all the potential for making new plants (offspring).

In this activity, you will conduct a thorough study of a flower. While dissecting the flower, you will locate and identify the structures involved in sexual reproduction in plants. You will make detailed observations in the process.

Materials

For each pair of students:

- 2 fresh flowers (from the same type of plant)
- colored pencils or pens (optional)
- 1 scalpel or single-edged razor blade
- 1 dissecting needle
- 1 hand lens
- paper towel or shallow tray

PROCEDURE

1. **STOP & THINK** Before you begin the dissection, look closely at one of the flowers. Draw and describe your observations of the flower in your notebook.
2. Use the scalpel and dissecting needle to carefully remove each part of the flower. Place it on a paper towel or tray.
3. Identify each component. Note how its location and structure relate to its function. Draw the flower in your notebook and label each component with its name and function. Compare your observations with those of your partner.
4. When you have completed the dissection, draw and describe each of the parts separately. Use a labeled diagram.

ANALYSIS

Record your responses to the following in your notebook.

1. Create a concept map that demonstrates the relationships among the structures of a flower, their functions, and the process of fertilization.
2. In nature, the pollen from male plants is often carried to female plants by insects. The insects are attracted to the nectar found in the brightly colored flowers. This method of mating results in random mixing of variants of traits of different plants. Plant growers often wish to breed plants to produce progeny with very specific characteristics. To do this, the mating or crossing of the parent plants must be done in a controlled manner. The growers must pay careful attention to which plants cross with which. Design a method that a plant breeder might use to create a new variety of plant. Use your understanding of plant reproduction. Describe each step of the process and the events that take place in the plant after pollination.

As you read "The Parson and His Peas," pay attention to the steps of Mendel's procedure to cross-pollinate the plants in his experiments.

The Parson and His Peas

Throughout history, farmers and gardeners have been interested in how traits are passed from generation to generation in their livestock and crops. Their goal was to produce plants and animals with specific characteristics. To do that, they studied patterns of inheritance and carefully chose the parents to be used in breeding. It was amid this interest in developing new varieties of plants and animals that a modern-day understanding of heredity began to emerge.

Gregor Mendel was not a scientist. Mendel was a monk who took a great interest in the plant varieties growing in the garden at the abbey where he lived. Some gardeners of the time bred plants to create new combinations of flower color, leaf shape, and hardiness. But Mendel was interested in breeding as a way to investigate how traits were passed from generation to generation. Mendel took a special interest in garden peas. With the help of the other gardeners at the abbey, Mendel isolated several strains of pea plants with distinct traits. One strain produced only tall plants, another only short plants; one produced only purple flowers, another only white flowers.

Mendel chose to follow seven traits in peas. Each trait showed only two variations. This made it easy for him to track the phenotypes. The phenotypes themselves were easy to observe with the naked eye. They were round or wrinkled seeds and yellow or green seeds. Table 2.8 shows the seven traits Mendel chose for his experiment and the two variations of each trait.

Other breeders had already observed that for some traits, one form seemed to show up much more frequently than the other. Mendel's experiment involved crossing plants with different variants of the same trait. He planned to observe and count which form showed up in the offspring and then analyze the inheritance of the variant.

Mendel wanted to breed a pea plant having round peas with another pea plant having round peas. How could he do it? Mendel used his understanding of plant reproduction to design an experimental approach. To follow patterns of inheritance, he needed to control which plants crossed with which to produce offspring.

Mendel knew that peas are self-pollinating (a process called **self-fertilization**). Because pea flowers develop male and female parts simultaneously, the plant can fertilize itself. It deposits the pollen from its anther onto its own stigma. In some plant varieties, however, the male and female parts mature at different times. In these cases, the flower does not pollinate itself. Instead, pollen is carried to the stigmas of other plants of the same species. This is done primarily by insects, but also by birds, other animals, or wind. As the insect feeds, the pollen from the anthers sticks to its body. As the insect moves from flower to flower, it leaves a "calling card" on each. This calling card is pollen, which attaches to the stigma. This initiates fertilization. The process by which pollen from one plant fertilizes the flowers of another plant is called **cross-pollination** or cross-fertilization.

The method that Mendel used to breed his pea plants involved several steps. First, he selected two pea plants he wished to cross. He removed the stamen in the flowers of the first plant to prevent self-pollination. Then, using a small brush, he removed pollen from the anthers of the flowers of the second pea plant that he wanted to cross with the first plant. He then placed the pollen on the stigma of the first plant (see Figure 2.40).

Table 2.8 Traits and Variations in Mendel's Peas

Trait	Variant	Variant
seed color	yellow	green
seed shape	round	wrinkled
flower color	purple	white
pod color	green	yellow
pod shape	inflated	constricted
flower position	axial	terminal
stem height	tall	short

The seven traits Gregor Mendel chose for his experiments. Each trait showed two variations.

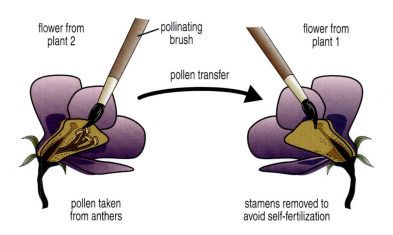

flower from plant 2 — pollinating brush — flower from plant 1

pollen transfer

pollen taken from anthers

stamens removed to avoid self-fertilization

Figure 2.40

Mendel carried out cross-breeding by brushing pollen from one plant onto the stigma of another.

In this way, he could carry out controlled pollination from one plant to another. After each cross, Mendel collected seeds and recorded the traits of the seeds that resulted from each cross. He then planted these seeds in his garden. When these plants matured, he determined the traits of the plants. These seeds and plants were called the **F_1 generation** (first filial). He then carried out controlled crossings of the F_1 plants and again noted which seeds came from each cross. The resulting plants were called the **F_2 generation**. Using this approach, Mendel collected and analyzed data on thousands of offspring through many generations.

ANALYSIS

1. Describe how the procedure you developed is similar to Mendel's procedure to cross-pollinate the plants in his experiments.
2. Describe how your procedure differs from what Mendel did in his experiments.

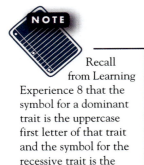

READING

My Parents Are Round and I'm Wrinkled—What Gives?

Before beginning his experiment, Mendel had observed many generations of plants. He did this to ensure that they always produced the same phenotype for a specific trait. For example, he made sure that plants with round peas always gave rise to new plants with round peas.

THE FIRST GENERATION

> **NOTE**
>
> Recall from Learning Experience 8 that the symbol for a dominant trait is the uppercase first letter of that trait and the symbol for the recessive trait is the lowercase letter.

To breed a first generation of pea offspring, Mendel took great care to cross-fertilize plants that had differing variants of traits. He began by crossing plants that only produced wrinkled peas with plants that only produced round peas. (The symbol for crossing is "×." Therefore, a cross between a plant producing a round pea and a plant producing a wrinkled pea would be represented by $R \times r$.)

Mendel took pollen from plants that produced wrinkled seeds to fertilize the flowers of a variant that produced round seeds. Then he did the reverse. He used the pollen from plants that produced round seeds to fertilize the wrinkled strain. One of his first observations was that the results did not change depending upon which plant contributed the pollen and which contributed the egg. In the first generation of offspring (the F_1), Mendel obtained the following data for the number of round seeds and the number of wrinkled seeds produced:

	round × wrinkled ("parents") ($R \times r$)	
F_1 generation	round seeds 7,300	wrinkled seeds 0

Mendel's published data did not indicate how many plants he crossed to produce all the seeds observed in the F_1 generation. What we know is that the flowers were carefully cross-fertilized, every pea pod was collected, and all the seeds were individually sorted and counted as either wrinkled or round. Mendel carried out these crosses many times in order to obtain statistically significant data.

THE SECOND GENERATION

To examine the second generation, Mendel crossed plants from the F_1 generation. He then collected and analyzed the seeds produced by this cross. His data from counting the shape of 7,324 F_2 generation seeds follow:

	round × wrinkled ("parents") (R × r)	
F_2 generation	round seeds 5,474	wrinkled seeds 1,850

One of Mendel's observations about seed shape was that one phenotype always appeared in the F_1 generation. This observation held true with all seven traits shown in Table 2.8. He called this the **dominant variant**. The other variant seemed to disappear in the F_1 generation and to reappear in the F_2 generation. He called this the **recessive variant**. With only the evidence of his garden pea crosses, Mendel established several important genetic principles. These include the following:

- There are pairs of factors (now called genes) that control heredity. In organisms that reproduce sexually, genes are inherited from each parent.
- Some organisms possess two forms of the gene for a single trait. In these cases, one form of the gene may be dominant and the other may be recessive. This is known as the **principle of dominance**.
- Two forms of each gene are separated (or segregated) during the formation of reproductive cells. Therefore, each reproductive cell (sperm/pollen or egg) has only one copy or allele of the gene. This is known as the **principle of segregation**.
- The genes for different traits may assort independently of one another. That is, any combination of alleles for each of the seven traits can take place in a reproductive cell. This is known as the **principle of independent assortment**.

Unfortunately, no one was ready to accept Mendel's work when it was completed in the 1860s. His paper, which detailed his results and conclusions, was generally ignored for more than 30 years after its publication. It is difficult for us to comprehend today just how incredible Mendel's achievement was. Mendel did his work prior to the knowledge or understanding of genes, chromosomes, DNA, and meiosis. Mendel's principles provide the basis for much of the current thinking in genetics.

Table 2.9   Traits and Alleles of Mendel's Peas

Trait	Alleles
seed color	**yellow**, green
seed shape	**round**, wrinkled
flower color	**purple**, white
pod color	**green**, yellow
pod shape	**inflated**, constricted
flower position	**axial**, terminal
stem height	**tall**, short

Note: The dominant trait is listed in bold print.

ANALYSIS

It is easier to answer question 4 if you write out the genotype of the F₁ generation from question 3. Then determine the genotype of the F₂ generation when the F₁ offspring are crossed. Explain your answer.

Record your responses to the following in your notebook.

1. Write the symbol for the allele of each trait listed in Table 2.9. Use the symbols geneticists use. (The letter to denote the allele is usually the first letter of the dominant trait. An uppercase letter indicates dominance and a lowercase letter indicates recessiveness.) For example, the symbols for seed color would be yellow Y, green y.

2. Select one trait (other than seed shape). Construct a flowchart or diagram of the steps Mendel used to collect his data.

3. What is the genotype of the yellow seeds in the "parent" generation? in the F₁ generation? of the green seeds in each generation? Remember, each seed has two genes for each variant. Be sure to use the correct symbols.

4. Do you think the genotype(s) of the yellow seeds in the F₂ generation might be the same as in the F₁ generation?

5. In the F₂ generation, 7,324 seeds were collected: 1,850 were green and 5,474 were yellow. What is the approximate ratio of these numbers? Why do you think there were many more round seeds than wrinkled seeds?

6. How does an understanding of meiosis explain Mendel's principles of segregation and independent assortment? Explain in a paragraph or in a diagram.

ACTIVITY

Sorting the Crosses

Are the patterns or ratios in inherited traits predictable or random? Assume that segregation and assortment take place the way Mendel thought they did. Then the possible gene combinations in the offspring that result from a cross can be predicted.

In the previous learning experience, you followed the segregation of genes during the formation of the reproductive cells (meiosis). Suppose the F₁ plants have one tall allele from one parent and one short allele from the other parent. The plant grows and forms flowers. The two alleles are segregated from each other when reproductive cells are made. Each F₁ plant will produce reproductive cells. Half of the reproductive cells will have the tall allele and half will have the short allele. What would be the result when two F₁ plants are crossed (see Figure 2.41)?

Geneticists use a **Punnett square** to help predict the results of crosses between organisms that have variants of a trait. Its design shows more clearly the possible gene combinations that result from a cross (see example in Figure 2.42). The square shows each possible gene combination for the offspring in the boxes that

NOTE

Punnett squares are named for an English geneticist, Reginald Punnett. He discovered some basic principles of genetics. He is also known for his work with the feather color traits of chickens. The color traits allowed Punnett to quickly separate the males from the females.

Figure 2.41

Segregation of paired alleles takes place during gamete formation. The alleles are paired up again when gametes fuse during fertilization.

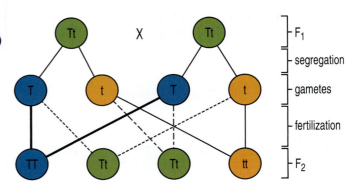

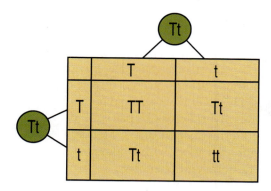

Figure 2.42

A Punnett square showing the cross between two heterozygous pea plants for stem height.

make up the square. The letters on the top represent the gamete alleles for one trait for one parent. The letters on the left side represent the gamete alleles for one trait for the other parent. The case of the letters indicates whether they are dominant or recessive alleles.

PROCEDURE

1. How can the Punnett square can be used to predict the outcomes of fertilization? Follow steps 1–7 below to predict the outcomes of Mendel's experiments. Cross a plant that has 2 dominant alleles (*RR*) for round seeds with a plant that has 2 recessive alleles (*rr*) for wrinkled seeds.

   Step 1   Make a key that represents the alleles in the cross.

   Step 2   Write the genotypes of the parents.
   Step 3   Determine the possible gametes that each parent can form.

   Step 4   Create a Punnett square.

   Step 5   Enter the possible gametes from one parent at the top of the Punnett square. Then enter those from the other parent on the side.

   Step 6   Complete the Punnett square by combining the gamete alleles in the appropriate boxes.

   Step 7   Compile the genotypes and phenotypes.

R = round
r = wrinkled

RR x *rr*

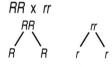

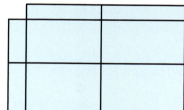

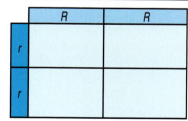

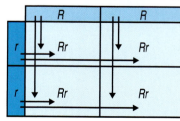

Phenotypes of the F_1 are all round. Genotypes of the F_1 are all *Rr*.

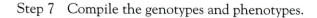

2. Are your results the same as Mendel's F_1 data?
   The predicted outcome was that all the peas would look round in the first generation. The square shows 2 organisms that are homozygous—1 dominant parent and 1 recessive parent. (Remember, organisms that are homozygous have 2 identical alleles for a particular trait.) When you cross those 2 organisms, all the offspring will have 2 alleles. They will have a dominant and a recessive allele for that trait. (This is a **monohybrid cross**.) That is, all the offspring are heterozygous. The square also confirms another one of Mendel's results. For each cross of a homozygous dominant variant with a homozygous recessive variant, all the plants showed the dominant phenotype.

3. Do the data from Mendel's F_2 experiments fit this model?
   The predicted ratio was 3 dominant phenotypes to 1 recessive phenotype. This ratio showed up consistently in Mendel's results. What would a Punnett square look like if you crossed peas from the F_1 generation shown above? Would the predicted phenotypic ratio appear? How is the genotype related to the phenotype?

4. **STOP & THINK** What are the probable genotypic and phenotypic ratios of a cross between a heterozygous round pea plant and a wrinkled pea plant?

5. **STOP & THINK** What would be the genotype of a homozygous tall plant with white flowers? What would be the genotype of a heterozygous tall plant with purple flowers? What alleles would be in the gametes of each parent?

ANALYSIS

Use a Punnett square to help you work through this Analysis. Record your responses to the following in your notebook.

1. You have a cat that has very long hair (H). Your friend has a cat with very short hair (h). You would like to breed your cat with her cat. But you don't know whether your cat is homozygous for long hair or heterozygous for long hair. Predict the genotypes and phenotypes of the F_1 generation in each case.

2. In the fruit fly *Drosophila melanogaster*, wings (W) are dominant over a lack of wings (w). Red eyes (R) are dominant over sepia (brownish) eyes (r). A wingless fly with sepia eye color is crossed with a fly that has wings and red eyes. (This is a **dihybrid** cross. A dihybrid cross consists of variants in two traits). What are the possible genotypes of each parent? What are the possible genotypes of the offspring? What are the phenotypes of the offspring?

3. You have a winged red-eyed fruit fly in your laboratory. Design a cross to determine whether the fly is heterozygous for both traits. Use a Punnett square to show all possible crosses.

4. Genetic counselors often use both Punnett squares and pedigrees to predict the probability of a trait variant taking place in a particular individual. **Albinism** is a recessive variant that results in a lack of pigmentation of skin and hair. Imagine that you are a genetic counselor with the following data:
   - Two couples—Harry and Theda T., and Jared and Emma A.—have normal pigmentation.
   - Harry and Theda have two daughters who are normally pigmented.
   - Jared and Emma have four children, three sons and one daughter. All four children are normally pigmented.
   - Harry and Theda's second daughter, Sally, marries Jared, Jr., one of Jared and Emma's sons.
   - Sally and Jared Jr. have two children. Their son is normally pigmented. But their daughter lacks pigmentation in her skin and hair, that is, she is an albino.

Sally and Jared Jr. wish to have another child and want to know the probability of this child being an albino.

   a. Create a pedigree of Sally and Jared Jr.'s families. Use the pedigree symbols found in Learning Experience 3 (Figure 2.14).

   b. Make a Punnett square with the genotypes for Sally and Jared Jr.

   c. What is the probability that their third child will be an albino?

   d. What is the probability that their third child will be a carrier?

5. The 23rd chromosome pair determines gender in humans. Determine the probabilities of a couple having a male baby (XY). Then determine the probability of the couple having a female baby (XX). A couple who has two daughters is planning to have a third child. What are the odds of this child being a boy? Explain your response.

A Growing Concern

CASE STUDY

Long before Mendel's work on pea plants, many farmers and gardeners were interested in how traits were passed on from generation to generation in their livestock and crops. The practice of agriculture arose in several areas of the world. The earliest evidence of agriculture dates back approximately 10,000 years in the Near East. It is not clear exactly what factors led early people to change from a life of foraging to a life of growing their own food in gardens and farms. But whatever the causes of the change, the key discovery in this change of lifestyle was that plants could be grown from seeds. Farmers soon learned that they could improve the quantity and quality of each succeeding year's harvest. They could do this by using only the seeds from crops that gave the highest yields, that were the most drought or disease resistant, that were easiest to harvest, or that tasted the best. Farmers bred cereal grains, such as wheat and rye, for characteristics of hardiness, drought resistance, and yield. Gardeners were interested in creating plants with different-colored flowers. They combined variant forms of the same trait.

In more recent years, scientists have developed genetic engineering techniques. These techniques are designed to bypass the vagaries (chanciness) of inheritance of traits. They enable scientists to insert genes from one organism into another organism. This, in turn, induces that organism to express new traits. Dozens of genetically engineered crops have already hit the market, and many more are on the way. Today you can buy Flavr Savr® tomatoes. These tomatoes have had flounder genes added to toughen up the fruit for shipping and to increase the shelf life. You can also buy soybeans that have had genes from petunia, bacteria, and cauliflower added to improve herbicide tolerance.

Topic: Genetic Engineering
Go to: www.scilinks.org
Code: INBIOH2261

A great deal of controversy has arisen over the production and use of genetically engineered crops. Proponents claim that the ability to add specific characteristics to fruits, vegetables, and cereal grains will provide nutritious food to more people year-round. The ability to make crops frost-resistant and herbicide-resistant may make food more affordable. Crops could be made resistant to damage by insects and fungi and to infection by bacteria and viruses. This would reduce the need for environmentally polluting pesticides and other chemicals.

Opponents, however, have a different perspective. Some members of consumer and environmental groups contend that it is impossible to predict the long-term consequences of the consumption of genetically engineered crops on human health. They worry about the insertion of genes into organisms in which they are not normally found. They think this may have serious consequences for the ecological balance of the environment, which laboratory and field-test trials cannot predict.

At the present time, the majority (about 93%) of genetic alterations are made to make food production easier and more profitable. The remaining 7% are engineered to improve taste or nutrition. What are the goals of modern techniques of creating new varieties of crops? Do the goals justify the means? The following article discusses the introduction of genetically engineered soybeans into the consumer market.

GENE ENGINEERED SOYBEANS GET FRIGID RECEPTION

In *The Gene Letter*, Volume 1, Issue 3, November 1996.

The first ship load of Monsanto's genetically engineered soybeans got a frigid welcome at the docks in Hamburg, Germany when it arrived in early November. Despite much scrutiny and regulatory approval from the FDA in the U.S. and the European Union, some food producers and supermarket chains have vowed they will not buy the beans or any product that contains them.

The fuss is over a single gene that Monsanto scientists transferred into the soybean plant so that it would be resistant to a major herbicide (also manufactured by Monsanto) called Roundup. Since Roundup kills all nonresistant leafy plants, the idea was to increase soybean crop yield by reducing weed encroachment.

Public opinion polls have showed [sic.] that Europeans are in general more concerned about bioengineered food products than are Americans. The Green Party has led the way in the attack against genetically engineered agricultural products. More than 80% of Europeans want such products clearly labeled as having been bioengineered. It is difficult to know the extent to which the tremendous fear generated by "mad cow disease" in the United Kingdom is influencing the reaction to the soybeans, but [the fears] must be making consumers generally more suspicious.

What is clear is that agribusiness giants like Ciba-Geigy, DuPont, Dow and Hoechst have made huge commitments to developing genetically engineered crops that will help to answer humanity's ever growing need for food. While Monsanto's new soybeans represent the first large scale entry of a genetically engineered crop into the European market, there are more than 50 food products in the U.S. product pipeline. Plans to introduce genetically engineered corn, chicory, and rapeseed in Europe are well underway.

Since the soybeans have passed all the necessary regulatory hurdles, the battle is likely to be fought at the checkout counters. If products using the modified plant are cheaper, economics is likely to determine acceptance. That, surely, is what Monsanto is betting.

 ANALYSIS

Record your responses to the following in your notebook.

1. You have a soybean selectively bred for a certain characteristic and one genetically engineered for a certain characteristic. Compare the similarities and differences between these two soybeans.
2. If a food has passed the necessary regulatory hurdles, should that food be labeled "genetically engineered"? Why or why not?
3. Would you eat foods that have been altered with bioengineering techniques? Include the reasons for your choice.
4. List four important values that influenced your decision in question 3.

There's a Mouse Gene in My Tomato!

ACTIVITY

You and your partner are part of a design team at Kerry's Chimeras, a biotechnology company. You have been assigned the task of designing a genetically modified food of your choice. The only guideline you have been given is this: The food should be designed to sell, sell, sell!

Materials

For each pair of students:

- poster board
- markers

PROCEDURE

1. Decide what food you will modify and how. (What new characteristic will it have?)
2. Explain why it is worthwhile to design this new product. Will it sell? Why? What benefit might it have for society?
3. Create an advertisement for this product on a poster board. Be sure to include the following:
   a. the name of the product,
   b. the new characteristic or feature,
   c. a description of why the food with this new characteristic is worth purchasing,
   d. potential benefits to society or to the customer of this new food, and
   e. a warning label if there are potential risks or problems to the customer or to society with this new food.
4. Be prepared to present your new food to the rest of the company (your class).

EXTENDING *Ideas*

▶ Reports have surfaced in recent years that Gregor Mendel may have altered his data. Some think he did this to have the numbers fit the expected monohybrid cross phenotype of 3:1 (dominant to recessive) and the dihybrid cross phenotype of 9:3:3:1. Research this controversy. State your opinion and provide your reasons.

▶ Five families, living in small villages close together in Colombia, have suffered as one member after another has fallen victim to an early onset of Alzheimer's disease. For generations, the families have regarded their affliction as a mystery, the subject of superstition. A team of Colombian and American researchers is creating pedigrees of the more than 3,000 living family members. The cause of this form of Alzheimer's is a mutation of a single nucleotide of a gene (PS1) on chromosome 14. The dominant form, called E280A, has spread through the Antioquia families. Research how scientists are solving this mystery and identifying the gene. Find out how the gene codes to produce the Alzheimer condition.

CAREER FOCUS

Nursery Worker   It is the middle of February in New England. But plants are flourishing in the warm, moist air at the Mountainview Nursery. Alan waters the orchids. His partner plants seeds for flowering perennials that will be sold as seedlings during the spring planting season.

Alan grew up in gardens. As a child, he helped his father with his landscaping business. He enjoyed working with his hands and learning about all of the different kinds of plants and the best conditions for growing them. As he grew older, he found he was very interested in the nurseries that supplied his father with different species of plants. His father would arrange those plants in customers' yards and gardens.

During Alan's high school years, he spent vacations working in a neighborhood nursery. He would water the plants, check them for insect damage or disease, prune them to create fuller foliage and more numerous blooms, and collect seeds for the next year's crop. He always felt proud when one of his seedlings or adult plants was sold. As a plus to his job, during the winters—when everyone else was complaining about the cold and the snow—he was always able to escape to his warm haven. Here he would surround himself with petunias, dahlias, azaleas, and roses; with greens like ivy, coleus, and ferns; and with many varieties of cacti.

As an adult, Alan owns his own nursery. He periodically takes courses to learn new techniques of nursery work. He finds out things like what different seeds are available and what technology exists for temperature control, watering, pesticides, and so forth. Alan has also taken numerous college courses in business management, horticulture, and biology. But his experience while growing up was the most important part of his training.

Besides maintaining and propagating small plants, shrubs, and trees, Alan keeps up a stock of gardening supplies for the nursery and for his customers. Other stock includes bird seed and feeders. Birds are considered an important ingredient in a successful garden. Alan follows gardening trends. He watches out for what plants are particularly popular during any year and brings in unique plants from around the world.

Alan recently made a new addition to the nursery. He set up a section for aquatic plants. Many of his clients have small ponds in their gardens and wanted to increase the amount of plants in and around them. This new area includes water lilies, blue flag irises, and several species of tall grasses.

To share all of the knowledge he has acquired over his years in the gardening and nursery business, Alan teaches regular seminars in his store. And he has made a practice of hiring a few high school students each year. He hopes to propagate his love and appreciation of the natural world through new generations.

Mapping Genetic Trails

Prologue

Mendel's observations of patterns in the inheritance of traits in peas led him to inferences that were later confirmed by research on chromosome movement during meiosis. Mendel inferred that alleles separate and segregate during gamete formation. He also thought that a gene for one trait did not influence the inheritance pattern for a different trait. That is, genes demonstrate independent assortment. However, there seems to be a problem. Think about the number of chromosomes in relation to the number of genes an organism has. A human, for example, has approximately 30,000 different genes. All of these genes are located on 23 pairs of chromosomes. Therefore, there are thousands of genes on each chromosome. (These are represented by the marker bands on your chromosome models.) The problem is this: If two genes are located on the same chromosome (**linked genes**), can they sort independently? If not, does this contradict Mendel's principle of independent assortment?

In this learning experience, you investigate how physically linked genes can sort. You also explore one of the major research efforts of the 20th century—the Human Genome Project. In this massive undertaking, scientists are using technologies developed from their understandings about chromosome segregation and assortment.

Brainstorming

Discuss the following questions with your partner, and record your thinking in your notebook. Be prepared to share your ideas with the class.

1. How do you think genes found on the same chromosome (linked genes) sort during meiosis?
2. Suppose that the data examining assortment of linked genes indicated that these genes could sort independently. How would this compare with Mendel's principles of segregation and independent assortment?
3. Can you think of any mechanisms by which genes on the same chromosome might sort independently?

265

ACTIVITY

I'll Trade You

What if segregation and independent assortment take place only in the ways Mendel proposed? Then the possible gene combinations in the offspring should be predictable. But geneticists soon discovered the concept of gene linkage. This concept states that all of the genes located on the same chromosome move together when that chromosome segregates during meiosis.

The fact of gene linkage seems to limit variation. What else might take place during meiosis that would increase variation? In this activity, you will examine the chromosomes found in gametes following meiosis. You will apply Mendel's principles to analyze the combination of alleles in the gametes.

Materials

For each pair of students:

- colored pencils or felt-tip markers (yellow, gray, brown, green, blue, red, and black)

TASK

1. A mythical mosquito has the following genotype:

   Hh Bb Rr Ll

   By chance, all of the dominant alleles came from the mother (maternal chromosome). All of the recessive alleles came from the father (paternal chromosome). Use the colored pencils or markers to create a drawing of the 3 chromosome pairs of your mosquito. Place the alleles in the appropriate locations. (The chromosomes and the location of the alleles on these chromosomes should be based on the model from Learning Experience 8. Draw 1 of each set of homologous chromosomes. Yellow represents the paternal chromosome; white represents the maternal chromosome.)

2. Determine the possible gametes for your mosquito. Then draw the chromosome contents of the gametes.

3. Use Table 2.10 to answer the following 2 questions. Record your responses in your notebook.
   a. If a gamete of this mosquito contains information for a black abdomen (*B*), which allele of wing shape would it have?
   b. If a gamete of this mosquito contains information for an orange abdomen (*b*), which allele of wing length would it have?

4. While examining the gametes of this mythical mosquito, a geneticist observed the genotypes shown in Figure 2.43. Describe the differences between the gametes you predicted in step 2 and the gametes in this figure.

5. In a short paragraph or a drawing, propose an explanation that could account for the unexpected genotypes.

Table 2.10   Genetic Information of the Mythical Mosquito

Trait	Phenotype	Symbol for Allele	Band Color	Chromosome (cm)
antenna texture	hairy smooth	*H* *h*	red	15
wing shape	round square	*R* *r*	green	30
wing length	long short	*L* *l*	black	22
abdomen color	black orange	*B* *b*	blue	30
unknown	not available	not available	brown	on all chromosomes

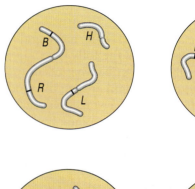

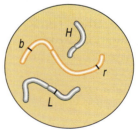
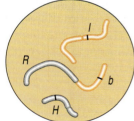
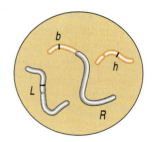

Figure 2.43

Some observed genotypes of gametes in the mythical mosquito.

Hairy, the Blue Tomato

ACTIVITY

The Jolly Blue Tomato Company specializes in producing novelty fruits and vegetables. They have found that consumers have become daring in their tastes. Consumers now crave new and exotic fruits and vegetables as a way of meeting the daily recommended intake of five servings.

Your team at Jolly Blue has been assigned the task of breeding a hairy, blue tomato that can be grown on a dwarf plant. In this way, many plants can be grown in a small space.

TASK

1. Your parent plants have the genotypes *Ss, rr, TT* and *ss, Rr, tt*. You also know that all 3 genes are located on the same chromosome. Use Table 2.11 to describe the phenotypes of your parent plants.

Table 2.11   Genetic Information of Parent Plants

Trait	Phenotype	Symbol
color	red blue	R r
texture	smooth hairy	S s
height	tall dwarf	T t

2. Your team has carried out many, many crosses. You have examined hundreds and hundreds of plants and their fruit. You have been able to produce plants and tomatoes with the following characteristics:
   - blue, smooth, and tall
   - blue, smooth, and dwarf
   - red, hairy, and tall
   - red, hairy, and dwarf

   However, you have not been able to produce a plant with blue, hairy, and dwarf characteristics. Write a report for the president of the Jolly Blue Tomato Company (who feels anything is possible). Describe what needs to happen to achieve the requested results. Your team is familiar with the modes to achieve variation, including that of crossover. **Crossover** takes place when there is an exchange of alleles between homologous chromosomes. Include a hypothesis in your report that might explain why producing a hairy, blue tomato may not be possible by conventional breeding techniques. Base your hypothesis on the team's understanding of variation.

3. Carefully examine the characteristics that seem to stay together. Think about how location on the chromosome might affect variation. Read "Home, Home on the Chromosome." Then revisit your explanation and see if it has changed.

READING

Home, Home on the Chromosome

The human **genome** consists of all of the genetic material present in a human's chromosomes. It is estimated that only about 2% of human DNA contains information for coding proteins. But even this small percentage consists of approximately 20,000–25,000 genes.

Think about this vast amount of DNA. How is it possible to determine the location of a single gene, which may be no bigger than a few thousand bases? Finding the location of specific genes on specific chromosomes has been the goal of many researchers of genetics. But this task is akin to locating individuals in the United States when you don't know their address, their city, or even their state of residence. Both tasks take a great deal of creativity, ingenuity, detective skills, plain hard work, and lots of money.

HOW DO YOU FOLD A GENETIC MAP?

The first gene to be located (mapped) on a chromosome was the gene responsible for red-green color blindness. Geneticists had observed that the inheritance of this disorder was passed from mothers who were able to perceive colors normally only to their sons. As you will recall from Learning Experience 7, females have XX sex chromosomes and males have XY sex chromosomes. Genes occur in pairs on the 22 pairs of autosomes. **Autosomes** are chromosomes other than sex chromosomes. But there is little or no homology between the X and the Y chromosome. Therefore, a gene on the male X chromosome (even a single recessive one) will be expressed. Females, however, with a normal allele on one X chromosome and a recessive allele on the other X chromosome would not show the recessive trait. This logic enabled researchers to map the gene for red-green color blindness. They mapped several other genes (including the gene for the blood clotting disease **hemophilia**), also on the X chromosome. Genes located on the sex chromosomes are known as **sex-linked genes**. The appearance of the associated phenotypes depends on the individual's sex.

In the 1960s, identification of genes on the autosomes began. Early mapping techniques involved joining or fusing in a test tube mouse and human cells into a new kind of hybrid mouse/human cell. This fusion had an interesting result: The newly created hybrid cell literally tossed out its human chromosomes until only a few remained. Scientists determined what human proteins still were being made in the hybrid after this chromosome-clearing process. As a result, they could assign the genes for these proteins to the human chromosomes that were still present in the hybrid cell. This approach, coupled with new staining techniques, enabled scientists to assign about 1,000 genes to specific chromosomes.

More precise approaches to gene mapping came with two key observations. The first was that genes on chromosomes tend to be inherited together unless crossover takes place. The distance between two genes can be determined by the frequency of crossover. In other words, how often are two genes on the same chromosome separated from one another. The closer two genes are, the less frequently they will be separated by crossover. Traits that often happen together, such as freckles and red hair, most likely are the result of gene linkage. As such, they are located close to each other on a chromosome. Genes that are linked show a very low frequency of crossover. Figure 2.44 gives an example of the relationship between the frequency of crossover between alleles and the location of the genes on a chromosome.

Topic: Genome Mapping
Go to: www.scilinks.org
Code: INBIOH2269

(a)

maternal chromosome

	A	B	C	D	E
A	0	.25	.10	.04	.41
B	.25	0	.31	.22	.60
C	.10	.31	0	.03	.32
D	.04	.22	.03	0	.35
E	.41	.60	.32	.35	0

paternal chromosome

(b)

B   A D C   E

Figure 2.44

Example of linked genes and the frequency of crossing over. (a) The numbers in the chart indicate the frequency of crossing over. The genes that are farthest apart, for example B and E, demonstrate greatest frequency of crossing over (.60). (b) The location of these genes on the chromosome, as determined by frequency of crossing over.

The second observation was made in the early 1980s. Scientists determined that individuals not only look different from one another, but that they also have distinctive chromosomes. Some of these distinctive features appear as variations in chromosome staining patterns (patterns of the DNA-binding proteins). Others are variations in the DNA sequence that may take place as frequently as every 500 bases. This happens primarily in stretches of DNA that have no coding function.

These regions of variation are called **genetic markers**. They can be used to follow inheritance of specific chromosomes or regions of a chromosome through many generations of a family. Scientists follow the inheritance of these markers and the inheritance of specific genetic diseases. In doing so, they have been able to find the chromosomal locations of genes responsible for disorders such as cystic fibrosis, sickle-cell anemia, Tay-Sachs disease, and fragile X syndrome.

This kind of genetic linkage map is used to locate the gene in a relatively small area of the chromosome. Once that is done, scientists can then construct a physical map that shows the actual position of a gene along the chromosome. The ultimate goal for creating physical maps of genes is to determine the DNA sequence.

THE HUMAN GENOME PROJECT

One of the major scientific initiatives of the 20th century has been to map, sequence, and identify the approximately 25,000 genes on the 24 human chromosomes (22 autosomes and two sex chromosomes X and Y). (To sequence means to determine the order of base pairs on the DNA.) In April 2003, this international effort, known as the **Human Genome Project**, made a major announcement. It had completed sequencing 99% of the gene-containing part of the human genome to 99.99% accuracy. This sequence information is already enabling scientists to identify genes related to specific diseases. By having the complete sequence of genes and their location on the chromosomes, scientists can interpret the functions of genes. They can also determine how the products of these genes—proteins—work together to organize and coordinate the chemistry of life.

Scientists hope that by having a complete genetic and physical map of the human genome, many medical problems can be solved and basic scientific questions answered. The potential medical benefits are enormous. By knowing the sequence of specific genes and the proteins that they encode, scientists can develop new tests for detecting disease. They can design new drugs for treatments. Perhaps they can even reach the ultimate goal of replacing faulty genes with normal genes (**gene therapy**). Individuals could become aware of a predisposition to certain diseases through genetic screening. As a result, they might be able to delay or prevent the onset of symptoms through changes in their lifestyle and habits. In addition, scientists could determine how specific environmental factors affect and alter genes. These factors include such things as chemicals, drugs, and pollutants.

Enormous benefits of unraveling some of the mysteries of human history and existence may also result. Scientists can compare the sequence of the entire human genome to the genomes of other organisms. This would help them clarify the evolutionary relationships among different species. Tracking the appearance of mutations will help establish a more precise evolutionary timeline.

With a map of the human genome in hand, scientists may be able to determine the mechanisms that control gene expression. This may also help them to understand the processes that regulate the careful timing of a cell's

Topic: Human Genome Project
Go to: www.scilinks.org
Code: INBIOH2270

growth and division. (And it may shed light on how the regulation of growth may fail in cancer patients.) Identifying certain genes and understanding how they are expressed can also lead to developing new strains of fruits and vegetables and new breeds of animals. Finally, it is hoped that by deciphering the human genome, we can understand one of life's greatest mysteries: How does a single fertilized egg grow and develop into a multicellular organism?

The Human Genome Project seems to promise a great deal in regard to curing disease and understanding many questions in biology. But many fear the consequences of such a project. From its beginning, the costs of the project have been enormous. More than 3 billion dollars from U.S. taxpayers has been spent. Add to that the costs of time and the numbers of individuals involved. There are those who feel that this is not a wise use of the taxpayers' money and that it is diverting resources from other important research.

Many are also concerned about the ethical considerations of the Human Genome Project. They think that once the human genome is sequenced and the genes identified, information about an individual's genetic makeup could become public knowledge. Following analysis of a drop of blood or a snip of hair, an individual's deepest genetic secrets might be available. Is that information that employers or health insurance companies should have access to, for example? Bioethical questions have already arisen as genes for genetic disorders are identified and diagnostic tests made available. Is it appropriate to diagnose a disease for which no cure is known, such as sickle-cell anemia and Huntington's disease? Will employers or insurance companies use these test results against the individual?

It is conceivable that one day every person might carry a DNA identification card rather than a driver's license. This card would identify an individual more precisely and thoroughly than any description or fingerprint. Who should have legal access to this card? Is this something you would feel comfortable having?

TASK

You are an aide to a congressperson. You have been assigned the task of preparing her for a vote in Congress on whether funding for the Human Genome Project should be continued. You need to write an informative position paper that can be used during a debate. Use the information in the reading "Home, Home on the Chromosome" and any other knowledge you have gained from Learning Experiences 7, 8, and 9. Your paper must include the following:

- the goals of the Human Genome Project;
- an explanation of the scientific concepts involved in the project;
- the potential benefits and abuses of the information derived from the project;
- the economic, legal, and ethical issues involved; and
- your recommendation as to how she should vote and why.

Your congressperson is somewhat uninformed about the basics of genetics. So be sure to include a clear and simple explanation of genes, genotype, phenotype, chromosomes, crossover, and genetic mapping techniques. Also make sure that your position paper is brief, concise, and very clear. Your congressperson does not have a strong understanding of biology and does not have much time to prepare for the vote.

● The distinctive characteristics of each individual's chromosomes have provided defenders of the law with a new weapon in the fight against crime. This weapon is DNA fingerprinting. DNA fingerprinting relies on the observation that the DNA of every individual creates a unique pattern when treated with enzymes. The enzymes cut the DNA into discrete fragments that can be visualized by various methods. This technique has been used to match the DNA of suspects with DNA isolated from blood or hair found at the crime scene. However, some critics question its validity and reliability. Research this technology and describe the principles behind it. Identify any high-profile cases in which it has been used. Explore the arguments for and against its use. Use your understanding of the science of DNA fingerprinting to explain which side you support and why.

● Treatment of genetic disorders includes recent technology in gene therapy. Two approaches are possible. In one instance, the appropriate gene is delivered to the specialized cells in which the altered protein is expressed. For example, in sickle cell, a functional β-globin gene would be delivered to cells resulting in normal red blood cells. This is called somatic gene therapy. Another possibility is to deliver the gene to the germline cells or gametes. In this approach, the altered gene would be "fixed" for all the progeny of that individual. Describe the differences between somatic and germline gene therapy in terms of long-range effects for both the individual and society. Serious concern has been expressed about the potential uses and misuses of germline gene therapy. Research the ethical issues involved in this technique and present both sides of the controversy.

● Gene therapy has been used in trials to treat the genetic disease cystic fibrosis. Research the molecular basis of cystic fibrosis. What are the current attempts to treat it through gene therapy?

CAREER FOCUS

Database Administrator   The door of the computer laboratory opened. Dr. Nadeau approached Mitra to discuss a presentation he was preparing, for which he needed her input. He was doing the presentation for an upcoming conference. The topic was on a recent cloning experiment his laboratory had attempted. This particular experiment was not successful. But Dr. Nadeau wanted to share the results of his research with the group of colleagues attending this conference. He needed Mitra to organize the data collected from this experiment and to illustrate the new knowledge obtained from the research.

Mitra's work is essential to the scientists with whom she works. She is often asked to run statistical analyses on the data and graph the results. Mitra is also responsible for keeping the database up-to-date and in good working order. To do this, she relies on her attention to detail. This is a highly competitive and fast-paced field. Because of this, Mitra needs to keep an eye on the security of the entire database system. There are people who would be very interested in having access to scientific data before they are published. Mitra has to make sure that access is available only to those scientists and technicians directly involved in the research.

Mitra learned computer basics in middle and high school. She always enjoyed working with numbers and data. She found it easy to use computers to perform the tasks she had in mind. Her first job after high school graduation was in a physician's office where she was exposed to medical terminology. Mitra became interested in biology and medicine, and enrolled in some undergraduate biology courses at a community college. Her computer background and willingness to learn more about biology, along with her experience in her first job, make this present position perfect for her. In addition, Mitra keeps up with the latest technological advances in computers and observes how technology is ultimately affecting the field of genetics.

When Dr. Nadeau returned from the conference, he said the tables and graphs Mitra had created for his presentation were very well received. Several scientists commented that the results were extremely clear. These results will be published in a medical journal. Then, perhaps, others will refer to this research for lobbying purposes or in courts of law. The news gave Mitra a strong sense of accomplishment and pride.

What Mendel Never Knew

Prologue

Look around you. The individuals in your class are a living illustration of how phenotypes are not always as straightforward as in Mendel's peas. Mendel made several fundamental observations about inheritance patterns in peas. He concluded that traits, such as the height of a pea plant, were determined by "discrete factors" (genes) that happen in pairs. One member of each pair was inherited from each parent. Mendel's crosses yielded offspring that were easily distinguished from each other. A plant was either tall or short. And the variant for tallness would dominate over the variant for shortness. These straightforward patterns are known as Mendelian genetics or Mendelian inheritance.

Scientists continued to investigate the patterns of inheritance in many different organisms. They discovered that Mendelian genetics was not sufficient to explain some phenotypic variations. In humans, dominant/recessive gene interactions are not frequently seen. For example, suppose one parent is tall and the other short. The phenotypes of their offspring do not follow the simple pattern of all tall. Nor will their F_2 generation (grandchildren) necessarily have a 75% chance of being tall and a 25% chance of being short. The pattern is much more complex. In this learning experience, you explore the traits that result from a variety of gene product interactions.

Brainstorming

Discuss the following questions with your partner, and record your thinking in your notebook. Be prepared to share your ideas with the class.

1. Look back to the list of traits and variations you made in Learning Experience 1, Finding the "Gene" in Genetics. Using that list, identify those traits that you think might have more than two variants. Next to the trait, list all the variants you can think of.
2. How do you think more than two variants of the same trait could occur? Describe any ways you can think of that this could happen.

Variation: It's Not That Simple

ACTIVITY

For many traits, variation is not the result of a simple dominant/recessive interaction between the products of two alleles of a gene. Rather, variation can result from different kinds of interactions. These interactions can take place among the products of two or more alleles. They can also be the result of the products of more than one gene. These interactions can result in a range of variations in that trait. In this activity, you will analyze several different traits. You will do this by using the information provided in six trait scenarios and in Table 2.12. You will then determine the kinds of interactions that take place among the gene products that result in the traits you observe.

TASK

1. Read each of the six trait descriptions that follow.
2. Use Table 2.12 to identify which mode of inheritance each trait exhibits.
3. In your notebook, record your response to the challenge found at the end of each trait description.

Table 2.12 Modes of Gene Product Interaction	
Mode of Inheritance	**Description of Interaction Resulting in Phenotype**
complete dominance	A gene has two alleles that may encode variant forms of that protein. This results in different phenotypes. When the two different alleles are present, only one phenotype will appear (dominate).
incomplete dominance	A gene has two or more alleles. The phenotype is the result of the interaction of the variant products of both alleles. The phenotype may appear as a blending of the two products. But the alleles continue to separate independently.
codominance	A gene has two alleles. The phenotype is the result of the action or interaction of both variant products of the alleles. This is similar to incomplete dominance. Except here the products are discrete rather than blended. The appearance of one phenotype over the other may be the result of environmental influences.
multiple alleles	A gene has more than two possible alleles. They all encode variants of the same protein. The phenotype is dependent on which two alleles are present in the organism. It also depends on the patterns in which the products of these alleles interact. The patterns may be dominant, incompletely dominant, or codominant.
pleiotropic	A single gene may have multiple effects on the phenotype of an organism. Both alleles of the gene encode a protein with an altered function. The failure to produce a functional protein alters many characteristics of the organism.
polygenic	The phenotype is the cumulative result of the interactions of the products of several genes and their alleles.

Trait 1

Sickle-cell anemia is the result of a change in the β-globin chain of hemoglobin. An individual who is homozygous for sickle-cell trait will show classic symptoms of sickle-cell anemia. These are intense joint pain, shortness of breath, anemia, and the characteristic sickle shape of the red blood cells. In an individual who is heterozygous for sickle cell, the alleles for both types of hemoglobin (A and S) are present in every red blood cell. But the sickling phenotype only appears under conditions of oxygen deprivation, such as during exercise at high altitudes.

Identify the mode of inheritance. Explain the phenotype of individuals who are homozygous and those who are heterozygous for this gene.

Trait 2

The so-called "blue" (actually gray) Andalusian variety of chicken is produced by crossing a black parent and a white parent. Color production in these chickens depends on a single gene. In the F_2 generation, black and also white chickens may reappear.

Identify the mode of inheritance. Describe how this gene product interaction produces the observed phenotype.

Trait 3

Human height is determined by a number of factors, including diet. But even if all individuals were fed the same diet, height among individuals would show continuous variation. That is, a gradation of small differences would still result within a certain range. Height is determined by a number of gene products. These include levels in production of hormones, such as growth hormone. They also include growth capacity of structural components, such as cartilage, connective tissue, skeletal muscles, and bone.

Identify the mode of inheritance for the height trait. Explain how this type of gene product interaction contributes to the variation of height.

Trait 4

The color of human skin is determined by genetic factors. But the shade may vary depending on environmental factors. Skin color is almost entirely the result of the amount of **melanin** pigment and its distribution in the outer layer of skin. The products of at least two genes have been shown to determine the levels of melanin produced. Several other genes appear to be involved in how this melanin is distributed in the skin. **Melanocytes** are special cells that produce melanin. They are much larger in darker-skinned individuals. They also have many more specialized structures that deliver the melanin to the outermost layer of skin cells.

Identify the mode of inheritance. Describe how this kind of gene product interaction might produce gradations in skin coloring.

Trait 5

There are four major blood groups in humans (A, B, AB, and O). These blood groups are determined by a gene that encodes an enzyme used in the synthesis of a polysaccharide (large sugar molecule). This polysaccharide is found on the surface of red blood cells. This gene has three alleles. Each encodes a variant of this enzyme. The variants result in the synthesis of the different forms of the polysaccharide that characterize the blood as being type A, B, AB, or O. Table 2.13 lists the phenotype (blood type) of an individual and the genotypes possible.

Identify the mode of inheritance for each genotype. Describe how the interaction of the products of each type of allele produces the resulting phenotype.

Table 2.13   Human Blood Types and Their Possible Genotypes

Phenotype (Blood Type)	Genotype (Alleles Present)	Polysaccharides on Surface of Red Blood Cell
O	OO	
A	AA, AO	
B	BB, BO	
AB	AB	

Trait 6

A single gene in rats controls the production of a protein involved in forming cartilage. Cartilage is the tough elastic tissue in vertebrate animals that provides some of the organism's structural support. A rat carrying two alleles with an altered protein displays a whole complex of birth defects. These include thickened ribs, a narrowing of the passage through which air moves to and from the lungs, a loss of elasticity in the lungs, blocked nostrils, a blunt snout, and a thickening of the heart muscle. These effects generally result in death.

Identify the mode of inheritance. Explain the effects of the gene products.

Playing Your Hand

Variation can be explained by the processes you have been exploring in the last several learning experiences. Think about Mendel's principles of segregation, independent assortment, crossover, and dominance, as well as the various modes of interactions of gene products. All these processes can account for the tremendous variation we observe among individuals. Once you have been dealt your DNA, however, is the outcome of the game predictable? What role does the environment play in the phenotypic expression of a genotype?

THE ONE AND ONLY YOU

The debate about nature versus nurture is an old one. This debate ponders the roles that genetic inheritance and the environment play in determining who a person is and will become. At the beginning of the 20th century, scientists were concluding that heredity is not destiny. Using daphnias (small freshwater organisms), they demonstrated that organisms with the same genetic makeup, raised under different conditions of temperature and acidity, displayed varying physical and behavioral characteristics. The phenotypic expression of their genotypes was influenced by their environment.

Identical twins separated at birth have provided fascinating insights into the roles played by heritable and environmental factors. These individuals are produced from a single fertilized egg. Thus, they share the same genetic makeup. Since 1979, traits of separated twins have been tracked in a study conducted at the University of Minnesota. In these studies, researchers measured physical and behavioral traits. These included handedness, fingerprint pattern, height, weight, intelligence, allergies, and dental patterns. They also compared twins' interests, fears, habits, and beliefs. The researchers found that identical twins separated at birth and reunited later were remarkably similar, right down to certain twitches and idiosyncrasies. However, enough variations in traits were also observed to indicate that the environment also makes a contribution.

For certain traits, the effect of the environment is readily apparent. In the past 100 years, the average height of humans has increased. This is mainly due to better nutrition. Although genetic inheritance plays a major role in determining height, diet can influence the final outcome. We can see another example of the effect of the environment in Himalayan rabbits and Siamese cats. The fur on their extremities—ears, nose, and paws—is much darker than the fur on the rest of their body. The color of the fur is determined by a gene encoding an enzyme that influences melanin production. An allele of this gene produces an enzyme that is sensitive to heat. In warm body regions, the enzyme is less active. So fur grows in lighter than it does at the cooler tips of the body.

For other traits, however, the link is less obvious. Imagine that at birth you were moved to an environment very different from your original one. How might you be different now? Would your genetic inheritance continue to make you "you"? Or would your environment have influenced you to become a very different person?

GENETIC JEOPARDY

The relationship between having a gene and how it is expressed is not as clear-cut as it seems. We see this most clearly in inherited diseases. The locations of genes for many heritable diseases are being mapped on chromosomes through the efforts of the Human Genome Project. Some of these are the genes for cystic fibrosis, Huntington's disease, sickle-cell anemia, and breast cancer. With this information, genetic counselors can, in theory, identify those individuals who have the gene. And those individuals, therefore, may have a genetic predisposition to the disease. But is having a faulty gene the same as having the disease? In cases such as sickle cell and cystic fibrosis, having one allele that encodes an abnormal protein does not result in disease. These are cases where the abnormal protein product is recessive. In other cases, such as Huntington's disease, the abnormal protein is dominant. So having a single copy, even in the presence of a normal copy of the gene, means that the individual will be affected.

Remember that a trait can be the result of the interactions of several alleles or gene products. Thus, the outcome of having an abnormal gene may not be easy to predict. Does having the breast cancer gene mean you are destined to develop breast cancer? Can maintaining a certain lifestyle reduce the risk of developing breast cancer? The answers are not clear at this time for some diseases. But for other diseases, much is known.

Hypertension is a cardiovascular disease. It appears to have both genetic and environmental causes. During the circulation of blood, the heart must pump blood against pressure in the arteries. Normally, the arteries are flexible and present little resistance to blood flow. However, as the pressure in the arteries rises (for example, when fat deposits clog the arteries), the work that the heart must do increases. In an individual with a high blood pressure (180/140), the heart must work twice as hard as the heart of an individual whose blood pressure is 100/70. The consequences of this extra work for the heart can be serious. The heart muscle can be damaged. This puts the individual at risk for a heart attack. Twenty to 50 genes may be involved in regulating blood pressure. One of the genes known to be involved encodes a protein, angiotensinogen. This protein controls blood vessel tone and flexibility. Some individuals with hypertension show variants in this protein. Some studies indicate that individuals can influence their blood pressure and propensity to heart attacks by controlling their diet and level of exercise.

The interplay between genetic and environmental factors is even more complex in mental and behavioral traits. Do these factors play any role in alcoholism, intelligence, sexual orientation, anxiety, and mental disorders? Headlines routinely proclaim that the genes for certain personality traits have been discovered. Even if these genes exist, unraveling the complexities of their interactions with other gene products and the environment will be a challenge for geneticists.

ANALYSIS

Record your responses to the following in your notebook.
1. The following factors appear to increase the risk of hypertension:
   - diet high in fat
   - diet high in salt
   - stress
   - family history
   - insufficient exercise
   - obesity
   - maleness
   - African ancestry
   - alcohol intake
   - age

Your latest medical examination indicates that your blood pressure is 190/140. Your doctor wants to know about the occurrence of hypertension in your family. She would like you to change some of your habits.

  a. Explain why your doctor thinks it is important to have information about your family.
  b. Describe what steps you can take to control your blood pressure.
  c. Do you think these steps will help even if you have a family history of hypertension? Why or why not?

2. It is now possible to identify a predisposition to certain diseases by testing to see whether an individual carries the allele for that disease. In some cases, such as breast cancer, a woman may or may not get the disease. But in other cases, such as Huntington's, the person will definitely get the disease if he or she carries a mutant allele. In each case, imagine the following: This disease runs in your family and you have the opportunity for **genetic testing**. Would you get tested? Why or why not?

EXTENDING *Ideas*

Ever since the decision was made to attempt to identify the approximately 20,000 genes in the human genome, the rate of discovery for individual genes has climbed steadily. Scientists have discovered an obesity gene that helps regulate weight. They have identified genes that cause or contribute to cancer and a gene that triggers the onset of Alzheimer's disease. Other research has suggested that traits that define important parts of our identity may also be written in our DNA. For example, genes may play a part in determining whether we are happy or sad or whether we are predisposed to alcoholism or schizophrenia. At the same time, scientists have uncovered some of the mechanisms by which the environment can influence genetic destiny by "turning on" or "turning off" various genes. This seems to strengthen the notion that nature and nurture are inseparable. Genes by themselves do not determine one's medical or behavioral fate. Research both sides of the debate. Do you think we are who we are because of the genetic traits passed down through the generations? Or do you think that environmental influences can and have altered our genetic destiny?

Archaeologist   The day has come. It is Ibrahim's first day working for the Cairo Museum. His supervisor leads him to a heavy locked door at the end of a long corridor. Ibrahim walks in and there she is. He's waited all these years. Mummy #46 lay on the table. She is awaiting his analysis. Ibrahim hopes to learn as much as he can about her while showing her the utmost respect, for she lived thousands of years ago.

Ibrahim grew up in the shadow of the pyramids. He dreamed of studying the pharaohs (kings) and queens who once ruled over his homeland. While in school, Ibrahim learned that more than 500 mummies and mummy fragments were rediscovered in storage at a Cairo university and moved to the Cairo Museum to be studied. Ibrahim was determined to be a part of the study to identify these mummies. Some of these mummies could have even been members of an Egyptian royal family.

Together with his courses in general archaeology, Ibrahim also studied genetics. He needed a background in genetics to work directly with the unidentified mummies. Ibrahim found that in the past, X-rays of skull measurements were used to establish relationships between mummies. But as the technology of DNA collections and testing becomes more and more advanced, it gives the best hope of successful identification.

In school, Ibrahim took classes in archaeology and anthropology. He was also fortunate to be able to travel around the world to take part in a number of different archaeological digs. Some involved excavating sites of ancient civilizations. At each site, Ibrahim and other students and scientists studied the architecture, pottery, furniture, artwork, and human remains. This helped them propose hypotheses about what life was like when that civilization thrived. The field experience was very important.

During his travels, Ibrahim learned that archaeologists are also very interested in the plant and animal life that surrounded the different sites of civilizations. Knowing what plant and animal life flourished in the surrounding regions helped his team learn about what the citizens of these communities used for food, clothing, and even shelter. For example, they might learn about a great drought that caused devastation to crops and farming. As a result, Ibrahim's team could possibly conclude that starvation brought the metropolis to a devastating end.

After receiving a bachelor's degree in archaeology, Ibrahim chose to continue his education. He earned a master's degree. Now he is part of an important study at the Cairo Museum.

He studies Mummy #46 carefully. Many hours of analysis lay before him. There are tissue scrapings and X-rays. He will then examine her teeth, the sparse hairs on her head, and even the position in which she lay. All of this will hopefully lead him to an identity. But finding one clear answer is sure to result in more questions as he continues his research within the maze of expressionless, nameless mummies.

For Further Study

The Anastasia Mystery

Prologue

If you were found wandering in a strange city with no papers or identification, how could you be identified? When there is an eyewitness to a crime, police artists can draw a composite sketch of the criminal and release it to newspapers and to television stations. But is just looking like the person in the sketch enough to convince authorities that they have the guilty person?

In this investigation, you read about a mystery that has intrigued the world since 1920. It was then that a woman appeared in Germany and claimed to be the Grand Duchess Anastasia, youngest daughter of the murdered Czar Nicholas and Czarina Alexandra of Russia. Citizens and scientists from around the world have attempted to determine her true identity. Books have been written and films have been made about whether this woman, known as Anna Anderson, was really Anastasia.

To investigate this mystery, you will use many of the concepts you have already explored in this unit. As you proceed, think about how the study of genetics has changed during the 20th century. How might this change, both in knowledge and the tools to apply this knowledge, help in solving this mystery?

Brainstorming

Discuss the following questions with your partner, and record your thinking in your notebook. Be prepared to share your ideas with the class.

1. What, if anything, do you know about Anastasia or the Russian royal family, the Romanovs?
2. How could you find out whether two individuals are related? What kinds of questions might you ask if you were trying to determine whether two people were related?

The Mysterious Woman

READING

She called herself the Grand Duchess Anastasia, daughter of Nicholas II, murdered Czar (Emperor) of Russia. There were those who believed her. How could anyone have survived that Siberian night in July 1918, when her parents, her three sisters, and her **hemophiliac** brother were massacred? Why did people believe her? She was, after all, in the Dalldorf Asylum for the Insane. People who are mentally unstable often think they are famous. So the question remains: Why would anyone believe her? But, believe her they did. Not everyone, but just enough people in enough high places to allow her to live out her entire life shrouded in mystery. Was this woman who became known as Anna Anderson really the youngest daughter of the last Russian Czar?

This story begins when a woman was found splashing in the icy cold waters of the Landwehr Canal in Berlin. It was February 17, 1920. The police and rescuers who pulled her sopping body from the canal couldn't get her to speak. She was pale and thin, looking no older than 20. They asked her numerous questions. Who was she? Why had she jumped? How old was she? Where was she from? She sat in silence until their threats of prosecution forced her to speak.

It is reported that she said, "I have asked for nothing," in German tinged with what some say was a vaguely Russian accent. She then fell silent once more. Unable to determine the mysterious woman's identity, the frustrated police took her to a local hospital.

When she awoke in the morning, more questions awaited. She again refused to answer. There were no clues to her identity. She carried no purse, no papers, no wallet. Her stubbornness and silence caused doctors to diagnose a mental problem and commit her to Dalldorf Asylum.

Fräulein Unbekannt (Miss Unknown), as they called her, lived quietly in Dalldorf, always refusing to answer questions of her identity. But the police pursued their job. They took pictures and circulated them. They tracked down the relatives of missing persons who fit her description. They inquired about escapees from prison and insane asylums. The answer was always the same—no one knew who she was.

Her doctors and nurses began to notice a somewhat aristocratic manner in the young woman. Clearly, she was not a working woman, they said. Her hands were too soft. She was too well mannered. She began to speak of travels in Scandinavia and of the German Kaiser (King) and the Crown Prince of England as if she knew them. The suspicions of the nurses were aroused.

Almost 2 years after her arrival at Dalldorf, she suddenly announced what some had already begun to suspect. She was Anastasia, the daughter of the Czar. Her admission turned on its head the world of the Russians living in exile in Germany. Many of them fervently hoped that a survivor of the tragic night that their Czar was assassinated could be found. People came to see her. Some determined that she simply knew too many intimate details of Czarist life to be anyone other than the Grand Duchess. Others flatly refused to acknowledge her claim.

The Russians who believed her tracked down a friend of Anastasia's mother to see if she could identify Fräulein Unbekannt. The friend became convinced that Fräulein Unbekannt was another of the Grand Duchesses, Tatiana. A maid of honor of the Czarina (the wife of the Czar and mother of the Grand Duchesses), Baroness Buxhoeven, was brought next to the hospital. She swore that the young woman was not Tatiana, for she was much too small. Fräulein Unbekannt spoke little and cowered under the covers of her bed during the many visits. This made it difficult to determine her identity.

The constant stream of visitors continued. One would say she was Anastasia and the next would declare she was not. She was released from the hospital into the care of a believer. The visits continued. All the while, the unknown woman firmly insisted that she was Anastasia.

She moved to the United States, married, and lived her entire life professing to be the Grand Duchess Anastasia. Two German courts rejected her claim. Nonetheless, she continued to maintain that her story was true. Even after her death, the debate about her true identity continued. How can it be proven who she really was?

NALYSIS

Record your responses to the following in your notebook. Be prepared to share your ideas with the class.

1. What other information would you need to determine whether Anna Anderson was really Grand Duchess Anastasia?
2. What characteristics might she have that would help you to determine her identity?
3. What questions would you ask? Of whom? What tests would you do?
4. Why do you think that people from several continents cared about this mystery?

What Runs in the Family?

Queen Victoria, who ruled for 64 years, had nine children. Her family tree has been researched in great detail. It has been a matter of great interest for two main reasons. First, many of her offspring married into the other royal houses of Europe, producing an extremely complex family tree. Second, a curious genetic trait appeared in the family.

TASK

Examine Figure 2.45, Queen Victoria's abridged pedigree. You may wish to refer to the symbols and notations from Figure 2.14 in Learning Experience 3. Discuss with your partner what patterns you see. Then devise an explanation for these patterns.

ANALYSIS

Record your responses to the following in your notebook.

1. What do the hatched squares represent? What **pattern of inheritance** do you see? (You might want to look for any similarities among those affected.)
2. Based on the information in the pedigree, identify the first individual affected with the **hemophilia allele**. From whom did he inherit it? Explain your response.
3. How do you think the change in this allele arose?

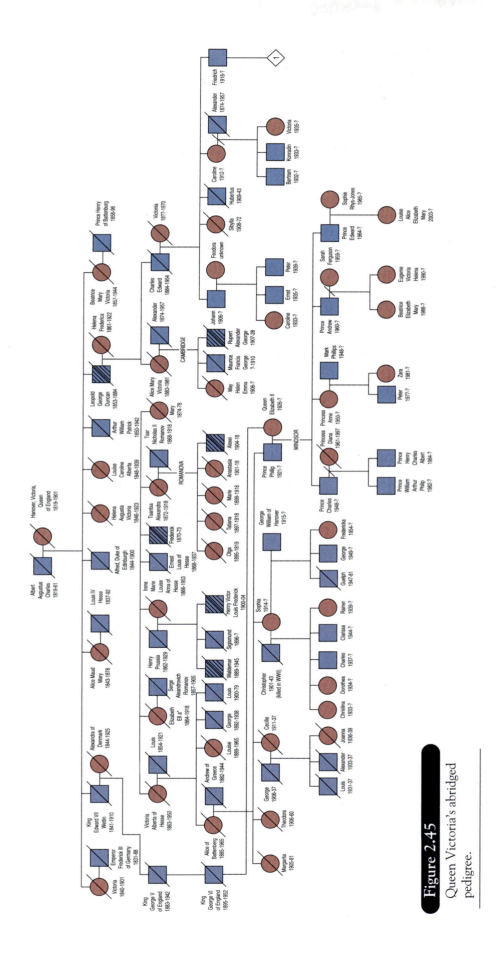

Figure 2.45

Queen Victoria's abridged pedigree.

4. Leopold George Duncan was affected, but his son was not. Only one grandson, Rupert Alexander George, was affected. Explain the pattern of inheritance for Leopold's children and grandchildren. Keep in mind that females are XX and males are XY. Also, the sex of the child is determined by the father, that is, whether the sperm that fertilized the egg contained an **X chromosome** or a **Y chromosome**.

5. Do you think any of the children of the current British royal family are at risk for this disease? Explain your response.

6. Are you able to determine Anna Anderson's identity from this pedigree? Why or why not?

READING

DNA Solves the Mystery

After the Bolsheviks murdered the Czar and his family, and the Russian Revolution took hold, Vladimir Lenin and then Joseph Stalin came to power as dictators. All mention of the royal family was forbidden. In May 1979, 12 miles from Ekaterinburg, Siberia, a Russian geologist located a grave he felt sure held the remains of the Romanov family. He kept quiet about it until 1989 when the announcement caused an international furor. In 1991, a Russian archaeologist was asked to assist in excavating the grave. She and others dug at the site. They found skeletal parts of nine people, although 11 were known to have been murdered early that July morning in 1918 (the seven Romanovs, their doctor, and three servants). Were these remains those of the Russian royal family? If so, where were the other two?

The first identification was done by computer superimposition of the skulls. But portions of the faces of some of the women were missing (they had been crushed by rifle butts). As a result, many scientists were not convinced by the identification of the remains as belonging to individual Romanovs. It also appeared that the skeletons of Alexis, the young son, and Anastasia, the youngest daughter, were missing.

The British Forensic Science Service was called in to do sophisticated molecular testing. Using **forensic science**, Doctors Gill and Ivanov took some bone and froze it in liquid nitrogen. They then ground it into a fine powder and dissolved it in various solutions. Lastly, they centrifuged it to release the DNA present in the bone cells. This extraction of bone released only a small amount of DNA. To obtain enough DNA to analyze, the DNA needed to be amplified (or increased in amount). The scientists used a technique called **polymerase chain reaction (PCR)**. This technique uses an enzyme that normally is involved in DNA replication to synthesize in a test tube segments of DNA of interest. Using this technique, they made enough DNA to be analyzed.

Using nuclear DNA (found in the nucleus), the team determined the sex of each of the skeletons by doing a comparison of base pairs on the X and Y chromosomes. They confirmed the earlier findings. The skeletons were those of four males and five females. By examining repeating DNA sequences, they found that skeleton numbers 3–7 were related. They also determined that number 4, a male, and number 7, a female, were the parents of numbers 3, 5, and 6.

At fertilization, the DNA from sperm and ovum come together. But only the cellular components of the ovum become part of the fertilized egg. Gill and Ivanov next extracted **mitochondrial DNA** from the nine skeletons. Mitochondria are cellular components found in the cytoplasm of all cells. They have their own DNA. Therefore, mitochondrial DNA is passed on from the

SCI LINKS
NSTA

Topic: Mitochondrial DNA
Go to: www.scilinks.org
Code: INBIOH2286B

mother to her offspring, a maternal line of inheritance only. The scientists used PCR again to amplify the samples. They found that they were of such excellent quality that scientists were able to put together DNA profiles for the nine bodies.

To make their identification foolproof, the scientists needed blood samples from living relatives of the Czarina. The forensic service studied genealogies and found that Prince Philip, the husband of Queen Elizabeth II of England, was a descendant of Czarina Alexandra's sister. He was Alexandra's grandnephew. Prince Philip agreed to give blood. His mitochondrial DNA was found to be a perfect match. He had the same sequence of DNA bases as did the mother (skeleton number 7) and her three daughters. In July 1993, Gill announced that the remains were those of the Romanovs. But what of Anna Anderson? She had died in 1984 and had been cremated. Was it ever going to be possible to prove her identity?

In one of those bits of unplanned luck, the researchers discovered that "Anastasia Manahan" had had surgery in 1951. Some of her excised tissue had been kept in formaldehyde in a laboratory in Charlottesville, Virginia. Once again, nuclear and mitochondrial DNA were extracted. These DNA were compared with the DNA of the bones of the Czar and the Czarina and with the blood of Prince Philip. What do you think was the result? Do you think that the woman who knew so much about incidents in the life of the royal family and who had been positively identified by knowledgeable Russians, was the Grand Duchess Anastasia?

On October 2, 1994, the (London) *Sunday Times* announced that genetic tests on tissue from Anna Anderson Manahan had removed, beyond all doubt, the possibility that she was the Grand Duchess Anastasia or in the maternal lineage of the Czarina Alexandra. The royal houses in Germany and in England were relieved at the news. Instead, her DNA profile matched that of Franziska Schanzkowska, a Polish peasant, and of her living grandnephew, Karl Maucher, a German farmer. Is this the end of the mystery?

ANALYSIS

Record your responses to the following in your notebook.
1. In what ways did knowledge of genetics and pedigrees help researchers decide which paths and clues to follow?
2. How did the development of modern technology allow researchers to pursue the artifacts (historical objects) and clues available to them?
3. Sometimes, people hold on to their "gut" feelings even in the face of scientific evidence. Has the scientific evidence convinced you? If not, what questions still remain for you? If yes, what was the most compelling evidence?
4. What other types of questions do you have about the Romanovs and the mystery? How might you go about finding answers to those questions?

The mystery of Anna Anderson's identity seems to have been solved. If you are interested in learning more about the politics and the science involved, read *The Romanovs: The Final Chapter* by Robert K. Massie (New York: Random House, 1995). This book fills in the details that were omitted from your reading.

Research a civil or criminal case in which DNA analysis helped identify an heir or apprehend a suspected criminal.

Genetics and Evolution: Making the Connection

Prologue

In his essay "The Wonderful Mistake" (Learning Experience 5), Lewis Thomas states that "The capacity to blunder slightly is the real marvel of DNA. Without this special attribute we would still be anaerobic bacteria and there would be no music." He goes on to suggest that if the design of DNA had been left to scientists, they ". . . would have found some way to correct this [capacity to blunder slightly], and evolution would have been stopped in its tracks."

What do DNA and genetics have to do with evolution? Organisms have come a long way since the first liposomal blob organized itself from a pool of organic material (recall Unit 1, Learning Experience 9). Today, Earth is inhabited by enormously diverse populations of different kinds of organisms. How did that happen? Is evolution still taking place today? In this learning experience, you explore how an understanding of the fundamental principles of genetics can explain the mechanisms by which change over time can take place.

Brainstorming

Discuss the following with your partner, and record your thinking in your notebook. Be prepared to share your ideas with the class.

In Unit 1, Learning Experience 9, you read and then explored this statement: "The ability to change with each new generation was an essential feature in the movement from the first cell-like structure to the complex organisms that have inhabited and continue to inhabit Earth. Without this ability to change, life on Earth today might still consist of little coalesced blobs of biomolecules. On a bigger scale, an additional characteristic of life is the ability to evolve."

With this statement in mind and using any prior knowledge you have, develop a definition of evolution. Identify at least three key components or essential ideas that relate to evolution.

ACTIVITY

Antibiotic Resistance: Evolution in Action

A sore throat may have required you to see a doctor at some point. Before prescribing an antibiotic, she probably took a swab of your throat with a long cotton swab that made you gag. A subsequent laboratory test would have revealed two things. First, was the discomfort you were suffering caused by a viral or bacterial infection? (You will learn more about the difference between viruses and bacteria in Unit 3.) Second, if bacterial, were the infecting bacteria resistant to any specific antibiotics? How do bacteria become resistant to drugs?

In Learning Experience 6, you investigated mutations in DNA as a mechanism for acquiring new traits. The DNA in bacteria, like the DNA in all organisms, is continually mutating. Many of these changes never show up as traits. Others, however, may affect the characteristics of the organism. In a population of bacteria, a very small percentage of the bacteria have mutations. But these mutations never show up in the larger population unless selective pressure from the environment is applied. A selective pressure is something in the environment that gives the organisms with a specific mutation a better chance of surviving and reproducing than organisms without this mutation. This phenomenon is known as **natural selection**.

In this activity, you will apply selective pressure to a bacterial population. You will then examine the outcome.

Materials

For each pair of students:

- 2 pairs of safety goggles
- 1 tube containing 2 mL of nutrient broth
- 1 tube containing 2 mL of nutrient broth with ampicillin (200 ug/mL)
- 1 beaker or test-tube rack to hold the tubes with the nutrient broth
- sterile pipette (1-mL) and bulb
- 2 nutrient agar plates without ampicillin
- 2 nutrient agar plates with ampicillin (200 ug/mL)
- 2 sterile cotton swabs
- 1 wax marking pencil

For the class:

- 1 37°C incubator (optional)
- culture of ampicillin-sensitive *E. coli* (25 mL)

PROCEDURE

SAFETY NOTE

1. Obtain 2 tubes of nutrient broth. One has no additives and one contains ampicillin ("A"). You will also need a beaker or rack to hold the tubes.
2. Either you or your teacher will inoculate each tube with the bacteria *E. coli*. Use a 1-mL pipette to place 1 drop of bacteria from the stock culture into each tube. Use a sterile technique. Shake gently to mix.
3. Place the tubes in the location indicated by your teacher. This will be either at 25°C (77°F) or 37°C (98.6°F).

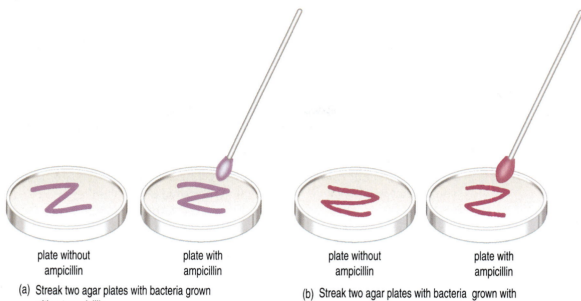

(a) Streak two agar plates with bacteria grown without ampicillin.

plate without ampicillin

plate with ampicillin

(b) Streak two agar plates with bacteria grown with ampicillin.

plate without ampicillin

plate with ampicillin

Figure 2.46

Streaking the agar plates.

4. When a tube becomes turbid (cloudy), place it at 4°C (about 40°F). When both tubes are turbid, the bacteria in the broth are ready to be grown on agar plates.

5. Obtain 2 agar plates without ampicillin and 2 agar plates with ampicillin.

6. Open the tube that contains the bacteria grown without ampicillin. Carefully dip 1 sterile cotton swab into the broth. Then streak the swab onto the plate without ampicillin (see Figure 2.46a). (Remember, you learned to streak agar plates in Unit 1, Learning Experience 8, Reap the Spoils.)

7. Repeat step 6, but streak this sample onto the plate *with* ampicillin (Figure 2.46a). Discard the swab as directed by your teacher.

8. **STOP & THINK** Why is it important to streak the agar plates in this order?

9. Repeat steps 6 and 7. This time use the tube that contains the bacteria grown in the presence of ampicillin (Figure 2.46b).

10. **STOP & THINK** What purpose do each of the different agar plates serve in the experiment?

11. Place your initials on the plates. Incubate them either at 25°C or 37°C until growth appears.

12. **STOP & THINK** What is the selective pressure in this environment?

13. Record your results in a written description or in a labeled diagram.

🔍 ANALYSIS

Record your responses to the following in your notebook.

1. Explain your results in terms of selective pressure.

2. What might be the difference between the bacteria that grew in the presence of the drug and those that did not?

3. Each colony (circle) of bacteria that appeared on your agar plate represents a single bacterium that has divided thousands of times. Therefore, each colony represents hundreds of generations produced from a single parent cell. Suppose you were to spread that colony onto a new agar plate containing ampicillin. Would each bacterium in that colony grow? What if you were to spread it onto an agar plate containing a different antibiotic. Would each bacterium in that colony grow? Explain your answers.

4. The doctor has determined that your sore throat is due to bacteria that are resistant to ampicillin. But these same bacteria are sensitive to erythromycin, another antibiotic. She has given you a prescription. You are to take the medicine for a full 7 days even if you are feeling better after 2 days. What do you predict will happen if you stop taking the drug after 2 days?

ACTIVITY

Teddy Graham Selection

Adapted from "Natural Selection with Teddy Grahams" by Robert R. Blake, Jr., Albert C. Wartski, and Lynn Marie Wartski. *The Science Teacher,* March 1993, pp. 64–65.

When you look at the natural world, you see easily that organisms are well adapted to their environments. Many have colors and textures that camouflage them from predators. Others have unique structures that enable them to feed efficiently, sense danger, or flee quickly. Trees in colder climates have narrow leaves that tend to remain year-round. Those in warmer climates have broader leaves that drop in the autumn. There are many such patterns in the living world.

However, an organism cannot change in and of itself to become better adapted. All such change happens at first by chance. The change is acted upon by the environment. Think about an animal being born albino (with white skin and fur). Albinism may have a selective advantage in the Arctic, but not along a riverbank in the tropics. Thus, those organisms having the advantageous variant of a trait will be selected for (survive) and will reproduce. Organisms may vary, but it is a population that evolves.

In this activity, you will be the environmental factor that applies selective pressure on the organism known as the Teddy Graham. There are two types of Teddy Grahams, the plain and the chocolate. You are a bear-eating predator who prefers to eat only chocolate bears. (It just so happens that the chocolate bears taste good and are easier to catch than the plain bears. The plain bears taste sour and are harder to catch.)

Materials

For each pair of students:

- 10 Teddy Grahams® in a plastic bag (Your teacher may provide samples other than Teddy Grahams.)
- 1 sheet of graph paper
- paper towels
- 1 small plastic bag

For the class:

- additional Teddy Grahams

Table 2.14　Data for Teddy Graham Selection Experiment

Generation	Chocolate Bears	Plain Bears	Total Bears
1			
2			
3			
4			

PROCEDURE

1. Obtain a mixed population of Teddy Graham bears from your teacher.
2. Copy Table 2.14 into your notebook.
3. Place your bears on a paper towel. Record the number of chocolate bears, plain bears, and the total population. This is generation 1.
4. Remove 3 chocolate bears and place them in a sandwich bag. (If you do not have 3 chocolate bears, make up the difference in plain bears. For example, if you have only 2 chocolate bears, remove also 1 plain bear.)
5. **STOP & THINK** What is the selective pressure in this environment?
6. Each surviving chocolate bear produces 1 new chocolate bear. Each plain bear produces 1 new plain bear. Obtain the new generation of bears from your teacher. Record these numbers as the start of generation 2.
7. Repeat steps 4 and 5 for 2 more generations.
8. Create a bar graph to show the totals of each type of bear in each generation.

ANALYSIS

Record your responses to the following in your notebook.

1. Use your understanding of natural selection to explain what happened to each population of bears over the four generations.
2. What do you think will happen to each type of bear over 10 or 20 generations? Why?

Changing Genes, Changing Populations

READING

In 1831, a young English naturalist by the name of Charles Darwin (see Figure 2.47) set sail on the H.M.S. *Beagle* for a 5-year journey around the world. At each stop along the way, Darwin went ashore to collect and classify organisms that few Europeans had ever seen before. As he observed, collected, and analyzed, Darwin was struck by the wide variation of characteristics in organisms. He noted these variations even among members of the same species. (A species is a group of similar organisms that can interbreed and produce fertile offspring; for example, horses are a species.) After studying thousands of examples of species and variation within them, Darwin reached several conclusions:

- Organisms produce more offspring than can be supported by the environment.
- These organisms display variations that can be inherited.

Figure 2.47

Charles Darwin.
© Bettmann/Corbis

- Organisms with certain variations are better suited for their environment. Therefore, these organisms may survive longer and produce more offspring. Others that are less well suited will produce fewer offspring or may die without leaving any offspring at all.
- The survival and reproduction of individuals with characteristics that make them better adapted to a particular environment is called natural selection.
- Natural selection over long periods of time may lead to the accumulation of so many changes in a population that a new species is formed. This process is called evolution.

SELECTING A NEW PAIR OF GENES

When Darwin proposed his theory of natural selection, he had no knowledge of Mendel's principles of inheritance or of genes and DNA. It would be more than 100 years before the connections between genetics and evolution were made. We learned how variations in the genetic makeup of an organism can produce variations in traits and how these traits are inherited. This provided the molecular explanation of how organisms could evolve. A mutation introduces a new allele of a gene into a population. (Recall from Learning Experience 7 that this mutation must take place in the egg or sperm in order to be inherited.) Say the phenotype of this new allele provides a survival advantage to a particular environmental condition or pressure. Then this individual will produce offspring that also bear this allele. Individuals without this allele will not survive and will not produce offspring. Thus, their genotype will eventually be eliminated from the population (see Figure 2.48).

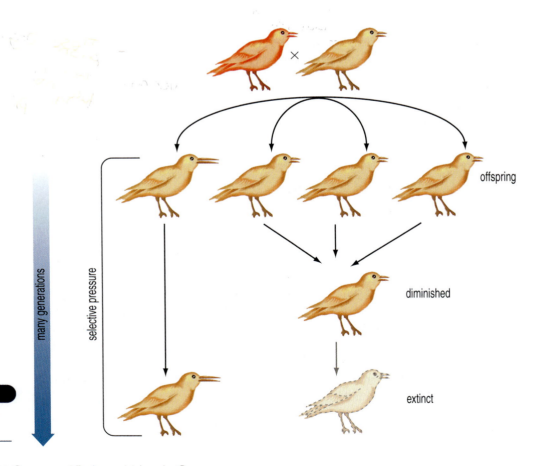

Figure 2.48

Effect of selective pressure on offspring.

Within a given population, the sum total of all its alleles is known as its **gene pool**. If the environment is stable, that is, if conditions do not change, then the gene pool is stable. If conditions change, selective pressure may result in the selection of a specific genotype that will increase in the population and change the gene pool. We saw an example of this in the experiment on antibiotic resistance. The starting gene pool in the bacterial population contained a gene that caused the bacteria to be ampicillin-sensitive. A small number of bacteria contained a mutation in that gene that caused them to be ampicillin-resistant. When ampicillin was present in the environment, the bacteria that possessed the resistance-allele were able to survive and reproduce. The sensitive bacteria died. Thus, the gene pool changed. The sensitive allele that was originally in the population disappeared, and the resistance-allele came to predominate.

STAYING AFLOAT IN THE GENE POOL

Not all alleles that survive in a gene pool are necessarily an advantage under all conditions. Recall in Learning Experience 3 when you read about sickle-cell anemia. Certain alleles are present in populations that can result in debilitating diseases and even death. Why do these alleles persist in a population? The first systematic study of this question was conducted in 1954. A scientist named Anthony Allison examined the distribution of the sickle-cell trait in Africa and Asia. He observed that the trait was mainly confined to tropical Africa. Here up to 45% of the individuals in certain tribes carried the allele. Populations in India, southern Arabia, and in parts of the Mediterranean also carried the allele. Recalling data on the patterns of distribution of malaria, Allison superimposed distribution maps of the two diseases. To his surprise, he found that they overlapped (see Figure 2.49). That is, wherever malaria occurred the sickle-cell trait was also found.

Malaria is a disease of the blood caused by a parasitic protozoan, *Plasmodium falciparum*. It is carried by a mosquito. The mosquito injects the parasite into the bloodstream during its meal of blood. The parasite infects red blood cells where it reproduces. This eventually bursts the cells, causing fevers, chills, nausea, headaches, and often death to the victim of the infection.

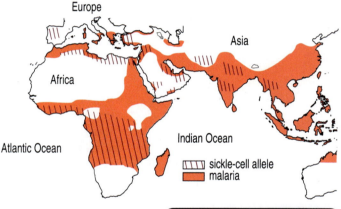

Figure 2.49

Geographic distribution of malaria and sickle cell.

Recall from Learning Experience 3 that sickle-cell anemia is also a disease of the blood. But sickle-cell anemia is an inherited disease. The hemoglobin made by the mutant allele causes the cells carrying this allele to collapse or assume a sickle shape. This, in turn, causes the cells to block the flow of blood through capillaries. Interestingly, a side effect of this sickling is that the collapsed red blood cell is resistant to infection by the malaria parasite. Because sickling cells cannot be infected, individuals who are heterozygous are more resistant to malaria. (These individuals carry one allele for normal hemoglobin and one for sickling hemoglobin.) Individuals who are homozygous for the normal hemoglobin allele are susceptible. In areas where malaria is prevalent, carriers of the sickle-cell allele are more likely to survive and produce offspring who carry this allele than individuals who have two normal hemoglobin alleles. The selective pressure of malaria keeps this recessive allele in the gene pool.

Thus, we see the dynamic nature of the organisms that inhabit Earth in the past, present, and future. Theirs is a balance among changing genotypes and phenotypes, and the changing environments in which these populations live. Although the kind of changes that will happen cannot necessarily be predicted, change will continue to take place. It is inevitable.

ANALYSIS

Record your responses to the following in your notebook.

1. Why do you think most organisms produce more offspring than the environment can support?
2. Explain the influence of natural selection on
   a. the color of the white Arctic rabbit,
   b. the bright colors of many flowers,
   c. the long necks of giraffes, and
   d. mosquitoes resistant to insecticide.
3. Breeders of domestic animals and plants have always used selection to produce plants and animals with new desirable characteristics that could be passed from generation to generation. For example, a cattle breeder might desire a cow that is a good milk producer but is of small stature. To breed such a cow, he might cross a large cow that is a good producer with a small bull. He would then screen the progeny for the desired traits. How is this "artificial" selection different from natural selection? Specifically, how is it different
   a. at the molecular level (that is, in the kind of variation),
   b. in the kind of "selective pressure," and
   c. in the time frame?
4. Hank has spent several years growing a bonsai tree. (This is a kind of miniature tree that is kept to a very small size by limiting its growth with wires and careful pruning.) He would like to start a business selling bonsai trees. He thinks that by collecting the seeds from his tree he can grow enough bonsai trees to sell. His friend Alicia asks him what planet he was on during the genetics part of their biology class. She claims that approach will never work. Who is right? Explain your answer.

READING

One Good Change Deserves Another

Organisms do not live isolated from one another. Rather, they exist in a balance in an ecosystem. What happens to one organism can affect the lifestyles or survival of other organisms. When one species' characteristics change through natural selection, these changes can affect other organisms that interact with it. These other organisms may also undergo change. They may respond to a different kind of natural selection, that of changes in a species they depend on. This evolution of two interacting species in which change in one species results in change in the other species is called **coevolution**. These changes can maintain or even strengthen the relationship between the two species.

On another collecting expedition in 1862, Charles Darwin visited Madagascar. Here he collected an unusual orchid that had a style 25 centimeters (10 inches) long. Recall from Learning Experience 9 that the style is the tube through which pollen must travel to reach the eggs in the ovary of a flower

Figure 2.50
Star orchid and Darwin's hawk moth.

(see Figure 2.50). Darwin knew that moths pollinated this species of orchid by feeding with their tongues on the nectar found in the ovary of the orchid. Based on his knowledge of orchids, moths, and evolution, Darwin made a prediction about the existence of a moth with a certain trait. He did this even though this particular moth had never been seen. Forty-one years later, well after Darwin's death, a moth with this exact predicted characteristic was discovered.

 **ANALYSIS**

Record your responses to the following in your notebook.

1. Describe the characteristic that Darwin predicted.
2. Explain the principles behind Darwin's prediction.

EXTENDING *Ideas*

▶ Before Darwin's voyage on the *Beagle,* a naturalist named Jean Baptiste Lamarck proposed his own theory of evolution. Lamarck based his theory on the observation that during the course of an individual's lifetime, parts of the body that are used extensively become larger and stronger. He suggested that these modifications acquired during an individual's lifetime could then be passed on to the next generation. Research Lamarck's theory of evolution. Compare it with Darwin's theory of natural selection.

▶ In 1858, Alfred Wallace was a young naturalist working in the East Indies. Wallace wrote to Charles Darwin, explaining his theory of natural selection. His theory was virtually identical to Darwin's yet to be published theory. Darwin quickly finished *The Origin of Species* and published it the next year. Research the work of Alfred Wallace. Why is Darwin credited with the theory of natural selection?

A Current Affair

Prologue

In the past 50 years, since the discovery of DNA, research about the underlying principles of genetics has led to the development of a number of technologies that have had an impact on everyday life. Daily, the newspapers and six o'clock news inform us of new strides in **genetically modified foods**, the potential of **stem cells** in curing disease, the hope of gene therapy, and the concerns about DNA testing in solving crimes. The knowledge you have gained in this unit should help you to better understand these reports. You should now be able to analyze them critically to determine whether the science supports the conclusions.

SCiLINKS®
NSTA

Topic: Stem Cells
Go to: www.scilinks.org
Code: INBIOH2298B

Brainstorming

Every day you hear about science discoveries in the media. Do you believe everything you read or see on TV? Do you ever question the information presented to you? Discuss the following questions with your partner, and record your thinking in your notebook. Be prepared to share your ideas with the class.

1. What do you usually read or watch that relates to science?
2. Have you ever questioned any information presented to you? If so, what was it? What made you question it?
3. What kind of questions might you ask to help you assess the credibility of information you are given?

ACTIVITY

Consider the Source

Newspapers, magazines, television, radio, and now the Internet are our major sources of information about emerging developments in scientific and technological fields. What do you think about when you read or hear these reports? What makes a story interesting and relevant to you? Has studying genetics made you more aware of the number of discoveries and technological advances being reported almost daily?

In this activity, you will select an article to serve as a starting point for your report. You will then research the science that relates to the topic and write a research paper that describes your ideas and conclusions. Your report should consist of science background, a case study, and a personal statement. This is an independent project that requires organization, creativity, and thoughtfulness. As you read through the following task, think of any questions or concerns you may have and discuss them with your teacher.

TASK

1. Search newspapers, magazines, and the Internet (if you have access) for an article on a genetics issue that you feel relates to your life either now or in the future. The article can deal with a **genetic disease**, genetics research, **genetic technology**, or environmental influences that can alter gene expressions.

   a. Be creative when thinking about how the topic in the article might relate to you now or in the future. The relationship can be direct or you can see the effects on your family or society. If you are a vegetarian, for example, you may be interested in the issue of whether a vegetarian would eat or drink products with animal genes in them. Or, perhaps your grandfather has a genetic disorder. You may want to find out what is known about the disorder and what it may mean for you. You may live on a farm or ranch where gene technology to enhance certain traits in plants or animals is important. These are just a few possibilities.

   b. As you read newspapers and magazines looking for a topic, focus your thinking on determining why a particular topic might be interesting to you. Once you choose an article, use your notebook to record relevant thoughts and ideas you have as you read your article. You might want to write down questions that the article raises or issues and concerns that might relate to the article. You may also want to record ways in which the article has meaning for you in your life and the ways the topic might affect your personal values.

2. Find more resources on the topic. Look for information on the science underlying the topic. Track down any research or technology that has been critical in uncovering information on the topic. Consider ethical issues or concerns related to the topic. Use the concepts in this unit as a resource for scientific information.

3. Write a research paper that includes the following:

   a. An overview of the article. Explain what it is about and the major points it makes.

   b. A clear explanation of the scientific knowledge behind the topic in the article. Explore the underlying science in more depth. If applicable, include a description of the technologies associated with this advancement in genetics.

   c. A critical analysis of the article. Include the source of the article and its reliability and the evidence presented in the article. Discuss why you think the conclusions in the article are valid or not.

   d. A case study that reveals the issues involved in this topic. Create a story or scenario to illustrate the particular situation or issue in genetics that your article addresses. You can design the case study to be an article that describes the issues and concerns that relate to the topic. Include your own decision-making process based on your analysis of the risks and benefits. Or your case study can be an original narrative. Describe an individual in a situation. What issues and concerns confront that individual? What decision you would choose?

   e. A short essay that describes how the topic you chose relates to your life. Include, if appropriate, what your topic might mean for society at large. Explore how the research for this activity may have influenced your opinions and concerns related to the topic.

   f. A bibliography of the references you used in writing the report. If you used quotes or ideas of other authors, be sure to document them by including the source.

4. Attach the following two appendixes to your paper:
   • a copy of the article you chose (include the source and date of publication), and
   • your notes (as described in step 1b).

5. Be prepared to give a 5-minute summary of your article. Include the major genetic principles involved and any ethical, personal, or societal issues that result.

 **ASSESSMENT**

Your report will be assessed on the following criteria:

• Have you gathered sufficient and appropriate scientific information?
• Have you reached logical conclusions about the issues and concerns that surround your topic?
• Does your case study reflect scientific insight and understanding? Does it include risks and benefits? Did you come to a decision?
• Does your final essay describe how the topic is related to your life and/or has meaning for society?
• Does your final essay clarify the values you bring to the topic and the ways in which your research may have affected your thinking about the topic?
• Is your report organized, clear, and complete? Does your report engage and interest the reader in your topic and the issues that surround it?
• Is your bibliography complete and accurate?
• Have you documented other authors' ideas and words?

 **CAREER FOCUS**

Science Writer   Geri has a deadline to reach. Her article for *In 2 Science,* a monthly science magazine, was supposed to describe the latest genetically engineered foods and their future repercussions. She has spent many hours interviewing scientists, nutritionists, and government officials so she could represent the different views and issues that result from these new edible creations. She feels that her article is scientifically accurate yet accessible to the public. *In 2 Science* is aimed at a high school audience.

   Geri started writing when she was very young. At first, she just wrote a personal journal. Then she wrote for her high school newspaper and even sent some articles into her local newspaper. She also loved science. Biology courses were her favorite. But instead of just a laboratory report, she found herself describing her experiments with journalistic vigor. When high school graduation approached, Geri wondered if there was a way to combine her two loves into one career. Should she major in journalism or in biology?

   A few weeks into her first college semester, she sat down with her adviser. He suggested that she major in biology and minor in English, although he acknowledged that there were other approaches to reach a similar goal. Her adviser used the term "niche journalism." This is where up-and-coming journalists are becoming more specialized in particular fields. Geri's specialized field would be the biological sciences. In addition to her coursework, she joined the staff of the college paper. Her regular column covered the discoveries taking place in the science laboratories on campus. She also wrote about certain scientific topics that may, in the near future, affect all people in some aspect of their lives. These included topics such as cloning or the availability of genetic tests.

During her senior year of college, Geri learned about internships in science journalism at a local newspaper or magazine. She found a position in the science division at the *Ledger*. Here she was expected to write articles that would be added to a monthly "Science in the News" insert. She also learned through the internship and further research that there were many places where she could use her skills after college. There were daily newspapers and science magazines, of course. But there were also specialized science and medical journals, television and radio stations, trade papers, and even popular magazines that reserved sections for reporting the latest advancements in science. Other options included working in public relations for medical firms where she could write press releases for new products and discoveries. Her internship created many opportunities for Geri to meet well-known writers and make numerous contacts with scientists, technicians, and other people associated with medicine, business, law, and other professions. Through this job, she met the editor-in-chief of *In 2 Science* who was very impressed with her work. After graduation, she accepted a position on the staff of the magazine.

For her own professional development, Geri hopes to continue her education and earn a master's degree in journalism. But for now, it's time to meet that deadline!

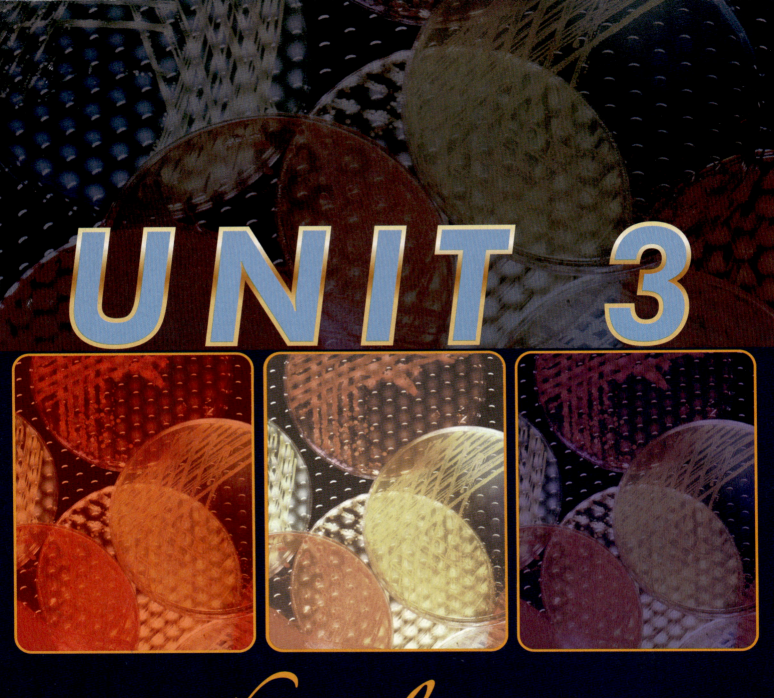

UNIT 3

The Blueprints of Infection

Contents

The Blueprints
of Infection

Introduction

On December 26, 2004, an enormous tsunami slammed into the coastlines and islands of South Asia. In a matter of minutes, it wreaked unparalleled destruction and loss of life. This monstrous wave swept people out to sea, crushed buildings, uprooted trees, and flung cars and appliances around like they were toys. The initial death toll exceeded 150,000. But in the days that followed this catastrophic event, the number of deaths continued to grow. The devastation caused by the tsunami resulted in the loss of fresh drinking water, the destruction of homes, the disruption of sanitation facilities, and changes in the ecology of the region. All of these conditions result in the spread of infectious diseases such as cholera, amebic dysentery, malaria, and dengue fever.

What are the causes of infectious diseases? How are they spread from one person to another? How do they cause sickness and death? Can these diseases be prevented or stopped? In this unit, you will explore the organisms that are the agents of infectious disease. You will determine how these organisms can cause disease by disrupting vital cellular processes in their hosts. By investigating how the body can defend itself against infection, you will determine ways in which infectious diseases can be prevented and cured. You will complete the unit by examining the personal and social ramifications of infectious diseases.

Disease Detectives

Prologue

. . . During an epidemic of 1918, according to medical lore, victims were struck down almost in midstride. Four women in a bridge group played cards together until 11 o'clock in the evening. By the next morning, three of them were dead. One man got on a streetcar feeling well enough to go to work, rode six blocks and died. During the single month of October, [this epidemic killed] 196,000 people in this country—more than twice as many as would die of AIDS during the first 10 years of that epidemic . . .

Excerpted from Robin Marantz Henig, "Flu Pandemic," *The New York Times Magazine,* November 29, 1992

Who were the victims? What set them apart from those who remained healthy? What caused all these deaths? Scientists, researchers, doctors, and public health officials study outbreaks of disease. They try to understand how each disease is spread, what is causing it, and how to stop it. In the case of the people described above, did anyone know how the disease spread? Could anything have been done to prevent it? How did the disease actually kill? We know now that by the end of the winter of 1918–1919, 2 billion people around the world had come down with influenza, also known as the flu. Between 20 and 40 million had died suddenly from a disease that seems common today. If it happened once, could it happen again?

Brainstorming

Discuss the following questions with your partner, and record your thinking in your notebook. Be prepared to share your ideas with the class.

1. How do you think diseases are passed from person to person? Give some examples.
2. What other epidemics do you know of that have happened more recently? How do you think they were spread among people? across countries?

Topic: Infectious Disease
Go to: www.scilinks.org
Code: INBIOH2306

In this first learning experience, you examine one of the early stories in the development of our understanding of **infectious disease**. Major discoveries in this field provided fundamental insights into how living organisms function. They also led to greater understanding in the control of disease and the maintenance of good health. These discoveries began with John Snow, an English surgeon. Snow traced cases of an outbreak of the highly infectious disease **cholera** in an effort to find the source. Use this first reading and excerpts from John Snow's writings to retrace this man's steps. Follow his work as he discovered preliminary answers to many of the questions about the source of the outbreak, who was affected, and what could be done to break the chain of transmission of disease.

READING

Cholera

In the early 1800s, England was in the throes of the industrial revolution. Until the late 1700s, most of England's workers lived in the countryside, laboring as farmers. But by 1830, the economic heart of England was in its cities. Here laborers, forced off of their farms, were competing for low wages in the new factory economy. Market towns could not change quickly enough to keep pace with their expanding populations. Cities had not yet invented police forces, and fire brigades services had to be bought. Housing was overcrowded. Because there was no system for collecting garbage, it piled up in streets, creating a breeding ground for vermin. Usually, raw sewage was thrown into the streets or into the nearest stream, which might be a source of drinking water. No city had an adequate clean water supply as yet. Of course, there was no gas or electric lighting at that time. In short, the infrastructure of the modern city had yet to be invented.

By 1830, the upper and lower social classes were divided dramatically. The desperately poor laborers struggled each day just to feed and clothe themselves. The newly rich factory owners who employed them were managing the world's most powerful empire for England and for their own profit. Poor laborers, who were paid starvation wages, feared and mistrusted the wealthy classes. In 1798, Thomas Malthus observed the overcrowding and miserable conditions in England's new cities. The economist wrote about the population explosion and argued that the growth in population guaranteed that poverty and starvation would become a severe problem.

The growing number of city-dwellers created a sudden increase in the demand for medical workers. At the same time, Britain's medical students were first being required to learn about human anatomy. To help institute this requirement, the dissection of a cadaver (a human corpse) was included in the required curriculum of medical schools. The only legal source of cadavers at that time was executed criminals. Unfortunately for medical students, the number of students far outnumbered the men and women who had been hanged from the gallows. So, medical schools began hiring grave robbers to provide them with an additional supply of corpses. Most of the graves poached were graves of the indigent. To the poor, it looked as though doctors used the bodies of the underclass to do their training, then used their training to benefit the upper class.

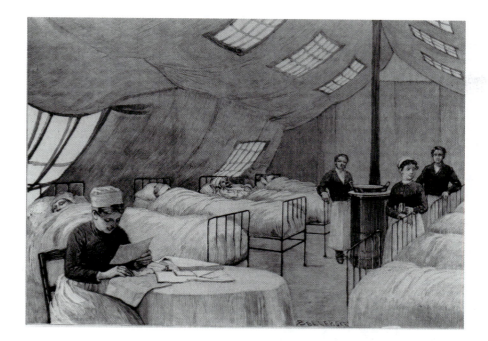

Figure 3.1
The flu epidemic filled hospitals in France.

In 1832, Parliament passed the Anatomy Act. This legislation provided doctors with the unclaimed bodies of people who had died in workhouses, prisons, and hospitals. This law guaranteed that all the cadavers for dissection would be poor. Poor people could not afford the services of doctors. For most of the working class, the only contact they could expect to have with a doctor happened if they were stricken in an epidemic and forcibly dragged to an unsanitary public hospital for treatment. In that case, they could expect to die in the hospital. With the passage of the Anatomy Act, it appeared to many of Britain's poor that the rich medical doctors were going to add insult to injury by interfering with their traditional, religious burial—literally by robbing their graves for science. The poor mistrusted the motives of the medical profession and the rest of the "better" classes. But the educated upper classes generally saw the attitudes of the poor toward the medical profession as proof of their ignorance and irrationality.

In 1826, a pandemic of the dreaded disease cholera had begun in India. (A **pandemic** is a disease that takes place among many individuals worldwide. This is in contrast to an **epidemic**, a disease that happens among individuals locally.) It was observed in India by British physicians and tracked as it made its way first to Russia by 1830, then to the Austro-Hungarian Empire by 1831. Cholera killed 100,000 people along the Danube River before making its way into Western Europe (see Figure 3.1). Then, in 1832 (the same year that the Anatomy Act was passed), cholera found its way to the shores of Britain.

At first, the reports of cholera aggravated English class tensions. Doctors reported that in Europe, cholera's victims were generally from the poorer classes. Conspiracy theories emerged. Some believed that cholera was a big profiteering hoax, drummed up by the grave-robbing doctors to scare people into buying medicine (see Figure 3.2). Others believed that cholera was not a disease at all. They thought that the government (which was, after all, in the hands of England's wealthiest citizens) had decided to poison the wells of the poor, to kill the surplus population, which Malthus had predicted.

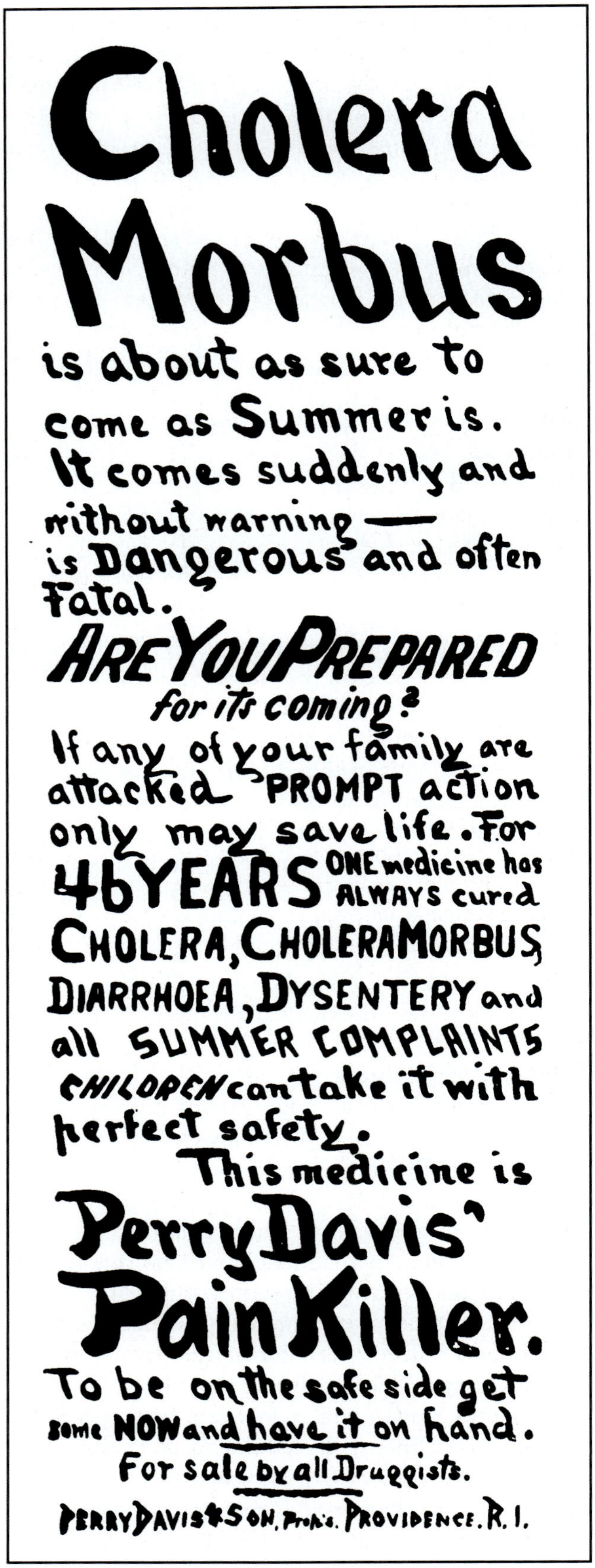

Figure 3.2

Was there a cure? "Morbus" was a synonym for disease.

Gruesome descriptions of the disease helped to fuel the panic and mistrust. Many victims died rapidly after experiencing terrifying symptoms. Often, the victim would feel absolutely healthy one minute, and the next, feel extremely nauseated. This nausea would be followed by a sudden and total evacuation of the bowels. From here, the victim would have the sensation of a great weight around the waist and a prickly sensation in the arms and legs. Cold, clammy sweats would begin, together with a suppressed pulse and severe headache. Within 1 hour of the disease's onset, a person's bowel movements would produce an odorless liquid, filled with ricelike pellets. (Doctors later determined that this "rice" was actually fragments of the victim's intestinal lining.) Soon, the patient's body would shrink and shrivel. Acute cramps would begin in the fingers and toes and then spread to the rest of the body. Skin would turn blue or black. Death generally occurred within 2–7 days.

No one knew the cause of the disease, but doctors had a variety of theories. Some believed that it was carried on the air by an unhealthy "effluvia." These effluvyists suggested that the effluvia was exhaled by those who were already ill. Others, miasmatists, believed that the garbage and feces covering the streets of the overcrowded cities produced some kind of deadly vapor or miasma, which, when inhaled, caused the cholera. Other theorists believed that an unhealthy diet was the cause. Still other beliefs included unclean water, or the "immoral drunkenness" and "dirty habits" of the poor. Some suggested that there might be a chemical contaminant causing the illness. Some said the disease was a punishment from God, and that there was nothing to be done to stop it. It was in this social and scientific context that John Snow, in 1832, an 18-year-old surgeon's apprentice, had his first experiences comforting the dying victims of cholera.

After the 1832 pandemic, cholera did not return to Britain until 1848. By the time it returned, Snow had become one of the most famous surgeons in England. He had become a leading pioneer in the use of surgical anesthetics (a brand new invention), and had become a personal physician of Queen Victoria. In the 16 years since 1832, the class tensions in England had, if anything, become worse. The medical profession was still arguing over the causes of cholera, and the public's feelings about it had not improved. But one major new idea had been introduced to the medical world. Though no one had yet proved it, a few radicals were suggesting that some diseases might be caused by **microbes**. John Snow knew of this idea, and he thought it might be true.

ANALYSIS

Record your responses to the following in your notebook.

1. Who were the victims of cholera in 1832? Why do you think that the disease happened primarily among this group of people?

2. Describe some of the theories about the cause of cholera. Where do you think some of these ideas came from? Was there any truth to these ideas about how diseases spread?

3. The cholera pandemic began in India in 1826. How do you think this disease spread across continents and oceans to affect Russia, the Austro-Hungarian Empire, and most of Western Europe?

4. Do you think the spread of epidemics takes place more or less frequently today than it did in the time of John Snow? Explain your response.

ACTIVITY

Investigating the Nature and Cause of Cholera

John Snow had three opportunities to study cholera. He first studied cholera in the pandemic of 1832, again in the epidemic of 1848–1849, and finally in the epidemic of 1853–1854. In 1854, he published "On the Mode of the Communication of Cholera." Here he outlined all of his discoveries. In his work, Snow presented the evidence he had collected and then used that evidence to draw conclusions.

You are going to begin a scientific analysis of data in order to solve the mystery of cholera. You will examine precisely the same evidence that was available to Snow in 1854. You will read six separate sets of excerpts from Snow's writing.

Materials

For each pair of students:

• 2 copies *Data Analysis* chart

PROCEDURE

1. As you read each data set, think about the following:
   • To solve the mystery as Snow did, you will have to use the tools of 1854. You will have no microscope.
   • In one respect, your job will be far easier than Snow's. Snow had to collect all of the evidence, sort through it, and figure out which evidence was relevant to his study. All you have to do is examine the evidence that he had determined to be relevant, and analyze it.
   • When Snow began, he had already heard 2 decades of medical debate about the possible causes of cholera. Like many scientists, he began with a hypothesis. Then he went out to find the evidence necessary to test his hypothesis.
2. In John Snow's day, doctors were searching for the answers to several crucial questions:
   • How did cholera spread?
   • Were the effluvia or miasma theories correct?
   • Was the disease spread by some other means?
   • Could the disease spread by a variety of methods?
   • Why did some of the people exposed to victims of cholera get sick, while others did not? Why were the poor especially vulnerable to the disease?
   • Could the spread of cholera be prevented? If so, how? Once a person had cholera, could he or she be treated? If so, how?
   • What was the underlying cause of the disease?

3. Read data set 1. Then fill in the *Data Analysis* chart by completing the following 2 steps:
   a. Determine which of the questions listed can be answered using the information given in the data set you have just read. Then write the answers that can be derived from the data in the row labeled "Hypothesis." In other words, answer the questions with your own hypotheses. (Possibly, your hypotheses will be similar to those developed by Snow.) If a question is not addressed in the data set, put N/A for not applicable in the appropriate box below the question.
   b. Think carefully about the information from the excerpted data. If possible, show how the data presented so far are inconclusive. (Even if the data point toward a particular answer to any of the 5 questions, other answers might still be possible.) Look for these gaps in the proof of your hypothesis. Record your ideas in the row labeled "Reasons data may be inconclusive."
4. Proceed to the second data set. Read it and then fill in that part of the chart. You may need to refer back to material you have already read. Follow the same procedure until you have finished data set 4.

Snow on Cholera: Data Collection

READING

Excerpts adapted from the original, as reprinted in *How We Know: An Explanation of the Scientific Process* by Martin Goldstein and Inge F. Goldstein, Plenum Press, NY, 1978

DATA SET 1

When it appears on a fresh island or continent, cholera always strikes first at a seaport.

It travels along highly populated areas, never going faster than people travel, and generally much more slowly.

It never attacks the crew of a ship sailing away from a country that is free of cholera.

DATA SET 2

I called recently to ask about the death of Mrs. Gore, the wife of a labourer, from cholera, at New Leigham Road, Streatham. I found that a son of the deceased had been living and working at Chelsea. He came home ill with a bowel complaint, of which he died in a day or two. His death took place on August 18th. His mother, who attended to him, was taken ill on the next day, and died the day following (August 20th). There were no other deaths from cholera registered in any of the metropolitan districts, until the 26th of August, within two or three miles of the above place . . .

* * *

John Barnes, aged 39, an agricultural labourer, became severely ill on the 28th of December 1832; he had been suffering from diarrhea and cramps for two days previously. He was visited by Mr. George Hopps, a respectable surgeon at Redhouse, who finding him sinking into collapse, requested an interview with his brother, Mr. J. Hopps of York. This experienced practitioner at once recognized the case as one of Asiatic cholera . . . He immediately began investigating for some probable source of contagion, but in vain; no such source could be discovered.

While the surgeons were vainly trying to discover where the disease could possibly have come from, the mystery was all at once, and most unexpectedly, unraveled by the arrival in the village of the son of the shoemaker, living at Leeds. He informed the surgeons that his uncle's wife (his father's sister) had died of cholera two weeks before that time, and that as she had no children, her clothes had been sent to Monkton by a common carrier. The clothes had not been washed; Barnes had opened the box in the evening; on the next day he had fallen sick of the disease.

During the illness of Mrs. Barnes, [the wife of John Barnes: she and two friends who visited Barnes during his illness also got cholera], her mother, who was living at Tockwith, a healthy village 5 miles distant from Monkton, was asked to attend her. She went to Monkton accordingly, remained with her daughter for 2 days, washed her daughter's linen, and set out on her return home, apparently in good health. While in the act of walking home she was seized with the malady and fell down in collapse on the road. She was carried home to her cottage and placed by the side of her bedridden husband. He, and also the daughter who lived with them, got ill. All three died within 2 days. Only one other case occurred in the village of Tockwith, and it was not a fatal case . . .

It would be easy by going through the medical journals and works that have been published on cholera, to quote enough cases similar to the above to fill a large volume.

* * *

Nothing has been found to favor the spread of cholera more than a lack of personal cleanliness, whether arising from habit or a shortage of water . . . The bed linen nearly always becomes wetted by the cholera evacuations, and as these do not have the usual color and odor of diarrhea, the hands of the person waiting on the patient [usually a woman, in England in 1850] become soiled without their knowing it. Unless these persons are scrupulously clean in their habits, and wash their hands before taking food, they must accidentally swallow some of the excretion and leave some on the food they handle or prepare, which has to be eaten by the rest of the family who, amongst the working classes, often have to take their meals in the sick room. Hence the thousands of instances in which, amongst their class of the population, a case of cholera in one member of the family is followed by other cases, whilst medical men and others, who merely visit the patients, generally escape . . .

On the other hand, the duties performed about the body, such as laying it out (for the funeral), when done by women of the working class, who make the occasion one of eating and drinking, are often followed by an attack of cholera . . .

* * *

When, on the other hand, cholera is introduced into the better kind of houses . . . it hardly ever spreads from one member of the family to another. The wealthy constantly use the hand-basin and towel, and their kitchens and bedrooms are separated.

DATA SET 3

Cholera invariably begins with the affliction of the (digestive) canal. The disease often proceeds with so little feeling of general illness, that the patient does not consider himself in danger, or even [ask] for advice, till the [illness] is far advanced . . .

In all the cases of cholera that I have attended, the loss of fluid from the stomach and bowels has been sufficient to account for death, when the poor diet and health of the patient was taken into account, together with the suddenness of the diarrhea, and the fact that the process of absorption of water in the digestive tract appears to be suspended during the illness.

A period of time passes between the time when the cholera poison enters the system, and the beginning of the illness. This period is called the period of **incubation**.

DATA SET 4

In 1849, there were in Thomas Street, Horseleydown, two rows of houses close together consisting of a number of small houses or cottages inhabited by poor people. The houses of the two rows were back to back . . . with a separating space between them, divided into small back yards in which were located the outhouses of both the courts. These outhouses drained into the same trench that flowed out to an open sewer that passed by the far end of both house rows. In one row of buildings, the cholera committed fearful devastation, while in the adjoining row, there was only one fatality and one milder case of the disease. In the former row of houses, the slops of dirty water poured down by the inhabitants into a channel in front of the houses and got into the well from which they obtained their water. In the latter house row, water was obtained from a different well.

* * *

Dr. Thomas King Chambers informed me that at Ilford in Essex in the summer of 1849, the cholera prevailed very severely in a row of houses a little way from the main part of the town. It had visited every house in the row but one. The refuse which overflowed from the outhouses and a pigsty could be seen running into the well over the surface of the ground, and the water had a nasty smell, yet it was used by all the people in the houses except for the one woman who escaped the cholera. That house was inhabited by a woman who took in linen to wash, and she, finding that the water gave the linen an offensive smell, paid a person to fetch water for her from the pump in the town, and this water she used for culinary purposes as well as for washing.

Snow on Cholera: Experimental Evidence

Continue with data sets 5 and 6. What are your ideas about the evidence presented so far? Do you feel it is adequate to accurately answer the questions posed at the beginning of this activity? John Snow did not feel he had enough evidence. He therefore carried out the following two separate experiments, which revolutionized medicine. Think about the following as you read data sets 5 and 6:

* What does the information Snow collected prove?
* What gaps remain in the data that are needed to support the hypothesis?

DATA SET 5

In 1849, a particularly terrible outbreak of cholera happened along Broad Street, near Golden Square, in London. Over a 10-day period, almost 500 people died there within 250 yards of the intersections of Broad and Cambridge streets (see Figure 3.3). At this intersection, there was a particularly popular public water pump. This pump was well-known for the good taste of its water. By the time of this catastrophe, Snow was more or less certain that cholera could be transmitted through the water supply. (This is based on the anecdotal evidence summarized in data sets 1–4.) He believed that the water at the Broad Street pump must have been contaminated (see Figure 3.4).

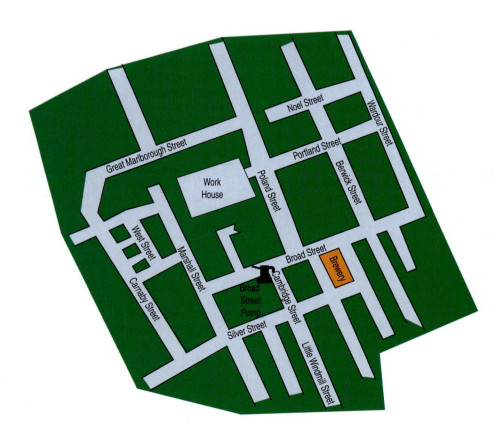

Figure 3.3

Map of the Broad Street area.

Figure 3.4

"Death's Dispensary" by George John Pinwell, 1866. Reproduced with permission from Philadelphia Museum of Art: The William H. Helfand Collection, 1985.

Table 3.1 Water-Drinking Habits of Cholera Victims					
83 deaths					
73 Living near Broad Street Pump			**10 Not Living near Pump**		
61	**6**	**6**	**5**	**3**	**2**
known to have drunk pump water	believed not to have drunk pump water	no information	in families sending to pump for water	children attending school near pump	no information

To prove his hunch, Snow went to the London General Register Office and got the names and addresses of the 83 people whose deaths had been recorded there. Then, going door to door, he collected information about the water-drinking habits of all the cholera victims in the area. Snow's findings are summarized in Table 3.1.

Snow next gave two sets of data that strongly support the role of the pump. There were two groups of people living near the Broad Street pump who had very few cases of cholera. These were the inhabitants of a workhouse (where homeless people were housed and given labor to do—as Oliver Twist was) and the employees of a brewery. Snow interviewed the manager of the brewery and discovered that the brewery gave free beer to its employees and had its own well. The manager was certain that his employees did not, in fact, use the Broad Street pump at all.

As soon as Snow informed the city officials of his data, they had the handle of the Broad Street pump removed. By this time, the cholera epidemic had more or less died down of its own accord. But the simple act of removing the pump handle was the first time in world history that a public health measure was taken as a direct response to scientific data.

DATA SET 6

Finally, in the epidemic of 1853–1854, Snow performed one more experiment. At this time, there was still no public water supply in London. However, since 1832, the city had grown tremendously, and entrepreneurs had begun to sell water door to door. Water companies ran pipes (sometimes wooden, sometimes lead) along streets in some neighborhoods. The residents could buy water that was brought through these pipes. If a homeowner bought the water, a pipe would be run from the street main into the front entrance of the home. This was much more convenient than having to run to the neighborhood pump as people had done on Broad Street. In many neighborhoods, two different companies competed door to door to sell their water. Thus, Snow could compare the relationship between water supply and cholera deaths both in different neighborhoods and within similar neighborhoods.

Snow did a tremendous amount of work. He went door to door to see if there was a relationship between the type of water a person drank and their risk of getting cholera. The results of his work are summarized in Table 3.2.

Table 3.2 Statistics on Drinking Water and Cholera Risk

	Number of Houses	Death from Cholera	Deaths per 10,000 Houses
Southwark and Vauxhall Co.	40,046	1,263	315
Lambeth Company	26,107	98	38
rest of London	256,423	1,422	55

Based on the chart, Snow went on to calculate the death rate per 10,000 for those persons receiving their water from the Southwark and Vauxhall Company. He did the same for those persons receiving their water from the Lambeth Company. See if you can make the calculations yourself. What do you conclude?

It turned out that after the 1849 epidemic, the Lambeth Company had moved the intake for its water pipes to a part of the Thames River upstream from where London's sewage poured into the river. The Southwark and Vauxhall Company had not—its pipes still brought in water containing London sewage.

ANALYSIS

Record your responses to the following in your notebook.

1. In the clearest language possible, write a hypothesis about how cholera spread. Use all the information accumulated by John Snow up to 1854. Explain how these data support your hypothesis.
2. After 1854, what important questions still remained to be answered about cholera?

A Proper Place to Begin

READING

It is appropriate that a discussion of the nature of disease begins with the story of John Snow. In fact, this is true for two reasons. First, Snow's work was a pioneering effort to combine scientific medical inquiry with statistics. This was already a critical innovation in the history of science and medicine. Second, Snow's study is one of the first recorded in the field of epidemiology. **Epidemiology** is a discipline that documents epidemics and attempts to determine the causes. Snow's research is also a proper place to begin our study of disease.

During the time of John Snow, cities lacked public sewage systems and clean water supplies. They also lacked police departments, fire departments, paved road systems, gas, and electricity. In other words, the urban world of the early industrial revolution was a dirty, chaotic place. Unless one had the money to purchase these services through a private company, life in the city was a dismal prospect.

But Snow's work was a **catalyst** to change all of this. We now had scientific, statistical proof linking disease to dirty drinking water and untreated sewage. This proof placed tremendous new pressures on city governments to manage these problems. To build citywide sewage disposal and treatment systems meant that the city governments in Europe and the United States had to be better organized. Taxes had to be raised to pay for new construction projects. A chain reaction began. Once city governments began to take responsibility for sewage and water, it was a natural step to garbage collection, police and fire protection, and to other services. The industrialized world now takes these services so much for granted that we refer to them as basic services.

The introduction of these infrastructure systems made urban life better for everyone. It reduced some of the class tensions in Britain. Finally, medicine and government made some changes that tangibly improved the lives of the working classes. Tensions did not disappear. But by the late 19th century, the unhealthy and miserable conditions of the urban poor had been substantially reduced.

Today, it is hard for Americans to imagine life without these necessities. Just 140 years ago, it was hard for most people to imagine life with them. Infrastructure has changed the deepest fabric of our lives.

But to suppose that such changes have been universal would be naive. While the vast majority of Americans no longer have to worry about the risk of cholera, outbreaks of the scourge continue to happen around the world. In much of the world, the wealth needed to build even the most rudimentary water supply and sewage disposal systems is lacking. Indeed, recent outbreaks of cholera in Latin America and Africa have spurred massive new efforts to build such infrastructure in many of the countries where these outbreaks took place. Perhaps history is repeating itself.

Outbreak in Pickle City

Desiduous, Kansas, is a small town, famous for its Desiduous pickles. In 2001, however, economic times were tough. Recession meant less money, and less money meant fewer pickles on the American plate. Economic problems were nothing new to Desiduous. Its town motto is, "As goes the American economy, so goes the pickle."

On Monday, July 20, however, Desiduous's distress was more than economic. Two previously healthy prominent male citizens, ages 35 and 42, had died mysteriously within 24 hours. Panic flowed through the town like juice from a shattered pickle jar.

Roscoe Clayman, the owner of the town multiplex theater, was a respected bowler and avid tuba player. Reginald Willowslip was unemployed, a retired pickle taster in the local factory who kept his taste buds in shape at the local saloons and pubs. The only thing these two men seemed to have in common was being avid philatelists (stamp collectors). Both had recently attended the annual stamp collectors' convention in Topeka, held at the beautiful and elegant Colossus Hotel.

In fact, across Kansas at this time, stamp collectors were falling ill and dying at an alarming rate. Within a 3-week period, 183 cases of the so-called stamp collectors' syndrome were reported. After the first week of this apparent outbreak/epidemic, the Centers for Disease Control and Prevention (CDC) in Atlanta was contacted and six young and eager **epidemiologists** rushed to the scene to begin intensive and extensive investigations.

TASK

You are part of this team of investigators. Your first task is to design a plan of action that will help you identify the cause of the outbreak. Your plan should include the following components:

- the question being asked,
- your hypothesis about the source of the epidemic,
- the kinds of data you need to collect,
- the kinds of questions you need to ask to obtain the data,
- the method for collecting and recording the data, and
- an approach for analyzing the data.

Outline your plan in your notebook and be prepared to discuss it in class. The goal of the class discussion is to develop a plan that is effective, thorough, and efficient. Remember, lives are at stake. Time is of the essence.

318   Learning Experience 1 Disease Detectives

EXTENDING *Ideas*

● Read stories about other disease detectives. Compare one of these stories to John Snow's story. Include the society in which it happened, the evidence, the techniques used, prior knowledge of the researcher, and what the impact of the discovery was on the spread of the disease. The powerful story of HIV, for example, is described in numerous books, magazines, and newspaper articles.

● Find out what the CDC does. What is its role? What techniques does it use? What kinds of jobs do people perform in the organization?

● Research the patterns of the spread and the cause of a recent epidemic. Describe how the source of the epidemic was determined.

CAREER FOCUS

Water Pollution Control Technician

Olivia and her coworker Elizabeth head out for a busy day on the job. Both women are water pollution control technicians employed by the town of Summersby. They have a long list of sites to visit before the day is through. They will take water samples at some sites; at other sites, they will inspect certain facilities. Their first stop is Sampling Station #58. Here they take a surface water sample to test for contaminants. They then visit Apex Manufacturing to ensure that the company is complying with state and local health and water pollution regulations.

As part of Summersby's pollution control program, Olivia works with environmental specialists in the Summersby environmental health department. Olivia's primary role as a water pollution control technician is to administer the town's water pollution control program. It's Olivia's responsibility to conduct inspections, tests, and field investigations to determine the extent of any water contamination, and try to find ways to control and prevent contamination. She collects and analyzes surface and groundwater samples for certain contaminants, tracks pollution sources, and ensures that they are abated. It's her job to set up, operate, and maintain environmental monitoring equipment and test instruments. Olivia and Elizabeth share responsibility for maintaining the records and data they collect and for preparing reports that document their results. They also conduct inspections such as the one carried out at Apex Manufacturing.

Growing up, Olivia loved exploring the outdoors. She appreciated nature and the science that explained how nature works. By the time she was in middle school, Olivia had already decided she'd become a wildlife biologist so she could work outdoors and study all kinds of animals. In the eighth grade, however, her science teacher had the class participate in a national watershed cleanup program. The class members mapped their local watershed, identified possible sources of pollution, and helped participate in cleanup efforts to improve the quality of the water in their area. Olivia was fascinated. She thought that working in water pollution control would enable her to help improve the environment, be involved in important scientific efforts, and get to spend time outdoors. In high school, Olivia took as many science classes as she possibly could. As she neared graduation, she researched several college programs and decided on a 2-year physical science program offered in Summersby. The program allowed her to study marine biology, ecology, chemistry, physics, and computers, which she now uses in her daily work. While working toward her degree, Olivia took on a part-time internship with the town of Summersby where she received valuable on-the-job training.

After graduation, the environmental health department offered Olivia a full-time job as a water pollution control technician. Today, she feels that her career is relatively stable since environmental protection is a nationally legislated priority. Habitat loss and point and nonpoint sources of pollution are adversely affecting environmental quality almost everywhere. The need for pollution control technicians will continue, if not increase, as the complexity of environmental problems increases. Olivia truly enjoys being directly involved with, and responsible for, changes that make a positive difference in the natural environment.

Learning Experience 2

Epidemic!

Prologue

Even before John Snow made his methodical, scientific study of how cholera spread, people were aware that certain illnesses could be passed from one individual to another. Common practices included avoiding contact with sick people, fumigating homes where sickness had taken place, and burning the bedding and clothing of sick individuals. In this learning experience, you examine the many ways that diseases can be transmitted (communicated). You then determine what, if anything, can be done to break the chain of transmission.

Brainstorming

Discuss the following questions with your partner, and record your thinking in your notebook. Be prepared to share your ideas with the class.

1. What data did John Snow collect that suggested that cholera was a disease that could be spread by some mechanism among groups of individuals? What data did he collect that suggested that cholera came from drinking contaminated water?
2. Might Snow have seen the same patterns of illness in the community with a disease such as heart disease or cancer?
3. What does it mean to "catch" a disease?
4. What diseases have you caught? How did you catch each one?
5. How are the diseases that you catch from other people different from a disease you might inherit?

The End of the World Is Nigh

The various outbreaks of cholera in London and in other cities such as New York and Boston during the 1800s are examples of the phenomenon known as an epidemic. An outbreak of a disease is considered an epidemic when it is prevalent and spreads rapidly among many individuals in a community at the same time. Epidemics of a disease that happen simultaneously around the world are considered pandemics. Epidemics and pandemics are part of life and of history. Some examples of these, past and present, are shown in Table 3.3.

Since Snow's time, epidemiologists and other scientists have determined that disease can be carried from one individual to another by a variety of methods. These methods are called **modes of transmission**. These modes of transmission

Topic: Disease
Transmission
Go to: www.scilinks.org
Code: INBIOH2322

Table 3.3   Examples of Epidemics and Pandemics through History

Disease	Mode of Transmission	Location/Date (CE)*	Infection Rate and/or Death Toll
smallpox	direct contact	Roman Empire (165–180)	25%–35% of population affected
bubonic plague	fleas on rats (vector)	Europe (1347–1350)	17–28 million deaths; 33%–50% of population affected
influenza	airborne	worldwide (1918–1919)	2 million deaths
polio	contaminated water	U.S. (1943–1956)	22,000 deaths; 400,000 affected
tuberculosis	airborne	worldwide (ongoing)	1 million deaths annually; 2 billion infected
diarrheal diseases (primarily enteric [intestinal] bacteria and rotavirus)	contaminated food and water	developing countries (South America, Africa, Asia) (ongoing)	10 million deaths annually
malaria	mosquitoes	developing countries (South America, Africa, Asia) (ongoing)	1.5 million deaths annually (80% children in Africa)
AIDS	direct contact	worldwide (ongoing)	40 million reported infections

*Note: CE stands for "of the common era"; it is also referred to as AD.

include spread resulting from direct, person-to-person contact or touching; from contaminated water and food (as Snow determined); through the air (see Figure 3.5); and through the **saliva** or feces of insects or other animals (called **vectors**). With the knowledge of how a disease is transmitted, perhaps we can take measures to reduce its spread or to avoid it ourselves.

In general, specific diseases are spread by only one mode of transmission. For example, flu is spread when saliva from an infected person is sprayed into the air during a sneeze. The flu is considered an airborne disease. Table 3.3 indicates how certain diseases are spread.

ANALYSIS

Record your responses to the following in your notebook.

1. Through what kinds of activities might individuals come in contact with each of these diseases?
2. What are ways people might try to avoid contracting these diseases?
3. List any infectious and noninfectious diseases that have occurred in your community during the past year. For each one, describe how you think it was transmitted.

Figure 3.5
Infectious diseases, such as a cold, may be spread when saliva droplets are sprayed into the air during a sneeze.
© Bettmann/Corbis

Outbreak

ACTIVITY

In this activity, you will participate in an epidemic without suffering any dire consequences. You will spread an **infection** by using one mode of transmission—direct contact. Then you will streak agar plates, a standard technique in the field of microbiology. (**Microbiology** is the study of **microorganisms**.) This will allow you to diagnose the presence of the infection and discover who has been infected. As you analyze your data, think about the kinds of preventative measures that might be used to halt the spread of this infection.

Materials

For each student:

- 1 pair of safety goggles
- 1 sterile cotton swab or inoculating loop
- 1 nutrient agar plate

For each group of eight students:

- 1 piece of contaminated candy (hard candy)
- 1 wax marking pencil
- 1 test tube containing nutrient broth

For the class:

- soap, detergent, or disinfectant
- warm tap water
- 4 sponges
- yeast solution
- sterilized tweezers or tongs
- disposal container or plastic garbage bags

Pre-laboratory Safety Check

When working with microorganisms, certain practices should be followed. These practices ensure that the materials you are working with do not become contaminated with microorganisms present in the air, on your hands and clothing, and on working surfaces. These practices are known as **sterile** or **aseptic** techniques. Sterile techniques also protect the investigator from becoming contaminated by the materials he or she is working with. Although all of the organisms you will be working with are harmless, sterile techniques should still be used. These include the following:

a. Wash hands thoroughly with soap and water before starting and at the conclusion of the experiment.
b. Wash the laboratory table with disinfectant or detergent before and after the experiment.
c. Use sterile media, glassware, and tools.
d. Keep hands away from the working ends of tools (such as inoculating loops, cotton swabs, and tweezers) and glassware. Do not touch the insides of agar plates.
e. Keep bottles, tubes, and flasks covered when not in use.
f. Do not mouth pipette.
g. Do not eat, drink, or smoke in the work area.

SAFETY NOTE

PROCEDURE

1. Count off within your group, and write your number on an agar plate using a wax pencil.
2. Remember, wash your hands thoroughly before you begin the experiment.
3. If your number is 1, your teacher will give you a piece of candy soaked in a contaminant, which is actually a **yeast** solution (a benign fungus). Roll it around in your right hand until your palm and fingers are very sticky. Put the candy in the disposal area designated by your teacher.
4. Shake hands with student number 2 in your group. Student 2 shakes hands with student 3, and so on, until all but the last person in the group has had a handshake.
5. Take a sterile cotton swab or inoculating loop and dip the cotton or loop end in the nutrient broth in the test tube. Then swab your right hand with it. Carefully open your agar plate and gently rub the loop or streak the swab across the surface of the agar. Do not press too hard. Roll the tip as you streak to transfer as much of the material gathered from your hand as possible to the agar. Swab in a zigzag pattern as shown in Figure 3.6. Dispose of the swab or loop as directed by your teacher.

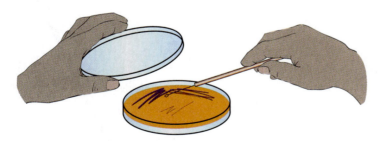

Figure 3.6

Streaking a plate. Make a zigzag pattern using an inoculating loop.

6. **STOP & THINK** What do you think is the purpose of the nutrient broth?

7. Cover the agar plate and turn it upside down (agar side up). Store it at room temperature (approximately 25°C [77°F]) to incubate for 24 hours.
8. Remember, wash your hands thoroughly after you finish the experiment. Then rinse with a dilute solution of disinfectant, if available.

9.  In your notebook, write a prediction of the results of this experiment.

10. After 24 hours of incubation, examine your plate and those of others in your group. Record whether or not there is growth on each of the plates.

ANALYSIS

Record your responses to the following in your notebook.

1. Which plate or plates have the most growth? the least? Make a chart that shows the range of growth on plates from your group.

2. Did the results agree with your prediction? If not, why do you think they differed?

3. Why was the last person in your group instructed not to shake hands with anyone? How is that person's plate different from the others?

4. What might these results tell you about the spread of infectious disease?

5. Do you think there is a danger in shaking hands with someone with smallpox? cholera? malaria? cancer? a genetic disease such as cystic fibrosis? Why or why not?

6. Headlines today frequently bear news of outbreaks of cholera in places such as Peru, Darfur, Chad, Afghanistan, and West Africa. But the last serious cholera outbreak in the United States took place in 1992. The article "U.S. Cholera Cases Set Record in 1992" describes this outbreak. Read the article and then answer the following questions:

   a. Why do you think the United States has not had the frequent outbreaks of cholera experienced in other countries?

   b. Explain why the advice in the article to "boil it, cook it, peel it or forget it" might have prevented the outbreak in 1992.

   c. Widespread international travel has been blamed for the rapid global spread of infectious diseases. Explain why this is the case.

   d. What precautions could an airline take to prevent the spread of infectious disease?

U.S. CHOLERA CASES SET RECORD IN 1992

Outbreak from Single Flight Accounted for 75 of 96 Incidents of Illness
New York Times, September 11, 1992

ATLANTA, Sept. 10 (AP)—A cholera outbreak aboard an Argentine airplane bound for Los Angeles helped push the number of travel-related cholera cases in the United States to an all-time high, Federal health officials said today.

The airplane cases resulted from a cholera outbreak that began in Peru in 1991 and has now spread to Mexico and the Caribbean, resulting in 5,000 deaths along the way, the Federal Centers for Disease Control reported.

Cholera is a severe diarrhea that can be accompanied by vomiting and dehydration. It is caused by contaminated foods and water, and can be fatal in cases of extreme dehydration. The centers said that 96 cholera cases had been reported in the United States since January and that 95 of those were travel related. The cause of the remaining case is unknown.

OUTBREAK FROM FLIGHT

The number of cases this year is higher than in any year since the Federal agency began monitoring cholera in 1961. In the 20 years through 1981, only 10 cholera cases were reported in the United States, the agency reported.

The bulk of this year's cases resulted in February from a cholera outbreak aboard an Aerolineas Argentinas flight from Argentina to Los Angeles. Seventy-five passengers developed cholera from a seafood salad served during the flight. Most of the remaining cases involved Americans traveling to Latin America or Asia to visit relatives, the agency reported.

Travelers should avoid drinking water that has not been boiled and avoid eating raw seafood, raw vegetables and food or drinks sold by street vendors, said Dr. Jessica Tuttle, a medical epidemiologist for the centers. She said the agency recommended that travelers follow a general rule of "boil it, cook it, peel it or forget it."

The centers also recommended that airlines traveling to and from cholera-affected areas be equipped with special medicine to treat cholera patients.

The agency also reported today that the 1991 cholera outbreak in Latin America had now spread to Mexico and the Caribbean. More than 600,000 cholera cases and 5,000 deaths have been attributed to the outbreak through Aug. 26, the centers said . . .

TASK

Propose a method of prevention that would be effective in stopping the spread of the classroom epidemic. Then design an experiment to test your proposal. Be sure to include the following in your design:

- the question(s) being asked,
- the hypothesis,
- your predictions about the experimental results,
- your experimental procedure,
- the method for data collection, and
- the broader implications that the results of your experiment might suggest about reducing disease transmission in everyday life.

EXTENDING *Ideas*

Analyze why and how prevention measures do or do not work. Trace the history of the treatment and prevention of diseases such as measles, bubonic plague, hepatitis, diphtheria, the common cold, polio, smallpox, rabies, Lyme disease, herpes, tuberculosis, malaria, influenza, or acquired immune deficiency syndrome (AIDS). Explain why methods of stopping the spread of the disease succeeded or failed.

The bubonic plague, or Black Death, originated in the Far East. It spread west to Europe during the 1300s through shipping trade routes. These ships brought plague-ridden rats and infected seafarers to seaport cities. The symptoms of the plague included swollen lymph glands, pain, fever, and coughing up blood. All of these symptoms preceded a painful death. Affected cities were filled with the unbearable stench from the bodies of the dead and dying. This nursery rhyme describes some of the symptoms and treatments of the time.

> Ring a ring of rosies, a pocket full of posies
> A-tichoo, a-tichoo, we all fall down

Determine the trade routes during this period of time. How did the path of the pandemic follow these routes? Explain how conditions during this time facilitated the spread of the disease. Describe the nature of the treatments available to people, and identify what finally ended the pandemic.

In some instances, the course of history has been shaped by the occurrence of disease. Smallpox facilitated the Spanish conquest of America; Charlemagne's conquest of Europe in 876 CE was slowed by an epidemic of influenza, which claimed much of his army; schistosomiasis is one of the reasons Taiwan is not part of mainland China today. Research one of these epidemics or another one that has played a role in historical events.

Are family pets factors in the transmission of diseases to humans? Is this a significant route of disease transmission? What precautions, if any, should pet owners take? Analyze local, regional, or state statistics to help answer these questions.

Public health is a field that addresses the problem of disease prevention by studying conditions of environment, culture, and society that affect the health of a group of people. Call your nearest state public health office and interview a public health officer about his or her job.

CAREER FOCUS

Public Health Microbiologist

It's first thing in the morning. The campus of Sierra College is deserted except for one person heading into the biology building. It's Liam, a research microbiologist and professor at Sierra College. He's starting his day early so he can work on a report of his research findings before he has to head to the microbiology course he is teaching. As a public health microbiologist, Liam studies bacteria and how they cause disease. Liam's report will detail his laboratory research, which focuses on various types of bacteria that cause stomach infections and lead to disease.

One of Liam's major career goals is admirable and ambitious. He wants to cure people or prevent them from getting sick by understanding the mechanisms that aid bacteria in causing disease. Liam feels his role, working toward understanding and curing diseases, is just as important as that of a doctor who works toward treating disease. He and his fellow public health microbiologists have an indirect impact on patients. They develop vaccines and ways to make disease-causing microbes less harmful. Liam's other important career goal is to pass on his enthusiasm to his students. In addition to teaching classes, he mentors students, giving them research assistant positions in his laboratory. In this way, he can show them what his work is really like and how they can contribute to scientific research.

As a child, Liam was fascinated by nature and was naturally curious about what makes life work. But it wasn't until he participated in a science fair in junior high school and won first prize that Liam realized he'd like to become a scientist. While taking a high school biology class and through his experiences in the science club, Liam found that he was deeply interested in biology. So he decided to attend Springfield University to study biology. He found that although his interests were mainly in biology, he had to take a lot of courses in chemistry and other life sciences.

During his summer breaks, Liam volunteered in various research laboratories. He thought that these practical and realistic experiences would provide him with a solid basis for making career decisions. He spent one summer in a microbiology lab. Here he saw how researchers were working to unravel the mysteries of diseases caused by bacteria. Liam loved examining bacteria under the electron microscope, which magnified the specimens thousands of times. He decided to pursue microbiology research as a career. His work in the lab also helped him realize that biology and chemistry are intertwined. He knew he would need knowledge of all the disciplines in the life sciences to be a successful researcher. He could see firsthand that all of the principles taught in the various science disciplines are used in everyday research in the lab. During his senior year, Liam was hired as a part-time research assistant in the microbiology lab. He was hooked!

After graduating with a Bachelor of Science degree in microbiology, Liam went on to a Ph.D. program. Here he studied toxins produced by bacteria and the roles they play in causing disease. During this time, he worked with other microbiologists and was mentored by an experienced researcher. After completing his Ph.D. in microbiology, Liam spent 2 years in postdoctoral training before becoming a faculty member at Sierra College. Liam finds it exhilarating when he's able to break through a challenge and unlock some of nature's secrets. Every time he discovers the answer to a problem, it seems to open up three or four more questions that need to be answered. Sometimes the answers to very difficult questions don't come easily. But Liam uses his best qualities—persistence and determination—to work toward solving these questions. Liam loves making new scientific discoveries and feels the changing world of microbiology helps him stay energized about his work. He's also energized by working with students and passing on his love for microbiology to a new generation of scientists.

Public Health Officer

Restaurants and cafes are great places to unwind and relax. But when it comes to these and other public buildings, it's work, not play, for Jasmine and her fellow public health officers. Food that hasn't been prepared hygienically is the perfect breeding ground for bacteria, like salmonella. As a public health officer for the state, Jasmine performs regular assessments of facilities that handle fresh food to minimize such community health risks.

Today, Jasmine is at Lucky's, a local restaurant, to inspect the premises. She checks that the utensils, procedures, and hygiene standards comply with regulations, and takes food samples for microbiological and chemical testing. During her inspection, Jasmine notices that one cook is handling food unhygienically. She talks with him and the restaurant manager about correct food-handling procedures and plans on conducting regular checks to ensure that the problem is corrected. In addition to examining the food preparation at Lucky's, Jasmine will also make sure the facility's ventilation is adequate and there is clear access to fire escapes.

It's Jasmine's responsibility to evaluate and monitor health hazards and to develop strategies to control risks in public places. Her goals are to ensure that members of the community abide by public health legislation and to educate the public on health issues. This involves many more duties than just monitoring facilities that handle food. By the end of the day, Jasmine will also investigate a construction site that has been reported as too noisy. This falls under the jurisdiction of the Public Health Office since prolonged exposure to noise is a nuisance and detrimental to one's hearing. She'll even visit Gnarly Tattoo, a tattoo parlor in town, to monitor tattoo and ear-piercing equipment to prevent the spread of blood-transmitted diseases.

Jasmine always knew she wanted a career that would enable her to work with people, but she wasn't sure what it would be. She excelled at science and loved biology in high school. On the weekends, she worked part-time in a local grocery store, stocking the produce shelves. During her first month on the job, the store was inspected by a public health officer. He took the time to talk with Jasmine and show her how she could handle the produce in a more sanitary, effective way. Over the next couple of years, she was able to talk with various public health officers that inspected the store. She listened to stories about the other types of activities they carry out in their day-to-day work. They told her that public health officers need to have good communication and negotiation skills since the people they work with aren't always receptive to their help. Jasmine felt that being a public health officer would enable her to combine her scientific knowledge with her desire to work with people to help ensure the public's health.

After graduating from high school, Jasmine decided to study public health at a 4-year college. Her program involved taking courses in biology, chemistry, math, computer science, and English. She also learned a variety of technical skills that she'd need to be a public health officer, like sampling and chemical analysis. She studied public health legislation. During the program, Jasmine met with her adviser several times to explore different career paths. He explained that most public health officers work for the state or federal government but that more opportunities were becoming available at major companies, such as food manufacturers and industrial plants. Jasmine felt that working for a state Public Health Office would allow her to have the most contact with the general public. So she pursued a position there after graduation.

Jasmine has been a public health officer for 6 years. She gets a great deal of satisfaction from helping to keep the public healthy and safe. She finds that being a public health officer is a perfect fit for her. She can apply her scientific background in a context that also requires her strong people skills— educating, negotiating, and communicating. Jasmine also tries to stay up-to-date with changes in public health legislation and takes professional development courses periodically to keep her skills sharp.

Options for Prevention

Prologue

Preventing the spread of disease is a major effort of public health workers around the world. How can the spread of a disease be prevented? The approach taken to prevent epidemics depends on the way the disease is transmitted. In this investigation, you design an experiment that will help answer this question for diseases that are transmitted by direct contact.

Brainstorming

Discuss the following questions with your partner, and record your thinking in your notebook. Be prepared to share your ideas with the class.

1. What diseases have you heard or read about that have been happening recently around the world?
2. How do you think these diseases are spread?
3. How do you think the spread of each of these diseases can be prevented?

ACTIVITY

Options for Prevention

Use the hypothesis and experimental design that you developed in the task at the end of the learning experience to answer the question posed in the Prologue above.

Materials

For each student:

- 1 pair of safety goggles
- 1 sterile cotton swab
- 1 nutrient agar plate

For each group of eight to ten students:

- 1 piece of hard candy
- 1 wax marking pencil
- 1 test tube with nutrient broth
- access to a heat source, such as boiling water, a flame, or an oven
- access to a cold source, such as a freezer or dry ice
- soaps, detergents, gloves
- any other materials required by your experiment

For the class:

- nutrient broth
- warm tap water
- yeast solution
- sterilized tweezers

PROCEDURE

SAFETY NOTE

1. Be sure you have recorded the following information in your notebooks:
   a. the specific question being asked;
   b. an appropriate hypothesis;
   c. the experimental procedure for investigating your hypothesis (include the materials you will use and the steps you will follow); and
   d. the method for collecting data.
2. Carry out the experiment. Make sure you observe all safety precautions.
3. Analyze your data. Describe your conclusions about what the results demonstrated.
4. After you have analyzed your data, prepare to present your hypothesis, procedure, results, and conclusions to the class.

Agents of Disease

Prologue

Long before microbes were identified as the causative agents of infectious disease, humans pondered the origins of disease. What caused the devastating epidemics that often decimated human populations? In trying to find a reason for this suffering, different cultures developed various explanations for disease: unknown poisons, bad air, evil spirits, divine retribution. Disease was often viewed as divine punishment for sins or aberrant behavior. Afflicted individuals were tortured or even executed.

Even without any knowledge of microorganisms, careful observation of patterns of disease led groups of people to understand that certain diseases were **communicable** (spread by contact with other humans or animals and through food and water). They learned that these diseases could be prevented by good hygiene and careful food preparation practices. But, what exactly was being communicated and causing disease?

In this learning experience, you explore the agents that cause disease. You will add what you have learned about the spread of disease to new information about causative agents. This combined knowledge will help you determine what is causing sickness and death among young adults in New Mexico. Like epidemiologists, you will examine data, apply your understanding, and then determine if there is a way to prevent the transmission of the disease.

Brainstorming

Discuss the following questions with your partner, and record your thinking in your notebook. Be prepared to share your ideas with the class.

1. What infectious diseases have you or anyone you know experienced?
2. How were these diseases identified as infectious?
3. Were these diseases caused by bacteria, viruses, or parasites? How were the causative agents identified?
4. How were the infections treated?

Bacteria and Viruses and Parasites, Oh My!

READING

Research in the late 1800s by a number of scientists provided evidence that many diseases were caused by microorganisms. The first conclusive demonstration that bacteria could cause disease was described in the work of Louis Pasteur and Robert Koch. Working independently, each scientist demonstrated that anthrax, a serious disease in domestic animals, was caused by bacteria found in the bloodstream. (Anthrax is also transmissible to humans.) The work of Pasteur, Koch, and other scientists in the field ushered in a new era of discovery. Bacteria, **viruses**, and **parasites** were now shown to be the causes of infectious diseases around the world.

In 1876, Koch proposed a set of criteria by which a microorganism could be determined to be an **infectious agent** (or **pathogen**). These criteria included the following:

- The microorganism must be present when the disease is present but absent in healthy organisms.
- It must be possible to isolate the microorganism.
- The isolated microorganism must cause disease when placed into a healthy organism.
- It must be possible to reisolate the microorganism from the second diseased host.

These criteria, called **Koch's Postulates**, are still used today to determine whether a disease is caused by an infectious agent. All organisms live in some kind of environment that provides them with nutrients and shelter in which to grow and replicate. In some cases, an infectious agent can survive in a number of different environments such as soil, water, a plant, or an animal. As a result, it is only a matter of chance where the agent finally appears. In other cases, an infectious agent, for one reason or another, can live only within another organism. This organism is called the **host**. Often, these pathogens require the nutrients that the host organism alone provides. The host becomes the environment from which the infectious agent derives everything it needs to survive. These organisms can only survive in one specific environment. This may be a plant, an animal, or a bacterium. In some cases, the specificity may even extend to the type of tissue or cell in which the pathogen must live.

Wherever it lives, an infectious agent must grow and replicate. To do this, it must locate a suitable environment, take up nutrients, and release by-products of its own metabolism. In carrying out these processes of life, the organism may deplete the nutrients in the environment, release toxic substances, and cause physical damage to its surroundings. The depletion of nutrients, damage from toxic substances, and mechanical damage can all contribute to causing the symptoms characteristic of the host's disease associated with that infectious agent. There are three major types of pathogenic (disease-causing) agents. These are bacteria, viruses, and parasites. (Although fungi are also important in some diseases, they will not be considered here.)

SC*i*LINKS®
NSTA

Topic: Pathogen
Go to: www.scilinks.org
Code: INBIOH2333

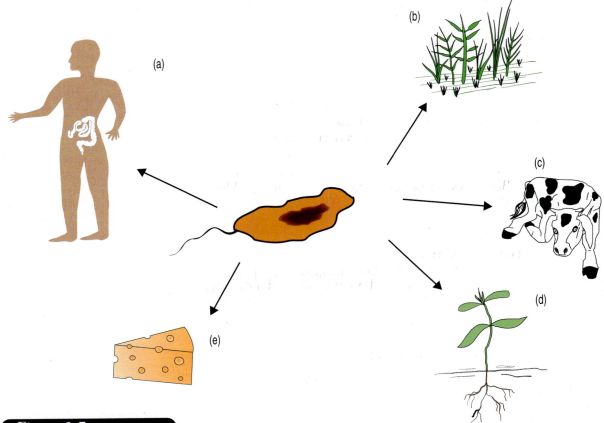

Figure 3.7

Bacteria carry out many roles in life. They (a) help animals make vitamins; (b) keep the soil fertile; (c) decompose dead matter; (d) fix nitrogen into nitrates; and (e) carry out processes that result in cheese.

BACTERIA—THE OLDEST ORGANISMS

For the first 2 billion years of Earth's existence, bacteria were its only tenants. Structurally, bacteria are the simplest of life-forms. They are single-celled prokaryotic organisms. Bacteria are capable of carrying out all of the cellular life functions. But they lack the internal structures, such as a nucleus and mitochondria, that are found in eukaryotic cells. Bacteria are also characterized by a cell wall that is made up of polysaccharides. This cell wall surrounds the cell membrane.

Bacteria constitute a large and diversified group of organisms. They are capable of growing in a remarkably wide range of habitats and conditions. Bacteria can be found just about anywhere—in the saltiest sea, in the hottest hot spring, and in the most acid or alkaline conditions. They make the soil fertile. In every gram of fertile soil, there exist about 100,000,000 living bacteria. This amounts to about 90–250 kg (about 200–550 lb) of bacteria for every acre of soil. Bacteria decompose dead organic matter, help plants obtain vital nitrogen from the air, and help us make vitamins and fend off undesirable microbes. They even provide us with some of life's pleasures, such as yogurt and cheese (see Figure 3.7). Most mammals are walking apartment complexes for a wide variety of bacteria. Some bacteria are essential to the well-being of the animal; most are just along for the ride.

Despite their abundance and diversity of species, bacteria are remarkably lacking in variety when it comes to shape and distinguishing structural features (see Figure 3.8). They can be spherical, as are the bacteria *Streptococcus pyogenes* (the causative agent of sore throats). They can be rod-shaped, as are *Salmonella typhi* (the cause of typhoid fever); *Vibrio cholerae* (the causative agent of cholera); and *Pseudomonas aeruginosa* (bacteria commonly found in soil). Or they can be helical or spiral-shaped, as are *Treponema pallidum* (the cause of syphilis) and *Spirochaeta picatilis* (large and harmless spirochete common in water).

Because bacteria have limited mobility, they must rely on carriers such as animals, water, or food. Insect bites and fecal material from birds, rodents, cats, and other animals can also transmit bacteria. Most people are scarcely aware of the bacteria around them. But life would be very difficult—if not impossible—without bacteria. Despite all the important things bacteria provide, people generally only recognize the existence of bacteria when they become ill. For this reason, bacteria are generally viewed as bad. Like all living things, however, bacteria are only carrying out the processes of life. And these processes include taking nutrients from their environment so that they can grow and reproduce. For the majority of bacteria, this environment is the soil or water. But for others, this environment is another organism. That organism may become diseased as a result.

The troublesome, pathogenic bacteria are only a small portion of the total bacterial world. Lewis Thomas in "On Disease" put it this way:

> It is true, of course, that germs are all around us; they comprise a fair proportion of the sheer bulk of the soil, and they abound in the air. But it is certainly not true that they are our natural enemies. Indeed, it comes as a surprise to realize that such a tiny minority of the bacterial populations of the earth has any interest at all in us. The commonest of encounters between bacteria and the higher forms of life take place after the death of the latter, in the course of recycling the elements of life. This is obviously the main business of the microbial world in general, and it has nothing to do with disease.
>
> It is probably true that symbiotic relationships between bacteria and their metazoan hosts are much more common in nature than infectious disease, although I cannot prove this. But if you count up all the indispensable microbes that live in various intestinal tracts, supplying essential nutrients or providing enzymes for the breakdown of otherwise indigestible food, and add all the peculiar bacterial aggregates that live like necessary organs in the tissues of many insects, plus all the bacterial symbionts engaged in nitrogen fixation in collaboration with legumes, the total mass of symbiotic life is overwhelming. Alongside, the list of important bacterial infections of human beings is short indeed.

Excerpted from "On Disease," copyright © 1979 by Lewis Thomas, from *The Medusa and the Snail* by Lewis Thomas. Used by permission of Viking Penguin, a division of Penguin Group (USA), Inc.

When bacteria do cause disease, they can do it in a variety of ways. These tiny invaders live in blood, on skin, on mucous membranes, and sometimes within cells. They may secrete toxic substances that damage vital tissues, feast on nutrients intended for the cell, or may form colonies that disrupt normal functions in the host's body. Directly or indirectly, their actions can cause extensive damage to the host.

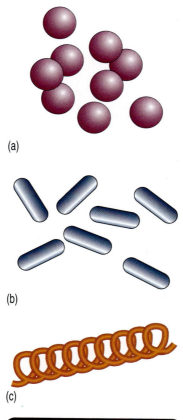

(a)

(b)

(c)

Figure 3.8

Three shapes of bacteria: (a) spherical; (b) rod-shaped; (c) helical.

The presence of bacterial cell walls makes some bacteria susceptible to treatment with antibiotics. **Antibiotics** are chemical compounds that either kill or inhibit the growth of bacteria. Certain antibiotics act by interfering with the synthesis of the cell wall. Because animal cells do not have a cell wall, antibiotics affect only the infecting bacteria. When first discovered in the 1920s, antibiotics were viewed as miracle drugs capable of saving humankind from the devastating diseases that had plagued them throughout history. However, almost as soon as a new antibiotic was discovered, certain bacteria with the ability to resist its killing effect were found. These were able to survive and multiply while the more susceptible bacteria were killed. Bacterial resistance to antibiotics is now one of the biggest challenges facing medical practitioners today.

VIRUSES—THE INVADERS

Viruses have an enormous impact on human beings. Like bacteria, they have been part of our lives since at least the beginning of recorded time. A bas relief from 1500 BCE Egypt depicts a priest with a shriveled leg, evidence of infection with polio virus. (BCE stands for "before the common era"; it is also referred to as BC.) A 13th-century manuscript shows a dog, mouth foaming, attacking a terrified man destined to die from the rabies virus transmitted from a dog bite. Smallpox is believed to have helped a small band of Spaniards under Cortés subdue the vast and powerful Aztec nation.

These microbes are too small to be visible even under the light microscope. They were discovered not long after bacteria were implicated as the causative agent in anthrax. Their existence was demonstrated in 1892 by the Russian scientist Dimitri Ivanovsky. Ivanovsky was investigating the cause of a disease in tobacco plants.

As perpetrators of disease, viruses have been viewed as one of the "bad guys" of the microbial world. They have been called pirates of the cell, viral hitchhikers, cellular hijackers, and pieces of bad news wrapped up in protein. These tiny microbes have been perceived as having evil intent. In reality, viruses are just simple microbes. They are genetic material (that is, nucleic acid) surrounded by protein. A virus is not a cell. It cannot maintain the characteristics of life on its own. It lacks the biochemical and structural components (cellular machinery) that enable an organism to carry out the life processes. It has no membrane, no nucleus, and no mitochondria, and thus no capacity to take up and use nutrients. It cannot reproduce, metabolize, or conduct any of the basic processes of life. A virus must seek out an environment that provides not only the nutrients it needs to carry out life processes, but also the cellular machinery required for these processes. That is, a cell. A virus cannot live outside a cell. Viruses exist for almost every kind of cell: bacterial, plant, fungal, and animal.

Viruses can be transmitted in a myriad of ways. These include by direct contact, through exchange of fluids such as blood, through the air (airborne), by insect and animal vectors, and in contaminated food and water. Viruses tend to infect specific kinds of cells. For example, the influenza virus prefers cells found in the lungs. The rotavirus that causes severe intestinal distress, however, is specific for intestinal cells. Human immunodeficiency virus, the causative agent of AIDS, grows specifically in cells of the immune system, T cells.

A typical virus is much smaller than any cell. It is comprised of a protein coat surrounding its viral genetic material (see Figure 3.9). This genetic material contains specific instructions for making identical copies of the virus. The proteins encoded by the viral genes must be able to take over the cellular machinery of the cell. This "commandeered machinery" is then used to aid the reproduction of the virus. And, in many cases, it is no longer available for the growth and reproduction of the invaded cell. A virus enters the cell. Using different mechanisms (depending on the kind of virus it is), it causes the cell to stop making what it needs for itself and instead makes what the virus needs to reproduce. A virus is like an unwanted guest who eats everything in the refrigerator, uses every clean towel in the house, and on leaving reduces your house to a pile of rubble. The virus uses the building blocks and energy stored that the cell has generated for its own growth and reproduction. The cell is depleted of the materials and energy it needs to repair the damage. The machinery the cell needs to make more of itself is no longer under its control. As a result, the cell often dies from this invasion.

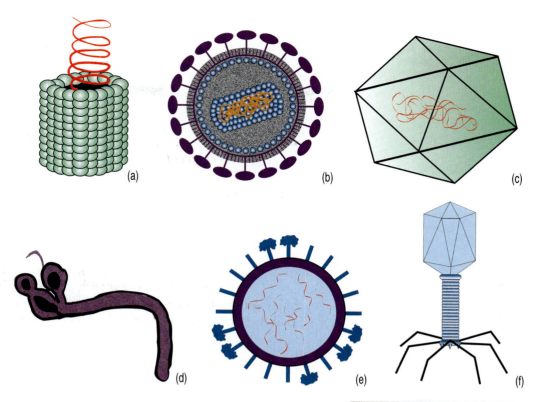

Figure 3.9

Various kinds of viruses: (a) tobacco mosaic virus; (b) human immunodeficiency virus (HIV); (c) polio virus; (d) Ebola virus; (e) influenza virus; (f) bacteriophage T4.

Viruses are not susceptible to antibiotics because they have no cell walls. Unlike the discovery of antibiotics for treating bacteria, no miracle drugs have been discovered for the treatment of viruses. In fact, to date, no truly effective **viricidal** (virus killing) drugs exist. In most instances, treatment of viral infections involves prevention (**vaccines**) or helping the body to help itself. This means sleeping, drinking plenty of fluids, and eating chicken soup.

PARASITES—A WAY OF LIFE

The parasitic way of life is highly successful. There are far more kinds of parasitic than nonparasitic organisms in the world. Those organisms that are not parasites are usually hosts. Even parasites are often hosts for other parasites. Or, in the words of Jonathan Swift:

> Big fleas have little fleas
> upon their backs to bite 'em,
> Little fleas have lesser fleas and so, ad infinitum

The parasitic way of life is one form of living relationship called **symbiosis**. A symbiotic relationship involves any two organisms that live together in close association. Often, this has mutually beneficial results, but sometimes not.

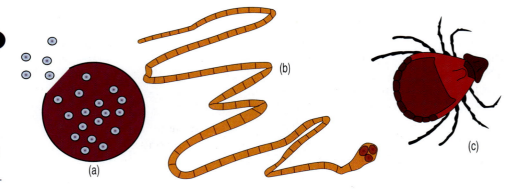

Figure 3.10

Various kinds of parasites: (a) plasmodia, microscopic parasites in a red blood cell; (b) tapeworm, a flatworm that can grow to more than 10 m (33 ft) in length; (c) tick, an insect the size of a pinhead.

Sometimes a **symbiont** actually lives at the expense of the host. That is, it uses nutrients required by the host. It is then called a parasite. Some parasites live their entire mature lives within or on the host. But others, such as fleas or mosquitoes, only visit for a meal. They eat and run (or fly).

Parasites can be unicellular **protozoa**, such as the plasmodia that live inside red blood cells. Plasmodia are the causative agent of malaria, the major infectious disease in the world today. Parasites can also be worms such as tapeworms, which live in the digestive tract, and schistosomes that inhabit the veins of the bladder or intestines and are the causative agents of schistosomiasis. Arthropods, such as fleas and ticks, are also parasites. These temporary parasites visit the host for frequent or occasional feedings (see Figure 3.10). There are also parasitic **fungi**. These include mushrooms, molds, and mildews, which feed on plants or animals. By this definition, certain bacteria and viruses can be considered to live as parasites. In the conventional definition, the term parasite refers only to eukaryotic organisms.

A parasite is often associated with damage to the host. A parasite may harm its host in any of a number of ways. It can do this by mechanical injury, such as boring a hole in it; by eating or digesting and absorbing its tissues; by poisoning the host with toxic metabolic products; or simply by robbing the host of nutrients. Most parasites inflict a combination of these conditions on their hosts. Of course, the parasite is only trying to survive. It is taking from its environment what it needs to sustain its life processes so that it can reproduce. Parasites do not have evil intent, any more than bacteria or viruses do.

Parasites are similar to viruses and bacteria in that they can be transmitted in a variety of ways. These include in contaminated food or water, by direct contact, or in the feces or saliva of an insect or other animal.

How we treat parasitic diseases reflects the great diversity of parasites. Many unicellular parasites can be treated with drugs such as quinine for malaria and arsenic derivatives for sleeping sickness. Tapeworms and nematodes (worms) can also be treated with drugs that interfere with their metabolism. No vaccines exist to date. But many parasitic diseases can be prevented by good hygiene, sanitary facilities, and effective programs of insect control. A simple change of habits, such as staying out of lakes and rivers, could prevent many serious and debilitating diseases.

THE HOST–INFECTIOUS AGENT INTERACTION

Despite their great diversity in structure and habits, all infectious agents have the same life requirements for survival: to grow and to reproduce themselves. These requirements, in fact, are shared with all living things. To fulfill these needs, all living things must obtain nutrients and live at appropriate temperatures and levels of moisture, pH, and oxygen. Organisms derive these essential components from their environment. In the case of infectious agents, however, that environment happens to be another living organism.

In many instances, the organism in which the infectious agent has taken up residence is not always a gracious host. Many host organisms have evolved ways to try to rid themselves of unwanted houseguests. Animals, plants, and even bacteria have developed a wide arsenal of physical, chemical, and biological strategies against invading organisms. In humans, the **immune system** has developed an elegant and complex response to infectious agents. Specific proteins called **antibodies** are made in response to almost every foreign substance that enters the body. (In fact, invading organisms can often be identified based on the kind of antibodies present in the body.) These antibodies bind to the foreign substance and mark it for destruction. If this substance is part of a virus, bacteria, or parasite, the organism may be doomed.

Antibodies are one kind of host response against infection; specialized cells are another. Certain cells of the immune system are mobilized and become an army of **white blood cells**. These cells circulate through the body and destroy the invaders. The function of these white blood cells is to engulf and destroy pathogens. They produce toxic substances designed to kill infected cells and invading organisms.

As with all living things, infectious organisms affect their environment as they grow. But it does not benefit the infectious agent to harm its environment in the process of living. The well-being of that environment or host is essential to the infectious agent's own well-being. Many host–infectious agent relationships exist in a balance in which the two partners have evolved to tolerance. The agent takes from the host what it needs without damaging the host, and the host tolerates the presence of the agent by not defending itself too vigorously. Other host–infectious agent relationships have not reached this level of tolerance, and the result is disease.

 NALYSIS

Record your responses to the following in your notebook.

1. What is meant when an organism is called an infectious agent?
2. Describe the following for the infectious agent that you read about (bacterium, virus, or parasite):
   a. the biological characteristics of this agent,
   b. the symptoms this agent might cause,
   c. how this agent might make you sick, and
   d. methods of treatment.
3. When a new disease appears, researchers first determine whether it is caused by an infectious agent. What would you need to do to prove this? Why is this not possible with certain diseases such as AIDS?

The Case of the Killer Congestion

Long-distance runner Merrill Bahe was on his way to his girlfriend's funeral on May 14, 1993, when he found himself gasping for air. Suddenly, and quite dramatically, Bahe was overcome with fever, headache, and respiratory distress. In the presence of his grief-stricken relatives, Bahe gulped desperately for air in their car, en route south to Gallup, New Mexico.

Minutes later the nineteen-year-old Navajo athlete was dead.

His twenty-four-year-old girlfriend had died in a small Indian Health Service clinic located sixty miles away from Gallup a few days earlier after an identical bout of sudden respiratory illness. And within the week her brother and his girlfriend, also young, athletic Navajos, who lived in trailers near Bahe's, fell mysteriously ill; the young woman died.

Excerpt from *The Coming Plague: Newly Emerging Diseases in a World Out of Balance* by Laurie Garrett. Copyright © 1994 by Laurie Garrett. Reprinted by permission of Farrar, Straus and Giroux, LLC.

Chilled by the sudden deaths of these apparently healthy, young adults, attending physician Bruce Tempest put out a call to other physicians and colleagues in the state. He described the symptoms and requested immediate notification if other cases were seen. By the end of the day he had compiled a list of five more healthy young people who had died of acute respiratory distress syndrome. Within the week, the list grew to 19 suspected cases, 12 of whom had died.

The disease seemed to follow the same pattern in every victim. It started with flulike symptoms of fever, muscle aches, and headaches. After a period of a few hours to 2 days, those symptoms worsened to coughing and irritation in the lungs. This seemed to be caused by leaks in the capillary network feeding the lungs with blood. This leakage of the plasma fluid from the blood filled the air sacs of the lungs. Shortly thereafter, the patients were unable to absorb oxygen from the air they took into their lungs. Starving for oxygen, the heart would slow down and death would soon follow.

TASK

What is causing this killer respiratory distress syndrome? How is it being transmitted? Can anything be done to stop the epidemic? Your group will act like a team of epidemiologists from the Centers for Disease Control and Prevention (CDC). You will familiarize yourselves with information about the characteristics of a wide range of diseases and with the data about the specific epidemic.

When researching epidemics, time is always of the essence. The disease continues to spread. The longer you take to solve the problem, the more deaths occur. You will have more than enough information. So think carefully about the data and identify which data give you information that will help you determine the causative agent. Then determine which data are still inconclusive.

Each team will need to complete a summary report. In this report, you will record the decisions and information that led to the identification of the causative agent. You will also outline your solutions for stopping the epidemic. Specifically, you will need to do the following:

1. Read the epidemiological, medical, and laboratory reports that follow.
2. Examine Table 3.4, Causes of Respiratory Distress. This table contains information about various causes of respiratory distress and hemorrhagic (bleeding) symptoms and their characteristics.
3. Discuss the data with your team. Use each of the three reports and Table 3.4 on pages 343–344 to eliminate candidates.
4. Record your rationale for each decision. For example, record how you decided whether the disease was infectious or noninfectious.
5. Review the information that the class shared in item 2 of the Analysis for the reading "Bacteria and Viruses and Parasites, Oh My!" This will help ensure that you have a complete picture.
6. Write a report that contains the following information:
   a. the nature of the epidemic (is it an infectious or noninfectious disease?);
   b. the probable causative agent of the epidemic, if infectious;
   c. the process by which you came to the decision about the causative agent;
   d. diagnostic procedures to use on a new patient demonstrating symptoms of the disease;
   e. potential treatment for the disease;
   f. the rationale for each decision; and
   g. recommendations for preventing further spread of the disease.
7. Be prepared to present the results of the data and your recommendations for stopping the epidemic to your fellow epidemiological teams.

Report One: Epidemiological Data

1. Data about infected individuals (victims):
   a. geographical distribution—lived in New Mexico and other parts of the Southwest, South, and northwest United States
   b. habits—worked in a variety of jobs; some held positions in maintenance or cleaning; no unusual hobbies
   c. living conditions—lived in trailers, small homes; generally in rural areas
   d. relationships—in some cases, victims were related; one instance of engaged couple as victims; primarily isolated cases of unrelated, uninvolved individuals
   e. travel—no pattern of foreign travel or association with anyone who has traveled
2. Data about environment:
   Recent rains and good growing conditions for seeds, nuts, berries, and insects had resulted in increase in rodent population.

Report Two: Medical Data

1. Symptoms—respiratory distress, flulike symptoms, fever, muscle aches, coughing, difficulty obtaining oxygen
2. Victims—range of ages; many young adults
3. Treatment—antibiotics ineffective; no response to antiprotozoal drugs (drugs that eliminate parasitic, single-celled organisms or protozoans)
4. Autopsy report:
   a. death by suffocation
   b. rapid occurrence of death after onset of symptoms
   c. air sacs in lungs filled with fluid, presumably from blood plasma leaking from pulmonary (lung) veins

Report Three: Laboratory Data

1. Mass spectral analysis (an assay for detecting chemical substances and heavy metals in blood and tissue)—negative for chemical toxins and heavy metals
2. Examination of lung tissue and blood smears by direct stain and light microscopic analysis—negative for visible pathogens
3. Growth in culture from blood and lung tissue—no growth demonstrated
4. **Immunology** report:
   a. large increase in number of white blood cells
   b. results of antibody detection assays:
      - negative for *Toxoplasma gondii*, *Streptococcus pneumoniae*, *Mycoplasma*, influenza virus
      - inconclusive for Ebola virus, hantavirus, pneumocystis, Legionella, *Pasteurella pestis*

Table 3.4 Causes of Respiratory Distress

Causes of Respiration Distress	Type of Agent	Mode of Transmission	Geographic Location	Symptoms	Main Target Population	Treatment	Nature of Immune Response	Location in Body	Method of Detection	Prognosis
phosgene	chemical toxin; poison gas	aerosol as gas	worldwide	coughing; fluid-filled lungs	all ages	NA*	NA	blood; lungs; other tissues	mass spectral analysis**	damage to lungs
paraquat	chemical toxin; herbicide	ingestion of treated plants	South America; Central America	cough; congestion; fluid-filled lungs	all ages; adult workers	NA	NA	blood; lungs; renal and skeletal tissue	mass spectral analysis	damage to lungs
influenza	virus	airborne; human to human	worldwide	fever, cough; muscle pain	all ages	bedrest; fluids	white blood cells; antibodies	intracell; lungs	antibody detection***	death in infirm; otherwise recovery
Ebola	virus	direct contact; human to human	Africa	internal bleeding; fluid loss	all ages	bedrest; fluids	white blood cells; antibodies	intracell; blood vessels	antibody detection	80% death rate
hantavirus	virus	airborne; aerosol; mice feces	Asia; U.S.	congestion; fever; fluid-filled lungs	all ages; adults between 20 and 60	bedrest; fluids	white blood cells; antibodies	intracell; blood vessels in lungs	antibody detection	70% death rate
plague	bacteria (*Pasteurella pestis*)	fleas living on rodents	worldwide	fever; swollen lymphs; cough; pain	all ages	antibiotics	antibodies	lungs; blood; lymph glands	direct stain of blood smears; antibody detection; culture†	generally fatal if untreated
Legionnaire's disease	bacteria (*Legionella*)	aerosol; scum water from appliances	U.S.	fever; muscle aches; congestion	all ages; older adults	antibiotics (often resistant)	antibodies	lungs; blood	direct stain of blood smears; antibody detection; difficult to culture	can be fatal if untreated

(continued)

Table 3.4 Causes of Respiratory Distress—continued

Causes of Respiration Distress	Type of Agent	Mode of Transmission	Geographic Location	Symptoms	Main Target Population	Treatment	Nature of Immune Response	Location in Body	Method of Detection	Prognosis
Mycoplasma pneumonia	bacteria	airborne; human to human	worldwide	persistent cough; fever; congestion	all ages	antibiotics	white blood cells; antibodies	intracell; lungs	antibody test; difficult to culture	generally complete recovery
bacterial pneumonia	bacteria (*Streptococcus* pneumonia)	airborne; human to human	worldwide	cough; fever; ear ache	children	antibiotics (often resistant)	antibodies	connective tissue; lungs; ear canals	culture; antibody detection	generally complete recovery; may persist
Toxoplasma	parasitic protozoan	cat feces; undercooked meat	worldwide	congestion; convulsion paralysis; heart disease	newborns; generally asymptomatic in adults	anti- protozoal drugs (?)	white blood cells; antibodies	intracell; lungs	antibody detection	eventual recovery; may cause birth defects
pneumocystic pneumonia	parasitic protozoan	believed to be airborne; human to human	Europe; U.S.	high fever in adults; air sacs filled with foam	malnourished children; weakened adults	anti- protozoal drugs (?)	white blood cells; antibodies	intracell; lungs	direct stain of sputum; antibody detection	often death

Notes:

*   NA means that the information is not available.

** Mass spectral analysis is an assay for detecting chemical substances and heavy metals in blood and tissue.

***Antibody detection is an assay in which the blood of victims is mixed with purified infectious agents. If antibodies specific to those organisms are present in the blood of victims, clumping will be seen in the sample. This indicates that the antibody has bound to the added microorganism. The person is most likely infected with that microorganism.

†   Culture is the growth of the organism on agar as you did in Learning Experience 2.

EXTENDING *Ideas*

▶ Describe a tradition, ritual, or custom that you think is based on an understanding of an infectious disease and its spread (for example, covering your mouth when you sneeze). Provide a possible explanation of what kind of infectious disease this custom might have been designed to prevent. Explain how this custom might achieve this.

▶ Parasitic diseases in developing countries are a great drain on the economic infrastructures of these countries. Research one disease caused by a parasite. Then describe the parasite's life cycle and the symptoms of the disease. Explain how this disease could cause financial loss in the country.

CAREER FOCUS

Epidemiologist   An outbreak of a mysterious illness in central Africa has been spreading rapidly, killing almost everyone who contracts it. Fatima and other epidemiologists from the Centers for Disease Control and Prevention (CDC), America's national public health agency, have been sent to the area to try to solve the mystery. The symptoms don't look like any other disease epidemiologists have seen before. Fatima and her colleagues may spend weeks or months in the region trying to determine the cause and how to stop it. All of their work must be done in this very remote setting. There is no running water, electricity, or phone, and the area is in the midst of a dangerous civil war.

Fatima is a disease detective, otherwise known as a field epidemiologist. She travels to remote places all over the world where outbreaks of disease are occurring. The outbreaks often happen in remote areas because many diseases are associated with animals such as mice, bats, or mosquitoes. These types of animals don't usually live in urban areas. Once she arrives at an outbreak location, her job is to try to figure out how people in the community are getting sick. She must determine what harmful microbe is causing the disease and how it is transmitted. Then she needs to help people avoid and treat their infections.

Fatima first tries to collect detailed information, much like pieces of a puzzle. She identifies who became sick first, who was second, and so on. She determines the relationships between the victims, if any, and tries to find out how they became infected. She carefully records this information and any other relevant medical information, and takes blood or other samples that she needs to analyze. Fatima then analyzes all of the data and tries to fit the puzzle together. She identifies possible causative agents and the mode of transmission so she can propose treatment and prevent further spread of the disease.

Fatima feels a sense of great satisfaction and accomplishment when helping a community overcome an outbreak. But she also admits that her job can be scary. Many of the diseases are deadly if contracted and rarely is there an existing treatment or vaccine. But when Fatima treats patients or draws blood, she takes precautionary measures to protect herself, such as wearing latex gloves, a plastic gown, and a mask. Sometimes the crew of epidemiologists will construct a portable lab in the field that is far away from as many people as possible and seal all the windows and doors. In this lab, Fatima and her colleagues take additional precautions, such as wearing body suits, masks, and respirators that provide clean air while they work on samples from the field.

At a young age, Fatima became interested in public health issues through her father, a public health nurse. He told her about his daily work experiences and about the people he met and assisted. When she was in high school, Fatima worked as a nursing assistant in a nursing home. The experience opened her eyes to the many opportunities medicine presents. She decided to major in public health science in college because she was interested in helping underserved populations get improved medical care. After graduating from college, she spent a year immunizing children in India. This experience influenced her decision to go to graduate school for a Ph.D. in epidemiology so she could combine her love of caring for people and treating illnesses.

Following her graduate studies, Fatima's mentor, who had worked for the CDC, recommended that she join a 2-year program run by the CDC. The program taught physicians and public health scientists to be disease detectives. She treasured the experience of traveling to communities that were experiencing an outbreak, and stayed on at the CDC. She finds epidemiology fascinating because it examines how the occurrences of diseases are affected by diverse factors. These factors can vary from microbial and physiological to environmental and behavioral. Fatima enjoys using her scientific knowledge to solve real-world problems in worldwide settings. She is enriched personally by working with different populations and learning about their culture. She gets tremendous satisfaction from knowing that her work is having a direct impact on the health of people all over the world.

Learning Experience 4

Search for the Cause

Prologue

In the previous learning experience, you were introduced to different causative agents of disease. Why are certain organisms pathogenic and others not? What special characteristics make these organisms harmful to their hosts? Is one factor responsible for the **virulence** (the capacity to cause extreme harm) of all these organisms? Or are many different factors responsible? These are some of the questions scientists ask as they investigate the causative agents of infectious diseases. In this learning experience, you analyze a classic experiment carried out in an attempt to answer these questions. You also conduct an experiment that investigates the factor or factors responsible for virulence in organisms.

Brainstorming

Discuss the following with your partner, and record your thinking in your notebook. Be prepared to share your ideas with the class.

In Unit 2, you explored the biomolecules and cellular processes responsible for the expression of traits. You should now understand these processes. Now try to imagine that you are a scientist in the early 1900s. You know that some organisms may express a trait that others do not. Your hypothesis is that there is something specific within a cell that is responsible for traits. You have one kind of bacteria that glows in the dark (the trait of phosphorescence) and another that does not. Design an experiment that would test your hypothesis.

Griffith's Search for the Cause

By the early 1900s, the notion that contagious diseases were the result of infectious agents had been accepted. From that time on, a major focus of research into infectious disease would be to understand the mechanisms by which these infectious agents caused the symptoms of disease in their hosts.

In 1928, a British bacteriologist named Frederick Griffith was investigating the way in which a certain type of bacteria, *Diplococcus pneumoniae*, caused pneumonia. Pneumonia is a serious and often fatal lung disease. Scientists already knew which type of bacteria caused the disease. They were trying to learn exactly *how* the bacteria caused the disease.

Griffith studied two strains of *D. pneumoniae*. Both grew very well in special culture media in his laboratory. But only one of them actually caused pneumonia when injected into mice. Griffith noticed that when he grew the bacteria on nutrient agar plates in the laboratory, he could distinguish one strain from the other simply by its appearance on the agar. The bacteria in the **virulent**, or disease-causing strain, secretes a polysaccharide (sugar) coat called a capsule around its cell wall. Bacteria grow in colonies on agar. (**Colonies** are discrete masses of cells that originate from a single cell.) Colonies of the virulent strain look smooth because of their capsules. Though Griffith did not know it then, we now understand that the capsules protect the bacteria from destruction by the host animal's immune response. This allows the bacteria to multiply and grow in the host. (You will learn more about the immune system in Learning Experience 12, Immune System to the Rescue.) The other, nonvirulent strain Griffith studied did not produce capsules. Instead, when grown on agar, the colonies appear to have rough, jagged edges. The lack of polysaccharide capsules make this strain vulnerable to the immune system. When it enters a host, it is destroyed by the immune response. This strain is, therefore, nonpathogenic (see Figure 3.11).

Griffith hypothesized that the capsule might be responsible for the disease in some way. What crucial pieces of information did Griffith have that enabled him to make this hypothesis and to design his experiment?

Figure 3.11

Characteristics of two strains of *D. pneumoniae*:
(a) nonpathogenic, rough-edged colonies and
(b) pathogenic, smooth colonies.

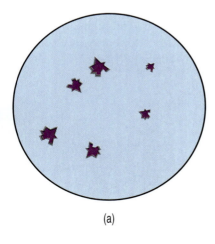

(a)

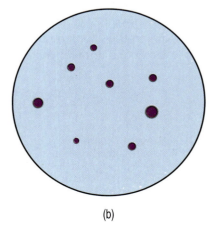

(b)

TASK

Carefully examine Figure 3.12, which illustrates Griffith's experiment. Discuss the following questions with your partner, and record your thinking in your notebook. Be prepared to discuss your responses with the class.

1. What simple question did Griffith pose in this experiment?
2. What parts of the experiment represented the controls? Describe how these served as controls.

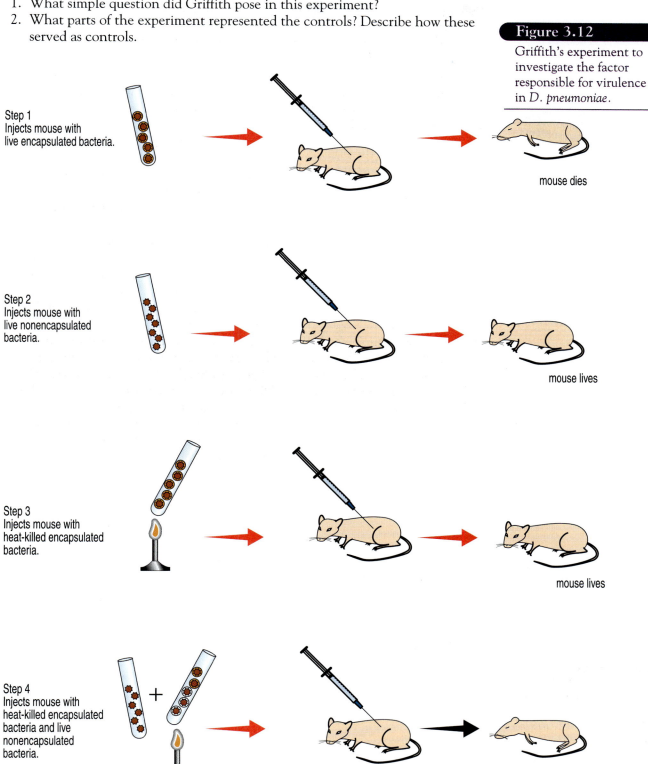

Figure 3.12

Griffith's experiment to investigate the factor responsible for virulence in *D. pneumoniae*.

Step 1
Injects mouse with live encapsulated bacteria.

mouse dies

Step 2
Injects mouse with live nonencapsulated bacteria.

mouse lives

Step 3
Injects mouse with heat-killed encapsulated bacteria.

mouse lives

Step 4
Injects mouse with heat-killed encapsulated bacteria and live nonencapsulated bacteria.

mouse dies

3. Say Griffith believed that the polysaccharide capsule of the encapsulated strain was responsible for its disease-causing characteristic. What do you think he predicted would be the result of injecting the heat-killed, encapsulated bacteria alone? Why?
4. Why do you think the mouse died when Griffith mixed and injected the dead, virulent strain with the live, nonvirulent strain?
5. Suppose you could isolate the bacteria that were injected as live, nonvirulent bacteria in the last step of the experiment. How could you determine whether they had changed characteristics and had become virulent?

ACTIVITY

In Isolation

Griffith reisolated the originally nonvirulent strain of *D. pneumoniae* from the dead mice in his experiment. He then observed that this strain no longer formed rough colonies on nutrient agar plates, but formed smooth colonies. When these were injected into mice, the mice died of pneumonia. Somehow the nonvirulent, nonencapsulated strain had been changed, or transformed, into the pathogenic, encapsulated strain. Some principle or factor had been transferred from the killed, virulent strain to the live, nonvirulent strain. This gave the harmless, nonvirulent strain the ability to make a polysaccharide capsule and cause disease.

For more than 15 years, researchers attempted to identify what had happened in Griffith's experiment. What had changed the harmless strain into a virulent form? In 1944, Oswald T. Avery, Colin MacLeod, and Maclyn McCarty tried to answer this question. They took the extract from dead virulent bacteria and one by one removed the biomolecules of the cell. First, they removed the proteins, then the carbohydrates, and next the lipids. This left the nucleic acids. Each time, they tested the ability of the remaining substances to make nonvirulent bacteria virulent.

In this laboratory experiment, you will isolate the factor that transformed the harmless strain of bacteria into a virulent form. To do this, you will use a procedure similar to that used by Avery, MacLeod, and McCarty. You will work with either thymus or liver (eukaryotic cells) or *E. coli* bacteria (prokaryotic cells). The same principles that Avery and his colleagues used to isolate the transforming factor apply to any living organism. Your teacher will ask you to follow either Protocol A or Protocol B.

Before beginning the experiment, read the entire procedure to determine the principles behind the experiment.

PROTOCOL A: ISOLATION FROM CALF THYMUS OR LIVER

Materials

For each pair of students:

- 2 pairs of safety goggles
- 1 mL of a homogenate of blended fresh thymus or liver (keep on ice)
- 2 mL salt (NaCl) solution
- 1 test tube (13 × 100 mm) with cap (or cover with plastic wrap)
- 1 test-tube rack (or small beaker to hold test tube)
- 5 mL ice-cold ethanol
- 1 pipette (optional)
- 1 glass stirring rod
- ice water bath (crushed ice and water in an insulated cup)
- plastic wrap
- 2 15-mL centrifuge tubes with lids (optional)

For the class:

- 1 tabletop centrifuge (optional)

PROCEDURE

Describe what is happening at the cellular level at each stage of the investigation. Use the Stop & Think questions in Table 3.5 and the diagram of the cell in Figure 3.13. Keep in mind that these are the same principles that Avery's team used when isolating the transforming factor from bacteria. (Although his team may have used different chemicals.) Table 3.6 provides the biomolecule composition of each cell part shown in Figure 3.13.

Table 3.5 Procedure and Principles Used for Isolating the Transforming Factor

Procedure	Principles Involved	STOP & THINK
*1. Blend together thymus with the buffer that contains • sugar • aspirin • Epsom salts • water • detergent solution (*This step is done either with the teacher or as a demonstration.)	Detergent dissolves lipids and denatures proteins. Epsom salts and aspirin inactivate enzymes that degrade nucleic acid (DNA).	What does the detergent do to the cell? What parts of the cell are affected? Why are aspirin and Epsom salts added? What does the blending do?
2. Pour homogenate into a beaker. Place 1 mL in test tube or centrifuge tube. Add 2 mL of salt solution (NaCl and water). Shake well for 2 minutes.	Salt breaks up membranes further.	What effect is the salt having on the cell? Describe what has happened to the cell in steps 1 and 2. Use the cell diagram in Figure 3.13.
3. If possible, spin tubes in a tabletop centrifuge for 7 minutes. (This step is optional.) Be sure the tubes are balanced. Remove your tube from the centrifuge and carefully pour off the liquid into a clean test tube. Be sure not to dislodge the pellet.	High-speed centrifugation separates larger structures, such as membrane fragments, from smaller, soluble biomolecules.	What is in the pellet? What is in the liquid?
4. Place test tube in an ice bath. Leave for 5 minutes.	Cold temperatures slow down the action of enzymes.	Why is it advisable to keep the liquid cold?
5. Carefully pour or pipette 5 mL ice-cold ethanol down the side of the tube to form a layer on top of the water layer.	Nucleic acid is soluble in water, but it is insoluble in ethanol.	What is happening when the ethanol is added?
6. Leave test tube undisturbed in ice water bath for 10 minutes.	N/A	
7. After 10 minutes, dip the end of a glass stirring rod into the cell/ethanol mix. Slide the rod back and forth between the layers while spinning the rod with your fingertips.	N/A	
8. Place the material attached to the rod on a piece of plastic wrap. Roll it, stretch it, and play with it.	N/A	What is the material on the glass rod?

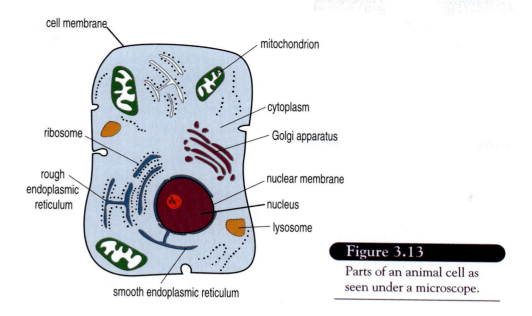

cell membrane

mitochondrion

cytoplasm

ribosome

Golgi apparatus

rough
endoplasmic
reticulum

nuclear membrane

nucleus

lysosome

smooth endoplasmic reticulum

Figure 3.13

Parts of an animal cell as
seen under a microscope.

Table 3.6 Biomolecule Composition of Animal Cell Parts

Cell Part	Biomolecule Composition
cell membrane	lipid, protein
endoplasmic reticulum	lipid, protein, nucleic acid
ribosome	protein, nucleic acid
Golgi apparatus	lipid, protein
lysosome	lipid, protein
cytoplasm	lipid, protein, nucleic acid, carbohydrate
mitochondrion	lipid, protein, nucleic acid, carbohydrate
nuclear membrane	lipid, protein
nucleus	lipid, protein, nucleic acid

ANALYSIS

Record your responses to the following in your notebook.

1. Draw a diagram of the components of a thymus or liver cell. Indicate where
   the transforming material is located.
2. In a flow diagram, show what you think happens to the cell during the
   following stages of the procedure:
   a. when adding the buffer solution and detergent,
   b. when blending, and
   c. when adding the salt solution.

3. What is on your glass rod? Avery's team isolated this very same kind of material from the *D. pneumoniae* bacteria. The team determined that it was responsible for transforming the harmless bacteria. Imagine that what you have on your glass rod has been isolated from bacteria instead of thymus. How would you determine that this material was responsible for transforming the nonvirulent strain into the virulent strain? Design an experiment to show whether the harmless bacteria would be changed by this material.

4. Avery's team isolated the material that could change an organism with one set of physical traits into an organism with a different set of physical traits. Explain how this material could be responsible for the transforming factor. Include what you know about this material and identify what you still need to know.

PROTOCOL B: ISOLATION FROM *E. COLI*

Materials

For each pair of students:

- 2 pairs of safety goggles
- 10 mL of *Escherichia coli* growth culture
- 2 test tubes (13 × 100 mm)
- 3 pipettes (1- to 5-mL)
- 5 mL Luria broth
- 1 mL liquid dishwashing detergent
- 1 g of proteinase K, or 6 g meat tenderizer solution
- ice water bath (crushed ice and water in an insulated cup)
- 15 mL ice-cold 95% ethanol
- 1 glass stirring rod

For the class:

- 1 plastic or glass pipette (5-mL)
- 1 tabletop centrifuge and appropriate tubes (15-mL centrifuge tubes)
- 1 water bath, 55°C–60°C (131°F–140°F) (or 60°C water in a large insulated cup)
- 1 small beaker or disposable cup (125- to 150-mL)
- plastic wrap

PROCEDURE

Describe what is happening at the cellular level at each stage of the investigation. Use the Stop & Think questions in Table 3.7 and the diagram of the cell in Figure 3.15. Keep in mind that these are the same principles that Avery's team used when isolating the transforming factor from bacteria. (Although his team may have used different chemicals.) Try to determine, on the basis of the experiment, what the transforming factor turned out to be. Table 3.8 provides the biomolecule composition of each cell part shown in Figure 3.15.

Table 3.7 Procedure and Principles Used for Isolating the Transforming Factor

Procedure	Principles Involved	STOP & THINK
1. Divide 10 mL of bacterial growth culture equally between 2 culture tubes.	N/A	
2. Place tubes in a tabletop centrifuge for 30 minutes or until a small pellet of cells forms at the bottom of the tube (see Figure 3.14a).	N/A	What is the purpose of spinning the bacteria out of the broth?
3. Carefully pour off the liquid from each tube into a beaker or disposal cup designated by the teacher. Be careful not to pour off your pellets (see Figure 3.14b). Your teacher may provide you with the pellets.	N/A	
4. Add 1 mL Luria broth to each pellet (see Figure 3.14c). Redissolve the pellets by tapping each tube with your finger. Mix the 2 solutions of bacteria resuspended from pellets together in 1 tube.	N/A	
5. Using a pipette, add 1 mL liquid detergent to the bacterial solution. Tap lightly (to avoid bubbling) for 5 minutes to mix.	Dishwashing liquid contains detergent. The detergent makes lipids soluble and denatures proteins.	What do you think the detergent is doing? What parts of the cells might be affected?
6. Place the tube in a 60°C (140°F) water bath for 10 minutes. (At this point, the reactions may be stored in the refrigerator for the next class session.)	Heat further denatures protein.	What is the purpose of heating the solution at this step? What parts of the cells might be affected?
7. Place the tube in an ice water bath for 5 minutes.	N/A	Why must you cool the solution down at this point (see step 8)?
8. Using a pipette, add 1 mL proteinase K or meat tenderizer solution. Mix gently by tapping. Place in a 60°C water bath again for 15 minutes to incubate.	Meat tenderizer is used to make meat easier to chew. It contains papain, which is found in papaya. Papain and proteinase K are both proteases. Proteases are enzymes that digest (or break down) protein into amino acids.	What does the proteinase K or meat tenderizer do?
9. After the incubation period, place the tube in an ice water bath once again for 5 minutes. Remove the tube from the ice water and tilt slightly. Gently add ice-cold ethanol to fill the tube. Do not shake or mix. (At this point, tubes may be stored in the freezer for the next class session.)	Nucleic acid is soluble in water, but it is insoluble in ethanol.	What happens after the proteinase K or meat tenderizer is used? What biomolecules remain intact? Refer to the diagram of the cell.
10. Allow the test tube to sit for 10 minutes. By then you should see a white precipitate form between the 2 layers.	N/A	What is the ethanol doing?
11. Dip your glass rod into white glue and then into the tube. Slowly rotate the rod, and move it up and down.	N/A	
12. Remove the rod. Place the attached material on a piece of plastic wrap. Roll it, stretch it, and play with it. Look at it under a microscope.	N/A	What is the material on the glass rod?

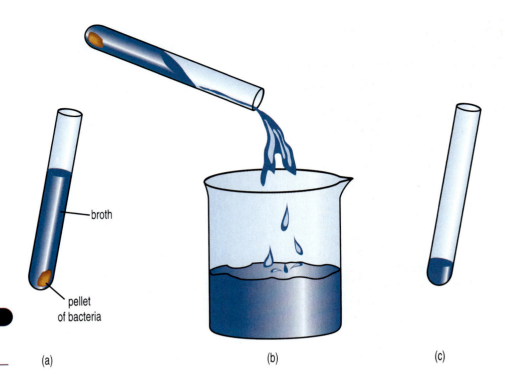

Figure 3.14

Procedure for isolating the
transforming factor.

(a)　　　　　　　　　　(b)　　　　　　　　　(c)

broth

pellet
of bacteria

Table 3.8 Biomolecule Composition of Animal Cell Parts

Cell Part	Biomolecule Composition
cell membrane	lipid, protein
cell wall	lipid, protein, carbohydrate
ribosome	protein, nucleic acid
cytoplasm	lipid, protein, nucleic acid, carbohydrate

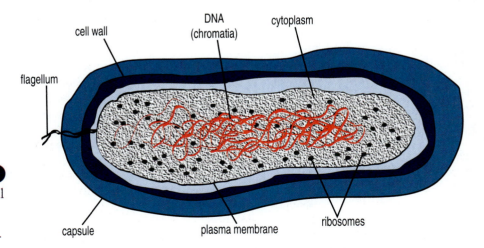

Figure 3.15

Diagram of a typical bacterial
cell, as seen through a
microscope.

flagellum

cell wall

DNA
(chromatia)

cytoplasm

capsule

plasma membrane

ribosomes

ANALYSIS

Record your responses to the following in your notebook.

1. Draw a diagram of the components of a bacterial cell. Indicate where the transforming material is located.

2. In a flow diagram, show what you think happens to the cell during the following stages of the procedure:
   a. when adding the detergent,
   b. when heating the mixture, and
   c. when adding the proteinase K or meat tenderizer.

3. What is on your glass rod? Avery's team isolated this same kind of material from the *D. pneumoniae* bacteria. The team determined that it was responsible for transforming the harmless bacteria. How would you determine that this material was responsible for transforming the nonvirulent strain into the virulent strain? Design an experiment to demonstrate that the harmless bacteria would be changed by the material.

4. Avery's team isolated the material that could change not only bacteria, but any organism, into an organism with a different set of physical traits. Explain how this material could be responsible for the transforming factor. Include what you know about the material and identify what you still need to know.

CAREER
Focus

Medical Bacteriology Laboratory Technician   It's a busy day for Owen, who works in the pathology laboratory at University Hospital. Four people have been rushed to the emergency room this morning complaining of similar symptoms. Doctors need Owen to conduct laboratory tests to determine what is making the patients sick. As a medical bacteriology laboratory technician, Owen investigates the microbes that cause illness in people and identifies the medication that can be used to fight them.

Specimens taken from the emergency room patients are immediately sent to the pathology lab. Owen then analyzes them for diagnostic purposes. He determines what bacteria may be causing the problem or illness and what antibiotics will help in treatment. He performs several laboratory procedures, such as urinalysis and immune assays. These tests help Owen identify the presence of bacteria in body fluids and the susceptibility to specific antibiotics. He must be aware that some strains of bacteria are developing a resistance to antibiotics. Owen then uses a microscope to view the bacteria. He's very efficient because quick identification is crucial to the health and, in some cases, the survival of the patient. During his analysis, he also consults with other technicians in the lab and the patients' doctors.

While growing up, Owen was drawn to science. But it wasn't until his high school biology teacher showed him different strains of bacteria under a microscope that he knew what career he wanted to pursue. She explained what each bacteria strain was and what illnesses they cause. His teacher mentioned that medical bacteriology laboratory technicians get to look at bacteria under the microscope for a living and help determine how patients should be treated. Owen thought this career would be ideal for him. He'd get to conduct scientific investigations in a hospital pathology lab setting and help people who are sick.

Owen researched laboratory technician programs of study and decided to attend a 2-year college medical laboratory science program. Through his program, Owen took courses in medical laboratory procedures, bacteriology, chemistry, and computer science. At the end of the program, he received a certificate and began searching for a job. Owen found that opportunities to work as a medical bacteriology laboratory technician were available all over the country and even internationally. Ultimately, Owen accepted a position at University Hospital. Someday, he'd like to take more courses to become a medical technologist, so that he can work on more complex projects and supervise a laboratory. But in the meantime, Owen tries to stay up-to-date on the latest techniques and issues in his field by attending conferences.

After several hours, Owen completes his analysis of the specimens. He discovers that the bacteria growing in culture is indicative of a very serious illness. His quick work in identifying the pathogen causing the sickness may save the patients' lives. His findings confirm that they have meningitis. He immediately reports these findings and includes a recommendation for an antibiotic treatment. At the end of the day, Owen is satisfied to have solved the puzzle and helped people to get well again.

Learning Experience 5

Language of the Cell

Prologue

Imagine that you have been asked to redesign your school building. You can rearrange rooms, knock down walls, and build new wings. The first stage in the remodeling process will probably involve drawing up a plan. This plan will guide how each of the new components fits together in the new design plan and, ultimately, how the new structures will work. The plan must be clear and accurate for builders to follow.

Other sorts of plans—the playbook for an athletic team, the musical score for a jazz group—work in much the same way. The information stored in the plan is read and translated into action. The information is used to construct a winning play or a melodious blend of instruments.

Avery and Griffith's work suggested that DNA might also be some sort of plan. This plan was thought to carry information. And, in some way, that information could direct the expression of new characteristics or traits, such as a polysaccharide coat on *D. pneumoniae.* But scientists did not know what this plan looked like or how it might work.

Often, the detailed workings of a biological phenomenon are a mystery. In these situations, a researcher needs to start thinking creatively about the possibilities. What could it look like and how might it work? How do other plans work? How do they encode information? How is that information used? In this learning experience, you begin by analyzing how information is deciphered and used in two sorts of plans. These plans are a musical score that produces a particular melody (see Figure 3.16) and a blueprint that produces a particular kind of house (see Figures 3.17a and 3.17b). These analogies are then applied to understanding DNA as yet another kind of plan.

Brainstorming

Discuss the following questions with your partner, and record your thinking in your notebook. Be prepared to share your ideas with the class.

1. What features do a blueprint and a musical score have in common?
2. How do you go about reading music? deciphering a floor plan? What do the plans mean? What information do you need to know to make sense of them?
3. What information do the symbols tell you about the music? the house?
4. What features remain constant within each plan? Which ones change?
5. How do the symbols relate to one another? How might the order or the placement of the symbols affect the code?
6. How might DNA be a plan for the cell? Explain your response using the analogy of a musical score or a house blueprint.

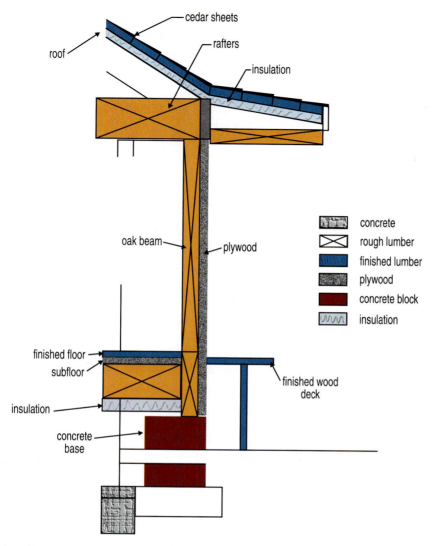

concrete
rough lumber
finished lumber
plywood
concrete block
insulation

cedar sheets
roof
rafters
insulation
oak beam
plywood
finished floor
subfloor
insulation
concrete base
finished wood deck

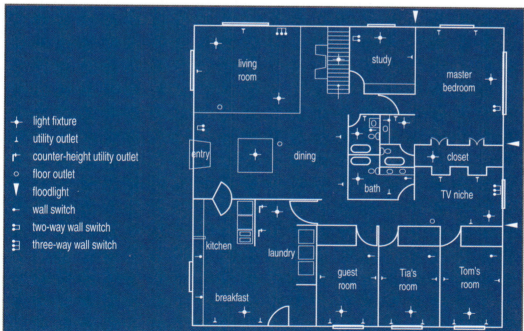

light fixture
utility outlet
counter-height utility outlet
floor outlet
floodlight
wall switch
two-way wall switch
three-way wall switch

living room
study
master bedroom
entry
dining
closet
bath
TV niche
kitchen
laundry
guest room
Tia's room
Tom's room
breakfast

Building DNA

Say DNA is responsible for giving the characteristic of virulence to *D. pneumoniae*. Can the next assumption be that DNA codes for all characteristics or traits of an organism? Does DNA itself have the characteristics necessary for such a task? How is it possible for the molecule to carry all the information necessary? Researchers recognized that whatever biomolecule they were looking for must have the capacity to carry an enormous amount of information. This information comprises all the instructions necessary for determining the biochemical activities and specific characteristics of the cell and the organism.

Two researchers investigating the role of DNA were James Watson and Francis Crick. In 1953, they proposed a model for the structure of DNA that gave some clues as to how it might work within the cell. Their model-building process was one of trial and error. Watson and Crick made important adjustments in their work as they added critical pieces of evidence from other researchers. For example, they learned about Maurice Wilkins and Rosalind Franklin's work with **X-ray crystallography**. This gave them critical information about the spiral architecture of DNA called the **double helix**.

The building blocks of DNA, called nucleotides, are composed of three kinds of molecules. These molecules are (1) a group of oxygen atoms clustered around a phosphorus atom (known as a phosphate group), and (2) a simple sugar, attached to a (3) **base**. The base may be any one of four rather similar nitrogen-containing bases: adenine (A), thymine (T), guanine (G), and cytosine (C). See Figure 3.18.

Erwin Chargaff discovered two key rules that helped in figuring out how the four nucleotides were put together. First, Chargaff found that in the DNA of any organism examined, the number of adenine bases was always equal to the number of thymine bases. He also found that the number of guanine bases was equal to the number of cytosine bases. This information suggested that adenine and thymine, and guanine and cytosine, might link to each other and travel in pairs. Second, Chargaff found that the amount of adenine and thymine bases, as compared with the cytosine and guanine nucleotides, varied considerably from species to species.

Many researchers at that time felt that the six molecules (the four bases and the sugar and phosphate groups) in DNA were too few to fit the task. Proteins were already known to play a central role in the vital processes of all living organisms. To many scientists, DNA could not be the hereditary "master" molecule. How could DNA carry all the instructions for life with only four kinds of variable subunits?

In this activity, you will construct a paper model of the DNA structure Watson and Crick proposed in 1953. As you piece the molecule together, keep this question in mind: How might this molecule encode all the information necessary for determining the biochemical activities and specific characteristics of all organisms?

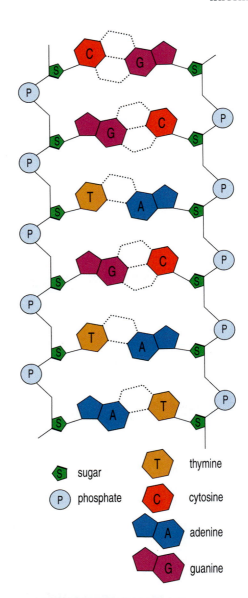

S sugar

P phosphate

T thymine

C cytosine

A adenine

G guanine

Figure 3.18

Components of a DNA molecule, including the bases and the sugar-phosphate backbone.

Materials

For each group of students:

- scissors
- tape, glue, or staplers (for fastening base pairs together)
- 1 m (about 3 ft) of string
- 2–3 drinking straws cut into 2.5-cm (1 in.) pieces (16 pieces)
- 1 paper clip
- large envelopes
- 6 small envelopes (for homework assignment)

For the class:

- 90 nucleotide base pair model pieces
  - 26 thymine-adenine (green)
  - 14 guanine-cytosine (pink)
  - 36 adenine-thymine (yellow)
  - 14 cytosine-guanine (blue)

PROCEDURE

1. Your class will work in 6 different groups. Each group will build a different portion of DNA from either molecule 1 or molecule 2 in Table 3.9.
2. Each group should collect the 15 model pieces of the nucleotide pairs as specified in the table.

Table 3.9 DNA Molecule Sequences

Molecule 1			Molecule 2		
Group A1	Group A2	Group A3	Group B4	Group B5	Group B6
CG	AT	AT	AT	CG	AT
GC	AT	AT	AT	AT	GC
AT	AT	GC	AT	GC	AT
CG	AT	TA	CG	TA	AT
CG	AT	GC	AT	CG	GC
AT	GC	AT	AT	AT	GC
AT	AT	AT	AT	AT	AT
CG	CG	GC	CG	GC	CG
AT	CG	TA	TA	CG	AT
TA	TA	AT	TA	TA	AT
TA	TA	CG	CG	TA	TA
TA	TA	GC	TA	GC	TA
TA	TA	AT	AT	TA	TA
TA	GC	TA	GC	TA	TA
AT	AT	TA	AT	TA	AT

3. Cut out the model pieces by following the instructions on each template as follows:
   a. Cut out each nucleotide pair that you will use around the solid outer lines. Each nucleotide pair will become 1 piece in the model you will build.
   b. Cut along the lines with arrows in the phosphate and sugar groups in each nucleotide pair. This will prepare the model piece for folding.
   c. Make a small hole at the X. This will prepare the model piece for placing it on the string.
4. Hold each model piece in front of you with the straight side of the figure to your right. (This is the side on which the letters specifying base pairs are written.) Study your model piece. Note that there is a phosphate group pictured on tab numbers 8–11, and another one shown on tabs 1–4. Tabs 12–14 and 5–7 each show a different sugar group. Each sugar is then linked to a different nitrogen-containing base (adenine and thymine, or cytosine and guanine). These bases in turn are linked by hydrogen bonds. (The hydrogen bonds are pictured as dotted lines on your model piece.)
5. Hold your model piece as directed in step 4. You are now ready to fold it and begin assembling your section of the model.
   a. Fold the phosphate group shown on tabs 8–11 up so that it stands straight up from the surface of the paper.
   b. Fold the sugar group on tabs 13–14 down so that it projects below the surface of the paper.
   c. Fold the phosphate and sugar represented by tabs 1–7 in the opposite way as follows: phosphate on tabs 1–4 should be folded so that it projects below the surface of the paper; the sugar on tabs 6–7 should be folded up so that it projects above the surface of the paper.
   d. Fold accordion style on the dotted lines between tabs 1–7. Make a staircase that rises from tab 1 to tab 7. The steps of the staircase will have symbols of different atoms in the model printed on them. The risers will have lines that symbolize bonds connecting each step.
   e. Fold accordion style on the dotted lines between tabs 8–14. Make a staircase that descends from tab 8 to tab 14. The steps of this staircase will also have symbols of different atoms printed on them. The risers will have lines that symbolize bonds connecting each step.
6. Repeat steps 5a–e with each model piece for your section of DNA.
7. Attach a string to a straightened paper clip. (The paper clip will serve as a needle.) String your group's model pieces together in the sequence listed in Table 3.9. Place a straw spacer between each model piece, much like beads on a string: model piece, straw, model piece, straw, and so on. Have the printed side of each model piece facing upward. The first nucleotide pair model piece should be at the top of the DNA sequence that you are building. The last (15th) piece should be at the bottom of the string. Tie a knot at each end of your model section so that the pieces will not fall off.

8. Join your group's model pieces together as follows:
   a. Orient your stack of model pieces as you did in step 4. Put the straight side (the one with the letters of the bases) to your right, and the pointed side of the paper to your left.
   b. Paste, tape, or staple tab 1 of the topmost model piece over tab 7 of the model piece directly below it. (You have just joined a phosphate group of the top model piece to a sugar group of the model piece below it.)
   c. Paste, tape, or staple tab 14 of the topmost model piece under tab 8 of the model piece directly below it. (You have just joined a sugar group of the top model piece to a phosphate group of the model piece below it.)
   d. Continue joining the remaining 13 pieces of your model section together until you have a twisted ladder shape. This shape molecule is known as a double helix.
9. Now join the 3 double helix sections (A1–3 or B4–6) of each group's molecule together consecutively. Follow the instructions that you used in step 7 for joining individual model pieces.
10. Suspend these models using string or wire from the ceiling of your classroom. Study them as you write responses to the Analysis questions that follow.

⊕NALYSIS

Record your responses to the following in your notebook.
1. Describe the basic features of a DNA molecule. What information do the letter symbols give you?
2. What features of the DNA molecule remain constant in various organisms? What features differ?
3. How might the order or the placement of bases affect the code?
4. Write the sequence of bases for the DNA strand you constructed.
5. Say 27% of the bases in a certain segment of DNA were adenine. What would be the percentages of thymine, cytosine, and guanine?
6. If DNA determines the characteristics of pneumococci, it seems possible that DNA could determine the traits of all living things. This means that DNA must be able to carry an enormous amount of information. How can a molecule composed of only four different kinds of subunits carry large amounts of diverse information?
7. How might DNA differ among different organisms? For example, how do you think mouse DNA or bacterial DNA differ from human DNA?

Writing the Book of Life

James Watson and Francis Crick announced their model of the double helix in 1953. In doing so, they described an extraordinary instruction book packed inside the nuclei of all our cells. Written in a language of few letters (four nucleotides), DNA contains all the information needed for the maintenance and perpetuation of life. The structure they described could explain how DNA could code for wrinkled and round peas, for hemoglobin, for virulence in bacteria, and for the variety of other traits seen in every organism.

What roles were played by each of the component pieces—the sugars, the phosphates, and the bases? This was the critical question Watson and Crick faced as they created and revised their DNA model. They knew they needed a pattern that could be written in thousands of variations. Yet a choice of only three pieces (sugar, phosphate, and base) did not initially seem to provide many options.

In the following excerpt, Crick describes his analysis of this elegant molecule.

The following passage is excerpted from *The Structure of the Hereditary Material* by F. H. C. Crick. Copyright © October 1954 by Scientific American, Inc. All rights reserved.

. . . It is now known that DNA consists of a very long chain made up of alternate sugar and phosphate groups. The sugar is always the same sugar, known as deoxyribose. And it is always joined onto the phosphate in the same way, so that the long chain is perfectly regular, repeating the same phosphate-sugar sequence over and over again.

But while the phosphate-sugar chain is perfectly regular, the molecule as a whole is not, because each sugar has a "base" attached to it and the base is not always the same. Four different types of bases are commonly found:
. . . adenine and guanine . . . thymine and cytosine . . . So far as is known the order in which they follow one another along the chain is irregular, and probably varies from one piece of DNA to another. In fact, we suspect that the order of the bases is what confers specificity on a given DNA.

. . . we found that we could not arrange the bases any way we pleased; the four bases would fit into the structure only in certain pairs. In any pair, there must be one big one [the purines adenine and guanine] and one little one [the pyrimidines thymine and cytosine]. A pair of pyrimidines is too short to bridge the gap between the two chains, and a pair of purines is too big to fit into the space.

Adenine must always be paired with thymine, and guanine with cytosine; it is impossible to fit the bases together in any other combination in our model. . . . The model places no restriction, however, on the sequence of pairs along the structure. Any specified pair can follow any other. This is because a pair of bases is flat, and since in this model they are stacked roughly like a pile of coins, it does not matter which pair goes above which. . . .

. . . the exciting thing about a model of this type is that it immediately suggests how the DNA might produce an exact copy of itself. The model consists of two parts, each of which is the complement of the other. Thus either chain may act as a sort of mold on which a complementary chain can be synthesized. The two chains of a DNA, let us say, unwind and separate. Each begins to build a new complement onto itself. When the process is completed, there are two pairs of chains where we had only one. Moreover, because of the specific pairing of the bases the sequence of the pairs of bases will have been duplicated exactly; in other words, the mold has not only assembled the building blocks but has put them together in just the right order.

Let us imagine that we have a single helical chain of DNA, and that floating around it inside the cell is a supply of precursors of the four sorts of building blocks needed to make a new chain . . . from time to time, a loose unit will attach itself by its base to one of the bases of the single DNA chain. Another loose unit may attach itself to an adjoining base on the chain. Now if one or both of the two newly attached units is not the correct mate for the one it has joined on the chain, the two newcomers will be unable to link together, because they are not the right distance apart. One or both will soon drift away, to be replaced by other units. When, however, two adjacent newcomers are the correct partners for their opposite numbers on the chain, they will be in just the right position to be linked together and begin to form a new chain. Thus only the unit with the proper base will gain a permanent hold at any given position, and eventually the right partners will fill in the vacancies all along the forming chain. While this is going on, the other single chain of the original pair also will be forming a new chain complementary to itself.

. . . We suspect that the sequence of the bases acts as a kind of genetic code. Such an arrangement can carry an enormous amount of information. If we imagine that the pairs of bases correspond to the dots and dashes of the Morse code, there is enough DNA in a single cell of the human body to encode about 1,000 large textbooks . . .

Figures 3.19, 3.20, 3.21 illustrate several important ideas about the structure of DNA that Crick suggested in his article.

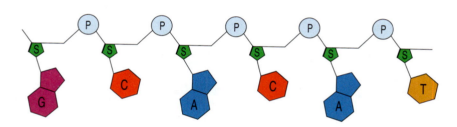

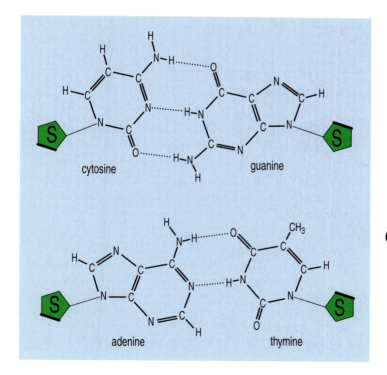

Figure 3.19

Crick's description of the DNA chain sounded much like a long chain made of links. This chain was formed by the sugar-phosphate backbone. From each of these links, bases were suspended. Each link with its base constituted a nucleotide subunit.

Figure 3.20

The relationship between the purines (adenine and guanine) and the pyrimidines (thymine and cytosine). Adenine always pairs with thymine; guanine always pairs with cytosine.

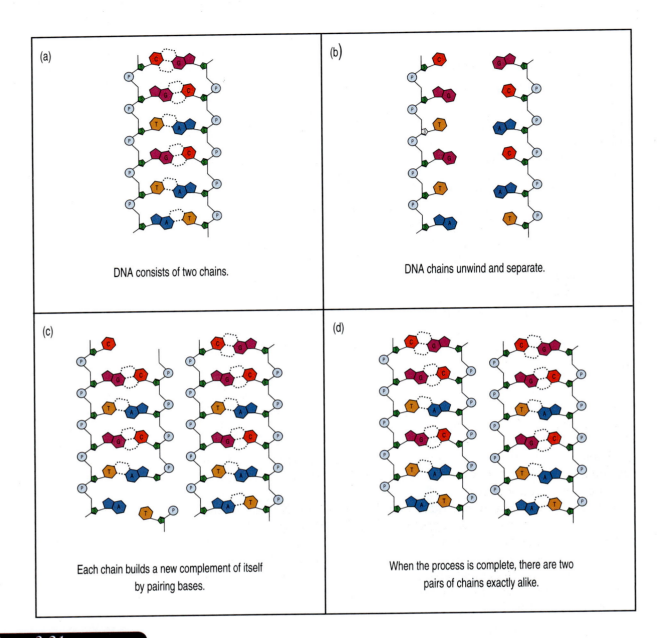

(a) DNA consists of two chains.

(b) DNA chains unwind and separate.

(c) Each chain builds a new complement of itself by pairing bases.

(d) When the process is complete, there are two pairs of chains exactly alike.

Figure 3.21

The model proposed by Watson and Crick suggests how DNA might produce an exact copy of itself.

Although Watson and Crick's model provided a giant leap in our understanding, a big question remained. How can a set of characters embedded in DNA actually determine what our bodies do? What could something like AGTCAT mean? In your own words, describe how the structure of DNA lends itself to replicating itself and providing enough information to code for "1,000 large textbooks."

DNA as a Coded Plan

You began this learning experience with questions about how DNA might work as a plan. Think back to the musical score and the blueprint for a house.

When Watson and Crick published their model, they suggested that the sequence of the bases in DNA might act as a code. However, they were not sure at that time what DNA coded for. But they thought it was intriguing that the structures of DNA and proteins were based on the same general plan. This plan included a regular, repeating backbone. The plan's variation came from the sequence of the bases of the nucleotides or in the order of the amino acids.

With this new knowledge, protein and DNA researchers thought back to Griffith's transformation experiment. The protein researchers had argued that making a polysaccharide coat required enzymes to put the right building blocks together in the right arrangement. They believed that nothing in the cell could be built without the enzymes directing and facilitating the construction work. If a polysaccharide coat were built, proteins must be involved. The DNA researchers stood behind Avery's evidence that DNA was the transforming material.

When DNA and proteins were found to have such similar chemical arrangements, these two fields of research came together. Watson and Crick suggested that the four bases of the DNA might code for the 20 amino acids that make up the proteins of cells. In this light, the change in characteristics of the pneumococci did require the work of proteins. But it was the plan of the DNA that determined the protein would be made. The plan carried the information that directed which protein would be produced. That protein set to work to make the polysaccharide coat.

How exactly could this happen? How do the symbols of DNA contain the information for proteins? Crick suggested that the base symbols of DNA could be similar to the dots and dashes of the Morse code. The Morse code uses only two symbols to represent all 26 letters, 10 numbers, and a few punctuation marks. Placed in combinations of one to six symbols long for each letter or number, a set of symbols can make words and phrases. In turn, an infinite number of messages can be created.

A	• —	N	— •	1	• — — — —
B	— • • •	O	— — —	2	• • — — —
C	— • — •	P	• — — •	3	• • • — —
D	— • •	Q	— — • —	4	• • • • —
E	•	R	• — •	5	• • • • •
F	• • — •	S	• • •	6	— • • • •
G	— — •	T	—	7	— — • • •
H	• • • •	U	• • —	8	— — — • •
I	• •	V	• • • —	9	— — — — •
J	• — — —	W	• — —	0	— — — — —
K	— • —	X	— • • —	.	• — • — • —
L	• — • •	Y	— • — —	,	— — • • — —
M	— —	Z	— — • •	?	• • — — • •

TASK

1. Write your name in code using the symbol system Morse set up.
2. Working in pairs, write a short sentence to your partner. When you are finished, swap sentences and try to decode your partner's message.

ANALYSIS

Record your responses to the following in your notebook.

1. What similarities are there between Morse code and DNA? How might this apply to the way DNA and proteins work?
2. In a short essay, explain what you know so far about the molecular languages of DNA and proteins. The following questions might help you to get started:
    a. Describe the makeup of these languages.
    b. How does one "speak" and make sense in each of these languages?
    c. How might the DNA alphabet be translated into the protein alphabet?
    d. How might DNA determine what a cell does?
3. Construct a concept map for DNA. Include the following terms: transforming factor, information, nucleotides, sugar, phosphate group, base pairs, building blocks, adenine, thymine, guanine, cytosine. Use additional terms as you need them.

CAREER FOCUS

Science Writer   Earlier this year, an outbreak of a new respiratory infection traveled the globe. It killed hundreds of people. Even though the outbreak is now under control, scientists are working to find out what happened and what can be done to prevent it from happening again. New infectious diseases and epidemics are happening around the world at an alarming rate. As a result, the job of a science writer has become similar to that of a war correspondent. Over the past several months, Lance has been traveling to the outbreak areas to gather information about the events that took place in those regions.

Lance is working on a book that will recount the story of the outbreak and inform the world of the scientists' findings. When the respiratory illness outbreak began, he approached several publishers with his idea to write a book. This book would involve readers in the drama of the moment while helping them to understand all the factors involved in the epidemic. Lance was hired by one publisher that was interested in publishing such a book.

Lance has spent countless hours interviewing scientists, researchers, government officials, and families. In this way, he can represent the different views and issues related to the outbreak. Lance is thrilled when he asks questions of scientists and they immediately reply, "That's a really good question." It means he's understood the issue well enough to know which parts of the research need further investigation. He also spends a great deal of time reviewing the published literature on the epidemic. In addition, Lance plans to visit the laboratories that are working on a cure and observing the scientists. Once he has conducted all of the background work, Lance's job is to translate technical scientific research into language that the general public will understand without oversimplifying it. His goal is to write a book that is scientifically accurate yet accessible to the public.

Ever since he was young, Lance wrote as a hobby. He began by keeping journals and writing short stories. In high school, he wrote for his school newspaper and even sent some articles into the local newspaper. But he also loved science and dreamed of becoming a medical researcher so he could contribute to the improvement of people's health. Biology courses were his favorite, so he decided to study biology in college. He never dreamed that his writing hobby would someday turn into a profession!

While in college, Lance interned in a laboratory. He soon realized that laboratory work was not for him. He met with his adviser and described all of his interests, including writing. She suggested he consider a career in science writing and that he also minor in English. In addition to his course work, Lance joined the staff of the college paper. He wrote a column about the discoveries taking place in the science laboratories on campus and about other scientific topics that affect the general public. During his junior year, Lance discovered that one of his professors was writing a textbook, so he volunteered to be her editorial assistant. He learned a great deal about science writing, as well as how to research photos and coordinate a large writing project.

After obtaining his bachelor's degree, Lance began a graduate science writing program where he discovered the many opportunities in which he could use his skills. Not only were writing jobs available at daily newspapers and science magazines, but also at companies that published specialized science and medical journals. In addition, writing positions were available at television and radio stations, as well as publishers of trade papers and even popular magazines. After completing his degree, Lance accepted a staff position at a weekly science magazine.

Lance feels fortunate that he's been able to combine his interest in science with his love of writing. His education in science helps him to understand the topic he's writing about as well as how to be analytical and methodical in his work. His job allows him to stay up-to-date with what's happening in science, and he's able to talk with scientists about their cutting-edge research. Lance tries to convey the excitement of science discoveries to others and gets a thrill from contributing to the public's understanding of science.

Nucleic Acid to Protein

Prologue

DNA stores the information of the cell. Proteins are the biomolecules that make the cell. What is the relationship between these two biomolecules?

Stored information is just that: information that is in storage, waiting to be used. Information in the blueprints for a house awaits the construction team that can translate the symbols and diagrams into the substance of a house. The notes in musical scores only come to life when the musician translates the notes into the complexity of musical sounds. How is the information in DNA, specifically in the sequence of its nucleotides, translated into proteins, which, in turn, carry out many functions?

In this learning experience, you explore the cellular processes in which the information in DNA is expressed as the protein the cell needs to carry out all of its functions.

Brainstorming

Discuss the following questions with your partner, and record your thinking in your notebook. Be prepared to share your ideas with the class.

1. What might be meant by the statement, "We are what we are because of our DNA"?
2. If DNA is made up of nucleotides and protein of amino acids, how do you think the information in the DNA can code for a protein that contains specific amino acids happening in the correct sequence? How might you relate this to the translation of Morse code symbols into letters and ultimately into words and sentences?
3. What is required to transform musical notes into a melody listeners can enjoy? a blueprint into a house where people can live? What do you think is required for the information in DNA to be transformed into protein?

The Messenger Tells All

READING

If DNA is found in the nucleus and protein is made in the **cytoplasm** (as we now know it is), a logistical problem seems to exist. In 1957, shortly after describing the double-helical structure of DNA, Francis Crick hypothesized that there needed to exist an intermediate translator of the information between DNA and protein. This translator would be something that could carry the information from the DNA in the nucleus to the site of protein synthesis in the cytoplasm. The **central dogma** (as it came to be known) stated that information stored in DNA was carried by another kind of molecule. In 1960, this other molecule was identified as another kind of nucleic acid. Scientists called it ribonucleic acid or RNA (see Figure 3.22). In later years, scientists learned that, in general, only one strand of the DNA double helix was copied into RNA.

The role of RNA is essential. Just as monks copied or transcribed writings of manuscripts for distribution in medieval times, the information in DNA is transcribed or copied into RNA molecules. These RNA molecules look very similar to the original but have several characteristics that distinguish RNA from DNA.

RNA almost always consists of a single strand, not a double helix. Another significant difference between RNA and DNA is the sugar. RNA contains the sugar ribose instead of the deoxyribose sugar found in DNA. The structures in Figure 3.23 show the difference in the sugar component of the two types of nucleic acids.

Another difference between RNA and DNA is in the composition of one of their bases. DNA has thymine. But instead of thymine, RNA has the base uracil. The difference in these bases is shown in Figure 3.24.

Transcription is the process by which information encoded in DNA is transferred to an RNA molecule. The information must be copied because DNA does not leave the nucleus. Think about how an architect might protect building blueprints from loss or damage by keeping them in a safe or locked place. Your cells protect DNA by keeping it safe in the nucleus. Instead, copies of the DNA are made and then sent into the cell's cytoplasm. These copies are the RNA. The RNA then directs the assembly of proteins.

The process of transcription is similar to replication. The DNA chains unwind and separate. The chain begins to build a complement of itself using RNA nucleotides present in the nucleus. Each DNA base is paired with its complementary RNA base.

SC*LINKS*
NSTA

Topic: Protein Synthesis
Go to: www.scilinks.org
Code: INBIOH2373

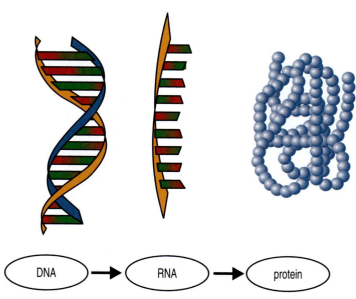

Figure 3.22

The information in DNA is used to assemble proteins.

Figure 3.23

RNA is chemically like DNA except for its sugars. Each ribose has an additional oxygen atom compared with deoxyribose. Note the presence and the location of the oxygen in the sugar of the RNA and DNA molecules.

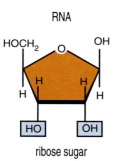

RNA

ribose sugar

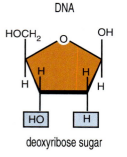

DNA

deoxyribose sugar

DNA

RNA

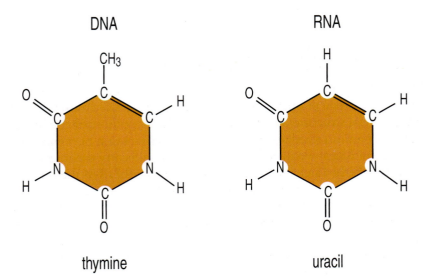

thymine

uracil

Figure 3.24

The difference between thymine (present in DNA) and uracil (present in RNA).

Cytosine is paired with guanine. But because RNA contains uracil instead of thymine, adenine is paired with uracil. In this way, the RNA strand is gradually built. In general, only one of the DNA strands has information to be used for the protein. Therefore, only this strand is copied into RNA. This DNA strand is called the **sense strand**. The other strand is called the **anti-sense strand**.

After transcription of the DNA is complete, the newly transcribed RNA leaves the nucleus. It passes through pores or openings in the nuclear membrane into the cytoplasm. Here it begins to direct the assembly of proteins in the process of translation. This molecule is called messenger RNA (mRNA). RNA also plays other roles in the cell, as you will see. Its chemical characteristics and structure enable it to move readily from the nucleus to the cytoplasm. RNA is also more easily degraded (broken down) than DNA. This feature gives the cell a great deal of flexibility and control in what information it expresses as protein. When the cell no longer needs the information encoded in a particular sequence of DNA, it stops transcribing it into RNA by various control mechanisms. The RNA already in the cell will eventually be degraded. The cell will no longer make that protein and, therefore, will not express that characteristic.

ANALYSIS

Record your responses to the following in your notebook.

1. Why do you think Crick proposed the need for an intermediate molecule between DNA and protein synthesis?
2. Identify which components of DNA (see Figure 3.25) differ from those of RNA. Describe how they differ.
3. Imagine an organism that has no DNA, but uses RNA only. How might such a system carry out the transfer of information? What might be the advantages of such a system? Would there be any disadvantages?

phosphate
group

base

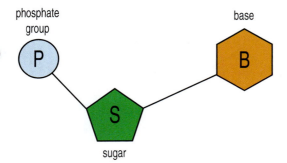

sugar

Figure 3.25

A DNA nucleotide is made up of a phosphate group bonded to a sugar. The sugar, in turn, is bonded to a base (adenine, guanine, cytosine, or thymine).

Cracking the Genetic Code

In 1961, Marshall Nirenberg figured out how information was stored in DNA. He "cracked the code." He did this by introducing an mRNA strand consisting solely of uracil nucleotides (as in UUUUUUUUU) into an extract of broken cells. (This extract was capable of making proteins in a test tube.) From this sequence, he obtained a protein made entirely of a single kind of amino acid. That amino acid was phenylalanine. He then placed an mRNA strand in the tube that contained the sequence AAAAAAAAA. He obtained a protein consisting of another single amino acid type, lysine. All possible RNA sequence combinations were tried. Using this approach, scientists determined that the nucleic acid code in DNA took place in triplets. A triplet is a series of three nucleotides in RNA (such as UGA) that specifies a particular amino acid. Each nucleotide triplet is called a codon.

Using Nirenberg's technique, scientists were able to decipher the code for all 20 amino acids. The result of all this work is the decoder of protein synthesis: the codon table (Table 3.10). With the aid of this table, we can identify the amino acids encoded in the RNA. The sequence of the bases in each codon determines which amino acid will be added next to a growing protein chain. In turn, the sequence of amino acids will determine the shape and, ultimately, the function of that protein.

ANALYSIS

Record your responses to the following in your notebook.

1. Nirenberg introduced UUUUUUUUU into his system and made the amino acid phenylalanine. What would have happened if he had used GGGGGGGGG? CCCCCCCCC?

2. Use Table 3.10 to decode the triplet AUG. Try decoding a few more by jotting down any triplet of RNA nucleotides and finding the corresponding amino acid. Can you write a triplet that has no corresponding amino acid?

   For ease of writing, the 20 amino acids can be abbreviated as follows:

ala	alanine	gly	glycine	pro	proline
arg	arginine	his	histidine	ser	serine
asn	asparagine	ile	isoleucine	thr	threonine
asp	aspartic acid	leu	leucine	trp	tryptophan
cys	cysteine	lys	lysine	tyr	tyrosine
gln	glutamine	met	methionine	val	valine
glu	glutamic acid	phe	phenylalanine		

3. All communication needs punctuation. Which codons represent punctuation?

4. Find the amino acids encoded by UCU, UCC, and UCA. What do you observe? What does this mean?

Table 3.10 The Codon Table: The Decoder of Protein Synthesis

G = guanine		C = cytosine		A = adenine		U = uracil	
codons		AGA						
		AGG						
	GCA	CGA						
	GCC	CGC						
	GCG	CGG	AAC	GAC	UGC	CAA	GAA	
	GCU	CGU	AAU	GAU	UGU	CAG	GAG	
abbreviations for amino acids	ala	arg	asn	asp	cys	gln	glu	
codons				UUA				
				UUG				
	GGA			CUA				CCA
	GGC		AUA	CUC				CCC
	GGG	CAC	AUC	CUG	AAA		UUC	CCG
	GGU	CAU	AUU	CUU	AAG	AUG	UUU	CCU
abbreviations for amino acids	gly	his	ile	leu	lys	met	phe	pro
codons	AGC							
	AGU							
	UCA	ACA			GUA			
	UCC	ACC			GUC		UAA	
	UCG	ACG		UAC	GUG		UAG	
	UCU	ACU	UGG	UAU	GUU		UGA	
abbreviations for amino acids	ser	thr	trp	tyr	val		stop	

Dances with Ribosomes

Think of DNA as the master blueprint of the cell. Imagine that the RNA molecules are the copies to be distributed as the guide to the building process. Then the components of the protein synthesis machinery are the construction team. The ribosome is the site of protein synthesis. It is the structure that holds all the pieces in place. Found in the cytoplasm, the ribosome is comprised of about 50 different kinds of proteins. These proteins are all wrapped up in a structural RNA. The ribosome has a special place where mRNAs bind.

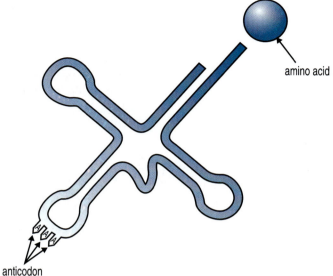

amino acid

anticodon

Transfer RNAs (tRNA) are the actual translators of the code. These are a group of RNAs that have a twisted loop structure made up of nucleotides. At the loop end, there are three nucleotides called anticodons. These anticodons match the sequence of a codon triplet in the mRNA. At the other end is an amino acid, bound to the tRNA. Figure 3.26 shows an example of tRNA. The codon sequence in the mRNA would be UUU. The anticodon on the tRNA is therefore AAA. And the amino acid at the other end would be phenylalanine. The sequence at the end of the tRNA loop matches the mRNA sequence and brings along with it its amino acid. (This happens much the way two strands of the DNA sequence match.)

Figure 3.26

The anticodon is a three-nucleotide sequence at one end of the tRNA. An amino acid is attached at the opposite end.

In this activity, you will model protein synthesis. You and your classmates will take on the various roles of the protein synthesis machinery. The classroom represents the cytoplasm, and the corridor outside the classroom represents the nucleus.

Materials

For the class:

- tape
- string
- balloons

ROLES

- mRNA: 2 or 3 students become the single strand of mRNA
- ribosome: 1 student is the ribosome
- enzymes that assemble amino acids into a protein chain: 2 students with tape and string
- transfer RNA (4 different types, multiple copies of each—GAC, CUU, AAA, and UUC—each of which holds an inflated balloon [amino acid] to which it is color coded): remaining students in the class

The Procedure describes the process of protein synthesis in detail. Once you have assumed your role, you and your classmates will create a protein as a class. It is important that you understand each step in the process. This central dogma of biology is essential to all living things. The information stored in DNA flows through RNA to protein. These proteins are essential for carrying out the functions and determining the characteristics of an organism. In the case of the bacteria D. pneumoniae, the DNA transferred from the virulent bacteria caused the nonvirulent bacteria to make a protein, which made it pathogenic to the host.

PROCEDURE

1. The mRNA starts in the nucleus (corridor) and enters the cytoplasm (classroom).
2. The mRNA attaches to the ribosome. The ribosome has been structured to reveal 3 nucleotide symbols (a codon) at a time. As mRNA moves through the ribosome, the person holding the ribosome calls out the revealed codon.
3. The appropriate tRNA with the complementary anticodon comes up to the ribosome bringing its attached amino acid (balloon).
4. The enzymes take the balloon from the tRNA and tape it to the string that they are holding.
5. The mRNA continues to move through the ribosome exposing each codon.
6. Appropriate tRNAs bring amino acids (balloons), which continue to be added to the protein chain. When tRNA gives up its amino acid balloon, it then goes to pick up the appropriate free amino acids until it will again be needed. Free amino acids (uninflated balloons) will be stored in the cytoplasm (a designated area in the room). Here they may be retrieved by a tRNA that has released its amino acid (balloon) and added to the growing protein chain on the ribosome.
7. When the complete chain of amino acids has been assembled, the enzymes will detach the chain from the ribosome and suspend it where it will be visible to the entire class.

ANALYSIS

Record your responses to the following in your notebook.

1. Create a concept map that summarizes protein synthesis (the process by which information is transferred from DNA to protein in the cell). Use the following terms in your map: nucleus, cytoplasm, ribosome, transcription, translation, DNA, mRNA, tRNA, amino acid, protein, enzyme. Be sure to include other terms as needed.
2. Suppose the mRNA message that leaves the nucleus and attaches to the ribosome were changed so that the final codon was GUA instead of the existing GAA. What would be the composition of the resulting protein chain?
3. What would be the nucleotide composition of the DNA sense strand that produced the change in mRNA?
4. What would be the nucleotide composition of the DNA sense strand that produced the original mRNA?
5. Explain the change that took place in the DNA to produce the new mRNA. Use your answers to questions 2, 3, and 4. What effect might this change have on the function of the new protein? Such a change in DNA is called a mutation.

TASK

Somatostatin is a hormone made in the **hypothalamus** that acts as an inhibitor of the growth hormone **somatotrophin**. It is a very small protein; it consists of only 14 amino acids. Because of its small size, scientists could determine its amino acid composition easily. From its amino acid sequence, they could then determine one of the possible sequences of nucleotides in DNA that encoded this gene. The worksheet *DNA Somatostatin Sequence* your teacher provides shows one of the sequences of DNA that could encode somatostatin. Using this sequence, transcribe the DNA into RNA and then translate that RNA into protein. Why is this sequence only one of the possible sequences for somatostatin? In your notebook, explain briefly in a sentence or two.

CAREER FOCUS

Geneticist   It's 9:55 AM and Harper just can't seem to tear herself away from the lab where she's studying the molecular genetics of cystic fibrosis. She's running late for her 10:00 human genetics course that she teaches to undergraduates, and she can't wait to tell them what she has been learning in her lab. Harper is a geneticist and professor at Wesley College. As a classical geneticist, Harper's job is to explore the patterns by which traits are transmitted through families, specifically the trait for cystic fibrosis. Her goal is ambitious. She wants to find a cure for cystic fibrosis. Harper plans to use the knowledge about the location of the cystic fibrosis gene to sequence that particular piece of DNA. Eventually, she wants to manipulate the gene sequence so it does not include a mutant gene.

Most of Harper's time is spent supervising the sizable research laboratory as well as the graduate students, postdoctoral fellows, and research technicians who work there. At other times, Harper is involved in the genetic evaluation of patients and in supervising their genetic counseling. As a faculty member of the college, Harper spends the remainder of her time teaching.

Growing up, Harper was always fascinated with science. She loved her high school biology course and decided to take an Advanced Placement biology class her senior year. When the class started to do an in-depth investigation in fruit fly genetics, Harper was captivated. One of her assignments was to read a paper by Watson and Crick that described the molecular structure of DNA. Thereafter, she was hooked on genetics.

Because of Harper's interest and enthusiasm, her teacher encouraged her to pursue genetics at the college level. During the summer between her junior and senior years, she worked as a research assistant in one of the genetics laboratories in the Biology Department. During Harper's senior year, she continued to work in the lab part-time and became passionate about research. She continued her lab work after graduation. But soon she realized that having only a bachelor's degree prevented her from being a major contributor in the lab. She just didn't have enough information to help the researchers come up with new ideas to pursue. Harper felt that more class work and training was necessary. So she decided to earn a Ph.D. and learn how to become an independent researcher. With additional postdoctoral training and mentoring from experienced genetics researchers, Harper became a professor of genetics and now runs her own laboratory.

Harper loves making new scientific discoveries. She feels the changing world of genetics helps her stay engaged in and energized about her work. She tries to pass on her energy and enthusiasm to the students she teaches. She uses the courses she teaches as an excuse to learn more about the latest discoveries. Harper also helps undergraduates and graduate students by mentoring them and giving them research assistant positions in her laboratory. In that way, she can show them what her work is really like and how they can contribute to scientific research.

Protein, the Wonder Ingredient

Prologue

The experiments of Griffith and of Avery and his colleagues demonstrated that DNA contained information enabling the bacteria *D. pneumoniae* to produce a polysaccharide capsule that allowed the bacteria to grow and flourish in the host. This growth produced the symptoms of pneumonia in the host. Later experiments demonstrated that the difference between the nonvirulent and virulent strains was actually a difference in just one protein. This was a specific enzyme that enabled the virulent strain to synthesize the protective polysaccharide capsule. The information that was transferred in Griffith's experiment was the gene for this enzyme. When the nonvirulent strain had incorporated this gene, it could then produce this enzyme, synthesize the polysaccharide coat, and become virulent (see Figure 3.27).

In the previous learning experience, you explored the processes involved in the translation of information from DNA into protein. Proteins are essential components of all living organisms. They carry out enormously diverse functions. How do proteins do what they do? What makes them uniquely able to carry out these functions, and thereby direct a great variety of chemical activities? In this learning experience, you explore the function of these wondrous molecules. You examine how their structure permits them to carry out these functions.

Brainstorming

Observe your teacher's demonstration. Then discuss the following questions with your partner, and record your thinking in your notebook. Be prepared to share your ideas with the class.

1. How is the physical appearance of the eggs different? What do you think caused the change?
2. What do you think are the major biomolecules in eggs?
3. Are the two eggs still made of the same biomolecules? If so, why do they look so different?
4. How do you think the heat may have affected the biomolecules? Which ones were affected? What other examples can you think of in which heat has changed the physical properties of biomolecules?

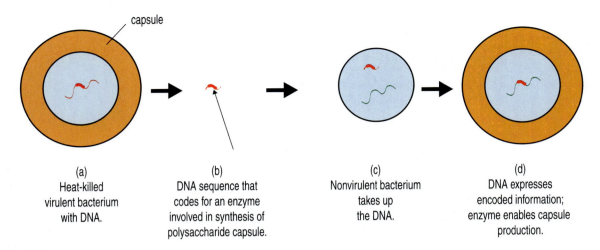

(a)
Heat-killed
virulent bacterium
with DNA.

(b)
DNA sequence that
codes for an enzyme
involved in synthesis of
polysaccharide capsule.

(c)
Nonvirulent bacterium
takes up
the DNA.

(d)
DNA expresses
encoded information;
enzyme enables capsule
production.

capsule

Figure 3.27

A nonvirulent strain
transformed to virulence.
The bacteria takes up DNA
containing the gene for an
enzyme involved in the
synthesis of the
polysaccharide coat.

READING

Protein, Protein, Everywhere

Living organisms contain an immense assortment of biomolecules. Bacteria, the simplest life-forms, contain about 5,000 different biomolecules. This includes 3,000 different kinds of proteins. In humans, the numbers and the variation are even greater. It is this diversity of protein biomolecules that enables cells to carry out the variety of activities involved in life processes. Proteins are a good example of the simplicity within diversity. They are all chains of amino acids. It is the number and order of the amino acid subunits that result in the diversity of proteins. This diversity then determines differences in characteristics of cells, and therefore of whole organisms.

Each type of protein is very efficient at one task. But how many proteins exist in the human body? No one knows; but a hundred thousand is not a bad guess. Although none of these protein molecules is identical to any found in bacteria, some of their functions are quite similar.

What are these proteins? Why are there so many different kinds? What do they do and how do they do it? Actually, you are probably more familiar with proteins than you think. They are the "wonder ingredients" in products you use every day. There are the laundry detergents that claim they can get out your toughest stains, and shampoos that are supposed to make your hair look terrific.

You may be most familiar with the proteins in the foods you eat. Proteins are an essential part of your daily diet. Plants can make their proteins from carbon dioxide, water, nitrates, sulfates, and phosphates. Animals, on the other hand, can synthesize only a limited number of proteins. They depend mainly on plants or other animals as dietary sources of protein. Protein intake is required regularly in animals because their bodies have little stored protein. If excess protein is taken in (more than the body can use), it is stored as fat.

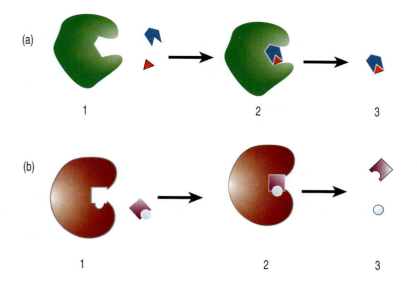

(a)

1   2   3

(b)

1   2   3

Figure 3.28
Enzymes facilitate anabolism by putting molecules together (a). They facilitate catabolism by taking molecules apart (b).

Proteins are essential to the structure and function of all living organisms. Next to water, protein is the most abundant substance in cells. Proteins make up half of the solid matter in cells (water makes up 70% of the cell). They perform a wide variety of tasks in organisms. These tasks can be classified by biological function.

The largest class of proteins consists of the enzymes. These are protein molecules that facilitate and enhance the rate of chemical reactions in the cell. That is, enzymes assist in chemical reactions so that the reactions proceed with speed and efficiency. Without enzymes, the metabolic reactions of the cell would still take place, but they would happen far too slowly to sustain life. It would take you about 50 years to digest your lunch. There are many reactions involved in the breakdown of food, the synthesis of cell components, or the transport and storage of energy. These reactions might take days or weeks or years to happen without enzymes. Instead, they happen in milliseconds in the cell because of the action of enzymes. Enzymes can bring two molecules together to form a new molecule (anabolism). Or they can bind a single molecule to break it down (catabolism) (see Figure 3.28). Examples of enzymes include **lactase**, which breaks down the milk sugar **lactose** into **glucose** and galactose; **catalase**, which degrades **hydrogen peroxide** to oxygen and water; **RNA polymerase**, which is responsible for transcribing the information in DNA into mRNA; and **diphosphoribulose carboxylase**, which fixes carbon dioxide (CO_2) into sugar in photosynthetic organisms. (Note that the suffix *-ase* is usually found in an enzyme's name.)

The second major class of proteins makes up the structural components of cells and tissues. Collagen is the major structural protein in connective tissue and in bone. It is also part of the "glue" that binds a group of cells together to form a tissue. Keratin is another structural protein. It gives strength to skin, hair, nails, horns, and feathers.

In addition, proteins carry out other essential types of functions. Actin and myosin are the two major proteins that enable muscles to contract. Some proteins have a transport function. Hemoglobin in blood carries oxygen around the body, myoglobin transports oxygen through muscle tissue, and serum albumin transports fatty acids through the blood to various organs. Hormones such as insulin (which regulates blood sugar) and somatotrophin (a growth hormone) are proteins. Proteins found in the immune system, such as antibodies,

SCiLINKS
NSTA

Topic: Proteins/Enzymes
Go to: www.scilinks.org
Code: INBIOH2383

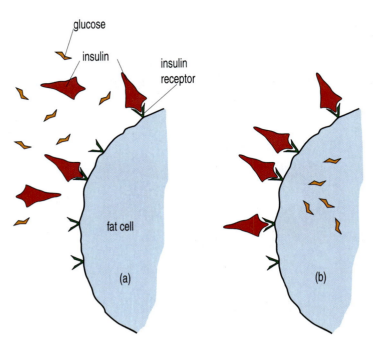

glucose

insulin

insulin receptor

fat cell

(a)

(b)

Figure 3.29

Insulin facilitates the entry of glucose into cells. (a) Insulin binds to a protein receptor on a fat cell. (b) The cell can then take up glucose from the blood.

protect us from infection. In contrast, toxins may do us great harm. Toxins are proteins made by organisms that include bacteria, plants, and snakes.

Many proteins act by binding to other proteins and triggering a specific cellular response. For example, the hormone insulin controls the level of glucose in the blood. Insulin acts by binding to specific proteins on the surface of muscle, liver, and fat cells. This binding causes a change in their cell membranes. This change results in the membranes taking up glucose from the blood, thus reducing the concentration of blood glucose (see Figure 3.29).

Proteins also can serve as a source of energy for cells. If the diet does not supply enough fat and carbohydrate, stored fat is broken down for energy. (Fat and carbohydrate are the primary sources of energy in the cell.) But stored fat can be used up, as in starvation or extreme dieting. Then proteins can be used for energy instead. This can happen even at the expense of building new cells and maintaining tissue structure.

How do proteins carry out all of these essential functions? How does the structure of a protein relate to its function? The shape of an individual protein is very important in its function. All proteins have a linear sequence of amino acids. But proteins are folded into complex three-dimensional structures. The shapes of these structures are determined by which amino acids make up the proteins and the sequence in which they occur. Just looking at the sequence of amino acids in a protein cannot tell us how it folds. It cannot tell us how growth hormone makes us taller or how a bacterial toxin can kill us. But the information in that sequence plays an essential role in determining how a protein folds and whether it is functional. We don't completely understand the rules governing protein folding. But we have figured out some of the pieces of the puzzle, as you will see in the activity Liver and Let Liver.

Record your responses to the following in your notebook.

1. Where do you find protein? Where is it in this room? in your house? outside the building? in your lunch? in some of the products you buy?
2. List four different functions of proteins. Give an example of each.
3. List some of the proteins you have learned about and describe their functions. Think back on what you have learned so far in Units 1, 2, and 3.
4. What might be meant by the statement, "We are what we are because of our proteins"?

Liver and Let Liver

Liver may not be one of your favorite foods. But the liver in your body should be one of your favorite organs. It plays the life-saving function of detoxification. Every day your body takes in toxic substances from the air and the food you eat. In addition, some of the by-products of your cells' metabolic activities are toxic to your system. The job of the liver is to neutralize and dispose of these toxic substances. It's a sort of hazardous waste disposal. Without a liver, hazardous products would soon build up and inhibit vital metabolic processes. This would result in death.

One of these toxic metabolic by-products in animal tissues is a molecule called hydrogen peroxide. You may be familiar with hydrogen peroxide as a substance that can be used for bleaching hair or for disinfecting wounds to prevent infection. Hydrogen peroxide (H_2O_2) is toxic to living things because it produces something called a superoxide radical, O_2-, from oxygen. This radical can destroy certain biomolecules such as proteins. Therefore, it is essential that organisms be able to dispose of hydrogen peroxide. Catalase is an enzyme present in liver cells (and other plant and animal cells) that neutralizes this hazardous waste product. It does this by breaking the waste product down into harmless molecules. In this activity, you will examine the effects of heat on the activity of this enzyme.

Materials

For each pair of students:

- 2 pairs of safety goggles
- 2 small pieces of liver (1 cooked and 1 raw)
- 2 flasks (125- to 250-mL) or test tubes (13 × 100 mm)
- 50–100 mL hydrogen peroxide

PROCEDURE

1. Place the raw liver in one flask or test tube and the cooked liver in the second flask.
2. Pour enough hydrogen peroxide into each flask to cover each piece of liver.
3. Observe the reaction for 5–10 minutes. Describe all your observations in your notebook. Then respond to the following Analysis questions.

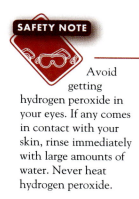

SAFETY NOTE

Avoid getting hydrogen peroxide in your eyes. If any comes in contact with your skin, rinse immediately with large amounts of water. Never heat hydrogen peroxide.

ANALYSIS

Record your responses to the following in your notebook.

1. The chemical formula for hydrogen peroxide is H_2O_2. What products do you think were formed in this reaction? Write a word equation that describes this reaction.
2. What happened when hydrogen peroxide was added to the raw liver? to the cooked liver?
3. What do you think caused the difference in these two reactions? Base your answer on what you learned from the reading "Protein, Protein, Everywhere."
4. How does this relate to the explanation you proposed about what happened to the egg at the beginning of this learning experience?

ACTIVITY

Getting into Shape

The first step in most protein reactions is for one protein to bind to another molecule. The molecule that an enzyme binds to is called a **substrate**. In the case of enzymes, this binding step brings the substrate into position so that the enzyme can act on it. This substrate could be another protein, a sugar, a lipid, or a nucleic acid. Transport proteins, such as hemoglobin and certain membrane proteins, bind molecules in order to move them from place to place. Structural proteins, such as collagen, may bind to one another to give shape and strength to the structure.

These binding interactions take place at specific sites on the protein molecules. These sites are called **binding sites**. The binding site on a protein is defined by the shape of the protein. The folding of the protein results in a groove, cleft, or pocket on its surface into which the second molecule fits. This is much like a key in a lock. If the shape of this binding site is altered, the ability of the protein to interact with the second molecule may be lost. This renders the protein unable to carry out its function. Once the second molecule binds to the protein, that enzyme can then do its job. That job can be an enzymatic reaction, a transport function, a structural function, or something else.

The principles of protein folding are one of the important, unsolved mysteries of science. We know that the amino acid composition and the order in which these amino acids happen in the protein play a central role in determining how a protein will fold. Amino acids have a characteristic structure. They differ from one another in their side groups, which may have a positive, negative, or neutral charge (see Figure 3.30). The positive and negative charges on the amino acids appear to be important in folding. Amino acids also demonstrate **hydrophobic** (water-fearing) and **hydrophilic** (water-loving) properties seen in lipids. These properties are also important in folding. The water-fearing parts tend to move to the interior of the molecule, away from the water. Another factor involved in folding is the ability of amino acids to form chemical bridges or bonds between each other.

In this activity, you will build a model that demonstrates the binding of a protein to another molecule. This is the first step in protein function.

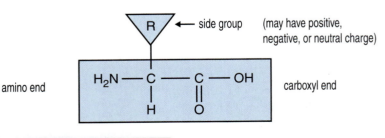

Figure 3.30

Structure of an amino acid.

Materials

For each pair of students:

- 4 extra-long pipe cleaners (chenille stems)
- 1 set of 50 colored beads that can be threaded on the pipe cleaners
  - 10 red beads, representing positively charged amino acids
  - 10 green beads, representing negatively charged amino acids
  - 30 beads of a third color, representing neutral amino acids
- 1 container to hold beads
- 1 small geometrically shaped object such as a ball, a triangular block, or a cube
- cellophane tape

NOTE Many forces are involved in determining protein folding. For the purposes of this activity, you will consider only the attractive forces of amino acids (positive, negative, and neutral charges) in determining how a protein folds.

PROCEDURE

1. Join 4 long pipe cleaners together securely, end to end. Be sure that you can't tug them apart.
2. Thread the beads along the pipe cleaners in random order. The protein molecule model must be built of pipe cleaners (representing peptide bonds) and no fewer than 25 beads (representing amino acids).
3. Twist your protein molecule model into a three-dimensional object. Form a pocket or groove around a small object (for example, a ball or triangular block). This represents the substrate. When twisting your molecule, 2 features are important:
   - The interaction of the protein molecule and the other molecule must show **binding specificity**. The binding molecule and the binding site should match in shape and fit together in a lock-and-key fashion. The goal is to make a space in the protein molecule into which the other molecule fits (relatively) precisely.
   - The protein molecule must be folded according to the principle of mutual attraction. Positively charged amino acids (red) will attract negatively charged amino acids (green). Neutral ones will have no effect on folding. When forming this pocket, be sure to have 2 or 3 locations where red and green beads come together. This represents what might happen in a protein in which the folding is dependent in part on interactions between positively and negatively charged amino acids. This may require some squeezing or sliding of beads. You may wish to stabilize this interaction with pieces of cellophane tape.
4. In your notebook, draw a diagram of your model. Indicate the following in words or drawings:
   - where the binding site is on your protein,
   - how the interacting molecule fits or binds at this site,
   - where the important interactions between the protein and the other molecule take place, and
   - how the structure of the protein defines the binding site.
5. Find a red bead that is important in forming the shape of the binding site. Substitute 1 green bead for it. What happens to the shape of your protein? What happens to the shape of your binding site? Record your responses in your notebook.

6. Replace the original red bead. Then substitute a neutral bead for 1 red or green bead that is important in forming the binding site. What happens to the shape of your protein? What happens to the shape of your binding site? Record your responses in your notebook.

7. Remove (delete) a section of your protein. (You may cut the protein molecule, remove the cut piece, and rejoin cut ends if you wish.) Does this change the protein shape or binding site? Does it matter where you delete a section? What happens to the shape of your protein? What happens to the shape of your binding site? Record your responses in your notebook. Be prepared to discuss your model in class.

ANALYSIS

Record your responses to the following in your notebook.

1. Describe the factors that determine the shape of your protein model.

2. How have changes in the shape of your protein influenced the protein's ability to bind to your other molecule? How might altering the shape of your protein change its function?

3. Describe the steps involved when the enzyme lactase breaks down lactose sugar into glucose and galactose. What would happen if the enzyme binding site were altered? What would be the consequences for the organism if this enzyme were altered?

4. Some molecules have more than one binding site. Take for example RNA polymerase, the enzyme that copies the encoded message in the DNA into mRNA. RNA polymerase has binding sites for the DNA molecule and for the RNA nucleotides. What would happen to the ability of this enzyme to carry out its function if one of the binding sites was altered or lost? What would be the consequences for the organism?

5. How might a change in the amino acid sequence of your protein take place? Base your answer on what you know about the transfer of information from DNA to protein.

6. The **endoplasmic reticulum** is a membranous system in eukaryotic cells. It is the site of many functions, including protein synthesis. Another process that takes place on these membranes is degradation of proteins that have not folded correctly after protein synthesis. Why is this activity an important function for the cell?

EXTENDING *Ideas*

◗ Investigate diseases that are the result of changes in the sequence of a protein. Examples include sickle-cell anemia, hemophilia, cystic fibrosis, Huntington's disease, or lactose intolerance. Describe the symptoms of the disease. Find out what protein is affected, what the function of that protein is (if it is known), what change has taken place to the protein, and how this is reflected in the DNA sequence (if it is known).

◗ Research how carbon monoxide poisoning happens. What effect does carbon monoxide have on animals? How does it bring about this effect? Describe how this is an example of the principle, "another key that fits the lock." What does carbon monoxide do to the lock?

◗ A permanent wave is an example of the altering, or denaturing, of proteins in hair. Explore the chemistry of a perm.

CAREER Focus

Chemical Technician   For some time now, the protein chemists at BioPro have been developing a new synthetic protein that can be used to attack and destroy pathogens in the human body. They're hoping that the protein will enhance the body's immune response. For months, scientists and technicians have been running various lab tests to collect information on the synthetic protein and its effects. Frequently, Dr. McDonald stops in at the lab to meet with Timothy, one of the lab's chemical technicians. They discuss the next steps in their research process. These steps include analyzing the data to determine if the protein was effective in destroying pathogens and at what levels it is most effective, and deciding whether the compound should be added to the line of products manufactured by BioPro.

Timothy has been involved with every aspect of the lab research. He helped organize tests and carefully conducted all of the chemical experiments and tests to gather data on the effectiveness of the protein. Timothy was extremely precise in how he collected the data and also in his computerized record-keeping. He needed the information in a format that made it easy to work with. Now that the testing phase is complete, Timothy spends his time updating the computerized data files and ensuring that they are accurate so that data analysis can begin. He will work with Dr. McDonald to perform computerized statistical analyses on the data and brainstorm possible interpretations.

Most positions as chemical technicians require a 2-year associate's degree. But Timothy was able to intern at BioPro when he was a high school senior. Timothy was a whiz at chemistry and computer science. So when he was preparing for his senior internship requirement, his chemistry teacher thought he should try to intern as a chemical technician. His guidance counselor and chemistry teacher helped him research companies and arranged his placement at BioPro. During his internship, Timothy learned many of the lab procedures, and he applied for a position as a chemical technician after graduating high school. When he was hired, he worked as a trainee under the direct supervision of a more experienced technician who continues to be his mentor.

Even though he had his dream job, Timothy felt that taking college-level math and science courses would help him advance professionally. He also wanted to develop his writing and communication skills for writing reports and making presentations. Now he's working toward his associate's degree by taking evening classes, which are paid by BioPro. But even when he has completed his degree, Timothy would like to keep up with new technologies by taking continuing education seminars and workshops through the American Chemical Society. Timothy feels that he has a very rewarding career. He's involved in the exciting world of science and discovery, and he can help improve the public's health even without an advanced scientific degree.

The Cholera Connection

Prologue

In the previous learning experience, you explored the many and diverse functions that proteins carry out in living organisms. The functions of some proteins are well-known, such as certain enzymes and structural components. The functions of other proteins are not so well understood.

One of these little-understood proteins is the **cholera toxin**. It is produced by the causative agent of cholera, *Vibrio cholerae.* The function of this protein in the bacteria is, as yet, not fully understood. Its consequences for humans, however, are all too clear in the symptoms of the disease *V. cholerae* causes.

How does the presence of an infectious agent in a host cause disease? There is great diversity in diseases and the pathogenic agents that cause them. There is also a wide variety of mechanisms by which the symptoms of disease are produced. In this learning experience, you investigate how one bacterial protein, cholera toxin, can cause the debilitating symptoms of disease. Based on your understanding of how the toxin affects cells, you will develop an approach to block its activity and prevent the symptoms.

Brainstorming

Discuss the following questions with your partner, and record your thinking in your notebook. Be prepared to share your ideas with the class.

1. Describe the different functions of proteins in an organism.
2. What makes proteins uniquely able to carry out their function?
3. What happens when a protein interacts with one or more substrates?
4. Describe what you think might happen when a toxin binds to a membrane protein.

A Debilitating Disease: A First Look

THE TOXIN THAT BINDS

Cholera is a serious disease that happens periodically in epidemic proportions. In 1995, epidemics of cholera in South America, Africa, and eastern Europe caused at least 384,000 cases of the disease. These epidemics resulted in about 11,000 deaths. In 2001, nearly 185,000 cases from 58 countries were reported to the World Health Organization (WHO).

V. cholerae, the bacteria that cause cholera, can be found in salt water or fresh water. Recent research suggests that V. *cholerae* may actually survive in the oceans of the world in a dormant or inactive form, coming to life when the oceans warm. The bacteria also grow in great numbers in human intestinal tracts. Within the intestines, V. *cholerae* attach to cells that line the intestine and begin to divide. During this growth, the bacteria secrete a protein, cholera toxin, into their immediate environment. Here the toxin binds to proteins in the membranes of the intestinal cells. In normal cells, certain proteins in the cell membrane regulate the flow of water in and out of the cell. Cholera toxin binds to one of these proteins. The result of this interaction is that water, salts, and other small molecules flow out of the cell into the intestinal lumen (passageway). This, in turn, causes the first main symptom of cholera—diarrhea.

A person with full-blown cholera can lose 20 liters (about 5 gallons) of water daily because of excessive diarrhea. Left untreated, patients rapidly become dehydrated, suffer from salt imbalances, and may die. One beneficial effect for the patient of this massive water loss is that it washes the bacteria out of the intestine. Thus, the disease can be cured spontaneously if the affected person can survive the acute phase of the disease. The most commonly used and effective treatment for cholera is oral rehydration therapy. This replenishes fluids and salts using a sugar-salt solution. This therapy treats the symptoms of the disease and leaves the cure to the host's immune system.

The Toxin Takes a Cell

ACTIVITY

How does cholera toxin interact with the host cells? In this activity, you and your partner will build a model of this interaction. To construct the model, use available materials and your knowledge about how proteins interact with other molecules. (Think back to your explorations in Learning Experience 7.)

Materials

For the class:
assorted materials for constructing model proteins and their binding sites:

- balloons
- solution of salt water (1%)
- long pipe cleaners (chenille stems)
- colored beads
- toothpicks
- construction paper
- gumdrops
- small marshmallows
- grapes

PROCEDURE

1. Before building your model, you should determine
   a. ways to show how protein binding sites interact with other molecules, and
   b. a way to show how these interactions might alter the shape of the biomolecules involved.
2. Build your model. As you work, be sure to consider the following:
   a. Proteins have a specific shape.
   b. The cholera toxin protein and the protein on the surface of the cell interact with one another.
   c. Each protein has 1 or more binding sites for substrates. The shapes of the binding sites on the protein and the substrates should fit together.
   d. Interactions of protein and substrate can cause a change in the shape of the protein or proteins. This change in shape results in some change in the components of the reaction.
   e. This interaction alters the ability of the cell to maintain water and salt contents.
3. Prepare to present your model to the class. In your presentation, be sure to indicate how

   a. the toxin interacts with components in the cell membrane,
   b. the interaction affects each reacting biomolecule,
   c. the interaction affects the cell, and
   d. the interaction produces the symptoms of cholera.

A Debilitating Disease: A Second Look

JUST TRYING TO GET A LIFE

V. cholerae bacteria do not produce toxin for the sole purpose of harming their host. To assume they do would be to assign the bacteria human characteristics that they do not possess. (This is called anthropomorphism.) Why, then, do *V. cholerae* (or any bacteria for that matter) produce a protein that is toxic? One explanation is that the protein serves a survival function for the bacteria by inducing diarrhea. The diarrhea induced by this protein provides a kind of escape mechanism. This theory suggests that the human intestine serves as a rich environment for bacterial growth. It provides an appropriate temperature and abundant nutrients, and acts as an incubator in which bacteria can multiply rapidly. The diarrhea provides the bacteria a means of escape and a return to the external environment where they can seek new hosts before the old host dies.

Another hypothesis suggests that the cholera toxin helps the bacteria obtain nutrients from damaged host cells. It does this by tapping into the energy, carbon, and other resources within the cell. By altering the properties of the membranes of intestinal cells, the toxin causes small molecules to leak out into the extracellular (outside the cell) environment. Since this is where the bacteria live, this leakage makes these resources available to the bacteria.

The explosive symptoms caused by the cholera toxin may, in reality, be a kind of "mistake" on the part of the bacteria. In an ideal host/bacterial relationship, the uninvited guest would like to take up residence for as long as possible. As many long-term guests know, the best way to do that is to be unobtrusive. For *V. cholerae*, that would mean quietly colonizing the gut for a long-term stay without being too obvious about it. With this strategy, it could continue to grow and reproduce, periodically passing its offspring out to seek new hosts. The devastating symptoms and mortality seen in many cases of cholera could reflect an unsuccessful attempt by the bacteria to colonize peacefully.

Even though we know what causes cholera, and the mode of transmission is well understood, epidemics of cholera continue to erupt around the globe. The reason for this is simple. Any conditions that foster crowding or poor sanitary standards can result in water contaminated with human fecal matter. This is a potential site of a cholera outbreak. Contaminated drinking water and unsanitary living conditions are facts of life in many areas of the world today. As a result, cholera continues to be a serious public health problem. Understanding the biochemistry, however, can help us to design ways to treat the disease and prevent the devastating symptoms.

ANALYSIS

Record your responses to the following in your notebook.

1. What possible functions might the cholera toxin have in the bacteria?
2. Not all *V. cholerae* bacteria produce a functional cholera toxin. Certain mutants (both natural and laboratory created) do not make a functional toxin. Do you think individuals infected with a mutant strain would display the symptoms of cholera? Why or why not?
3. Another possible function of the cholera toxin in *V. cholerae* is that this protein enables the bacteria to stick around, literally. This suggests that the toxin may serve as an adhesive, enabling the bacteria to form colonies on the inner surface of the host's intestinal lining. Recent investigations indicate that mutants that do not make cholera toxin can colonize the intestinal lining just as efficiently as those that do make the protein. Do these results support or disprove the adhesive model? Explain your answer.
4. Propose a model (starting at the DNA level) to explain why the toxin in these mutants (question 3) might no longer function. Use your understanding of information transfer in the cell and the importance of protein shape.

Design That Drug

ACTIVITY

You are a member of the scientific team of the pharmaceutical company Drugs R Us. Your company manufactures many designer drugs. These are chemical compounds that are specially designed for specific purposes. Once scientists understand how molecules such as toxins interact with each other, they can design drugs that can compete for the active sites used by these molecules. In theory, this would prevent the symptoms of the disease that these molecules can cause.

TASK

1. Your current assignment is to develop a designer drug for cholera that will block the action of the cholera toxin. Be sure to consider the following:
   a. how proteins interact with each other,
   b. how other biomolecules might be involved in these interactions, and
   c. how different biomolecules might compete for the same binding site.
2. As well as being a scientist in this company, you are also head of the Advertising Department. (Drugs R Us is a small company.) Your next task is to design a full-page advertisement for a medical journal that describes your product. Be sure to include the following:

   a. how the product is to be administered and why (orally, injected, in the water source, etc.);
   b. what symptoms the product eases;
   c. the biochemical basis for its activity;
   d. how its effectiveness in treating the symptoms of cholera has been determined; and
   e. a memorable name for your product.

Cholera: A Grim By-product of Squalor

CHOLERA: A GRIM BY-PRODUCT OF SQUALOR

BOSTON GLOBE [STAFF PRODUCED COPY ONLY] by Richard Saltus. Copyright 1994 by GLOBE NEWSPAPER CO (MA). Reproduced with permission of GLOBE NEWSPAPER CO (MA) in the format Textbook via Copyright Clearance Center.

The dreaded news that cholera has begun a lethal rampage among starving masses of Rwandan refugees was no surprise to infectious disease specialists, who said yesterday that unless relief workers can restore some measure of sanitation to the crowded camps, the epidemic could spread indefinitely.

And cholera—a bacterial infection that causes diarrhea so severe that it can cause death in hours—may only be the beginning.

"We're concerned about a whole range of diseases: cholera, dysentery, food-borne illnesses, measles," said Robert Howard, a spokesman for the federal Centers for Disease Control and Prevention in Atlanta. "You have here a whole breakdown in sanitation and public health. This is potentially one of the largest-scale epidemic situations we have seen in many years."

With forecasts yesterday of up to 50,000 cases of cholera among the millions of Rwandans huddled in eastern Zaire, officials of the CDC's International Health Program were preparing to send not only doctors but also at least one engineer to the refugee zone to give advice on the enormous sanitation problem, Howard said.

Virtually unknown in industrialized countries, cholera is endemic in parts of Asia, Africa and the Middle East where poverty and inadequate sanitation expose people to water or food contaminated by human waste. The bacterium that causes it, known as *Vibrio cholerae*, can spread rapidly whenever the social order breaks down and masses of people crowd together, making sanitary disposal of wastes impossible. This is the case now in Zaire.

Once infection begins, a toxin produced by the bacterium in the small intestine triggers uncontrollable diarrhea that quickly depletes the body of water and vital minerals called electrolytes.

"The disease produces massive amounts of stool that contain the organism, and it can get into food and water," said Dr. Mary Wilson, an infectious disease specialist at Mount Auburn Hospital in Cambridge and the Harvard School of Public Health.

The huge influx of refugees from war-torn Rwanda into Zaire, with its few facilities for housing, health care or sanitation, "created an ideal environment" for diseases to spread rapidly once the organisms got a start, Wilson said. "One could predict that other food-borne diseases, like shigella, will become a problem, and measles also can be devastating, especially to children, in situations like this."

Sometimes cholera causes only mild symptoms, but it can be so severe that "people can lose many gallons of water in a 24-hour period," said Dr. Leo Liu, a specialist in infectious disease at Harvard Medical School and Boston's Beth Israel Hospital.

Pregnant women, children and the elderly are especially prone to the life-threatening consequences of losing so much fluid. Untreated, victims become unbearably thirsty, stop producing urine, and suffer weakness and muscle cramps. Their circulatory system may simply collapse. Up to 50 percent mortality has occurred in some epidemics, though it can be as low as 1 percent if health care resources are available.

In large epidemics, Liu added, health workers place the weakest, sickest patients on "cholera cots"—canvas cots with a hole beneath the buttocks, so that the continuous outpouring of watery diarrhea can be caught in basins or cans. "You have to dispose of all this contaminated water, or the bacteria will just spread," Liu said.

Antibiotics can help rid the body of the cholera bug, but the mainstay of treatment is replacing fluids and salts in patients. If they can be "rehydrated" quickly, cholera patients generally recover in a few days with no long-term effects. How to do this now in Zaire is what the international relief effort must figure out.

(Reprinted courtesy of the *Boston Globe*)

ANALYSIS

Record your responses to the following in your notebook.

1. Compare the cholera epidemic in Rwanda with the cholera epidemic in London during the 1830s (Learning Experience 1 in this unit).
   a. What are the differences in living situations?
   b. What might have brought on the disease in each population?
2. Compare what was known about the disease during the London epidemic with what was known in Rwanda.
   a. What was known about how to treat the victims? How was this information used?
   b. What was known about how to halt the epidemic? How was this information used?
3. Why do you think that epidemics of cholera still occur even though research has identified how the disease is spread, the causative agent, the molecular basis of the symptoms, and methods for alleviating the symptoms and curing the infection?

EXTENDING *Ideas*

● Toxins are also produced by other kinds of bacteria, including the bacteria of tetanus, *Bordetella pertussis,* and a pathogenic *Escherichia coli*. Research one of these pathogens. What do we know about the mode of action of the toxin? How does it affect its host? What are the symptoms of the disease? Compare this pathogen with what you have learned about the cholera bacteria and cholera toxin.

● Toxins from bacteria have been studied as part of programs in biological warfare. Research what toxin-producing bacteria have been considered for biological warfare and how some countries would use it. How would these countries protect their own populations from the bacteria? Write an essay that speculates on the practicality and ethical considerations of countries developing such programs.

One way to determine the effect of a drug on a disease is to test it on animals. Human testing of drugs and vaccines, called a clinical trial, is often carried out after the effectiveness and the potential side effects of the materials have been determined in animal models. Call your local hospital, university, drug companies, or branch of the Food and Drug Administration to determine whether any clinical trials are underway in your area. Find out what drugs are being tested and against what diseases. What is the protocol or way the trial is being conducted? What are the anticipated outcomes?

Human experimentation has been a part of the history of scientific investigation in the United States. In some cases, the course of a disease was followed in patients even though a cure was available. Investigate the Tuskegee experiments on syphilis in humans. Prepare an essay on why this was done and what was learned. Why have the ethics of this approach come under scrutiny? Were any other experimental alternatives available?

Infectious agents of plants also produce toxins. Some fungi that infect plants produce toxins called mycotoxins. When humans and other animals eat the plants, they may contract diseases called mycotoxicoses. One such disease is ergotism. Ergot is produced by a fungus, *Claviceps purpurea,* which infects rye and other grasses. Throughout recorded history, people have occasionally consumed fungus-infected rye. This happened especially in times of famine when every last bit of grain was needed. The alkaloids produced by this fungus cause a wide range of devastating symptoms. These include memory loss, blindness, double vision, confusion, hallucinations, abortions, gangrene, and muscle spasms. In France, the disease was called "sacred fire" because the afflicted individuals felt as though they were being burnt. Research ergot and its biological activity. Determine the impact of this disease economically and socially during the Middle Ages in Europe. Describe methods that are taken today to avoid this disease.

CAREER FOCUS

Research Pharmacologist   Jackie's afternoon lecture involves the effect of antibiotics on strains of bacteria that cause illness in humans. This is her area of research, so she has lots of information to share with her graduate students. Jackie is a research pharmacologist at Southern University, where she also teaches pharmacology courses to graduate students. (Jackie is not a pharmacist who prepares and dispenses drugs to patients.)

   After her lecture, Jackie returns to her lab on campus to continue working on her research. Like all research pharmacologists, her goal is to study and understand the effects of drugs. She studies how they change the normal processes that take place in living animals. She also studies how drugs produce these effects by mimicking or interfering with the action of other substances normally found in the body. But Jackie specializes in clinical pharmacology. Clinical pharmacology is the study of therapeutic and toxic actions of drugs in humans. Jackie's lab research focuses on the effects of antibiotic compounds and how they can be used to create medications. She studies how the chemical structure of the substance interacts at the cellular and molecular levels. Jackie hopes that her research will help in standardizing drug dosages and discovering how they should be used most effectively.

As a student, Jackie excelled in biology. She particularly enjoyed learning about anatomy. Jackie was spellbound when a high school teacher taught a unit on microbiology and how different bacteria respond to the presence of antibiotics. One day after class, Jackie asked her teacher what kind of scientists study such things for a living. Her teacher told her that the field of science was called pharmacology and that it required a lot of schooling. But she thought that it might be a good fit for Jackie.

While taking a pharmacology course in college, Jackie discovered that it was a fascinating field that would allow her to branch out into many different disciplines. The course required her to apply what she learned in her other courses in biochemistry, microbiology, microanatomy, and physiology. She decided that after graduation she would pursue a Ph.D. in clinical pharmacology from a medical school. To be considered a clinical pharmacologist, Jackie needed specialized training. This training involved using drugs for treatment, assessing their side effects, monitoring their levels in patients, preventing or treating overdoses, and determining the consequences of interactions with other drugs. While working toward her doctorate, Jackie assisted research pharmacologists. She learned how to design and carry out experiments to determine how drug concentrations in the body change over time. She also learned how to test newly discovered or manufactured substances for their safety, activity, and possible use as drugs.

After completing her graduate studies, Jackie had several career paths to choose from. Although she could have pursued positions in industry or in government, Jackie wanted to pass her knowledge on to others. She felt that working at a university would be the best fit for her. She began by doing several years of postdoctoral work for another pharmacology researcher before eventually taking a faculty position at Southern University. Jackie loves working in a field that is challenging yet allows her to help others. She does this both through her pharmacological research and the teaching and mentoring of students at the college.

Public Health Nurse

Henry has a busy day ahead of him. He's headed to the City Community Center where he's organized a free immunization clinic for infants and children. Not only will he administer the immunizations, Henry will also distribute literature and talk with parents about disease prevention and the importance of immunization. Henry is a public health nurse at the Lakeville County Health Department. Here he serves as the immunization coordinator. It's Henry's job to organize such events and make sure that as many people as possible are given the opportunity to be immunized. Henry loves that he can meet so many different people and actually teach them about health issues. He sees himself as a teacher as well as a nurse. And the fact that his work directly affects the health of people in his community gives Henry great satisfaction.

Growing up, Henry always thought that he would become a teacher because he loved working with children. He spent his summers working as a counselor at a local camp. But when he reached high school, he enjoyed his science courses so much that he reconsidered teaching. Henry met with his guidance counselor. They discussed his interests and possible career paths that would be a good fit. His counselor pointed out that nurses work in the field of science and medicine but also spend much of their time teaching people about health issues. At his teacher's suggestion, Henry volunteered at the local hospital to see nurses in action. His work at the hospital convinced Henry that pursuing a nursing career would be the right fit for him. He was accepted to a nursing school at a nearby college. Henry loved learning all of the scientific information that is required to become a nurse. But he also enjoyed applying that information by working with people.

During the last year of his training, Henry was able to work in a variety of settings. It was then that he decided which type of nursing was right for him. Working with a nurse in the health department helped Henry decide that public health nursing would be best for him. He was excited by how many different settings public health nurses work in and how many people they can reach and influence to lead healthier lives. Upon graduation and certification, Henry sought a public health nurse position at a hospital. After working at the hospital for 3 years, Henry accepted his position in the Lakeville County Health Department. Now Henry cannot imagine doing anything else!

Emerging Diseases, Emerging Problems

Prologue

In the mid-20th century, medical science seemed to have made tremendous advances against the scourges of infectious disease. Predictions were commonly made that infectious diseases would soon be relegated to science history as public health measures and technology seemed to eliminate the problems globally. Improved sanitation, effective mosquito control, an arsenal of antibiotics, and global vaccination appeared to ensure a world free from infectious afflictions.

Sadly, however, these predictions were premature. Infectious diseases today remain the major cause of death worldwide. They are also a leading cause of illness and death in the United States. Since the early 1970s, more than 30 diseases with symptoms never before described have appeared. These include acquired immune deficiency syndrome (AIDS), hepatitis C, Ebola hemorrhagic fever, encephalitis-related Nipah virus, and West Nile fever. More than 20 diseases once thought vanquished have been routinely reported worldwide. These include cholera, malaria, tuberculosis, and rabies. These new diseases are caused by a wide range of organisms including viruses, bacteria, fungi, protozoa, and helminthes (worms) (see Figure 3.31).

What are the origins of these so-called new diseases that are reported in the news with increasing regularity? Are they really new diseases caused by new pathogens? Or does a new set of circumstances allow a disease to appear in the population? Why are some diseases, once thought to have been conquered by modern medicine, reappearing in new, and sometimes even more virulent forms?

In this learning experience, you begin a research project in which you investigate in depth the circumstances, biological and social, that can result in the emergence or reemergence of a disease.

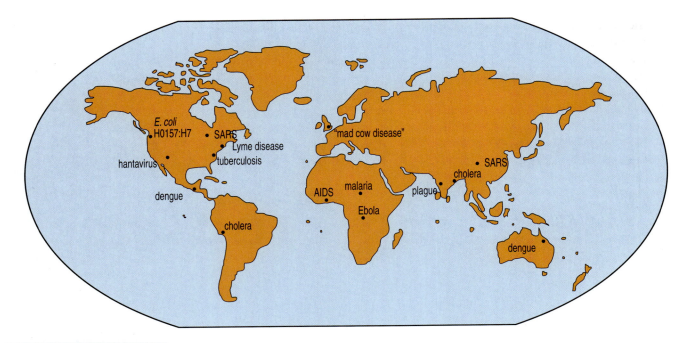

Figure 3.31

Examples of outbreaks of
emerging diseases worldwide.

Brainstorming

Discuss the following questions with your partner, and record your thinking in
your notebook. Be prepared to share your ideas with the class.

1. What new infectious diseases have you read or heard about?
2. Describe what you know about these diseases. Where did they happen?
   What caused them? How were they spread? What are their symptoms?
3. Do you think that diseases that emerge thousands of miles away from the
   United States should be of concern to the general public? to our scientists?
   to our government? Why or why not?

Diseases: New and Old

The emergence and reemergence of infectious diseases in the past three decades
is unprecedented in the annals of medicine. Much of the blame for this alarming
state of affairs rests squarely on the shoulders of humans and their activities.
Most of the causative agents of these new diseases are in themselves not new at
all. But rather, they have long been part of the animal world. Often they have
been found in regions of the world previously inaccessible to humans. Many
factors have contributed. These factors have created conditions that give
microorganisms already present in the environment a selective advantage. This
enables those microorganisms to jump from species to species and from human to
human, creating and spreading new diseases. These factors include the following:

- changes in climate that result in increased global warming, which results in
  increases in populations of microorganisms and their vectors;
- changes in ecological systems that provide new habitats for organisms, bring
  different organisms into direct contact, and increase the range of insects
  carrying disease;

- the development of previously inaccessible areas such as rain forests, bringing humans in contact with new species of animals and insects;
- changes in lifestyles that bring large numbers of people into cities where population growth outpaces the supplies of clean water and overextends the sanitation systems; and
- overuse of antibiotics and insecticides that once controlled populations of disease-carrying vectors, which has led to drug resistance in bacteria and insect populations.

Changes in the microorganisms or the vector that carries them can also result in the emergence of a new disease or reemergence of an old one. In 1978, for example, an epidemic of distemper in dogs was the result of a mutation in a virus that normally only infects cats. Mutations in *Mycobacterium tuberculosis,* the causative agent of tuberculosis, have resulted in resistance to a broad range of antibiotics. Tuberculosis has returned with a vengeance. New discoveries have revealed that certain diseases, once thought to be noninfectious, are actually caused by infectious agents. For example, the bacteria *Heliobacter pylori* have been identified as the causative agent of peptic ulcers. Certain infections *in utero* (in the womb) are caused by a parasite, *Toxoplasma gondii.* These infections can result in mental retardation.

In this research project, you and your partner will select an emerging or reemerging disease to investigate. You will need to apply the concepts that you have explored in this unit to understand the factors involved in the emergence or reemergence of this disease. At the end of the unit, you will present the findings of your research to the class. You will structure your presentation as a public health policy that you have developed for creating strategies to reduce the risk of future outbreaks of this disease.

You and your partner will be responsible for becoming experts in this disease. At this point, you may not have all the understandings and concepts required to address some of the issues relating to this disease. These will be acquired in the remainder of the unit and through your own research.

TASK

1. Decide on the disease you and your partner want to research. You may select from the list in the reading "Emerging and Reemerging Diseases," or you may pick another emerging or reemerging disease of your own choosing. The list provides a brief background on each disease.
2. Gather information on the epidemiology, environmental and social factors, and biological data of your disease. Use resources such as the library, Internet, public health policy groups, local health professionals, and national organizations such as the Centers for Disease Control and Prevention (CDC) and the National Institutes of Allergies and Infectious Diseases. When conducting research, look for information that will help you address the questions listed in Table 3.11. We do not know or understand everything about these infectious agents yet. So you may not find the answers to all of the questions in Table 3.11. If this is the case for your disease, explain in your presentation that certain data are unavailable, or have not yet been identified by the experts. Be aware that information about diseases and their agents changes continually. Today's facts are sometimes tomorrow's fiction due to new findings and discoveries in research.

Table 3.11 Questions for Research Project

Epidemiology

- When and where was this disease first recognized?
- Why is this disease considered emerging or reemerging?
- How many documented outbreaks have there been?
- What are the **mortality rates**? (How many individuals have died?)
- What are the **morbidity rates**? (How many individuals were taken ill?)
- What population has been affected by this disease?
- What characteristics did this population share that may have contributed to the outbreak? (Think about habits, travel, work, relationships, gender, cultural practices, etc.)
- What methods were used to trace the outbreak?
- Who has done the research? What is the story behind their research and investigation into the outbreak?

Environmental and Social Factors

- In what kind of environment did the disease first appear?
- Describe the communities that have been affected. Did any social customs, economic factors, or political difficulties take place or change that might have provided the pathogen with a new host or might have facilitated the spread of the disease? If so, explain what happened. How did these factors create an opportunity for the pathogen?
- Did any changes take place in medical practices? (Were there changes in drug use, new procedures, loss of health care facilities, or reduction in prevention programs, for example?)
- Did any changes take place in the local or global environment that might have caused new opportunities for the host/pathogen contact? (Think about deforestation, reforestation, drought, famine, global warming.) If so, explain what happened. How did these factors create an opportunity for the pathogen?

Biological Data

- Describe the mode of transmission of the disease. How was this determined?
- What is the nature of the causative agent (virus, bacteria, parasite)? How was this determined?
- Describe what is known about the biology of the pathogen. Where in the host does it grow? What requirements does it have to maintain its own life functions? How does it affect the host's ability to maintain its life functions? Which biological functions in the host does the pathogen disrupt?
- What characteristics of this pathogen enable it to enter a new host?
- What kind of immune response does this organism provoke in its host?
- What are the symptoms it produces? What is the biological basis of these symptoms?
- Is it related to other familiar or unfamiliar pathogens? Did any changes take place in the pathogen to cause this new or reemerging disease? (Think about changes in virulence, development of drug resistance, changes in tissue or host specificity.) If so, describe these changes. How did they contribute to the appearance of this disease?

3. Develop a public health policy. Once you have gathered your information, design a public health policy that proposes strategies for reducing the risk of future outbreaks. This policy must consist of strategies that are realistic. Take into account the biology of the infectious agent, the context of the local social conditions in which they are to be carried out, the living conditions, the economic status of the area, and the political situation. Also note any changes that are taking place in the area. For example, do not propose a high-cost solution to problems in a desperately poor developing nation. Do not try to change centuries-old social customs and habits. Instead, try to gain a perspective of the culture and economic situation in which this disease is happening.

   Your policy should include the following:
   - a brief description of the disease (include its epidemiology, the nature and biology of the causative agent, and the events that led to the outbreak in the area);
   - strategies for reducing the occurrence of this disease (such as developing programs for education in behaviors to reduce risk, implementing changes in sanitation infrastructure, expanding health care and public health services, developing vaccines or drugs, and developing programs to determine risks involved in certain environmental development programs; include an explanation of why these strategies would be effective); and
   - methods for identifying and containing future outbreaks should they happen (surveillance systems for the early detection, tracking, and control of the disease).

4. Prepare your presentation. The final presentation should take about 10 minutes and should include the following:
   - appropriate information and background materials on the disease;
   - a description of your public health policy, the rationale behind it, and an explanation of how it takes into account the specific social and economic conditions of the community in which the disease takes place; and
   - visual aids that enhance your presentation.

   The presentations will take place at the end of the unit. At the close of each presentation, your teacher will ask some follow-up questions. Then the class will discuss your public health policy proposal. Each presentation and follow-up discussion should take about 20 minutes.

5. Compare the emergence of the different diseases. As you listen to the other presentations, take notes on the following:

   - common themes that have been observed about emerging diseases;
   - how the problem of infectious diseases should be addressed in making public policy; and
   - what strategies could be put in place for anticipating the rise of new diseases.

   A discussion at the end of the presentations will address these issues.

EVALUATION

Your final presentation will serve as an assessment. The presentations will be evaluated by your teacher and fellow students on the following criteria:

- Have you gathered sufficient and appropriate information?
- Have you reached logical conclusions about your emerging or reemerging disease based on the information and ideas you have gathered?
- Does your presentation reflect insight and understanding of the reasons for the emergence or reemergence of the disease?
- Does your public policy proposal demonstrate knowledge about the local conditions at the site of the outbreak? Does it show a thoughtful and feasible response to those conditions? Does it reflect an understanding of the problems posed by the pathogen that you have been studying?
- Is the presentation organized, clear, and effective? Does the presentation engage the audience? Is the class interested in your topic?
- Can you respond concisely and clearly to questions from the audience?

READING

Topic: Emerging and
 Reemerging Diseases
Go to: www.scilinks.org
Code: INBIOH2406

Emerging and Reemerging Diseases

In this reading, we present brief descriptions of diseases that have been classified by the CDC as emerging or reemerging infectious diseases. These are diseases that have shown increased occurrence in humans within the past three decades. With your partner, read through the list and choose the disease that you would like to investigate. You may also select a disease of your own choosing. But you must confirm that this disease is considered emerging or reemerging and verify it with your teacher.

ACQUIRED IMMUNE DEFICIENCY SYNDROME (AIDS)

Caused by the human immunodeficiency virus (HIV), AIDS was first recognized as a new and distinct clinical disease in 1981. AIDS is thought to have originated when a virus was transmitted from African wild monkeys to humans by an as yet unknown mode of transmission. Initially, AIDS was identified as a disease of homosexual men. It now has developed into an increasing threat to all populations. AIDS is transmitted by sexual contact or by blood contact. Researchers estimate that more than 36 million persons are currently infected with the virus, with 16,000 new infections happening every day. Early infection with HIV shows no detectable symptoms. But because it grows in the white blood cells of the immune system, HIV makes the infected individual susceptible to a variety of rare and not-so-rare diseases. Since no cure or treatment is presently available, death is the inevitable outcome of infection. Death is generally caused by one of the diseases that result from a compromised immune system rather than directly by the virus.

HEMORRHAGIC FEVER

In 1976, a terrifying disease made its appearance in Zaire. It apparently materialized out of the rain forest from an unknown host. Caused by the Ebola virus, hemorrhagic fever is one of the deadliest and most contagious viral diseases known. Characterized by massive internal bleeding, it kills nine out of 10 individuals infected. The disease reappeared in Zaire in 1995. Since then, it has laid claim to lives in Sudan, the Ivory Coast, Uganda, and Gabon, killing more than 800 people. Epidemics of this disease have resulted from transmission by direct contact with infected individuals or laboratory monkeys. The most recent epidemic in Zaire was believed to be spread by the funeral practices of the people. Ebola virus spreads through the blood. It replicates in many organs, causing extensive damage, which results in bleeding, shock, and death. No cure or vaccine exists.

LYME DISEASE

Lyme disease was first described as a disease during an outbreak in Lyme, Connecticut, in 1975. It is now found in all 50 states, wherever deer and human populations live in close proximity. Caused by spirochete bacteria, it is transmitted from deer to humans by a tiny tick. In the earliest stages of the disease, the symptoms resemble the flu. These symptoms can include chills, fever, joint pain, and fatigue, accompanied by swollen **lymph nodes** nearest the bite. Left untreated, the bacteria move into other parts of the body, including the muscles, nerves, joints, and brain. Late-stage Lyme disease is debilitating. It causes severe arthritis, mental confusion, numbness of the arms and legs, and heart problems such as arrhythmia.

HEMORRHAGIC COLITIS (FAST-FOOD SYNDROME)

In 1993, children in the state of Washington were coming down with bloody diarrhea and severe abdominal cramping (hemorrhagic colitis). Since then, multiple outbreaks have taken place across the world. In 1996 alone, major outbreaks were reported in Germany and Scotland. The largest recognized outbreak, affecting approximately 5,000 persons, happened in Japan. The causative agent has been identified as *Escherichia coli* 0157:H7. Infection has most commonly been linked to eating undercooked beef such as hamburgers. Initially associated with foods served in fast-food restaurants, contaminated beef has begun to appear in supermarkets. The bacteria can also be transmitted through poor hygiene practices.

TUBERCULOSIS

Tuberculosis was one of the leading causes of death prior to the introduction of antibiotics in the 1940s. Also known as consumption and the great white plague, tuberculosis is caused by rod-shaped bacteria. Between 1953 and 1984, the number of new cases of tuberculosis dropped from 84,000 to 22,000. Public health workers foresaw the end of tuberculosis in the 21st century. But in 1985, the case rate began to increase at an alarming rate due to the appearance of multiple drug-resistant strains. Today, it ranks among the top 10 causes of death in the world. About one-third of the world's population is infected with *Mycobacterium tuberculosis*. Every year, approximately 8 million people develop the active disease and 2 million die. Tuberculosis is transmitted through droplets formed during coughing by infected individuals. The symptoms include fatigue, loss of weight and appetite, fever, and a persistent cough. If the disease is left untreated, death is common. A vaccine known as BCG confers some protection, but it is not readily available in the United States.

Toxic Shocklike Syndrome

Headlines such as "New Flesh-eating Bacteria Stalks Population" flashed across newspapers and tabloids in the early 1990s. Individuals who had suffered minor wounds or injuries were experiencing symptoms of severe invasive infections. These infections were causing extensive damage to soft tissue, and in many instances resulting in death. The infecting agent was identified as *Streptococcus pyogenes*. This pathogen has been long known as the causative agent of a childhood disease, scarlet fever. Scarlet fever, which is characterized by a diffuse rash and fever, had been a common disease prior to the 1950s. At that time, it virtually disappeared. This was most likely due to the use of penicillin to treat sore throats, which are also caused by *S. pyogenes*. In recent times, however, this pathogen appears to have returned with a vengeance. It appears first as a skin or wound infection. It then develops into bloodstream infections that send the patient into shock.

Malaria

Unlike many of these new infectious diseases, malaria has been around for many hundreds of years. It is caused by the parasitic protozoan plasmodium, which is transported by a mosquito vector. Malaria causes widespread disease and death in Africa and Asia. At various times in history, malaria was thought to be a conquered disease. Eradication of the vector brought relief to the United States and many parts of Asia. But malaria is back. Misuse of antibiotics and insecticides has resulted in drug-resistant strains of the parasite and insecticide-resistant mosquitoes. Malaria is on the rise, and the arsenal with which to combat it has diminished. Approximately 500 million of the world's people are afflicted with the disease. Each year, 1 to 1.5 million die, most of them children. Symptoms include fever, shivering, pain in the joints, and headache.

Bovine Spongiform Encephalopathy (Mad Cow Disease)

Bovine spongiform encephalopathy (BSE) became a significant problem in Great Britain in the early 1990s. It was at that time that this neurological disease began affecting significant numbers of cattle. An alarm was sounded in the mid-1990s when several young men and women in Great Britain died of a rare (particularly in young people) neurological disease. The disease affected the brain and spinal cord, causing spongelike lesions. Oddly enough, these symptoms resembled those found in cattle infected with BSE. The question was raised as to whether the infectious agent could be transmitted by ingesting contaminated beef. (This infectious agent is a somewhat mysterious agent called a **prion**, which appears to be made up entirely of protein.) The possibility of such an epidemic raised a serious threat both to the health of beef-eating individuals and to the British economy, which depends on the export of beef.

SEVERE ACUTE RESPIRATORY SYNDROME (SARS)

In November 2002, a new highly transmissible and lethal respiratory disease emerged from China. It traversed the globe, carried on the wings of international travel. Initial attempts to contain the disease failed. By 2003, outbreaks were being reported in Hong Kong, Singapore, Vietnam, and Canada. These outbreaks involved 8,100 cases and 774 deaths. SARS is caused by a virus. It is transmitted by close person-to-person contact through respiratory droplets produced when an infected person coughs or sneezes. The disease begins with a high fever followed by headache and body aches. Most patients develop pneumonia.

WEST NILE FEVER

Identified in 1937 in Uganda, West Nile fever first appeared in New York City in 1999 following a drought and heat wave. It disappeared until 2002. After a long, hot, dry summer, it reappeared in 44 states, infecting 4,161 and killing 284. The causative agent of the disease is West Nile virus. It is transmitted by mosquitoes that become infected when they feed on infected birds, the natural reservoir of the virus. Infected mosquitoes then spread the virus to humans and other animals during a meal of blood. While 80% of individuals infected show no symptoms, serious neurological effects happen in about 1 in 150 infected people. These symptoms can include high fever, headache, neck stiffness, stupor, disorientation, coma, tremors, convulsions, muscle weakness, vision loss, numbness, and paralysis. These symptoms may last several weeks, and the neurological effects may be permanent. The remaining individuals infected will display milder symptoms. These include fever, headache, body aches, nausea, vomiting, and sometimes swollen lymph glands or a skin rash on the chest, stomach, and back.

Behold the Conquering Pathogen

READING

Despite all the technological and medical advances made in the 20th century, today's physicians, policymakers, and scientists sometimes find themselves in a position reminiscent of the one John Snow found himself in, back in 1854. In the last 30 years, medical researchers and physicians have been confronted with unfamiliar and sometimes terrifying diseases.

David Satcher is former director of the CDC in Atlanta and was Surgeon General under President Clinton. In the following article, he describes some of the lessons and challenges that emerging and reemerging diseases present. Use this article and the Analysis questions that follow as a guide to thinking about your own research and in planning your policy and presentation.

LESSONS AND CHALLENGES OF EMERGING AND REEMERGING INFECTIOUS DISEASES

David Satcher, *ASM News*. vol. 62, No. 2, 1996

In 1821 . . . Americans had an average life span of well under 50 years, and the vast majority of deaths were due to infectious diseases. In the first half of the 19th century, problems such as malaria, yellow fever, and cholera were present even in the mid-Atlantic states, and respiratory diseases such as diphtheria, pneumonia, and rheumatic fever were the routine killers of children and adults. Even at the turn of this century, infectious diseases remained the leading cause of death, with tuberculosis leading the entire list in the United States.

Now that is no longer the case. Over the course of the 20th century we have made tremendous progress in our efforts to control infectious diseases. Perhaps the best-known accomplishment in this area is the eradication of smallpox, with the last case occurring in Somalia in 1977. Smallpox thus became the first disease in history to be completely eradicated from the world. As a result, millions of people around the planet will no longer needlessly suffer a painful death and disability from this dreaded disease.

Following on the heels of the smallpox success, polio is well on its way to eradication. Over a period of only 40 years, we have gone from a situation in which millions of children were stricken with this terrible disease every year to the recent certification of the western hemisphere as free of polio.

Major advances have also occurred on a number of other fronts; the number of measles cases in the United States reached a historic low in 1994, and *Haemophilus influenzae type B* disease is rapidly fading as a leading cause of childhood meningitis and sepsis as a result of introduction of conjugate vaccines in the late 1980s.

These spectacular successes have occurred for a number of reasons, including improvements in the standard of living (including basic sanitation and hygienic measures), the development and introduction of vaccines, and the development and introduction of antibiotics.

These successes have taught us some important lessons. First, combating disease requires a strong collaborative effort between the basic sciences, clinical medicines, and public health. Polio provides an example: basic scientists developed vaccines to protect against disease; clinicians diagnosed disease, cared for patients, and delivered vaccines; and public health implemented vaccination campaigns and monitored for the occurrence of cases. None of these entities can perform alone and expect success. The second lesson is that when we put our minds to it, we can achieve spectacular results in the area of infectious disease control and prevention.

Not so many years ago, many of the best scientific and public policy minds in the country were ready to close the book on infectious diseases. Essentially we were victims of the very successes that I just mentioned. These experts believed that our vaccines and antibiotics would solve all of our problems and we could easily control any new problem that arose. As events of recent years have shown, these pronouncements were premature.

In the 1990s, infectious diseases account for more than 50% of deaths throughout the world, and we are increasingly faced with new and reemerging disease challenges. Examples of these threats include the worldwide AIDS epidemic, which is now 15 years old and growing; the resurgence of tuberculosis in the late 1980s; the new hantavirus first detected in the southwestern United States in 1993; the 1994 epidemic of plague in India; diphtheria sweeping across the former Soviet Union; a new cholera strain in south Asia; and the frightening reemergence, for the first time since 1979, of Ebola virus last year [1995] in Zaire.

Virtually every year brings information on a newly recognized pathogen, such as the herpes virus responsible for Kaposi's sarcoma and the morbillivirus, which killed horses and their trainer in Australia. Compounding the problem, our microbial foes have developed an amazing capacity to resist our control efforts, particularly through the development of drug resistance, and we are helping them by injudiciously prescribing and taking antibiotics. Probably more than anything else, emerging antibiotic resistance threatens to reverse many of the hard-fought gains made in the control of infectious diseases in the last century.

Why is this happening? There are many factors responsible for the resurgence of infectious diseases, including human behaviors, and demographic changes, technologic and industrial advances, changes in the environment, international commerce and travel, and a breakdown of public health control measures.

LESSONS FROM EMERGING AND REEMERGING DISEASES

We have learned and are learning several lessons from emerging and reemerging disease. First, we must never take for granted the adaptability of the microbial and parasitic coinhabitants of this planet with whom we compete for space and resources, including food. Just as we have the ability to create new weapons such as vaccines and antibiotics and pesticides, these coinhabitants have demonstrated the ability to develop new defenses, new pathways, and new armamentaria [inventory of resources] for survival and growth. We see it in the drug-resistant *Streptococcus pneumoniae* organisms or the enterococci. We see it in the drug-resistant malaria that is now ravaging parts of Africa. This ability to survive, to change, and to grow is a major force of our coinhabitants that we cannot afford to underestimate.

Second, just as human behavior, demographics, and lifestyles have been shown to be major factors in chronic disease epidemiology, it is increasingly clear that they are major factors in emerging and reemerging infectious disease. Examples include antimicrobial misuse and resistance, the role of sexual behavior in AIDS transmission, the role of cooking practices in *Escherichia coli* O157:H7 transmission, the role of funeral practices in the spread of Ebola virus in Africa, and the role of human-rodent interaction in many parts of the world in supporting diseases such as the plague in India or the hantavirus in the southwest.

The third lesson is that progress in modern technology and changes in ecology and land use often bring with them unintended and undesirable consequences. Examples include the invasion of the rain forest in South America and Africa and the appearance of new viruses such as Bolivian hemorrhagic fever virus, Guanarito virus, and Ebola virus and air handling systems, and the emergence of Legionnaires' disease.

The fourth lesson is that increasingly we live in a global community and public health, in order to be effective, must be global in nature and outlook. We are today less than 24 h [hours] away from almost any community in the world, and people who encounter an infectious disease agent in one part of the world today may be in a totally different part of the world tomorrow. We must remember that viruses, bacteria, and parasites do not need visas to cross borders and they even occasionally ride first class.

The last lesson is that prevention of infectious diseases makes economic sense in addition to medical sense. A dose of measles vaccine saves $17 [for each dollar spent on treatment] in health-care expenses. Once polio is eradicated, it is estimated that the global savings will be >$1.5 billion per year. And in the mid-1980s we estimated it would take about $40 million in federal expenditures to eradicate tuberculosis from the United States. Now we are spending over $100 million annually as a result of its resurgence and the emergence of multiresistant forms. As is true of most medical problems, prevention of infectious disease pays.

If we keep these lessons from emerging infections in mind, they will serve us well in years ahead as we attempt to be a healthier people in a healthier world through prevention.

ANALYSIS

Record your responses to the following in your notebook.

1. What is meant by a new or emerging disease? Where might a new disease come from?

2. Describe some of the biological, social, political, and economic issues that might be involved in the emergence or reemergence of a disease.

3. Many social and economic endeavors have unintentionally resulted in the emergence of infectious diseases. In 1960, for example, the Aswan Dam was constructed in Egypt to control flooding of the Nile. It was also built to store water for times of drought and to provide much needed hydroelectric power. However, an unforeseen result of this endeavor was a change in the ecology of the area. This change resulted in epidemics of yellow fever and schistosomiasis. Another example occurred when the Peace Corps introduced water pumps in African villages. These pumps created new breeding grounds for mosquitoes that resulted in new outbreaks of malaria. What do you think is the trade-off between progress and disease happening in an area? Do you need more information to decide? If so, what kind of information will help you? What should designers of major projects such as the Aswan Dam take into consideration as they design projects that may change the ecology in an area? What information might be needed to predict such an outbreak?

EXTENDING *Ideas*

▶ Chronic fatigue syndrome (CFS) is a disorder characterized by profound tiredness and weakness. Patients with CFS become exhausted after mild physical exertion and are often unable to conduct the routine tasks of life. This has been a difficult illness to diagnose since incapacitating fatigue is associated with a wide range of well-defined diseases. But CFS was officially given disease status in 1988. It occurs most often in white women between the ages of 25 and 45. The cause of the disease has not been determined. No evidence exists that CFS is communicable through person-to-person contact, or even that it is a communicable disease. But numerous lines of research have implicated the possible involvement of several well-characterized viruses. Research CFS. Find out its clinical aspects, demographics, and possible causes. Then decide whether you think CFS is an infectious disease. Support your decision with evidence from your research.

Learning Experience 10

Viral Hitchhiker

Prologue

Someone who is sick will often say that she "caught a bug" or "picked up a germ" somewhere. As you explored in Learning Experience 3, Agents of Disease, the infection can be caused by bacteria, viruses, or parasites. These infectious agents are known to infect and cause disease in every kind of organism. Even these infectious agents can have infectious agents that disrupt their life functions. In other words, even bugs can get bugs.

No one with a runny nose or an upset stomach is likely to care whether the infection is bacterial, viral, or parasitic. They just want the symptoms to go away. In reality, though, there are huge differences among these organisms. And why you are getting sick is, in part, a reflection of these differences. As you have discovered in previous learning experiences, bacteria can cause symptoms inadvertently with the by-products of their metabolism. Viruses cause symptoms, in part, because of their total dependence on the host's cellular machinery.

In the next three learning experiences, you investigate the effects of viruses on their hosts. You also examine how these effects can result in disease in the hosts. This learning experience provides two alternative investigations for exploring viral infections. In Experiment 1, you design an experiment to determine the effects of tobacco mosaic virus on plants. In Experiment 2, you examine the effects of a bacterial virus (bacteriophage) on bacteria. Your teacher will tell you which experiment to carry out.

Topic: Virus
Go to: www.scilinks.org
Code: INBIOH2413

Brainstorming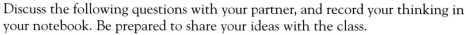

Discuss the following questions with your partner, and record your thinking in your notebook. Be prepared to share your ideas with the class.

1. What diseases have you or anyone you know had that were caused by a virus? How do you know these diseases were viral as opposed to bacterial or parasitic?
2. Describe the symptoms of any of these diseases.
3. How do viruses differ from bacteria and parasites?

4. Describe the structure of a bacteriophage. Use your understanding of viruses from Learning Experience 3.
5. What do prokaryotic and eukaryotic cells have in common that make them both susceptible to infections by viruses?

Experiment 1

READING

Invasion of the Cell Snatchers: A First Look (Experiment 1)

In the late 1800s, the tobacco crop in Russia was being destroyed by a disease that left the plants mottled and spotted. The leaves of afflicted plants looked like a mosaic of light- and dark-green areas. In 1892, a Russian biologist, Dimitri Ivanovsky, carried out experiments to determine the cause of the blight.

The existence of bacteria as causative agents of disease had already been determined by Louis Pasteur and Robert Koch. Pasteur had developed a technique for isolating bacteria and determining whether they were able to cause disease. He tested infectious fluids by passing them through a filter. Pasteur checked to see if the material that was retained on the filter was able to cause infection but the **filtrate** (the liquid that passed through the filter) was not. If this were found, the presence of a bacterial agent of infection in the original fluid was indicated.

Ivanovsky applied Pasteur's technique. But he used an infectious extract from tobacco plants suffering from the mottling disease. To his surprise, he found that the filtrate rather than the material retained on the filter was fully infectious when applied to healthy plants (see Figure 3.32). Because the filtrate was able to satisfy Koch's Postulates (recall from Learning Experience 3), it must have contained an infectious agent. Up until this experiment, all known infectious agents were too large to pass through a filter. This observation led to the recognition of the existence of a whole new class of infectious agents. These agents were much smaller than any previously known organisms.

The actual nature of the causative agent remained a mystery until 1935. It was then that advances in technology made it possible for Wendell Stanley, an American biologist, to isolate and identify the cause of the mottling disease. He squeezed the juice from 2,000 pounds of tobacco leaves. From this juice, he extracted a residue that could be purified to form pure needlelike crystals. When the crystalline form was dissolved and applied to tobacco leaves, it could cause disease. The particles were named tobacco mosaic virus (TMV). Later tests showed TMV to be rod-shaped particles composed of more than 2,000 identical protein molecules. These molecules formed a coat around a core of RNA.

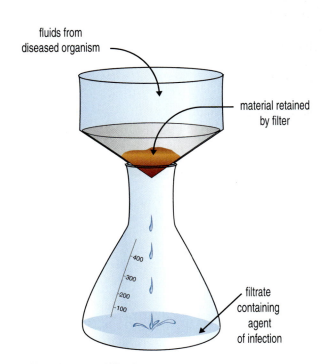

fluids from diseased organism

material retained by filter

filtrate containing agent of infection

Figure 3.32

Isolating the causative agent from infected tobacco plants.

ANALYSIS

Record your responses to the following in your notebook.

1. How did Ivanovsky apply Koch's Postulates to prove that the disease in tobacco plants was caused by an infectious agent (recall Learning Experience 3)?
2. Why were Ivanovsky's results an unexpected outcome at that time?
3. What was the significance of Ivanovsky's discovery to the study of infectious disease?

A Pox (or TMV) upon Your Plant (Experiment 1)

ACTIVITY

What happens to a plant when it is infected by a virus? In fact, what happens when any organism is infected by a virus? After Wendell Stanley isolated TMV, he dissolved the crystalline form, applied it to tobacco leaves, and found that it could cause disease. TMV, which is found worldwide, can infect more than 150 kinds of **dicotyledonous plants**. (These plants include tobacco, tomato, begonia, pea, bean, and petunia.) The virus is very stable. It can survive in dried, infected plant material (such as cigarettes, cigars, and chewing tobacco) for many years.

The symptoms caused by TMV can be either **systemic** or **localized**. In a systemic infection, the virus spreads throughout the plant. This causes the plant to have the mottled, mosaic effect observed by Ivanovsky with the leaves becoming a patchwork of light- and dark-green areas. In addition, the leaves are stunted in growth and parts of the plant may be distorted. In other cases, the infection may be localized. The virus remains at the site of infection in small necrotic lesions (areas of tissue breakdown). In a localized infection, the virus does not spread throughout the plant. None of the systemic symptoms are observed. The kind of infection that takes place depends on the kind of plant that is infected.

In this activity, you will design an experiment to study infection in a plant. You can use any of the materials provided.

Materials

For each group of four students:

- 4 pairs of safety goggles
- 2 tobacco or tomato plants, 4–6 weeks old
- 2 pinto bean plants, 2–3 weeks old
- 1 mortar and pestle
- 0.1 M dibasic potassium phosphate buffer, 10 mL
- 1 emery board
- 2–4 cotton swabs
- 1 test tube
- 4 eyedroppers
- 1 graduated cylinder or pipette (5–10 mL)
- 1 small cup

For the class:

- tobacco from several different brands of cigarettes
- additional dicotyledonous plants (petunia, geranium, etc.)
- monocotyledonous plants (corn, different grasses, irises, etc.)
- 500 mL distilled water
- access to a gram scale
- 1 graduated beaker or measuring cup (500-mL)
- access to a heat source
- soap or detergent
- 1 L (1 qt) household chlorine bleach
- spray bottles (atomizers)
- stock of pure tobacco mosaic virus (optional)

PROCEDURE

1. Formulate a question about the disease-causing capacity of TMV based on the readings and on the following information:
   a. TMV can be found in cigarettes. The amount may vary according to brand.
   b. TMV will infect certain kinds of plants but not others.
   c. TMV will cause one type of symptoms in some kinds of plants and other kinds of symptoms in different kinds of plants.
   d. TMV cannot enter plants directly through the leaf. To infect the plant via the leaf, the leaf must be abraded (rubbed gently with an emery board).
2. Discuss with your group what you would like to find out about TMV in plants. Agree on 1 specific question you want to try to answer by conducting an experiment. Write down your question and discuss it with your teacher.
3. Propose a hypothesis based on what you know so far about TMV.
4. Design an experiment that would address this question and that you can carry out using materials from the materials list. Outline the specific steps in the procedure that you will use in your experiment. Carefully think through the order in which you will carry out your experiment. You should take note of the following procedural techniques:
   a. If you are using tobacco from a cigarette, it will need to be ground into a slurry, or solution. Place 2 pinches of tobacco in the mortar. Measure 5 mL of buffer in a graduated cylinder. Pour the buffer into the mortar. Grind the mixture with the pestle until it is a fine slurry. Use as needed in your experiment.
   b. When using the emery board on a leaf, gently abrade (scrape) the surface of each leaf you want to infect. If you infect a plant in more than 1 location, note the position of each leaf on the plant and the age of the leaf. You may do this by sketching a picture in your notebook and labeling it appropriately.
   c. Use a cotton swab dipped in the slurry to infect the abraded leaves of the plants. After inoculating the leaves, gently rinse the leaves by running water over them using an eyedropper. Have a cup under the leaf to catch the rinse water.
   d. Be sure to include a negative control (and a positive control, if possible) in your experimental design.

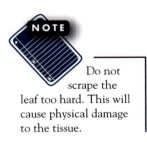
Do not scrape the leaf too hard. This will cause physical damage to the tissue.

5. Indicate how you will collect and record the following data and observations:
   a. the appearance of the plant and leaves on any control plants;
   b. the appearance of the plant and leaves on the experimental (infected) plants;
   c. when symptoms of the disease first appeared on each plant;
   d. the severity of symptoms during the incubation period for each leaf;
   e. the total number of leaves infected and the degree of infection;
   f. how the experimental plants compared to one another in terms of symptoms;
   g. location of infection, rate of the appearance of symptoms, severity of symptoms; and
   h. any other differences or similarities that you have observed.
6. Show your procedure to your teacher before starting your experiment.
7. Collect materials for your group. Set up your experiment. Be sure to label your experimental and control plants clearly.
8. Place the plants in a sunny or well-lit area for 5–7 days. Observe your plants and record your observations every day. Set up a data chart to describe the condition of leaves and plants.

SAFETY NOTE Always wash your hands thoroughly with soap and water after handling tobacco or infected plants to avoid inadvertent contamination of plants with TMV.

ANALYSIS

Record your responses to the following in your notebook.

1. Analyze your data with your group. Discuss the meaning of the results and the conclusions that you can draw from them. (Be sure to take notes on the group discussion to use in writing your laboratory report.)
2. Plan your presentation. Include in your planning, individual responsibility for preparing any illustrations, graphs, and text to be used in the presentation. The presentation should include the following:
   a. the project title;
   b. the names of the research group members;
   c. the question that your group asked;
   d. a clearly summarized procedure;
   e. the data clearly presented, including graphs or tables where appropriate, and at least one diagram (a series of diagrams showing the changes you observed is preferable);
   f. a summary of your conclusions;
   g. the most significant information that you wish to share with the other groups; and
   h. any unanswered questions, new questions, and at least three suggestions for further study.
3. Write your own individual report. Include the following:
   a. the question being asked,
   b. the hypothesis,
   c. the design of the experiment,
   d. the procedure,
   e. the data and observations,
   f. the conclusions from the data,
   g. a discussion of whether the data answered the question (and if not, why not),
   h. any sources of possible error, and
   i. any new questions that arose as a result of this experiment.

Invasion of the Cell Snatchers: A Second Look (Experiments 1 and 2)

Many viruses have been identified since the discovery of TMV (Experiment 1) and bacteriophages (Experiment 2). Viruses come in a wide variety of shapes and sizes (see Figure 3.33). Most viruses are hundreds of times smaller than bacteria or eukaryotic cells. Viruses are essentially genetic material wrapped up in a protein. They lack the cellular machinery required to carry out the basic life processes for growth, reproduction, and response to stimuli. Many viruses carry no enzymes to replicate their genetic material or transcribe nucleic acid into mRNA. None have the protein synthesis machinery (ribosomes, tRNAs) to translate this information into protein. Viruses are inert until they enter a host cell. Here they come to life by redirecting the host's cellular machinery to make multiple copies of the virus.

The genetic material of a virus can be either DNA or RNA. Viruses that have DNA as their genetic material include the causative agents of smallpox, chickenpox, and mononucleosis. In general, we tend to think of the genetic material as DNA. But many viruses (such as poliovirus and influenza virus) have RNA as genetic material. Since the genetic material of a virus is generally small, it can encode only a small number of proteins. Generally, these proteins are those that make up the viral coat and enzymes that enable the virus to reproduce.

The proteins in the coat of the virus protect the viral genetic material outside of the host cell. These proteins also assist viral entry into the cell. Each virus has a unique set of proteins that interacts with surface molecules, usually proteins, on the membranes of the host cell. The viral proteins (like keys in a lock), enable the virus to gain entry into the host by binding to the host protein, or **receptor**.

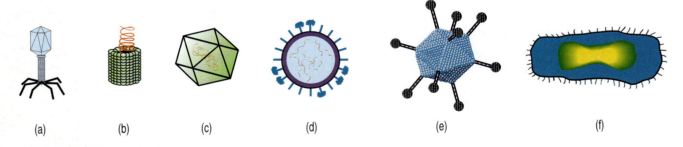

(a) (b) (c) (d) (e) (f)

Figure 3.33

Examples of various viruses. (a) T4 bacteriophage infects bacteria and contains DNA; (b) tobacco mosaic virus (TMV) infects plants and contains RNA; (c) poliovirus contains RNA and causes polio in humans; (d) influenza virus contains eight RNA segments and infects a variety of animals; (e) adenovirus is a DNA-containing virus that causes colds in humans; (f) vaccinia virus infects animals, contains DNA, and is a close relative of the smallpox virus.

In some cases, the proteins on the surface of the virus are very specific for binding. These proteins only permit the virus to infect certain types of plant, animal, or bacterial cells. For example, poliovirus will only infect human and monkey cells. In other cases, the viruses can infect a wide variety of cell types. Influenza virus can infect humans, pigs, and ducks.

The following list describes the steps involved in a viral infection. These steps are correlated to the numbers in Figure 3.34.

1. A virus attaches to an appropriate cell type.
2. The virus, or its genetic material, enters the cell. If the whole virus enters, the protein coat is removed to expose the genetic material.
3. a. The information in the viral genetic material is read and translated into viral protein. These proteins may include enzymes specific for making more viral nucleic acid and viral enzymes (for example, a viral DNA or RNA polymerase). These proteins may also include structural proteins used to assemble new viruses.
   b. Many copies of viral nucleic acid are made. Anywhere from hundreds to thousands of copies are made in each infected cell.
4. Viral structural proteins assemble around each copy of the nucleic acid. This forms a new virus.
5. The new viruses formed from the original infecting virus are released from the infected cell. These viruses attack new cells and repeat the process. Viruses escape the cell either by bursting (**lysing**) the cell or by "budding" out of the cell membrane.

For a time, viruses were thought to be the smallest infectious agent. During the 1980s, however, an even smaller disease-causing agent called a prion was identified. The nature of prions remains a mystery. But they seem to be agents of deadly diseases of the central nervous system. These diseases include Creutzfeldt-Jakob disease and Kuru, which cause dementia and death

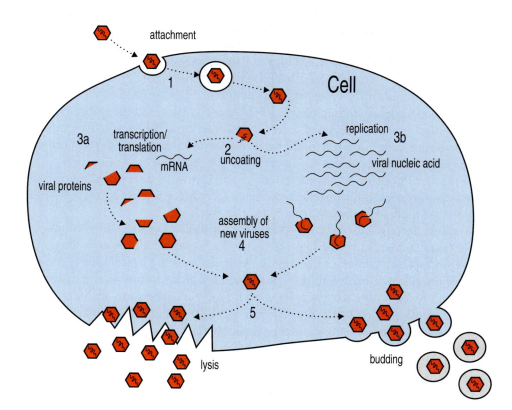

Figure 3.34

Steps involved in a viral infection.

in humans, and bovine spongiform encephalopathy or mad cow disease, which appeared as an epidemic in cattle in Great Britain in the early 1990s. Surprisingly, prions seem to be entirely protein, with no detectable nucleic acid. How they infect, replicate, and cause disease is the subject of investigation in many laboratories.

 **ANALYSIS**

Record your responses to the following in your notebook.

1. To survive, all organisms must have the capacity to grow and reproduce. What are the difficulties that confront a virus in carrying out these life processes?
2. How does a virus make more of its nucleic acid and more protein? Where does it get the enzymes, cellular machinery, and building blocks to carry out these processes?
3. The proteins found in the coat of viruses interact with proteins on the surface of their host cell. Describe how this interaction might make it possible for a virus to infect only certain kinds of cells. Use your understanding of protein binding. Use words and/or diagrams to explain.
4. Viruses are often referred to as "nonliving." Do you agree or disagree with that statement? Explain your answer.

 READING

To the Eater of the Spoiled, Belongs the Disease (Experiment 1)

Salmonella are medically important bacteria that are responsible for two different diseases in humans. These bacteria are transmitted by improper handling procedures during food preparation and/or poor sanitation. One species, *Salmonella typhimurium*, causes a self-limiting, localized infection. It is one of the most common causes of food-borne infections. When a human ingests this pathogen in contaminated food or water, a localized infection takes place in the gastrointestinal tract of the unlucky diner. Symptoms of food poisoning include nausea, vomiting, localized lesions in the intestine, abdominal pain, and diarrhea. Symptoms usually appear 6–24 hours after ingestion of the contaminated food and may last from a day to a week.

The other species, *Salmonella typhi*, causes an invasive, systemic infection. Typhoid fever is the result. The bacteria enter the bloodstream through the intestine and spread throughout the body. After multiplying in the spleen and liver, they are released back into the bloodstream. The symptoms of the disease include high fever, a flushed appearance, and anorexia, sometimes accompanied by chills, convulsions, and delirium. If left untreated, typhoid fever can be fatal.

Why does *S. typhimurium* remain a localized infection and *S. typhi* invade the intestinal wall and enter the bloodstream to become a systemic disease? We don't know the answer at this time. But we do know that the most virulent *S. typhi* strains produce a polysaccharide capsule. What role this capsule plays in the ability of the bacteria to invade systemically remains a question.

Interestingly, when mice are infected with the less severe *S. typhimurium*, it causes a systemic infection in the mice that resembles typhoid fever in humans. In contrast, *S. typhi*, which causes typhoid fever in humans, does not even infect mice.

ANALYSIS

Record your responses to the following in your notebook.

In a short essay, compare localized and systemic infections of different hosts and different strains as exemplified by the diseases caused by tobacco mosaic virus and salmonella. Use diagrams or tables where helpful. In your discussion, include the importance of the type of host and type of infecting agent in determining whether the disease will be systemic or localized. Propose a model or hypothesis based on your understanding of bacteria and viruses. Think about how they infect organisms as to the factors that might determine whether an infection is systemic or local.

Experiment 2

Invasion of the Cell Snatchers: A First Look (Experiment 2)

READING

Viruses that infect bacteria were discovered at the beginning of the 20th century. In 1915, Felix d'Herelle, a Canadian scientist, was investigating an epidemic of dysentery. Dysentery is a disease caused by shigella bacteria. He grew bacteria from the feces of infected individuals on agar plates to isolate them. As he carried out his experiments, d'Herelle observed that sometimes he saw clear, circular spots where no bacteria grew. He called these spots plaques. He determined that the cause of these plaques were viruses that infected bacteria and killed them. He named these viruses bacteriophages, or bacteria-eating agents. Unknown to d'Herelle, at the same time Frederick W. Twort, working in London, had also identified a virus that was capable of killing bacteria. Generally, both men share the credit for this important discovery.

One of the questions d'Herelle pursued in his work was whether a bacteriophage could be used as a treatment for bacterial diseases in humans. In the 1920s, researchers pursued this form of therapy as an important possibility. Despite hundreds of reports in scientific literature, however, this form of treatment failed to be effective in treating bacterial infections.

Despite this failure, d'Herelle and Twort's discovery led to a revolution in the biological sciences. By examining the processes involved in bacteriophage infection, scientists were able to formulate an entirely new approach to studying life processes at the molecular level. Research on bacteriophages led to fundamental understandings of DNA, transcription, and protein synthesis. Bacteriophages provided the tools for understanding how genetic information is stored, how it is expressed, how it changes, and how it is passed on to succeeding generations.

ANALYSIS

Record your responses to the following in your notebook.

1. Why do you think that d'Herelle thought that bacteriophages could be used as a treatment for bacterial infections?
2. Was it a concern that the bacteriophage might infect human cells?

ACTIVITY

Even My Bugs Have Bugs (Experiment 2)

What happens to bacteria when they are infected by a bacteriophage? In this activity, you will determine the effects of viruses on bacteria.

Materials

For each group of four students:

- 3 test tubes (13 × 100 mm)
- 3 agar plates
- 3 pipettes with 0.1-mL gradations
- 1 pipette with 5-mL gradations
- 1 wax marking pencil

For the class:

- 500 mL tryptone broth
- 100–150 mL tryptone soft agar overlay
- 37° C (98.6° F) incubator
- access to a heat source
- 1 thermometer
- 500 mL nutrient agar
- 1 L (1 qt) household bleach
- 1 set of diluted bacteriophage
- 10 mL overnight growth of *E. coli* B

SAFETY NOTE

PROCEDURE

1. Use a wax marking pencil to label 3 test tubes "0," "10^{-6}," and "10^{-10}." Label 3 agar plates the same way. Also label the plates with your group name.
2. Obtain a sample of the *E. coli* overnight growth culture from your teacher. Add 0.1 mL of the culture to each of the 3 test tubes.
3. Add solutions to the 3 test tubes as follows:
   a. Add 0.1 mL tryptone broth to the tube labeled 0.
   b. Add 0.1 mL of the 10^{-6} bacteriophage dilution to the tube labeled 10^{-6}.
   c. Add 0.1 mL of the 10^{-10} bacteriophage dilution to the tube labeled 10^{-10}.
4. Add 5.0 mL of soft agar overlay to each tube. Mix well. (The overlay should be no warmer than 45°C [113°F].)

5. Pour the contents of each tube into the appropriate agar plates. Tilt the plates gently back and forth and side to side to cover the plate completely with the agar. Replace covers on each plate.
6. Place the plates right side up on a flat table. Allow the agar overlay to harden. Invert each plate. Place in a 37°C incubator and leave overnight.
7. After 24 hours, remove your group's plates from the incubator. Examine them carefully. Describe the appearance of each in your notebook.

ANALYSIS

Discuss the following questions with your group. Record your responses in your notebook in preparation for a class discussion.

1. Describe what has happened on your plates. What differences do you observe from plate to plate? Why do you think there are differences?
2. What was the purpose of the sample to which only broth with the bacteria was added? What do you think has happened on an uninfected plate? on the other plates?
3. Why do you think that plaques appear as clear zones or holes? How has the bacteriophage affected the growth of the bacteria?
4. Say an infectious agent kills every host cell available. What would happen then to the infectious agent?
5. Why do you think attempts to use bacteriophages for therapy might have failed?
6. Why would bacteriophages be important tools for studying fundamental life processes in living organisms? Why might they prove better to work with than animal or plant viruses?
7. In words or drawings, describe the steps of infection of the bacteria by the bacteriophage that led to the result you have observed. Be sure to include each step of what the bacteriophage is doing and what is happening to the host cells.
8. Use your data and information from the class discussion to write your own individual report. Include the following:
   a. the question being asked,
   b. the hypothesis,
   c. the design of the experiment,
   d. the procedure,
   e. the data and observations,
   f. the conclusions from the data,
   g. a discussion of whether the data answered the question (and if not, why not),
   h. any sources of possible error, and
   i. any new questions that arose as a result of this experiment.

At this time, read "Invasion of the Cell Snatchers: A Second Look" (Experiments 1 and 2) on page 418. Complete the four Analysis questions that follow the reading.

Kuru is a slow, fatal infection of the nervous system that has only been seen in natives of the New Guinea Highlands. It appears to be the result of the practice of cannibalism during funeral rites. Symptoms include the loss of mental ability, speech and vision problems, and paralysis. But these symptoms may not appear for 30 years or more after contact. These symptoms are very similar to those of Creuzfeldt-Jakob disease in humans and bovine spongiform encephalopathy (BSE or mad cow disease). Prions have been implicated as the causative agent in all of these diseases. Research prions; describe their biology and mode of transmission. How do they reproduce themselves with no apparent nucleic acid as part of their makeup?

In some people, *Salmonella typhi* hides out in the gallbladder. These people can shed bacteria in their feces for years without showing any symptoms of the disease. Such chronic carriers cause major public health problems, especially when they are employed as food handlers. The classic case of a chronic carrier took place in the early 1900s. By tracing a number of typhoid cases back to their probable source, health officials first identified Mary Mallon. Mallon, a professional cook in New York City, was a carrier who had caused several outbreaks. She came to be known as "Typhoid Mary." Mallon was offered a gallbladder operation as a way of eliminating the source of the bacteria. (Antibiotics had not yet been discovered. So an operation was the only feasible solution to resolving her carrier state.) When she refused the operation, she was imprisoned for 3 years. She was then released, after promising not to cook for others. Apparently, she did not take the allegations about her carrier state very seriously, because she changed her name and resumed her profession as a cook. She was subsequently employed by hotels, restaurants, and hospitals, and managed to spread typhoid fever to many more people before she was finally apprehended. After her second apprehension, she was imprisoned again. This time she was imprisoned for 23 years, until her death in 1938. The identification and quarantine of individuals infected with contagious diseases has led to much discussion and controversy. Legislation has been proposed barring immigration by individuals known to carry the human immunodeficiency virus (HIV), the causative agent of AIDS. Outbreaks of pneumonic plague in 1994 led to restrictions on international travel in and out of India. In an essay, discuss the moral and legal implications of such identification of and restrictions on individuals carrying contagious diseases.

Read the following excerpt:

Salmonella has served many purposes. It has been used as a model organism for studying bacterial metabolism and genetics and bacterial virulence. As a major cause of food-borne disease, it serves as an indicator of how safe a country's food and water supplies are. It is also the basis for many of the new oral vaccines. And now, believe it or not, someone has come up with a new use for Salmonella—as a means for honoring an admired public figure. Shortly after Michael Jordan announced his intended retirement from basketball, Dr. Stanford Shulman, Chief of Infectious Diseases at a Chicago, Illinois hospital revealed to the press that he was naming a new strain of Salmonella after Michael Jordan: Salmonella mjordan. We will probably never know whether Michael Jordan, in his heart of hearts, felt honored or otherwise by having a strain of diarrhea-causing bacteria named after him (would you?). One wonders how Mr. Jordan will represent this honor in his trophy room (if he has one), and how it will be handled by the Basketball Hall of Fame. Just keep it far away from the snack bar, guys.

From *Bacterial Pathogenesis: A Molecular Approach* by Abigail A. Salyers and Dixie D. Whitt, ASM Press, 1994, p. 230

How might you react if you were being "honored" by having some dreadful disease named after you? Why would you react this way?

Diseases that affect plants have had a profound impact on human lives. When crops that normally sustain populations are destroyed by epidemics of disease, famines are often the result. In 1733, 12,000 people on an island in Japan perished when rice stunt, a viral disease of rice, destroyed the crop. A fungal blight of potatoes in 1845 and 1846 decimated this primary staple food of the Irish people. The blight caused a million deaths and a mass emigration of 1.5 million people, many of them to the United States. In 1942, a fungal disease of rice in Bengal caused the deaths of 2 million people. Research one of these famines or another famine caused by a plant disease. Describe the characteristics of the infectious agent and the effect on the plants. Explore the social and economic ramifications of the disease on the population.

Humans and other animals may be the victims of several degenerative disorders of the central nervous system. These disorders appear to be caused by "proteinaceous infectious particles," or prions. Although these particles appear to be completely devoid of nucleic acid, they can cause transmissible diseases. The diseased state seems to be the result of a change in a normal cell protein. Research prions; describe what we know about how these infectious agents might be transmitted and how they can cause disease. (For a review article, see "The Prion Diseases" by Stanley B. Prusiner, *Scientific American,* January 1995, pp. 48–57.) In his novel *Arrowsmith* (written in the 1920s), Sinclair Lewis used the idea of treatment with a bacteriophage to cure a bacterial infection as the main plot in his novel. He described a fictional outbreak of bubonic plague in the West Indies where the young doctor Arrowsmith attempts treatment with a bacteriophage. The novel presents well-researched insights into the understandings of the time about this form of therapy. It raised the ethical issue of who should get treatment (and who should not) when new medicines are being tested. Read the novel. Describe the scientific theories that are presented and the ethical issues that are raised. How are these ethical issues still a problem today?

Pathologist   It's a busy day for Kerry, a clinical pathologist who works in the pathology laboratory at Mountain Medical Center. Five people have been rushed to the emergency room this morning complaining of similar symptoms. Kerry needs to conduct laboratory tests to determine what is making the patients sick. Specimens taken from the emergency room patients are immediately sent to the pathology lab.

Kerry uses the lab's equipment to examine samples from the skin, organs, blood, or other body fluids to identify possible sources of infection. She identifies the presence and stages of disease in order to provide physicians with a diagnosis. This includes information about the likely sources of the patients' infections and the way they should be treated. Kerry also formulates a plan to ensure that the infectious disease is not spread throughout the hospital.

Upon examining specimens from the patients, Kerry finds that four of the five patients are suffering from meningitis. She makes a relatively quick diagnosis because she has been conducting treatment studies for meningitis and community-acquired infections and resistance patterns for these diseases in the laboratory. Occasionally, this involves going down to the mortuary to get specimens of tissue from people who have died.

Growing up, Kerry was fascinated by medicine and anatomy. In the second grade, she saved her allowance money to buy herself an anatomy set. Kerry always wanted to be a doctor, even though, as a child, she did not know any women doctors. She excelled in her science courses in high school and decided to pursue medical school. During college, she took pre-med courses such as biology, chemistry, anatomy, physiology, math, and Latin. But the course that intrigued her most was a microbiology class where she learned about bacteria and other agents that can cause disease. She loved examining specimens under the microscope and connecting their structure and behavior to the expression of disease.

Once she graduated from college, Kerry went on to medical school for 2 years of course work and 2 years of hospital training. During her studies in medical school, Kerry learned more about pathology and became convinced that this was the right specialty for her. After medical school, Kerry went on to further training, called a residency, in order to specialize in pathology. Six years after completing her medical degree, Kerry was finally certified as a clinical pathologist. It was a long haul, but she loves studying pathology in depth.

Investigating infectious diseases is fascinating for Kerry. She finds it intellectually challenging to keep up-to-date with a field that's constantly changing. She enjoys looking through a microscope for insights into the germs that infect people. She likes following up to make sure the patients at the medical center are getting the best possible treatment. Kerry realizes that there is a lot of responsibility in her job because the doctors rely heavily on the information she discovers in the laboratory. But she is proud of her dedication to her work.

I Opened the Window and In-flew-enza

*I had a little bird
And its name was Enza.
I opened the window
And in-flew-enza.
(a nursery rhyme)*

Prologue

Organisms rarely live a singular, uninvaded existence. To paraphrase Jonathan Swift (Learning Experience 3), big organisms have little organisms ("upon their backs to bite 'em"). Most living things serve as habitats for other living things. Some organisms can live together, one in or on the other, in perfect harmony (such as common intestinal bacteria in humans). In these cases, the invader produces no ill effects in the host. At times, it is even beneficial. The life processes of pathogens, however, can produce discomforting and sometimes fatal effects in their hosts. As you investigated in previous learning experiences, the toxin produced by the bacteria *Vibrio cholerae* provides some function (as yet undefined) for the bacteria. When carrying out this function for the bacteria, the toxin binds to a membrane protein in the intestinal cells of its host. This causes the devastating symptoms of cholera. Other pathogenic bacteria and parasites may cause symptoms when their life processes interfere with a biological function of the host. These life processes can also deprive the host of vital nutrients or cause structural damage to the host.

What, then, makes a virus pathogenic? Viruses lack the cellular machinery necessary for maintaining the characteristics of life. What happens when a virus enters the host organism? How can a virus make more of itself if it lacks all the necessary cellular machinery to carry out the life processes? What causes the symptoms of viral infection in a host?

An important approach to answering those questions employs a technique called **polyacrylamide gel electrophoresis (PAGE)**. This technique enables scientists to analyze the protein content of a cell and determine the events that take place when a virus invades a cell. In this learning experience, you use data generated by PAGE to determine what happens when a virus takes up residence in a cell.

Brainstorming

Discuss the following questions with your partner, and record your thinking in your notebook. Be prepared to share your ideas with the class.

1. What function does the genetic information (DNA or RNA) of a virus serve?
2. In what ways might the information in the viral genome differ from the information in the cellular genome?
3. What do you think happens to the proteins in a host cell when it is infected by a virus?

ACTIVITY

Pop Goes the Cell!

In earlier learning experiences, you explored the role of proteins in cells. You saw that cells contain hundreds and hundreds of proteins. A distinguishing characteristic of the identity and function of a cell is its protein content, or **protein complement**. The proteins in a cell determine what activities the cell can carry out. A red blood cell, for example, must contain hemoglobin to transport oxygen. A muscle cell must have the proteins actin and myosin to be able to contract. And a liver cell has many proteins for getting rid of toxic substances that accumulate in an organism. (Catalase is an example of one such protein.) In addition, proteins in all of these cells enable them to carry out activities referred to as housekeeping functions. These are the functions necessary for maintaining life and carrying out the cellular processes of life.

Suppose you wanted to examine the protein complement a cell was making. How could you go about it? One way to examine the proteins would be to separate them from one another so as to distinguish them. Electrophoresis is one method for separating and examining proteins. Electrophoresis depends, in part, on the fact that proteins come in a wide range of masses or sizes. (The size depends on the number of amino acids that make up the protein.) Thus, proteins can be separated from one another based on these differences.

If you want to examine the proteins in a cell, you first need to lyse (break open) the cell to release the proteins. Then you place the proteins into a gel matrix. You pass an electrical current between a negative electrode at one end of the gel and a positive electrode at the other end. Many biomolecules have a net negative charge. As a result, they will move toward the positive electrode.

The gel matrix acts like a sieve (much like a colander or strainer). It has pores of a specific size. These pores allow certain-size molecules to pass freely but slow down the passage of larger molecules. The denser the matrix, the smaller the pore size, and the more the matrix slows down the progress of the proteins toward the positive electrode. Thus, the smaller the protein, the farther down it can move into the gel.

In this activity, you will simulate the process of gel electrophoresis. You will compare the protein complements of two cells, one of which has been infected with influenza virus.

Materials

For each group of four students:

- 2 paper bags representing 2 cells:
  - 1 normal, uninfected cell
  - 1 cell infected by influenza virus

PROCEDURE

1. Obtain 1 healthy cell and 1 infected cell from your teacher.
2. Devise a method to lyse or release the proteins in your cells. Be sure that you do not cross-contaminate (mix) your samples.
3. Use your desk or table to represent the gel matrix. Straighten out the proteins of each cell type. (Extend them to their full length.)
4. Stack the proteins at the top of your gel (table) in 1 pile for each sample. (Place the 2 stacks side by side.) Indicate where the positive and negative electrodes of your gel setup would be.
5. Move the proteins down the table in a single column for each sample. Simulate how you think the proteins might move in the actual gel matrix.
6. Describe or draw the protein complement of each cell. Indicate how the proteins moved in the gel.
7. **STOP & THINK** Describe the differences between the protein content of the infected cell and the uninfected cell.
8. **STOP & THINK** What do you think the protein patterns tell you about the effects of the influenza virus on the cellular processes of the host cell?

A Protein Guide to the Cell

READING

Polyacrylamide gel electrophoresis permits the analysis of all the proteins being synthesized by a cell. To be able to visualize these proteins, we first need to mark or label the proteins that are being made. This must be done in a way that not only makes the proteins visible but that also labels only those proteins being made at one specific point in time. Proteins in a cell can be labeled with radioactivity by using radioactive amino acids. Amino acids can be made radioactive by substituting a radioactive element for a nonradioactive one. For example, the amino acid methionine is made radioactive by substituting radioactive sulfur (^{35}S) for nonradioactive sulfur. ^{35}S methionine can be added to cells. The cells then incorporate this radioactive amino acid into the cellular proteins they are synthesizing. Any proteins containing this amino acid will also be radioactive (see Figure 3.35). After the proteins of the cells are labeled in this way, the cells are broken open or lysed by detergent. This releases the proteins and other biomolecules. (The mixture that is released when cells are lysed is called a **cell extract**.)

The next step is to separate the proteins from one another to distinguish them. As described in the opening paragraphs to the activity Pop Goes the Cell!, the cell extract is placed in a gel matrix. An electrical current is applied to the matrix, and the proteins separate, or fractionate, according to mass or size (see Figure 3.36).

Think back to your exploration of protein shape in Learning Experience 7, Protein, the Wonder Ingredient. Proteins in the cell are folded into shapes that are determined by their amino acid sequences. Proteins can be unfolded or lose

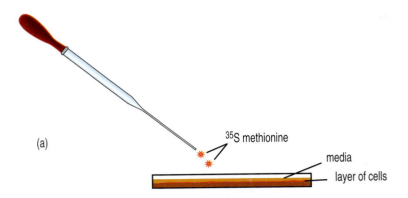

(a)

³⁵S methionine

media
layer of cells

Figure 3.35

Preparation of samples for polyacrylamide gel electrophoresis. (a) Molecules of methionine (a kind of amino acid) containing the radioactive element sulfur are added to media in which cells are growing. (b) The cells take up the amino acids. They then incorporate the amino acids into proteins being made on ribosomes.

cell
ribosomes
mRNA
³⁵S methionine
(b)
radioactive protein

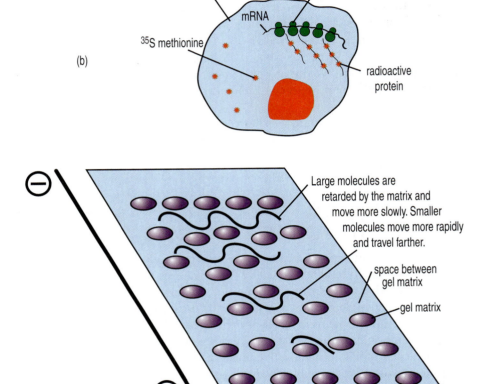

⊖

Large molecules are retarded by the matrix and move more slowly. Smaller molecules move more rapidly and travel farther.

space between gel matrix

gel matrix

⊕

Figure 3.36

Biomolecules of different sizes moving through a gel matrix.

their shape in a process called **denaturation**. When you boil an egg, the albumin protein (white) of the egg becomes denatured. This changes its physical characteristics dramatically. Heating a protein in a detergent also causes denaturation. To separate proteins by their true size, the proteins need to be unfolded. To do this, proteins are generally heated in a solution of a sodium dodecyl sulfate (SDS). This solution is an **anionic** (negatively charged) detergent that binds to most proteins. By binding to the protein, SDS has two effects. First, the detergent and heat interfere with the interactions that cause the folding in a protein. This disrupts the three-dimensional structure of the protein. This, in turn, causes the protein to assume the shape of a linear polypeptide chain. Second, the SDS masks any charge the protein may have (as a result of its amino acid content). It does this by saturating the linear chain with its own negative charge. Figure 3.37 illustrates a protein in the presence of an anionic detergent.

   The basic procedure for analyzing the proteins in a cell by gel electrophoresis is summarized in Figure 3.38.

1. To label the proteins, cells are grown in a small culture dish in the presence of radioactive amino acids.
2. The cells are placed in a test tube. Detergent is added to break open the cells and to release the cell extract. The extract may be heated to facilitate denaturation with the detergent.
3. The cell extract is removed from the test tube with a pipette.
4. The extract is placed on top of a gel matrix and an electrical current is applied.
5. The proteins move through the matrix and are separated by size.
6. The proteins are visualized by exposing the matrix to film. When a film is exposed to the radioactive protein in the gel matrix, the radioactivity causes the emulsion in the film to precipitate or come out of solution. This happens much the same way as when film is exposed to light.
7. When the film is developed, a black spot or band is seen wherever the film has been exposed to radioactivity. Therefore, wherever a radioactive protein is present in the gel matrix a corresponding black band will appear on the film.

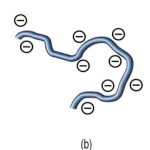

(a)   (b)

Figure 3.37

In the presence of SDS and heat, a compact folded protein (a) is denatured. The protein then assumes the structure of a linear polypeptide chain (b) because it is saturated with negative charges.

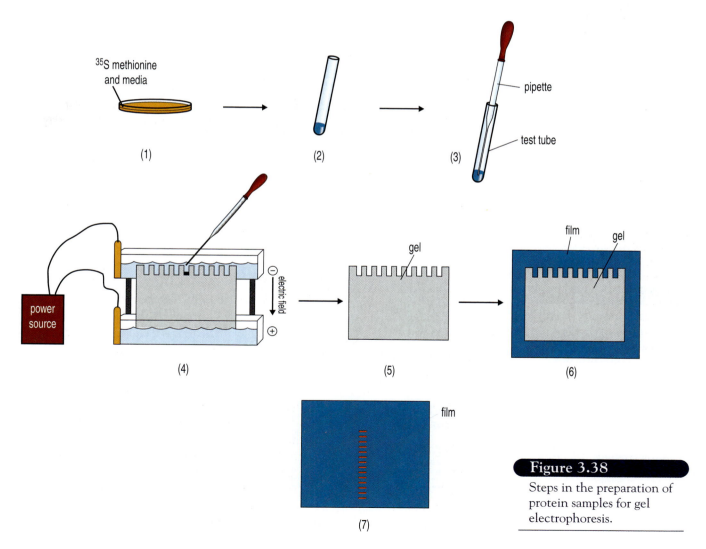

Figure 3.38

Steps in the preparation of protein samples for gel electrophoresis.

Many different kinds of biomolecules (most commonly, nucleic acids and proteins) can be separated using this technique. The ability to separate biomolecules in a gel matrix provides a way to analyze the molecular components of cells, tissues, and organisms. This method is the central technique in sequencing the human genome. It is one of the most widely used techniques in molecular biology.

 ANALYSIS

Record your responses to the following in your notebook.

1. Explain what is happening at each of the following steps in the activity Pop Goes the Cell! Use your understanding of protein analysis by gel electrophoresis (refer to Figure 3.38).
   a. Releasing the chenille stems or paper strips from the paper bags.
   b. Straightening the crumpled chenille stems or strips of paper.
   c. Stacking the stems or strips together on the gel.
   d. Ordering them in a column according to size.
   e. Comparing the two columns.
2. What other biomolecules would you expect to be present in your cell extract?
3. Follow along as a scientist investigates what happens to a cell and its proteins when a virus infects it. Our scientist sets up two dishes of lung cell cultures. One dish contains only the nutrients (in a media) required by the cells for growth and a radioactive amino acid. The other dish contains media, the radioactive amino acid, and the influenza virus. As the cells grow, the radioactive amino acid is incorporated into the proteins being made. After 24 hours, the cells are removed from the dishes. The cells are placed in separate test tubes, lysed with detergent (SDS), and heated. The extract is then placed in separate wells (indentations) on top of a gel matrix. An electric current is passed through the matrix for several hours. The gel matrix is then removed and exposed to photographic film for several days. The film is developed, and the patterns shown in Figure 3.39 are observed.

   a. What biomolecules do the bands on the gels represent? Why are other biomolecules not seen?
   b. What property or properties of the biomolecules caused them to separate in the observed patterns?

There was no step in the activity equivalent to labeling the proteins with radioactivity or exposing them to film.

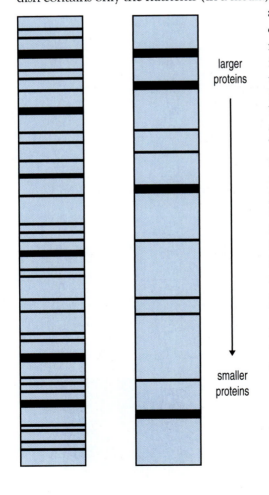

(a)   (b)

larger proteins

smaller proteins

Figure 3.39

Polyacrylamide gel analysis of (a) noninfected cells and (b) cells infected for 24 hours with the influenza virus. Cells were grown in the presence of ^{35}S (sulfur-35) methionine. They were lysed in detergent (SDS) and fractionated on a polyacrylamide gel. After fractionation, the gel was exposed to film for 5 days. (The illustration represents the results seen on the film.)

c. What do the bands in Figure 3.39a represent? in Figure 3.39b? What does the difference in the protein patterns tell you about what is happening in the infected cell?

d. Imagine that you wanted to force a cell to make certain proteins in large quantities. Describe one way in which a virus might stop a host cell from synthesizing its own proteins and make only viral proteins. Base your description on your understanding of viruses, the patterns in Figure 3.39, and the transfer of information in a cell from nucleic acid to protein. Draw or diagram how this might take place. Be prepared to share your thinking with the class. Be sure to include all the steps required for a virus to make more of itself.

SCLINKS
NSTA

Topic: Viral Diseases
Go to: www.scilinks.org
Code: INBIOH2433

Influenza: The Inside Story

READING

Almost everyone has had or knows someone who has had the influenza virus. Commonly known as the flu, influenza travels from host to host through the air. Flu enters the body through the gateways of the nose and mouth. It attaches to receptors on the surface of the host cells in the lungs.

As it enters the cells, flu releases its nucleic acid, which consists of eight pieces (segments) of RNA. Within the cell nuclei, these RNA segments are transcribed into mRNA. It is at this point that our virus becomes a kind of "pirate."

Influenza has evolved a very clever and efficient mechanism for commandeering the protein synthesis machinery of its host cell. In normal, uninfected cells, every mRNA has a sequence at one end called a cap. This cap is required for the mRNA to bind to the ribosome and have its sequence translated into protein. Without the cap, no translation can take place. The influenza virus carries with it into the cell an enzyme that can cut the cap sequences. This enzyme cuts the sequences from the host mRNAs and attaches them to the viral mRNAs. As a result of this pirating, the host mRNAs can no longer be translated, but the viral messages can (see Figure 3.40).

The viral nucleic acid then proceeds to direct the synthesis of enzymes and proteins required for the virus to reproduce itself. The eight segments of viral RNA encode 10 proteins. Eight proteins are part of the virus itself; two are enzymes used in synthesizing viral components. The virus proteins and nucleic acids are then assembled into virus particles that exit the cell by a process of budding. During the infection process, two proteins are inserted into the host cell membrane. These two proteins are part of the final viral particle. As the virus escapes from the cell, it is encased in a lipid protein coat containing these two viral proteins. These proteins are embedded in lipids from the host membrane.

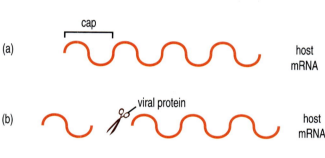

(a) host mRNA — cap

(b) host mRNA — viral protein

(c) viral mRNA

Figure 3.40

Virus-stealing caps from host mRNA. (a) The host mRNA contains a sequence at one end of the molecule that is required for protein synthesis. (b) A viral protein cuts this sequence from the end of the host mRNA. (c) This sequence is attached to the end of the viral mRNA. The host mRNA can no longer be translated into protein, but the viral mRNA can.

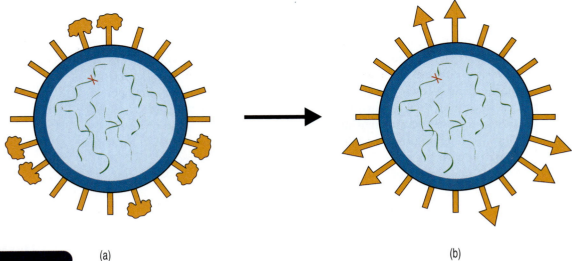

(a)   (b)

Figure 3.41

(a) The influenza RNA
sequence mutates. (b) The
change in sequence results in
a change in one of the coat
proteins. The × represents a
change in one nucleotide.

RNA is less stable than DNA. As a result, RNA viruses are 100 times as likely to mutate or change their sequence as DNA viruses are. Any group of RNA viruses, therefore, contains a large number of mutants. Most of them do not survive. This is either because the mutants have proteins that do not function correctly or because they have no particular selective advantage over the unchanged virus. If the environment changes, however, some of the mutants may have an advantage. This genetic flexibility enables RNA viruses to move into new environmental niches, new geographical locations, and new populations. One potential result when the RNA virus mutates is that the proteins that make up the viral coat may alter. This change in coat protein may result in the virus being able to infect a new kind of host or evade the immune response of its normal host (see Figure 3.41).

The influenza virus has an additional evolutionary advantage over most other RNA viruses. Its genetic material consists of eight very loosely connected pieces (or segments) of RNA. The influenza virus has a broad host range. In other words, most flu viruses can infect a wide range of animals, including humans, pigs, and ducks. When two influenza viruses from different animals enter the same host, segments of the viruses of both types can mingle. Say, for example, a virus from a human infects a pig that is already infected with a pig influenza virus. The pig can serve as a mixing vessel for the creation of a new and deadly (to humans) influenza virus. The human virus may pick a viral segment of the RNA genome from the pig virus that encodes a completely different set of viral coat proteins. The result would be as if the human virus took off its cloth coat and put on a pigskin leather jacket (see Figure 3.42).

This kind of exchange can result in the emergence of a very new and different virus, which is part pig virus and part human virus. Fortunately, this kind of event happens rarely, about once in every 10–40 years. But when it does, the ramifications for the human population can be severe. The flu pandemic of 1918, which killed 20 million people, was the result of one such occurrence.

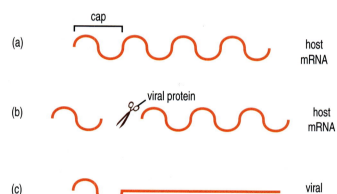

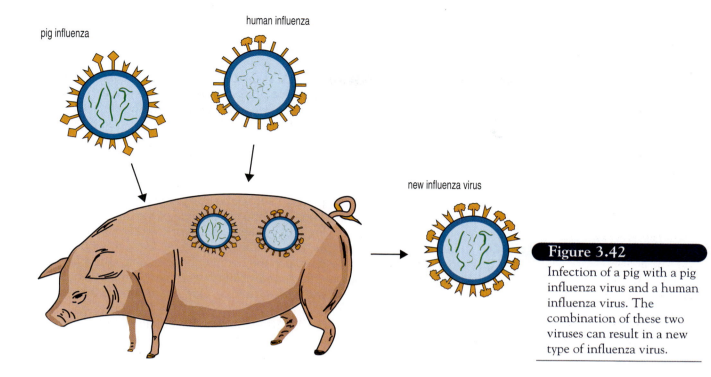

pig influenza

human influenza

new influenza virus

Figure 3.42

Infection of a pig with a pig influenza virus and a human influenza virus. The combination of these two viruses can result in a new type of influenza virus.

 **ANALYSIS**

Record your responses to the following in your notebook.

1. Draw or create a three-dimensional model of the steps involved when an influenza virus takes over a host cell. Use the information provided in this reading. Explain how this model is supported by the data you analyzed in the activity Pop Goes the Cell! and in the protein patterns you observed in Figure 3.39 (reading Analysis question 3c).

2. How do you think the influenza virus might spread from an infected cell to a noninfected cell in the lungs?

3. Describe an experiment you could carry out to investigate the events involved in the infection of a cell by tobacco mosaic virus. How would you use the technique of polyacrylamide gel electrophoresis in this experiment?

EXTENDING *Ideas*

▶ The influenza epidemic of 1918 killed millions of people around the world. Research how and why that happened. Do you think this could happen again? Provide evidence to support your decision.

Public Health Educator   Gus's work mission is ambitious. He wants everyone in the state to be educated about HIV and AIDS. He wants everyone to realize what they can do to ensure that they don't contract the deadly virus. As a public health educator, Gus tries to promote health and prevent disease within the population. He helps people change their behavior and adopt a healthier lifestyle. He helps them learn how to use health services and to be aware of preventative measures that can protect against disease, specifically AIDS. Gus works for the state's HIV/AIDS program. This program was set up to increase public awareness about HIV/AIDS prevention and treatment.

Growing up in a poor community, Gus witnessed poor health conditions all around him. His family wasn't aware of the importance of the long-term health benefits of good nutrition and regular exercise. Several members of his family had health problems, like diabetes, as a result. Even though they needed medical care, many people in the community, including Gus's family, avoided going to the doctor. Oftentimes, children were not brought to the doctor for routine checkups and immunizations. Gus saw diseases like AIDS spread through his community.

As he grew older, Gus knew that he wanted to do something to improve the health of people living in impoverished communities like his own. He loved the health courses he took in high school, as well as learning about the science behind health problems. He met with his guidance counselor to discuss his college and career options. Gus's counselor suggested public health education as a field that might fit Gus's interests. She also pointed out that with his high grades, he might qualify for a scholarship. Gus found a college public health program that he wanted to attend. His counselor helped him land scholarships that would pay for his tuition and expenses.

During college, Gus took many courses in health and science, such as biology and chemistry. One of his public health courses focused on the HIV and AIDS epidemic. Gus was struck by how uneducated much of the population is about AIDS prevention. Gus felt that to be most effective in his work as a public health educator, he would also need to complete a master's degree.

Upon completing his degree, Gus sought a position working on an AIDS prevention education project. He found out about a project being run by his state and was hired as a public health educator. Gus helps to organize the project's initiatives. This involves doing a lot of administrative tasks like managing the project budget, coordinating services, and communicating with all parties involved with the project. He has to make sure that he's up-to-date on the latest research and health findings in the field so that he gives the public the most recent information. But the time that Gus finds most satisfying is when he is out in the community, running educational events. That is when he can see firsthand the positive effect his work can have on people's health.

Fractionating Hemoglobin

Prologue

Proteins determine the functions and characteristics of living cells. As a result, scientists can gain insight into the activities of a cell by analyzing cellular proteins. Gel electrophoresis facilitates this characterization by using the properties of proteins to separate them for analysis. In this investigation, you examine the protein content of red blood cells from different animals by gel electrophoresis.

Brainstorming

Discuss the following with your partner, and record your thinking in your notebook. Be prepared to share your ideas with the class.

In Unit 2, you read about Denzel who had his blood tested for the sickling trait. Explain how this test might have been carried out. Use your understanding of polyacrylamide gel electrophoresis and sickle-cell anemia.

Fractionating Hemoglobin

Materials

For each pair of students:

- 2 pairs of safety goggles
- 2 small test tubes (or 1.5-mL reaction tubes) with caps
- 1 test-tube rack
- 7 micropipettes (25 μL)
- 1 pipetting bulb or micropipettor
- toothpicks
- samples of blood from 2 different animals (5 μL each)
- 10 μL distilled water
- 1 test-tube clamp or forceps
- 1 ruler
- 1 wax marking pencil

For the class:

- boiling water bath
- 10 mL bromophenol blue gel loading solution
- 10 mL of a 10% solution of sodium dodecyl sulfate (SDS)
- 1 electrophoresis box and gel bed
- 1 power pack
- chart paper

PROCEDURE

1. Label 2 test tubes, each with the different blood sample from those available.
2. Use a micropipette to place 5-μL samples of blood in the test tubes. (Use a clean micropipette for each sample.)
3. With a clean micropipette, add 5 μL of distilled water to each sample. Stir each sample with a different toothpick. Describe the appearance of your samples in your notebook.
4. With a clean micropipette, add 5 μL of the SDS solution to each sample. Put a cap on each tube and flick the tubes gently with your finger to mix the contents.
5. Place the test tubes in a boiling water bath for 2 minutes. Be sure the tubes are capped, or the samples will evaporate.
6. With a clean micropipette, add 5 μL of loading solution from the class supply to each sample.
7. Your teacher has already placed an agarose gel in the electrophoresis running chamber. The gel contains 1X TBE (Tris-Borate-EDTA). Be sure the gel is oriented correctly with respect to the electrodes. The top of the gel should be near the negative electrode.
8. Load your samples with a micropipette into individual wells. Be sure to keep track of which sample went into which well and where your samples are on the gel. Describe or draw this location in your notebook.

9. **STOP & THINK** What do you think the proteins in your samples will look like? Describe or draw your predictions in your notebook.
10. Run the gel until the tracking dye in the loading solution reaches the bottom.
11. Your teacher will remove the gel from the chamber and then stain and destain the gel.

ANALYSIS

Examine your gel with your partner. Record your responses to the following in your notebook.

1. How many bands are present on each gel? What do these bands represent?
2. Is any one band darker than any others? What does it mean when a band is dark? What do you think this band is?
3. Using a ruler, measure how far this band migrated in each sample.
4. Compare the patterns of your two samples. How are they similar? How do they differ? Did the predominant band in each sample migrate differently? What might that mean?
5. What happened to the samples when you added water? when you added the SDS? when you boiled the sample? What was happening to the cells and the proteins at each step?
6. What property of these proteins determined how far they migrated? What steps did you take to ensure that the proteins migrated because of this property only?
7. Are there any observable differences in the migration patterns of the hemoglobin from the different samples of blood? Why or why not?

Immune System to the Rescue

Prologue

The world we live in teems with microbial life. Every breath we take, every inch of our skin, every bite of food that enters our mouths, every surface we touch is covered with an enormous array of microscopic organisms. Fortunately, the majority of these microbes pose no threat. But a small number of these life-forms can cause disease. We call these life-forms pathogens. Do we have any way to defend ourselves against these potential biological hazards in our environment? How is it that we usually stay healthy when agents of disease are everywhere?

In this learning experience, you explore some of the components of the immune system. This is our body's intricate and extraordinarily efficient defense against disease. The immune system is a diverse collection of specialized proteins, cells, organs, and structures designed to identify and destroy invaders before they destroy the host. You will model several events that take place when this system is confronted with pathogenic organisms.

Brainstorming

Discuss the following questions with your partner, and record your thinking in your notebook. Be prepared to share your ideas with the class.

1. Your body has several lines of defense against infectious agents. Which mechanisms are you currently familiar with?
2. In most cases, if you had chicken pox once you cannot get it again. Why do you think you are protected against a second infection?
3. The symbiont of one species is the pathogen of another. That is, an organism can infect one species and coexist peacefully. But when the same organism infects another species, it produces symptoms of disease. How do you explain this?

The Competition

Your body is on constant alert for trouble from the outside world. Not only does this trouble come from microorganisms, but it can also come from toxins, pollutants, pollen, and any number of foreign substances that might gain entry and be disruptive. In many ways, the immune system is like a security system. It sends out alarms and keeps you well protected when something potentially harmful enters. To get a sense of how this line of defense works, you will design a security system of your own.

Imagine that your pharmaceutical company Drugs R Us has made several amazing breakthroughs. Not only has your research team developed a drug that prevents the symptoms of cholera, but the group has also designed vaccines that promise to bring a halt to several diseases including malaria, AIDS, and the common cold. The potential in profits is staggering. As a consequence, you have had serious problems with attempts by your competitors to sabotage your equipment and steal your drug and vaccine designs.

You are concerned that the security measures you have taken to protect the work that goes on inside your 700,000 square-foot building are not adequate. You and your crackerjack team are meeting to try to solve this problem before something happens. As part of your brainstorming strategy, you need to define the problem and come up with some solutions. The following task defines the steps you will need to take to attend to your security concerns.

TASK

As a team, work through the following steps:
1. Identify the ways that your competitors could get into your building.
2. Identify the ways that they might gain access to your equipment and secret files.
3. Create a plan for protecting your corporate headquarters against the possibilities you identified.
4. Prepare a list of roles and job descriptions for your security team.
5. Describe how these efforts will work together and back up one another to ensure tight protection against invasion.

The Pathogens Are Coming!

The body's first defense against pathogens is simply to try to keep them out. The skin, for example, acts as a physical barrier to the pathogens. It also carries out chemical warfare against infection by secreting oils and sweat that acidify the surface of the skin. This makes it difficult for potential pathogens to grow. Openings in the skin, such as the mouth and nostrils, provide easy portals of entry for infectious agents. These entryways into the body are protected by a modified type of skin called a mucous membrane. The mucous linings of these passageways physically trap microbes and debris. Some also contain antimicrobial enzymes that can break down or digest microorganisms (see Figure 3.43).

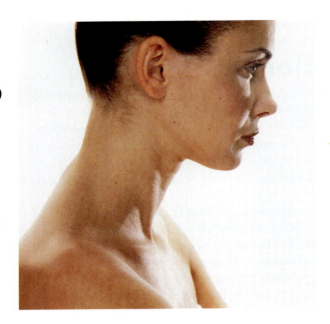

Figure 3.43

The body's first lines of defense against infection. Openings such as the mouth and nasal passages are lined with a mucous membrane. This membrane can trap microbes or actually destroy them with enzymes. The skin provides a physical barrier. It secretes oils and sweat that rinse the surface clean of microorganisms.
© Royalty-Free/Corbis

Topic: Immune System
Go to: www.scilinks.org
Code: INBIOH2442

When microorganisms manage to get past the first line of defense, your body activates another set of defenses. Invaders enter the body and find their target tissues (for example, lung cells, epithelial cells, intestinal cells). They now begin their confrontation with components of the immune system. The immune system is made up of many specialized cells that work in a cooperative effort of ordered reactions. These reactions recognize and defend the body against foreign invaders.

The immune response relies on proteins and their interactions. As you have seen throughout this unit, proteins play many essential roles in maintaining life. Proteins are also key players in the recognition and communication processes that enable the immune system to stop an invasion. Cells, bacteria, viruses, and parasites all have proteins on their surfaces. Just as you recognize your friends and relatives by their physical characteristics, your immune system recognizes substances as friends or foes by these proteins. They act as a type of identity card. In human cells, these proteins are called major **histocompatibility complex (MHC)** markers. These markers enable the immune system to recognize self from nonself. They also make it unlikely that the immune system will attack proteins of its own body.

As you saw in Learning Experiences 7 and 8, the shape of a protein determines its function or activity. In this case, the shape of the protein marker tells the immune system if the shape is foreign or one of its own. If the shape is foreign, the immune system goes into action. Proteins synthesized by specialized cells of the immune system are sent out into the body through the circulatory system. They act as a call to arms for other cells of the immune system to initiate actions that help to defend the body. The circulatory system and the lymphatic system enable components of the immune system to travel to wherever they are needed in the body. The **lymphatic system** is a specialized network of vessels that eliminates products of cellular and bacterial breakdown. It does this by transporting excess fluids away from interstitial (nonspecific) spaces in body tissue and returning those fluids to the bloodstream. The lymphatic system is also involved in white blood cell and antibody production.

Molecules recognized by the immune system as foreign are called **antigens**. They may be carbohydrates and proteins on viruses, bacteria or parasites, pollen particles, or proteins inserted into the cell membrane during infection. In response to these antigens, other proteins called antibodies are produced by cells of the immune system. As you will discover in this learning experience, these antibodies provide powerful protection against infection. The response of the immune system depends on the specific interactions among cells and proteins. These specific interactions enable the immune system to recognize what does not belong and to take action to eliminate it.

ANALYSIS

Record your responses to the following in your notebook.

1. List the components of the body's defense system. (Include those components described in this reading and any others that you know about.)
2. Next to each component, explain what you think it does as part of this system.
3. Match each component to the part of the security system listed in the table that you made in class.

You Make Me Sick (But I Still Need You): A First Look

The alarm clock sounded with its usual too-early-morning shrill. As Flora tried to open one eye and then the other to face another school day, she realized something was wrong. She felt . . . sick. Her throat was scratchy and sore and her body ached all over. She felt hot and sweaty, yet at the same time she was shaking from chills. She was frighteningly weak. In a nutshell, she felt really lousy. When her mom entered Flora's room for the morning knock-down-drag-out battle about getting out of bed, she stopped in her tracks. She could tell at a glance that Flora was not well. A trip to the doctor confirmed that Flora was sick and probably had the flu that was going around her school. Flora wanted to know why she ached so and felt so hot and weak. The doctor responded, "Well, of course you ache; of course you have a fever; of course you're weak. You're sick!"

But why do you feel so awful when you are sick? How can the influenza virus, which grows primarily in the lungs, make you feel so terrible all over? As you saw in Learning Experience 3, Agents of Disease, many diseases have the same symptoms, even when the disease is caused by very different things. What causes these symptoms? What do infectious agents that bring them on have in common so that they would produce the same symptoms? The answer is the host—you. More specifically, the common factor is your immune response to these infectious agents.

As you know, the immune system is made up of highly specialized cells and proteins whose main job is to keep you from harm. The first kind of cell that a pathogen such as a virus or bacterium encounters after entering the body is the **macrophage**. Large, amorphous, and amoeba-like, the macrophage engulfs the invader. It digests the pathogen and adds some of the pathogen's antigens to its own surface proteins. These viral or bacterial antigens on the macrophage surface serve as a red flag. They signal the rest of the immune system that attackers have entered the body and it's time to get busy. A chain of events begins in which **helper T-cells** and **killer T-cells** are called to active duty to quell the invasion. This kind of response is called a **cell-mediated response**. A second kind of immune response known as the **humoral response** may also be drafted into action. **B-cells** are stimulated to divide and to produce antibodies. These proteins can also neutralize and destroy the infectious agents. You will explore both of these immune responses in greater detail in the activity Confrontation!

 **NALYSIS**

Record your responses to the following in your notebook. This analysis will help you understand the tasks you will do in the next activity.

1. Identify the players in the two different kinds of immune responses, cell-mediated and humoral. Use the descriptions from the reading.
2. Using diagrams or drawings, indicate how the players interact.

ACTIVITY

Confrontation!

As you explored in the reading "You Make Me Sick (But I Still Need You): A First Look," the immune system has two responses to infection. The cell-mediated response and the humoral response work together to quell invasions of pathogens. In this activity, you and the members of your team each represent a different component of the immune response. As such, you will determine how the components of the immune system work together to defend against infection by viruses. The information you have to work with for the task on page 451 includes the following tables and diagrams:

- a list of components of the cell-mediated response (Table 3.12),
- a diagram of the cell-mediated response to infection (Figure 3.44),
- a list of components of the humoral response (Table 3.13),
- a diagram of the humoral response to infection (Figure 3.45),
- a list of the characteristics of viral invaders (Table 3.14), and
- a diagram of the immune response to an infection by the virus that causes chicken pox (Figure 3.46).

Table 3.12 Components of the Cell-Mediated Response (see corresponding Figure 3.44)

Player of the Immune System	Role: What It Does	What It Interacts With
macrophage	• Found circulating in the blood. • When a macrophage encounters a foreign antigen (a protein from a foreign invader), it engulfs viruses, bacteria, infected cells, or cell remnants that display the antigen on the surface. • Macrophages display the engulfed viral antigen (protein) on their own surfaces. They do this by inserting viral antigen into its own cell membrane. • When a macrophage engulfs a virus, it calls other immune cells to the scene. (This is called the cell-mediated response.) • When macrophages that have engulfed invaders encounter helper T-cells, the T-cells bind to the viral antigen on the macrophage surface. • When helper T-cells bind to the antigen, the macrophage releases a protein called **interleukin**. As an activating factor, this protein stimulates helper T-cells to divide. • Macrophages engulf viruses, bacteria, or infected cells coated in the antibody.	• viruses • bacteria • an infected host cell displaying viral antigen on its surface • a cell remnant displaying viral antigen on its surface • helper T-cells • viruses, bacteria, or infected cells with antibodies bound to antigens
helper T-cell	• Originates in bone marrow; matures in the thymus gland (thus the "T" in T-cell). • Found circulating in the blood. • First to arrive at infection scene when macrophages send out alarm. • Has protein receptors on its surface. These distinguish foreign substances, bacteria, and viruses by the proteins found on their surfaces. • Recognizes viral and bacterial antigens on macrophage's surface. • Binds to viral and bacterial antigens on a macrophage. This causes the macrophage to release the chemical substance interleukin. This, in turn, stimulates helper T-cells to divide. • Releases activating factor (interleukin). This stimulates T-cells and B-cells to divide and activates killer T-cells. • Part of cell-mediated response.	• macrophages • killer T-cells • B-cells
killer T-cell	• Originates in bone marrow; matures in the thymus gland (thus the "T" in T-cell). • Found in circulating blood. • Can attack and destroy cells infected with active virus displaying viral antigens on their surface. It does this by injecting toxic chemicals into them. • Part of cell-mediated response; arrives at infection when macrophages send out signal. • Activated by interleukin released from helper T-cells.	• infected host cell displaying antigen on its surface

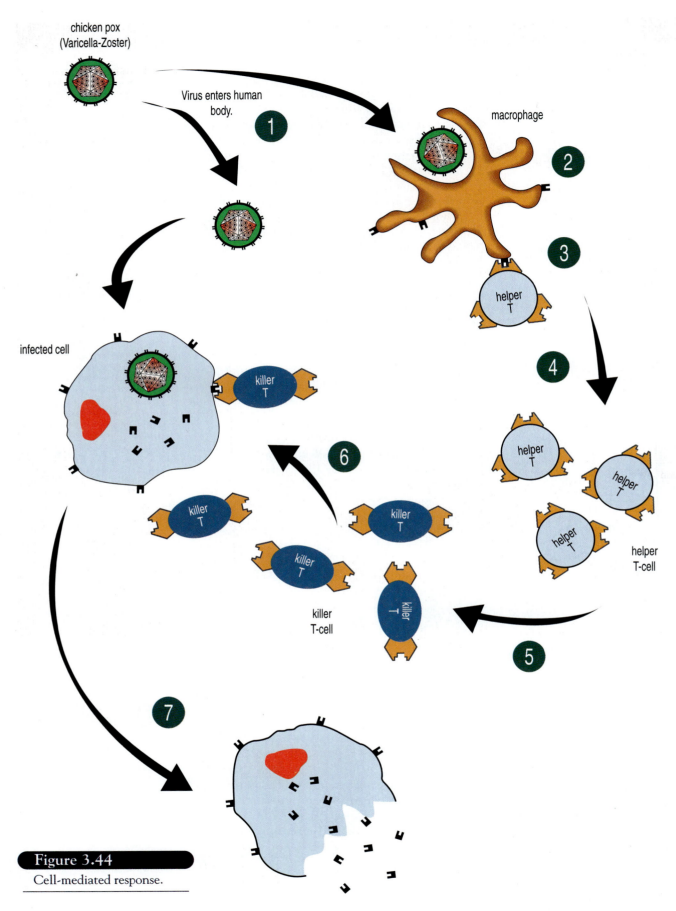

chicken pox
(Varicella-Zoster)

Virus enters human body.

macrophage

helper T

infected cell

killer T

helper T

helper T

helper T

helper T-cell

killer T

killer T

killer T

killer T

killer T-cell

Figure 3.44

Cell-mediated response.

Table 3.13 Components of the Humoral Response (see corresponding Figure 3.45)

Player of the Immune System	Role: What It Does	What It Interacts With
B-cell	• Found in the bloodstream; originates in bone marrow (thus the "B" in B-cell). • May bind to viruses or bacteria using receptors on the surface of the B-cell called antibodies. These antibodies recognize a specific antigen. • May bind with viral fragments found on infected cell surface. • B-cells begin secreting antibodies that recognize viral and bacterial antigens. • Interleukin molecules are released from activated T-cells. These molecules stimulate B-cells to divide.	• viruses • bacteria • host cell with viral antigens displayed on its surface
antibody	• Produced by B-cells. • Is a protein that has a precise recognition of an individual antigen. • Binds to viruses. This prevents viruses from infecting cells. • Binds to bacteria. • Binds to viral antigens on the surface of the infected host cells and tags those cells for destruction. • Macrophages engulf viruses, bacteria, and cells with antigens that have antibodies bound to them.	• viruses • bacteria • antigens on infected cells
memory B-cell	• A B-cell activated by interactions with antigens differentiates into a memory cell. • Remains after infection. • Ready to respond rapidly should the body ever encounter the same antigen again. If identical viruses or bacteria invade the body later, the antibody on the memory B-cell binds to the virus or bacteria and marks them for destruction. The virus is halted before infection is established.	• viruses and bacteria that have infected the body before

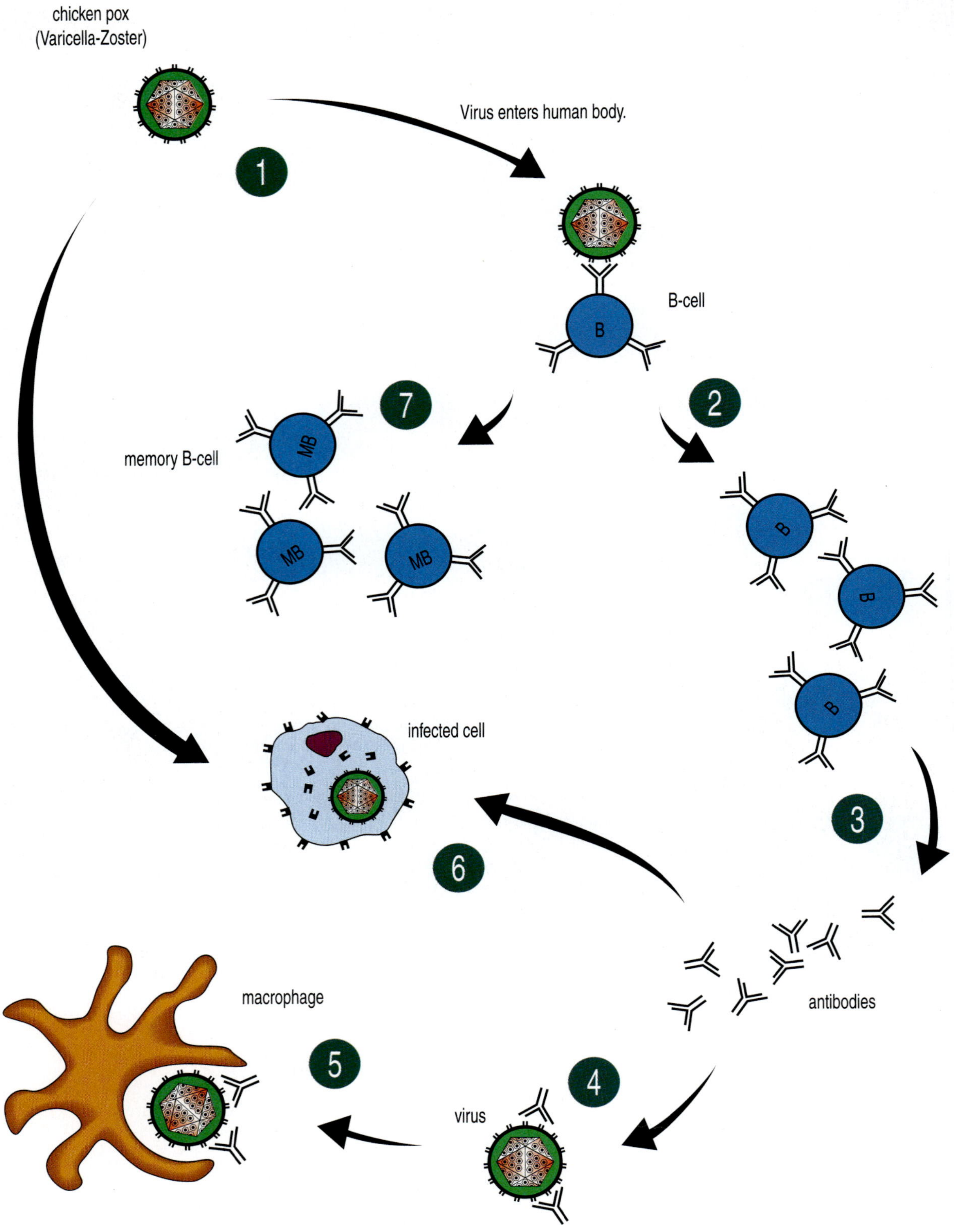

chicken pox
(Varicella-Zoster)

Virus enters human body.

1

B-cell

B

7

2

memory B-cell

MB

MB   MB

B

B

B

infected cell

3

6

macrophage

antibodies

5

4

virus

Figure 3.45

Humoral response.

Table 3.14 Characteristics of Viral Invaders

Invader	What It Does

chicken pox virus	• May infect a host cell. Viral antigens are inserted into the cell membrane. The shape of the antigen expressed is unique.
	  –Viral DNA, which codes for viral proteins, is injected into the host cell.
	  –The cell begins making viral proteins instead of cell proteins; DNA is replicated.
	  –These proteins and DNA assemble into new viruses.
	  –The cell is disabled or killed. Hundreds to thousands of new viruses are released.
	• May be ingested by a macrophage.
	• May bind to memory B-cell, which has receptors that recognize specific chicken pox antigens.

influenza virus	• May infect a host cell. Viral antigens are inserted into the cell membrane. The shape of the antigen expressed is unique.
	  –Viral RNA, which codes for viral proteins, is injected into the host cell.
	  –The cell begins making viral proteins instead of cell proteins; RNA is replicated.
	  –These proteins and RNA assemble into new viruses.
	  –Hundreds to thousands of new viruses are released by budding; cell dies.
	• May be ingested by a macrophage.
	• May bind to a memory B-cell, which has receptors that recognize specific influenza antigens.

human immunodeficiency virus (HIV)	• Infects helper T-cells.
	  –Binds to receptor molecule on the surface of the T-cell.
	  –Genetic material (RNA) is taken into the cell.
	  –Makes viral RNA and proteins that are assembled in virus particles.
	  –Virus particles bud out of the T-cell and enter the bloodstream.
	  –Kills host T-cell in the process.
	• May also infect macrophages without being destroyed. Can grow and reproduce slowly without killing the macrophage.

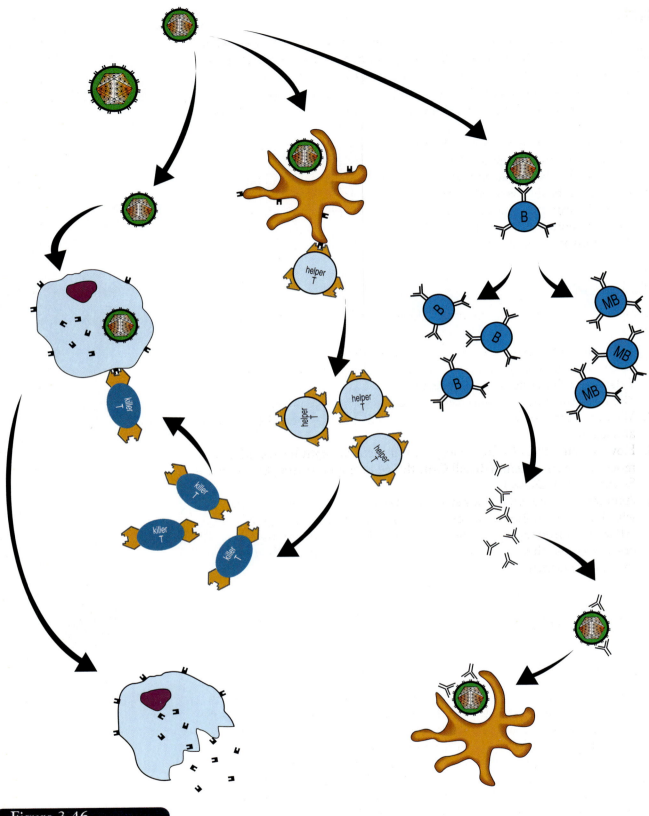

Figure 3.46

Summary of cell-mediated
and humoral responses to
chicken pox infections.

TASK

Using the information in the preceding tables and figures, you and your team will take on four challenges to describe the immune response to different viral infections. Record your responses to the following in your notebook.

1. The body is infected with the chicken pox virus. List the steps of the immune response. (Use Figure 3.46 as a guide.) Include a labeled diagram of the process.
2. The body is now reexposed to the chicken pox virus. List the steps of the immune response. Include a labeled diagram of the process.
3. The body has been infected with HIV. List the steps of the immune response. Include a labeled diagram of the process.
4. While fighting the chicken pox virus (for the first time), the body is infected with influenza virus. List the steps involved in the immune response to this double invasion. Include a labeled diagram of the process.

ANALYSIS

Record your responses to the following in your notebook. Draw a diagram to illustrate each response.

1. What would happen if a person were infected by a chicken pox virus but had no macrophages? Say mounting an effective antibody response takes 5 to 7 days, and the virus needs 2 to 3 days to establish a thriving infection. What are the possible outcomes for a person with this deficiency?
2. Why do most people get chicken pox just once, but they get the flu again and again?
3. How do you think Griffith's encapsulated bacteria might have eluded the mouse immune system? (Recall Griffith's work from Learning Experience 4, Search for the Cause.)
4. Acquired immune deficiency syndrome (AIDS) is the disease associated with human immunodeficiency virus (HIV) infection. Many people with AIDS suffer from opportunistic infections. These are infections from organisms that their bodies could normally fight off. Explain how you think this might happen.

You Make Me Sick (But I Still Need You): A Second Look

READING

What is happening in Flora's body to make her feel so lousy? In a sense, Flora's body has turned into a battleground. The immune system is waging a war with the influenza virus and, as in any fight, someone is bound to get hurt. In this case, that someone is Flora. As you have seen, the immune response is an incredibly complex system. It is comprised of trillions of highly specialized cells interacting through a number of different kinds of proteins. In addition, the immune response is taking place all over the body. Cells are flashing around to sites of infection like police to a crime scene. In order to be effective and efficient, these cells must be able to communicate with each other.

This communication is carried out by a set of chemical messengers called **cytokines**. These messengers travel around the body through the bloodstream and lymphatic system. Interleukin-1(IL-1) is one kind of cytokine. After the macrophage has encountered and engulfed a pathogen, it releases IL-1. IL-1 interacts with T-cells and stimulates them to divide. IL-1 has another effect, and this is where you start to feel sick. IL-1 can affect the regulation of body temperature. Normally, the human body is kept at a comfy 37°C (98.6°F) by a part of the brain called the hypothalamus. (Think of the hypothalamus as the body's thermostat.) If the temperature of your body drops below this mark, you will begin to shake and shiver as a way of generating heat in an attempt to warm up.

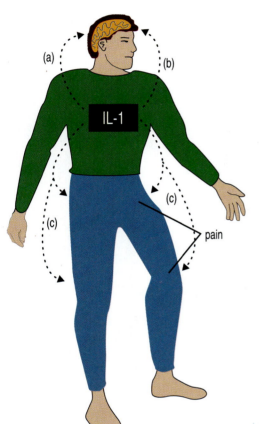

Temperatures above this mark cause the body to sweat as a way of dissipating heat before you cook. IL-1 somehow fiddles with the hypothalamus; it sets the thermostat higher than normal. The end result is that you feel cold at 37°C. You begin to shiver in an attempt to raise your body temperature; you now have a fever.

As if that weren't bad enough, IL-1 also causes the hypothalamus to release a substance called corticotrophin-releasing factor (CRF). CRF is a stress signal. It prepares your body to deal with stressful emergency situations such as taking a biology exam or escaping a herd of stampeding cattle. In the presence of CRF, energy storage is blocked. Instead of sending lipids into storage as fat, or sugar into storage as glycogen (recall Unit 1, Learning Experience 4), these molecules are sent to the muscle to be used immediately for energy. This enables you to ace that test or outrun those cattle. CRF also dampens sexual drive, appetite, and reproductive processes. These are activities that become superfluous in a cattle stampede (or biology test).

With the release of IL-1 from the macrophage and, in turn, CRF from the hypothalamus, energy is made available for fighting the infection. But you also lose your appetite and your interest in the opposite sex, and you feel pretty low in general. As if that were not enough, IL-1 also seems to be responsible for making the nerve pathways in your body more sensitive. Enter the aches and pains (see Figure 3.47).

So is IL-1 worth all the trouble it puts your body through? As you have just learned, IL-1 is essential in initiating the cascade of events that make up cell-mediated immunity. But the actions of IL-1 may also be part of another line of defense against infection. By redirecting the energy available from activities such as eating, making fat cells, and reproducing, IL-1 is helping in another way. It is making more energy available for immune cells to divide, migrate around the body, synthesize new proteins, and wage the good fight against infection. Studies have suggested that the immune system may work better at higher-than-normal body temperatures. Some viruses and bacteria grow more slowly at elevated temperatures. So despite how poorly a fever may make you feel, it is probably helping you recover. And all those other symptoms may indicate that your body is pulling all its resources toward making you well.

Flora's doctor suggested she go home, take two aspirin to reduce the symptoms, and not call him in the morning. But perhaps the best treatment for feeling lousy is to feel lousy and let your body handle it.

Figure 3.47

IL-1 causes many of the symptoms of disease. It (a) raises the temperature setting in the brain, causing the body temperature to increase; (b) stimulates CRF production in the brain, reducing the appetite; (c) excites neurons in the nerve pathways, giving that achy, breaky feeling to every inch of the body.

ANALYSIS

Record your responses to the following in your notebook.

1. Create a concept map from the reading. Show how components of the immune system cause the symptoms of a disease. Be sure to include at least 10 concepts or words from the reading.

2. The immune system is a finely tuned, highly responsive system. However, it is also responsible for many of the symptoms of disease. Often, the reason you feel so crummy when you are sick is the result of the immune system doing its job. Write a short essay describing how the symptoms of illness increase your survival advantage. Then explain why you would or would not use symptom-reducing drugs (such as aspirin) when you are sick.

Can't Catch Me

The complexity of the immune responses enables the body to protect itself against a vast array of microbial invaders. But if the immune system keeps the body in such a state of defensive preparedness, why do 17 million people a year still die of infectious diseases, and millions more suffer the symptoms of these infections? Let's examine one answer to this question by exploring various strategies that different parasites have evolved to evade the immune response.

Any two organisms, generally of different species, that live in close association are considered symbionts. **Parasitism** is a form of symbiosis in which one of the organisms, usually the smaller of the two, is metabolically dependent on the other partner. It is an obligatory relationship, for the parasite at least. The parasite cannot normally survive if it is denied access to its host. In some cases, the parasitic relationship may cause harm to the host.

The establishment of a successful parasite-host relationship is not easy. When a parasite enters a host, it is confronted by a barrage of obstacles. Entry across the skin barrier in itself can be a problem. If the organism seeks entry through the mouth, it must survive the tumultuous passage through the digestive system. Once it has gained entry inside the body, it must travel to the site where it has access to the nutrients and shelter that it needs to survive. This could be a red blood cell, a vein, the intestines, a muscle, or liver cells. Once there, it must be able to remain there and not be washed out, digested, absorbed, or otherwise ejected by the immune response of the host.

During the course of their evolution, parasites have developed specific adaptations that have enabled them to survive in their environments. Tapeworms have developed hooks to hang on in the intestinal lumen (tube) so that they can absorb the nutrients they require. The plasmodium agent of malaria spends part of its life in the mosquito, which injects the parasite into the bloodstream of its host while feeding. The causative agent of amebic dysentery forms cysts that allow it to survive for long periods in water or contaminated food until some hapless traveler comes along and ingests it.

Perhaps some of the most remarkable adaptations that any organisms have made are the mechanisms parasites use to evade the immune system. You have already seen one example of immune response evasion in your investigations of *Diplococcus pneumoniae* (Learning Experience 4). As you recall, the virulent strain of this pneumococcus is encapsulated in a polysaccharide coat. This enables the bacteria to (literally) slip past the first line of defense of the immune system, the macrophage. Although it may be caught later by the humoral response, the encapsulated strain has a distinct advantage over the nonencapsulated strain because of this ability to avoid engulfment by the macrophage. This tactic has given the virulent strain of pneumococcus a selective advantage in growing in the host environment.

Parasites have evolved a wide array of strategies for evading the host's immune response. Most parasites appear to use one or more of the tactics listed in Table 3.15.

Parasites can evade the immune system by these strategies as long as the immune system does not change. But over time, the immune system also evolves and develops counterstrategies in an attempt to expel the intruder. An example of this is the host-parasite interaction in leishmaniasis. This is a disease caused by a parasitic protozoan that lives inside macrophages. Having developed the ability to live within a macrophage, leishmania has eliminated a major line of defense by the host. The host, however, in a game of evolutionary one-upsmanship, has evolved a strategy of its own. This counterstrategy involves transporting some of the parasite proteins that are being synthesized as the parasite grows within the macrophage to the cell surface. Here they will be recognized as foreign antigens by T-cells. Recognition of these antigens results in the destruction of the infected macrophage. This somewhat self-destructive (for the macrophage) strategy enables the immune system to fight back.

Table 3.15 Strategies for Evading the Immune Response

Strategies	Evasion Tactics
anatomical seclusion	The site at which a parasite grows is not very accessible to components of the immune system. Or the site is located where antibodies and white blood cells may not be able to recognize its antigens, such as inside a cell.
antigenic variation	The population of parasites is made up of subpopulations with different antigens on their surfaces. One such population will dominate until it is eliminated by the immune response. Then a second subpopulation will increase in number until it is eliminated by the immune response and is replaced by a third antigenic type.
shedding and renewal	A parasite can shed the antigens/antibody complexes on its surface. Once shed, the parasite replaces them with new antigens of the same type.
antigenic disguise	The parasite hides its own antigens under a "coat" of host antigen. The parasite adsorbs the host antigen on its own surface, and the host sees the invader as self.
protective coat	The parasite develops a cyst wall, which is antigenically inert. The wall contains no antigens to which the host immune system can respond.
immune suppression	Many parasites can suppress the immune responses of their host. They do this by using mechanisms we don't clearly understand.
circulating immune complexes	The parasite can induce a nonspecific antibody response that floods the host with antibodies. None of these antibodies, however, are directed specifically toward parasite antigens.

Think of the relationship between host and parasite as a kind of balancing act. The host exerts considerable effort in ridding itself of the parasitic interloper. The survival of the host may depend on how successfully it does this. The parasite, on the other hand, requires the nutrients and shelter that the host provides. And to survive and reproduce, it must avoid the effects of the immune response. To survive, each must adapt or accommodate the other in a process known as coevolution.

In coevolution, two populations interact so closely that each evolutionary change in one population has an effect on the other population. In other words, natural selection for a specific change in one takes place as a response to a change in the other. Perhaps the best examples of coevolution are seen in the relationships between flowers and the insects that pollinate them. Many flowering plants and insects have formed a partnership over millions of years. The partnership helps plants reproduce when insects bring pollen from another plant for fertilization. The plants, in their turn, provide food (nectar) for the insects. This relationship has coevolved. That is, changes have taken place and been selected for in plants and insects that enhance this partnership. Recall the story of Charles Darwin, the moth, and the orchid that you read about in Unit 2. When Darwin discovered an orchid in Madagascar whose flower had a foot-long tube leading to the nectar at the base, he made a prediction. He predicted that somewhere nearby there was a moth with a proboscis long enough to reach the nectar. Many years later a moth with a suitably long proboscis was discovered. Darwin based this prediction on the concept of coevolution.

Parasites and their hosts live in intimate association. As a result, they exert strong selective pressures on the evolution of each other. To survive, parasites have had to evolve ways to avoid the host's immune response. The host, in turn, in order to survive infection, has had to respond to these changes by evolving ways to restrain the growth of the altered parasites. In a "successful" host-parasite interaction, the parasite can grow and reproduce. But it does not grow and reproduce so extensively that it weakens and kills the host. This would only serve as a dead end for the parasite. The host can restrain the growth of the parasite enough that, in many instances, the host will show no signs of its "dual existence."

 **ANALYSIS**

Table 3.16 describes several parasitic diseases of humans. The table includes the causative agent, the site of infection, the symptoms, and the strategies the agent of infection has evolved to avoid a particular immune response.

For each disease, speculate about how each parasite's strategies enable it to avoid the immune response. Include in your description the tactics each parasite appears to use (from Table 3.15). Then explain in your own words why this is effective. Base your explanation on your understanding of the cell-mediated and humoral immune responses.

Table 3.16 Parasitic Diseases: Their Agents, Symptoms, and Evasion Tactics

Disease	Causative Agent	Site of Infection	Symptoms	Evasion Tactics
amebiasis (dysentery)	*Entamoeba histolytica* (amoeba)	mucosal lining of large intestine	• diarrhea • cramps • vomiting • malaise	• antigen shedding and renewal
African trypanosomiasis (sleeping sickness)	*Trypanosoma brucei* (protozoan)	blood (extracellular)	• swollen glands • apathy • lack of coordination • mental apathy • convulsions	• antigenic variation • immunosuppression
leishmaniasis	*Leishmania donavani* (protozoan)	macrophage red blood cell	• enlarged liver and spleen • anemia • emaciation	• anatomical seclusion • immunosuppression • circulating antibodies
malaria	*Plasmodium falciparum* (protozoan)	red blood cell	• chills and fever • anemia • blood in urine	• anatomical seclusion • antigenic variation • antigen shedding and renewal • immunosuppression
schistosomiasis	*Schistosomma japonica* (fluke)	veins of small intestine	• fever • skin rash • abdominal pain • bloody diarrhea • damage to the small intestine • enlarged liver and spleen	• antigenic disguise • antigen shedding and renewal • immunosuppression • circulating antibodies
trichinosis	*Trichinella spirilis* (worm)	juvenile stage in intestine; adult stage in muscle tissue	• intestinal inflammation • pneumonia • meningitis • deafness • brain and eye damage (juvenile stage) • muscle pain • difficulty in breathing • heart damage (adult stage)	• antigen shedding and renewal • protective coat • immunosuppression

EXTENDING *Ideas*

- Research the immune response to a bacterial infection. Compare the immune response evoked by a bacterial infection to that of a viral infection.

- Research the immune response to cancer cells.

- An important feature of the immune system is the ability to distinguish foreign invaders from the body's own cells. What happens during the immune rejection of organ transplants? Research drugs designed to stop rejection. How do these drugs work?

- Research the biology of an autoimmune disease. Some examples of autoimmune diseases include diabetes, multiple sclerosis, lupus, and arthritis. What happens in the immune system to cause the symptoms manifested by one of these diseases? Look for any recent research that is trying to develop ways of alleviating these symptoms.

- Some research suggests that the psychological state of an individual may play a role in his or her ability to fight off disease. The implication is that mental functions may be interconnected with the immune system. Some think that the number of lymphocytes may actually increase with a positive outlook. Describe the evidence from sources that suggest this. Evaluate the data.

- When a person becomes sick with an infectious disease, a common symptom is swollen glands or lymph nodes. Lymph nodes are part of the lymphatic system of the body. When pathogens enter the body, they eventually make their way into the lymphatic system. Here white blood cells live and wage their wars. The lymphatic system also serves as a waste disposal system. It filters out the detritus of the battle. Research the lymphatic system and its components. How does the lymphatic system carry out its functions?

- Do long-time associations of an infectious agent with a particular species of host bring about tolerance, loss of virulence for the infectious agent, and fewer symptoms of disease for the host? Or does the battle just intensify over time? Is the truly successful parasite the one that can reproduce prolifically and get its offspring into the world, even if it means leaving behind the wasted carcass of its host? These questions are hotly debated by evolutionary biologists and parasitologists. Research this debate. What is the scientific evidence that favors each side? Which theory would you support? Explain your decision.

- The parasitic way of life has resulted in the evolution of some strange and interesting structural adaptations. Tapeworms have developed a mouth part that consists primarily of a hook to grasp the intestine. This hook allows them to absorb nutrients from the intestine. They have lost their own digestive powers since they have no need for them in their environment. Fleas and lice have lost their wings, and in some cases, their eyes, since their lifestyle does not require them. Research parasite adaptations to their specific environments. Describe how, through natural selection, these changes may have taken place.

- In the early 19th century, the catalog of a well-known department store advertised tapeworms for sale as a guaranteed way to lose weight. Research tapeworms. Why might this have been considered a feasible approach? Would this be permitted today? Why or why not?

CAREER FOCUS

Physician Elijah, a young man in his mid-20s, has come to Sydney's office for help. He's suffering from symptoms she's very familiar with: runny nose, sneezing, and watery and puffy eyes. Sydney is a physician who specializes as an allergist-immunologist. She sees patients who have a disease or condition caused by allergies, a problem related to the immune system, or are undergoing surgical transplantation of an organ that may be rejected by their bodies. In Elijah's case, it's a fairly straightforward seasonal allergy.

As with any physician, Sydney's job is to diagnose and treat diseases and disorders of the human body. She must educate patients, letting them and their families know what's going on and explaining the possibilities for treatment. But Sydney finds that there really is nothing quite as rewarding as making her patients feel better after suffering with an allergy or immunology problem.

Growing up, Sydney was always interested in anything having to do with biology and helping people. She figured that medicine was probably the best combination of her interests. She was fascinated by how living things functioned and what they could do. During high school, Sydney took as many math and science classes as possible. Her guidance counselor also suggested she take Latin. He reminded her to study hard in English class, as this experience would help her when writing papers in college. After graduating high school, Sydney was accepted to a pre-med college program. Although she enjoyed her courses, she really wanted to gain some hands-on experience working with patients. Her adviser suggested that she become a certified nurse assistant or an EMT. She thought that becoming an EMT would be exciting. So she completed the training and was able to get valuable experience while she worked her way through school. As an EMT, Sydney got a taste of medicine. But she felt driven to delve deeper by pursuing a medical degree and becoming a physician.

Sydney went on to medical school, but she wasn't sure which field of medicine she would pursue. One day while riding the elevator of one of the buildings on campus, Sydney noticed a poster advertising a talk about allergy and immunology. She went to the talk and was intrigued—enough to seek out the allergist-immunologist who gave the talk. Over the course of her 4 years in medical school, Sydney developed a mentor relationship with him and decided to specialize in allergy and immunology.

After medical school, Sydney completed her residency, during which time she enjoyed making patients feel better. When her patients showed their appreciation and thanked her, she knew she had made the right decision. Although her work was not nearly as glamorous as what she'd seen on television shows, she still found it very rewarding. Upon finishing her residency, Sydney chose to complete 3 more years of training to become an allergist-immunologist. Her training took many years and a lot of hard work. But making a difference in people's lives motivated her to continue.

Sydney feels that one of the major benefits of being a doctor is the opportunity to develop meaningful and lasting relationships with patients and their families. She loves that there's never a dull moment in her job. Sydney is constantly challenged to keep up with the latest findings in her field so that she can give her patients the best care. And she's found that there is nothing more rewarding than helping someone feel better.

Search for the Cure

Prologue

Reports of infectious diseases appear in the media with great regularity. It is perhaps unavoidable, at times, for us to view the world as a place teeming with microbes of all shapes, sizes, and ferocities. Sometimes it feels like these guys are just waiting for a suitable host—you—to cross their paths so that they can take up residence and literally parasitize the life processes out of you. There are reports of outbreaks of age-old diseases, such as cholera and dysentery. We have the appearance of never-before-identified diseases, such as AIDS, SARS, and hantavirus. And we are seeing the recurrence of diseases once thought conquered, such as tuberculosis and staphylococcal and streptococcal bacterial infections. How does anyone remain healthy? It's enough to make you avoid eating, drinking, breathing, or touching anything. It's certainly enough to make you keep your distance from another person who might be a walking repository of microscopic menaces.

And yet, many individuals never contract any of these diseases. Many others survive them with few or no physical consequences other than immunity to reinfection. Clearly the immune system of individuals plays a role in determining whether, and how sick, a person may become from an infection. But are there other ways to minimize the debilitating and costly impact of infectious diseases?

In this learning experience, you explore the various ways in which infectious diseases can be prevented and, once contracted, treated. You also explore the advantages and disadvantages of preventative medicine, such as vaccines, as compared to therapeutic medicine, such as treating the disease with drugs once contracted.

Brainstorming

Discuss the following questions with your partner, and record your thinking in your notebook. Be prepared to share your ideas with the class.

1. Are there any behaviors or habits that you might change based on what you have learned in this unit? If so, what are they? Why might you change them?
2. Describe any experiences you or anyone you know has had with different kinds of preventative habits or medicines. How could you determine whether this behavior or medicine prevented the disease? Explain.
3. Describe any treatments you have experienced or know about for curing an infectious disease.
4. What do you think is the difference between preventing a disease and treating a disease? Which do you think is preferable? Why?

READING

An Ounce of Prevention . . .

"An ounce of prevention is worth a pound of cure." This adage speaks directly to the two major approaches taken in a search for dealing with any disease, prevention and treatment. Concern about disease and how to deal with it far predates our modern understanding of the causative agents of disease. Before we understood how infectious diseases were spread, prevention was practiced largely on the basis of superstition and tradition. Sometimes this approach was effective. When it was, it was most likely because traditions and superstitions are often based on generations of observations about what constitutes sensible and healthy behavior. We then discovered that diseases were caused by microbes, and that microbes could be transmitted through food and water systems. This led to a major breakthrough in the prevention of disease. Public health practices have contributed enormously to reducing epidemics of infectious disease. Think about providing clean water and adequate sanitation facilities, regulating procedures for handling food, and educating people about personal hygiene and behavior. These practices have greatly lowered the incidence of countless diseases, such as plague, cholera, sexually transmitted diseases, and tuberculosis, that decimated populations before the 20th century. Technological advances in medicine, such as the development of vaccines, have greatly aided in the prevention of infectious diseases.

Topic: Vaccinations
Go to: www.scilinks.org
Code: INBIOH2460

VACCINES: FOOLING MOTHER NATURE?

In 1796, Edward Jenner, an English physician, made an observation that led to the development of the first vaccine. Smallpox was a terrible disease, widespread throughout history and around the world Survivors of smallpox were often left with disfiguring pockmarks on their skin. These were the result of lesions caused by the infecting virus. Because of the prevalence of this disease, scarred individuals were commonplace. Jenner noticed that milkmaids, on the other hand, rarely had pocked skin. He observed that these milkmaids were often in contact with cows infected with a related disease, cowpox. He hypothesized that this contact protected them from contracting smallpox. Jenner tested his theory by scratching the skin of healthy individuals (starting with his own son) with scrapings from cowpox lesions. Crude though they were, these first vaccinations

Figure 3.48

An 1802 cartoon "The Wonderful Effect of the New Inoculation!" satirizes Edward Jenner and his vaccine against smallpox. (From *Viruses* by Arnold J. Levine, Scientific American Library, New York, 1992.)

provided effective protection against smallpox (see Figure 3.48). Modern scientific investigations have demonstrated that those scrapings from cowpox lesions contained a virus closely related to the variola virus, the causative agent of smallpox. Jenner is credited in the Western Hemisphere with the initial observations about cowpox and with the development of vaccines. But the Chinese were carrying out a form of intranasal (up the nose) vaccination for smallpox 1,000 years ago. **Scarification** (scratching the surface of the skin) in India a few centuries later served as Jenner's model for vaccination.

Today, smallpox has been eradicated and has been declared a conquered disease (Figure 3.49). This is the result of an extensive and aggressive vaccination plan around the world. The only remaining smallpox viruses are samples found in freezers in two laboratories at the Centers for Disease Control in Atlanta, Georgia, and in Moscow, Russia. Much scientific and ethical debate has taken place over whether these stocks of virus should be destroyed. Some scientists feel that there is much to be learned about viruses and immunity by studying this virus. Other scientists express great concern for the risk should the virus be released accidentally or on purpose. Much of the world's population is no longer being vaccinated. No decision has been reached, and the stocks remain.

Figure 3.49

Ali Maow Maalin is the last person to contract smallpox naturally.

Modern science and technology have developed vaccines for a number of different diseases. Many individuals have been vaccinated against such childhood diseases as measles, mumps, rubella, polio, diphtheria, pertussis, tetanus, hemophilus influenza, and hepatitis. Vaccination is based on the principle that once the immune system has encountered an infectious agent, the system can respond much more rapidly to a repeat exposure to that agent. After the first exposure, it takes about 5 to 7 days for antibodies to appear, and nearly 2 weeks for a full antibody response to develop. A person who has been exposed previously to the agent, however, mounts an antibody response within 1 or 2 days. This is because the memory B-cells are ready and waiting. Vaccines are designed to confer the benefits of this rapid antibody response without the individual having to endure a full-blown infection and accompanying disease symptoms. A vaccine can be made up of one of several different kinds of materials:

- It may be an infectious agent that has been killed and therefore cannot cause a disease.
- It may be an agent whose virulent properties have changed, or mutated, such that the organism can grow but cannot cause symptoms of the disease.
- It may consist of specific proteins of the infectious agent. These are the antigens to which the immune system responds during an actual infection.

In each of these cases, the immune system recognizes the antigens and responds as though the vaccine material were an actual infection.

Although developing a vaccine may sound easy in theory, it can be very difficult in practice. The immune system may recognize that the material in the vaccine is not quite the real thing. It might then develop a weaker immune response than it would in a real infection. In some cases, components or contaminants of the vaccine cause the individual to feel sick and suffer side effects. Identifying the proteins that evoke an effective immune response to a specific infectious agent can be very difficult and time-consuming. The development of an effective vaccine can be very expensive ($100–$200 million for each vaccine). If vaccines are to make a substantial contribution to public health, they must be available cheaply and readily to millions of people. Despite the obvious long-term gains of preventing disease, at times, economics can block the development and use of vaccines.

ANALYSIS

Record your responses to the following in your notebook.

1. Why was inoculating an individual with the cowpox virus an effective method in preventing smallpox? (Cowpox and smallpox are caused by different but related viruses.) Think about what you know about protein interactions and the immune response.
2. Describe how a vaccine against cholera might be developed. How would it work? Use your understanding about the immune response.
3. What kinds of vaccines do you think we need to develop today? Explain your choices.
4. In 1796, Jenner tested his vaccine on healthy individuals, including his own young son. Do you think such an experiment would be carried out today? Would you volunteer for such an experiment? Explain your responses.

When Good Things Happen to Bad Bacteria

When preventative measures are not available or fail, disease sometimes happens. In many cases, the response of the immune system is sufficient to fight back and defeat the invader. But in many other cases, the immune system receives help in the form of treatments with drugs. One class of drugs used to treat bacterial infections is antibiotics. This group of chemical compounds is synthesized naturally by certain kinds of microorganisms.

Before the discovery of antibiotics, bacterial infections simply ran their courses. Sometimes the immune system of the patient successfully fought off the infection and the patient lived to tell the tale. Sometimes the patient died. With the discovery of antibiotics, we felt we had triumphed over microbes. However, the feeling of superiority did not last long.

Within 1 or 2 years of the discovery of the antibiotic penicillin, the first drug-resistant strain of staphylococci appeared. As fast as new antibiotics were discovered, strains of microbes resistant to that antibiotic were also discovered. Nearly all disease-causing bacteria known to medical science have become resistant to at least one antibiotic. Our medical miracle is now a medical dilemma.

In this activity, you will compare the effect of three antibiotics on two nonpathogenic strains of the Gram-negative bacteria *Escherichia coli*. The Gram stain technique is a first step in identifying bacteria. The results of this technique will place bacterial cells in one of two groups. In one group, Gram-positive bacteria stain deep purple. In the other group, Gram-negative bacteria stain red. The two distinctive stains reflect differences in the cell walls in these organisms. The cell walls of Gram-negative bacteria have a high lipid content. But the cell walls of Gram-positive bacteria have no lipids. The differences in the two groups of bacteria are also reflected in their sensitivity to certain antibiotics (see Table 3.17).

Table 3.17 Bacteria Sensitivity to Certain Antibiotics

Antibiotic	Effect on Bacteria*	Mode of Action	Effective Against
ampicillin	bactericidal	inhibition of cell wall synthesis	broad spectrum (Gram-positive and Gram-negative)
tetracycline	bacteriostatic	inhibition of protein synthesis	broad spectrum
erythromycin	bacteriostatic	inhibition of protein synthesis	Gram-positive

*Bacteriostatic means the antibiotic prevents bacteria from growing. Bactericidal means the bacteria are killed directly.

Materials

For each pair of students:

- 2 pairs of safety goggles
- 2 nutrient agar plates
- 1 inoculating loop or sterile cotton swab
- 1 sterile forceps or tweezers
- 1 Bunsen burner or candle
- 1 wax marking pencil
- tape
- distilled water
- 1 ruler

For the class:

- 2 different strains of *E. coli* bacteria (labeled 1 and 2)
- paper disks soaking in distilled water, or 1 of 3 antibiotic solutions
- 3 antibacterial solutions
- sponges
- 37° C incubator (optional)

PROCEDURE

1. Before conducting this experiment, read through the entire procedure. With your partner, design a control for the experiment.
2. Review the safety procedures described in the Pre-laboratory Safety Check for the activity Outbreak in Learning Experience 2.
3. Obtain 2 nutrient agar plates. Label one "1" and the other "2."
4. Sterilize an inoculating loop in a flame or use a sterile cotton swab. Dip the loop or swab in *E. coli* bacteria culture 1. Remove the cover on a sterile nutrient agar plate. Use the sterile loop or swab to inoculate the agar plate with the bacteria. Streak the bacteria by following the techniques you used in Learning Experience 2. Streak the whole plate. Use Figure 3.50 as a guide to the streaking pattern.
5. Repeat the process in step 4 for *E. coli* culture 2.

Figure 3.50

Procedure and pattern for streaking a plate.

6. Use tweezers to remove 2 paper disks from each of the 3 antibiotic solutions. Remove 2 disks from the distilled water. Place 1 of each treated disk and 1 untreated disk in a different part of each of the bacteria-streaked sections of the nutrient agar plates. (Be sure to place the disks on areas that you have streaked with bacteria.) Replace covers and secure with tape.

7. Use a wax pencil to mark the location and name of each antibiotic disk on the cover of each plate. Make a drawing of each plate with appropriate labeling in your notebook.

8. Leave the plates at room temperature to incubate for at least 24–48 hours. Or place in a 37° C incubator overnight.

9. After 24–48 hours, look for abundant growth on the nutrient agar plates. Examine each plate. Describe and record your observations on each part of the plate. Compare the amounts of growth around the 4 disks. Measure and record the size of any clear zone, and examine it for any bacterial growth. Record the location and appearance of any growth that you observe inside the clear zone.

ANALYSIS

Prepare a laboratory report for this experiment in your notebook. Be sure to include the following:

a. the question being asked,
b. the experimental approach you used,
c. the controls you included and why,
d. the results that you observed,
e. any possible sources of error,
f. your conclusions based on your observations, and
g. your explanation of what happened at the molecular level.

Use the information in the reading and in Table 3.17 to analyze your data. Remember that the bacteria you used are both strains of *E. coli*.

. . . Is Worth a Pound of Cure  READING

For a variety of reasons, the prevention of disease may not be possible or may not be the method of choice. In many countries where the majority of people live at a subsistence level, the cost of installing good sanitary facilities, even to prevent the spread of water-borne diseases, is prohibitive. In some instances, a change of behavior could prevent disease. But changing the personal habits of a lifetime or the cultural habits of generations can be difficult. The process of vaccinating large populations can be very difficult even in cases where effective vaccines exist. (And for many diseases, there are no vaccines.) Often simply getting individuals to sites where the vaccine can be administered is a challenge. In addition, many vaccines require two or more sequential injections. Finding the same individuals again to complete the series of injections poses problems, particularly in rural areas. Obtaining sterile needles and providing storage facilities and refrigeration can be a logistical nightmare in many developing countries. (Refrigeration is needed to preventing the denaturation of the protein components of the vaccine.)

meadowsweet: origin of aspirin; reduces pain.

rosy periwinkle: origin of vinblastine; fights cancer.

poppy: origin of codeine; reduces pain. Also a cough suppressant.

foxglove: origin of digitalis; used with slow heartbeats or fainting spells.

ipecacuanha: origin of ipecac; induces vomiting.

Figure 3.51

Plants are the source of many commonly used medicinal drugs.

Another, less-acknowledged problem with prevention of disease is its lack of drama. Prevention, which results in the absence of disease, is often difficult to appreciate. The herbal healer or internist, however, who snatches a patient back from the jaws of death is highly praised, appreciated, and rewarded. With prevention is always the question, "Did that treatment or behavior really keep me from getting sick?" In many societies, the motivation for the development of preventative measures may be less rewarding than discovering the cure.

The search for the cure for diseases is as ancient as humankind. Indeed, the healing arts are most likely as old as the martial arts. Almost every society has revered its healers, from the honored medicine men and women in early tribes to the near worship of physicians in modern society. Early healers usually turned to the natural world for the plant and animal products that seemed to be effective in preventing and treating certain ailments. Even today, modern science still shops at nature's pharmacy. Many of the drugs in common usage have been developed based on the chemical constituents of plants used by traditional healers (see Figure 3.51).

NEED A HANKY, ALEX?

The cure generally takes the form of medicinal drugs. Drugs, in this case, are defined as substances given to humans or other animals for the treatment of a disease. A drug may be designed to alleviate the symptoms, or it can be used to cure the disease. A drug of the former type can be as simple as a water, sugar, and salt solution, which is the most effective way of treating cholera. This simple solution rehydrates the body and enables the individual to survive the course of the infection by treating the symptoms. Treating the symptoms rather than the cause enables the immune system to establish a response that can clear the infection. For certain viral diseases—colds, influenza, and chicken pox, for instance—bed rest, fluids, and perhaps an occasional bowl of chicken soup are the best and only effective treatments known to date. By taking in nutrients and conserving energy, stricken individuals can assist their immune systems to overcome the unwelcome invader.

Mother's Best

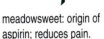

Chicken Soup

Some drugs work directly on the causative agent. In many cases, this happens by blocking some specific metabolic function of the organism. The best-known example of this type of medicinal drug is the class known as antibiotics. (You encountered antibiotics in Learning Experience 3, Agents of Disease.) Antibiotics are chemical compounds that kill or inhibit the growth of bacteria. They are produced by microorganisms such as bacteria and mold. The story of antibiotics began in 1929, with the British bacteriologist Alexander Fleming. Fleming found that a culture dish in which he was growing *Staphylococcus* bacteria had become contaminated by the fungus *Penicillium*. (Legend has it that Fleming had a bad cold while he was conducting these experiments, and the original contaminating organism dripped from his nose.) Rather than just ditching his culture plate in frustration, Fleming took a closer look. He noticed that growth of the staphylococci had been inhibited in the region bordering the mold. This seemed to be the result of some chemical substance diffusing outward from the mold (see Figure 3.52).

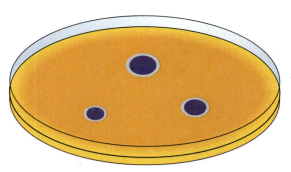

Figure 3.52

Fleming saw a clear region in the bacterial growth around the mold. He thought the mold was producing a chemical substance that could kill bacteria.

This observation led to the isolation, purification, and full-scale production of penicillin. When the full potential of such an antibacterial agent was realized, scientists initiated a systematic search for other antibiotics. Within a few years, a whole medicine chest of different antibiotics was discovered. Many of the antibiotics were isolated from a wide variety of molds and bacteria. Medical practice was revolutionized. The bacterial infections that had been among the most dreaded scourges of humankind, such as tuberculosis, syphilis, bacterial pneumonia, and bubonic plague, became treatable. Many scientists and medical practitioners thought that tales of bacterial infections would soon be relegated to the history of science. Little did they realize . . .

ANTIBIOTICS: PROBLEM SOLVERS OR PROBLEM CAUSERS?

How do antibiotics work? How do bacteria become resistant? Penicillin kills bacteria by binding to an enzyme that helps bacteria synthesize cell walls during growth and cell division. The binding of the antibiotic to the enzyme prohibits the bacteria from dividing properly, and the bacteria die. Other antibiotics have other targets. Erythromycin binds to a protein of the bacterial ribosome and blocks protein synthesis. Tetracycline also interferes with bacterial protein synthesis by binding to the site on the ribosome where tRNAs normally bind. Sulfonamides inhibit an enzyme in a synthetic pathway for a compound essential to the synthesis of nucleic acids in bacteria. These compounds bind specifically to bacterial proteins, leaving the host molecules unaffected.

In 1945, Fleming correctly predicted that human behavior leading to misuse and abuse of penicillin would create serious medical problems involving the development of bacterial resistance to the antibiotic. He had already demonstrated in the laboratory that mutants present in populations of bacteria were resistant to penicillin. These mutants could be selected for by growing the bacteria in increasingly higher concentrations of the drug. It was later shown that bacteria can develop resistance to penicillin in two ways. First, a bacterial mutation in an enzyme involved in cell wall synthesis can occur. In this case, the enzyme can still perform its function but no longer binds penicillin. Second, some bacteria have acquired the capacity to destroy the antibiotic before it destroys them. This can happen when the bacteria acquire new DNA from their

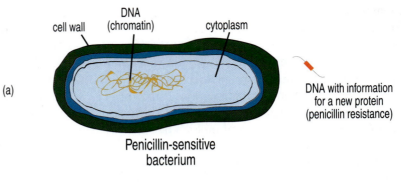

(a)

cell wall

DNA (chromatin)

cytoplasm

DNA with information for a new protein (penicillin resistance)

Penicillin-sensitive bacterium

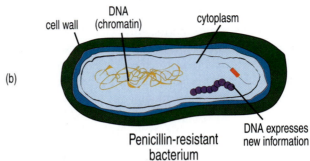

(b)

cell wall

DNA (chromatin)

cytoplasm

DNA expresses new information

Penicillin-resistant bacterium

environment. This DNA has information for antibiotic-destroying enzymes encoded in it. Where would this DNA come from? Bacteria that make antibiotics would most likely carry genes encoding proteins to protect themselves against the effects of that antibiotic. A current theory hypothesizes that fragments of DNA can contaminate preparations of antibiotics because they are isolated from the organisms that produce them. The DNA is carried along as the drug is prepared and ingested. The DNA fragments are taken up by the bacteria in the body (see Figure 3.53).

What constitutes the misuse of antibiotics? We are seeing a resurgence of tuberculosis and the appearance of multidrug-resistant forms of the bacteria that cause it. Scientists attribute this to the failure of infected patients to take antibiotics for the entire period of time recommended. When antibiotics are prescribed, an indicated course of treatment is given. Often, upon feeling better, a patient will stop taking the drug. This can set the scene for a selection of drug-resistant forms of the bacteria.

Drug misuse also arises out of the view that these drugs are a cure for all ills. The patient who has the flu yet insists on a prescription for antibiotics is a common occurrence in doctors' offices around the United States. In many countries, antibiotics are available without prescription. As such, they are commonly used as self-prescribed cures for all kinds of aches and pains, or even as preventative medicine. All of these situations have led to a potentially deadly scenario—that of drug-resistant bacteria causing unstoppable, lethal infections.

Will bacteria rule the world in the end? One might imagine that this is a possibility with their ability to mutate so readily and with the capacity to shuttle DNA-encoding multidrug resistance back and forth among themselves. But medical science has marshaled its forces and is taking up some of the same weapons the bacteria use: modification and change.

The search for new and effective drugs against disease continues. Some scientists systematically screen many different kinds of microbes looking for substances that demonstrate antibacterial activity. Others use a "pull everything off the shelf and try it" approach. Both have proven effective, though tedious and time-consuming. With either method, finding any substance that is even slightly effective gives chemists a place to start. But they may as well be trying to unlock a lock by using every possible key they can find and hoping one works. These approaches have been shown to be expensive and labor-intensive. For each successful drug developed, thousands more have been made, tested, and rejected. In the quest for new antibiotics, however, a combination of these approaches has led to the discovery that certain frogs, moths, pigs, jellyfish, and sharks all produce powerful antibiotics. Researchers are studying these compounds and modifying them. They are testing them to determine whether these drugs will serve as a new source of artillery against bacterial diseases.

DESIGNER DRUGS

Another, more rational approach is being used in the development of **designer drugs**. (Recall Learning Experience 8, The Cholera Connection, in which you designed a drug against cholera toxin.) This approach is based on an understanding of the infectious agent, and more specifically of the target molecules within that agent. These molecules might be enzymes, for example, that are required for an essential function. Scientists seek to understand the structure of the target protein and the process by which it interacts with another molecule. Based on this understanding, a drug can be designed to compete for the binding site on the target.

This technique is being used in attempts to develop effective drugs against AIDS. An HIV protein, a protease, is required for the virus to process or cut its proteins to the proper size. Drugs are being designed to compete for the binding site of this protease and thereby inactivate it. The proteins required for virus growth would not be available, and the virus would be eradicated. Clinical trials have indicated that this drug, in combination with other drugs aimed to fight against HIV, are effective in reducing or eliminating the virus from infected patients. Many people with AIDS are now living longer and living symptom-free lives.

A designer drug approach to developing new antibiotics might involve understanding how an enzyme capable of destroying the antibiotic works. One then designs a molecule that fits into the binding site of the enzyme. This incapacitates its antibiotic-destroying ability.

The causative agents of disease contain many potential target molecules that are unique to that organism. This makes it possible to develop drugs that kill the agent but leave the host untouched. However, this approach requires in-depth understanding of the biological and biochemical mechanisms of these causative agents and how they cause disease. In addition, the cost of developing these designer drugs is high. Inevitably, this cost is reflected in the final price of the product. This could make the cost of such drugs to affected individuals living in developing countries prohibitive.

TAKE TWO FLOWERS AND CALL ME IN THE MORNING

For centuries, the study of plants has led to the discovery of medicines effective against a variety of ills. Curare is used by natives in the Amazon to make deadly poison arrows. Surgeons use it as a muscle relaxant. To shrink cancer tumors, young leukemia victims are treated with vincristine and vinblastine, isolated from the rosy periwinkle plant of Madagascar, and taxol, derived from the Pacific yew tree. Derivatives of quinine, isolated from the cinchona plant, are effective against the parasite responsible for malaria. Even the common dandelion, soaked in a little honey, can be eaten to help combat the flu. The croton plant is a colorful plant of Central America commonly used decoratively in American homes. It has been used in many parts of South and Central America to make a medicinal tea for colds and flu. (One U.S. drug company has isolated an active compound from the croton plant. The company is testing it as an oral drug for respiratory viral infections and as a topical ointment for herpes infections.) Garlic is used routinely in China to fight viral infections.

The microbial world will forever be a part of the human world. For the most part, the relationship between these two worlds is beneficial. For adversarial interactions, however, the battle will be ongoing. We have immune systems equipped to defend, vaccines designed to protect, and drugs developed to destroy microbes. In spite of all this, the microbial world is constantly evolving, changing, and surviving.

ANALYSIS

Record your responses to the following in your notebook.

1. Describe how bacteria might develop resistance to the drug tetracycline.
2. Describe how bacteria could acquire the trait of drug resistance by taking up DNA from its environment.
3. Some scientists argue that humankind will always be plagued by bacteria. They say that drugs offer only a temporary reprieve from suffering, and that the only rational approach to defeating infectious disease is with vaccines. Do you agree or disagree with this statement? Explain your answer.

READING

A Shot in the Dark?

To be vaccinated or not to be vaccinated. That is the question faced by many individuals today. Although vaccines have been shown to be very effective against many diseases of childhood, some parents harbor anxieties over whether to have their children vaccinated. In some cases, they worry about the side effects. In others, the problem is not recognizing the importance of prevention. Many of these diseases, such as whooping cough, measles, and mumps, are not often seen today due to the availability of vaccines. As a result, many parents fail to recognize them as diseases that can cause sickness and sometimes death.

In the following article, writer Diane White suffers over making her own decision about whether to be vaccinated against the flu. Read her arguments and then carry out the task in the Analysis.

FLUMMOXED BY THE FLU

This year I decided not to get a flu shot. Last year I skipped it. In late winter I came down with something that may have been a kind of flu, but it wasn't bad.

Some people really need flu shots, people in high-risk groups—health-care workers, the chronically sick, elderly people. I'd read the news stories reporting a shortage of flu vaccine this year; some people who need shots can't get them. I hated to think I'd be depriving someone who really needed the vaccine.

Then one evening, skimming a magazine and half-watching the news on TV, I heard a voice edged with panic cry, "The worst flu season in two decades!" It was an ad for some patent nostrum alleged to relieve flu symptoms. Night after night I kept seeing the same ad, and the more I saw it, the more difficult it was not to leap to my feet and run to the nearest drugstore to stock up, assuming I could find any. The ad is so persuasive—or manipulative—I wouldn't be surprised if the stuff sold out as soon as the spot aired.

No wonder there's a shortage of vaccine, I thought. No wonder people are clamoring for it. They've all seen that ad.

I decided I'd better get a flu shot.

Watching the ad had made me recall the Hong Kong flu of 1968–69, one of the worst in recent memory. I remembered lying in bed with a high fever, too weak to move, my throat so sore I couldn't talk, every millimeter of my body aching. If the Hong Kong flu did that to me when I was young and healthy, what would it do to me now that I'm middle-aged and broken-down?

Flu shots were being given free at work. The company had a supply, so it wouldn't be as though I were taking it from people who might die if they didn't get it. But how could I be sure? And then I remembered I'd been sick for three days after the last time I'd had the vaccine. Not desperately sick, the way I was with the Hong Kong flu, but sick enough.

I decided maybe I wouldn't get a flu shot.

I'd take a chance. I'd been reading the flu-related stories in the paper. This year's indeed may be the worst in 20 years. Then again, it may not be. Each year scientists try to predict the exact nature of the influenza virus so a vaccine can be formulated to neutralize it. But the virus mutates so quickly that, by some estimates, they have only a 50–50 chance of being right. So it's a gamble. Flu roulette.

And I'd been reading *A Dancing Matrix: Voyages Along the Viral Frontier* by Robin Marantz Henig, a book both fascinating and humbling. It's fascinating because the subject is compelling and Henig is a superb storyteller, humbling because it puts to rest any notion that human beings control their environment.

Henig writes that many researchers believe we're in for a pandemic of influenza in the next few years. A pandemic occurs when a higher than expected rate of disease strikes several continents at the same time; in an epidemic the higher than normal disease rate is confined to one area. The last pandemic was the Hong Kong flu of 1968–69, which killed 28,000 people, a terrible toll but nothing compared to the 1918–19 pandemic, when between 20 million and 40 million people died.

I decided to get a flu shot.

But then I heard Henig in a radio interview. She said that people not in the high risk groups shouldn't get flu shots because the vaccine provides only temporary immunity to a particular strain of flu virus. But if you get the flu, she said, then you'll be immune for life to that strain.

Maybe I wouldn't get a flu shot after all.

Because if I got the flu, I'd be immune for life. Assuming I survived. And what's a week or so of feeling absolutely miserable, with fever and chills and aching all over and coughing and sneezing, compared to a lifetime of immunity to a strain of flu that may or may not come around again?

The next day I got a flu shot.

ANALYSIS

Diane White's dilemma over whether or not to get a flu shot is a problem faced by millions of Americans every flu season. In her article, she outlines the pros and cons of obtaining a shot. Her arguments acknowledge biological, economic, sociological, and psychological issues. Like Diane White, you are going to weigh the advantages and disadvantages, or the costs and benefits, of getting a flu shot.

One way to approach making a decision is to weigh the possible costs or risks of an action versus the possible benefits. Listing the ideas, actions, or outcomes that fall into the two categories can help you decide which plan of action to pursue. It can also help you identify areas where you don't know enough to make a good decision and need more information.

In this type of cost/benefit analysis, remember that a cost might not be strictly an amount of money. An action that wastes your valuable time is a cost. Doing something that would make you sick would be a cost. Similarly, a benefit may be more than having money or a guarantee of good health. A benefit might be something as simple as feeling happy or not having to do something you don't want to do. A benefit might also be a gain for the greater good rather than for an individual gain.

Set up a table of costs versus benefits on a sheet of paper. Reread Diane White's article. Look for the costs and benefits she weighed in making her decision. Fill in your list with costs and benefits using what you learned about the influenza virus in Learning Experience 11 and about the immune system in Learning Experience 12. For example:

Costs	Benefits
Vaccines can make you sick.	Vaccines can keep you from becoming seriously ill.

Make a decision about whether you would get a flu vaccine. Defend your decision. Be prepared to discuss your lists and to address the following in class:

1. I was vaccinated for measles and now I'm immune for life. Why doesn't a flu shot protect me that long? Why do they say I need to have one every year?
2. If I take medicines that relieve the symptoms, then I should be fine. Except they never seem to work very well, and I'll still miss school/work/fun.
3. Diane White may be able to get a flu shot free at work, but I have to go to the doctor. It costs a lot of money. Why does it cost so much?
4. I had the flu and my doctor wouldn't give me antibiotics. Why don't antibiotics work against the flu? He told me the only thing to do was to go home, get lots of bed rest, and drink plenty of fluids. My mother could have told me that.
5. I guess I should get a flu shot. Everyone else is getting one.

▶ Your research team at Drugs R Us Pharmaceutical Company has been given the assignment to cure influenza once and for all. You have a budget of several million dollars and the latest in up-to-date technology and equipment. But the team has been deadlocked in a tiny office for weeks arguing over whether the effort should be spent on developing a vaccine or designing a drug. The team is split pretty much in half, and the arguments are strong on both sides. Describe the costs and benefits of each approach. Then make the deciding vote on which way the team should go. Why did you vote as you did?

▶ Research the arguments for and against destroying the stocks of smallpox virus. How would you vote? Justify your decision.

▶ Mr. C. was a respected businessman from Buenos Aires, who had accumulated a fortune from his family inheritance and personal investments. An energetic man, he spent more than two-thirds of his day pursuing business ventures. He did not like to be held back by sore throats and mild cold symptoms. He generally treated himself with readily available drugs that he bought at the local pharmacy. On one occasion, however, Mr. C. had an exceptionally bad cough and fever on and off for several weeks. During this time, he took several different antibiotics, but nothing seemed to help. Mr. C.'s doctor was concerned and asked him what he had taken. Mr. C. mentioned several things, including chloramphenicol, which has been implicated in shutting down blood production in the bone marrow and even causing leukemia. Mr. C. was flown to Boston where he was diagnosed with acute leukemia. He was treated for leukemia using drugs that destroy many of the white blood cells in the body (including T-cells and macrophages). Even as the leukemia was being brought under control, his infection raged out of control. The intern told Mr. C. that a common intestinal bacterium, *E. coli,* was circulating in his blood and it was resistant to eight antibiotics. (Normal *E. coli* would be killed readily by any one of the eight.) On the twenty-second day after admission, with his bone marrow free of detectable leukemia, Mr. C. died of bleeding and overwhelming infection. An autopsy revealed that the resistant *E. coli* had produced multiple sites of infection in his liver and other organs. What happened to Mr. C. and why? (Adapted from *The Antibiotic Paradox* by Stuart B. Levy, Plenum Press, 1992.)

▶ In recent years, antibacterial soaps have become very popular. Some researchers think that these soaps are effective in preventing the transmission of disease. Others feel they are just a gimmick, doing no more than regular soaps. Design and carry out an experiment that would address this controversy.

▶ Every year a new flu vaccine is designed and distributed in an attempt to prevent a flu epidemic. In 2004, something went drastically wrong in the production of the vaccine. The United States experienced a massive shortage of the vaccine. Research what went wrong in the production of the vaccine. Propose a method for preventing future shortages.

Technology Transfer Specialist

It's going to be a hectic day for Cora Jones. A biotechnology company, Klone-a-Kitty, Ltd., needs a licensing agreement for techniques developed by a professor at Cora's university. Cora then needs to draft a legal agreement with a local hospital for clinical trials that are about to begin on a new drug developed at the university. She is also scheduled to meet with another professor who needs to file a patent application for his newly developed artificial skin. And a pile of scientific and legal journals are sitting on her desk. This reading will update Cora on the latest cutting-edge developments in science and on the latest in legal procedures relating to technology and patents.

Crazy days—but that is what Cora loves about her job. Each day is different and exciting. The challenges require her to be knowledgeable about a wide range of topics. She must be able to communicate with a wide variety of people and solve problems quickly. Cora feels that her work is very valuable. She helps to move discoveries and inventions from the laboratory to other researchers, to companies for development, and ultimately, to the public to improve and even save lives.

Cora is a technology transfer specialist (TTS). This is a relatively new career that involves facilitating the transfer of materials among different organizations. A TTS must understand the science, the legalities, and the business aspects of these transfers in order to protect the interests of everyone involved. In her day-to-day work, Cora will prepare legal documents that involve the transfer of materials, confidentiality, collaborations, patents, and clinical trials. She will prepare for these demands by meeting with scientists and reading journals, proposals, and business plans. She also meets with other technology transfer specialists and attorneys to negotiate agreements.

Cora liked science in school and went on to graduate-level work in biology. She had always been fascinated by inventions and scientific discoveries but never really wanted to do the experimental work herself. While never formally trained in law, Cora has acquired broad legal experience as well as an understanding of business. It is a combination that she finds exciting and challenging every day!

Insistence on Resistance

Prologue

How do organisms acquire new traits? One way is in the mutation of DNA encoding a protein. A change in the nucleotide sequence of the DNA can result in the elimination or altered ability of a protein to carry out its function. This change, in turn, can produce different characteristics in the organism. Another way that organisms might acquire new traits is in the acquisition of new DNA.

Under normal conditions, bacteria will take up free DNA molecules from the environment. And, in many instances, they express the encoded information. However, this is a relatively rare event. Only at certain points in their growth cycles do the cell walls of some bacteria in a population become quite permeable and allow the entry of molecules that would not normally enter the cell. This small percentage of cells is said to be competent. The process of taking up the free DNA is called transformation. In some cases, bacteria take up DNA from their environment. This DNA contains information that, when expressed as proteins, results in the characteristic of antibiotic resistance. In this activity, you investigate the way in which bacteria become resistant to antibiotics.

Brainstorming

Discuss the following questions with your partner, and record your thinking in your notebook. Be prepared to share your ideas with the class.

1. What examples of organisms acquiring new traits have you seen in the course of this unit? Where did the information for the new traits come from?
2. What advantage might an organism gain with the capability of taking up foreign DNA?

ACTIVITY

Teaching Old Bacteria New Traits

In genetic engineering work, most bacterial strains can be made competent by treating them with calcium chloride and a heat shock treatment to make the cell walls more permeable. Many biotechnology companies rely on this technique of cell transformation. In this experiment, you will introduce competent bacteria to a small circular piece of DNA (a **plasmid**.) You will then look for the expression of a new characteristic encoded by this plasmid. The plasmid has several characteristics. These include the following:

- the gene for resistance to the antibiotic ampicillin (a form of penicillin);
- the ability to be taken up by bacteria; and
- the ability to replicate once inside a bacterial cell.

Materials

For each group of four students:

- 4 pairs of safety goggles
- 10 mL nutrient broth
- 2 nutrient agar plates without ampicillin
- 2 nutrient agar plates with ampicillin (200 µg/mL)
- 4 small test tubes (70 × 75 mm)
- 4 sterile glass spreading rods
- 2 pipettes (1-mL)
- 1 pipetting bulb or pipettor
- 1 wax marking pencil
- 1 ice bath (ice and water in an insulated cup)
- 42°C (about 108°F) water bath (warm water in an insulated cup)
- 1 thermometer

For the class:

- 1 tube of competent *Escherichia coli*
- 1 tube of plasmid DNA containing the gene for ampicillin resistance
- tape
- 37°C incubator (optional)

PROCEDURE

1. Read through the entire procedure carefully before conducting the experiment. It is critical that you work quickly and efficiently. Be sure that every step is carried out as described.
2. Design an experiment to answer this question: Can bacteria take up DNA containing a gene encoding ampicillin resistance? Be sure to include controls that will ensure the following about your experiment:
   a. The ampicillin is capable of killing antibiotic-sensitive bacteria.
   b. The competent bacteria (with and without the plasmid) can grow under normal conditions (in the absence of ampicillin).

3. Create a table that describes the purpose of each sample in your experiment. You should have 3 control conditions and 1 experimental condition.

4. Carry out the procedure that begins with step 5. Use a wax marking pencil to label each plate (such as numbering them from 1–4). Record these numbers and the condition each represents in your notebook. Label the 4 test tubes the same way.

5. Obtain a sample of approximately 1 mL of competent *E. coli*. (The bacteria are competent because they have been treated with calcium chloride and are competent to take up DNA.) Also obtain a 1 mL sample of the plasmid DNA containing the ampicillin-resistance gene.

SAFETY NOTE

6. Using a 1-mL pipette, add 0.2 mL of *E. coli* to each tube.

7. Using a second pipette, add 0.1 mL of nutrient broth to the tubes labeled 1 and 3. Using the same pipette, add 0.1 mL of plasmid DNA to the remaining 2 tubes (tubes 2 and 4). Swirl each tube gently.

8. Place all 4 tubes in an ice bath for 20 minutes. Near the end of that time, prepare a warm water bath by placing warm tap water in an insulated cup. Be sure the water temperature is between 40° C and 44° C (104° F–111° F).

9. At the end of the 20 minutes on ice, move the 4 tubes to the warm water bath. Incubate 5 minutes. Then return to the ice bath.

10. Plate out your bacteria from the test tubes onto the appropriate plates. Do that as follows:
    a. Select your first tube (for example, number 1—bacteria without plasmid). Remove the cover from plate 1, and carefully pour the contents of the tube onto the plate.
    b. Using the flat bottom part of a spreading rod (the bottom of the "hockey stick"), spread the bacteria over the entire surface of the plate. Replace the cover and secure with tape.
    c. Allow the bacteria to soak into the agar for a few minutes, then invert. Use a wax marking pencil to mark the bottom of each plate to identify your group's plates.

11. Repeat step 10 with the other 3 tubes. Be sure to follow your experimental design. Put the correct tubes of bacteria in the appropriate plates. Use a new spreading rod each time.

12. Leave the plates at room temperature to incubate for at least 24–48 hours. Or place them in a 37° C incubator overnight.

13. After 24–48 hours, look for abundant growth on some of your plates. Examine each plate. Describe and record your observations of each plate in the table you set up in step 3.

ANALYSIS

Record your responses to the following in your notebook.

You and your colleagues have been asked to develop a business plan for a new biotechnology company. The mission of this new company is to produce large quantities of gluease, an enzyme found in a rare mollusk. This is the only enzyme known to dissolve super-bonding glue, and it is in great demand. Your task is to develop a scientific plan for making large quantities of gluease based on your understanding of transformation. Write up your experimental design, and explain how your design will enable the company to generate the needed amounts of gluease. Include in your experimental proposal a method (an assay) for determining how you will know that you are making the product. (You may assume that the gene for gluease has already been identified and isolated.)

Citrus growers in Florida are subject to capricious weather. A killing frost early in the season can destroy an entire crop. In the past few years, the gene for frost resistance has been identified and isolated. Using techniques similar to those described for getting foreign DNA into bacteria, scientists have been able to insert this gene into oranges. This makes the oranges impervious to the destruction of an early freeze. Some people, however, are opposed to the large-scale use of such technology. Investigate the research that enables this technology to exist. Discuss the pros and cons of using this technology for large-scale citrus growth. Decide how you feel about its use. Explain your thinking.

Learning Experience 14

Stopping the Epidemic

Prologue

Sometime in January 1991, a Chinese freighter arrived in Peru and moored in Lima's harbor. The freighter unloaded its cargo. Then, like so many other vessels in hundreds of other ports around the world, in the quiet of the night it dumped the raw sewage stored in its bilge into the waters of the harbor.

Perhaps it was this Chinese vessel—or another vessel from another part of the world—whose bilge water was teeming with a newly mutated strain of cholera. Perhaps the cholera bacteria were ingested by shellfish in the harbor. Perhaps those shellfish were harvested by local fishermen and then consumed by people in the streets. How the bacteria found their way into the destitute shanty towns of Lima is a matter of speculation. We will never know for certain. What we do know is that by February 23, 1991, Peru's first confirmed case of cholera in almost a century had appeared in a Lima hospital. Physicians christened the new strain *Vibrio cholerae* 01, serotype Inaba, biotype "El Tor." By the end of 1993, El Tor had caused close to 1 million cases of cholera, and more than 8,600 deaths.

Although cholera has made a new home for itself in Latin America, it has always been a part of life in Southern Asia. For generations, it has been **endemic** (prevalent in or native to a particular location) to regions of India. In more recent decades, it has become endemic throughout Africa as well. Since 2001, outbreaks have been reported in many countries. These include Ecuador, Peru, Colombia, India, Bangladesh, Liberia, South Africa, Zimbabwe, and Burundi, to name a few.

As you have learned in this unit, John Snow and Edward Koch solved the mysteries of cholera more than a century ago. Snow's research showed conclusively that cholera was a waterborne disease. He identified ways in which its spread could be halted. Koch isolated and identified the agent that caused it. Surely, it seems, in the age of antibiotics and high-tech sanitary facilities, prevention of this disease should be within our capabilities. After all, cholera was the very first disease to be understood using the techniques of modern epidemiology. So why is cholera a permanent plague in so much of the world? Why is it still causing so much misery, from Asia and Africa to Mexico and Argentina? Can these outbreaks be prevented?

Seeking the answers to these questions is, of course, worthwhile. The answers would improve conditions and save countless human lives. But seeking answers reveals the extraordinarily complex relationships between the discoveries of science and the human societies in which those discoveries are used, misused, or lost. The story of cholera in Latin America says a great deal about modern medicine. At the same time, it says even more about the economic, social, political, and organizational contexts that complicate the way that medicine is practiced.

In this learning experience, you role-play various individuals attending a public health conference in Tumaco, Colombia. Tumaco was the site of another cholera outbreak in 1991. The goal of this conference is to hear from individuals with different ideas and different interests. Conference attendees then attempt to address these different perspectives in designing strategies for resolving the epidemic.

ACTIVITY

The Time of Cholera

It is fall 1991, and the city of Tumaco, Colombia, is in the early stages of a cholera outbreak. In an attempt to bring resources and attention to his people's plight, the mayor of the city has initiated a public relations strategy. He has convened Tumaco's first-ever public health conference. Never expecting them to say yes, he has brazenly invited powerful officials from the World Health Organization (WHO), the Pan American Health Organization (PAHO), the Centers for Disease Control and Prevention in Atlanta, Georgia (CDC), the World Bank, pharmaceutical corporations, and politicians from the Colombian National Assembly.

To the mayor's surprise, he receives a phone call from a vice president of the World Bank shortly after sending out invitations. The World Bank official wants to know if the conference could be redesigned to focus not just on Tumaco's local problems, but on the spread of cholera throughout Latin America. The mayor responds that the crisis in Tumaco could naturally serve as a model of the problems confronting any country in which cholera was endemic. He states that a focus on Tumaco's local situation would not prevent the conference from also examining the larger issues. He is delighted when the World Bank official answers that in that case, she plans to attend. The mayor is amazed when, after the World Bank official has agreed to attend, one after another, the other powerful invitees phone to say that they, too, will be coming.

Although the facilities will be extremely modest, Tumaco now finds itself playing host to a high-powered conference. During this three-day meeting, participants will examine international data about the epidemic, debate strategies for resolving Latin America's cholera epidemic, and develop action plans.

INVITATION TO ATTEND THE FIRST CONFERENCE ON THE PREVENTION AND TREATMENT OF CHOLERA IN LATIN AMERICA

The citizens of Tumaco, Colombia, request your presence at the First Conference on the Prevention and Treatment of Cholera in Latin America. This conference brings together representatives of various groups concerned with the outbreak of cholera in Latin America. The goals of the conference are twofold:

- Develop an accurate picture of the public health challenges facing Latin America, with particular emphasis on cholera.
- Formulate a plan of action to address those challenges.

CONFERENCE AGENDA

Day One: Opening Statements

What are the challenges facing Latin American countries during a cholera epidemic?

Speakers present their perspectives on the issues that surround a cholera outbreak. These perspectives represent a broad range of social, economic, political, and scientific interests in the community and throughout the world.

Day Two: Action Plans to Address the Prevention and Treatment of Cholera

What strategies can be developed to treat cholera epidemics and prevent future outbreaks?

Speakers present their action plans from the perspective of their expertise and interests. Plans will take into consideration the issues of the other speakers.

Day Three: The Future

Where do we go from here?

Speakers use the information, perspectives, and action plans presented during the conference to summarize the conclusions of the conference and determine the next steps.

PREPARING YOUR OPENING STATEMENT

To prepare for Day One of the conference (during which the first goal will be addressed), you must do the following:

1. Read the *Washington Post* article, "The Time of Cholera: One Latin American Town Battles an Epidemic." Take notes on any information you think is important. Use this reading as a resource for your opening statement and your action plan.

2. Read the character role profile that your teacher gives you. Your character will represent issues from one of the following perspectives:
   - medical issues,
   - large-scale national or international economic and political issues, or
   - local economic and social issues.

   Keep your role profile a secret. Prior to the conference, nobody else should know who you are or what your point of view will be. Maintain a little suspense and mystery before the conference. This will make the event more exciting for everyone involved.

3. Write a thoughtful 2–3-minute opening statement for the conference. In this speech, you will share your character's knowledge and concerns with the other conference members. The character profile your teacher gives you is a superficial sketch. Your job is to develop that sketch into a complete person, with an identifiable voice and perspective. As you develop your character, consider all of the following questions:
   - What are the messages that your character is eager to share at this conference?
   - Why does your character want to share these messages? (Your messages may be based on logic, evidence, idealism, and/or the institutional or economic interests of the group you represent. Some of the people at this conference have a vested interest in particular outcomes. Having a vested interest, however, does not mean a person is wrong or bad.)
   - What kind of information is your character interested in finding out at the conference?
   - What sort of people is this character likely to choose as political allies? Why?

4. Think about preparing visuals such as graphs, charts, and pictures to help you get your point across. But keep in mind that you have only 3 minutes in which to make your points. So choose wisely.

It is important that you give careful thought to the nature of your character. In preparation for Day Two of the conference, your character will develop an action plan. This plan will take into consideration what you learned as you listened to the opening statements of others in Day One. But remember, your plan must still be consistent with the perspective of your character. This does not mean that your character cannot change his or her mind. But say your character came to the conference planning to advocate for children or to seek government contracts. In that case, your character should not leave having made a speech about saving the environment and forgetting his or her other issues.

THE TIME OF CHOLERA: ONE LATIN AMERICAN TOWN BATTLES AN EPIDEMIC

Tumaco, Colombia—One-year-old Sandra Moreno lay motionless in the stifling heat, oblivious to the tube in her arm as her mother gently swept flies away from the baby's gaunt face. In make-shift hospital beds nearby, a dozen listless women, some moaning, lay with intravenous lines protruding from their arms. The cholera ward in the San Andrés Hospital in this rural Pacific coast town is already filled to overflowing; at times, patients are forced to lie on metal stretchers that line the walls. Built as an annex to the hospital auditorium, the 15-bed women's ward is made of cinder block. Its windows are narrow slits without screens; there are neither electric lights nor fans.

Sandra Moreno is among the more recent victims of the cholera epidemic that has killed more than 1,000 people and infected more than 150,000 in Latin America since January. An acutely infectious and potentially fatal disease virtually unknown in developed countries, cholera is spread when food—especially raw fish—and drinking water are contaminated with fecal waste. It is characterized by severe diarrhea, vomiting and fever, which lead to rapid dehydration and wracking cramps.

If too much body fluid is lost, the victim dies, sometimes within hours. Because of the poor sanitary conditions necessary to spread cholera, which is rarely transmitted by person-to-person contact, it is widely known as a disease of poverty.

San Andrés, which treats patients for free, is the only hospital in this high-risk, sparsely populated area of 300,000 people spread over 250,000 square miles. Its resources are already strained to the breaking point although, remarkably, none of the 56 cholera patients who have made it to the hospital so far has died. Local officials attribute its success to the dedication and preparation of the hospital staff.

After a month in which only 40 cases of the disease were reported, in Colombia the number of confirmed cases in the past week jumped to 113, according to health ministry officials; health experts say the epidemic is growing exponentially. "Things are rapidly getting worse, and this is only the beginning, because of the conditions people live in," said Alberto Vargas, director of medicine at San Andrés Hospital. "The water is not fit to drink, the poverty is absolute, and these conditions make Tumaco an area of cultivation of the bacteria. I do not know how we will manage."

Since the epidemic began in Peru last January, Colombia, with more resources and more time to prepare, has been working on teaching its citizens preventive measures, stockpiling rehydration solutions of salts and purified water and making contingency plans to slow the spread and limit the number of deaths, according to Colombia's Health Minister Camilo Gonzalez. Along with educational campaigns that urge people to boil drinking water for 10 minutes, to wash their hands after defecating and to abstain from eating raw fish, the ministry has designed several programs that are just now being implemented.

These include plans to distribute thousands of buckets to be used as toilets, chlorine to purify drinking water and rudimentary treatment of fecal waste.

Although Colombia is better prepared than was Peru, experts agree the epidemic is likely to wreak havoc here and spread through most of the rest of the continent before the year is over. The reason: widespread poverty.

"Without urgent steps taken in the environment, we will get cholera and more," said Luís Sanchez, an environmental health specialist for the Pan American Health Organization (PAHO). "The technology [of sewage treatment] is available to eradicate these problems, but we do not have the political will or the resources."

THE POOREST REGION IN AN IMPOVERISHED COUNTRY

Tumaco, located on an island, is the center of activity for the Pacific coast region. Its population is predominately black, composed of the descendants of slaves brought over during the nineteenth century to work washing gold scooped from the tropical rivers that crisscross this area.

This is the poorest region of Colombia. In this city of 60,000 only 8 percent of the houses have any type of sewage treatment, and only about 30 percent have running water. People make their living from fishing, curing hardwoods along the jungle rivers and panning for gold.

San Andrés, a 30-year-old 70-bed hospital is not equipped to handle the new flood of cholera cases, no matter how hard its staff works.

One recent Sunday, a single doctor and two nurses were on duty, tending not only to the nine newly arrived cholera cases but to the many other emergencies that occur in an area already suffering from the peak of the annual malaria season. Health minister Gonzalez said there were 28,000 cases of malaria, a potentially fatal disease borne by mosquitoes, reported along the Pacific coast so far this year.

Even in normal times, the lack of resources makes medical care here difficult. Behind the hospital, where laundry is done by hand, dirty bedding and clothing are piled high. Washing is impossible because the city's faulty water supply often leaves the hospital without water. And when it rains heavily, as it did this month, there is no way to dry clothes, sometimes forcing doctors to delay surgery.

While cholera cases can be fatal and take both time and resources to treat, once a patient starts to be rehydrated, he or she can be cured quickly. Most cholera patients are able to leave after two to three days in the hospital, but that depends on how far dehydration has progressed when they arrive for treatment.

One of the most severe cases to arrive at San Andrés was Pola Quinones, an elderly woman who had suffered from severe diarrhea for three days before her family embarked on the 30-minute canoe ride across the open sea in a driving rain to get her to the hospital. She had been unable to speak for two days, most of her vital signs were extremely weak and her color was a pallid gray.

When she arrived in the hospital, doctors and nurses immediately began rehydrating her through intravenous lines in both arms. As her daughter collapsed in tears in an empty wheelchair, two nurses flanked Quinones and, by hand, squeezed plastic bags filled with fluid to force it into her body more quickly.

After forcing two quarts of fluid into Quinones in less than two hours, they wheeled her to the cholera ward. Two days later, she was able to sit up and drink liquids on her own after receiving almost five gallons of fluid.

"We have to be very aggressive when we get patients like that, or they will die," said Manuel Angulo, a physician at the hospital. "Cholera itself is easy to treat, but the state of shock is what is difficult. If they arrive here with even a little bit of life left, we can save them."

But the Quinones case, along with a dozen others from outlying rural areas, has heightened doctors' fears about the rapid spread of the epidemic.

"We are seeing more and more cases from rural areas, and as that spreads, the difficulty will be in transporting them to where they can be treated," said one medic who asked not to be identified. "That is where we will begin to see our deaths. People can only travel by canoe or on foot and will not make it for treatment."

To help combat the epidemic, the hospital had 30 special beds built. Most are made of wooden planks with a hole cut in the middle and no mattress. That allows patients suffering from acute diarrhea to defecate directly into a plastic bucket, which is then emptied into a special sterilizing solution. To make the beds more comfortable, the hospital experimented with canvas cots with holes cut in them, but the fabric ripped and is costly to replace.

WHY CHOLERA IS FLOURISHING

Three blocks from the hospital, the living conditions that give rise to the epidemic are evident and help explain why cholera is flourishing here.

Houses made of wooden planks sit on platforms far enough above the water to avoid flooding at high tide. At low tide, the beach is piled with trash, which pigs root through while swarms of flies feast on excrement.

In the Las Americas neighborhood, Alfonso Palacios, 60, said he and his family have begun boiling their drinking water, although many of his neighbors have not.

To help explain the difficulties the neighborhood faces, he led visitors on a precarious wooden walkway built on 10-foot stilts over the garbage and water, past crowded houses, to a cement structure missing most of its roof and part of its walls, perched over the ocean.

Palacios explained that the building, which contains eight stalls, is the neighborhood bathroom used by dozens of people. Feces and urine fall straight into the ocean below and are then washed ashore. A few yards away, children splash in the ocean.

"The children love to play in the water," Palacios said. "Often, they get sores on their arms and legs from the swimming, but we cannot stop them."

While many people here say they are boiling their drinking water—in accordance with an announcement broadcast repeatedly on radio and television—others, having received little help from authorities for decades, are suspicious of the measure or simply refuse.

Because diarrhea from parasites and malnutrition is so widespread, Vargas, the medical director of San Andrés Hospital, said that many people here cannot distinguish cholera as a more severe disease than the usual ones with which they are afflicted. Other health experts say that many more victims than the number officially reported may have died without being diagnosed or treated.

"It is difficult for people to accept change here," he noted. "You cannot change centuries of culture in two or three days. It will take years."

In the Vientos Libres neighborhood, two elderly women who sat in the doorway of their raised house chewing sugar cane stalks illustrated Vargas's statements.

"I do not boil my water, and I never will because boiled water tastes different," said the owner of the home, who declined to give her name. "If God wants me to get cholera, I will get it, and if He wants to cure me, then I will not die."

In Las Flores, as with most of the poor neighborhoods, drinking water comes through half-inch water pipes at ground level settled in the permanent mud; when not in use, the pipes are covered with a screw-on plastic cap. Water can only be gathered in buckets during low tide. The houses are built on seven-foot stilts, and when the tide comes in carrying garbage and fecal waste, it covers and fouls the water pipes.

Nearby, three children standing in the mud fill tin pans with ocean water, which they drink, as adults lounge on catwalks above.

"This is the way we live," said Andres Lopez, a local resident. "We have no resources to change."

"ONLY CATASTROPHE GETS THE GOVERNMENT'S ATTENTION"

While the health of Pacific coast residents has long been precarious, the cholera epidemic has now plunged the economy into decline and has also become a political issue.

Because one of the main ways cholera bacteria is spread is by eating raw fish, Colombia's internal seafood market has collapsed. Scientists say that cooking seafood carefully completely kills the bacteria, but the fear of eating any fish or seafood persists.

Because no evidence of contamination has been found in deep-sea fish or carefully controlled shrimp farms, exports have not suffered.

Dario Garces, owner of Inpespa, one of the largest fish processing plants in Tumaco and president of the city's chamber of commerce, said he had shut down his plant and was precariously close to bankruptcy. He said a recent study by the chamber of commerce showed that Tumaco was losing $167,000 a day in fish sales and the subsequent ripple effect through the small economy.

Ernesto Kaiser, Tumaco's mayor, who is widely respected for his efforts to bring aid to the city, said that he would push the government to commit the millions of dollars necessary to end the threat of cholera by building sewage and water treatment systems. But, Kaiser acknowledged, his chance of success was a long shot.

"Only catastrophe gets the government's attention," Kaiser said. "We need to seize the moment and get the resources now, before we are forgotten again."

Even if Tumaco officials manage to draw attention to their plight, the rest of the coast is far less fortunate, as the experience of the village of Salahonda, an hour ride by launch across the bay, demonstrates.

Roberto Castillo is the only doctor in the swampy town of 6,000 who treats cholera cases that arise among residents who live upriver. "Our case load is doubling every week," said Castillo, who recently treated 25 cases in his 12-bed clinic. "I am exhausted, I have no time to sleep."

Because of the lack of resources, each patient has to bring bedding and food, although treatment is free. There is electricity only from 7 p.m. to 11 p.m., when the generator is working. Just two houses have septic tanks, and raw sewage runs through a ditch in the middle of town.

"My biggest fear is that we will see cholera stay as an endemic disease, as malaria is," Castillo said. "Right now, it costs us about $120 to treat each patient, and the government, because of the emergency, has given us the resources. But that will not last indefinitely, and then what will we do?"

In the nearby hamlet of La Playa, fishermen cut up the day's catch to salt and dry, then sell upriver. Because the fish companies stopped buying fresh fish since the epidemic began, the fishermen work twice as hard for less money.

One old man, sitting on a wooden bench under a shade tree with three friends, said he does not understand why everyone is talking about cholera. "They say that cholera can kill us, and that we can get it from the fish," he said, while his friends nodded in agreement. "But if that were true, then, if the fish had cholera they would die, wouldn't they? That is why I do not believe them."

Asked if he is boiling his water, he laughed. "Boiled water does not quench your thirst," he said. "It is the same as drinking nothing."

Castillo said such responses are normal. Many people here blame cholera not on bacteria but on the "evil eye" or another curse inflicted by an enemy.

"That is why cholera will advance as far as hygienic conditions permit it to go," he said. "And here, that is very, very far."

CONFERENCE PROTOCOL

Day One: Presenting Opening Statements

Today, each participant will present his or her opening statements. The presentations will be made in three groups: medical issues, large-scale issues, and local issues. Following each set of statements (for example, when the medical issues speeches have all been given), conference participants will have a chance to ask questions of the speakers.

During these proceedings, be sure to take careful notes on the issues that the other presenters discuss. What they say will influence the action plan that you develop. Note any information or ideas and pose questions that may help you to develop your character's action plan.

Day Two: Preparing an Action Plan

Today, each participant will present an action plan. This action plan should address how cholera epidemics can be prevented and/or treated based on the particular perspective of each character. Each speaker will again have 3 minutes to present his or her ideas. This is a more challenging exercise than preparing your opening remarks. Now you must synthesize the sea of information you heard at the conference. Basing your thoughts on that information, you will develop an argument for attacking the cholera crisis from your perspective as an expert or a representative of a certain group. For example, say you are an expert on large-scale economic and political issues. Your action plan should deal exclusively with these aspects of the crisis.

When preparing your plan, address the following questions. In the debate segment of the conference, you must also be prepared to articulate the rationale for each of your policy recommendations.

1. What actions do you think should be taken?
2. Of these measures, which should be done first, second, third, and so on?
3. Prioritize your recommendations. Which measures are most important? Which are least important? Could any of these actions be skipped to save money and/or time?
4. Identify the obstacles that might prevent you from carrying out your action plan. If your action plan is to go forward successfully, what pitfalls must be avoided?
5. Identify the likely beneficiaries of your action plan.
6. Who will most likely have to pay for the measures you suggest in your action plan?

Again, consider adding visuals such as graphs, charts, and pictures to help you communicate your plan to others. But keep in mind that you have only 3 minutes in which to present your plan. So choose your points wisely.

CONFERENCE EVALUATION

Your role playing will be evaluated on the following criteria.

Day One
- Is your opening statement clear? Is it informative? Is it engaging?
- Does your opening statement present an accurate picture of the character and concerns of the individual you are role-playing?

Day Two
- Is your action plan complete?
- Are your ideas logical and realistic?
- Does your plan take into consideration the relevant data that were presented during Day One of the conference?
- Is there a rationale for the sequence of actions that you will recommend?
- Have you prioritized your suggestions?
- Have you identified potential obstacles to success, those likely to pay, and the likeliest beneficiaries?

Day Three: Thinking about the Future

Today, participants will wrap up the conference by summarizing the ideas that were presented and by planning follow-up activities. It is important for you as conference attendees to think about the message you will take back to your constituencies. How will you answer the question, What can we do next to control the reemergence of cholera in Latin America?

OVERALL ACTIVITY EVALUATION

You will also receive an overall evaluation for your performance throughout the conference. This will be based on how carefully you listened to the ideas and arguments of others and how they influenced your thinking. In particular, you will be evaluated on the following:

- Did your character listen carefully to the ideas and arguments of others?
- Have your character's primary goals or concerns remained true to the issues and groups he or she represents while still taking into consideration other perspectives?

Your participation in the conference will also be evaluated on these factors:

- Did you ask questions of other speakers?
- Did you challenge views that contradicted your own or seemed to make no sense?
- Did you respect the other conference members?
- Did you respect the conference process?

UNIT 4

What on Earth?

Contents

What on Earth?

Introduction

Earth is populated by millions of different species of organisms. It is a place where change is the norm. The relationships among organisms and their environments are constantly shifting and adjusting. The science of ecology focuses on the interactions among living things and their relationships to the environment. These connections link the concepts of ecology to other sciences such as biology, chemistry, physics, and geology. An understanding of the complex interactions among the structures and functions of the natural world is necessary for interpreting the impact of humans on the environment. Since Earth's formation approximately 4.5 billion years ago, countless complex interrelations have slowly evolved among its inhabitants and their habitats. In addition, natural events, such as earthquakes, volcanoes, asteroids crashing into Earth, and climatic fluctuations, have led to vast changes in the kinds of microorganisms, plants, and animals that inhabit Earth. From such events, new organisms and interrelationships have evolved. As a result, new relationships between living and nonliving factors have been established.

This unit focuses on the interactions among organisms and on the dependence of organisms on the nonliving factors in their environment. In this unit, you will develop an understanding of the dynamic responses of living things to changes in their environment.

Home Is Where the Habitat Is

Prologue

The natural world surrounds us, but most of the time we are not aware of it. Think about your journey to school today. What living things did you see? Why are those particular organisms living there? How and where do they get the resources to stay alive? In what ways do these organisms interact with one another and with the environment?

Living things are linked to their habitat by many factors. These factors include the nonliving or physical conditions in the environment. They also include the number and kinds of organisms present in the area. The science of ecology focuses on the interactions among living things and their relationships to the environment.

In this learning experience, you begin an exploration of ecological systems (ecosystems) and the organisms that inhabit them. You will observe an area in your school yard and identify the organisms that live there. You will also look for other less visible components that are present in your school yard habitat. Using these observations and your analysis of the interactions among those organisms, you will design and create a mini-ecosystem. This ecosystem will be used as a model for the principles you will study in this unit. Finally, you will consider the political, economic, and environmental issues surrounding the reintroduction of wolves into areas where they once lived. You will speculate about how replacing an organism might affect the structure or function of that ecosystem.

Brainstorming

Discuss the following questions with your partner, and record your thinking in your notebook. Be prepared to share your ideas with the class.

1. What is a habitat? Give some examples.
2. What is an ecosystem? Give some examples.
3. What are some of the features and/or components of an ecosystem?

ACTIVITY

Life in a Square Meter

Grass, weeds, trees, birds, insects. Living things surround you. In any environment, each plant or animal lives in its own special place, its habitat. This is where it carries out its life functions. Every organism uses its environment to obtain what it needs and, in turn, affects the environment.

In this activity, you will observe some organisms that live above and below the ground within a square-meter area. What are these organisms? How do these plants and animals obtain food? Where are the inorganic materials they need, and how do they obtain them? As you think about these questions, begin to consider the relationships of organisms to the environment within an ecosystem.

Materials

For each group of four students:

- 1 large bag or box (for carrying materials)
- 1 meterstick or tape measure
- 4 large nails or golf tees
- 1 hammer, mallet, or fist-sized stone
- 5 m (about 16 ft) of string
- 1 thermometer
- 1 trowel, spade, 5-cm pipe, or small bulb planter
- 1 sheet of graph paper
- 1 pencil
- 1 sheet of newspaper
- 2 hand lenses or magnifying glasses
- 1 soil test kit (optional)

PROCEDURE

1. Designate a recorder and an illustrator for your group.
2. Have 1 member of your group collect a hammer, mallet, or large stone; 5 m of string; and 4 nails or golf tees for your group. Follow your teacher outdoors.
3. Choose an area that is as diverse as possible. For example, look for a spot that might have a tree or shrub, a variety of weeds, and grass. This area should not be right next to another group's area. But you must be within the sound of your teacher's voice.
4. Hammer 1 nail (or tee) into the ground. Measure 1 m (about 3 ft) from this nail and hammer in a second nail. Continue in this way until you have a square with a nail at each corner.
5. Attach string to the 4 nails to rope off your square-meter plot (see Figure 4.1).
6. Have the illustrator draw a top view of the plot to scale on graph paper. Label the plant life, soil covering, and debris. Include rocks, leaves, or pine needles, and any other features of your square meter. Write the names of all your group members at the bottom of the drawing.
7. In your notebook, record the date, time, temperature, weather conditions, and the location of your plot.

SAFETY NOTE

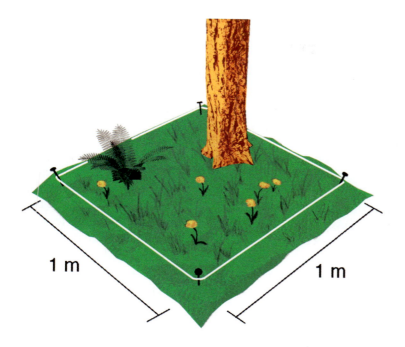

Figure 4.1

Square-meter plot.

8. Create a data chart to record the following: organisms (plant and animal) observed, their locations, and their numbers (or percentage of the plot they occupy).
9. Kneel next to one side of your area, and look carefully at each type of plant. Record each plant name in your data chart. If you cannot identify a plant, draw a picture of its shape and leaves.
10. Continue your observations by looking carefully for each type of animal in your area. Record your findings in your data chart. If you cannot identify an organism, draw a picture of it. (If applicable, include the number of legs.)
11. Spread a sheet of newspaper on the ground outside the square-meter area.
12. Dig straight down into the soil in one part of your plot to get a soil core. Use a trowel, a 5-cm pipe, or small bulb planter. Remove the soil intact and place it on newspaper. Use a hand lens or magnifying glass to find and count all the organisms (including any eggs) living in the soil. Record your findings in your data chart. Note any soil layers you see.
13. Place the lower part of the thermometer in the hole, burying the bulb if possible. Let it stand in the hole for 3–5 minutes to adjust to the soil temperature. Record the temperature.
14. If a soil test kit is available, test the pH of the soil according to the directions in the kit. Record the pH level in your data chart.
15. Replace the soil.
16. Return all materials to the classroom.

ANALYSIS

Record your responses to the following in your notebook.

1. Describe what you think the interactions might be between the plants and animals in your plot.
2. What nonliving factors might affect the organisms in your plot?
3. Do you consider your plot an ecosystem or part of an ecosystem?
4. In a short paragraph, describe what information you might need to better understand the connections between the organisms and their environments.

The Factors of Life

THE LIFE OF A POND

Beneath the surface of the water, the amount of light lessens. The colors darken rapidly from a light blue at the top to a dark green near the bottom. Thin, light-colored stems bearing long, slender leaves reach toward the surface, poking through a mat of green algae that covers the surface. A school of small, black-banded silvery fish swims through these stems as a frog follows their progress through bulging eyes. A large insect uses its long pointed legs to grasp one of the fish. The fish struggles and then is still. Tiny shrimplike animals swim through the water. A large number of much smaller living things dart and tumble around them. The mud at the bottom vibrates with life. Some of these living things are visible to the eye. Some can only be seen by scooping up a sample and viewing them through a microscope.

This pond comprises a naturally occurring group of organisms that live in a particular area and depend on and sustain each other. We call this a **biotic** (living) community. A biotic community is influenced by and dependent upon **abiotic** (nonliving) factors. These factors include sunlight, soil, topography, wind, temperature, moisture, and minerals. The combination of the biotic and abiotic factors creates an **ecosystem**. The pond described above is an example of an ecosystem. The web of interacting factors within an ecosystem is so tightly knit that, should one factor change, all the rest of the relationships may be affected to some degree.

In a pond, for example, some fish eat algae and excrete organic waste. Bacteria then use this waste as a nutrient and break it down into inorganic materials. Algae use the inorganic materials for making food. Thus, a group of organisms within the community is affected by the activities of the other organisms. It is a cycle of life and death (see Figure 4.2).

A change in one abiotic factor can trigger changes throughout the ecosystem. For example, an increase in available nitrogen can lead to an overgrowth of algae. Too much algae in the water can block the passage of sunlight. Without sunlight, the algae cannot make food. They will die, sink to the bottom, and become organic waste fed on by bacteria. The resulting explosive growth of the bacterial population will deplete the amount of oxygen in the water. The fish may increase in number temporarily in response to excess food (the algae). But the low oxygen may eventually lead to the death of the fish.

THE MATTER OF LIFE

At the core of every organism's interaction with its environment is the organism's need for energy and nutrients. Energy powers its life processes, and raw materials build and maintain living tissue. In a continuous cycle, plants and animals exchange the chemicals necessary for building materials.

Organisms in an ecosystem can be named according to how they obtain food. Those organisms capable of making their own food are called **autotrophs**. Autotrophs manufacture sugar from solar energy and simple chemicals found in the environment through the process of photosynthesis. Organisms that get their

Topic: Biotic/Abiotic
Factors
Go to: www.scilinks.org
Code: INBIOH2496

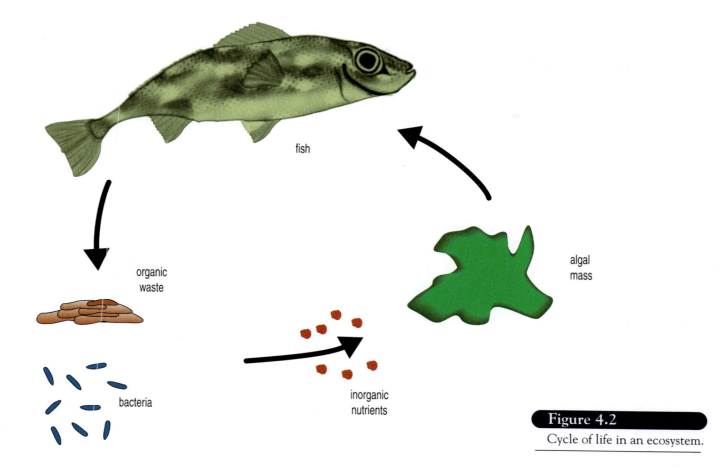

fish

organic
waste

algal
mass

bacteria

inorganic
nutrients

Figure 4.2

Cycle of life in an ecosystem.

energy by consuming other organic matter are called **heterotrophs**. For life to
cycle, a third group of organisms, the decomposers, are necessary. **Decomposers**
break down organic material into inorganic materials that autotrophs use to
build biomolecules.

In an ecosystem, the biotic and abiotic factors are interconnected. A shift in
any of the factors will affect some part of the community. In healthy ecosystems,
these changes are self-correcting. Only sudden and/or extreme change can
disrupt the interactions in an ecosystem and lead to serious consequences.

ANALYSIS

Record your responses to the following in your notebook.

1. Explain three different ways that organisms in an ecosystem are dependent
   upon the abiotic factors in the environment.
2. List the organisms in the opening paragraph of this reading. Decide whether
   each is an autotroph, a heterotroph, or a decomposer. Explain your decision.
3. Explain how autotrophs, heterotrophs, and decomposers interact to
   maintain an ecosystem.
4. Is a tree considered an ecosystem? Why or why not? Base your answer on
   your understanding of ecosystems.

Topic:
Autotrophic/Heterotrophic
Go to: www.scilinks.org
Code: INBIOH2497

ACTIVITY

Life in a Jar

What can a jar full of mud, leaves, and water tell us about life on Earth? Can you create an ecosystem in a jar that mimics how living things interact with their environment? In this activity, you will develop a small ecosystem that will serve as a model for the interactions within any ecosystem. We will call our jar ecosystem an "ecocolumn." What would the jar need to contain? What are the important components necessary for this mini-ecosystem?

Materials

For each group of four students:

- 3 or more clear plastic, 2-L soft drink bottles (same brand, with caps)
- 1 wax marking pencil or felt-tip marker
- 1 razor blade or scalpel
- 1 scissors
- 1 awl or nail
- clear, waterproof tape
- 1 darning needle or large safety pin
- silicone sealant
- soil, water, plants, compost, fruit flies, spiders, snails, and/or other small organisms
- wick (cotton rope or other absorbent material)

For the class:

- 2 or 3 large shoebox tops (to hold the bottles when cutting)

PROCEDURE

1. What type of ecosystem do you want to model? Determine the number of chambers you would need to create a functioning ecocolumn. (Each chamber can represent a different habitat.) See Figure 4.3 for one idea about creating and filling chambers.
2. Identify the abiotic conditions for the ecocolumn (for example, temperature, humidity, soil type, light). How will you provide these conditions?
3. Identify the materials and specimens you will need to collect to create the ecocolumn. What kinds of plants, animals, insects, and other living things will you use? Each group member should bring one of these materials or specimens to the next class.
4. Draw a plan of the chambers. List the organisms and other materials you plan to include in each habitat.
5. Remove the labels from each of the bottles as follows. Fill the bottle one-quarter full with hot water (50° C–65° C [122° F–149° F]). Make sure the water is not too hot (see Figure 4.4a). Screw the cap back on the bottle to keep the pressure inside. Tip the bottle on its side so that the water warms the area where the label is attached to the bottle. Gently peel off the label (see Figure 4.4b).

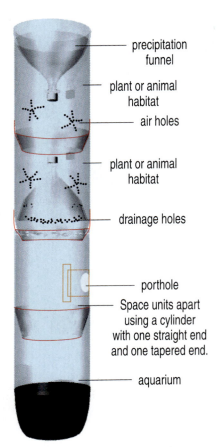

precipitation funnel

plant or animal habitat

air holes

plant or animal habitat

drainage holes

porthole

Space units apart using a cylinder with one straight end and one tapered end.

aquarium

Figure 4.3

An example of a multichambered ecocolumn. Create one or more habitats for your own column. (*Ecocolumns were developed by the Bottle Biology Project, Department of Plant Pathology, College of Agricultural and Life Sciences, University of Wisconsin—Madison.*)

(a)

(b)

Figure 4.4

(a) Add hot water. (b) Tip the bottle on its side. The water will warm and soften the glue.

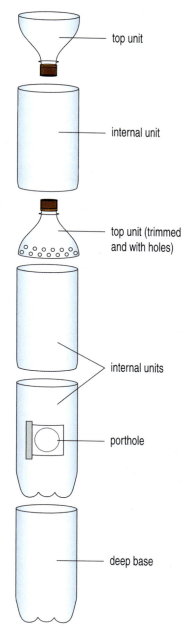

top unit

internal unit

top unit (trimmed and with holes)

internal units

porthole

deep base

6. Use a felt-tip marker or wax pencil to mark the bottles for cutting. Make sure the bottle is dry before making your marks. You can cut each bottle above or below the curve near the neck, or above or below the bottom. Figure 4.5 shows the different parts of a cut bottle that can be used to make the internal chambers. The number of bottles you need to cut will be determined by the number of chambers you want.

7. Lay a marked bottle in a shoebox top to stabilize it (Figure 4.6a). Cut each bottle along the lines you drew in step 6. Use a cutting blade or razor to start the cut. Make a slit large enough to insert the top arm of a scissor (Figure 4.6b). Snip around the bottle following the marked line (Figure 4.6c).

8. Add the biotic and abiotic components to the appropriate chambers. Record these specimens and materials and their placement in your notebook.

9. Connect the chambers by taping them together in the arrangement you designed. Use the appropriate bottle pieces you cut. Be sure the connections are tight. Any chamber with water must be leakproof.

10. Determine the number and height of the drainage holes. These holes will affect the environment in a soil-filled chamber. Poke air holes in any chambers that contain living organisms. Make the holes small enough to prevent any organisms from escaping but large enough to add water when needed. Make enough holes to provide adequate ventilation. You can make holes using a pin, a needle, a nail stuck into a cork, or an awl or paper punch. (It will be easier to make the holes if you heat the hole-making tool.)

11. Observe your ecocolumn daily. Note any changes and describe them in your notebook.

12. Determine if and when you will need to add food or water. If you include predators, such as spiders or carnivorous plants, be sure to maintain a food supply for the organisms.

    Also, make sure to take into account the light and temperature needs for the different sets of organisms. Water plants in the ecosystem very lightly, as an accumulation of water will leave the soil soggy and plants may rot.

13. Keep a record in your notebook. Are there any other variables you need for your functioning ecocolumn? Is there anything else you would like to keep track of during the experiment?

Figure 4.5

Parts of the bottle used to form the ecocolumn.

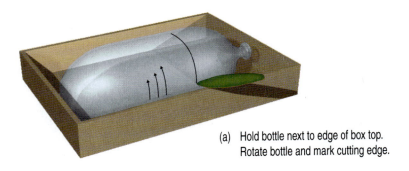

(a) Hold bottle next to edge of box top. Rotate bottle and mark cutting edge.

(b) Begin cut with razor blade.

(c) Insert scissors and cut along the marked line.

Figure 4.6

Cutting bottles for ecocolumn chambers.

ANALYSIS

Record your responses to the following in your notebook.

1. Prepare a laboratory report for this experiment in your notebook. Be sure to include the following:
   a. a labeled diagram of the ecocolumn (include the organisms in each chamber, as well as the abiotic factors);
   b. a description of the changes you observed;
   c. a data chart that summarizes the data you collected, any trends you observed, and notations of when organisms were added and when organisms appeared to die;
   d. a diagram of food chains or food webs within the ecocolumn;
   e. an analysis of your observations and data using concepts from the unit; and
   f. conclusions you were able to draw from the experiment (include your responses to the Analysis question that follow).

   You may wish to discuss with your group the responses to the Analysis questions.

2. How is your ecosystem similar to a large, natural ecosystem on Earth?
3. Suppose you placed a cap on the ecocolumn and omitted the air holes. This would create a closed system. How would this ecosystem be similar to and different from an ecosystem on Earth?
4. Picture an aquarium that contains plants, animals, and decomposers, and has a sealed glass top. Is it possible for life to be maintained indefinitely in such an aquarium? Explain your response.

Wolves

CASE STUDY

AFTER 50 YEARS, FABLED PREDATORS ARE BACK HOME

Excerpted from Michael Milstein, *The Boston Globe.* Monday, January 23, 1995, pp. 25–26.

HINTON, Alberta, Canada—

. . . Fifty years after the gray wolf was poisoned out of existence—with the aid and encouragement of the US government—federal biologists were returning the storied predator to its original place in two wild remnants of the American West.

In Idaho, the return came on January 14, when four beleaguered animals left their crates timidly and then darted into the thick timber of one of the largest roadless regions in the West.

In Yellowstone two days earlier, the wolves had emerged over several hours, cautiously stepping out into one-acre, chain-link pens, where they will stay for six to eight weeks. Biologists hope that transition period will persuade them to become permanent American immigrants, rather than high-tail it back to Canada.

Stretching their stiff legs after the long trip, the wolves nibbled on elk and deer meat left for them, paced along the fences of their pen and tugged at the heavy wire, seeking a way out.

In Canada, meanwhile, wildlife workers were pursuing the rest of the 30 animals that will be brought south and turned loose this winter—15 each in Yellowstone and Idaho. The intent is to capture and release 30 animals annually over the next three to five winters. By then, biologists say, Yellowstone and Idaho should each have 10 fruitful wolf packs, or about 100 animals, enough to sustain their population but few enough to be controlled by regulated hunting (see Figure 4.7).

The wolves' return to Yellowstone fills a missing patch in the diverse biological quilt of the world's first national park. Not only do wolves belong there, park biologists say, but the sly hunters provide a check on the thousands of elk, deer, and bison that in places eat the spring grasses down to bare ground.

"This extraordinary creature creates for us a complete portrait of what a national park should be," said Interior Secretary Bruce Babbitt, noting that his own ranching ancestors had joined in the systematic poisoning and trapping that erased wolves from Yellowstone and the West early in the century.

Since then, lone wolves have occasionally wandered into Yellowstone, but none stayed. In the lower 48 states, wolves lived only in Minnesota and far northern Montana.

The wolves' return to Yellowstone came slowly. As far back as 1980, the US Fish and Wildlife Service, overseer of endangered species, proposed transplanting wolves to the 2.2-million-acre park. But the plan was repeatedly stalled by political wrangling, by studies costing $6 million so far and by a series of legal challenges that continued even after the first of the wolves had been captured.

Along the way, the Fish and Wildlife Service received 160,000 public comments, the most ever generated by any federal action.

Most wanted the wolf back.

And so early this month, sharp-shooting biologists armed with tranquilizer guns and riding in helicopters scoured Canadian forests so cold that fumes from pulp plants hung in valleys like soup in a bowl. One wolf died when a dart accidentally punctured its lung, but otherwise the capture went smoothly . . .

Soon after Yellowstone Park was established in 1872, hunters—with government encouragement—began lacing elk carcasses with strychnine to poison wolves that preyed on the majestic elk and bighorn sheep that tourists were coming to see. Such was the loathing for wolves that early eradication efforts included shoving explosives into dens of newborn pups. From 1914 to 1926, park rangers killed at least 136 wolves.

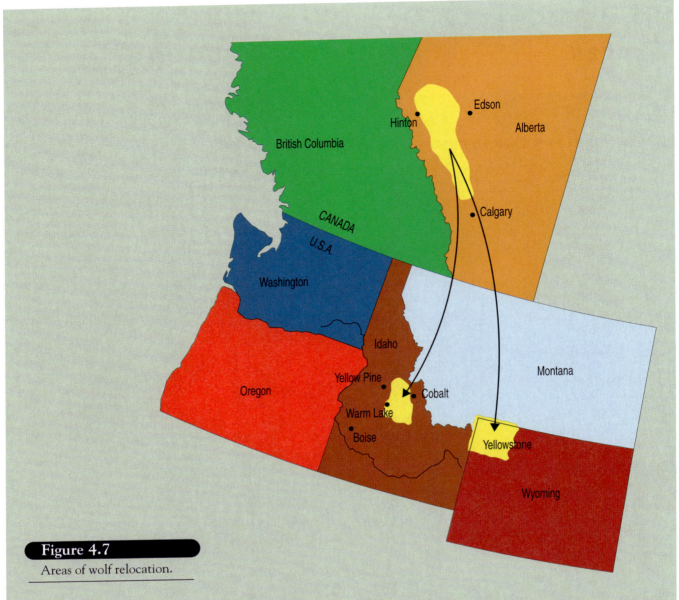

British Columbia

Hinton

Edson

Alberta

Calgary

CANADA

U.S.A.

Washington

Idaho

Montana

Oregon

Yellow Pine

Cobalt

Warm Lake

Boise

Yellowstone

Wyoming

Figure 4.7

Areas of wolf relocation.

"Gray wolves are increasing and have become a decided menace to the herds of elk, deer, mountain sheep and antelope," a park superintendent reported in 1915. "An effort will be made the coming winter to capture or kill them."

The effort took several decades; the last known Yellowstone wolf was killed in 1944. And while the government has changed its thinking in the years since, many ranchers and farmers have not. The coyotes, cougars, bears and eagles that stalk their livestock are predators enough, they say, but they concede that they are in the minority.

"We lost the battle," said Stan Flitner, who grazes cattle near Shell [Wyoming], 150 miles from Yellowstone's boundary. "It seems to be the law of the land that we've got to reintroduce an animal that's going to cause nothing but problems."

Biologists agree that a healthy wolf population might kill perhaps 20 cattle and 70 sheep in a year. But studies suggest that wolves could attract millions of new tourist dollars, more than offsetting the economic loss to ranchers or hunters that compete with wolves for game . . .

To ease any hardships, Defenders of Wildlife has created a private fund to compensate ranchers who lose livestock to wolves. So far, more than $100,000 has been collected, part of it in contributions from children. The fund has paid out $17,000 for cattle and sheep killed by the few wolves that have migrated from Canada into northwest Montana.

"If there's a price to making sure future generations get to see a wolf, making its living where it belongs, we're willing to foot it," said Defenders president Rodger Schlickeisen.

The opponents, however, have not given up. Even while wolves prowled their pens in Yellowstone, the Wyoming legislature considered a symbolic bill that would put a $500 bounty on the federally protected animals. In another last-ditch effort, the American Farm Bureau Federation last month sued the government to stop the reintroduction, and now, to send any released wolves back to Canada . . .

"It's unfortunate our people have to bear this burden while everyone else gets this warm fuzzy feeling," said Jake Cummins, a rancher and vice president of the Farm Bureau's Montana chapter.

Instead of attacking livestock, though, biologists expect that the wolves will prey mainly on elk, bison, and other big herbivores that have overrun Yellowstone in the absence of the predators.

"If these wolves realize they've got a buffet sitting right here, they'll have no reason to go anywhere else," said Yellowstone biologist Michael Phillips, who will watch over the park's newest residents. . . .

Computer models foresee wolves culling Yellowstone's 40,000 elk by 5-to-30 percent. That influence may well be healthful, limiting elk numbers that now swing wildly from boom to bust and leave thousands to die during hard winters.

Wolves should also stabilize the growing herds of bison, which now are shot if they leave the park.

In the absence of wolves, coyotes have taken over [parts of their] ecological niche. Wolves should retake their position atop the food chain, driving off the coyotes and leaving more room for the foxes and raptors that compete with coyotes.

"It may be hard on coyotes," said Robert Crabtree, an independent ecologist specializing in coyote behavior, "but wolves may be the critical link that increases diversity and gets this ecosystem back on track."

ANALYSIS

Record your responses to the following in your notebook.

1. What results followed the removal of wolves from the Yellowstone ecosystem?

2. The reintroduction of the wolves to Yellowstone is controversial. Identify at least two important issues on each side of the controversy.

3. Suppose you had been in charge of this project. What decision would you have made about whether to introduce the wolves into Wyoming and Idaho? Discuss the reasons for your decision.

4. List three important beliefs or values that influenced your decision about reintroducing wolves. Explain how they influenced you.

EXTENDING *Ideas*

- Read *The Return of the Wolf to Yellowstone* by Thomas McNamee (New York: Holt, 1997). Write an essay describing how the presentation of the issues in the book affected your own point of view. How did the book inform you about ecology and human nature?

- Research the ecological and political issues that surround other species, such as the peregrine falcon, the California condor, or the bison. What factors determined their reintroduction to their once-native habitats? What have the results been?

CAREER FOCUS

Park Ranger   Search planes flew low over the trails near the top of the mountain. Groups of trained individuals trudged up the tough incline. All were in search of two teenagers who had separated from their school hiking group and had not returned to the base camp. There was still daylight by which to search, but snow was expected overnight and winds near the summit were known to reach 70 mph and beyond. These are conditions that could surely prove fatal for two youngsters not prepared for an overnight stay.

Curtis is a park ranger with the National Park Service. Although lost hikers are not an everyday occurrence on the popular mountain, it happened often enough for him to be trained in survival techniques and to be physically fit. He enjoys being outdoors and knows his job is important for keeping natural recreational areas such as this safe for travelers.

Curtis grew up in the middle of a big city. His apartment complex was surrounded by concrete and steel. His experiences with wildlife were limited to occasional squirrel sightings and numerous encounters with stray dogs and cats. Curtis longed for trees and ponds, and frogs and snakes. He knew that when he grew up, he would work outdoors to be as close to nature as possible.

A boy scout growing up, Curtis had his sights set on learning everything he could about the outdoors. After high school, he chose to go to a community college. He did this in spite of knowing that a person needs only a high school diploma, a driver's license, and experience or knowledge of the outdoors to start a career as a park ranger. In college, he concentrated in recreation and tourism, while taking general and field science courses. The summer after his first year, he worked as a camp counselor. He also became a member of the Sierra Club, taking trips to different sites for hiking, canoeing, and skiing. When he graduated, he began a 6-month training program with the National Park Service. This eventually led to his job at the popular hiking and camping site.

No day was typical for Curtis, though some were less strenuous than others. There were days when he stayed at the base camp, talking with hikers before and after their climbs. He was available for questions and was sure to warn visitors of any particular dangers they might encounter while hiking. When not in base camp, Curtis could usually be found hiking the trails. He would direct people to trails that were, perhaps, easier or more challenging. He was watchful that everyone was respecting the natural areas. He made sure that they were not doing anything to endanger others. This included starting fires or, in winter, causing avalanches. Sometimes he might encounter someone acting suspiciously or causing destruction to the trees or other areas of the mountain. Curtis then took charge of the situation in the safest way possible. His job was to be aware of the land and the people in his surroundings.

Curtis was always on call for emergencies, and this day was one of them. After searching the mountain for several hours, the students were found near the base of a ravine, cold and hungry, but all right. Another day with a happy ending.

Learning Experience 2

Oh, What a Tangled Web We Weave

Prologue

Did you know that there may be up to 2 million earthworms under a football field? Or that vacant lots are not just areas filled with dirt, litter, and broken glass, but can be the home of countless numbers of plants and animals? As you may have observed in your square meter, even your school yard, no matter how barren it may appear, supports life. What living things are out there? What are their roles? How do they interact with one another? Why are they there and not in some other type of environment?

In this learning experience, you examine the organisms found in a specific environment and consider the roles they might have in that environment. You then examine the complex feeding relationships that exist among organisms in a marsh ecosystem.

Brainstorming

Discuss the following with your partner, and record your thinking in your notebook. Be prepared to share your ideas with the class.

1. Describe the habitat in which you live.
2. List all the interactions you have in a day with the biotic and abiotic factors in your habitat. Base your response on what you learned in the previous learning experience.

ACTIVITY

Mystery Soil

An organism does not live in isolation. The survival of any organism depends on its interactions with other organisms within its habitat. It also depends on the abiotic factors that define the living conditions of that habitat. *How* that organism lives within that specific habitat defines its ecological niche. An organism's **ecological niche** is the sum of all its activities and the relationships it needs to survive and reproduce. These include its

- habitat—where it lives in the ecosystem;
- relationships—all its interactions with other kinds of organisms in that ecosystem; and
- nutrition—what it eats and how it gets it.

Earth is divided into millions of ecological niches. Each represents a "home" and a way of living for the life within it.

In this activity, you will observe a soil sample, collect data about that sample, and speculate about the niche of each type of organism you see. As you proceed, you will need to think like an ecologist in order to begin to understand this community of living organisms. Ask questions such as, Is the soil an ecosystem? What lives there? What do these organisms do in this ecosystem? What resources do they need to live? What interactions take place in soil?

Topic: Niche
Go to: www.scilinks.org
Code: INBIOH2507

Materials

For each group of four students:

- 1 zippered plastic bag containing a sample of soil
- 2 hand lenses or magnifying glasses
- 2 tweezers
- 2 dissecting needles (or coffee stirrers)
- 1 sheet of newspaper
- 1 petri dish
- dissecting microscope
- rotting log (if available)

For the class:

- invertebrate field guides (optional)

PROCEDURE

1. Spread a sheet of newspaper on your laboratory table. Place the bag containing the soil sample on the newspaper. Do not shake or mix the soil.
2. Open the bag and smell the soil. Discuss with your group how you might describe the smell of the soil. Write your description in your notebook.
3. Observe the soil's color, texture, and any organisms it contains. Record your observations in your notebook.
4. Use the tweezers and needles to probe through the soil. Be careful not to mix the layers. Carefully observe the organisms you find and take notes on your observations. Describe each life-form in detail. Take note of its shape, color, number, kind of appendages, and so on. Remember, plants, fungi, and mold are organisms as well. So be sure to carefully describe all the different kinds of life you observe. Include eggs or any other unusual signs of life. Note the number and in which layer(s) organisms are found.
5. Place the organisms in a petri dish for further study with a hand lens or dissecting microscope. Expand on the observations you made in step 4.
6. If field guides are available, have group members take turns trying to determine the type and name of each organism.
7. **STOP & THINK** Try to identify the resources that you think the organisms found in your soil sample might use. How might each kind of organism

SAFETY NOTE

obtain its nutrition? For example, do the organisms eat other organisms within the soil sample? Do they require sunlight, humidity, and so on? Record your thinking and the rationale for it.

8. Go to a group that looked at a soil sample taken from a different location. Describe how the organisms in the two samples are similar and how they differ.

ANALYSIS

Record your responses to the following in your notebook.

1. Describe the relationships among the plants, the animals, and the soil in the mystery soil you examined.
2. What characteristics or factors did you use to determine the resources that the organisms required?
3. Suppose two different populations of organisms with similar resource needs moved into the same habitat? What do you think might happen?
4. Recall the reading in Learning Experience 1 about the wolves in Yellowstone National Park.
   • Describe the ecological niche of the wolves.
   • What happened to the ecosystem when the wolves were removed?
   • Why do you think coyotes eventually came into Yellowstone?
5. Think about your understanding of an ecological niche. Describe the niches for the organisms in the bottle ecosystem you built in Learning Experience 1.

TASK

One interesting way to visualize interactions in the biological world is to create analogies. For example, imagine that the soil ecosystem from the activity Mystery Soil is analogous to a supermarket or grocery store. Each type of organism in the soil community represents a different type of store employee. With your group, use the following questions to brainstorm the types of supermarket jobs and how they relate to one another. Then create a chart, concept map, or diagram to illustrate the interrelationships inside and outside the grocery store.

• What types of jobs are there in a grocery store?
• How do these jobs relate to one another?
• Which employees can work independently?
• Which employees are dependent? In what ways are they dependent?
• Are there other types of jobs that are done outside the store that are necessary to what goes on inside it?

ACTIVITY

What's for Lunch?

Many of the interactions in an ecosystem involve food. Food provides living things with the building blocks and the energy they need to carry out the processes of life. Think about what you have eaten today. Can you trace it back to its original source? If you ate an egg, you know it came from a chicken that fed on corn. And the corn used sunlight, air, and water to make food. This is a simple example of a **food chain**, a linked feeding series. (Another food chain is

snapping turtle

duckling

duckweed

SCLINKS.
NSTA

Topic: Population
Go to: www.scilinks.org
Code: INBIOH2509

Figure 4.8
A food chain.

shown in Figure 4.8.) In natural ecosystems, food chains may be simple or complex. They include producers (autotrophs that make their own food by photosynthesis); consumers (heterotrophs that eat other organisms); and decomposers (organisms that break down the remains of other organisms into simpler substances).

In this activity, you will examine how individual food chains become interconnected. A consumer in one food chain often consumes organisms in another food chain. This forms a **food web**. Working with descriptions of organisms found in a freshwater marsh ecosystem, you will connect them according to their feeding relationships and the transfer of energy. Each of the biota cards in this activity represents a population. A **population** is a group of individuals of the same kind living in a particular area within a community of organisms.

Materials

For the class:

- 17 biota cards
- 1 cardboard "sun"
- lengths of yarn or string
- scissors
- tape

PROCEDURE

Part A: Creating a Food Web

1. Read through the entire Procedure before beginning this activity.
2. Read the information on your biota card.

3. Place the sun and the producer cards on a large table or on an open floor space.
   a. Connect each producer to the sun with yarn or string and tape.
   b. Using yarn or string and tape, connect each consumer to the producer(s) on which it feeds.
   c. Continue making connections until all the biota cards have been linked.
4. **STOP & THINK** Look at the arrangement. You have just created a marsh food web. Find all the food chains that make up this food web. What do they have in common? Record your response in your notebook.

Part B: Simulating Local Extinction

An insecticide that kills mosquitoes and leaf beetles has been sprayed over this marsh ecosystem. What do you think will happen? Follow steps 1–4 to simulate the effect of the insecticide on this community of organisms.

1. Locate and remove the mosquito card. Trace the yarn pieces that connect to it, and remove each piece of yarn along with the mosquito card. As these yarn links are removed, note the food source(s) of each organism that eats the mosquito.
2. Locate and remove the leaf beetle card. Trace and remove all the connecting yarn pieces as you did in step 1.
3. Continue the simulation by looking at the remaining consumers. Have any of these consumers lost their food source in this ecosystem? If so, they must be removed as well.
4. Continue the simulation until the full impact of the event is visible.
5. **STOP & THINK** Which organisms remain? Describe in your notebook how this event affected the food web as a whole. How did it affect the separate food chains? How might the ecosystem recover?

🔍 ANALYSIS

Record your responses to the following in your notebook.

1. Describe the consequences of removing a single organism from an ecosystem.
2. Suppose the American black duck disappeared instead of the insects. What do you think would happen to the rest of the community? Explain your reasoning.
3. Where do decomposers fit into the food web? Why is their role necessary for life?

READING

Managing Mosquitoes

Malaria is a serious infectious disease in the tropics that can cause high rates of mortality, especially among children. During the early 1950s, malaria was a serious problem to the Dayak people of Borneo. In an effort to stop this epidemic, the World Health Organization (WHO) decided to rid Borneo of malaria by killing the mosquitoes that spread this disease. WHO used a potent insecticide called DDT. The mosquito population was soon wiped out, and the incidence of malaria greatly reduced. But the consequences of this treatment were much more far-reaching than anyone could have predicted.

Not too long after the spraying of DDT, the thatched roofs on the houses began to collapse. More distressfully, outbreaks of two new infectious diseases, sylvatic plague and typhus, began to appear in the villages. Was there a relationship between getting rid of the mosquitoes and the new problems in the villages? The answer lay in food webs. DDT is an insecticide, so it affected not only mosquitoes but other kinds of insects in the sprayed area, including roaches. The roaches accumulated the DDT in their bodies, even though it did not kill them outright. Roaches are a favorite food of a small lizard called a gecko. When the geckoes ate the DDT-laced roaches, the insecticide accumulated in their bodies. It did not kill them either. But it made these normally lightning-fast lizards slow down and, thus, become much easier prey to the village cats. When the cats ate the lizards, they did die from DDT poisoning. With no cats to control them, rats flourished, bringing with them the diseases that they carried, plague and typhus.

But what caused the roofs to collapse? In addition to roaches, geckoes also enjoy dining on a species of thatch-eating caterpillars, thus keeping their numbers in check. Without the lizards to eat them, the caterpillars multiplied out of control. This resulted in large numbers feasting on the thatch roofing material of the village houses.

Realizing the problems that its program had created, WHO parachuted hundreds of cats into Borneo in an attempt to repair the damage.

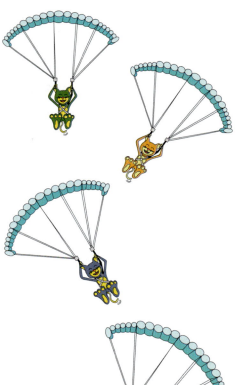

NALYSIS

Record your responses to the following in your notebook.

1. Draw a food chain that describes the relationships among the roaches, geckoes, caterpillars, rats, and cats in Borneo.
2. In your own words, explain what happened when the DDT was sprayed in the area. How was removing mosquitoes in Borneo different from what happened when you removed mosquitoes from the food web in the activity What's for Lunch?
3. What might WHO have done before it began its mosquito removal program?
4. What conclusions can you draw about the importance of any one species in an ecosystem? Base your answer on your understandings from the activity What's for Lunch and the reading "Managing Mosquitoes."

EXTENDING *Ideas*

 In early spring of 1963, a quiet aquatic biologist and science writer was interviewed in her Maine coastal home for a CBS television show. The program would be called "The Silent Spring of Rachel Carson." Before the show could be aired, three of the five original sponsors withdrew their support, and CBS received more than a thousand letters about the upcoming show, most criticizing it. When the program was broadcast as scheduled, it also included presentations by four United States government

representatives and a prominent chemist of a chemical manufacturing company. What science topic could be that controversial?

Six months previously, Rachel Carson's book *Silent Spring* had been published. She had carefully and scientifically documented the destructiveness of chemical pesticides to the natural environment. Carson stated that their widespread use was potentially as damaging to life as nuclear explosions. She urged scientists and government officials to conduct further research to determine the effect of DDT and other pesticides on soil, water, animals and their food webs, as well as on human health and life.

Read *Silent Spring.* Chapters 1, 6, and 8 are particularly relevant to the concepts you are studying in this unit. Then write an essay that addresses any or all of the following:

• the relevancy of Carson's ideas and concerns then and today;

• whether her ideas have influenced current thinking, and if so, how;

• the place of pesticides in the modern world (developed and developing countries); and

• what interested and/or surprised you in the book.

Every June, approximately 2,200 amateur ornithologists and bird-watchers across the United States and Canada join in an annual bird count called the breeding count survey. This survey, which began in 1966, has uncovered some interesting trends in bird populations. Birds such as robins, starlings, and blackbirds prosper around humans. But many other populations of colorful forest birds have severely declined. What is causing the devastating losses? Destruction of critical habitats is clearly a major issue; predation and parasitization also present a growing threat. Research the various ways in which humans and other organisms may be contributing to the decline in the bird populations. How are people attempting to reverse the trend? You may also want to join some bird-watchers in your area who participate in the annual breeding count survey and contribute to the research.

Owls, hawks, and eagles all belong to a group of birds called raptors, or birds of prey. They actively hunt small vertebrates for food, particularly voles, shrews, and mice. Raptors consume bones, feathers, and hair when eating prey. After the bird has digested its meal, this undigestible material is rolled and compacted in the raptor's digestive tract to form a pellet. This pellet is then passed through its body. Since owls tend to swallow their prey whole, their pellets are apt to contain whole skeletons.

Obtain an owl pellet from the field or local Audubon reservation. Wearing latex gloves, measure and record its mass, length, and diameter. Place the pellet in a petri dish, and carefully dissect it with teasing needles. Place the bones in the cover of the dish. Sort the pieces and assemble the skeleton. Try to identify the prey.

Zookeeper   The young Siberian tiger, Sheba, has just arrived at the zoo. As the zookeeper in charge of large cats (lions, tigers, and so on), Miguel will be overseeing the tiger's care during her stay. Sheba is on loan to the zoo in order to mate with a male Siberian tiger already on site. Because of the rarity of Siberian tigers today, Miguel's zoo is taking part in a global project to strengthen the gene pool of the Siberian tiger. This is being done by mating females from some zoos with unrelated males from other zoos.

Nearly every child loves animals and waits expectantly for a visit to the zoo. Miguel spent many hours at the zoo as a child because his mother was a staff veterinarian at a large metropolitan zoo. She often brought Miguel to work with her and allowed him to tag along with different zoo workers—provided he not get in their way. He usually ended up helping Mr. Polk, the senior zookeeper, with his everyday tasks.

In high school, Miguel enjoyed his biology courses and made sure to take plenty of math and other science classes. He followed up in college with a major in zoology and a minor in communications. Miguel studied communications because he knew that a zookeeper is the first line of public relations for an animal park. The university he attended included a teaching zoo where students could earn credits for hands-on experience with animals. Not many schools offer this opportunity, but he specifically wanted as much hands-on work as possible.

The time Miguel will spend caring for Sheba will be only a small part of each busy day. He is in charge of the daily cleaning and maintenance of all the large-cat enclosures, and of the proper feeding of the animals under his care. As the keeper of many animals, and having other responsibilities as well, Miguel does not have time to do all of the work himself. He supervises other staff members and student interns as they complete some of these tasks. The animals' daily care requires Miguel to work weekends and holidays. Because of the hands-on aspect of his job, he has to make sure he is physically fit. Some tasks entail lifting heavy food bags and constructing different structures.

When new animals arrive or a new exhibit is planned, Miguel helps to design and build any new enclosures. He helps to choose and care for the plants in and around the enclosures. He makes sure that the new homes closely resemble the animals' natural habitats. At the same time, he has to be primarily concerned for the safety of zoo visitors. He has to be sure that no one can get into the enclosures and that warning signs are posted where needed.

Miguel also has the pleasure of introducing some of the animals under his care to the visiting public. A couple of times each week, he presents an animal showcase. He brings a few of the smaller animals onto a stage and explains a little about them to the audience. For instance, he often brings the youngest members of his cat entourage onto the stage. The children gasp and the adults look on with interest. He describes the cub's life in the wild, what it eats, how it hunts, and then answers any questions the audience might have.

Miguel has to be extremely familiar with all the cats at the zoo so that he can detect any subtle changes in their behavior caused by illness or increased stress. Shortly after Sheba's arrival at the zoo, he noticed some changes in her behavior. And, after 4 months, Miguel was thrilled to witness the birth of her cub. Named Tomorrow, the cub was the first step toward keeping the Siberian tiger from extinction.

Round and Round They Go

Prologue

Where do the elements that make up your body come from? Where do you get the energy you need to make it through the day? As you explored in both Unit 1 and in the previous learning experience, the energy and building blocks you need come from the food you eat. Energy and building blocks pass from organism to organism, and eventually back to the earth, air, and sea. Here they are recycled again through food chains and food webs. That means almost all of the atoms in your body have been around the block, so to speak, many, many times. The carbon atoms in your muscles may have been part of the molten rock deep in Earth's interior, or found in the bones of a *T. Rex.* The energy in the ATP molecules in your muscles that once came from the sun may have powered the flight of a bird. How do elements and energy cycle through the ecosystem of Earth? What roles do food webs play in this recycling process?

In this learning experience, you examine the flow of energy through the feeding levels of a typical food chain. You then identify the essential resources needed for the preservation of life and see how these resources are cycled through the larger ecosystem that is planet Earth. These biogeochemical cycles transfer materials (organic and inorganic) among organisms, from organisms to the abiotic environment, and back to the organisms, thus sustaining life on Earth.

Topic: Biogeochemical Cycles
Go to: www.scilinks.org
Code: INBIOH2514

Brainstorming

Discuss the following with your partner, and record your thinking in your notebook. Be prepared to share your ideas with the class.

1. Make a list of everything you have eaten for the past 2 days.
2. Next to each item write the word *animal* or *plant* depending on the origin of the food. Some items might be both such as a cake in which the flour would be "plant" but the eggs would be "animal." Determine whether you are primarily a herbivore (vegetarian), carnivore (meat eater), or omnivore (both plant and animal eater).
3. Give three reasons why eating food from plants is a good idea. Give three reasons why eating food from animals is a good idea.

Going with the Flow

Think about the number of blades of grass it takes to feed a prairie dog, and the number of prairie dogs to feed a coyote. Why is there such a difference? Why are there fewer consumers in each successive level in a food chain?

All of life's processes require energy. After a consumer obtains nutrients from its food source, it processes the nutrients to obtain energy and building blocks. The energy and building blocks are then used by the organism for growth, movement, and a variety of other activities.

Does the amount of energy available in a food source depend on its trophic level? **Trophic level** is the level in a food chain where an organism is found. Plants are considered the first trophic level, herbivores the second, animals that eat herbivores the third, and so forth. In the process of photosynthesis, plant producers convert light energy (from the sun) to chemical energy (in the form of sugar). **Herbivores** (plant eaters) are consumers that use the chemical energy harnessed by producers as their food source; **carnivores** consume herbivores. In this activity, you will investigate the flow of energy through organisms in successive trophic levels of a food chain. You will also determine what happens to the amount of available energy at each level.

*SCI*LINKS®
NSTA

Topic: Trophic Levels
Go to: www.scilinks.org
Code: INBIOH2515A

TASK

1. Sunlight provides energy to the primary producer—20,000 kilocalories (kcal) per square meter. A **calorie** is the unit of measurement for the energy produced by anything when burned or oxidized. A kilocalorie is equal to 1,000 calories. Foods oxidized in the body produce so much energy that when we speak of the calories of energy in foods, we are actually referring to kilocalories.

   When the producer is consumed by the primary consumer, some of the energy is used during metabolic activities of the producer, or released as heat. Calculate the kilocalories (assuming starting kilocalories of 20,000) used by each trophic level and the kilocalories available to be used in the next trophic level. Use the percentages from Table 4.1.

2. Construct a line graph that shows the energy transfer in this ecosystem. Be sure to represent the energy in a way that makes clear the amount of energy being transferred.

*SCI*LINKS®
NSTA

Topic: Photosynthesis
Go to: www.scilinks.org
Code: INBIOH2515B

Table 4.1 Energy Released along a Food Chain

Trophic Level	Energy Source	% Energy Released during Metabolism	% Energy Released to Waste
primary producer*	sunlight energy	60%	20%
herbivore**	primary producers	65%	20%
primary carnivore***	herbivores	70%	25%
secondary carnivore****	primary carnivores	70%	25%

*Primary producer—an organism that synthesizes food molecules from inorganic compounds by using an external energy source.
**Herbivore—an organism that eats only plants.
***Primary carnivore—an organism that eats an herbivore.
****Secondary carnivore—an organism that eats a primary carnivore.

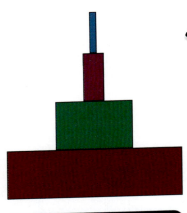

Figure 4.9

Symbolic representation of amounts of energy at each trophic level.

 ANALYSIS

Record your responses to the following in your notebook.

1. How much of the original 20,000 kcal of energy is available for the secondary carnivore? How much energy would be available to a tertiary carnivore? Explain your calculation.
2. Explain what happens to energy as it passes through the different trophic levels.
3. Is there more energy transferred to the consumer after eating a pound of rice or a pound of meat? Explain your response.
4. Explain the concept that is illustrated by the pyramid in Figure 4.9.
5. Examine Table 4.2. In a diagram, arrange the organisms represented in the table into trophic levels. Label the organisms as producers or primary, secondary, and/or tertiary consumers. Use arrows to show the energy flow. Justify your labels and arrows in a sentence for each organism.

Table 4.2   Organisms and Their Food Sources

Organism	Major Food Sources
algae	photosynthesis
swamp milkweed	photosynthesis
Japanese beetle	swamp milkweed
freshwater clam	algae, mosquito larvae
spring peeper (tree frog)	beetles
little brown bat	mosquitoes, beetles
muskrat	cattails, bulrushes, spring peepers, freshwater clams

 ACTIVITY

It's Elemental

What resources do plants and animals need to maintain life? In this activity, you will use snails and a simple freshwater plant, *Elodea*, to explore the interrelationships among animals and plants, and the resources found in the environment. The chemical indicator bromthymol blue turns green or yellow in the presence of an acid. It will help you determine the presence of carbon dioxide. When carbon dioxide is dissolved in water, a weak acid called carbonic acid is formed.

Materials

For each group of four students:

- 4 pairs of safety goggles
- 4 culture tubes or test tubes with tight-fitting covers or stoppers
- 1 test-tube rack
- 1 wax marking pencil
- 100–200 mL distilled water (or "aged" tap water)
- 1 eyedropper
- 1–2 mL of 0.1% bromthymol blue solution (aqueous)

- 4 small water (pond) snails
- 2 sprigs of *Elodea*
- access to a fluorescent lamp

PROCEDURE

1. Obtain 4 test tubes and place them in a test-tube rack. With a wax marking pencil, label the tubes 1, 2, 3, and 4. Then pour distilled water into each of the tubes until they are three-quarter full.
2. Using an eyedropper, add 4 drops of bromthymol blue solution to each tube.
3. Tightly seal tube 1 with a stopper and return the tube to the test-tube rack.
4. Tilt tube 2 slightly and gently add 2 snails. Place the stopper in the tube and put the tube in the rack.
5. Add 1 sprig of *Elodea* to tube 3. Stopper the tube and place it in the rack.
6. Add 2 small snails and 1 sprig of *Elodea* to tube 4. Place the stopper on the tube and put the tube in the rack (see Figure 4.10).
7. **STOP & THINK** What do you think will happen in each of the tubes. Write your predictions in your notebook.
8. **STOP & THINK** What is the purpose of tube 1? Record your response in your notebook.
9. Set the test-tube rack under a fluorescent lamp.
10. Observe the tubes daily for 1–2 weeks. Each time note the color of the water and the apparent health of the organisms. Record these data in a chart in your notebook.
11. At the end of the experiment, dispose of any dead organisms. If possible, place your live organisms in an existing aquarium or prepare an aquarium tank for them.

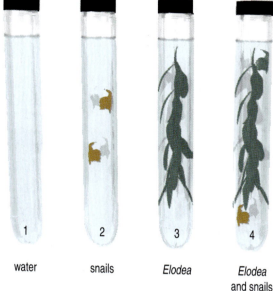

water   snails   *Elodea*   *Elodea* and snails

Figure 4.10
Closed living systems.

ANALYSIS

At the completion of the experiment, record your responses to the following in your notebook.

1. In which tube(s) did you note a color change? What caused the change in each tube?
2. Which organisms remained healthy? Which, if any, did not remain healthy? Why do you think that was the case?
3. What gases are involved in tubes 2–4? How do you know?
4. Draw a picture of what you think is happening to the gases in this experiment. Base your drawing on your conclusions from this experiment.
5. What do you think would happen in each of the four tubes if they were placed in the dark?

ACTIVITY

An Infinite Loop

Organic nutrients such as carbohydrates, proteins, and lipids are made up of elements including carbon, oxygen, hydrogen, and nitrogen. These elements, however, are also present in the environment in inorganic forms.

The amounts of carbon, oxygen, and nitrogen in the present atmosphere have remained nearly the same since life came into existence about 3.8 billion years ago. That means that the oxygen you breathe could also have been inhaled by your great-grandparents or by George Washington. And the carbon in the food you ate for dinner last night might once have been part of a dinosaur! How is that possible?

In this activity, you will be assigned to follow the flow of one of the following cycles: carbon-oxygen, nitrogen, or water. You will read some information about that cycle and discuss it with a partner to help clarify your understanding. Then you will diagram the cycle.

Materials

For each group of three students:

- 3 sheets of unlined white paper (legal-size, 11 × 14 in.)
- felt-tip markers or colored pencils

PROCEDURE

1. Separate from your group of 3 and join other students who have been assigned to the same cycle. With a partner from this new group, read the information given. Then discuss how to draw this cycle.
2. Create a labeled diagram of the cycle on a legal-sized sheet of paper. Include all applicable biotic and abiotic factors. Add arrows to show the cycling.
3. Return to your group of 3 and explain the cycle to the other group members.

CARBON-OXYGEN CYCLE

1. These two linked cycles provide plants and animals with energy and the materials for the basic building blocks of life. Carbon and oxygen have independent cycles, but often travel together. Carbon, oxygen, nitrogen, and hydrogen are bonded together and form biomolecules. That is, they form carbohydrates, proteins, and lipids. Carbon (C) is found in all living things in biomolecules. It is also found in the atmosphere as carbon dioxide (CO_2). Oxygen (O_2) makes up 21% of Earth's atmosphere and is found dissolved in fresh and ocean waters.
2. In the process of photosynthesis, plants take in water (H_2O) from the soil and carbon dioxide from the air. The water and carbon dioxide are converted into biomolecules such as sugars or carbohydrates. The by-product—oxygen—is released into the air.
3. In the process of respiration, all living things (including plants) use oxygen to "burn" sugars. This produces water and releases carbon dioxide as a by-product into the air.

4. Animals eat plants or other animals and break down the consumed organism's complex biomolecules into simpler biomolecules. This releases energy that is now available for the consumer.

5. As land animals and plants die, decomposers use oxygen from the air or soil to break down the dead organisms' carbon-containing biomolecules. Carbon dioxide is released into the atmosphere.

6. Over long periods of time, pressure from overlying soil or water can compress carbon from dead organisms into peat. It can then become fossil fuels such as coal, natural gas, or oil. When humans burn fossil fuels, the carbon in the fuel combines with oxygen in the air. This releases carbon dioxide into the air.

7. Photosynthetic phytoplankton in the ocean take carbon dioxide from the air or ocean water and incorporate the carbon into biomolecules. This releases oxygen.

8. As aquatic animals and plants die, decomposers oxidize the dead organisms' carbon compounds. This releases carbon dioxide into the ocean water. Organic material also sinks to the aquatic floor where, over time, the carbon can be compressed into fossil fuels.

NITROGEN CYCLE

1. Nitrogen gas (N_2) makes up 78% of Earth's atmosphere. Plants and animals cannot use nitrogen in this gaseous form. Nitrogen is also found in ocean water and in nitrogenous compounds located in soil.

2. **Nitrogen-fixing** bacteria in the soil, and cyanobacteria in the ocean, can convert nitrogen gas into ammonium (NH_4) or ammonia (NH_3). Ammonia in soil also comes from excreted animal waste.

3. Other **nitrification** bacteria take the ammonia in the soil and combine it with oxygen from the air or soil. This forms nitrites (NO_2) and then nitrates (NO_3). Plants convert these nitrogen-containing compounds into biomolecules such as proteins, amino acids, or nucleic acids. Some nitrates in the soil are leached into groundwater and eventually carried into waterways leading to the ocean.

4. Both on land and in the ocean, consumers eat other animals or plants and use the nitrogen in the protein of these organisms. The nitrogen is incorporated into other proteins the consumer can use. Or the proteins are broken down to produce energy. The nitrogen combines with hydrogen to form ammonia and is excreted as waste.

5. Decomposers in the soil and in the ocean break down the nitrogen-containing biomolecules in dead organisms. This releases nitrogen gas into the air and water. This process is known as denitrification.

6. As aquatic plants and animals excrete waste or die, this organic material sinks to the ocean floor. Some bacteria that decompose nitrogen compounds convert nitrates to nitrites; others convert nitrates back to molecular nitrogen (N_2), thus completing the (aquatic) cycle. Seasonal ocean currents bring water and nutrients back to the surface of the ocean (a process called upwelling). Here nitrogen gas is released into the air or converted into ammonia by bacteria.

7. Other types of bacteria in the ocean do the following: convert nitrogen gas into ammonia, convert ammonia into nitrites, or convert nitrites into nitrates.

WATER CYCLE

1. The oceans are the reservoir for 97% of the water on Earth.
2. The heat from the sun is the force that drives the water cycle. The sun heats the ocean water, which evaporates into the air. Salt remains in the ocean. The sun also causes evaporation from lakes and rivers.
3. The evaporated water in the air condenses into clouds. When cooled, the clouds release rain, snow, and other forms of precipitation back into the ocean and onto land.
4. Water is released into the air from leaf surfaces during photosynthesis. During respiration, all living things release water vapor into the air.
5. When precipitation falls on land areas with vegetation, the plant roots hold the water in the soil. This water (called groundwater) is available for use by plants and animals. When precipitation falls on land areas without vegetation, excess water can wash away topsoil into lakes or rivers.
6. Precipitation can also fall on lakes, rivers, or the ocean.
7. Water in lakes and rivers can eventually return to the ocean.
8. Water that does not flow into lakes or rivers, and is not used by plants and animals, moves through the ground. Large underground reservoirs (aquifers) are located beneath Earth's surface. This water slowly makes its way back to the ocean.

ANALYSIS

Record your responses to the following in your notebook.

1. Draw a carbon cycle using a black marker or crayon. On the same sheet of paper, draw an oxygen cycle using a blue marker or crayon. At what point are these cycles unlinked?
2. Choose one major biotic or abiotic factor in each of your cycles. Describe the consequences if this factor were not present. Explain your response.
3. Kamo no Chomei, a Japanese author, wrote, "The flow of the river is ceaseless and its water is never the same." Use your knowledge of the water cycle to explain this quotation.
4. All of the elements in these cycles are finite (of limited amounts). How is this fact important in your thinking about the cycles?

EXTENDING *Ideas*

- There are approximately 36 chemical elements that cycle through the biosphere. Research one or two others (such as phosphorus, sulfur, or calcium) to see how their cycles complement the cycles you already explored.
- Conduct a soil analysis of your square meter. Test for the presence of water or nitrogen.
- The burning of fossil fuels—coal, oil, and natural gas—is constantly adding carbon dioxide into the air. As a result of excess carbon dioxide, a greenhouse effect on Earth is taking place. The carbon dioxide in the air traps the sun's energy, not allowing the heat to escape. Determine why the greenhouse gases might be a cause for concern. Research the current thinking about the link between burning fossil fuels and global warming.

Each year, the streams and rivers of the United States carry away 4 billion metric tons of sediment. Wind blows away another 1 billion metric tons. This loss of topsoil reduces soil fertility and crop production. Once it is lost, soil cannot easily or quickly be replaced. Soil erosion has become a serious environmental and economic problem. Research some of the methods currently being used for reducing soil erosion.

CAREER FOCUS

Meteorologist "There is a hurricane warning in effect for coastal Alabama, Mississippi, and Louisiana. Hurricane Katrina is traveling northwest at 15 mph and carrying sustained winds in excess of 120 mph. She is expected to make landfall just before 8 o'clock tonight, Residents should evacuate all coastal areas . . ."

Melinda turned off the microphone. In her position as a meteorologist with the Mobile, Alabama, branch of the National Weather Service, she has been at work for hours. Melinda is tracking what might be the strongest, most dangerous hurricane to hit the Gulf coast in decades. Surrounded by all of the latest weather forecasting equipment, Melinda watches closely for any changes. Although severe weather means long hours of work, it always renews her love and respect for the forces of nature.

Melinda grew up in the Midwest, where hurricanes were never a problem but tornadoes were much feared. She saw the humbling destructiveness of a tornado just once. As much as the ferocity of storms excited her, the calmness of a clear day with white puffy clouds gliding overhead was just as intriguing. It was this intrigue that lead her into the field of meteorology.

While in high school, Melinda researched meteorology. She learned that most jobs in that field were with the National Weather Service (NWS), a branch of the National Oceanic and Atmospheric Administration (NOAA). Melinda chose a college that offered a degree program in the field. She also could have attended other schools and taken college courses required by the NWS. Those courses include meteorology-specific classes such as weather analysis, forecasting, and dynamic meteorology. General courses required include calculus, physics, computer science, and statistics. Melinda also discovered that forecasting the weather was not her only option. Some meteorologists spend their days doing research on the physical and chemical properties of the atmosphere and on factors that affect the formation of clouds, rain, snow, and hail. Others study long-term weather patterns in specific regions in order to provide advice about building design and agriculture.

But Melinda was most excited about the prospect of forecasting the weather. After receiving a bachelor's degree, she landed a job with the NWS in Mobile. Her entry-level position entailed collecting atmospheric data from weather balloons and from other technological data sources such as Doppler radar. Doppler radar can detect rotational patterns in violent storm systems. Melinda was asked to analyze the data collected to aid the other forecasters. After spending a little over a year in that position, she started her climb toward being the primary meteorologist in the Mobile branch. Now she is doing what she loves.

Hours later, Katrina hit, causing millions of dollars in damages to cities and towns along the coast. Lives were lost, but many more people would have died if not for Melinda's skills and those of other meteorologists in tracking the storm and alerting people to the grave dangers.

Investigate Locally, Think Globally

Prologue

What does what you are learning in biology have to do with real life? Throughout the previous units, you have seen how understanding fundamental concepts in biology can help you deal with issues and problems that you may confront in your life. This is also true in ecology. You may become interested in issues on a global level, such as the destruction of the rain forest. Or you may become involved personally on a local level, such as with the impact a local industry is having on the air and water quality in your community. In both situations, you will want to be able to think about these issues using your understandings of ecology.

In this extended learning experience, you carry out an investigative study in your community. You identify a problem or question, design the experimental approach, collect data, and apply your understandings about ecology to analyzing a local environmental issue.

Brainstorming

With your partner, identify three questions, problems, or studies relating to your local environment that you would like to investigate. Record your thinking in your notebook, and be prepared to share your ideas with the class.

ACTIVITY

Investigating Your Own Environment

Have you ever wondered about what animals inhabit the woods near your school, or how certain plants can grow through sidewalks. Do you think about whether the factory upstream from your town is affecting the river near your house? In this activity, you have the opportunity to explore questions about your own neighborhood and community.

522

PROCEDURE

1. With your class or group, identify a question or problem you want to investigate over the course of the unit.

2. Design an experiment or investigative process that will enable you to answer the question or problem you posed. The procedure should include how you propose to investigate the question; a hypothesis, if appropriate; how and what kind of data you will collect; and how you will record the data. The project will extend over the next 5–7 weeks. So you will also need to develop a plan and a schedule for collecting information and data.

3. Show your project design to your teacher for approval.

4. At the end of the project, develop an individual field-study report that contains the following components:
   - the topic being studied;
   - the question being asked;
   - the hypothesis (if applicable);
   - the design of the field study (if applicable);
   - the procedures (include materials);
   - the data and observations;
   - the conclusions from the data;
   - concepts from the unit that relate to the data and conclusions;
   - possible sources of error; and
   - new questions as a result of the field study.

5. You may also be responsible for participating in a poster session or preparing a formal presentation.

Students Rescue Pond After Years of Murky Mud

READING

The following news article demonstrates the kind of impact you can have on your own environment through your project.

Mr. Fred Bottle's tenth-grade biology class was on a mission. Their assignment was to identify a problem in their environment, investigate it, collect data on it, and come up with a solution. Robin Roberts, Chris Brown, and Kerry Alexander knew exactly what they wanted to do. They had been best friends since first grade and their favorite place to go, Pennypacker Pond, had, over the years, become a murky, smelly, weedy puddle of pestilence. They decided for their project that they would investigate exactly why this was and find a way to restore the pond to the pristine clarity of their youth.

Their first step was to don big boots and wade into the pond to take pictures, map the area, and determine whether there was any flow of water in and out of the pond. They hit the town library to learn the history of the pond and to see if they could find old maps of the area. Using this information, they created two profiles of the pond, one from 15 years ago and one for the present day.

The next step was to collect samples of life in the pond, such as plants, insects, and invertebrates. Armed with nets, microscopes, and field guides, and using various Web sites, they identified the pond wildlife, counted them, and determined their lifestyles and life cycles. With this data, they were able to construct a food web for the pond. Using a water-quality kit, they assessed the quality of the water and the level of pollution.

The students were able to determine that the pond had become overgrown and murky due to leakage from the school sewer system, a situation that created ideal conditions for bacterial and algal growth. The students wrote letters to the Town Council, causing the town to allocate money to repair the sewer pipes. The students enlisted their friends, parents, and neighbors to help remove the overgrowth that was choking the pond and to clear the pond of algal scum. Within a few months, the pond was clear. The town, then, stocked the pond with several different kinds of freshwater fish. Robin, Chris, and Kerry could once again enjoy their pristine pond.

Population Pressures

Prologue

In the previous learning experiences, you have been investigating the interactions and interdependencies that take place in ecosystems. An important factor in the stability of any ecosystem is the size of the populations that inhabit it.

What factors influence population size? Although populations may generally stay about the same size from year to year, changes in environmental conditions or in biotic factors may cause a resultant change in population size. Among prairie meadow mice, for example, a cold summer may result in an increase in reproduction. As the number of mice increases, the numbers of their **predators**, such as the hawks and coyotes that feed on mice, will also start to increase. If normal weather patterns return in subsequent years, reproduction of the mice will decline. The hawk and coyote populations will begin to decline in turn as their **prey** decrease in number. This restores the system to equilibrium over time. If cool summers persist for long periods of time, however, the populations might shift to a new equilibrium. When ecologists examine the populations of organisms, they look for trends in how populations increase and decrease over time. They then use this information to analyze the dynamics of the populations and the entire ecosystem.

In this learning experience, you begin to examine the different patterns of population growth and determine the significance of these patterns over time. You evaluate how the factors that influence the growth or reduction of populations interact. This interaction determines the population size at any given time. Finally, you look at populations of organisms in northeastern forests. Specifically, you will examine how interacting factors influence both Lyme tick-borne disease epidemics and outbreaks of gypsy moths.

Brainstorming

Discuss the following questions with your partner, and record your thinking in your notebook. Be prepared to share your ideas with the class.

1. What resources would a male mouse and a female mouse in a cage need to stay alive?
2. Suppose you placed a male mouse and a female mouse in a cage with the appropriate resources. What do you think would happen?
3. Suppose you left the mice in the cage for a very long time, but gave them only the same amount of resources that they started with. What do you think would happen then? Explain your response.

ACTIVITY

Unsupervised

Say a population could live under ideal conditions—have all the food, space, and other resources it needs; no competition for resources; and no predators. Such a population would show its **biotic potential**. Existing organisms would reproduce to their fullest, as would subsequent generations. Such a large increase in numbers is called **exponential growth**. When placed on a graph, this type of growth produces a **J-shaped curve** (see Figure 4.11).

Conditions in nature are seldom ideal, however. Predator-prey relationships are the norm. In addition, a variety of other environmental factors hinders such unlimited growth. In this activity, you will examine one population, that of yeast, growing undisturbed in a sugar culture for 5 days. What will happen to this population over time? What factors will influence changes in the yeast population?

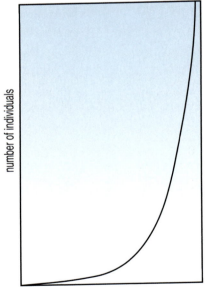

Figure 4.11

The J-shaped curve shows the exponential growth of a population under ideal conditions.

Materials

For each pair of students:

- 1 sheet of graph paper

PROCEDURE

1. Examine Figure 4.12. The graphic represents samples of yeast cells taken over time from a yeast population growing in a nutrient-rich culture flask. The samples were placed on a glass slide with a grid (to make counting easier), and viewed through a microscope.
2. **STOP & THINK** What type of growth curve do you predict we will see over a 5-day period?
3. Create a data chart in your notebook to record the number of yeast cells in each of the samples in areas A, B, and C. Include the time intervals. Insert another column for the average number of yeast cells in all areas.
4. Count the yeast cells (represented as small circles) on each slide.
5. Record your data in the chart you created. Calculate the average of the 3 areas to 1 decimal point. Check your numbers with your partner.
6. Construct a graph of your data. (Only about 1/1000 of the original yeast population was placed on the counting slides. Note this sampling limitation on your graph.)

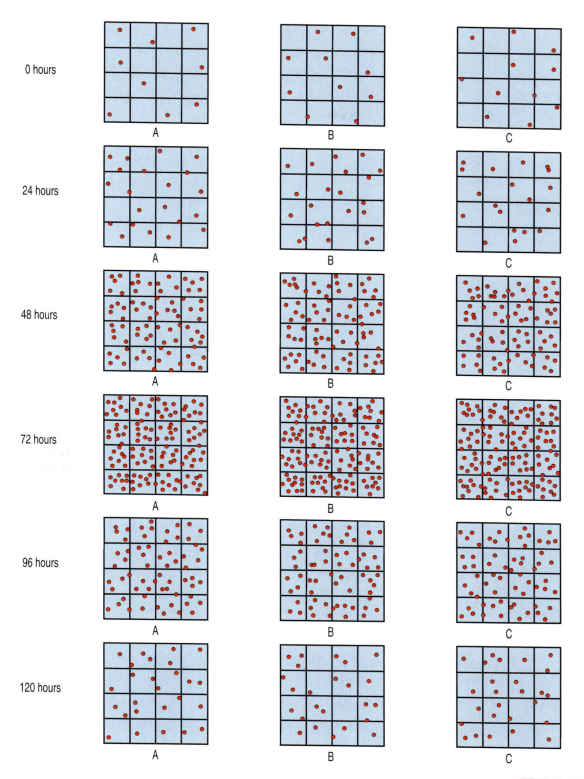

0 hours

A B C

24 hours

A B C

48 hours

A B C

72 hours

A B C

96 hours

A B C

120 hours

A B C

Figure 4.12

Yeast population growth in a nutrient-rich culture.

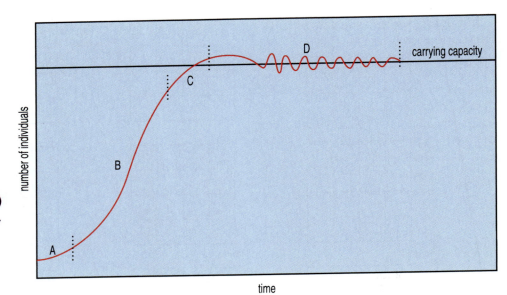

Figure 4.13

Growth curve stages: (a) slow growth; (b) exponential growth; (c) slowing growth; (d) growth leveling off near the carrying capacity.

Topic: Carrying Capacity
Go to: www.scilinks.org
Code: INBIOH2528A

Topic: Limiting Factors
Go to: www.scilinks.org
Code: INBIOH2528B

ANALYSIS

Record your responses to the following in your notebook.

1. During which time intervals was the population growth most rapid? Why?
2. What was happening during the other time intervals?
3. Use Figure 4.13 to identify and label the stages of growth on your graph.
4. Suppose the yeast were started in a larger flask with more media. Would the graph be different? In what way?
5. How is the yeast growth curve similar to and different from an exponential growth curve? Why might it be different?
6. The **carrying capacity** of a habitat or environment is the maximum number of organisms an area can hold and the number at which the population remains for a period of time (see Figure 4.13). What might cause the carrying capacity of a population to change?

The Lynx and the Hare

Is the boom-and-crash pattern you saw in the yeast culture typical of all populations? Remember, no animal, plant, or insect exists in total isolation in the real world. Even within a small community, there are hundreds, even thousands, of different populations. Each has positive and negative effects on the others.

A variety of biotic and abiotic factors both stimulates and reduces population growth. For example, predators, disease, parasites, and competition with other organisms are biotic factors that reduce population size. Abiotic factors such as weather and lack of food, water, or shelter are also known to reduce population size. These **limiting factors** generally balance reproductive rates and keep natural populations below their biotic potential. What is the relationship between these limiting factors and growth factors?

In this activity, you will explore the relationship between populations of lynx and their prey, snowshoe hares. In nature, both predator and prey have evolved structures and behaviors to counterbalance each other. Thus, they coexist in a moderately stable relationship. In the following simulation, you determine what happens to each population over many years.

Lynx and hare.

Materials

For each group of four students:
- 100 hare cards, 5 × 5 cm (2 × 2 in.)
- 25 lynx cards, 10 × 10 cm (4 × 4 in.)
- 1 ruler or tape measure
- masking tape
- 1 sheet of graph paper

PROCEDURE

1. Use masking tape to outline a 50 × 50-cm (20 × 20 in.) square on a flat surface. This will represent the boundaries of an ecosystem.
2. Create a 3-column table to record the following: round number (each round equals 1 year), the number of hares, and the number of lynx. You will begin with 6 hares and 1 lynx.
3. Take 6 hare cards and scatter them randomly within the ecosystem.
4. Take 1 lynx card and drop it from a height of 10–15 cm (4–6 in.) above the hares. Try to drop the lynx onto as many hares as possible.
5. Remove all of the hares "caught" by the lynx. A hare has been caught if the lynx card touches the hare card in any way.
6. If the lynx catches 3 or more hares, the lynx will survive and reproduce 1 kit (baby). When this happens, get another lynx card. If the lynx catches fewer than 3 hares, the lynx will die. In this case, remove a lynx card. If the number of lynx in the ecosystem falls to zero, 1 new lynx immigrates into the area for the next round.
7. Each surviving hare reproduces 1 baby. To simulate this, scatter 1 new hare card in the ecosystem for each surviving hare. Six is the smallest number of hares that will ever be in your ecosystem. If the number of hares in the ecosystem falls below 6, then more hares immigrate into the area for the next round. This ensures the minimum of 6 hares in the population.
8. This is the end of round one. Record the numbers of hares and lynx living in the ecosystem.
9. Use the new number of lynx cards and repeat steps 4–8 until you have completed 25 rounds.
10. Create a graph that illustrates the change in the lynx and hare populations over time (the rounds).

At the completion of the activity, record your responses to the following in your notebook.

1. Describe your graph in words.
2. How is the population of hares dependent upon the population of lynx? How is the population of lynx dependent upon the population of hares?
3. What would happen if all of the hares were removed from the ecosystem? Explain your response.
4. What do you think would happen if all of the lynx were removed? Explain your response.
5. What other factors could affect the size of the hare population? What other factors could affect the size of the lynx population?

CASE STUDY

A Friendly Warning

TICKS AND MOTHS, NOT JUST OAKS LINKED TO ACORNS

MICE THRIVE ON ACORNS AND DEER TICK LARVAE THRIVE ON MICE

by Les Line, *The New York Times,* April 16, 1996.

A tangled cycle of events in northeastern forests that gives a reason for both Lyme disease epidemics and outbreaks of gypsy moths has been unraveled by ecologists. They have traced both events to the bumper crops of acorns that are produced every three or four years and to the white-footed mice that feed on them.

The bumper acorn crops influence the life cycles of mice and deer as well as the gypsy moths and the spirochetes that cause Lyme disease. Based on their theory, the two ecologists, Dr. Richard S. Ostfeld and Dr. Clive G. Jones of the Institute of Ecosystem Studies in Millbrook, N.Y., predict that the gypsy moth population in the Northeast will undergo one of its periodic explosions beginning this year. They expect it to build to a major defoliation in 1999 that will rival the devastating caterpillar blight of 1979–81 unless one of the moth's natural enemies, like a fungus or parasite, intervenes.

The two ecologists also warn that there will be tremendous numbers of deer tick nymphs, the vectors of Lyme disease, in the oak-dominated woodlands of New York and New England this spring and summer.

What the two ecologists call "the acorn connection" is laid out in the May issue of the journal *Bioscience* in an article written by them and Dr. Jerry O. Wolff, a biologist at Oregon State University. The study's principal findings come from long-term studies of gypsy moths and white-footed mice at the Mary Flagler Cary Arboretum, site of the Institute of Ecosystem Studies, and a 14-year study by Dr. Wolff of mouse populations at the Mountain Lake Biological Station in southwestern Virginia.

The forests at both sites are dominated by oaks, which have evolved a cunning strategy for reproduction. Their acorns are rich in the proteins and fats that give them a head start over other tree seeds, but that also make them a favorite food of mice and deer. So instead of producing large crops each year, which would foster a steady population of acorn consumers, the oaks have evolved a feast-and-famine regimen: occasional bumper crops, separated by years in which the consumers starve.

"The evolutionary response of oak trees appears to have been to produce such large crops of acorns that the

Orbiting satellites enable people to forecast the weather, make phone calls from their cars, and choose from hundreds of television channels. How can these same satellites be used to predict outbreaks of deadly diseases? In an area of research called landscape epidemiology, scientists use features of a landscape to identify where and when infectious diseases might happen. This approach has been used to identify areas at risk for outbreaks of Lyme disease. Researchers analyze vegetation patterns and examine animals for antibodies to the bacterial agent responsible for the disease. The resulting data allow them to identify regions posing the greatest danger of infection.

Research the theory behind landscape epidemiology. Describe how it can be used to predict outbreaks of infectious diseases, such as Lyme disease, cholera, or leishmaniansis (a disease caused by protozoan parasites).

CAREER FOCUS

Statistician   There was a constant hum in the office. Bureau workers were gathering incoming data and watching readouts on their computer screens that were scrolling numbers and demographics of millions of people. Louis was excited to start working with the new information and to see how accurate and efficient the latest survey process was.

The United States census, instituted in 1790 by George Washington, was to be carried out once every 10 years. That first year, the information requested consisted of the number of people living in the country. Little was asked about the inhabitants except their ages and who the head of the household was. The information was to be used primarily for two purposes: to allocate seats in the House of Representatives (the number of seats depends on the population in a state) and to provide a record of the country's military potential (at that time, males over the age of 16) in case of war.

Much has changed since the beginnings of the process, from technology to (most obviously) the number of people in the United States. More than two hundred years after the first census, the information requested of the growing, diversifying population has increased to include wealth, race, education, means of transportation, and so on. When all of the information was collected from the 2000 census takers, it was time for Louis to begin using the data to create some understanding of the U.S. population. How many people live in the United States and its territories? What is the poverty rate? How many children are growing up in single-parent households? What state has had the greatest influx of residents since 1990?

The collection of data is tedious and the U.S. population is mobile. As a result, Louis and the other statisticians with the Department of Commerce must use the returned data (sometimes coming from only 50% of an area's inhabitants) and, with different statistical techniques and formulas, create a profile of the U.S. population that is as close as possible to reality. This information is in demand from many different public and private enterprises, not only for its present value, but for forecasting future trends. For example, if it looks as though more and more people are moving into particular areas, how can those areas accommodate the increased traffic, demand for resources, and so on?

Louis has always enjoyed math. He took part in his high school's math club, attending many contests where he was thrilled to compete with his peers. It was only natural for him to follow a mathematical path while attending college. He majored in statistics and rounded out his education with a minor in sociology, reflecting his interest in people. While attending a job fair before graduation, he spoke with a representative from the Census Bureau and was excited by the possibility of a career that included both of his interests.

Between the actual census years, Louis spends his time working with the latest data. He analyzes and arranges it for different uses, and studies ways to make the next census even more accurate. Not only does Louis enjoy his job because of the mathematics involved, but also because of what he learns about the U.S. population as an ever-changing, evolving, mobile society.

Be Fruitful and Multiply?

Prologue

How does the human population growth curve compare to that of other organisms you have studied? Is Earth capable of supporting everyone and everything? What factors influence this growth? On January 1, 2005, the world population reached 6,409,765,942. About 92 million more people are added to the world each year. But what do these numbers mean?

As you have seen, there are many factors involved in studying the population dynamics of a single species. The addition of 92 million people each year cannot be studied out of context. What are some of the factors that regulate the human population? Are they the same factors that influence other organisms?

In this investigation, you explore human population dynamics by examining the factors that influence the shape of the growth curve for the human population. You also begin to investigate the carrying capacity for humans on Earth.

Brainstorming

Discuss the following question with your partner, and record your thinking in your notebook. Be prepared to share your ideas with the class.

What kind of problems might occur if the human population on Earth continues to increase at its present rate?

Is More Better?

ACTIVITY

Do you think there is a world population problem? A population grows for as long as the number of births exceeds the number of deaths. Babies born each year increase the population by their own number. But they also further enlarge the population when they grow up to have children of their own. Think about this in your family. How many children are in your family? How many children do you and your siblings think you would like to have? Now, what about the rest of your class? Think about the number of people in their families, and the number of children they think they will have, and so on for a few generations. If

Table T4.3 Human Population Growth

Year (CE)	Population (in millions)
1	170
200	190
400	190
600	200
800	220
1000	254
1100	301
1200	360
1300	360
1400	350
1500	425
1600	545
1700	600
1750	629
1800	813
1850	1,128
1900	1,550
1950	2,555
2000	6,080
2025*	7,871
2050*	9,190

*projected population
Sources:
U.S. Census Bureau, Population Division, International Programs Center Historical Estimates of World Population (2004)
http://www.census.gov/ipc/www/worldhis.html
U.S. Census Bureau, International Data Base. Total Midyear Population for the World: 1950–2050
http://www.census.gov/ipc/www/worldpop.html

you were to think about this for the whole United States, you would see a trend toward increasing population. When considering population dynamics, however, one must also factor in death rates.

What can we learn by studying the human population growth curve? What is the projected size of the human population in the year 2025? In this activity, you will graph human population levels through history. Based on your understanding of the growth curves you investigated earlier in this learning experience, you then speculate on the factors that influence human population.

Materials

For each student:

- 2 sheets of graph paper
- cellophane tape

PROCEDURE

1. Tape 2 sheets of graph paper together.
2. Using the data in Table T4.3, make a graph of the world population from the year 1 CE to the present. Then extend your graph to include the projected data to 2050 CE.

ANALYSIS

Record your responses to the following in your notebook.

1. How does this growth curve compare to the growth curves you investigated earlier in this learning experience?
2. When do you notice a sharp rise in the curve?
3. What do you think caused such a rise?
4. Do you think the world population will ever reach 12 billion? What human and environmental factors do you think would be necessary to allow for the world population to reach that number?
5. Do you think there is a world population problem? If yes, what potential solutions might you suggest? If no, at what point do you think there might be a problem? Why then?

Putting the Bite on Planet Earth

Excerpt from "Putting the Bite on Planet Earth" by Don Hinrichsen, *International Wildlife*, September/October 1994, pp. 36–41.

Each year, about 90 million new people join the human race. This is roughly equivalent to adding three Canadas or another Mexico to the world annually, a rate of growth that will swell human numbers from today's [1994] 5.6 billion to about 8.5 billion by 2025.

These figures represent the fastest growth in human numbers ever recorded and raise many vital economic and environmental questions. Is our species reproducing so quickly that we are outpacing the Earth's ability to house and feed us? Is our demand for natural resources destroying the habitats that give us life? If 40 million acres of tropical forest—an area equivalent to twice the size of Austria—are being destroyed or grossly degraded every year, as satellite maps show, how will that affect us? If 27,000 species become extinct yearly because of human development, as some scientists believe, what will that mean for us? If nearly 2 billion people already lack adequate drinking water, a number likely to increase to 3.6 billion by the year 2000, how can all of us hope to survive?

The answers are hardly simple and go beyond simple demographics, since population works in conjunction with other factors to determine our total impact on resources. Modern technologies and improved efficiency in the use of resources can help to stretch the availability of limited resources. Consumption levels also exert considerable impact on our resource base. Population pressures work in conjunction with these other factors to determine, to a large extent, our total impact on resources.

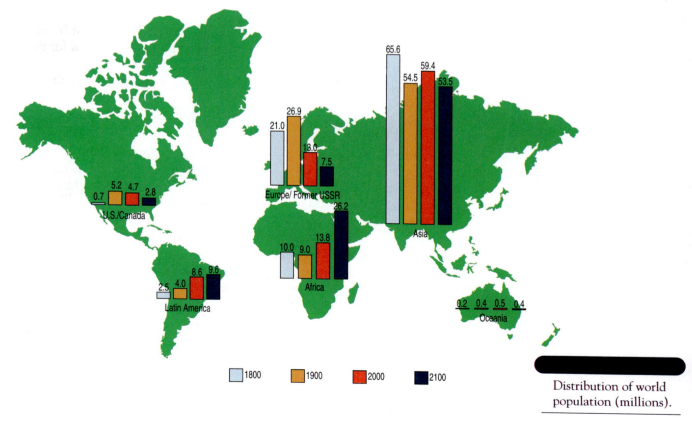

Distribution of world population (millions).

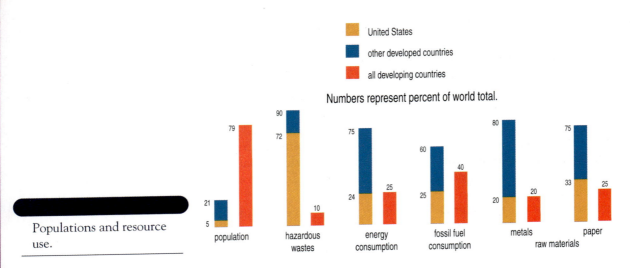

Populations and resource use.

For example, although everyone contributes to resource waste, the world's bottom-billion poorest and top-billion richest do most of the environmental damage. Poverty compels the world's 1.2 billion bottom-most poor to misuse their environment and ravage resources, while lack of access to better technologies, credit, education, health care and family-planning condemns them to subsistence patterns that offer little chance for concern about their environment. This contrasts with the richest 1.3 billion, who exploit and consume disproportionate amounts of resources and generate disproportionate quantities of waste. One example is energy consumption. Whereas the average Bangladeshi consumes commercial energy equivalent to three barrels of oil yearly, each American consumes an average of 55 barrels. Population growth in Bangladesh, one of the poorest nations, increased energy use there in 1990 by the equivalent of 8.7 million barrels, while U.S. population growth in the same year increased energy use by 110 million barrels. Of course, the U.S. population of 250 million is more than twice the size of the Bangladeshi population of 113 million, but even if the consumption figures are adjusted for the difference in size, the slower growing U.S. population still increases its energy consumption six or seven times faster yearly than does the more rapidly growing Bangladeshi population.

In the future, the effects of population growth on natural resources will vary locally because growth occurs unevenly across the globe. Over the course of the 1990s, the Third World's population is likely to balloon by more than 900 million, while the population of the developed world will add a mere 56 million. Asia, with 3.4 billion people today, will have 3.7 billion people by the turn of the century; Africa's population will increase from 700 million to 867 million; and Latin America's from 470 million to 538 million. By the year 2000, the Third World's total population is expected to be nearly 5 billion; only 1.3 billion people will reside in industrialized countries.

The United Nations estimates that world population will near 11.2 billion by 2100. However, this figure is based on the assumption that growth rates will drop. If present rates continue, world population will stand at 10 billion by 2030 and 40 billion by 2110 . . .

Perhaps the most ominous aspect of today's unprecedented growth is its persistence despite falling annual population growth rates everywhere except in parts of Africa, the Middle East and South Asia. Annual global population growth stands at 1.6 percent, down from 2 percent in the early 1970s. Similarly, the total fertility rate (the average number of children a woman is likely to have) has dropped from a global average of six only three decades ago to slightly more than three today.

Population continues to grow because of tremendous demographic momentum. China's annual growth rate, for example, is only 1.2 percent. However, the country's huge population base—1.2 billion people—translates this relatively small rate of growth into a net increase in China's population of around 15 million yearly. Clearly, any attempt to slow population growth is a decades-long process affected by advances in medicine, extended life spans and reduced infant, child and maternal mortality.

ANALYSIS

Record your responses to the following in your notebook.

1. Look at the map on page 537. What is the most populous region in the world? Which area is expected to show the greatest increase in world population?
2. What percentage of the world population lives in the United States?
3. Look at the bar graphs on page 538. Which countries consume only 25% of the world's energy and contribute only 10% of the hazardous wastes? What does this mean?
4. What observations can you make about the relationships among population, industrialized/developed nations, and resource consumption?
5. Pick one day out of your life. Think about what you eat, what you wear, what you own, and other things you come in contact with, including the places you go. What natural resources do you rely upon on a daily basis?
6. Would you consider lowering your standard of living to make more resources available to your children and grandchildren? to people in developing countries? What would you choose to give up? Why?

Variation . . . .
Adaptation . . . .
Evolution

Prologue

So far in this unit, you have been exploring the interactions among organisms and the relationships of organisms to their environments. Living ecosystems are incredibly complex. A variety of plants and animals of different sizes and shapes lives distinct but connected lives. Why is there such an enormous assortment of organisms? How did this diversity come about? What might we expect in the future?

Between 1849 and 1860, the English naturalist Henry W. Bates wandered through the forests of the Amazon capturing and identifying butterflies. After grouping together the butterflies with similar characteristics, Bates found he had 94 separate types. We now know that there are more than 100,000 different types of butterflies and moths on Earth. This makes butterflies and moths the second largest group of insects. (The largest group is that of the beetles, with more than 250,000 different types.) How did so many different kinds of insects come to be? What distinguishes one kind of butterfly from another? Does each kind have a separate ecological niche in the ecosystem that is Earth? How could such a great diversity of life on Earth come into existence?

In this learning experience, you continue to explore the principles of evolution (changes in populations of organisms over time). In particular, you explore Charles Darwin's theory of natural selection. It has been more than a century and a half since Darwin published *On the Origin of Species.* Evolutionary biologists have accumulated many lines of evidence that support the process of evolution as the explanation for diversity on Earth. In addition, they have carried out intense research to determine how organisms evolve. Scientists may not be able to explain all the processes that allow evolution to take place. But they accept the general process of evolutionary change just as gravity is accepted even if physicists cannot completely explain it either.

Brainstorming

Discuss the following questions with your partner, and record your thinking in your notebook. Be prepared to share your ideas with the class.

1. Since the early 1800s, scientists and naturalists have observed that the coloration of the peppered moth populations living in the industrialized regions of Great Britain had gradually turned from light gray to dark gray. These same moths in rural areas, however, remained a light gray. Explain this observation. Use your understanding of natural selection and genetics from Unit 2, Learning Experience 12, and the following information:
   a. In the early 1700s, the Industrial Revolution began in London. This revolution resulted in the rise of many industries, such as textile manufacturing, iron production, beer brewing, and the forging of great steam engines. Industrialization soon became the life force of major urban areas in Britain.
   b. Coal was the major source of energy for most industries of the time.
   c. When coal is burned, great quantities of soot are released into the air. The soot coats buildings, roadways, trees, and everything else in a city in a thin black film.
   d. Peppered moths tend to rest on the trunks of trees.
2. How does the story of the peppered moth relate to the discovery of so many different kinds of butterflies?

What Is This, Anyway?

In recent years, new products have been introduced, such as compact discs and cellular phones. In many basements or garages, people are tinkering, trying to invent a new device that can be patented and produced and will, they hope, make them rich. An important consideration for inventors is that the structure (shape, size, features) of the object they invent must be related to the function it will perform. For example, if you invent a high-tech, futuristic lamp, it still needs to carry out its original function of delivering light. Similarly for organisms, their structures must help them carry out their life processes, from getting food to reproducing. Their structures must help them function in their unique environments. In the following activity, you will explore the relationship of structure to function. This is an integral concept to the continued existence of all organisms.

Materials

For each student:

- 1 sheet of lined notebook paper
- 1 pencil

PROCEDURE

1. Number a lined sheet of paper according to your teacher's instructions.
2. Go to your assigned station and observe the mystery object. What do you think its function is? Write your response next to the corresponding station number on your sheet.

3. At your teacher's signal, move to the next station. What is the function of this object? Write your response next to the proper number on your sheet.
4. Continue, at the signal, until you have examined all the objects and recorded your predictions.

 **ANALYSIS**

Record your responses to the following in your notebook.

1. What general principle or concept do you think this activity illustrates about the relationship between structure and function?
2. What might be the importance of this principle in the plant and animal world? Explain by using several examples.
3. Can you group two or more objects together? Base your response on the structure or perceived function of each object. Explain your reasoning for the grouping.

 READING

Collectors Classify

Have you ever made a collection of objects such as seashells, dolls, car models, or baseball cards? When people collect things, they often like to organize them into categories in order to keep track of them or to see how the objects relate to one another. Someone might arrange seashells by size, shape, color, or where they came from. Dolls might be arranged by size, country of origin, or age they are supposed to be, whereas baseball cards can be organized by team or by position on the field.

Scientists have a need to organize and classify the huge diversity of life that they see collected on Earth. Classification of these organisms enables scientists to communicate in a common language about specific organisms. They can determine relationships among organisms and characterize newly identified organisms by comparing them to others in a systematic way.

Aristotle was the first to classify organisms as either plant or animals. Plants were categorized by the kind of stem they had, whereas animals by where they lived—in the air, in the water, or on land. As more and more organisms were discovered, it was clear that these categories were not sufficient. There needed to be a simple way to identify organisms and their relationships to other organisms.

In the 1700s, a Swedish naturalist, Carolus Linnaeus, devised a system to group organisms using structural features. He put organisms with structural similarities into **species**. He then grouped similar species into a larger group called **genus**, which were then grouped again into a **family**. Similar families were placed into **orders**; similar orders into **classes**. Similar classes were grouped into phyla, which were then placed in either the animal or plant **kingdom**. The person sitting next to you would be classified as follows:

Species	sapiens
Genus	Homo
Family	Hominidae
Order	Primates
Class	Mammalia
Phylum	Chordata
Kingdom	Animalia

As you can see, every step of classification is more inclusive. That is, family would include all kinds of humanlike organisms (today, there is only one—us). But the order includes all primates, the class includes all mammals, the **phylum** includes all vertebrates, and the kingdom all animals. To simplify the naming of organisms, Linnaeus decided to use only the genus and species. Thus, humans are *Homo sapiens*.

With the discovery of microscopic organisms, this system of classification needed expanding. Today, taxonomists identify five kingdoms. **Taxonomists** are scientists who study the groupings of organisms and determine their relationships. The criteria for these five groupings include cell structure, tissue structure, nutritional requirements, and patterns of development. At present, the kingdoms are organized as follows:

- **Monera**—prokaryotic organisms that obtain nutrients either by absorption or by photosynthesis or chemosynthesis such as bacteria.
- **Protista**—unicellular eukaryotes that lack specialized tissues and obtain their nutrients by absorption, or photosynthesis such as euglena and planaria.
- **Fungi**—unicellular and multicellular eukaryotes with tissue differentiation that obtain their nutrients by absorption such as mushrooms and slime mold.
- **Plants**—all multicellular and autotrophic organisms with tissue differentiation.
- **Animals**—all multicellular heterotrophic organisms with tissue differentiation.

Recently, a new kind of taxonomy has been developed called **molecular taxonomy**. This approach uses the similarity between organisms at the molecular level to group organisms. Taxonomists make comparisons among nucleic acids common to all organisms, such as ribosomal RNA, or among proteins found in most organisms, such as cytochrome c. (Cytochrome c is a protein involved in cell respiration.) The closer the sequences, the more closely related are the organisms. Thus, members of the same species would have identical ribosomal RNA sequences. Whereas, the more distantly related the organisms, the more divergent their sequences would be.

ANALYSIS

Record your responses to the following in your notebook.

1. Recall the classification system described in the reading for classifying the person sitting next to you. Describe the characteristics of organisms at each step of the classification. For example, what are the common characteristics in the family Animalia?

2. Do you think that the genus *Homo* ever had more than the one species *sapiens*? Explain your response.

The Evolving Understanding of Evolution: A First Look

READING

In Unit 2, Learning Experience 12, you read how a young naturalist, Charles Darwin (see Figure 4.14), spent 5 years collecting, sorting, observing, and analyzing enormous numbers of different organisms from around the world. Darwin was struck by the incredible variation among the different organisms in

Figure 4.14

Charles Darwin shortly after he returned from his voyage on the H.M.S. *Beagle. Photo Researchers, Inc.*

structure, form, and physical characteristics. He spent the next 20 years of his life analyzing his own observations and the findings of other naturalists. In 1859, he published his conclusions about how this enormous diversity of organisms came to be.

In *On the Origin of Species by Means of Natural Selection*, Darwin set forth ideas that would revolutionize scientific thinking and influence how we look at life on Earth. His theory of natural selection includes the following precepts:

- Organisms reproduce others of their own kind.
- In nature, there is an overproduction of offspring.
- There are variations (differences) among offspring, and some of these variations will be inherited.
- Some organisms have "favoured" variations, such as slightly longer legs (for speed) or outer coloring that better matches their surroundings (for camouflage). These organisms are more likely to survive and pass on these adaptations to their offspring ("the survival of the fittest").
- The process of natural selection enables those organisms whose adaptations allow them to survive in their environment to reproduce.
- Over time, the survivors with the favorable adaptations will make up most of the population.

Topic: Charles Darwin
Go to: www.scilinks.org
Code: INBIOH2544A

I Came, I Saw, I Inferred

Some of Darwin's ideas have been modified since 1859. But his basic ideas that organisms undergo evolutionary change and are selected by their environments have been supported and reaffirmed by several lines of evidence. Sometimes, understanding exactly what evolution is may be hard. It is a difficult if not impossible phenomenon to observe, since in general it takes place over a very long time (millions of years). In addition, the evidence is indirect and based on reaching conclusions by deduction, much like how a detective would use clues.

In the following activity, you will make observations and draw conclusions based on inference. **Inference** is reaching a conclusion based on assumptions and deductions made from observations.

TASK

Topic: Natural Selection
Go to: www.scilinks.org
Code: INBIOH2544B

Imagine one of the following two scenarios (see Figure 4.15):

- A storm has dumped 10 inches of beautiful powdery snow on your town overnight. School is cancelled, so you decide to take a walk before the snow is trampled by sledders and hikers. As you emerge from your house, you see the following patterns in the snow.
- It's a hot night and you haven't slept well. Just as the sun is creeping over the horizon, you kick off the covers, get out of bed, and walk down toward the shore. The tide is out, and the mud is smooth as glass. Under the lightening sky, you observe the following patterns in the mud.

Discuss the following with your partner, and be prepared to share your ideas with the class.

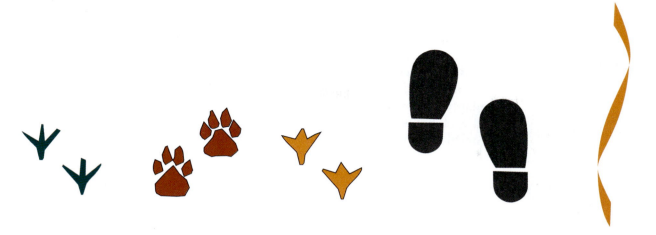

Figure 4.15

Animal footprints.

READING

1. Describe what kind of organisms passed through the area while you slept. Explain your reasoning.
2. What features can you identify about each organism based on the evidence you have? What features can you not identify?
3. Explain why your observations and conclusions in this example are based on inference.

The Evolving Understanding of Evolution: A Second Look

Evidence that organisms have evolved over time comes from five sources. When plants and animals die, sometimes a record of their existence is embedded in sedimentary rock deposits as fossils. This **fossil record** enables scientists to reconstruct by inference how organisms have changed over time. The record also shows that there has been a tremendous variety of living things during the history of Earth, and that organisms come and go. Many organisms existed millions of years ago but no longer exist today. Those organisms, however, may be the ancestors of organisms alive today.

A second line of evidence can be seen in anatomical similarities or **morphology** among very different kinds of organisms. Many different kinds of organisms share similar types of body structures or body parts. Figure 4.16 shows

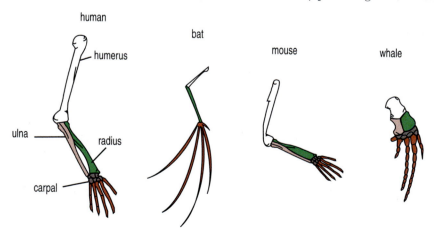

Figure 4.16

The five-digit structure and forearm structure of various animals.

the five-digit structure and forearm structure of a variety of different animals. These anatomical similarities suggest that these organisms all shared a common ancestor and that they diverged over the course of evolution into different species.

In the way that anatomical similarities suggest a common ancestor, biochemical and molecular similarities suggest this even more strongly. These similarities form a third line of evidence. As you saw in your investigations in Unit 1, all living things, right down to the smallest virus, share the exact same chemical makeup in all their biomolecules. Comprised primarily of six elements, all biomolecules share the same structures and functions. Nucleic acids are made up of purines, pyrimidines, phosphate, and sugar groups. Proteins are made up of the same 20 amino acids. Many carbohydrates, such as glucose, are identical no matter where you find them. And lipids share common structures throughout all living things.

Many of the proteins found in very different organisms, such as in yeast and in humans, are very similar (**homologous**) in their amino acid composition. Many metabolic processes of anabolism and catabolism are often indistinguishable from bacteria to human. And the transfer of information from DNA to RNA to protein is so universal that it was called the central dogma. (Recall, however, that there are exceptions to this central dogma.) The presence of cells is one of the characteristics of life as you defined it in Unit 1. Across all living things, cells retain a remarkable family resemblance. This incredible molecular unity of life provides compelling evidence that all life on Earth is related.

A story is told about the eminent embryologist Kark von Baer. (An embryologist is a scientist who studies the development of embryos.) In 1828 von Baer wrote, "I have two small embryos, preserved in alcohol that I forgot to label. At present I am unable to determine the genus to which they belong. They may be lizards, small birds, or even mammals." The similarities between a 4-week-old human embryo and the early embryos of fish, salamanders, turtles, chickens, pigs, sheep, and mice are so striking that it is difficult to tell them apart. The retention of the embryonic pattern of development in so many organisms suggests that this pattern was found in an earlier, common ancestor. The pattern may have been retained because it formed a strong foundation from which a variety of organisms could develop (see Figure 4.17). As Darwin wrote, "the embryo is the animal in its less modified state," and that state "reveals the structure of its progenitor." **Embryology** forms the fourth line of evidence.

In his travels around the world on the H.M.S. *Beagle,* Darwin observed patterns in the clustering of what he called "closely allied" species. These are organisms with very similar body plans. For example, Australia has a wide variety of marsupials such as kangaroos and koala. Before the arrival of humans, Hawaii and New Zealand had no land mammals, but instead had an incredible diversity of plant, insect, and bird life found nowhere else on Earth. Adjacent areas in South America were occupied by two similar species of large flightless birds. But these birds were not ostriches, which are found only in Africa, or emus found only in Australia. These **biogeographical data** suggested to Darwin that life in isolated areas has evolved over millions of years. These observations constitute the fifth line of evidence.

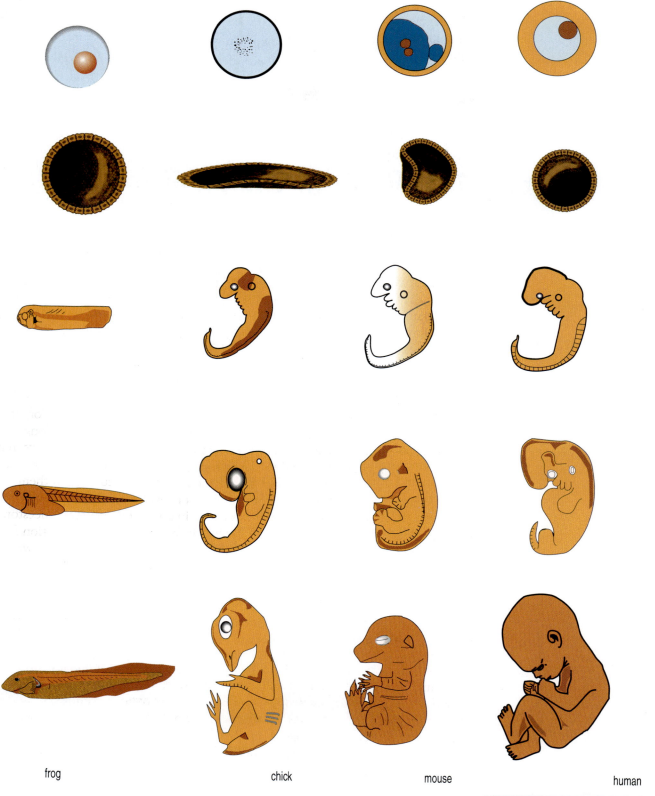

frog   chick   mouse   human

Figure 4.17

The early embryonic stages of vertebrates resemble one another.

 **ANALYSIS**

Record your responses to the following in your notebook.

1. Giraffes are graceful creatures with the striking feature of very long necks that enable them to feed on the leaves of tall trees. Describe the evidence you would look for in investigating the evolution of the modern-day giraffe. Use your understanding of natural selection and the evidence for evolution.

2. What evidence might suggest the molecular basis of this evolution?

 ACTIVITY

The Beak of the Finch

Evolution takes place over a long period of time. As a result, it can be difficult to observe directly, but it is not impossible. In Unit 2, Learning Experience 12, you observed evolution and natural selection in action in the development of antibiotic-resistant bacteria. In 1973, two scientists, Rosemary and Peter Grant, began a study of finches, the same kind of bird that Darwin studied. During his visit to the Galápagos Islands, Darwin collected 13 different species of finches. He speculated that the finches originated from the mainland of South America and colonized the islands. Once there, the finches could not easily fly away from the islands. But the environment was in a state of constant change, and therefore the sources of food available to the finches were changing constantly.

Like Darwin, the Grants found that the finches and the island locale provided ideal conditions for study. By catching, measuring, and keeping track of virtually every bird on the Galápagos Island of Daphne Major, the Grants were able to study more than 20 generations of birds. They observed evolution in action and reconfirmed that natural selection is the major force in evolution. In addition, they demonstrated that evolution can take place at a much faster pace than Darwin and others had ever imagined.

In this activity, work with a partner to examine the relationships among the structure of the finches' beaks, their food source, and the changes in food source due to environmental conditions. Determine how this affected the changes in the finch population that the Grants observed.

PROCEDURE

1. Figure 4.18 shows the beaks of 6 different kinds of finches. It also describes the food and habitat of each kind of finch. In your notebook, explain how you think the shape and size of the bill is well adapted to the food source of the finch.

	Vegetarian Tree Finch	Large Insectivorous Tree Finch	Woodpecker Finch	Cactus Ground Finch	Sharp-beaked Ground Finch	Large Ground Finch
Shape of bill	parrotlike bill	grasping bill	uses cactus spines	large crushing bill	pointed crushing bill	large crushing bill
Main food	fruit	insects	insects	cactus	seeds	seeds
Habitat	trees	trees	trees	ground	ground	ground

Figure 4.18

Beaks of Darwin's finches and finches' food.

2. Figure 4.19 shows graphs of the rainfall and temperature on Daphne Major between 1965 and 1984. Examine the graphs. Describe the variations or lack of variations in the environment that these graphs indicate.

3. Figure 4.20 shows three graphs that indicate rainfall, number of birds, and the biomass of seeds. Focus on the year 1977. Describe what happened to the rainfall, the number of birds, and the seeds. One observation in the seed population was that bigger seeds survived the environmental conditions of 1977. Based on your understanding of these graphs, which birds from Figure 4.18 do you think would not have survived the conditions in 1977? Which would have survived? Explain your responses.

4. The Grants studied the characteristics of the birds that survived the conditions of 1977. These data are shown in Figure 4.21. Describe the changes that took place. Explain why this happened.

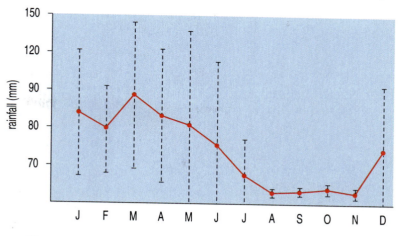

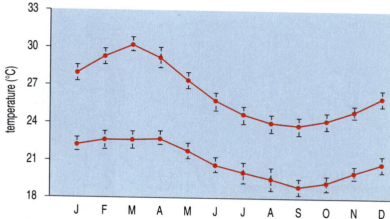

ANALYSIS

Record your responses to the following in your notebook.

1. Explain how the beaks of the finches illustrate a structure/function relationship.
2. How did the environment of Daphne Major vary between 1965 and 1984? What impact might that have had on the finches' food source? How did this in turn affect the finch population?
3. What surprising conclusion did the Grants reach when they analyzed the data collected in the years after 1977? Why was this surprising?
4. The years following the conditions of 1977 brought a flip-flop in environmental conditions. The rains poured down and caused flooding on the island. In response, plants that produced small seeds flourished. Describe the impact you think this had on the finch population on the island.

Figure 4.19

Mean monthly precipitation and temperature on the Galápagos Islands between 1965 and 1984. Grant, Peter R. *Ecology and Evolution of Darwin's Finches*. © 1986 Princeton University Press. Reprinted by permission of Princeton University Press.

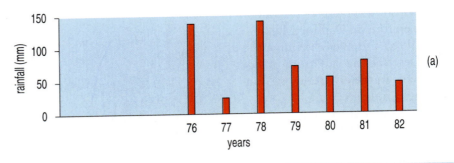

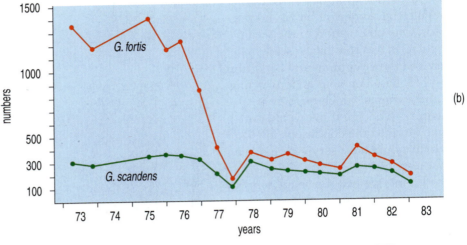

Figure 4.20

(a) Rainfall on Daphne Major. (b) Population size of two resident species of finches on Daphne Major. (c) Biomass of small seeds on Daphne Major.
Grant, Peter R. *Ecology and Evolution of Darwin's Finches.* © 1986 Princeton University Press. Reprinted by permission of Princeton University Press.

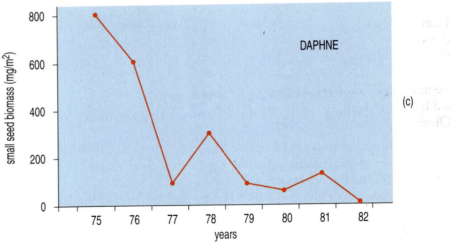

Figure 4.21

Bill depth of surviving finches in 1978.
Grant, Peter R. *Ecology and Evolution of Darwin's Finches.* © 1986 Princeton University Press. Reprinted by permission of Princeton University Press.

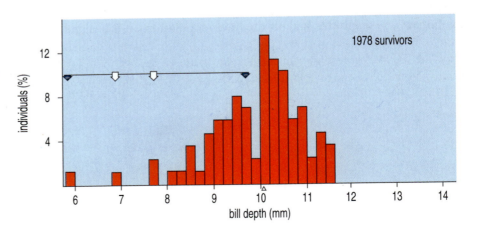

Variation Is the Spice of Life

ACTIVITY

As you saw with the finches, for evolution to take place, there must be variations among individuals. For it is these variations that allow populations to change as the environment changes. Do these variations come about to ensure survival? Or are they the unplanned consequences of changes in the DNA and of random mating? In the following simulation, you will explore changes in individuals that make up a population.

Materials

For each pair of students:

- 1 paper bag with movement directions
- 2 sheets of graph paper
- 2 pens or pencils (of different colors)

PROCEDURE

1. Fill in the center square of the graph paper grid with a pencil.
2. Shake the paper bag to mix the contents.
3. Without looking in the bag, draw out a single strip of paper. Fill in your grid according to the instruction on the strip of paper. (Figure 4.22 lists all the possible movements you will make on your grid.)
4. Place the strip of paper back in the bag. Repeat this sequence 20 times, using the same pencil.
5. Circle the last square you filled in. Then wait for your teacher's instructions.
6. If your "organism" did not survive, join a pair whose organism did survive.
7. Beginning with the last square (the one you circled), repeat steps 2–5 using a different-colored pencil or pen.
8. Observe the grids of the other groups.

ANALYSIS

Record your responses to the following in your notebook.

1. What does the central square of the grid represent?
2. In evolutionary terms, what were you showing as you followed the directions on the strips?
3. Why did some grids not survive?
4. Explain why your completed grid was different from the grids of other groups. Use your understanding of Darwin's theory of natural selection.
5. How might this simulation illustrate the principle that individuals vary but do not evolve, but that populations evolve?

ONE LEFT	ONE RIGHT

TWO LEFT	TWO RIGHT

ONE UP	ONE DOWN

TWO UP	TWO DOWN

REPEAT LAST STEP	REVERSE LAST STEP

NO CHANGE	NO CHANGE

DIAGONAL LEFT-UP	DIAGONAL RIGHT-UP

DIAGONAL LEFT-DOWN	DIAGONAL RIGHT-DOWN

Figure 4.22

Movement directions.

Ornithologist   Leah cringed on her couch, hiding her head behind a pillow until the credits to Alfred Hitchcock's *The Birds* scrolled up the TV screen. The fictitious birds in the movie were stalking the residents of a small town, waiting on rooftops, power lines, and other perches before attacking them. Although Leah was terrified throughout the film, she found herself greatly interested in the birds—so interested that this film led Leah into a career as an ornithologist.

When Leah saw *The Birds,* she was in high school. She was sure that birds did not act like they did in the film, but she wanted to learn more about them. After visiting the library and thumbing through numerous books on the subject, she decided to change her path in school so that she could continue to learn more about birds and their behavior. That meant adding more science courses, especially biology, to her course load. She joined the National Audubon Society, and sometimes found time on weekends and after school to volunteer at a local bird sanctuary. There she clerked in the bookstore, filled the bird feeders, and took notice of all of the different species of birds (and their unique behaviors) that visited the feeders.

Leah's family was very proud when she was accepted into a top university and when, 4 years later, she graduated with a bachelor of science degree in wildlife management. Not wanting to stop at an undergraduate degree, she continued on to get a master's degree in environmental biology.

Having already been involved with the National Audubon Society's Christmas bird counts, Leah became a bird researcher. She spends most of her time on a study of the piping plover. She and her coworkers set a goal of increasing the population of this shore-nesting bird by protecting their nesting sites from human encroachment. In the past, many plover nests have been tampered with or destroyed because of automotive and all-wheel-drive beach access. Leah's days are filled by trips to the beaches to check the status of the nesting pairs. Sometimes she visits other nesting sites on the East Coast to compare notes with other researchers. During these visits, she counts and measures eggs, makes sure that nesting sites are cordoned off from the public, and counts the nesting pairs. This might mean banding birds that haven't yet been identified. But there is cause for celebration. Within a few years after Leah and her coworkers started this project, they noted a marked increase in the numbers of nesting pairs.

During the winter months after the piping plovers move south, Leah spends a lot of time in front of a computer, analyzing her data and getting ready for the next nesting season. Even though her job keeps her very busy, Leah still makes time to volunteer at her local bird sanctuary. She still fills bird feeders, but also leads seminars to educate the public about its feathered friends and how best to live harmoniously among them.

Must Like Long Walks, Dining by Candlelight, and Be of Same Species

Prologue

Throughout this unit, you have investigated different populations of organisms. You have explored those in your square-meter environment, some in food webs, and still others in your study of growth curves and biogeochemical cycles. You have seen and used the word *species* in different activities and readings. But what is a species exactly? As you read in the Prologue to Learning Experience 6, Henry W. Bates grouped butterflies of similar appearance together. He called them separate species, as did most collectors of the time. But is there more to the concept of species than meets the eye? In this learning experience, you determine the criteria that are used to define a species.

Brainstorming

Discuss the following questions with your partner, and record your thinking in your notebook. Be prepared to share your ideas with the class.

1. What is a species?
2. What criteria would you use to identify an organism as belonging to a species?

Of Fish and Dogs

Consider the cichlids, perchlike fish found in the fresh waters of South America, Africa, Sri Lanka, and India. Cichlids have been of great interest to researchers for several reasons. One reason is their parenting behavior. Cichlids hatch their young in their mouths (mouth brooding), and both parents show strong nurturing and protective ties to the young. This is unusual behavior for fish.

Dogs are . . . well, dogs.

In this task, you will examine diagrams that show a collection of cichlids found in Lake Victoria in Africa and a collection of dogs. How many different species can you identify in each figure?

TASK

Examine the two groups of animals shown in Figure 4.23 and Figure 4.24. Determine how many different species you think are in each group. List the reasons (criteria) that you used to separate species within each collection. Be prepared to explain your criteria to the class.

Figure 4.23

How many different species of dogs do you see?

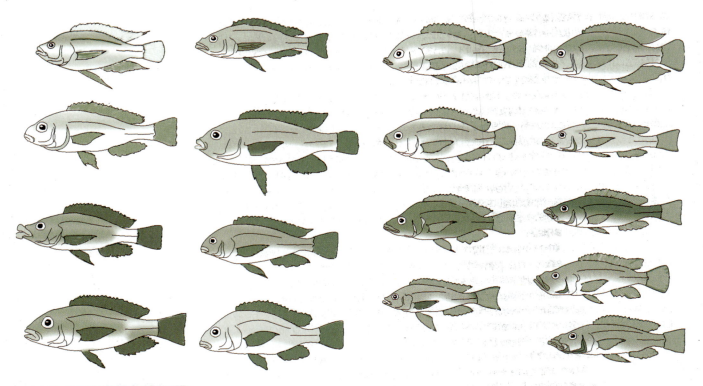

Figure 4.24

How many different species of cichlids do you see?

Topic: Species/Speciation
Go to: www.scilinks.org
Code: INBIOH2556

READING

The Fundamental Unit

Reprinted by permission of the publisher from *The Diversity of Life* by Edward O. Wilson, pp. 38–39, 51–52, 55, 56, 59, 62, 74, Cambridge, Mass.: The Belknap Press of Harvard University Press, Copyright © 1992 by Edward O. Wilson.

. . . I will try to cut to the heart of the matter with the "biological-species concept": a species is a population whose members are able to interbreed freely under natural conditions. This definition is an idea easily stated but filled with exceptions and difficulties, all interesting . . . I must add at once that not all biologists accept the biological-species concept as sound or as the pivotal unit on which the description of biological diversity can be based. They look to the gene or the ecosystem to play these roles.

. . . I think they are wrong, but in any case will return shortly to the difficulties of the biological species to give voice to their misgivings.

For the moment let me go on to expand the definition, which is accepted at least provisionally by a majority of evolutionary biologists. Notice the qualification it contains, "under natural conditions." This says that hybrids [that is, the descendants of different kinds of animals] bred from two kinds of animals in captivity, or two kinds of plants cultivated in a garden, are not enough to classify them as a member of a single species. To take the most celebrated example, zookeepers have for years crossed tigers with lions. The offspring are called tiglons when the father is a tiger and ligers when the father is a lion. But the existence of these creatures proves nothing, except perhaps that lions and tigers are genetically closer to each other than they are to other kinds of big cats. The still unanswered question is, do lions and tigers hybridize freely where they meet under natural conditions?

Today the two species do not meet in the wild, having been driven back by the expansion of human populations into different corners of the Old World. Lions occur in Africa south of the Sahara and in one small population in the Gir forest of northwestern India. Tigers live in small, mostly endangered populations from Sumatra north through India to southeastern Siberia. In India, no tigers are found near the Gir forest. It would seem at first that the test of the biological-species concept, free interbreeding in nature, cannot be applied. But this is not so: during historical times the two big cats overlapped across a large part of the Middle East and India. To learn what happened in these earlier days is to find the answer.

At the height of the Roman Empire, when North Africa was covered by fertile savannas—and it was possible to travel from Carthage to Alexandria in the shade of trees—expeditions of soldiers armed with net and spear captured lions for display in zoos and in coliseum spectacles. A few centuries earlier, lions were still abundant in southeastern Europe and the Middle East. They preyed on humans in the forests of Attica while being hunted themselves for sport by Assyrian kings. From these outliers they ranged eastward to India, where they still thrived during British rule in the nineteenth century. Tigers ranged in turn from northern Iran eastward across India, thence north to Korea and Siberia and south to Bali. To the best of our knowledge, no tiglons or ligers were recorded from the zone of overlap. This absence is especially notable in the case of India, where under the British Raj trophies were hunted and records of game animals kept for more than a century.

We have a good idea why the two species of big cats, despite their historical proximity, failed to hybridize in nature. First, they liked different habitats. Lions stayed mostly in open savanna and grassland and tigers in forests, although the segregation was far from perfect. Second, their behavior was and is radically different in ways that count for the choice of mates. Lions are the only social cats. They live in prides, whose enduring centers are closely bonded females and their young. Upon maturing, males leave their birth pride and join other groups, often as pairs of brothers. The adult males and females hunt together, with the females taking the lead role. Tigers, like all other cat species except lions, are solitary. The males produce a different urinary scent from that of lions to mark their territories and approach one another and the females only briefly during the breeding season. In short, there appears to have been little opportunity for adults of the two species to meet and bond long enough to produce offspring.

Wilson's criterion of a species is whether members of that group can interbreed. This definition has been extended by others to include the idea that this interbreeding must result in the production of fertile offspring. That is, the offspring must be capable of bearing offspring themselves. In some instances, this is physically impossible. But size and structure are not the only physical limitations. Even organisms of similar structure may have differing numbers of chromosomes that would make production of a viable embryo impossible. Even in cases in which it is physically possible for mating between two species to take place, it will not usually occur in the wild. As you have seen from Wilson's description of tiglons and ligers, the definition of species is complex. The key phrase is, "under natural conditions." Habitat isolation is another reason that two species capable of breeding may not do so. If two organisms are not introduced, they have no chance to court and mate. And even if they do meet, other features will indicate to potential suitors that the mate in question is of a different species and not an appropriate mate. Some of these features include species-specific coloration, scent, variation in reproductive timing (such as when the female is in heat), and courtship behavior. Even though all cichlids in Lake Victoria may look pretty much alike to us, the fish themselves are clearly quite aware of which fish is which, and will only breed with fish of the same species.

ANALYSIS

Record your responses to the following in your notebook.

1. Explain why cichlids are considered different species, but dogs, the same species. Be sure to include in your explanation factors that would or would not influence hybridization.

2. How do you think the concept of separate finch species is related to separate cichlid species?

3. The term *hybrid* is often used to describe the offspring of different species that have been bred under artificial circumstances in laboratories, zoos, or farms. A technique called crossbreeding allows the breeder to produce new organisms with very specific traits. An example of such crossbreeding is the mating of a horse and a donkey, which produces a mule. A horse (*Equinus caballus*), which has 64 chromosomes, will mate with a donkey (*Equinus asinus*), which has 62 chromosomes. Their mule offspring will have 63 chromosomes and will be sterile. Explain what you think this means in terms of species. How does this extend your understanding of the definition of species?

READING

Cichlids Past and Present

The cichlid fish of Lake Victoria in East Africa are remarkable not only for their variations in color and in their parental attentiveness as mouthbrooders, but also for their ancestral origins. Within this one (albeit very large) lake live 300 or more distinct species of cichlids. The cichlids are distinctive in color, structure, and feeding habits. Some are bottom-feeding algae-eaters; some eat snails, others mollusks, others fish; some only eat fish scales; and still others prefer only the eyes of fish. In spite of these differences, the cichlids are astonishingly the same at the level of their DNA. In some cases, they differ by only one nucleotide. All of the different species of cichlids in Lake Victoria have evolved from a single ancestral species within the last 750,000 years.

In 1959, British colonists introduced the Nile perch to the lake. The Nile perch is a sport fish that grows to almost two meters (more than six feet) in length. A voracious predator, this fish is responsible for undoing thousands of years of evolution in a single gulp by decimating the cichlid population and eliminating many species. In doing so, this large fish has also upset the ecosystem balance of the lake by removing the algae-eating cichlids. In the absence of the cichlids, algal blooms fill the lake. When these blooms die and decompose, the oxygen content of the lake is reduced. This results in a decline in the population of other fish, crustaceans, and other biotic members of the ecosystem.

ANALYSIS

Construct a diagram or drawing in your notebook that shows how the introduction of the Nile perch affected the ecosystem of Lake Victoria.

EXTENDING *Ideas*

▶ Why are mules sterile? Breeding a horse with a donkey produces offspring called mules. Research the genetic make-up of horses, donkeys, and mules. Explain why horses and donkeys are considered separate species even though they can mate and produce offspring.

Learning Experience 8

The Diversity of Life

Prologue

Throughout this unit, you have seen the enormous diversity of life on Earth. You have witnessed diversity in your field study, in food-web explorations, in your ecocolumn, in population studies, and in your readings. There are many aspects of diversity. But in most cases, the term refers to the number of species on Earth. Scientists and naturalists have described about 1.8 million species of living organisms and estimate that there are 5 to 100 million in all. Most of the undiscovered kinds of life are thought to be in the ocean depths, in the soil, and in the tropical rain forest canopy. Sometimes, species are discovered by scientists, but they are already known to the native population. (An example is the tree kangaroo of New Guinea "discovered" in 1994.) In addition to the tremendous diversity of life found on Earth today, many more millions of species that once lived on Earth have died out. But how have new species appeared (speciation)? What can explain so many different species of cichlids or so many changes in species over time? In this learning experience, you explore the origin of and the changes within the diversity of life.

Brainstorming

Discuss the following questions with your partner, and record your thinking in your notebook. Be prepared to share your ideas with the class.

1. Figure 4.25 shows a representation of the number of species among life-forms. Insects, for example, account for half of all known species (approximately 800,000 species). What principle or concept is this illustration demonstrating?
2. Why is the elephant so small? Why is the insect so large?
3. What surprises you about this figure? Why?

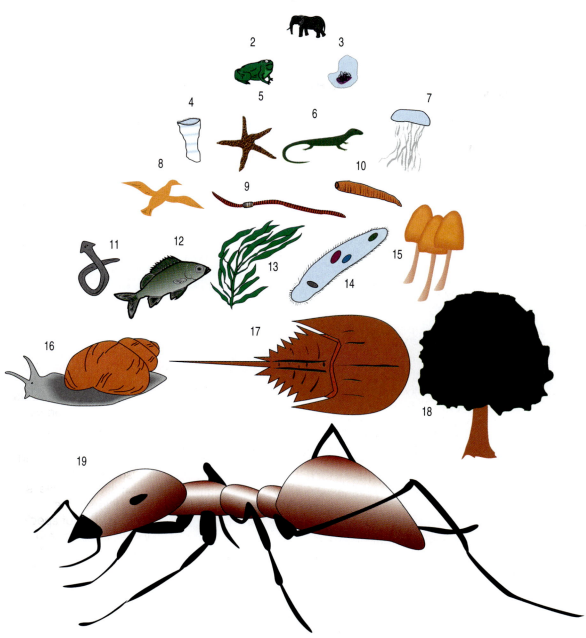

Figure 4.25

Each drawing represents a
major group of organisms
and the number of species
in that group.

1. mammals
2. amphibians
3. bacteria
4. sponges
5. echinoderms
6. reptiles
7. coelenterates
8. birds
9. earthworms
10. roundworms
11. flatworms
12. fish
13. algae
14. protozoa
15. fungi
16. mollusks
17. noninsect arthropods
18. plants
19. insects

Reprinted by permission of the publisher from *The Diversity of Life* by Edward O. Wilson, pp. 38–39, 51–52, 55, 56, 59, 62, 74, Cambridge, Mass.: The Belknap Press of Harvard University Press, Copyright © 1992 by Edward O. Wilson.

New Species

What is the origin of biological diversity? This profoundly important problem can be most quickly solved by recognizing that evolution creates two patterns across time and space. Think of a butterfly species with blue wings as it evolves into another species with purple wings (Figure 4.26). Evolution has occurred but leaves only one kind of butterfly. Now think of another butterfly species, also with blue wings. In the course of its evolution it splits into three species, bearing purple, red, and yellow wings respectively. The two patterns of evolution are vertical change in the original population and speciation, which is vertical change plus the splitting of the original population into multiple races or species. The first blue butterfly experienced pure vertical change without speciation. The second blue butterfly experienced pure vertical change plus speciation . . . The origin of most biological diversity, in a phrase, is a side product of evolution.

Vertical change is mostly what Darwin had in mind when he published his 1859 masterwork. The full title tells the story: *On the Origin of Species by Means of Natural Selection, or the Preservation of Favoured Races in the Struggle for Life*. In essence, Darwin said that certain hereditary types within a species (the "favoured races") survive at the expense of others and in so doing transform the makeup of the entire species across generations. A species can be altered so extensively by natural selection as to be changed into a different species, said Darwin. Yet no matter how much time elapses, no matter how much change occurs, only one species remains. In order to create diversity beyond mere variation among the competing organisms, the species must split into two or more species during the course of vertical evolution.

blue wings

purple wings

Figure 4.26

An example of vertical evolution. A blue-winged butterfly species may evolve over time and space and become purple-winged.

. . . Any evolutionary change whatsoever that reduces the chances of producing a fertile hybrid can yield a new species . . . Consider a male of species A and a female of species B trying to create a fertile hybrid offspring. Because they are genetically different from one another, things can go wrong. The two individuals might want to mate in different places. They might try to breed at different seasons or times of the day. Their courtship signals could be mutually incomprehensible. And even if the representatives of the two species actually mate, their offspring might fail to reach maturity, or attaining maturity, turn out to be sterile. The wonder is not that hybridization fails but that it ever works. *The origin of species is therefore simply the evolution of some difference—any difference at all—that prevents the production of fertile hybrids between populations under natural conditions.*

. . . But wait: I have been speaking of the origin of species in paradoxical language. In the traditional language of biology, the "mechanisms" have "functions." Yet they represent whatever can go wrong, not what can go right. In other words, beauty arises from error. How can both of these apparently contradictory perceptions be true? The answer, based on studies of many populations in the wild, is this: *the differences between species ordinarily originate as traits that adapt them to the environment, not as devices for reproductive isolation.* The adaptations may also serve as intrinsic isolating mechanisms, but the result is accidental. Speciation is a by-product of vertical evolution.

To see why this strange relationship holds, consider the special but widespread mode of diversification called *geographical speciation*. Start with an imaginary population of birds—say, flycatchers—that was split by the last glacial advance in North America. Over several thousand years, the population living in what would today be the southwestern United States adapted to life in an open woodland, while the other population, in the southeastern United States, adapted to life in swamp forests. These differences were independently acquired and functional. They allowed the birds to survive and reproduce better in the habitats most readily available to them south of the glacial front. With the retreat of the ice, the two populations expanded their ranges until they met and intermingled across the northern states. One now breeds in open woodland, the other in swamps. The differences in their preferred habitats, based on hereditary differences acquired during the period of enforced geographical separation, makes it less likely that the two newly evolved populations will closely associate during the breeding season and hybridize. The adaptive difference in habitat thus accidentally came to serve as an isolating mechanism.

. . . The two populations have turned into distinct species because they are reproductively isolated where they meet under natural conditions. The single ancestral, pre-glaciation species has been split into two species, an entirely incidental result of the vertical evolution of its populations while they were separated by a geographical barrier (Figure 4.27).

. . . Great biological diversity takes long stretches of geological time and the accumulation of large reservoirs of unique genes. The richest ecosystems build slowly, over millions of years. It is further true that by chance alone only a few new species are poised to move into novel adaptive zones, to create something spectacular and stretch the limits of diversity. A panda or a sequoia represents a magnitude of evolution that comes along only rarely. It takes a stroke of luck and a long period of probing, experimentation, and failure. Such a creation is part of deep history, and the planet does not have the means nor we the time to see it repeated.

blue wings

yellow wings

purple wings

red wings

Figure 4.27

An example of divergent speciation. A blue-winged butterfly species may evolve over time and space into purple-, yellow-, and red-winged species.

ANALYSIS

Record your responses to the following in your notebook.

1. How would you define speciation?
2. Create and label a flowchart that diagrams and explains Wilson's two examples about the blue butterflies. Be sure to indicate where mutation, adaptation, and natural selection play roles.
3. How do geographic isolation and reproductive isolation lead to speciation? Give an example.
4. Do you think speciation is evolution? Explain your response.
5. Discuss the meaning of the quotation, "The environment is the theatre and evolution is the play."

ACTIVITY

SCiLINKS
NSTA

Topic: Biodiversity
Go to: www.scilinks.org
Code: INBIOH2564

Mapping the Gradient across the Americas

The term **biodiversity** (a contraction of biological diversity) in part refers to the variety of life-forms on Earth. Biodiversity, often referred to as **species richness**, is the number of species in an area or habitat. Confronted with the vast numbers and diversity of species, one might ask, What is the distribution of various species? What are the factors that influence where plants and animals can be found? How are evolution and speciation related to biodiversity?

In this activity, you will identify patterns in the distribution of species and determine general principles that help explain species distribution.

Materials

For each group of three students:

- 1 set of species richness maps
- assorted colored pencils

For the class:

- reference material, including atlases, encyclopedias, and geography books

PROCEDURE

1. Examine the maps in Figures 4.28, 4.29, and 4.30. The numbers indicate different species, and the lines help you follow the distribution.
2. Color each map so that patterns in each species become more apparent. For example, leave all the spaces between lines 0–99 white, color red between lines 100–199, and so on.
3. Create a color code. Place it in the corner of the sheet for reference. Be sure to use the same code in each map.
4. Discuss the following Analysis questions with your group members.

NALYSIS

Record your responses to the following in your notebook.

1. List the areas in each map that have the greatest number of species of mammals, of trees, and of birds. List those areas with the fewest.
2. Analyze your lists. Which of the areas have the same diversity patterns? Which are different? What might be some reasons for this?
3. Examine the maps that show the topographical, landform, and climatic regions of North and Central America in the atlas. What patterns do you see that might explain the reasons for greater or lesser species diversity?
4. List several general principles that explain how geography plays an important role in species diversity.
5. Examine Figure 4.31. Explain the reasons for and possible consequences of the changes shown in Costa Rica. Use your understanding of natural selection, mutation, adaptation, speciation, and the impact of environment on evolution.

Figure 4.28

Species richness: mammals.

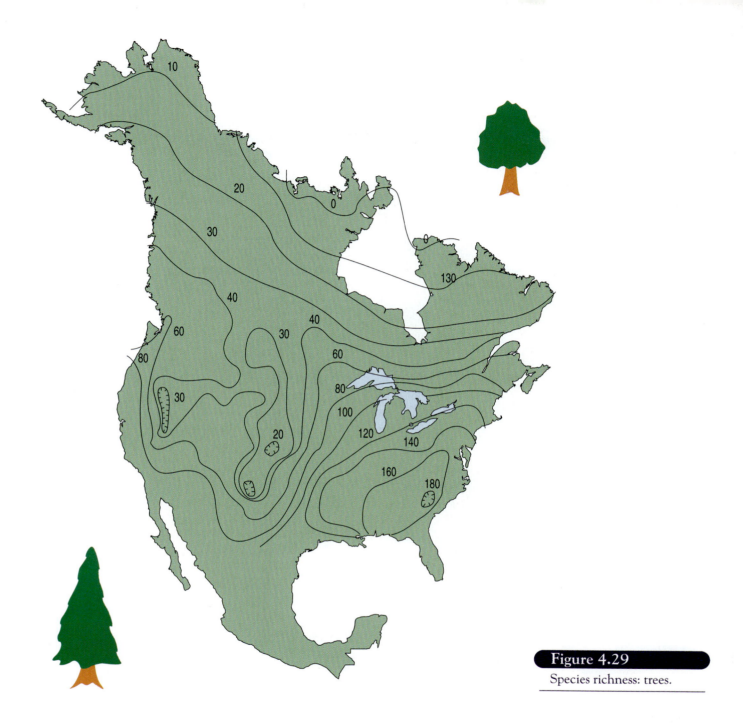

Figure 4.29

Species richness: trees.

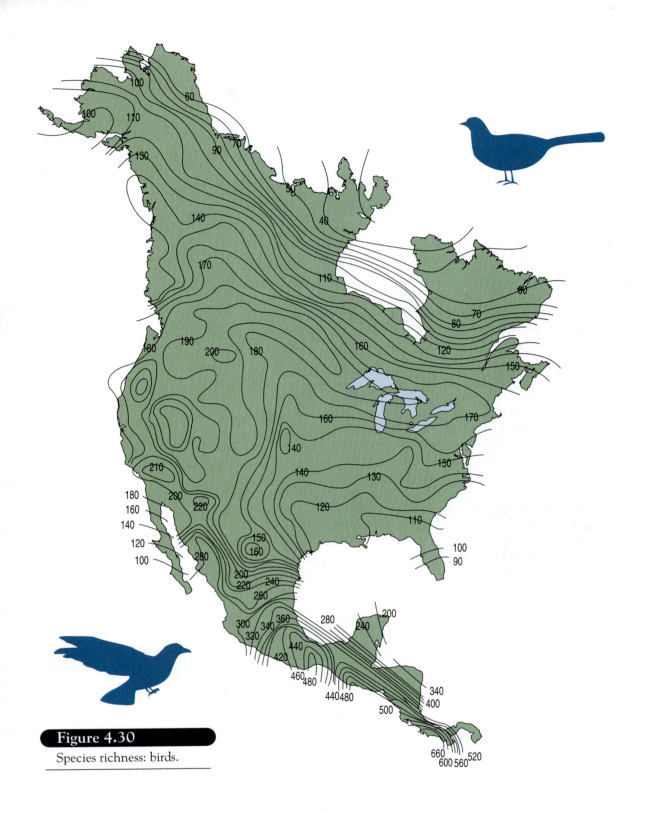

Figure 4.30

Species richness: birds.

Figure 4.31

Forest areas (green) in Costa Rica from 1940 to 1983.

1940 1950 1961 1977 1983

EXTENDING *Ideas*

- Investigate and visit your local branch of the National Audubon Society and/or other nature/conservation societies in your area. These groups sponsor many events including bird watching, nature walks, and other outdoor activities.

- In *After Man: Zoology of the Future* (New York: St. Martin's Press, 1981), Dougal Dixon has created an interesting "zoo of the future." He contemplates future evolution on our own planet. He waves a time wand, sets his scenario 50 million years from now, and eliminates today's dominant species. In their place, he creates new animals that might take over as the major occupants of Earth's surface. Dixon uses these new animals to show some of the basic principles of evolution and ecology. He does not make firm predictions that this is what the animals would look like, but instead offers an exploration of the possibilities. Design your own critter (herbivore or carnivore) that might appear in the future. Place it in its specific environment, describe its niche, and explain how it is adapted to its environment.

- Evolution is a dynamic process. Species and groups of related species are emerging while other species are dying out. Madagascar is an island in the Indian Ocean off the east coast of Africa. Thirty species of lemurs live on the island. (A lemur is a type of primate found nowhere else in the world.) These 30 species originated from one or two ancestral species. Research the evolution of lemurs and the speciation that resulted from changes over time.

- The history of humans on Earth is an example of evolution, speciation, and extinction. The earliest hominid known from the fossil records is *Australopithecus afarensis,* which lived in Africa about 3–5 million years ago. This species, thought to be the only hominid species around at that time, was 1.4 meters (about 5 feet) tall, walked upright (was bipedal), and possibly lived in family groups. Their cranial capacity (brain size) was about the same as the modern-day chimpanzee, and their teeth remains indicate they were mostly vegetarian. About 2 million years later, speciation of hominids occurred, which resulted in at least three distinct species. Research and diagram human evolution from *Australopithecus* to modern-day *Homo sapiens sapiens.*

CAREER FOCUS

Cartographer

"Marsha's Maps. May I help you?"

"I hope so. I am interested in adding a detailed, interactive road map of Hopedale to our town's Web page. I am especially interested in showing street names and major building landmarks."

"Well, you've contacted the right place!"

Marsha is a cartographer. A few years ago, she started her own business. With recent leaps in technology, she has been able to cater to a larger clientele than she had ever dreamed. She has created maps for magazines, tourism guides, government agencies, municipalities, and Web sites.

Marsha's interest in maps began with the treasure maps that her father created for her when she was a child. She soon began manually mapping out her neighborhood, including all of the popular hangouts and spots of interest (such as the local burger joint).

In high school, Marsha took courses in algebra, geometry, trigonometry, drafting, mechanical drawing, and computer science to help her toward her goal of becoming a cartographer. Once out of high school, she began working toward a 4-year degree in engineering at the university. When her financial aid fell through after 2 years, she became concerned that she would not reach her goal. But Marsha learned that she could still get an associate's degree from a 2-year college, then become an apprentice to an established mapmaker, and still become a cartographer. With technological advances, she also knew that her computer training would be an important aspect of her career.

Marsha began her career as a surveyor, doing hands-on data collecting using theodolites (tools used to measure horizontal and vertical angles) and electronic equipment used to measure distances. Sometimes she even found herself using a simple tape measure.

After working for a number of years and getting an adequate feel for the field of cartography, Marsha felt ready to start her own company. Her maps have included relief maps, which show landforms such as hills, mountains, and trees from above; city maps, which she finds challenging because of the amount of information needed to fit clearly into a small space; tourism maps, which need to be informative, yet make an area inviting to visitors; and many others for special projects. Her data usually come from digital data received from Geographic Information Systems (GIS). For much larger projects, she depends on data from the Global Positioning System (GPS). The GPS is a satellite system that can precisely locate points on Earth using radio signals transmitted for satellites. These systems have made it possible for Marsha to create interesting, informative, and artistic maps using little more than her computer and her knowledge of surveying and mapping.

Marsha works closely with clients, making sure to create exactly what they expect before hiring her. One client recently asked her to create a map of some hiking trails in a popular state park. Because this information was not readily available, she hired a consultant surveying company to help her. By carrying handheld systems, the surveyors were able to receive GPS signals as they walked and rode over the trails. They located each point along the paths and stored the information for Marsha to use. Combining the trail data with existing maps of the state park, Marsha created a layered map of the trails, hills, and overhanging trees. This type of information made it possible to produce printed maps of the trails for visitors. These maps also could be extremely helpful to the park rangers should they ever need to locate someone lost on the trails.

"Marsha," called one of her associates from her work station. "Hopedale's Web site is active and your map looks spectacular! The mayor called and said she has already received wonderful feedback from residents and visitors!"

Learning Experience 9

Going . . .
Going . . . Gone!

Prologue

Belayed 2,000 feet above Kauai's Kalalau Valley, botanists Ken Wood and Steve Perlman risk their lives to rescue Hawaii's imperiled plants from extinction. Out of reach from goats and other alien invaders, such cliffs are among the last strongholds of the state's native flora. With the unhappy distinction of being the country's endangered species capital, the Hawaiian Islands have already lost hundreds of original life-forms while hundreds more teeter on the verge of oblivion.

(Excerpted from "On the Brink: Hawaii's Vanishing Species" by Elizabeth Royte, *National Geographic,* September 1995, p. 2.)

Why would anyone risk his or her life in an attempt to save a plant or animal species? Why are these organisms becoming endangered and going extinct? Does it really matter if they do?

As you learned in Learning Experience 5, extinction is part of the natural cycle of life. It plays an important role in evolution and the continuing diversity of life on Earth. In this learning experience, you explore some of the factors that result in the endangerment and loss of species and some of the factors that surround the preservation and protection of species.

Brainstorming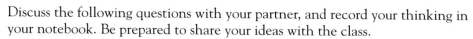

Discuss the following questions with your partner, and record your thinking in your notebook. Be prepared to share your ideas with the class.

1. What do the terms *endangered species* and *extinction* mean to you?
2. Do you think that extinction is a positive process or a negative process? Explain your thinking.
3. What kinds of things do you think cause extinction?

Return to the Past

The Endangered Species Act, passed by Congress in 1973 and reauthorized in 1988, regulates a wide range of activities that involve plants and animals designated as endangered or threatened. The act defines an **endangered species** as a plant or animal that is rare and in immediate danger of extinction. A *threatened species* is any plant or animal that may become endangered in the foreseeable future. The act prohibits the following activities involving endangered species:

- importing them into, or exporting them from, the United States;
- taking (which includes harassing, harming, pursuing, hunting, shooting, wounding, trapping, killing, capturing, or collecting) the species within the United States and its territorial seas;
- taking them on the international high seas;
- possessing, selling, delivering, carrying, transporting, or shipping any such species if unlawfully taken within the United States or on the high seas;
- delivering, receiving, carrying, transporting, or shipping them in interstate or foreign commerce in the course of a commercial activity; and
- selling or offering the species for sale in interstate or foreign commerce.

Violators of this act are subject to fines of up to $100,000 and 1 year of imprisonment. Organizations found in violation may be fined up to $200,000.

TASK

1. Examine the graphs in Figures 4.32 and 4.33. Compare the data presented.
2. Write responses to the Analysis questions, and be prepared to discuss your views.

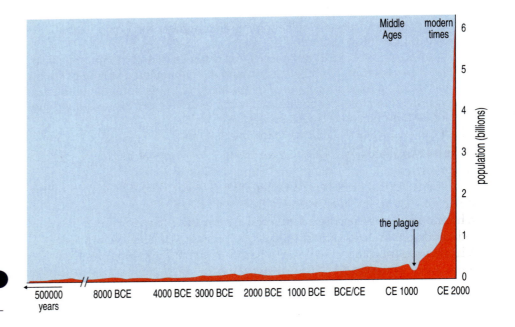

Figure 4.32

World population curve.

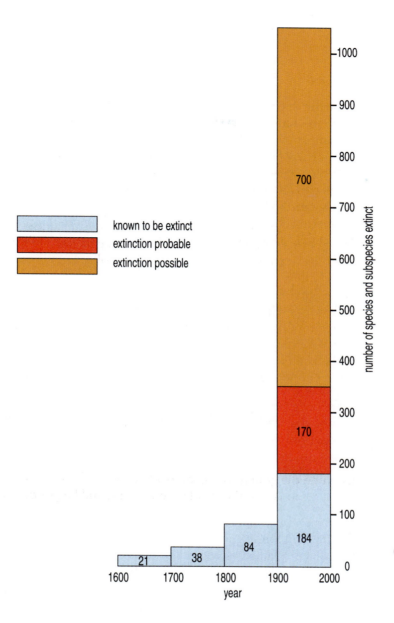

Figure 4.33

Number of vertebrate species lost.

ANALYSIS

Record your responses to the following in your notebook.

1. What resemblance do you see between the human population curve and the extinction graph?
2. How are the extinctions caused by humans different from extinctions that took place before the appearance of humans on Earth?
3. What human behaviors are causing the acceleration of species endangerment and extinction?
4. What do you predict will happen to both human and other species populations in the future? Why do you think so?

What Good Is It, Anyway?

Over the last 200 million years, about 90 species per century, or less than 1% per year, have become extinct. Judging from the fossil record, the natural average life span for an entire species is about 4 million years. If there are perhaps 10 million species on Earth today, the extinction rate as a result of natural extinction would be about four species per year. According to some estimates, however, the annual rate of species loss is as many as 50,000 species per year.

Does it matter if a certain species becomes extinct? Are all species "equal" when thinking about this, or are some more "valuable" than others? Who decides which to save and which to let go? What are the criteria for such a decision?

The rosy periwinkle (see Figure 4.34) has become a symbol of the untapped resources that lie within the dense growth of the rain forests and whose habitat is threatened by humans leveling rain forests. Found in the rain forests of Madagascar, this small plant with dark green leaves and a pink flower is a member of a large group of plants called *Vinca*. It has long been used in folk medicine for a range of ailments including dysentery, menstrual disorders, diabetes, and toothaches. Researchers have found substances in the roots, stems, and leaves of this plant that are extremely effective against two forms of cancer that were once fatal to children. These are Hodgkin's disease, a cancer primarily of young adults, and acute lymphocytic leukemia. The discovery of these substances (vinblastine and vincristine) in rosy periwinkle was a fortunate accident—a side result of the search for a cure for diabetes—but it has saved thousands of lives. Such discoveries enforce the concern that by deliberately or inadvertently destroying species, we may be destroying sources of products that could enhance or even save our own lives.

The loss of the rain forest is of extreme concern to many people. The Amazonian rain forest in Brazil, for example, is a massive tropical ecosystem that covers 5 million square kilometers (almost 2 million square miles). It is the largest continuous expanse of tropical rain forest in the world. Although rain forests cover only 7% of the planet's land surface, they contain 50% of the plants and animals found on the globe. The plants of the rain forest, whose potential medicinal value remains unknown, also serve as a source of oxygen for the planet's animal population.

Many scientists seem resigned to the fact that most of the rain forests will eventually be cut down. At the present rate of destruction of 1,800 hectares (about 4,500 acres) per hour, this seems inevitable. E. O. Wilson calculates that 27,000 species are slated for extinction every year.

ANALYSIS

Using *rain forest* as the central concept, create a concept map in your notebook that shows the relationships within this ecosystem and the possible consequences from the destruction of the rain forest.

Figure 4.34

Rosy periwinkle.

Save the Fly? Are You Kidding?

"If you see one flying, you won't forget it. It's spectacular."
"I'm talking about jobs. How can you equate a fly with people's livelihoods?"
"When it's gone, it's gone forever. We want to save the habitat and the fly."
"The dinosaurs and the passenger pigeons are gone and I don't miss them."

What organism is causing such heated debate in San Bernadino County in southern California? It is the Delhi Sands flower-loving fly, which, in 1993, became the first fly to be put on the endangered species list for protection (see Figure 4.35). There are so few left that they can almost be counted individually.

Delhi Sands is the largest remaining inland sand dune system in the Los Angeles basin. Its habitat supports not only the fly but pocket mice, butterflies, an unusual cockroachlike cricket, and rare flowers. Of the original 103 square kilometers (40 square miles), 120 hectares (300 acres) are available for the fly's needs. In effect, however, only 18 hectares (45 acres) actually support it. It appears to be heading quickly for the same fate—extinction—as its sister subspecies, the El Segundo fly. This fly was buried under the tarmac of the Los Angeles International Airport.

Many factors have led to the loss of this fly's habitat and to its reduction in numbers. Some of these include construction, off-road vehicles, spraying for weeds, bulldozing for fill, and the dumping of manure from local dairies. Because the fly is protected, a hospital under construction has been moved a few hundred feet, construction of a subdivision has been stalled, and the plans for a massive industrial development have been halted with a potential loss of thousands of jobs. A lawsuit filed to end the federal government's protection of the fly was dismissed but has been appealed.

The obscure fly spends most of its life underground during its larval stage as a maggot. The entomologists who study the fly are not sure what the maggots eat. The adults emerge from the earth in the summer and fly for a few days, hovering like hummingbirds above flowers and extracting their nectar with a long strawlike mouthpart. (This structure is an example of adaptive evolution. Recall Darwin's orchid and moth from Unit 2.) The males fly over the dunes in the heat of the day looking for females with which to mate. No one is sure how the flies mate, but the females then lay fertilized eggs deep in the sand; the eggs hatch in a week. Entomologists consider the Delhi Sands fly an interesting creature in an important habitat, each worthy of protecting.

The debate on saving species seems less controversial when it involves species appealing to humans, such as cuddly looking baby seals, Bambi-like deer, or songbirds. But this fly, like the snail darter and the northern spotted owl before it, is generating political, moral, and biological debate. On one side are those who want to weaken the Endangered Species Act. They see the protection of this supposedly insignificant creature as an example of the absurdity of saving all endangered species. On the other side are entomologists (those who study insects) and others who support the act to its fullest. They want to protect creatures great and small. Is there a middle ground?

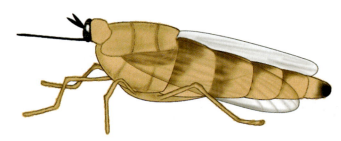

Figure 4.35

Delhi Sands fly.

Can one support the protection of some organisms, but not others? What would be the criteria? Would the criteria change depending on the species? What would be the basis for such a change in view?

 ANALYSIS

In a short essay in your notebook, respond to the following questions:

- What is your reasoned opinion about whether the Delhi Sands fly should be protected? Explain your thinking.
- What beliefs or values do you have that helped to shape your decision?
- Does your view hold true for all endangered species? Why or why not?

Be prepared to share your ideas with the class.

EXTENDING *Ideas*

If you are fascinated by the extinction of the dinosaurs, you may wish to read *T. Rex and the Crater of Doom* by Walter Alvarez (Princeton, NJ: Princeton University Press, 1997). This is a highly readable scientific book that gives insights into how discovery leads to more riddles that need to be solved. Alvarez shows the dynamic nature of research and of the personalities of the scientists who are involved in the mystery of the death from above.

Learning Experience 10

Back to Nature

Prologue

Is it possible to reverse the current trend of destroying natural habitats and the organisms in them? For many years, people have tried to save the environment by conserving resources and reducing pollution. But until recently, few people were thinking about recovering lost ecosystems. Environmentalists, politicians, and business people are now working on restoring selected environments. The goal in **restoration ecology** is for the habitat and its resources to be physically repaired, and, if necessary, its missing components replaced.

There are many types of restoration projects. Some projects improve depleted farmland soil. Some, like the return of the wolves to Yellowstone National Park, restore populations of plant or animal species. Others employ techniques for using natural resources without depleting them. And still other projects convert vacant lots in urban areas into miniparks or gardens.

Restorations are never perfect reproductions of past ecosystems, however. The restorations are different because of what is not there any longer. These are the species that have become extinct or have moved to other areas. They are also different because of what is there now. Perhaps a bird, insect, or plant newcomer has invaded the ecosystem or occupied a vacated ecological niche and succeeded in making itself at home. As you have learned in this unit, even ecosystems that exist undisturbed by humans change too, sometimes dramatically. Planners of any restoration project must, therefore, choose both the place and the time in the past that they are attempting to restore.

A major project is now underway in Florida to restore the Everglades. The story of the Everglades reveals the complex relationships between humans and the environment. But the outcome of this ambitious project is still uncertain. Upon completion, this project will be the largest water-system restoration in history.

In this learning experience, you explore the concept of restoration ecology—and what this could mean for the future—by looking into the issues that surround the Everglades Restoration Project. To understand the issues and complexities, you will need to research the biological and social issues surrounding the restoration of the Everglades system and reflect on the possibilities of restoring an ecosystem.

Brainstorming

Discuss the following with your partner, and record your thinking in your notebook. Be prepared to share your ideas with the class.

1. What kinds of restoration projects can you envision?
2. Why might a group want to restore an ecosystem that has been damaged or destroyed? Use examples from question 1.

CASE STUDY

Anything We Want

Either intentionally or by accident humans have disturbed or damaged many of Earth's ecosystems. Yet, with our current ecological knowledge and experience, it may be possible to restore or repair some of these ecosystems. Restoring an ecosystem that has deteriorated is complicated. You first need to know what the original looked like and how it functioned. Next, you need to determine what might be missing. Then you need to plan, and finally, you need to pay for the project.

Begin by reading the article "Bringing Back the Everglades." Then, with your partner, carry out the task.

TASK

1. Using the information in the reading, identify and list all the ecological, political, social, and economic issues surrounding the restoration of the Everglades. You may want to categorize your list by type of issue. You could then keep a related list of groups, individuals, and organizations involved in specific aspects of the restoration project.
2. With your partner, decide on one issue to research in depth from the list you made. At the end of the research project, you will present your findings and conclusions in a mock congressional committee hearing that has been set up to evaluate the status of the project. You and your partner should focus your research and report on the following:
   a. the ecological principles that need to be taken into consideration, including the organisms affected by the project;
   b. the views of the companies, groups, or individuals affected by your particular issue;
   c. your views and your analysis of the pros and cons of the issue; and
   d. your own educated opinion about what should be done.
3. Develop an opening statement for the committee. The intent of this short speech is to share with the committee members your knowledge and concerns about the issue you and your partner have researched. The speech should last about 3 minutes. As you develop your speech, consider the following:
   a. What messages are you eager to convey to the members of this committee?
   b. What other issues affect the subject of your research? What do you need to know about them?

4. Take careful notes on the issues that the other students present. You will need their expertise to make an informed decision. Following the committee hearing, there will be a discussion of the issues that were presented and of the status of the Everglades Restoration Project.

5. Prepare an independent comprehensive paper in which you describe what you would do if you were on the committee. Include the rationale behind the restoration project, all major issues, the arguments presented, and your own educated opinion. This paper will be evaluated by your teacher.

BRINGING BACK THE EVERGLADES

Amid great scientific and political uncertainty, ecosystem managers in Florida are pushing ahead with the boldest—and most expensive—restoration plan in history.
by Elizabeth Culotta

Reprinted with permission from *Science*, June 23, 1995: 268, 1688–1690. Copyright 1995, American Association for the Advancement of Science.

When steamships plied central Florida's Kissimmee River early in this century, passengers on ships traveling [toward each other] would spot each other across the marshes in the morning, then traverse the serpentine waterway for a full day before meeting. But in the 1960s, the U.S. Army Corps of Engineers straightened out the Kissimmee. In the name of efficiency and flood control, they dug 56 miles of straight canal to replace 103 miles of meanders—and destroyed at least 1.2 million square meters of wetlands in the process. The river was once home to flocks of white ibis; today it boasts the cattle egret, accompanying herds of cows grazing on the canal's linear banks.

But at one spot on the central Kissimmee, boats must again follow the twists and turns of the old river channel. The Corps is slowly putting the kinks back into the Kissimmee. By working with the state of Florida to restore the wetlands, they hope to bring back the invertebrates, fish, and, eventually, the wading birds that once nested here. With an estimated price tag of $370 million, this is the most ambitious river restoration in U.S. history.

It is, however, a mere drop in the watershed compared to plans for the rest of south Florida. Over the next 15 to 20 years, at a cost of roughly $2 billion, the Corps and state and other federal agencies plan to replumb the entire Florida Everglades ecosystem, including 14,000 square kilometers of wetlands and engineered waterways. It's an urgent task, planners say. For after decades of drainage, altered water flow, and pollution, the Everglades is dying, and as they go, so goes the region.

If wetlands that once replenished underground aquifers stay dry, cities may face future water shortages. Anoxic conditions threaten fish in Florida Bay, saltwater intrudes into marshes and drinking wells, and wildlife—including 55 endangered or threatened species—is at risk. "This is not rescuing an ecosystem at the last minute. This is restoring something that has gone over the edge," says George Frampton, assistant secretary of the Department of the Interior and chair of the federal interagency South Florida Ecosystem Restoration Task Force.

More than the ecology of southern Florida is at stake. Wetlands managers from Australia to Brazil are keeping a close eye on the project as they search for ways to restore their own ravaged regions. If planners can pull it off, the Everglades restoration will become a world model, says wetlands expert Joy Zedler of San Diego State University, who notes that most restorations "are the size of a postage stamp compared to the Everglades." James Webb, Florida regional director of the Wilderness Society and a member of the Governor's Commission for a Sustainable South Florida, puts it another way: "If we can't do it in the Everglades, we can't do it anywhere."

The Everglade snail kite is one of many endangered species that inhabit the Everglades.

Map of the Florida Everglades.

The overall goal of the restoration is to take engineered swampland riddled with canals and levees and transform it into natural wetlands that flood and drain in rhythm with rainfall. Planners hope the entire ecosystem—plants and animals—will blossom as a result. "Wet it and they will come" is the unofficial motto. But because no one understands all the complex ecology involved, planners must accept a hefty dose of scientific uncertainty. "We really don't know what we're going to get out there," says biologist John Ogden of Everglades National Park. And the Corps and the South Florida Water Management District (SFWMD), cosponsor of the restoration, still haven't come up with a final blueprint for the replumbing.

The other big unknown in the Everglades is political. Would-be rescuers represent a surprisingly broad coalition of interests and money, from federal and state agencies to environmentalists and urban developers, who want a steady water supply. But holding such a diverse coalition together over the planned life of the project will be tricky. Moreover, the steep price tag—of which one third is supposed to come from the federal budget—and extensive federal involvement run counter to Washington's current budget-cutting mood. Indeed, some of the agencies now contributing expertise and money, such as the National Oceanic and Atmospheric Administration, are high on the list of candidates for political extinction (*Science*, 19 May, p. 964). "We have the technical knowledge to do the restoration," says Ogden. "But I worry about sustaining the political will."

A RIVER OF GRASS

In the late 1800s, when fewer than 1000 people lived in what are now Dade, Broward, and Palm Beach counties, water spilled over the banks of Lake Okeechobee in the wet season and flowed lazily southward to Florida Bay. This was the "River of Grass," a swath of saw grass and algae-covered water 50 miles wide and only a foot or two deep. People found the vast swamp inhospitable—too wet and too many bugs—but its mosaic of wetland habitats supported a stunning diversity of animals and plants, including huge colonies of wading birds.

Then the human migration to Florida began. In order to make the River of Grass and adjacent marshlands suitable for cities and agriculture, about half of the Everglades was drained in successive waves of development starting early this century. The mammoth flood-control project, built by the Corps at the behest of the state of Florida, transformed the hydrology of both public and private lands. Today, water is channeled swiftly through 1600 kilometers of canals and 1600 kilometers of levees, stored in parks called "water conservation areas," and partitioned by countless water-control structures. The River of Grass is interrupted by the world's largest zoned farming area, the Everglades Agricultural Area (EAA), south of Lake Okeechobee. To prevent flooding, "extra water" is diverted east and west to the Gulf of Mexico and the Atlantic Ocean. The whole system is completely artificial, says Lewis Hornung, a Corps engineer responsible for undoing much of the work of his predecessors on the Kissimmee.

The old Corps engineers recognized that their work would alter the natural world, says Hornung. But no one predicted the devastating effects. For example, hundreds of thousands of birds once nested around the headwaters of the Shark River in the southern Everglades. But as water was drained away further north, the marshes dried out more often, salinities rose—and the birds left. Throughout the Everglades, wading-bird populations are down by 90%. All other vertebrates, from deer to turtles, are down from 75% to 95%, says Ogden. "What we have out there is not the Everglades," he says. "It's a big wet area with spectacular sunsets, but functionally it's not working at all. The animal life in many places is no better than you'd see in roadside ditches in Florida in the summer."

THE BEST LAID PLANS

The good news is that hydrological damage may be reversible, explains ecologist Lance Gunderson of the University of Florida. "It's all there except the water . . . If we redo the hydrology, it will explode," says Richard Ring, superintendent of Everglades National Park.

But will the flora and fauna come back? Anecdotal reports from marshes in the northern part of the park suggest that the wetlands do indeed revive when fresh water returns, says Steve Davis, senior ecologist at the SFWMD. "And it's sort of common sense," adds Robert Johnson, chief hydrologist at the national park. "Wetlands need to be wet." Still, to date scientists can't cite the results of any large-scale reflooding study to prove this point. Says Ogden: "Hydrological restoration doesn't equal ecological restoration. This is a big uncertainty, and we need to design flexible plans to deal with it."

Plans are already shifting. In late 1994, the Corps released a preliminary study that outlined six alternatives for revamping the hydrology, although they didn't endorse any specific option. Planners now say none of the six is likely to be the solution, admits Stuart Appelbaum, who directs the Corps' Everglades planning process. There's simply no consensus yet on exactly how to increase water storage and flow while guarding against

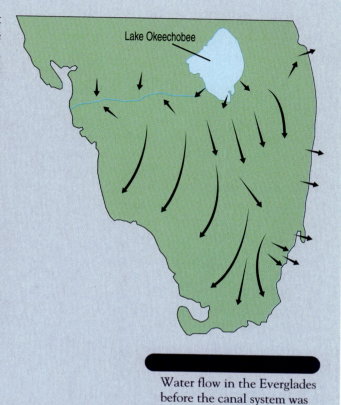

Water flow in the Everglades before the canal system was built.

floods. Nor have restorers made tough decisions about which lands to acquire from private owners for water management. The Corps has gone back to its planning; Appelbaum says a coordinated restoration blueprint is due in 6 years.

Frampton and others want a plan sooner. But in the meantime, restorers point to three smaller, independent hydrological efforts that are already entering construction. One is the Kissimmee. A second project will funnel more water to Shark Slough in the northeastern part of Everglades National Park, and a third will create a buffer strip between wetlands and drained crop fields along the park's eastern border. "At least there are three projects you can point to that are more than just words or paper, where things are actually happening," says Colonel Terrence "Rock" Salt, executive director of the federal task force.

These planners are using an approach they call "adaptive management," which basically means learning by doing. For example, as part of reflooding Shark

Slough, Hornung's crew needs to move water from one water-conservation area to another. To do so, he could either build a canal—which models say is more efficient—or simply tear down the levee between the areas. He's experimenting by degrading part of the levee and watching what happens.

To researchers, such experiments are nothing out of the ordinary, but admitting that the outcome is unknown is a new idea for engineers accustomed to having a plan and sticking to it, says Salt. "In our legal system (and there have been many lawsuits over the Everglades already), uncertainty is an admission," says Davis of the SFWMD. "And now here we are starting off up front admitting and defining it."

QUALITY CONTROL

One thing ecologists do know is that water quality, as well as quantity, will be a crucial part of any restoration. Reflood the swamps with polluted water, and the historic system is unlikely to return. Says biologist Douglas Morrison of the National Audubon Society in Miami: "You can say, 'Wet it and it will grow'—but then the next question is what will grow?" In the Everglades, the answer is often cattails. These tall plants were once only a small part of Everglades vegetation, cropping up around high-nutrient areas like alligator holes. But today in some places, cattails nearly 4 meters tall completely blanket the wetlands, says ecologist Ronald Jones of Florida International University. "It's a massive conversion at the landscape level," agrees biologist Wiley Kitchens of the National Biological Service in Gainesville, Florida.

The culprit: phosphorus. The historic Everglades had extremely low concentrations of this nutrient, says Jones. Today, extra phosphorus enters the system from the EAA, where water used to irrigate fertilized sugarcane fields picks up a load of phosphorus, then is swiftly channeled to the water-conservation areas. There it spurs nutrient-loving vegetation like cattails and blue-green algae. Jones argues that to be true to the historic system, the Everglades needs very low levels of phosphorus—perhaps as low as 10 parts per billion. "The sugar growers say we want it cleaner than Perrier—and that's true, for phosphorus. That's just the character of the Everglades," he says.

Not surprisingly, the sugar growers are unconvinced. "Ten parts per billion—what's the basis for that? Parts of the Chesapeake Bay watershed are at around 400 ppb," says Peter Rosendahl, vice president of

environmental communications at Flo Sun, one of the major sugar companies. He points out that no one really knows how much phosphorus the Everglades can handle; studies are under way now. "There's no real reason to believe that extra nutrients are the cause of the decline in the Everglades," he says.

A partial solution to the problem, one mandated by an act passed by the state legislature last year, calls for a ring of artificial marshes around the EAA to filter phosphorus from the water. A test marsh full of cattails is already up and running.

There are other thorny water quality issues, however. Chief among them is mercury, which is mysteriously contaminating fish and wildlife in the heart of the remote Everglades, to the point that fishers are advised not to eat their catch. So far, no one knows where the mercury is coming from or just how much damage it's causing, says Dan Scheidt, south Florida coordinator at the Environmental Protection Agency. But whether the issue is phosphorus or mercury, it's increasingly clear that specific goals for water quality will have to be addressed in the coordinated restoration plan. "We have some movement on the hydrology," says Salt. "But we haven't yet looked at water-quality issues holistically—and we need to."

SUPPORTING THE SWAMP

The depth of the political backing for the plan also concerns planners. In the current political climate, it's hard to count on ongoing federal commitments. Webb of the Wilderness Society worries that popular support is "like the River of Grass itself—miles wide and only a few inches deep." There's also the small matter of aligning dozens of government agencies and interest groups, from sugarcane growers to Indian tribes. For example, sugarcane researcher Barry Glasz of the Department of Agriculture says he doesn't even like the word "restore," because to him it suggests turning the clock back to a time before agriculture. Indeed, many environmental groups would like nothing better than to reduce the sugar industry's presence in South Florida. "The EAA has about half a million acres of sugar. We'd like to see maybe one third of that taken out of production and become wetland or water-retention areas," says Ron Tipton of the World Wildlife Fund.

On the other hand, surveys have shown strong public support for saving the Everglades, says Davis of the SFWMD. And urban planners and utility officials—who want to guard the water supply—agree with environmentalists that some hydrological restoration is needed. In the historic system, wetlands cached rainfall for months and so recharged the ground water of the Biscayne Aquifer, which supplies the thirsty cities of Florida's southeast coast, explains Tom Teets, water supply planner for the SFWMD. Now much of the rainfall is shuttled out to sea long before it seeps into the ground. Water supplies are adequate for the 4.1 million people who lived in Florida's urban southeast coast in 1990, but Teets and others worry about the 6 million expected to live there by 2010. "We get 60 inches of rainfall, but we can't retain it because the water has been managed poorly," says Jorge Rodriguez, deputy director of the Miami-Dade Water and Sewer Department. "So we feel everyone can benefit from restoration."

Adjacent to the test fill in the central Kissimmee, water is once again flowing through the ancient oxbow turns. The area affected is too small to see a large influx of wildlife, says Louis Toth of the SFWMD, the Kissimmee's resident biology expert. But vegetation is slowly colonizing the filled-in canal, and game fish are spawning in the newly restored flood plain. Whether uncertain science and precarious political support can engineer a similar recovery for the whole Everglades, however, is still too far downstream to see clearly.

Appendix A

Nutrient Content of Food

The following table is a list of calorie, protein, fat and carbohydrate values by common serving sizes. All calorie values have been rounded to the nearest five calories. Values for the remaining nutrients are rounded to the nearest gram. The abbreviation (Tr) means there is a trace amount of that nutrient present in the quantity described. This table has been abstracted from *Nutritive Value of Foods* (Home and Garden Bulletin Number 72) available from the Superintendent of Documents, U.S. Government Printing Office, Washington, D.C. 20402.

Food	Amount	Calories	Protein	Fat	Carbohydrate
Almonds, unsalted	1 oz.	165	6	15	6
Apple	1 medium (2¾-inch diameter)	80	0	0	21
Apple Juice (Cider)	1 cup	115	0	0	29
Applesauce:					
sweetened	1 cup	195	0	0	51
unsweetened	1 cup	105	0	0	28
Apricots:					
dried	1 cup (28 halves)	310	5	1	80
fresh	3 medium	50	1	0	12
Asparagus, raw/cooked	4 spears	15	2	0	3
Avocado	1 8-ounce avocado	305	4	30	12
Bacon:					
regular	3 slices	110	6	9	0
Canadian	2 slices	85	11	4	1
Banana	1 medium	105	1	1	27
Bagel	1 (3½ inch diameter)	200	7	2	38
Barley, pearl	1 cup, raw	700	16	2	158
Beans:					
green, fresh	1 cup	30	2	0	7
kidney, canned	1 cup	230	15	1	42
snap, canned	1 cup	45	2	1	10

Food	Amount	Calories	Protein	Fat	Carbohydrate
Beef:					
cooked, lean meat only	2.8 ounces	175	25	8	0
flank, uncooked,	4 ounces	165	24	65	0
lean meat only					
porterhouse, uncooked,	4 ounces	185	24	9	0
lean meat only					
rib roast, cooked,	2.2 ounces	150	17	9	0
lean meat only					
round, cooked,	2.6 ounces	135	22	5	0
lean meat only					
rump, uncooked,	4 ounces	180	24	9	0
lean meat only					
sirloin, broiled,	2.5 ounces	150	22	6	0
lean meat only					
uncooked, as purchased,	1 pound	1,510	74	132	0
no bone					
Beef, dried	2.5 ounces	145	24	4	0
Beef Stew	1 serving (1 cup)	220	16	11	15
Beets	2 (½ cup, diced)	30	1	0	7
Biscuits w/baking powder	1 (2-inch diameter)	100	2	5	13
& enriched flour					
Blackberries, fresh	1 cup	75	1	1	18
Blueberries, fresh	1 cup	80	1	1	20
Bologna	2 slices	180	7	16	2
Bouillon cubes (all types)	1 packet	15	1	1	1
Brazil Nuts	1 ounce	185	4	19	4
Breads, fresh or toasted:					
Boston brown	1 slice	95	2	1	21
cracked wheat	1 slice	65	2	1	12
French	1 slice	100	3	1	18
Italian	1 slice	85	3	0	17
rye, light	1 slice	65	2	1	12
white, enriched	1 slice	65	2	1	13
raisin	1 slice	65	2	1	13
whole wheat	1 slice	70	3	1	13
Bread Crumbs, soft	1 cup	120	4	2	22
Broccoli, fresh cooked	1 cup	45	5	0	9
Brussels Sprouts	1 cup	60	4	1	13
Butter	1 tablespoon	100	0	11	0
Buttermilk	1 cup (8 ounces)	100	8	2	12
Cabbage:					
cooked	1 cup	30	1	0	7
raw	1 cup shredded	15	1	0	4
Cakes:					
angel-food	¹⁄₁₂ of 10-inch cake	125	3	0	29
cheesecake	¹⁄₁₂ of 10-inch cake	280	5	18	26
devil's food cake w/	¹⁄₁₆ of 9-inch cake	235	3	8	40
choc. frosting					
cupcake, frosted	1 medium	120	2	4	20
fruitcake	¹⁄₃₂ of 8-inch loaf	165	2	7	25
poundcake	¹⁄₁₇ of 8-inch cake	120	2	5	15
yellow cake, choc.	¹⁄₁₆ of 9-inch cake	235	3	8	40
frosting					

Food	Amount	Calories	Protein	Fat	Carbohydrate
Candy:					
caramel, plain	1 ounce	115	1	3	22
chocolate, milk	1 ounce	145	2	9	16
fudge	1 ounce	115	1	3	21
gum drops	1 ounce	100	0	0	25
hard candy	1 ounce	110	0	0	28
Cantaloupe	½ (5-inch diameter)	95	2	1	22
Carrots:					
fresh cooked	1 cup, sliced	70	2	0	16
raw	1 cup	45	1	0	11
	1 whole	30	1	0	7
Cauliflower					
cooked	1 cup	30	2	0	6
raw	1 cup	25	2	0	5
Celery, raw	1 cup, diced	20	1	0	4
	1 stalk	5	0	0	1
Cereals, cooked:					
corn grits, enriched	1 cup	145	3	0	31
farina, enriched	1 cup	105	3	0	22
rolled oats, oatmeal	1 cup	145	6	2	25
Cereals, ready-to-eat:					
All Bran	⅓ cup (1 ounce)	70	4	1	21
Corn Flakes	1¼ cup (1 ounce)	110	2	0	24
Rice Krispies	1 cup (1 ounce)	110	2	0	25
Shredded Wheat	⅔ cup (1 ounce)	100	3	1	23
Cheese:					
American, processed or natural	1 slice (1 ounce)	105	6	9	0
Camembert	1 wedge	115	8	9	0
Cheddar	1 ounce	115	7	9	0
cheese spread	1 ounce	80	5	6	2
cottage, creamed	1 cup	215	26	9	6
uncreamed	1 cup	125	25	1	3
cream	1 ounce	100	2	10	1
Mozzarella, whole milk	1 ounce	80	6	6	1
Parmesan	1 tablespoon	25	2	2	0
Ricotta, partially					
skimmed milk	1 cup	340	28	19	13
whole milk	1 cup	430	28	32	7
Roquefort or blue	1 ounce	100	6	8	1
Swiss	1 slice (1 ounce)	105	8	8	1
Cherries					
canned, red sour, pitted	1 cup	90	2	0	22
fresh, sweet	10 cherries	50	1	1	11
Chicken, fried w/skin					
breast	4.9 ounces	365	35	18	13
drumstick	2.5 ounces	195	16	11	6
roasted, flesh only					
breast	3 ounce	140	27	3	0
drumstick	1.6 ounce	75	12	2	0
Chicken Pot Pie	1 3-inch pie	545	23	31	42
Chili Con Carne, canned	1 cup	340	19	16	31

Food	Amount	Calories	Protein	Fat	Carbohydrate
Chocolate:					
milk	1 ounce	145	2	9	16
semi-sweet	1 ounce	145	1	10	16
unsweetened (baking)	1 ounce	145	3	15	8
Chocolate Milk Drink 1%	1 cup	160	8	3	26
Chocolate Syrup	2 tablespoons	85	1	0	22
Chop Suey	1 cup	300	26	17	13
Clams, uncooked	3 ounces, meat only)	65	11	1	2
canned	3 ounces	85	13	2	2
Cocoa powder	¾ ounces	75	1	1	19
Cocoa, prepared with milk	1 serving	225	9	9	30
Coconut, fresh shredded	1 cup	285	3	27	12
Coffee, brewed	6 ounces	0	0	0	0
Cola Drinks	12-ounce bottle	160	0	0	41
Cookies:					
chocolate chip, commercial	4 cookies	180	2	9	28
fig bar	4 squares	210	2	4	42
oatmeal w/raisins	4 cookies	245	3	10	36
sandwich-type	4 cookies	195	2	8	29
sugar	4 cookies	235	2	12	31
Corn					
canned, whole kernel	1 cup	165	5	1	41
fresh	1 ear	85	3	1	19
Cornmeal, uncooked, enriched	1 cup	500	11	2	108
Crabmeat, canned	1 cup	135	23	3	1
Crackers:					
graham	2 crackers	60	1	1	11
saltine	4 crackers	50	1	1	9
rye wafers	2 wafers	55	1	1	10
Cranberries, raw	1 cup	45	0	1	11
Cranberry Juice Cocktail	1 cup	145	0	0	38
Cranberry Sauce canned	1 cup	420	1	0	108
Cream:					
half-and-half	1 tablespoon	20	0	2	1
heavy	1 tablespoon	50	0	6	0
	1 cup	820	5	88	7
light	1 tablespoon	30	0	3	1
	1 cup	470	6	46	9
sour, commercial	1 tablespoon	25	0	3	1
Cucumbers, raw	6 slices (⅛-inch thick)	5	0	0	1
Custard, baked	1 cup	305	14	15	29
Dandelion Greens, cooked	1 cup	35	2	1	7
Danish Pastry, plain	4¼ inch piece	220	4	12	26
Dates, whole, pitted	10 dates	200	0	0	180
Doughnuts (cake type)	1 doughnut	210	3	12	24
Eggs					
fried	1 egg, margarine	90	7	10	1
scrambled	1 egg, milk and margarine	100	7	7	1
shirred or poached	1 egg	75	6	5	1

Food	Amount	Calories	Protein	Fat	Carbohydrate
Eggplant, steamed	1 cup	25	1	0	6
Figs, dried	10 figs	475	6	2	122
Fish Sticks	1 fish stick	70	6	3	4
Flounder, baked	4 ounces	80	17	1	0
Flour:					
all-purpose, enriched	1 cup, sifted	420	12	1	88
cake, unenriched	1 cup, sifted	350	7	1	76
whole wheat	1 cup, sifted	400	16	2	85
Frankfurters	1 frankfurter	145	5	13	1
French Toast	1 slice (no syrup)	155	6	7	17
Fruit Cocktail, canned	1 cup fruit and syrup	185	1	0	48
Gelatin Dessert	½ cup prepared	70	2	0	17
Gelatin, unflavored, dry	1 envelope	25	6	0	0
Ginger Ale	12 oz. bottle	125	0	0	32
Gingerbread	⅑ of 8-inch cake	175	2	4	32
Grapefruit	½ medium	40	1	0	10
Grapefruit Juice:					
sweetened, canned	1 cup	115	1	0	28
unsweetened	1 cup	95	1	0	22
Grapefruit Sections	1 cup with syrup	150	1	0	39
Grape Juice	1 cup	155	1	0	38
Grapes	10 grapes	35	0	0	9
Gravy:					
canned beef	1 cup	125	9	5	11
brown from mix	1 cup	80	3	2	14
Haddock, breaded, fried	1 fillet (3 ounces)	175	17	9	7
Halibut, broiled w/but.	3 ounces	140	20	6	0
Herring, pickled	3 ounces	190	17	13	0
Honey	1 tablespoon	65	0	0	17
Honeydew Melon	⅒ of 6½ inch melon	45	1	0	12
Ice Cream, vanilla	1 cup (11 percent fat)	270	5	14	32
	1 cup (16 percent fat)	350	4	24	32
Ice Milk	1 cup (4% fat)	185	5	6	29
Jam	1 tablespoon	55	0	0	14
Jelly	1 tablespoon	50	0	0	10
Kale, cooked	1 cup	40	2	1	7
Ketchup	1 tablespoon	15	0	0	4
Lamb:					
chop, lean, braised	1.7 ounces	135	17	7	0
leg, lean, roasted	2.6 ounces	140	20	6	0
rib roast, lean	2 ounces	130	15	7	0
Lemon Juice	1 cup	60	1	0	21
Lettuce, iceberg	1 cup	5	1	0	1
	1 head	70	5	1	11
Liver	3 ounces	185	23	7	7
Macaroni and Cheese	1 cup	430	17	22	40
Macaroni, cooked, enriched	1 cup	155	5	1	32
Mangos	1 medium	135	1	1	35
Margarine					
80% fat	1 tablespoon	100	0	11	1
40% fat	1 tablespoon	50	0	5	0
Marshmallows	1 ounce	90	1	0	23
Mayonnaise	1 tablespoon	100	0	11	0

Food	Amount	Calories	Protein	Fat	Carbohydrate
Milk:					
buttermilk, cultured	1 cup	100	8	2	12
condensed, sweetened	1 cup	980	24	27	166
evaporated whole	1 cup	340	17	19	25
liquid, skimmed	1 cup	85	8	0	12
liquid, 98% fat-free	1 cup	120	8	5	12
liquid, whole	1 cup	150	8	8	11
nonfat dry milk, instant (dry powder)	1 envelope	325	32	1	47
Yogurt (made with partially skimmed milk): plain	1 cup	145	12	4	16
fruit flavored	1 cup	230	10	2	43
Molasses, light	2 tablespoons	85	0	0	22
Muffins:					
blueberry	1 muffin	135	3	5	20
bran	1 muffin	125	3	6	19
corn	1 muffin	145	3	5	21
English	1 muffin	140	5	1	27
Mushrooms:					
canned	1 cup	35	3	0	8
fresh	1 cup	20	1	0	3
Noodles, egg, cooked, enriched	1 cup	200	7	2	37
Oils:					
corn, cottonseed, olive, peanut, and soybean	1 tablespoon	125	0	14	0
Olives:					
green	4 medium	15	0	2	0
ripe	3 small	15	0	2	0
Onion, raw	1 cup	40	1	0	8
Orange	1 medium (2⅝-inch diameter)	60	1	0	15
Orange Juice, fresh, frozen or canned	1 cup	110	2	0	26
Orange Sections	1 cup	85	2	0	21
Oysters, raw	1 cup (meat only)	160	20	4	8
Pancakes, from mix	1 (4-inch diameter)	60	2	2	8
Parsley, raw	10 sprigs	5	0	0	1
Peaches:					
canned, syrup pack	1 cup	190	1	0	51
fresh, uncooked	1 medium	35	1	0	10
Peanuts, roasted	1 cup	840	39	71	27
	1 ounce	165	8	14	5
Peanut Butter	1 tablespoon	95	5	8	3
Pears:					
canned, syrup pack	1 cup	190	1	0	49
fresh, uncooked	1 medium	100	1	1	25
Peas:					
green, canned	1 cup	115	8	1	21
split, dried, cooked	1 cup	230	16	1	42
Pecans	1 ounce	190	2	19	5
	1 cup	720	8	73	20

Food	Amount	Calories	Protein	Fat	Carbohydrate
Peppers, green, raw	1 medium	20	1	0	4
Perch (ocean), breaded, fried	1 filet	185	16	11	7
Pickles:					
dill	1 medium	5	0	0	1
sweet	1 small	20	0	0	5
Pie Crust:					
homemade, double crust	1 9-inch shell	1,800	22	120	158
homemade, single crust	1 9-inch shell	900	11	60	79
packaged mix, double crust	1 (8- or 9-inch shell)	1,485	20	93	141
Pies:					
apple, double crust	⅙ of 9-inch pie	405	3	18	60
custard	⅙ of 9-inch pie	330	9	17	36
lemon meringue	⅙ of 9-inch pie	355	5	14	53
pecan	⅙ of 9-inch pie	575	7	32	71
pumpkin	⅙ of 9-inch pie	370	6	17	37
Pineapple:					
canned, crushed	1 cup	200	1	0	52
juice, unsweetened	1 cup	140	1	0	34
sliced, canned	1 slice	45	0	0	12
fresh, diced	1 cup	75	1	1	19
Pizza, cheese	⅛ of 15-inch pie	290	15	9	39
Plums, fresh	1 (2⅛-inch diameter)	35	1	0	9
Popcorn, popped, with oil	1 cup	55	1	3	6
Pork:					
ham, roasted	3 ounces	160	20	8	0
loin chop, uncooked	4 ounces (lean meat only)	210	22	13	0
Potatoes:					
baked	1 medium	220	5	0	51
boiled	1 medium	120	3	0	27
French-fried in oil	10 pieces	160	2	8	20
mashed	1 cup, milk and margarine	225	4	9	35
sweet, baked	1 medium	115	2	0	28
sweet, candied	1 piece (2½ inch × 2 inch)	145	1	3	29
Potato Chips	10 medium	105	1	7	10
Pretzels	10 sticks (2¼-inch long)	10	0	0	2
Prune Juice, canned	1 cup	180	2	0	45
Prunes, dried	5 large	115	1	0	31
Pudding, chocolate	5 ounce can	205	3	11	30
Pumpkin, canned	1 cup	85	3	1	20
Pumpkin Seeds dry, hulled	1 ounce	155	7	13	5
Radishes, raw	4	5	0	0	1
Raisins, seedless	1 cup	435	5	1	115
Raspberries, red fresh	1 cup	60	1	1	14
Rhubarb, cooked with sugar	1 cup	280	1	0	75

Food	Amount	Calories	Protein	Fat	Carbohydrate
Rice:					
brown, cooked	1 cup	330	5	1	50
white, enr., uncooked	1 cup	670	12	1	149
cooked	1 cup	225	4	0	50
Rolls, dinner	1 (2½ inch diameter)	85	2	2	14
Salad Dressings:					
blue or Roquefort	1 tablespoon	75	1	8	1
French	1 tablespoon	85	0	9	1
Italian	1 tablespoon	80	0	9	1
Thousand Island	1 tablespoon	60	0	9	2
Salmon:					
baked (red)	3 ounces	140	21	5	0
canned (pink)	3 ounces	120	17	5	0
Sauces:					
barbecue	¼ cup	80	1	0	16
Hollandaise	1 cup	240	5	20	14
(w/water) spaghetti, canned, tomato puree	1 cup	105	4	0	25
white (w/milk)	1 cup	240	10	13	21
Sauerkraut, canned	1 cup	45	2	0	10
Sausage, pork link					
cooked	1 link (16 per pound)	50	3	4	Tr
brown and serve	1 link	50	2	5	1
Scallops, breaded, frozen	6 scallops	195	15	10	10
Sherbet	1 cup (2% fat)	270	2	4	59
Shortening, solid	1 tablespoon	115	0	13	0
	1 cup	1,810	0	205	0
Shrimp, French fried	3 ounces	200	16	10	11
canned	3 ounces	100	21	1	1
Soups (canned soups are prepared according to label directions):					
beef broth	1 cup	15	3	1	0
chicken, cream of (with milk)	1 cup	190	7	11	15
chicken-noodle	1 cup	75	4	2	9
chicken with rice	1 cup	60	4	2	7
clam chowder, New England	1 cup	165	9	7	17
mushroom, cream of	1 cup	205	6	14	15
onion (from packet)	1 cup	20	1	0	4
pea, green	1 cup	165	9	3	27
tomato, clear	1 cup	85	2	2	17
cream of	1 cup	160	6	6	22
vegetable	1 cup	70	2	2	12
Spaghetti, cooked	1 cup	190	7	1	39
w/meatballs & sauce	1 cup	330	19	12	39
w/sauce & cheese	1 cup	260	9	9	37
Spinach, fresh, cooked	1 cup	40	5	0	7
Squash:					
summer, sliced	1 cup	35	2	1	8
winter, baked	1 cup	80	2	1	18
Strawberries, fresh	1 cup	45	1	1	10

Food	Amount	Calories	Protein	Fat	Carbohydrate
Sugar:					
brown	1 cup	820	0	0	212
granulated	1 tablespoon	45	0	0	12
	1 cup	770	0	0	199
powdered (confectioners')	1 cup	385	0	0	100
Sunflower Seeds, dry, hulled	1 ounce	160	6	14	5
Sweet Potatoes	See Potatoes				
Syrup:					
maple	2 tablespoons	122	0	0	32
table (corn)	2 tablespoons	122	0	0	32
Tangerine	1 (2⅜-inch diameter)	35	1	0	9
Tomato Juice, canned	1 cup	40	2	0	10
Tomatoes:					
canned	1 cup	50	2	1	10
fresh	1 medium	25	1	0	5
Trout, broiled	3 ounces	175	21	9	0
Tuna:					
canned in oil	3 ounces	165	24	7	0
canned water pack	3 ounces	135	30	1	0
Turkey, roasted (white and dark meat)	3 ounces	130	18	5	3
Turnips, white, cooked	1 cup	30	1	0	5
Veal:					
cutlet, broiled	3 ounces	185	23	9	0
Vegetable Juice, canned	1 cup	45	2	0	11
Vinegar	1 tablespoon	0	0	0	1
Waffle	1 7-inch waffle	205	7	8	27
Walnuts, chopped					
black	1 cup	760	30	71	15
English	1 cup	770	17	74	22
Watermelon	1 wedge, 4 inch × 8 inch	155	3	2	35
Yeast:					
Baker's dry, active	1 package	20	3	0	3
Brewer's dry	1 tablespoon	25	3	0	3
Yogurt	See Milk				

Molecules of Life Information Sheets

PROTEINS

Functions

Except for water, **protein** is the most abundant class of molecules in most living organisms. Proteins make up many of the structural components of organisms. Examples include collagen, keratin, and glycoproteins. (Collagen holds tissues together; keratin gives strength to hair, skin, nails, horns, and feathers; and glycoproteins lubricate joints.) Enzymes are protein molecules that enable the chemical reactions of living organisms to take place. The enzyme lactase breaks down milk sugar (lactose) into its subunit sugars. Proteins also carry out other essential types of functions for living organisms. For example, hemoglobin carries oxygen around the body; serum albumin transports lipids to various organs; and somatotropin, a hormone, stimulates growth.

Subunit Structure

Proteins are made up of subunits called **amino acids**. There are 20 different amino acids that make up the proteins of most organisms. All amino acids have a characteristic backbone structure (see Figure AppB.1). This structure is made up of carbon, hydrogen, nitrogen, and oxygen. One end of this backbone structure is the **carboxyl** group (COOH). The other end is the **amino group** (NH_2). These ends are joined by a carbon atom to complete the backbone.

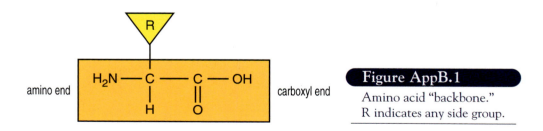

Figure AppB.1

Amino acid "backbone."
R indicates any side group.

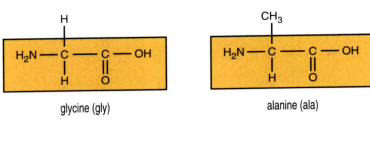

glycine (gly)

alanine (ala)

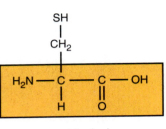

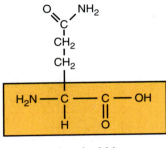

cysteine (cys)

glutamine (gln)

Branching from the central carbon atom is another atom or group of atoms called the "side group." This side group distinguishes one amino acid from another. These side groups can be made up of different arrangements of carbon, hydrogen, oxygen, sulfur, and nitrogen (see Figure AppB.2).

Forming Proteins from Amino Acids

When two amino acids join together, the hydrogen (H) from one end of one amino acid bonds to the hydroxyl group (OH) from the end of another amino acid. This reaction results in the formation of a molecule of water and two amino acids linked by a **peptide bond** (see Figure AppB.3a). The linkage can continue by the same process to form a long string of amino acids. A protein, then, is a large biomolecule formed by linking amino acids together through peptide bonds (see Figure AppB.3b). The type of protein, and thus its function, is determined by the kind of amino acids joined together. It is also determined by the sequence or order in which those amino acids are arranged.

(a)

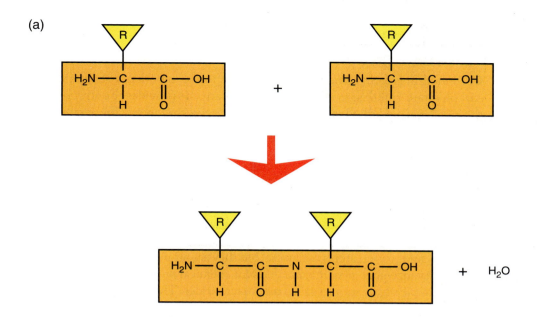

(b)

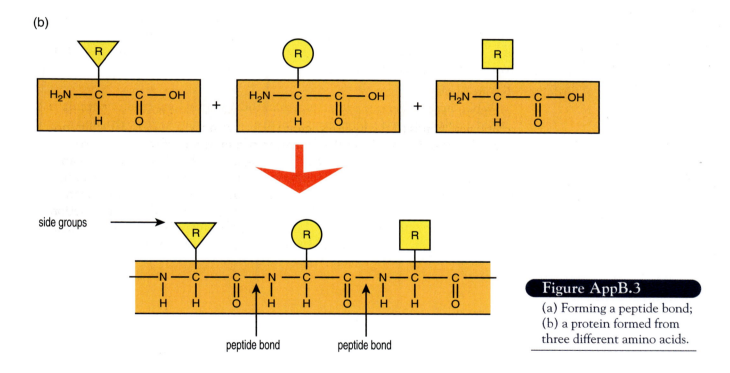

side groups

peptide bond   peptide bond

Figure AppB.3

(a) Forming a peptide bond;
(b) a protein formed from
three different amino acids.

CARBOHYDRATES

Functions

Carbohydrates form some of the major structural components of organisms. The carbohydrate cellulose is manufactured by plants. It provides the structure of their cell walls. Carbohydrates are the major source of energy for organisms. Energy is stored in the form of sugars and complex carbohydrates such as starch, glycogen, and cellulose.

Subunit Structure

The simplest carbohydrates are sugars. Sugars are molecules that contain anywhere from three to eight carbon atoms. These atoms are arranged in either an open chain or a ringlike structure. Glucose is an important sugar in energy storage. Fructose is a simple sugar found in fruit (see Figure AppB.4). It has the same number of carbon, hydrogen, and oxygen atoms as glucose, but they are arranged slightly differently. This different arrangement gives fructose different chemical properties (and a different taste!). Simple sugars are also called **monosaccharides**. This means "one sugar."

Forming Complex Carbohydrates from Simple Carbohydrates

Simple sugars can be joined together to form large biomolecules of carbohydrates. When two simple sugars are joined together, they form a **disaccharide**. This means "double sugar." Sucrose is ordinary table sugar. It is formed when glucose and fructose are linked together by covalent bonds. Lactose is another disaccharide. It is formed from galactose and glucose (see Figure AppB.5).

When many sugars are joined together, the resulting long-chain molecule is called a **polysaccharide**. This means "many sugars." Starch, glycogen, and cellulose are three examples of polysaccharides formed from the same sugar, glucose. But these polysaccharides are linked together in different ways to form different complex carbohydrates. Starch is a highly branched structure that is used in food storage by plants. Animals store food in the form of glycogen. Glycogen is also made up exclusively of glucose, but it is more highly branched than starch. Cellulose is yet another polysaccharide made up exclusively of glucose. It is joined together in yet a different way from starch and glycogen (see Figure AppB.6).

Figure AppB.4

Examples of simple sugars with their carbon atoms arranged in a ringlike structure.

glucose   fructose

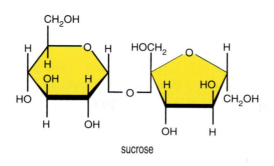

sucrose

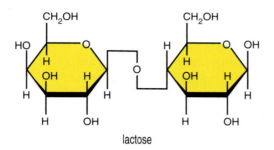

lactose

Figure AppB.5

Some disaccharides.

cellulose

Figure AppB.6

Examples of polysaccharides.

LIPIDS

Functions

Lipids are made up of a variety of molecules that do not dissolve in water. Fats are the most abundant family of lipids. They are an important source of stored energy for organisms. Lipids also form a structural component of our cell membranes. **Steroids** are another form of lipids. They perform many different functions in organisms. Some steroids are vitamins, hormones, cholesterol, and chlorophyll.

Structure of Fats

Fats are composed of two different kinds of molecules. These molecules are fatty acids and glycerol. Fatty acids are long hydrocarbon chains that end in a carboxyl (COOH) group. In these chains, carbons are bonded together along the chain; hydrogens are bonded perpendicular to the chain. Some chains consist entirely of carbons that are each bonded to two hydrogen atoms. In these chains, the fatty acid is described as **saturated**. This means that the carbon atoms are each bonded to four other atoms. Some fatty acids contain one or more carbon atoms that have only three neighboring atoms (two carbon atoms and one hydrogen atom). In this fatty acid, a double bond forms between the two carbons. This fatty acid is described as **unsaturated**. Fatty acids differ from one another primarily in length. In other words, they differ in the number of carbons joined together (see Figure AppB.7).

In a fat, three fatty acids are joined to a glycerol molecule that serves as a backbone (see Figure AppB.8). Saturated fats (containing only saturated fatty acids) can be found in butter, cheese, chocolate, beef, and palm and coconut oils. Unsaturated fats can be found in olives, peanuts, almonds, corn, fish, and avocados.

Other Lipids

Some other lipids contain fatty acids, such as **phospholipids**. Phospholipids form an important component of the cell membrane. They are made up of fatty acids joined to a phosphate group through the glycerol molecule. Cholesterol has quite a different structure (see Figure AppB.9; note the phosphate group). It has an intricate ring structure that joins a chain of carbon and hydrogen atoms. This ring structure is also characteristic of steroids.

palmitic acid
saturated fatty acid

oleic acid
unsaturated fatty acid

Figure AppB.7

Examples of saturated and unsaturated fatty acids.

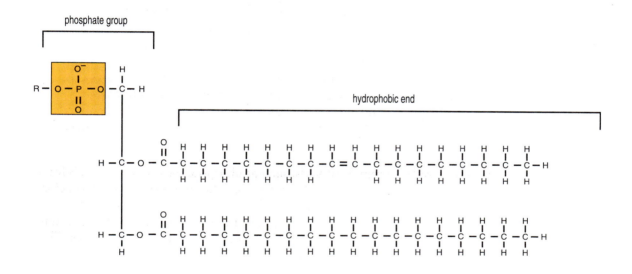

glycerol   +   fatty acids

Figure AppB.8

Structure of a fat.

phosphate group

hydrophobic end

phospholipid

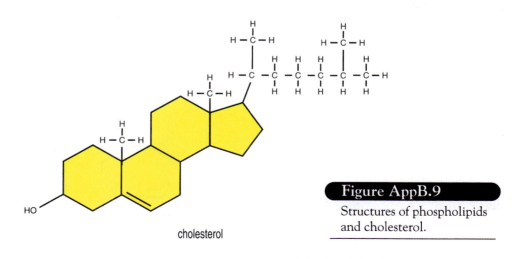

cholesterol

Figure AppB.9

Structures of phospholipids and cholesterol.

NUCLEIC ACIDS

Functions

Nucleic acids are the essential information storage molecules of living organisms. Deoxyribonucleic acid (DNA) stores all the information that a living organism requires in order to carry out the processes of life. The DNA contains the instructions used to form nearly all of an organism's proteins. The information is translated into proteins using another kind of nucleic acid. This acid is called ribonucleic acid (RNA). One kind of RNA forms a copy of the information in the DNA. This RNA, with other kinds of RNA, is used in the actual assembly of proteins from amino acids (protein synthesis). Some viruses use RNA as the information storage molecule instead of DNA.

Subunit Structure

Nucleic acids are assembled from subunits called **nucleotides**. The nucleotide is made up of three molecules: a sugar, a phosphate group, and a base.

- The sugar contains atoms of carbon, hydrogen, and oxygen. In DNA, the sugar is **deoxyribose**. Deoxyribose has one less oxygen than the **ribose** sugar in RNA (see Figure AppB.10).
- The **phosphate group** consists of one phosphorus atom surrounded by four atoms of oxygen.
- The base is a ring of molecules containing nitrogen, carbon, oxygen, and hydrogen. A DNA nucleotide can have one of four bases. These bases are adenine, guanine, cytosine, or thymine. An RNA nucleotide will have the base uracil instead of thymine.

When these three basic molecules are put together, they form the nucleotide (see Figure AppB.11).

Figure AppB.10

Deoxyribose and ribose; sugars with carbon atoms arranged in a ringlike structure.

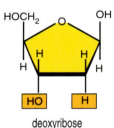

deoxyribose

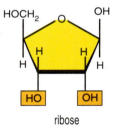

ribose

Figure AppB.11

A generic nucleotide.

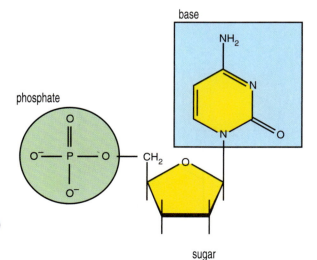

Making Nucleic Acids from Nucleotides

Both RNA and DNA are made by joining the nucleotide subunits together in a specific way. DNA is assembled by joining nucleotides in a long chain in which the phosphate and sugar molecules alternate to form a ladder. The bases hang off the side. Usually DNA consists of two such strands joined by interactions between bases of the strands. Only adenine can bond with thymine, and only cytosine can bond with guanine. This is because of the arrangement of the atoms within the base and the constraints of the molecule.

RNA is formed in a similar joining of the nucleotide subunits. But RNA usually occurs as a single strand (see Figure AppB.12).

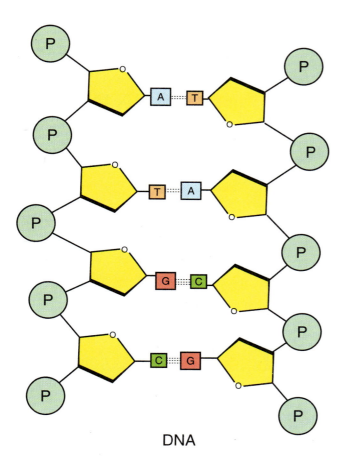

DNA

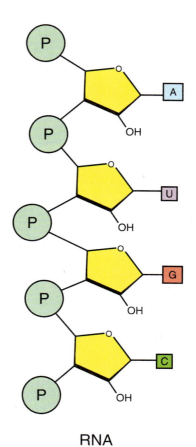

RNA

Figure AppB.12

Nucleic acids.

Glossary

A

abiotic   Nonliving factors in an environment that affect ecological systems; such as temperature, humidity, pH, geographical features, pollutants.

active transport   The movement of molecules across a membrane that requires the input of energy. Often involves the movement from an area of lower concentration to an area of higher concentration.

adenine   A purine base found in DNA and RNA. Pairs with thymine in DNA and uracil in RNA.

adenosine triphosphate (ATP)   A high-energy molecule containing three phosphate groups. Is used to store energy in cells.

albinism   A recessive variant that results in a lack of pigmentation of skin and hair.

allele   Alternative form of a specific gene located in the same position on homologous chromosomes.

amenorrhea   Cessation of menstruation.

amino acid   A small molecule made up of carbon, hydrogen, oxygen, nitrogen, and sometimes sulfur. Is joined together with other amino acids to form proteins.

amino group   A chemical group (NH_2) at one end of the protein backbone.

amniotic fluid   The fluid surrounding a fetus. Contains shed fetal cells and therefore can be sampled for karyotyping.

anabolism   Chemical reactions involved in the synthesis of new biomolecules.

androgen   A male sex hormone produced in the testis. Regulates the development and maintenance of male secondary sex characteristics (such as increased muscle mass and strength and facial and body hair), male organs, and spermatogenesis. The major androgen is testosterone.

anionic   Having the properties of a negatively charged ion.

anorexia nervosa   An eating disorder that is a form of self-starvation. Has serious debilitating effects on organs and organ systems.

anther   The part of the stamen in a flower that produces the pollen (or sperm).

antibodies   A group of protein molecules. Produced by B-cells in the immune response that bind to and neutralize foreign antigens.

antibiotics   A group of compounds produced by microorganisms. Capable of killing or inhibiting the growth of other microorganisms.

anticodon   A group of three nucleotides on the transfer RNA. Pairs with the complementary codon on the messenger RNA during protein synthesis.

antigen   A substance that induces an immune response.

anti-sense strand   The strand of DNA that is not transcribed and contains no genetic information.

apical stem   The growing point of a plant at the tip of its stem. Contains actively dividing cells.

apoptosis   Programmed cell death.

aseptic   Free from pathogenic organisms.

asexual reproduction   A form of reproduction involving only one parent and no fusion of gametes or specific reproductive organs. Takes place in unicellular organisms by cell division or fission and in plants by vegetative propagation of stems, leaves, or roots. The progeny have the same genes as the parent.

autosome   Any chromosome in a cell other than the sex chromosome (X or Y).

autotroph   An organism whose principal source of nutrition is inorganic materials. Organic materials (biomolecules) are synthesized from inorganic starting materials such carbon dioxide. May occur using light energy (photosynthesis) or chemical energy (chemosynthesis).

auxin   A class of plant growth hormones made in the apical stem. Promotes growth by causing cells to enlarge and elongate.

axillary   Located near the axil, which is the area between the upper side of a leaf or branch and the stem or branch from which it springs.

B

B-cell   A cell of the immune system that produces antibodies.

bactericidal   A substance capable of killing bacteria.

bacteriophage   A virus that infects bacteria. Made primarily of protein and DNA.

bacteriostatic   A substance capable of inhibiting the growth of bacteria.

base   A nitrogenous molecule. Either a purine or pyrimidine.

binding sites   Sites on cells or proteins that interact specifically with other proteins.

binding specificity   A state in which only a certain protein or proteins bind to another protein.

biodiversity   The number and variety of different organisms found within a specific geographic region.

biogeographical data   Data relating to the geographical distribution of organisms

biomolecule   A class of large molecules found in living organisms.

biotic   Biological factors in an environment that affect ecological systems; includes all living organisms in an ecosystem.

biotic potential   An estimate of the maximum level that living things can survive and reproduce under optimal environmental conditions.

bulimia nervosa   An eating disorder characterized by binge eating followed by vomiting and/or the use of laxatives.

C

calorie   The unit of measurement for the energy produced by anything when burned or oxidized; a kilocalorie is equal to 1000 calories. Foods oxidized in the body produce so much energy that "calories" of energy referred to in foods are actually kilocalories.

carbohydrate   A biomolecule made of carbon, hydrogen, and oxygen. Can serve as the major source of energy or form important structural components of organisms.

carboxyl group   A chemical group (COOH) at one end of the backbone structure of protein.

carcinogen   An agent known to cause cancer.

carnivore   An animal that uses flesh as its primary source of nutrition.

carrier   An individual or organism that carries a recessive allele for a disease or defect, which is usually masked by a dominant allele. Also used to describe an individual infected with a pathogenic organism but does not show signs of the disease yet is infectious.

carrying capacity   The maximum number of organisms that an environment can support without damaging that environment.

catabolism   Chemical reactions involved in the breakdown of biomolecules. Results in the release of building blocks for anabolism and energy that is stored in ATP.

catalase   An enzyme that catalyzes the breakdown of hydrogen peroxide.

catalyst   A substance that increases the rate of a chemical reaction without being changed by that reaction.

catalyze   To increase the reaction rate of a chemical reaction.

cell extract   The internal components of a cell that are released when a cell is lysed, or broken open.

cell-mediated response   The immune response that takes place involving T-cells.

cellular respiration   A series of chemical reactions that use oxygen to transfer the chemical energy in molecules formed during catabolism to ATP.

central dogma   The convention that states that DNA is transcribed into RNA and RNA is translated into protein. Often written DNA → RNA → protein.

centromere   The region of a chromosome that links two sister chromatids together after chromosome duplication. Also attaches to the spindle fibers during meiosis and mitosis. Appears as a constriction in the chromosome.

chemical reaction   A reaction between two or more substances. Results in the formation of a different substance or substances.

chlorophyll   A group of molecules that absorbs energy from the sun or light. These pigments give plants their green color.

cholera   An infectious disease caused by a bacterium *Cholera vibrio*. Spread through contaminated water.

cholera toxin   A substance produced by the bacterium *Vibrio cholera*. Is poisonous to other organisms.

chorion   One of three embryonic membranes surrounding a fetus.

chromatid   One of the two halves of a duplicated chromosome. Consists of DNA, histones, and other proteins.

chromosomal aberration   An abnormality in the structure or number of chromosomes in a cell.

chromosome   A threadlike structure consisting of DNA, RNA, and protein. Carries the genetic information of the organism in discrete segments on the DNA (genes).

class   In the taxonomic classification of organisms, a collection of similar orders.

codominance   A mode of variation in which a gene has two alleles that are equally dominant. The phenotype is the result of the action or interaction of both variant products of the alleles.

codon   A sequence of three nucleotides in the DNA or RNA. Codes for a specific amino acid.

coevolution   The evolution of two or more interacting species in which change in one species results in change in the other species. Often, the changes reinforce the relationship between the organisms.

colony   A discrete mass of cells that originates from a single cell.

communicable   Capable of being spread from organism to organism.

complementary   Matching.

complete dominance   A mode of variation where a gene has two alleles. These two alleles may encode variant forms of that protein, resulting in different phenotypes. When the two dissimilar alleles are present, only one phenotype will appear (dominate).

cross-fertilization   The transfer of pollen from one plant to fertilize the ova of another plant of the same species.

crossover   Recombination between two homologous chromosomes. Results in the exchange of corresponding genetic material. This mode of variation takes place during meiosis.

cross-pollination   *See* cross-fertilization.

cytokine   Small regulatory protein molecules released by cells of the immune system. Act to communicate among the components of the immune system.

cytokinesis   The division of cytoplasm and organelle distribution between daughter cells during cell division in meiosis and mitosis.

cytoplasm   The internal component of the cell that contains the organelles. Where metabolic activity takes place. Is comprised of water, salts, and small molecules.

cytosine   A pyrimidine base in DNA and RNA. Pairs with guanine.

D

decomposer An organism that feeds on dead organisms, breaking them down into simpler substances, thus recycling nutrients for other organisms. Examples include bacteria and fungi.

denaturation The act of changing the structure of proteins by heating or adding a detergent.

deoxyribonucleic acid (DNA) A large biomolecule that contains most of the information needed by organisms to maintain the processes of life and to pass this information on to their progeny.

deoxyribose The sugar component in DNA.

designer drug A drug designed for a specific purpose. Often designed based on an understanding of its mode of action and chemical interactions.

dicotyledonous plant Plant with two embryonic leaves.

digestion The process by which food is broken down to smaller molecules that can be absorbed.

dihybrid cross A cross that involves two different alleles of two different genes. For example, a cross between a winged, red-eyed homozygous fruit fly (WWRR) with a wingless brown-eyed homozygous fruit fly (wwrr).

diphosphoribulose carboxylase The enzyme in plants that fixes carbon dioxide into sugar.

diploid An organism having two copies of each chromosome, one derived from each parent.

disaccharide A molecule containing two separate sugar molecules. For example, the sugars fructose and glucose join together to form sucrose.

dominant variant The variant trait of an allele. Expressed when an organism has two variant alleles of a gene.

double helix Two helical polynucleotides coiled around each other. Usually used to describe DNA.

Down's syndrome A condition in humans caused by trisomy at chromosome 21. Characterized by anomalies in physical development and mild to severe mental retardation.

E

ecological niche The place of an organism in an ecosystem or community as defined by its feeding sources, the resources it uses, its habitat, and its interactions with other members of the community.

ecosystem An entity made up of all living and nonliving factors that interact, exchange materials, and affect one another.

electrolyte Ions, such as sodium or chloride. Required by cells to maintain the osmotic balance in cells and to regulate the electric charge in a cell membrane.

electron A negatively charged subatomic particle that surrounds the nucleus of atoms.

element A substance made up of one kind of atom.

embryology The study of the development of organisms from conception to birth or hatching.

endangered species A species present in such small numbers that it is at risk of extinction.

endemic Of or belonging to a particular place or people.

endocrine system In animals, the endocrine system comprises the glands that produce hormones. The glands of the endocrine system release the hormones directly into the bloodstream. Where they are transported to organs and tissues throughout the entire body.

endocytosis The process by which a cell engulfs and internalizes large extracellular substances. The cell surrounds the substances with its membrane and forms an intracellular vacuole.

endoplasmic reticulum (ER)   A system of membrane-bound sacs in the cytoplasm of cells. Some ER support the ribosomes and protein synthesis. Other ER support lipid biosynthesis.

endosperm   A food source that is in a separate structure within the seed of a plant.

enzyme   Protein molecules that catalyze the chemical reactions that take place in organisms.

epidemic   The occurrence of an outbreak of a disease in larger numbers than expected in a given area over a defined period of time.

epidemiologist   Someone who studies epidemiology.

epidemiology   The study of the outbreaks of disease, especially with regard to their causes and ways to control them.

essential nutrient   A nutrient that an organism cannot synthesize but must obtain from its environment.

estrogen   Hormones that are secreted by the ovaries, placenta, and adipose tissue. Stimulates the development of female secondary sex characteristics (such as breasts and body hair) and promotes the growth and maintenance of the female reproductive system.

eukaryote   A cell that contains a nucleus and membrane-bound organelles.

evolution   The process by which changes take place in living organisms over long periods of time. These changes manifest themselves as new characteristics in a species. Can lead to the accumulation of so many changes in a population that a new species is formed.

exponential growth   A type of growth in which the rate of increase in the size of the population is proportional to the number of organisms in the population. For example, when the numbers are small, the rate of increase is slow, but as the population increases, the rate of growth increases.

extracellular   Outside of the cell.

F

F_1 generation   The first generation. Results from a cross between two parents.

F_2 generation   The second generation. Produced by crossings within the F_1 generation.

facilitated diffusion   The movement of molecules from an area of high concentration to an area of lower concentration through channels in the cell membrane. This process requires no input of energy.

Fallopian tubes   A pair of ducts in females. Carries the egg (ovum) from the ovary to the uterus.

family   In the taxonomic classification of organisms, a collection of similar genera (genus).

fat   A class of biomolecules made up primarily of long-chain fatty acids. They form the most abundant class of lipids and are an important source of stored energy.

fatty acid   A class of biomolecules that contains long hydrocarbon chains. May be saturated (contain no double-bonded carbon) or unsaturated (contain double-bonded carbon).

fertilization   Fusion between a male gamete (sperm, pollen) and a female gamete (egg, ovum). Forms a zygote.

filament   In flowers, the stalk of the stamen that supports the anther where pollen is formed.

filtrate   The fluid that passes through a filter.

flagellum   The whiplike tail of the sperm. Facilitates movement through the ducts and toward the egg.

follicle-stimulating hormone (FSH)   A hormone produced by the anterior pituitary gland. Acts on the ovary to stimulate the growth and maturation of follicles and ova.

food   Substances that provide building blocks and energy for organisms.

food chain   The relationships among organisms defined by the transfer of energy in food. Each organism in the chain obtains energy by eating the organisms preceding it and is in turn eaten by the organism following it.

food web   the network formed by the interconnections among food chains in a community when organisms consume more than one type of food.

forensic science   Investigative methods that use modern technology, such as DNA analysis, to gather objective information that can be used to solve a crime.

fossil record   The evidence for evolution found in the remains or impressions left in rocks by organisms that died a long time ago in the Earth's geological past.

fungi   A diverse group of organisms separated from other plants by a lack of chlorophyll. Generally unicellular or composed of filaments that may form a compacted mass, as in a mushroom.

G

gamete   A cell (egg or sperm) containing single copies of chromosomes. Can fuse with a gamete of the opposite sex to form a zygote. Also called sex cells.

gene   A sequence of DNA. Encodes information that, by itself or with information encoded in other genes, results in a visible characteristic or trait of an organism.

gene pool   The sum total of all the alleles within a given population at any one point in time.

gene therapy   The replacement of a gene encoding a defective protein with a gene encoding a normal protein. Corrects a genetic defect or disease.

genetic disease   A disorder that is inherited. Is the result of an error in a gene or chromosome.

genetic marker   An allele or region of DNA that can be detected phenotypically or by molecular techniques. Is used to follow inheritance of specific chromosomes or regions of a chromosome through many generations of a family.

genetic technology   Using genetic principles to cure disease, create new products, and develop solutions to problems.

genetic testing   Medical test used to determine whether an individual carries the allele for a particular disease.

genetically modified foods   Plant and animal food products that have been modified to possess new traits by the introduction of DNA from other organisms.

genetics   The study of inheritance, variation, and the molecular basis of traits.

genome   All the genetic material and information present in the cells of an organism.

genotype   The combination of genes and/or alleles in the DNA of an organism.

genus   In the taxonomic classification of organisms, a collection of similar species.

germination   The initiation of growth and development of a plant. Happens when the embryonic plant breaks out of its seed coat.

gibberellic acid   A substance that stimulates plants to grow taller by causing stem elongation.

gland   An organ that produces a specific chemical substance, such as a hormone. Is distributed around the body through ducts or via the bloodstream.

glucose   A monosaccharide found in nature as glycogen, starch, and cellulose. Involved in energy storage and energy release.

glycogen   A carbohydrate comprised of glucose. Serves as the major energy storage in animals.

glycolysis   The first set of chemical reactions that takes place in the breakdown of carbohydrates, usually glucose, into smaller molecules.

gonad   The reproductive organ in which gametes (egg or sperm) are produced; the ovary in females and the testis in males.

growth   The orderly increase of all the components of an organism that is dependent on the uptake of nutrients. Often results in the increase in size of an organism.

guanine   A purine base found in DNA and RNA. Pairs with cytosine.

H

haploid   A cell containing one copy of each chromosome.

helper T-cell   A white blood cell that recognizes antigens on the surface of macrophages. Releases chemical substances that stimulate other cells of the immune system to divide and activate.

hemoglobin   A protein found in solution in red blood cells. Binds oxygen and transports it throughout the body.

hemophilia   Any of several inherited diseases in which normal blood clotting is impaired due to a defect in one of several blood-clotting genes.

hemophilia allele   An allele of gene coding for a blood factor that has a mutation. Codes for a defective protein that is involved in blood clotting.

hemophiliac   A person who suffers from the blood-clotting disease hemophilia.

herbivore   An animal that uses plant material as its primary source of nutrition.

heritable   Able to be inherited or passed from generation to generation.

heterotroph   An organism whose principal source of nutrition is organic materials from which they obtain biomolecules and energy.

heterozygous   An organism that has two different alleles for a trait.

histocompatibility complex.   A protein complex on the surface of cells that identifies that cell as self and not foreign.

histone   A group of basic proteins that forms a complex with DNA and is a major component of chromosomes. Believed to be involved in regulating gene expression.

homologous   Describing parts of organisms of different species that are similar in structure.

homologous chromosomes   Chromosomes that carry the same genes and pair at meiosis. One member of the pair is inherited from the father and the other from the mother.

homozygous   Having two identical alleles for a particular trait.

hormone   Molecule in plants and animals. Regulates metabolism, growth, and sexual development.

host   An organism that is used by another organism for food or shelter.

Human Genome Project   A scientific initiative in the 20th century. Designed to sequence (determine the order of base pairs on the DNA), and identify the approximately 30,000 genes on the 24 human chromosomes.

humoral response   The immune response mediated by the production of antibodies from B-cells.

hydrogen peroxide H_2O_2; a by-product of metabolism that is toxic to living things.

hydrophilic   Water loving. Will interact with water.

hydrophobic   Water fearing. Does not solubilize with water.

hypothalamus   A region of the brain responsible for regulating the physiological state of the body. Influences the release of hormones from the pituitary gland. Regulates body temperature, heart rate, blood pressure, appetite, drinking, excretion, and other metabolic activities.

hypothesis   An opinion or guess as to the probable answer to a question. Usually based on prior knowledge, observations, and experience.

I

immune system A system in the body comprised of cells and proteins. Designed to protect the body from foreign substances or substances that may cause disease.

immunology The study of the immune system.

incomplete dominance A mode of variation that takes place when a gene has two or more alleles. The phenotype is the result of the interaction of the variant products of both alleles. The phenotype may appear as a blending of the two products. Although the alleles continue to separate independently.

incubation The time between the initial infection of a host by an infectious agent and the time that symptoms appear.

indicator A chemical compound. Used to detect the presence of specific compounds.

indole acetic acid A kind of auxin that promotes growth in plants by causing cells to elongate.

infection A disease resulting from the establishment of an infectious agent in a host.

infectious agent An organism capable of causing disease.

infectious disease A disease or illness that can be transmitted from organism to organism. Usually caused by viruses, bacteria, or parasites.

inference The process of deriving logical conclusions from indirect evidence.

interleukin Another type of protein messenger of the immune system. Protects against viruses and cancer cells.

intermediate A product of catabolism that can serve as the starting material for the synthesis of biomolecules.

intracellular Inside the cell.

J

J-shaped curve The shape of the curve when exponential growth is graphed.

K

karyotype A chart or display of the complement of chromosomes of an organism. Ordered by number, size, and morphology.

killer T-cell A white blood cell of the immune system. Attacks and destroys infected cells by injecting toxic chemicals into them.

kingdom In the taxonomic classification of organisms, the highest classification into which organisms are grouped, based on fundamental similarities and common ancestry.

Koch's Postulates A set of criteria used to determine whether a microorganism is the cause of a disease.

L

lactase An enzyme that catalyzes the breakdown of milk sugar to glucose and galactose.

lactose A disaccharide found in sugar. Made up of glucose and galactose.

limiting factors The biotic and abiotic factors in an environment that determine the population size.

linked genes Genes found on the same chromosome.

lipid A biomolecule made of carbon, hydrogen, and oxygen. Is insoluble in water. Lipids are an important source of stored energy. They form structural components of membranes, and make up steroids.

liposome A membranous sack made up of fatty acid.

localized Taking place at a specific site on a body or organism.

luteinizing hormone (LH) A hormone secreted by the pituitary gland. Stimulates the production of estrogen and eggs (ovulation) in females. In males, it stimulates the testes to produce androgens.

lymph node   A part of the lymph system. Responsible for transporting lymph around the body.

lymphatic system   A system of vessels and nodes. Carries tissue fluid (lymph) around the body and transports white blood cells.

lysing   Breaking open, as in a cell.

lysosome   A vacuole within the cell. Contains digestive enzymes that break down substances within it.

M

macrophage   A white blood cell of the immune system. Engulfs antigens, viruses, and bacteria, and displays the antigens on the surface. Interacts with helper T-cells.

malaria   A disease of the blood caused by a parasitic protozoa, *Plasmodium falciparum*. Is carried by a mosquito.

maternal   Of the mother.

meiosis   The process that produces sex cells (gametes). Results in the reduction of the chromosome number to half.

melanin   A group of pigments that determines skin, eye, and hair color.

melanocytes   Specialized cells that produce melanin.

menopause   In females, the time when reproductive hormone production slows and ovulation ceases.

menstruation   A discharge of blood, secretions, and tissue debris from the uterus. Recurs in nonpregnant human and other primate females of breeding age. Takes place following an ovulation that does not result in pregnancy.

messenger RNA (mRNA)   A class of nucleic acid. Carries the information in the DNA code to the ribosome for translation into polypeptides.

metabolic processes   The chemical reactions involved in the breakdown and transformation of food into useful nutrients, new biomolecules, and energy.

metabolism   The sum of all the chemical reactions that take place in the cell.

metamorphosis   The transition from the juvenile to adult stage in insects and amphibians. Is also controlled by hormones.

microbe   An organism too small to be seen with the naked eye. Includes viruses, bacteria, fungi, protozoa, and some algae.

microbiology   The study of microorganisms.

microorganism   Microbe.

mitochondrial DNA   DNA found in the cellular organelle mitochondria. Is inherited exclusively from the mother.

mitosis   The process in which chromosomes are duplicated in a cell and separated into two nuclei. This process is followed by cell division in which two daughter cells are formed.

modes of transmission   The variety of ways that disease can be carried from one individual to another.

molecular taxonomy   Classification of organisms based on the structure and function of biomolecules.

molecule   A particle consisting of two or more atoms of the same or different types bonded together.

monohybrid cross   A cross between two individuals who are heterozygous (dominant and recessive) for a single trait.

monosaccharide   A sugar that cannot be broken down further to a simpler carbohydrate. Examples are glucose and fructose.

morbidity rate   A measure of illness that a disease causes.

morphology   The form and structure of an organism or one of its parts.

mortality rate   A measure of death that a disease causes.

multiple alleles A mode of variation in which a gene has more than two possible alleles. All alleles encode variants of the same protein. The phenotype depends on which two alleles are present in the organism and the patterns in which the products of these alleles interact. The patterns may be dominant, incompletely dominant, or codominant.

mutagen A chemical known to cause mutations.

mutation A change that takes place in the sequence of DNA of an organism. Can result in an altered protein and a change in phenotype.

N

natural selection The survival and reproduction of individuals with characteristics that make them better adapted to a particular environment.

negative control A sample in an experiment, such as water, that does not react with an indicator reagent. Used to ensure that any positive results are real.

neutron A subatomic particle without charge that is found in the nucleus of atoms.

nitrification The process carried out by bacteria in the soil by which ammonia is converted to nitrite and nitrite to nitrate in the nitrogen cycle.

nitrogen-fixing A kind of microorganism that converts gaseous nitrogen (N_2) to nitrates that can be used by plants.

nucleic acid A class of biomolecules made up of carbon, hydrogen, oxygen, nitrogen, and phosphorus. Important in storing information for all cellular processes and transferring this information into proteins.

nucleotide A molecule found in nucleic acids. Consists of one phosphate group, one sugar (deoxyribose or ribose) molecule, and one attached nitrogenous base (adenine, cytosine, guanine, or thymine).

nucleus In eukaryotic cells, the membrane-bound organelle that contains the genetic material DNA. Encodes most of the information needed to maintain the processes of the cell.

nutrient A substance required by the body to maintain the characteristics of life.

O

oocyte A reproductive cell in the ovary. Gives rise to an egg or ovum during meiosis.

oogenesis The process by which ova or eggs are formed in meiosis.

order In the taxonomic classification of organisms, a collection of similar families.

organelle A discrete membrane-bound structure within a cell that carries out specific functions.

organic Describes substances that contain carbon.

ovary The female reproductive organ that produces ova or eggs.

ovulation The release of a secondary oocyte from a follicle in response to hormonal stimulation. Maturation of the oocyte is completed during its passage to the uterus.

ovum A female reproductive cell (gamete, egg).

oxidized The state of a molecule when it has lost electrons.

P

pandemic A disease taking place over a wide area (several countries or continents). Affects large numbers of the population.

parasite An organism living in close association with another organism. Derives food and/or shelter, often at the expense of the other organism.

parasitism An association between two organisms in which one, the parasite, benefits from the other, the host. This happens often at the host's expense.

passive transport   *See* facilitated diffusion.

paternal   Of the father.

pathogen   An organism capable of causing disease.

pattern of inheritance   The systematic way in which a gene is transmitted from parent to offspring.

pedigree   A chart that depicts family relationships and the patterns of inherited traits.

peptide bond   The type of bond that joins two amino acids together to form a protein.

phenotype   The observable characteristics of an organism. Results from gene expression.

phloem   Specialized tissue in the stem of plants. Transports sugar, the products of photosynthesis, and other molecules throughout the plant.

phosphate group   A molecule made up of one phosphoric atom and four atoms of oxygen. Is part of a nucleotide.

phospholipid   A class of lipids that contains fatty acids joined to a phosphate group. Important components in membranes.

photosynthesis   The chemical reactions involved in the conversion of sunlight, carbon dioxide (CO_2), and water (H_2O) to energy and sugar in plants and photosynthetic microorganisms.

phototropism   A directional growth pattern in response to light.

phylum   In the taxonomic classification of organisms, a collection of similar classes.

pistil   The female structure of a plant located in the center of the flower. Consists of a vase-shaped ovary (where the eggs are produced) and a stigma. The stigma connects to the ovary through a tubular style.

pituitary gland   A gland located beneath and controlled by the hypothalamus region of the brain. Produces many different hormones, which, in turn, control the production of hormones produced in other glands of the endocrine system.

plasmid   An extrachromosomal segment of DNA found in bacteria as a circular double-stranded DNA. Carries genes for antibiotic resistance, toxins, and certain enzymes.

pleiotropic   A mode of variation in which a single gene may have multiple effects on the phenotype of an organism. Alters many characteristics of the organism.

polyacrylamide gel electrophoresis (PAGE)   A method used to separate biomolecules by size and/or charge. Uses a gel polymer matrix and an electric field.

polygenic   A mode of variation in which the phenotype is the cumulative result of the interactions of the products of several genes and their alleles.

polymerase chain reaction (PCR)   A technique that uses an enzyme that normally is involved in DNA replication to synthesize in a test tube segments of DNA of interest. Using this technique, quantities of DNA can be produced for different kinds of analysis.

polypeptide   A growing chain consisting of amino acids.

polysaccharide   A biomolecule containing sugar molecules joined together in long chains. For example, starch consists of many glucose molecules joined together.

population   A group of individuals of the same kind (or species) living in a particular area within a community of organisms.

positive control   The sample in an experiment in which the outcome is known because there is no variable. Used to ensure that the reagents in the experiment are working.

predator   An organism that lives by hunting and eating other organisms.

prey   An organism that is hunted or caught for food.

principle of dominance   In cases in which an organism possesses two forms of the gene for a single trait, one form of the gene may be dominant and the other may be recessive.

principle of independent assortment   The genes for different traits may assort independently of one another. That is, any combination of alleles for each of the seven traits can occur in a reproductive cell.

principle of segregation   Two forms of each gene are separated (or segregated) during the formation of reproductive cells. Each reproductive cell (sperm/pollen or egg) has only one copy or allele of the gene.

prion   A protein particle. Implicated in being the agent of infection in certain neurological diseases.

probability   The likelihood or chance that a trait or variant will happen in a particular individual.

progeny   Offspring or children.

prokaryote   A cell that has no distinct nucleus or membrane-bound organelles.

protein   A class of biomolecules made up of carbon, hydrogen, oxygen, nitrogen, and sulfur. Make up many of the structural components of organisms. Enzymes are also proteins.

protein complement   The kinds of proteins that make up an organism.

proton   Positively charged subatomic particle found in the nucleus of atoms. The number of protons in the nucleus determines the type of atom.

protozoa   A phylum of single-celled organisms. Ranges from plantlike forms (*Euglena*) to animal-like forms

puberty   The period of adolescence during which humans become sexually mature and capable of reproduction.

Punnett square   A diagram used to help predict the results of crosses between organisms having variants of a trait. Shows more clearly the possible gene combinations resulting from a cross. The square shows each possible gene combination for the offspring.

purine   A molecule that occurs in DNA. Is characterized by two nitrogen rings and pairs with pyrimidines during DNA replication, transcription, and translation.

pyrimidine   A molecule that occurs in DNA. Is characterized by one nitrogen ring and pairs with purines during DNA replication, transcription, and translation.

pyruvate   A 3-carbon intermediate formed by glycolysis. Enters a second metabolic pathway, which generates more ATP and other intermediates for the synthesis of new biomolecules.

R

receptor   Proteins on the surfaces of target cells that will receive or bind only certain hormones.

recessive variant   A variant is expressed in the phenotype only when the individual inherits two recessive alleles from both parents. This variant disappears in the F_1 generation and reappears in the F_2 generation.

restoration ecology   the interdisciplinary study of restoring and repairing habitats that have been damaged or destroyed.

ribonucleic acid (RNA)   A class of nucleic acids involved in the process of transferring the information from DNA to protein. Consists of nucleotides, each of which is made up of the sugar ribose; a phosphate group; and one of four bases: adenine, cytosine, guanine, and uracil.

ribose   The ring sugar found in RNA.

ribosome   An organelle consisting of RNA and protein. Provides the structural support for protein synthesis.

RNA polymerase   Enzyme responsible for transcribing DNA into RNA.

S

saliva Secretion produced by the salivary glands of animals. Used to moisten food and break down certain kinds of food by enzyme action.

saturated Any organic compound that contains only single bonds between carbon atoms and has the maximum number of hydrogen atoms; often used to describe fatty acids.

scarification Scraping of a surface such as a leaf or skin to allow the passage of a substance.

selective permeability The uptake of only specific substances by a cell.

selective pressure Factors in the environment that affect survival rates of organisms. Can cause organisms with a specific mutation to have a better chance of surviving and reproducing than organisms without this mutation.

self-fertilization The process in plants in which pollen is transferred from the anther to the stigma on the same flower.

self-pollination *See* self-fertilization.

sense strand The strand of DNA that is transcribed and contains the genetic information.

sepal Leaves that support a developing bud on a plant.

sex-linked gene A gene found on the sex chromosomes of organisms.

sickle-cell anemia A disorder of red blood cells that can run in families. Causes the red blood cells to collapse into shapes resembling sickles when the oxygen level of the blood is low.

simple diffusion The mixing of two or more substances by the random motion of molecules. Requires no input of energy.

solar energy Energy from the sun.

somatic gene therapy The treatment of genetic disorders where the appropriate gene is delivered to the specialized cells in which the altered protein is expressed. For example, in sickle cell, a functional β-globin gene would be delivered to cells that eventually form red blood cells.

somatostatin A hormone that regulates the release of other hormones such as growth hormone.

somatotropin A hormone in the pituitary gland. Helps to regulate metabolic activity.

species In the taxonomic classification of organisms, a population of organisms that can breed amongst themselves and produce fertile offspring.

species richness Biodiversity; the number of different species in an area or habitat.

spermatocyte The male reproductive cell that gives rise to sperm through meiosis.

spermatogenesis The process by which sperm are produced from the spermatocyte by meiosis.

stamen The male reproductive organ in plants. Consists of the filament and the anther.

starch Long-chain molecule made up of glucose molecules linked together. In plants, is the major energy-storage molecule.

stem cell An undifferentiated cell that has the capacity to give rise to cells with highly specialized functions.

sterile *See* aseptic.

steroid A group of lipids that is comprised of four carbon rings. Examples include some vitamins, hormones, cholesterol, and chlorophyll.

stigma The female reproductive structure in plants. Connects to the ovary through a tubular style.

stomata Tiny holes, or pores, in leaves. Allow gases to pass in and out of the plant.

style The tube through which pollen must travel to reach the eggs in the ovary of a flower.

substrate   A substance that is acted upon by an enzyme.

sugar   A class of sweet-tasting carbohydrates. Soluble in water and consist of linked carbon atoms with hydroxyl groups (–OH) attached.

symbionts   Two organisms living in close association, usually for mutual benefit.

symbiosis   The state of living in close association with another organism, often for mutual benefit.

systemic   Not localized in one particular part of the body or organism. Takes place throughout.

T

target cell   A cell that can bind hormones through specific receptors on its cell membrane. This binding of the hormone initiates specific processes in cells. These processes include the production and maturation of gametes.

taxonomist   A scientist who studies the principles and procedures of classification.

testis   The male reproductive organ in which sperm mature and where testosterone is produced.

testosterone   The male hormone that is produced by the testes (and in small amounts by the adrenal glands). It controls the development of internal reproductive structures in the fetus and the appearance of secondary sexual characteristics during puberty.

thymine   A pyrimidine base found in DNA. Pairs with adenine.

toxin   A poisonous substance produced by the metabolic activities of a living organism.

trait   A physical characteristic of an organism that can be observed.

transcription   The process that copies information from DNA to RNA.

transfer RNA (tRNA)   A small RNA molecule that transports a specific amino acid to the ribosome during protein synthesis. It base pairs its anticodon sequence to the codon in the mRNA.

translation   The process that produces an amino-acid chain or polypeptide from the information carried by mRNA.

translocation   The exchange of portions of genetic material between nonhomologous chromosomes. Results in phenotypic anomalies.

trisomy   The condition in which three copies of a chromosome are present.

trophic level   The level in a food chain at which an organism is found. Organisms found at the same number of steps or levels from the primary producers (plants) are at the same trophic level.

U

unsaturated   Any organic molecule that contains one or more double bonds between the carbon atoms; often used to describe fatty acids.

uracil   A pyrimidine base found in RNA. Pairs with adenine.

uterus   A muscular structure in female animals. Is the site of growth of a fetus if fertilization of the egg occurs.

V

vaccine   An antigen introduced deliberately into the body to produce a protective immune response to a pathogen.

vacuole   An organelle in eukaryotes surrounded by a single membrane. Separates a variety of materials from the cell cytoplasm.

variable   The condition being tested in an experiment.

variant   A difference in characteristics or traits.

vector   An organism that carries and transmits agents of infectious disease.

viricidal   Able to kill viruses.

virulence   The relative ability of an organism to cause disease.

virulent   Capable of a severe course of infection.

virus   An extremely small infectious agent. Generally comprised of nucleic acid and protein. Capable of infecting plants, animals, and bacteria, and may cause disease.

W

white blood cell   A cell of the immune system involved in the cell-mediated response.

X

X chromosome   The larger of the two sex chromosomes in mammals. Carries specific sex-linked genes. Females have two X chromosomes.

X-ray crystallography   A method of using X-ray diffraction by crystals to determine the atomic structure in crystal molecules.

xylem   Specialized tissue in the stem of a plant. Conducts water and dissolved substances drawn from the soil through the roots up to the leaves.

Y

Y chromosome   The smaller of the two sex chromosomes in mammals. Carries a small number of genes, some of which are involved in determining maleness. The male has one X and one Y chromosome.

yeast   A unicellular fungus whose metabolic activities are used to produce bread and beer.

Z

zygote   Results from the fusion of an egg and a sperm. Contains a full complement of 46 chromosomes. Is the starting place in the development of a complex, multicellular organism.

Index

S

Saliva, 65, 323
Salmonella mjordan, 424–425
Salmonella typhi, 420, 424
Salmonella typhimurium, 420
Salmon sperm DNA, 179
Salt curing, 116
Saltus, Richard, "Cholera: A Grim by-
Product of Squalor," 396–397
Salyers, Abigail A. and Dixie D. Whitt,
*Bacterial Pathogenesis: A Molecular
Approach*, 425
Sand dollar chromosomes, 209
SARS. *See* Severe acute respiratory
syndrome, 409
Satcher, David, 409
"Lessons and Challenges of Emerging
and Reemerging Infectious Diseases,"
410–411
Sayre, Anne, *Rosalind Franklin*, 186
SBEI. *See* Starch-branching enzyme I
Schanzkowska, Franziska, 287
Schistosomiasis, 456
Science writers, 300–301, 370–371
Scientific illustrators, 78
Scrotum, 219
Search for Life on Other Planets
(Jakosky), 7
Sea urchins
DNA, 179
fertilization and, 233–236
Secondary sex characteristics, 241–244
in boys, 242
in girls, 243
See also Puberty
Seeds, 253
biochemistry of seed development,
168–170
peas, 165–170
Seed selection, 155
Selective permeability, 107
Self-fertilization, 254
Self-pollination, 253
Self-starvation, 38–39
Sepal, 252–253
Serum albumin, 383
Severe acute respiratory syndrome
(SARS), 409
Sex cells. *See* Gametes
Sex-linked genes, 269
Sex testing, 213
Sexual reproduction, 215–232
age of procreation, 250
chromosomes and, 216–232
cloning, 231–232

fertilization, 218, 228–229
gametes (sex cells), 215–217, 228
meiosis, 217–219, 224–230
mosquitoes, 216, 220–227
oogenesis, 217–218
ovaries, 216–219
in plants, 251–263
spermatogenesis, 218–219
testes, 216–219
See also Hormones; Human
reproductive system; Puberty
Shulman, Stanford, 424
Sickle-cell allele, 295
Sickle-cell anemia, 170–172, 276
Arabs and, 174
symptoms of, 171
Silent Spring (Carson), 511–512
Single-celled bacterium, 11–13
Single-celled organisms, 99–100, 239
Sleeping sickness (African
trypanosomiasis), 456
Slime mold, 13–14
Smallpox vaccination, 460–461
Snails, *Elodea* and, 516–517
Snow, John, 309–317, 479
Sodium dodecyl sulfate, 430–432
Sodium hydroxide, 24, 118
Soil erosion, 521
Solar energy, 22, 73
See also Sunlight
Somatostatin, 379
Somatotrophin (growth hormone), 241,
379, 383
South Asia tsunami, 304
Soybeans, genetically engineered, 262
Speciation, 560
See also Diversity of life
Species, 542, 554–559
cichlids, 555–556
dogs, 555
extinction of, 571–576
interbreeding, 556–558
new, 562–564
See also Diversity of life
Species richness, 564
See also Diversity of life
Sperm, 218–219, 253
production, 244
Spermatocyte, 218–219
Spermatogenesis, 218–219
Spinal cord injuries, 125
Spleen, 200–201
Spontaneous generation theory, 85
Stamen, 252
Staphylococcus, 467